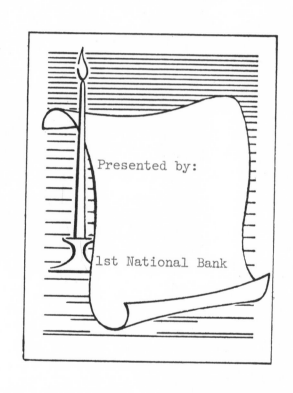

Presented by:

1st National Bank

ROMAN POLITICS
220-150 B.C.

COIN TYPES
DEPICTING
Portraits and Activities of some Politicians
(*See Notes, p. xiii*)

ROMAN POLITICS

22O-I5O B.C.

BY

H. H. SCULLARD

OXFORD
AT THE CLARENDON PRESS
1973

Oxford University Press, Ely House, London W. 1

GLASGOW NEW YORK TORONTO MELBOURNE WELLINGTON
CAPE TOWN IBADAN NAIROBI DAR ES SALAAM LUSAKA ADDIS ABABA
DELHI BOMBAY CALCUTTA MADRAS KARACHI LAHORE DACCA
KUALA LUMPUR SINGAPORE HONG KONG TOKYO

First Edition 1951
Second Edition 1973

Printed in Great Britain
at the University Press, Oxford
by Vivian Ridler
Printer to the University

PREFACE

THE main purpose of this work is to examine the political activities of the men who shaped the destinies of Rome in the half-century or so during which she became the dominant power in the Mediterranean world. Despite the varying influences exercised upon historical development by economic and geographical factors, policy and history are made by men, and during the period of her expansion Rome's policy was in the last resort determined by a small circle of senators, drawn from a limited number of families. The Senate as a whole, influenced in varying degree by public opinion, might govern the State, but a handful of nobles dominated the Senate, and it is the purpose of this work to examine the careers of this inner ring of senators in an attempt to estimate the contribution made by individuals and groups of individuals towards moulding public life.

It is a natural tendency of all governing bodies to fall into groups or cliques, the nature of which may be determined by social, economic, or political factors. In early Rome, where the structure of society rested upon the family and clan, groupings tended to follow these social cleavages and resulted in a division not merely into Nobles and Commons but also into rival groups within the nobility striving for office and power. Various attempts have been made to estimate the extent and influence of such groupings. Here the pioneer work of F. Münzer, who has skilfully attempted to reconstruct their pattern, is fundamental, but it stands somewhat *in vacuo*. Any attempt to apply such results to the continuous development of Rome's domestic and foreign policy must involve travelling over much-worn paths, but only by the cumulative effect of small pieces of evidence can a picture of the whole be built up. The result must inevitably be scrappy and unsatisfactory since so many pieces of the jig-saw are lost, but this should not, I think, prevent the attempt from being made.

Most of Rome's statesmen are known to us by name, but before the time of the Gracchi many of them unfortunately are little more than the impersonal embodiment of the list of offices which they held, and their personalities evade us. Amid this somewhat arid array of phantoms who were once men, one naturally tends to turn to those few in whom Clio has allowed later generations to see some semblance of flesh and blood or even of vivid personality. Two such are Scipio Africanus and Cato the Censor. The achievements and personality of the former have received some attention from scholars of this century, but it is strange that Cato has found no full-scale biographer and that little has been written about him in English. One reason may be that any investigation of his activities must involve the wider question of the nature of the political life of his day. I have therefore thought it more profitable to attempt to concentrate on the background as a whole in order to see how a *novus homo* fitted into the scheme of family politics rather than to focus attention primarily upon all the varied activities of the man. But although Cato and Scipio rightly have been regarded as personifying the two main cultural developments of their day, it is well to remember that, however eminent their contribution, Roman policy was shaped by a wider circle of consuls and ex-consuls: their names are recorded and some of their military and administrative achievements are known, yet as men they must remain obscure and the majority could repeat the words of Tennyson's Ulysses with more bitter meaning, 'I am become a name'.

Lack of information prescribes the chronological limits within which such an inquiry can be conducted in any detail, since for the mid-Republic there is no such wealth of literary and epigraphical evidence as has rendered prosopographical studies of the late Republic and Early Empire so fruitful. The extant books of Livy, our primary source, cover only the years 219–167 B.C.; for the decades before and after we have no continuous account of the elections at Rome and no praetorian *fasti* to show which families after reaching the penultimate stage of an official career failed to gain the crowning glory of the consulship. But if 167 B.C. marks the effective end of such an inquiry because chance has robbed us of the later books of Livy, the date will not seem entirely meaningless to those who recall that Polybius at one time considered that it would form a suitable limit to his history.

It is with very sincere gratitude that I record my great obligation to the friendly help of Professors F. E. Adcock, M. Cary, and A. H. McDonald, who have been generous enough to read through the substance of this work, each at a different stage in its production, and have encouraged me to continue with it. Their criticisms and suggestions have been of the highest value to me: I am very grateful. It is hardly necessary to add a reminder that I am alone responsible for the imperfections of this work, nor is it feasible to attempt here to record my debt to the work of historians of this period in general— that, I hope, will be clear from the bibliographical references—but I should like to express my obligation in particular to three writers on the internal history of Rome: F. Münzer, P. Fraccaro, and A. H. McDonald. Finally, I am greatly indebted to the Delegates of the Clarendon Press for their willingness to undertake the publication of this book, and in particular to Professor R. Syme for his helpful suggestions for pruning an overladen growth. Thanks to his expulsive, but constructive, advice, reinforced by that of Professor A. H. McDonald, much dead wood has been removed; if any is judged to remain, I alone must be held accountable.

H. H. S.

KING'S COLLEGE, LONDON

September, 1949

PREFACE TO SECOND EDITION

I AM grateful to the Delegates of the Press for offering to reissue this book which has been out of print for some years. For practical reasons it is desirable that, apart from a few minor corrigenda, it should be reprinted as it stands: thus it remains essentially a book of 1951. However, I welcome the opportunity to make some additions in a Foreword. These take the form of (i) a reproduction of part of a paper which I read at the end of 1954 at a Colloquium at the Institute of Classical Studies in London, in which I replied to some points raised by reviewers (it appeared in the Institute's *Bulletin*, 1955, 15 ff.), (ii) mention of some later discussions of the problem of factional politics, and (iii) some further bibliographical references to works which deal with more specific points.

I would add that naturally I do not believe that all the groupings that I have suggested can be regarded as established in detail and many may have been more fluid than I have postulated, but on the other hand I still feel that Roman political life worked this way, namely on a basis of personal alliances which as between members of the governing nobility rested to a great extent upon the claims of family and 'friendship', and as between the governing class and the rest of the electorate upon the relationship of patronage and *clientela*. A noble knew to a considerable extent upon whose votes he could count, and this support crystallized in his mind and in that of his friends and rivals as a 'group' or faction, unofficial but not unreal.

H. H. S.

LONDON
April, 1972

CONTENTS

NOTES ON FRONTISPIECE

THE coin types, here reproduced, illustrate various aspects of this period of history: portraits and achievements of Roman statesmen and soldiers, and the strong feeling of family tradition evinced in the moneyers' choice of types. I wish to express my thanks to Mr. E. S. G. Robinson, Keeper of Coins at the British Museum, and to Mr. R. A. G. Carson, for their kindness in supplying me with the casts.

1–2. SCIPIO AFRICANUS (?). *Obv.* Male head. *Rev.* Horse and palm-tree (a normal Carthaginian type). Silver coin, minted at Carthago Nova. For the portrait see pp. 119; 255.

3. SCIPIO AFRICANUS (?). Male head. Bronze coin of Canusium. *BMC, Italy*, 135 n. 5. See p. 255.

4. CN. CORNELIUS BLASIO (?), *cos.* 270. *BMC Rn. Rep.* II. 294 f. (hereafter quoted as *BMC*). *Denarius*, 105 B.C. (the dates of *denarii* mentioned here are those given by the late E. A. Sydenham in his forthcoming work on Republican coinage). The portrait is usually thought to be that of Scipio Africanus, but see p. 255.

5–6. FLAMININUS. *Obv.* Head of Flamininus. *Rev.* Nike crowning his name. Gold stater. See pp. 119; 255.

7–8. M. CLAUDIUS MARCELLUS, *cos.* V 208 B.C. *Obv.* Head of Marcellus. The triskeles, a symbol of Sicily, refers to his capture of Syracuse. Marcellinus, moneyer, probably *cos.* 18 B.C. *Rev.* Marcellus dedicates *spolia opima* in temple of Iuppiter Feretrius (222): see p. 58. *BMC*, I. 567. *Den.* 38 B.C.

9–10. CATO. *Obv.* Female bust. *Rev.* Victory seated, referring probably to the *aedicula* which Cato dedicated to Victoria Virgo in 193 (L. xxxv. 9. 6). Cato must remain without a portrait. For his views on portraiture see p. 156. *BMC*, II. 303. *Den. c.* 92 B.C.

11–12. EARLY DIDRACHM. *Obv.* Bust of Hercules. *Rev.* Wolf and twins. For a symbolic reference to the *amicitia* of the Fabii and Ogulnii see p. 34. *BMC*, II. 134. Silver didrachm, *c.* 269 B.C.

13. VOTING SCENE. Interior of Comitium, with *pons* in foreground. Voter on l. receives a *tabella* from a *rogator*; voter on r. drops vote in box; three parallel lines denote tribal enclosures (*saepta*); in background, the tribune's seat. After introduction of ballot in 139 B.C. See p. 19. *BMC*, II. 274. *Den.* 106 B.C.

14. PROVOCATIO. Togate figure, soldier, and lictor. See p. 96. *BMC*, II. 301. *Den.* 104 B.C.

15. SERGIUS. Sergius on horseback, holding sword and barbarian's head in l. hand. See p. 282. For his exploits see Pliny, *NH*, VII. 104–6. *BMC*, II. 269. *Den.* 108 B.C.

16. SULPICIUS GALBA. Naval trophy; two figures wearing the petasus, one a naked captive, the other clothed. This probably refers to Galba's naval operations against Aegina (209–208), the prisoners being sold *sub hasta* and then bought back by their fellow-citizens. *BMC*, I. 488. *Den.* 54 B.C.

17. M. SERVILIUS GEMINUS. Servilius on horseback (M. on shield), spearing another horseman. He is said to have been wounded in 23 victorious single combats (Plut. *Aem. Paull.* 31). *BMC*, I. 179. *Den.* 85 B.C.

18. M. AEMILIUS LEPIDUS. Equestrian statue of Lepidus. A statue on the Capitol recorded how as a youth he had saved a fellow-citizen's life in battle (Val. Max. III. 1. 1.). *BMC*, I. 447. *Den.* 66 B.C.

19. M. AEMILIUS LEPIDUS. Lepidus placing a wreath on head of Ptolemy V. See pp. 94; 237. *BMC*, I. 449. *Den.* 66 B.C.

20. Q. MINUCIUS THERMUS. Minucius protects fallen comrade from a barbarian. This probably refers to his Ligurian campaigns (193–1). *BMC*, II. 302. *Den. c.* 95 B.C.

21. Q. FABIUS PICTOR. Fabius, Flamen Quirinalis, holds a flamen's cap and wears a praetor's armour. See p. 136. *BMC*, I. 181. *Den.* 110 B.C.

22. L. SCIPIO ASIAGENUS. Iuppiter in *quadriga*. Refers to Scipio's triumph over Antiochus. See p. 139. *BMC*, I. 206. *Den.* 101 B.C.

23. Q. MARCIUS PHILIPPUS. Horseman in Greek armour; behind, a Macedonian horned helmet. Refers to Philippus' campaign against Perseus (169); horseman might be Perseus. *BMC*, I. 175. *Den. c.* 125–120 B.C.

24. L. AEMILIUS PAULLUS. Paullus on r. of trophy; on l., Perseus and his two sons. TER refers probably to Paullus' three victories in Spain (190), Liguria (181), and Macedonia (168). *BMC*, I. 418. *Den.* 55 B.C.

LIST OF ABBREVIATIONS

AJA, American Journal of Archaeology.

AJP, American Journal of Philology.

Aymard, *Premiers rapports*, G. Aymard, *Les premiers rapports de Rome et de la confédération achaïenne (198–189 av. J.-C.)* (1938).

BCH, Bulletin de Correspondance Hellénique.

Beloch, *Röm. Gesch.*, K. J. Beloch, *Römische Geschichte bis zum Beginn der punischen Kriege* (1926).

Bilz, *Scipio Aemilianus*, K. Bilz, *Die Politik des P. Cornelius Scipio Aemilianus* (1936).

Bloch–Carcopino, *Hist. rom.*, G. Bloch and J. Carcopino, *Histoire romaine, II: La République romaine de 133 à 44 avant J.-C.* (1935).

BM Coins Rn. Rep., H. A. Grueber, *Coins of the Roman Republic in the British Museum* (1910).

Bull. Com. Arch., *Bullettino della commissione archeologica comunale di Roma.*

CAH, Cambridge Ancient History.

CHJ, Cambridge Historical Journal.

CIL, Corpus Inscriptionum Latinarum.

Class. et Med., Classica et Mediaevalia.

CP, Classical Philology.

CQ, Classical Quarterly.

De Sanctis, G. De Sanctis, *Storia dei Romani* (1907–23).

Dessau, *ILS*, H. Dessau, *Inscriptiones Latinae Selectae.*

Dittenberger, *Syll.*, W. Dittenberger, *Sylloge Inscriptionum Graecarum* (3rd ed. 1915–24).

Econ. Surv., T. Frank, *Economic Survey of Ancient Rome* (1933–40).

FGH, F. Jacoby, *Fragmente der griechischen Historiker.*

FHG, C. Müller, *Fragmenta Historicorum Graecorum.*

Fraccaro, *Processi*, P. Fraccaro, *I processi degli Scipioni* (1911).

Gelzer, *Nobilität*, M. Gelzer, *Die Nobilität der römischen Republik* (1912).

Groag, *Hannibal*, E. Groag, *Hannibal als Politiker* (1929).

Haywood, *Scipio*, R. M. Haywood, *Studies on Scipio Africanus* (1933).

IG, Inscriptiones Graecae.

Inscr. Ital., Inscriptiones Italiae.

Janzer, *Cato*, B. Janzer, *Historische Untersuchungen zu den Redenfragmenten des M. Porcius Cato* (1937).

Jordan, *Cato*, H. Jordan, *Catonis quae extant* (1860).

JRS, Journal of Roman Studies.

Kahrstedt, *Gesch. Karth.*, U. Kahrstedt, *Geschichte der Karthager* (1913).

Malcovati, *ORF*, H. Malcovati, *Oratorum Romanorum Fragmenta* (1930).

Maxis, *Prätoren*, E. Maxis, *Die Prätoren Roms* (1911).

Meyer, *ORF*, H. Meyer, *Oratorum Romanorum Fragmenta* (1842).

Mem. Linc., Memorie della r. Accademia nazionale dei Lincei.

Mommsen, *Dr. publ.*, *Le Droit public romain* (French translation of *Röm. Staatsr.*).

Mommsen, *Röm. Forsch.*, *Römische Forschungen* (1864–79).

Mommsen, *Staatsr.*, *Römisches Staatsrecht*, ed. 3 (1887–8).
Münzer, *RA*, F. Münzer, *Römische Adelsparteien und Adelsfamilien* (1920).
Not. Scav., *Notizie degli scavi di antichità.*
OCD, Oxford Classical Dictionary.
Otto, *Gesch. Zeit VI. Ptol.*, W. Otto, *Zur Geschichte der Zeit des VIten Ptolemäers* (1934).
Peter, *HRF*, H. Peter, *Historicorum Romanorum Reliquiae* (i, 2nd ed. 1914).
Philol., *Philologus.*
Proc. Brit. Acad., *Proceedings of the British Academy.*
PW, Pauly–Wissowa–Kroll, *Real-Encyclopädie der classischen Altertumswissenschaft.*
Regibus, *Processo*, L. de Regibus, *Il processo degli Scipioni* (1921).
Rev. Ét. Gr., *Revue des études grecques.*
Rev. Ét. Anc., *Revue des études anciennes.*
Rev. Ét. Lat., *Revue des études latines.*
Rev. Hist., *Revue historique.*
Rev. Phil., *Revue de philologie, de littérature et d'histoire ancienne.*
Rhein. Mus., *Rheinisches Museum für Philologie.*
Riv. Fil., *Rivista di Filologia.*
Schur, *Scipio*, W. Schur, *Scipio Africanus und die Begründung der römischen Weltherrschaft* (1927).
Scullard, *Scipio*, H. H. Scullard, *Scipio Africanus in the Second Punic War* (1930).
Scullard, *Roman World*, H. H. Scullard, *A History of the Roman World from 753 to 146 B.C.* (1935).
SEG, Supplementum Epigraphicum Graecum.
SGDI, Sammlung der griechischen Dialektinschriften.
Stud. Stor., *Studi storici per l'antichità classica.*
Syme, *RR*, R. Syme, *The Roman Revolution* (1939).
TAPA, Transactions of the American Philological Society.
Taylor, *Party Politics*, Lily R. Taylor, *Party Politics in the Age of Caesar* (1949).
Thiel, *Roman Sea-Power*, J. H. Thiel, *Studies on the History of Roman Sea-Power in Republican Times* (1946).
Walbank, *Philip V*, F. W. Walbank, *Philip V of Macedon* (1940).
Willems, *Sénat*, P. Willems, *Le Sénat de la république romaine* (1885).

SHORTER ABBREVIATIONS

L., Livy
P., Polybius (edited by T. Büttner-Wobst)
cos., consul
pr., praetor

FOREWORD[1]

IN this book I have argued that during the years 220 to 150 B.C.
effective political control at Rome rested in the hands of twenty or
fewer noble families, who owed this virtual monopoly partly to
their adroit control of the elections. Their power was based on birth
and family tradition, political alliance, and above all on patronage,
economic, legal, and political. Although occasionally constrained by
popular action, the nobles in the main skilfully controlled the People,
and the chief domestic struggles raged less between nobles and commons than within the ranks of the nobility itself, which would naturally tend to fall into rival groups. These, granted the strong Roman
feeling for family ties and *patria potestas*, would normally rest upon
the family and *gens* or upon groups of families and *gentes* allied by
kinship, by marriage, or by political convenience. Thus emerged rival
groups which did not develop into anything like modern political
parties because their leaders did not normally proclaim political programmes when seeking electoral support but rather appealed for
personal backing.

Most historians admit the existence of such groups, but differences
of opinion arise when any attempt is made to assess in any detail their
interrelationships and permanence: were they continually forming
and dissolving, were they merely supporters of an individual leader,
no longer recognizable after his political eclipse or death, or can they
legitimately be regarded as real political entities, though unofficial and
undefined? Some historians may well have been tempted to over-
emphasize the results which can legitimately be drawn from the Livian
evidence by Münzer's pioneering methods. Since some reviewers of
my book would include me in this class and indeed doubt the whole
interpretation, we may now briefly consider four of these.

F. Hampl, if I understand him aright, refuses to go beyond the
obvious fact that certain men had supporters, friends, and enemies.[2]
To envisage groups or interrelationships involves danger; to assign to
a group a particular policy is to invite disaster. We must be content
with Livy at his face value. A. Bernardi also doubts the legitimacy of

---

[1] Section (1) comprises the substance of part of 'Roman Politics', *Bulletin of the Institute
of Classical Studies of the University of London*, 1955, 15 ff.

[2] *Anzeiger für die Altertumswissenschaft*, 1953, 89–97.

any detailed analysis, because 'the life of any society is so complex, the interaction of forces so obscure . . .; the difficulty of entering intimately into human intentions in so distant and imperfectly documented an epoch, is like trying to reconstruct a complicated mosaic design with only a few tesserae.'[1] With this view all who have worked in this field will have much sympathy, and I myself had used the metaphor of a jigsaw puzzle with many lost pieces (P. v). But I think our metaphors reveal our differences: odd *tesserae* can scarcely be put together so as to reconstruct an unknown design, but a few pieces of a jigsaw puzzle can often be fitted together to form a coherent, and possibly a revealing part of the whole. I am not convinced that we have not got sufficient outline knowledge of the period to get some general idea of the pattern and make sense of some of the pieces.

More serious is the attack of M. Gelzer[2] and Mrs. M. I. Henderson,[3] who unite in questioning the existence of electoral blocs or coalitions at this period on the ground that they are not specifically mentioned in the sources. The unity of their criticism, however, is not maintained when they examine the annalistic tradition for second-century domestic politics. While Mrs. Henderson believes that no *historia contexta* existed in pre-Sullan annals (i.e. presumably it was created by men like Valerius Antias and Claudius Quadrigatus), Gelzer on the other hand traces the Livian election accounts back to the older annalists with less Sullan elaboration. But the fact remains that these accounts afford little direct evidence of the existence of political groups, and if Gelzer is right (as, in view of the plain factual style of much of these records, he probably is), his criticism is the more damaging since much in the accounts will derive from the time of the Gracchi, only a generation or two after the events that they describe.

If then these postulated political groups had no Latin name (a point Mrs. Henderson labours), and if they do not figure clearly in reliable sources, how then can we maintain that they existed? To this we could reply by asking two questions. First, whether we could expect a clear nomenclature when even in Cicero's day political groups were referred to with considerable lack of clarity.[4] Unofficial bodies are less likely

---

[1] *Rivista storica italiana*, 1953, 105–11.

[2] *Historia*, i. 4. 634–42 (reprinted in *Kleine Schriften* (1962), i. 201–10).

[3] *JRS*, 1952, 114–16.

[4] In the later Republic personal labels were sometimes used, such as Mariani or Sullani. The precise meaning of *factio* and *partes* in different contexts is not always easy to pin down. Cicero and Caesar avoid using *factio* in discussing day-to-day politics, while Livy uses it only once for second-century politics (xxxviii.55), although the *Periochae* refer to the *factio* of a Marius or Sulpicius. Only Sallust uses it often, for the clique that controlled the Senate. *Partes* is used by Cicero, Sallust, and Caesar for opposing groups, but whereas Sallust and Caesar avoid a personal use, Cicero, the *Bell. Hisp.*, *Alex.*, and *Afric.*, and Livy's *Periochae* for the revolutionary period do speak of the *partes* of individuals. *Coitio* is used of a very temporary electoral compact, often of a dubious nature bordering on *coniuratio*. Cf. L. R. Taylor, *Party Politics in the Age of Caesar* (1949), 9 ff.

to be clearly labelled than official organs of the State: thus it is salutary to be reminded that later even the imperial councils lacked precise definition, and J. A. Crook can write, 'a study of the names by which imperial councils are referred to in different documents leads to this important negative result: during the whole period from Augustus to Diocletian they never had an official name. The phrase *consilium principis*, in particular, never occurs at all.'[1] Secondly we might ask whether the groupings are really the kind of organization to which we should expect any reference in the early annalistic accounts. These accounts may not always have been as barren as Cato's sarcastic reference might suggest, but the fact that from the time of Sempronius Asellio policy ('quo consilio quaque ratione gesta essent') was included in the subject-matter of history,[2] does not mean that such descriptions of policy must have included internal politics in the sense of factional struggles within the nobility.

The difficulty, I think, arises partly from the question of definition. Historians who try to trace the development of such groups naturally have to mention them often, and the name itself (be it faction, group, coterie, party) by mere repetition suggests a more rigid and permanent unit than is perhaps intended or justified. By such a group I would suggest only (*a*) a noble and those of his fellow nobles whom ties of family or friendship bound to him, and (*b*) the actual men who on a given occasion recorded their votes for him. But elections came once a year, there were (after 197 B.C.) at least eight senior magistrates to be elected, and candidates normally came from a very limited number of *gentes*. When during the year after a specific number of voters had supported for instance a Scipio, a friend or relative of his stood for office, it would be singular indeed if a majority of the votes cast for the second man were not cast by the same individuals who had voted for the first in the previous year (though doubtless there was a fringe of floating votes which had to be wooed at each election). This is labouring the obvious, but I want to suggest that there must normally have been a large number of voters on whom a given noble could count, and that therefore a considerable part of the electorate would tend to vote on traditional lines. If then various blocs of the electorate tended to vote over considerable periods of time for candidates of certain families, little harm should be done by describing such a group of voters as a Scipionic or Fabian group, provided that it is realized that its allegiance had a purely personal basis.

Such groups, personal and unofficial and remote from the possibility of exact constitutional definition, being based on the nature of Roman society rather than of Roman public law, would scarcely

---

[1] *Consilium Principis* (1955), 104.
[2] Cf. J. P. V. D. Balsdon, *CQ*, 1953, 158 ff.

receive mention by ancient annalists, who would be more concerned
with leaders than with followers. In so far as, and for as long as, a
Roman noble or his relations could continue to count on certain votes,
it would seem that a political entity was in existence. Such a group did
not spring full-born into existence on the eve of an election: though
its detailed composition must have altered at times, and its expectation
of life remained uncertain, it yet provided the basis of a noble's political power. And in the competition for place, it would be strange if
such groups did not on occasion unite to form coalitions: the fact is
attested in the late Republic. Thus, to me at any rate, it does not appear
unduly to strain credulity to believe that such unofficial coteries
formed the unadvertized background of those friendships and rivalries
which, as our sources record, enlivened the political scene of the
second century.

False emphasis may also arise, I think, from conceiving such groups
as self-conscious corporate personalities: it was in fact the leaders that
would normally think in terms of groups, while the rank-and-file
voters would be more conscious of recording their votes for an individual than the *de facto* link that bound them to others voting for the
same man (apart from their more immediate contact with the members
of their own centuries or tribes). A shorthand phrase, as 'the Fabian
group', may sometimes suggest a greater self-conscious cohesion in a
group than perhaps existed. It was the small coterie of nobles and
their friends that by organization and planning gave its essential
existence to the wider group of those who could be induced to vote
for them.

But I do not want to seem to be going too far to meet my critics.
Gelzer, for instance, objects to the suggestion that a Fabian group
lived on after the death of the Cunctator in 203. Here I mean that the
same group of families continued to work together for their mutual
advantage (e.g. to secure a praetorship for Fabius Buteo in 201) and
that they would have mustered for such an election much the same
voters as had previously voted in line with the Cunctator's wishes.
After all it is not only material goods that are inheritable. As
Wirszubski wisely reminds us: 'unlike honos, which is limited in time,
and gloria, which is transient, dignitas attaches to a man permanently,
and devolves upon his descendants . . . being inheritable, dignitas is
closely allied with nobilitas.'[1] Political and group loyalties, no less, may
have survived the death of a princeps.

It is not possible here to enter into any detailed discussion of source
criticism, where the main task is to try to separate the earlier reliable
tradition from later false additions, a process that inevitably involves
a considerable subjective element. But an example or two may be

[1] *Libertas as a Political Idea at Rome* (1955), 36.

taken in order to illustrate the nature of the difficulties, e.g. Livy's account of the elections for 216 B.C. (xxii. 33–5), which Gelzer believes I have misinterpreted.[1] He rightly urges that Polybius' account should be given priority. But this does not take us very far, since Polybius merely names the new consuls and gives no hint of the elaborate electoral struggle which Livy records. Why should he? The result, but not normally the process, of an election might influence universal history (here through its effect on the battle of Cannae). Livy describes how Veturius, who was appointed dictator to conduct the elections, was forced, with his Magister Equitum, to resign as *vitio creatus*. Gelzer accepts this as good pontifical tradition, but he objects to any suggestion that Fabius might have been behind this move and have been using the religious machinery against the Aemilian Veturius. The ground of Gelzer's objection is twofold: he believes that it is doubtful (*a*) whether Fabius' religious scruples would have allowed him to have acted thus, and (*b*) whether he would have thought so much of group-politics in time of national need. Now some may feel that the first point can scarcely be determined with confidence since we may seem to lack sufficient evidence really to evaluate the genuineness of Fabius' religious outlook (though it must be admitted that his known religious manœuvres resulted in his own advantage).[2] As to the second point, strategy was involved on this occasion as well as possible group-interests, and Fabius' motives in fiddling with the elections may well have been to keep out his political rivals in an attempt to maintain his own strategy of *cunctatio* against the wishes of both the Aemilian–Scipionic group, now dominant in the Senate, and of the People, since both of these wanted a decisive battle. But, says Gelzer, I support this view by reference to the speech of the tribune Baebius (L. xxii. 34. 3–11), which is late annalistic, and such eclectic criticism is not justified. Now I do not accept the speech itself, but I would accept Livy's introductory summary of it (that Baebius accused . . . 'non senatum

---

[1] On these elections see now E. S. Staveley (*Historia*, 1954, 205 ff.), who accepts my interpretation as fundamentally correct. He argues cogently in support of A. Schwegler's old but neglected view that an *interrex* enjoyed a peculiar prerogative when conducting a consular election which may therefore have been decided in accordance with the wishes rather of the presiding officer than the *populus*.

[2] I remain unconvinced by the arguments of Ilse Müller-Seidel (*Rhein. Mus.* 1953, 241 ff.) that Fabius' conduct must be explained by his genuine traditional religious feelings and not by political considerations (*a*) when he stepped into Marcellus' place in the elections for 215 B.C., i.e. he respected the thunder and the augurs' wishes, and (*b*) when he stopped the election of Aemilius for 214 because the latter as *flamen* could not leave Rome and a consul was needed in the field, with the result that Fabius himself was elected. It is possible that I may have exaggerated Fabius' lack of religious fears (p. 61), but if Müller-Seidel is right in her interpretation of Fabius' motive, one may wonder why it did not occur to him, as presiding officer for 214, to refuse to accept the *professio* of Aemilius, rather than to allow the election to start and then stop it. The application of a 'cui bono' argument remains very awkward for her thesis since the fact remains that Fabius himself *twice* stepped into a vacancy created by these religious scruples—or wire-pulling.

modo sed etiam augures, quod dictatorem prohibuissent comitia perficere') *because* it merely amplifies the earlier observation of Livy (which Gelzer accepts as good priestly tradition) about Veturius and his Magister Equitum Pomponius: 'iis vitio creatis iussisque se magistratu abdicare, ad interregnum res rediit' (33. 12). This sentence implies action by the augurs, which has merely been made more explicit by the Baebius references and has obviously been elaborated by the later annalists. Thus both the augural action and its implications should go back to the earlier annalists. Where I do go beyond the written evidence is to draw attention to the composition of the College of Augurs in 216 and point out that Fabius was its head. Thus all the evidence, including not dissimilar action by Fabius in 215 and 214, seems to me to point in one direction.

In regard to the elections themselves Gelzer rejects Livy's list of candidates and therewith the whole story of the reluctant Aemilius. The matter obviously turns on the reliability of the list of five unsuccessful candidates, which may well in fact be genuine since two possible sources of information were available: (*a*) unofficial family archives might well retain proud records of the noble competitors that a man's ancestor had beaten at the polls, and (*b*) official records of candidates may have been filed as early as this in the State archives, while we certainly cannot be sure that the *tabulae pontificum* did not record the names of *all* candidates, unsuccessful as well as successful. Thus I should be chary of believing that the whole of this part of Livy's narrative is late annalistic with no earlier nucleus, and that therefore, as Gelzer believes, it should be cast into the historian's waste-paper basket, though quite obviously in its present form it has been highly elaborated, perhaps by Valerius Antias.[1]

Another potential danger, that of the possible distorting influence of later events or feelings, can be illustrated from the division of opinion which, as recorded by Livy (xlii. 47), divided the Senate in 171 B.C. on the question of Philippus' diplomacy towards Perseus which the old-fashioned denounced as deceitful. A. Bernardi (op. cit.) rejects this: he argues that the passage in Livy is not from Polybius who would not blame methods that were common in the Hellenistic world, and he believes that the remonstrances of the older senators in Livy merely reflect the moral attitude of Livy himself: thus we must not look for contemporary groupings here. But since Livy's chapter is embedded in a long passage (chs. 36–67) which is Polybian, there seems no good reason to single out chapter 47 as an annalistic

---

[1] If Staveley's views (op. cit.) are accepted, Livy's account of two elections on successive days will have to be rejected, but Staveley still accepts the list of candidates, 'which wears every appearance of being authentic'; it will have been that published by the dictator before his resignation rather than by the *interrex*.

insertion (F. W. Walbank, *JRS*, 1941, 86 n. 37, accepts it as Polybian). Further, the emergence of a new group of plebeian leaders at this time is attested by the Fasti, and the fact that some of them employed unscrupulous methods which angered many senators is clear from the activities of men like M. Popillius in Liguria and C. Cassius Longinus in Illyricum. Livy's long accounts of their continued disobedience to senatorial orders can scarcely lack a kernel of truth. Rather, the quarrels of these men with the Senate seem to support the reliability of the division of opinion reported in chapter 47. Further, there is evidence that Aemilius Paullus exemplified some of the more rigid aspects of the *mos maiorum* and objected to the methods of these newer plebeian leaders. Polybius, who knew Paullus' son so intimately, is not likely to have been unaware of this. Such considerations certainly would not weaken the case for a Polybian origin of chapter 47, a passage which I should take (*pace* Bernardi) as confirmatory evidence of a division of senatorial opinion at this time.

But the fact remains that, whatever may be felt about the evidence for certain episodes, Livy's accounts of elections do not normally contain references to *partes*. Here all modern historians may unite in asking 'why should there be such references?', but for different reasons: some because they do not believe that such groups existed, others because they regard them as too unofficial and personal to receive formal notice by the annalists. The latter class resemble the astronomers whose assessment of their existing evidence leads them to believe that something is missing, as the planet Neptune before its discovery; the former apparently feel that no such links are missing. It is difficult to see how the question can be settled, even if Egypt or Herculaneum yield further papyri, since few authors are likely to have recorded precisely the sort of evidence we need. A complete text of Cato's speeches or Lucilius' satires would obviously illuminate further the *amicitiae* and *inimicitiae* of the nobles; but how far would they really take us behind the scenes? Nevertheless the critic who accepts as true the general picture of political life in the late Republic as it is envisaged by, for instance, R. Syme, and who yet remains sceptical about earlier groupings (e.g. Mrs. Henderson, who admits that 'within the post-Sullan nobility we can trace real groups'), such a critic may be asked to what extent he would expect to find the party intrigues of the nobles reflected in the later books of Livy, if these were ever recovered. If he would not expect to find them there, why should we expect to find them in the earlier decades? If Livy is unlikely to have revealed the *arcana imperii* of the late Republic, why should we demand more from him for the mid-Republic?

II

It may be useful to mention some of the more recent works (i.e. after 1954) that deal to a greater or lesser extent with the nature of Roman politics.

First, J. Hellegouarc'h, *Le Vocabulaire latin des relations et des partis politiques sous la République* (1963), which analyses in great detail the vocabulary of politics. This is a valuable study, but although Hellegouarc'h recognizes that the sources reflect a vocabulary that was developing to match the needs of the complex growth of practical politics, especially in the late Republic, his treatment tends to be formal and linguistic rather than linked closely to the vagaries of historical evolution. His first part deals with 'La notion de groupe politique'; after considering the concepts of *fides* and *amicitia*, he turns to the use of *factio* and *partes* (pp. 100–15) before going on to discuss terms of political agreement and disagreement. On *factio* he concludes:

> il nous apparaît que *factio* ne s'applique pas exclusivement à la *nobilitas*. Il s'agit d'une déformation de la notion d'*amicitia*; le mot désigne l'ensemble des gens unis par des liens divers et particulièrement par les liens de parenté ou de clientèle à celui qui en est le chef. A l'origine, il présente un sens surtout familial et social et ne comporte aucune nuance péjorative [p. 109].

On *partes* he concludes:

> les *partes* sont d'une façon générale des groupes beaucoup plus vastes que les *factiones*. Dans ces derniers, ce qui domine, c'est la notion de l'union étroite autour d'un chef ou d'un petit nombre de chefs, de personnes qu'ils utilisent à la défense de leurs intérêts personnels; le groupe désigné par *partes* exerce son activité dans le domaine de la politique générale du pays [p. 113] .... On constate d'ailleurs que cet emploi du pluriel [sc. *partes*] n'est sans doute apparu que tardivement dans l'histoire de la République et qu'il s'applique presque exclusivement à des groupes postérieurs à l'époque des Gracques [p. 114].

'*Amicitia* in the late Roman Republic' is the subject of a paper by P. A. Brunt (*Proc. Camb. Phil. Soc.* 1965, 1 ff.) in which he emphasizes that the use of *amicitia* does not of necessity imply any political relationship, but may often involve only private and personal affection. Few would cavil at this view, but at the same time it allows for a political usage. Indeed Brunt writes '*amici* might form a political faction', but he hastens to add that 'we must beware of assuming that it was necessarily long lasting' (p. 16). This view is also underlined in his criticism of D. Earl's *Tiberius Gracchus* (and of *Roman Politics*) in *Gnomon* (1965, 189 ff.) where he writes of the hypothesis that groups of families might remain fairly stable for generations, 'no such stable groups are explicitly attested at any period, and in the late Republic ... both major and lesser politicians are found in all sorts of combinations, changing almost from year to year, as differences of principle or personal advantage, gratitude or rancour might dictate . . . we should be ready to study the conduct of individuals rather than hypothetical groups [p. 190] . . . individuals must always be considered as such, and not simply as members of kinship groups' (p. 191). This viewpoint is maintained by Brunt (*Didaskalos*, 1971, 281) in reference to the remark by E. Gruen (*Roman Politics and the Criminal Courts, 149–78 B.C.* (1968) p. 3) that 'the workings of back-stage manœuvers would not usually find their way into the works of extant authors. It hardly follows that the Romans refrained from organizing for political purposes.' Brunt finds that 'this is unconvincing. Even today we might be ignorant of back-stage manœuvres in the Conservative and Labour party, but the existence of these parties is an overt fact. The whole theory under consideration presupposes that the existence of e.g. the Metellan faction was no less well known.' Whether Brunt is right or wrong in his general position, this particular criticism seems to me misdirected. The whole point is that the Conservative and Labour parties are well-known parts of the constitutional machinery of the country, while Roman factions were private groupings around an individual: this man, rather than his policy or his other supporters, was generally the first consideration of the voter.

From *amicitia* it is natural to turn to *clientela*, and here one of the most influential books of recent years is E. Badian's *Foreign Clientelae, 264–70 B.C.* (1958). It is only partly relevant here since, as its title indicates, it is not concerned primarily with the struggle for power within the Roman nobility, but it has emphasized once again the fundamental role played by the workings of the patron-client relationship in the whole of Roman life and society. How Badian regards the play of internal political tensions can be seen e.g. in his article on Caepio and Norbanus which is dedicated to Münzer and applies his methods to the decade 100–90 B.C. (*Historia*, 1957, reprinted in *Studies in Greek and Roman History* (1964), 34 ff.). His remarks on prosopography and *factio*, and on Münzer and Gelzer should be noted: they appear on p. 218 of his discussion of Gelzer's *Kleine Schriften* (3 vols. 1962–4) in *JRS*, 1967, 216–22. Incidentally, the value of having these papers by Gelzer collected together is immense, not least because they include his work on the nobility, which has now most usefully been translated into English by R. Seager, as *The Roman Nobility* (1969).

I gruppi politici romani nel III secolo a. C. (1962) by F. Cassola comprises a detailed study of the years 232–201 which is set in historical perspective by a very substantial review of the period 342–232; this is preceded by an introductory assessment of the nature of political life. His general view is that political groups existed, but were relatively ephemeral, since they consisted of the following of an outstanding

individual who was temporarily linked to others through the acceptance of a common policy, and such loyalties and obligations did not
normally outlast the leader: thus he would deny the existence of a
Claudian–Fulvian bloc or a Scipionic–Aemilian group. His interpretation, however, is determined and dominated by his belief that the
nobility was forced to respond to two pressure-groups which had
mutually contradictory interests: the small farmers, who were interested in the fertile lands of north Italy, and the commercial traders,
who looked to south Italy and overseas. But although trade was
undoubtedly increasing and some Roman nobles may have had more
concern with it than the traditional limitation of their interests to
agriculture might suggest, many historians would deny that commercial interests could seriously influence senatorial policy at this early
period. In general, no doubt, some individual senators can be identified
as supporters of an 'Italian' policy, others of a more expansionist
(though not necessarily commercial) policy, but it is more doubtful
whether the supporters of such ideas fell into two opposing groups
(the patrician Claudii, the Metelli, Cornelii Scipiones for the mer-
chants, and Flaminius, Claudius Marcellus, and the Fabii for the
contadini) as Cassola argues. (Incidentally the picture of Flaminius as
political ally of Q. Fabius Maximus scarcely rings true.) It may be
helpful to mention some of the reviews of Cassola's book: E. S.
Staveley, *JRS*, 1963, 182–7; J. Briscoe, *CR*, 1963, 321 ff.; A. Lippold,
Gnomon, 1963, 595 ff.; S. I. Oost, *Cl. Phil.* 1964, 55 ff.; E. T. Salmon,
AJP, 1965, 197 ff.; H. H. Scullard, *Riv. storica italiana*, 1963, 382 ff.

Much of the ground covered by Cassola is traversed by A. Lippold,
*Consules. Untersuchungen zur Geschichte des römischen Konsulats von
264 bis 201 v. Chr.* (1963). He lays emphasis on the individual rather
than on the family or group because he finds a basic change during the
third century: the old Roman aristocratic *Kollektivmoral* gives place
to a new individualistic *Adelsideal*; the individual leader had greater
opportunities for personal advancement and he seized them eagerly
in the pursuit of glory. Lippold therefore tries to establish the contribution made by leading magistrates to the formation of policy.
However, in general some may feel that any serious relaxation of
traditional attitudes belongs to a period after the latter half of the
third century. Lippold, who was not able to use Cassola's book until
his own work was finished, has added a dozen or so pages, indicating
points where he dissents from it. See E. S. Staveley's review in *JRS*,
1964, 197 ff.

In *Re Publica Amissa* (1966) Ch. Meier deals primarily with the last
decades of the Republic. For this period he goes further than many
in denying solid political groupings. He believes that senators had such
conflicting ties and claims that their small coteries were continually

forming and dissolving in kaleidoscopic style in reaction to the day-to-day problems that arose; personal ties (*necessitudines*) rather than programmes (*partium sensus*) are important; where traces of faction raise their heads, Meier would dismiss them as exceptions that prove the rule. (With the growth of Pompey's opposition, the scene changed somewhat when the Senate, in opposition, became more a party than a government.) Indeed Meier believes that 'Die Faktionsthese, die heute vor allem vom Ronald Syme, H. H. Scullard, Lily Ross Taylor und E. Badian vertreten wird, scheint damit für die späte Republik widerlegt zu sein' (p. 182; cf. pp. 187 ff.). His interpretation goes much further than the point of view of Brunt, who himself writes 'Meier has probably taken his contention too far, for instance in denying that *gentes* often combined with their *amici* to promote the election of one of their members or that candidates often acted in concert' (*JRS*, 1968, 231). Naturally Meier is not attracted to the idea of close family links in the field of politics in an earlier period, but (and perhaps here I may be allowed to quote a sentence from a letter of his to me) 'aber ich würde auch Ihren Kritikern nicht einfach zustimmen, die oft genug doch wohl das Kind mit dem Bade ausgeschüttet haben'. For two long reviews of this work see P. A. Brunt, *JRS*, 1968, 229 ff.; E. W. Gray, *CR*, 1969, 325 ff.

A very different point of view is taken by D. C. Earl in *Tiberius Gracchus. A Study in Politics* (1963), which examines the political basis of Tiberius Gracchus' power. This he finds in the backing of the Claudii Pulchri and Mucii Scaevolae, who with the Sempronii Gracchi formed a 'political group of the classic Roman type . . . a *factio* with bonds of *amicitia* strengthened by those of marriage', and led by Appius Cladius, the princeps senatus; they were 'favourably regarded by Fulvii, Calpurnii Pisones and, possibly, Manlii' (pp. 12, 14). This interpretation is supported by an analysis of earlier similar groupings, including a full assessment of the elder Tiberius Gracchus. Such an interpretation is, of course, rejected by those who do not believe in 'family politics' (cf. P. A. Brunt, *Gnomon*, 1965, 189 ff., reviewing Earl), and indeed Gracchus the social reformer is rather overshadowed by Gracchus the politician, but that he was supported by a powerful group of nobles can scarcely be denied.

A. E. Astin reveals what Roman politics mean to him, both in historical terms in his *Scipio Aemilianus* (1967), and in principle in an inaugural lecture entitled *Politics and Policies in the Roman Republic* (Belfast, 1968). In his book he reviews:

Scipio's friends and enemies, and such political groupings as can be discerned. Modern scholarship has made it abundantly clear that in the Roman governing class personal and political relationships were inextricably entangled, with the consequence that the consideration of 'family group' factions and of motivation by factional rivalry is indispensable to the understanding of Roman politics . . . it is necessary to bear in mind that there were other political considerations besides factional advantage . . . political groupings cannot be assumed always to have been completely separate entities, tempting though it often is to think of them as simple units [p. 80].

In particular, Astin believes that Aemilianus gave his support to Cato on the issue of war with Carthage in 150 (cf. *Latomus*, 1956, 176 ff.), examines the political activities between his African and Spanish campaigns, and has a most valuable survey of the Gracchan crisis. In regard to Tiberius' associates in this last episode he reaches much the same conclusions as Earl ('Earl . . . offers an assessment similar to the present one in several respects', p. 191, n. 1) and concludes that 'the cumulative evidence for division along factional lines . . . is quite considerable' (p. 199) without, however, endorsing Earl's view of previous patterns of similar groupings. In his lecture Astin has directed attention primarily to the period 200–167 B.C. He rehearses some of the criticisms that have been brought against the concept of 'family-based politics' (pp. 7 f.), and has 'no doubt that much of this attack is well-directed'; nevertheless he concludes that 'if political activity in the early second century was much more fluid, more complex and sometimes more individualistic than some of the prosopographers have allowed, I remain convinced that family solidarity was a major factor, and hence that the groupings and rivalries of families, as well as of individuals, were often a significant feature of the political scene.' He then goes on to argue that, although exceptions can be found, political groupings and struggles were generally unrelated to matters of policy: 'issues of policy need not have been, and in my opinion were not, primary factors in the determination of political groupings' (p. 17). Astin has also illustrated how a family could act as a political unit from the fortunes of the very minor Atinii, who flashed into a brief prominence between 197 and 186 (*Hommages à M. Renard* (1969), ii. 34 ff.).

Part of the period studied by Astin falls within the limits of E. S. Gruen's book, *Roman Politics and the Criminal Courts, 149–78 B.C.* (1968), in which factional politics are considered less in the light of electoral struggles than of political trials. Not that these two facets are mutually exclusive, but we lack Livy's detailed account of the elections after 167 and although Cato's numerous appearances in the law-courts emphasize that political trials were not infrequent in the earlier period, the courts took on a new aspect after the creation of the first permanent criminal court in 149. At the same time in Gruen's period violence increased, as did pressures from the urban plebs, the business classes, the peasants, and the army. He adopts a moderate position: 'The structure of Roman politics remains difficult to grasp. Although it does not consist of neat, insulated and consistent patterns, neither is it to be dismissed as a totally unsystematic, and ad hoc set of arrangements' (p. 4). Again, 'the prudent historian eschews dogmatism or slavish adherence to a scheme. Yet the foregoing discussion undeniably reveals a strikingly consistent structure of political alliances for the 140s and 130s . . . the factional structure of senatorial politics admits of no doubt' (p. 25). But new political issues 'cut sharply across old factional lines. The senatorial groups of the 140s and 130s were barely recognizable in 123. A more fluid and shifting structure was the order of the day' (p. 78); 'the rules were different but the game of factional politics continued to be played' (p. 95).

Two books handling more limited themes should be mentioned. In *Cato der Zensor* (1954) D. Kienast finds some five to ten loose groupings in the Senate, mostly very ephemeral (p. 138), and though Cato had friendly relations with the Marcelli, Licinii, and Aemilii, he was essentially politically independent (p. 135). Nor, incidentally, did he wage a systematic war against Scipio (p. 134). In *Regnum in Senatu. Das Wirken römischer Staatsmänner von 200 bis 191 v. Chr.* (1968), Ursula Schlag examines the first decade of the second century and there finds few traces of 'family politics': rather, the chief feature was *Individualismus*, not a 'bellum omnium contra omnes' (as H. Strasburger has characterized my viewpoint, *Gnomon*, 1955, 208), but a *bellum* between individuals who ruled the Senate like temporary monarchs. The book, which was begun before the appearance of Lippold's work, thus develops a similar interpretation for the next decade. The support of *amici* is so vague in the Livian tradition that they can only really be understood as an anonymous majority in the Senate; an exception to this is a small group which formed around Flamininus, but it had only a short existence and was the creation of Flamininus himself, not a family group (p. 14, and developed in ch. 2). This view of individualism is worked out especially in relation to two fields: the desire for triumphs and Eastern politics.

Four books deal with more strictly constitutional aspects. *Greek and Roman Voting and Elections* (1972) by E. S. Staveley is an important study of the mechanics of their activities, extremely relevant to the theme of this book, but he does not deal in any detail with the more personal political rivalries to attain glory through election to the higher magistracies. L. R. Taylor's *Roman Voting Assemblies* (1966) concentrated even more on the machinery. On the other hand in her basic study, *The Voting Districts of the Roman Republic* (1960), political repercussions are considered, especially in the final chapter where she discusses the purpose of those responsible for creating and settling the voting districts, a process in which the censors had a controlling influence: 'these were the men who controlled Roman politics, men of senatorial and particularly noble families, who to enter into the pacts that were the Roman substitute for the political party, had to be able to deliver the vote of their own tribes.' While the censors were frequently activated by the common good, nevertheless 'considerations of family advantage in the exercise of suffrage could never have been entirely absent. Sometimes it was undoubtedly the major factor in determining assignments to tribes' (p. 297). This is illustrated in particular by the attempt of Scipio Africanus to obtain power in rural tribes in 189–188 in an effort to re-establish his political fortunes: 'no other noble seems to have been as successful as Scipio in creating new divisions of tribes' (pp. 306 ff.). (This view of Scipio's manœuvring is rejected by E. Badian in a long review of this important book: *JRS*, 1962, 200 ff.). A not dissimilar view of the years 189–188 was put forward independently by J. Bleiken, *Das Volkstribunat der klassischen Republik* (1955) in a section (pp. 68 ff.) which shows how the Scipiones Africani made use of the tribunate. The book examines the tribunate in the period from 287 to 133 when the tribunes were less independent, and consequently their initiative might derive from the Senate or magistrates or even a coterie of nobles: thus they helped to build up the predominance of the nobility.

Reference may be made to a few further reviews of *Roman Politics*. A full-blooded rejection of factional politics comes from A. Heuss (*Historische Zeitschrift*, 1956, 593 ff.), a more moderate one from H. Strasburger (*Gnomon*, 1955, 207 ff.). Two which are more favourable to the idea of family groupings should be noted for their critical discussion of some points of detail: J. W. Swain, *Class. Phil.* 1953, 33 ff. and L. R. Taylor, *AJA*, 1952, 302 ff. The latter makes a different assessment of the relations of the Fabii, Manlii, and Fulvii, and believes that 'although at times, as for instance in the censorial elections of 189, candidates are clearly divided into three blocks, there is no ancient evidence for long-term divisions of the nobles into three groupings.'

In contrast to such shorter contributions a great work of reference requires grateful acknowledgement: T. R. S. Broughton's *Magistrates of the Roman Republic*, i (1951). If it had been published before this book was written, it would have made the task very much lighter. With this may be mentioned another great work, F. W. Walbank's *Historical Commentary on Polybius*, i– (1957–), which is partly relevant here, as also is A. J. Toynbee's *Hannibal's Legacy* (1965), especially vol. ii. It is very useful to have many of P. Fraccaro's papers collected in three volumes of *Opuscula* (1956–7); many of those on Cato and on the trials of the Scipios are to be found in volume i.

ADDENDUM. *Aufstieg und Niedergang der römischen Welt*, i (ed. H. Temporini, 1972) has just reched me. Note especially T. R. S. Broughton, 'Senate and Senators of Roman Republic: the Prosopographical Approach' (250 ff; with select bibliography, 261 ff.); E. Badian, 'Tiberius Gracchus and the Roman Revolution' (668 ff., esp. 674 ff. on prosopography); B. Twyman, 'The Metelli, Pompeius and Prosopography' (816 ff., esp. 827 ff. on the structure of politics). Two other items have just come to my notice: F. Serrao, 'I partiti politici nella repubblica romana' in *Ricerche storiche ed economiche in memoria di C. Barbagallo*, i (1970, ed. L. De Rosa), 503 ff., which deals more with larger groups of conflcting interests than with family groupings, but see esp, 510 ff. and 535 ff.; and secondly. A. Weische, *Studien zur politischen Sprache der römischen Republik* (1966) of which the first chapter on 'parties' is also more concerned with Populares and Optimates than struggles within the nobility.

III

Finally, I append a list of some other articles and works which are relevant to the theme of this book but do not, of course, constitute a complete bibliography of the work published during the last twenty years on the period involved. They are arranged roughly in the chronological order of their content.

G. V. Sumner	'Roman Policy in Spain before the Hannibalic War', *Harvard Stud. Class. Phil.*, 1967, 205 ff.
——	'Rome, Spain, and the Outbreak of the Second Punic War',*Latomus*,1972,469 ff.(refutes Errington's criticisms).
R. M. Errington	'Rome and Spain before the Second Punic War', *Latomus*, 1970, 26 ff.
A. E. Astin	'Saguntum and the Origins of the Second Punic War', *Latomus*, 1967, 577 ff.
Z. Yavetz	'The Policy of C. Flaminius and the Plebiscitum Claudianum', *Athenaeum*, 1962, 325 ff.
T. A. Dorey	'The Dictatorship of Minucius', *JRS*, 1955, 92 ff. (before 218 B.C.).
——	'The Elections of 216 B.C.', *Rhein. Mus.*, 1959, 249 ff.
J. E. A. Crake	'Roman Politics from 215 to 209 B.C.', *Phoenix*, 1963, 123 ff. (events not effected by groups).
H. H. Scullard	*Scipio Africanus: Soldier and Politician* (1970) (more general treatment than in earlier works).
F. W. Walbank	'The Scipionic Legend', *Proc. Camb. Phil. Soc.*, 1967, 54 ff.
T. A. Dorey	'Scipio Africanus as a Party Leader', *Klio*, 1961, 191 ff. (Scipio ineffective).
D. E. Hahm	'The Roman Nobility and Three Major Priesthoods 218–167 B.C.', *TAPA*, 1963, 73 ff. (age and status of men co-opted into the colleges).

J. Bleiken	'Kollisionen zwischen Sacrum und Publicum', *Hermes*, 1957, 446 ff. (cf. pp. 345 ff.).
A. H. McDonald	Review of G. Klaffenbach, *Der römisch-ätolische Bündnis-vertrag vom Jahre 212 v. Chr.*, *JRS*, 1956, 152 ff.
E. Badian	'Aetolica', *Latomus*, 1958, 197 ff.
——	'Sulla's Augurate', *Arethusa*, 1968, 26 ff. (changes in priesthoods in 210, 204, and 174).
J. P. V. D. Balsdon	'Rome and Macedon, 205–200 B.C.', *JRS*, 1954, 30 ff.
B. Ferro	*La origine della II guerra macedonica* (1960). Cf. A. H. McDonald, *JRS*, 1963, 187 ff.
F. Cassola	'La politica di Flaminino e gli Scipioni', *Labeo*, 1960, 105 ff. (two groups, but similar aims: hence collaboration on occasion).
J. P. V. D. Balsdon	'T. Quinctius Flamininus', *Phoenix*, 1967, 177 ff. (upholds F. against charges of dishonesty).
E. Badian	'The Family and Early Career of T. Quinctius Flamininus', *JRS*, 1971, 102 ff.
E. Badian	*Titus Quinctius Flamininus. Philhellenism and Realpolitik* (Univ. of Cincinnati, 1970. Two lectures. Rejects Balsdon's defence of F.).
——	'Rome and Antiochus the Great: a Study in Cold War', *Class. Phil.* 1959, 81 ff. (reprinted in *Studies in Greek and Roman History* (1964), 112 ff.).
R. M. Errington	*Philopoemen* (1969) (for Flamininus in Greece).
S. I. Oost	*Roman Policy in Epirus and Acarnania* (1954).
J. P. V. D. Balsdon	'L. Cornelius Scipio: a Salvage Operation, *Historia*, 1972, 224 ff.
I. Shatzman	'The Roman General's Authority over Booty', *Historia*, 1972, 177 ff.
A. E. Astin	'Professio in the Abortive Election of 184 B.C.', *Historia*, 1962, 252 ff.
J. Gagé	'La rogatio Petillia et le procès de P. Scipion', *Rev. phil.* 1953, 34 ff. (refuted by E. Siena, *Riv. fil.*, 1957, 175 ff.).
J. Briscoe	'Fulvii and Postumii', *Latomus*, 1968, 149 ff. (on view of Astin, *Scip. Aem.*, pp. 342 f. about these families during 181–168 B.C.).
——	'Q. Marcius Philippus and *Nova Sapientia*', *JRS*, 1964, 66 ff.
——	'Eastern Policy and Senatorial Politics, 168–146 B.C.', *Historia*, 1969, 49 ff.
R. L. Calvert	'M. Claudius Marcellus, cos. II, 155 B.C.', *Athenaeum*, 1961, 11 ff.
D. C. Earl	'The Calpurnii Pisones in the Second Century B.C.', *Athenaeum*, 1960, 283 ff. (relations with Fulvii and Claudii).
——	'M. Octavius, trib. pleb. 133 B.C.', *Latomus*, 1960, 157 ff. (earlier alliances of the Octavii).

L. R. Taylor	'Forerunners of the Gracchi', *JRS*, 1962, 19 ff.
H. H. Scullard	'Scipio Aemilianus and Roman Politics', *JRS*, 1960, 59 ff.
F. W. Walbank	'Political Morality and the Friends of Scipio Aemilianus', *JRS*, 1965, 1 ff.
W. Hoffmann	'Die römische Politik des 2. Jahrhunderts und das Ende Karthagos', *Historia*, 1960, 309 ff.

C

INTRODUCTION

IN England in the eighteenth century, when the aristocracy was paramount, commoners seldom reached the Cabinet, but in the first half of the next century there was this advance: 'it was not necessary to be a peer in order to be a cabinet minister, but birth and connexion were almost indispensable to Cabinet rank',[1] and Sir Robert Peel could exclaim in 1835, 'Damn the Whigs, they are all cousins!' In like manner at Rome the age when the patricians monopolized the highest offices of the State gradually passed, but only to be followed by a period when a mixed patricio-plebeian governing class maintained a traditional exclusiveness and closed its ranks against all who lacked birth or connexion. Many a Roman, whom birth had set outside the exclusive circle of *nobiles* and who yet aspired to high office early in the second century B.C., must have been enraged and discouraged by a sentiment similar to that expressed by Sir R. Peel.

The Roman aristocracy, however, which formally wielded its political power through the magistracies and Senate and presented a formidable aspect to the would-be intruder, was often far from harmonious in its internal policies and was torn by dissensions which arose between both individuals and groups. But such discord did not give rise to a system of party politics as understood in modern parliamentary democracies. Political life at Rome was not organized on a basis of parties which proclaimed definite programmes. Indeed, there was less need for such a system in a Republic where every citizen had the right to record a personal vote on all important measures, and where the Senate was not elected directly by the People. It is true that the magistrates from whom the Senate was normally recruited were elected by the People, but when seeking office they did not appeal to the electorate on party lines as government or opposition candidates. There was no party organization, no party ticket. Rather, 'men who stood for high office announced their own programmes and gathered for the occasion such social or economic groups to their support as they could'.[2] 'The Roman politician had to be the leader of a faction',[3] and this faction had to be organized by the candidate, or by the great noble who might wish to introduce him to public life.[4]

---

[1] O. F. Christie, *The Transition from Aristocracy, 1832–1867*, p. 114.

[2] Tenney Frank, *Proc. Brit. Acad.* 1932, 123.

[3] R. Syme, *The Roman Revolution*, 16.

[4] For a discussion of the meaning of the words *factio* and *partes* see Lily R. Taylor, *Party Politics in the Age of Caesar*, 8 ff., who also compares a Roman election campaign, not with a Presidential election, but with the preparatory manœuvring at the national nominating convention within the Democratic or Republican party: 'the groups that form about candidates for the nomination emphasize personalities and make few pretenses of

The primary support on which a rising politician depended for electoral success was the influence of his family or clan. If he could not always count on the help of his whole *gens* because of internal political divisions (e.g. a Cornelius Lentulus might not always support a Cornelius Scipio, while a plebeian Claudius Marcellus might not be favoured by the patrician branches of the Claudian *gens*), he would at any rate expect the loyal backing of his sub-*gens*. Then marriage-connexions might secure him help from other families: the nobles were often closely linked by intermarriage, probably more intimately than a superficial glance at the surviving records suggests, because lack of information about the women of the noble families often precludes a detailed study of the links.[1] Marriages of political convenience, which are more obvious during the last century of the Republic, are unlikely to have been confined to that period alone. Thus, the influence of the clans, whose ramifications were widespread and often evade detection, would be mustered in support of junior members seeking political careers and of senior members aiming at the highest offices.

Where family connexion failed, personal obligation might impose support. Patronage extended its tentacles widely, reaching far beyond a noble's personal dependents. In early days a patrician family might strengthen its position by backing the interests of a struggling plebeian house, or by championing the cause of a family which had recently settled in Rome from another part of Italy. A relationship not unlike that of patron and client would thus be established between some of the greater and lesser houses and would tend to be transmitted to later generations. As Roman influence spread throughout the Mediterranean world and life became more highly organized, political support might be sought by a successful general from his soldiers. Long before the time when the shadow of the legions darkened political life and when armies provided the weapon by which an aspiring politician cut down his rivals, a military leader who had given his troops victory and spoils might well hope to engage their votes after their return to civilian life. Nor will a landed aristocracy always have disdained help from successful business men or groups of financiers, while the able lawyer would have an influential following of clients who might seek to repay help received in the courts by supporting the political interests of their advocate. In the provinces also the successful soldier, governor, or financier would create a body of men devoted to his interests.

providing programs, and the final result depends largely on the strength of the friends whose support each of the candidates can muster' (p. 8).

[1] Compare the complaint of Asconius (p. 10 Clark): 'socrus Pisonis quae fuerit invenire non potui, videlicet quod auctores rerum non perinde in domibus ac familiis feminarum, nisi illustrium, ac virorum nomina tradiderunt.'

Above all, individuals and families might unite for mutual political benefit. 'Politicians formed compacts. Amicitia was a weapon of politics, not a sentiment based on congeniality.'[1] A classic example of such political friendships is seen in the First Triumvirate of Caesar, Pompey, and Crassus, who, by agreeing to work together in order to further their own political ambitions, sounded the death-knell of the Roman Republic. As Quintus Cicero reminded his brother in the *Handbook of Electioneering* which he wrote for the guidance of a *novus homo*: 'in ipsa petitione amicitiae permultae ac perutiles comparabantur', and again 'omnes centurias multis et variis amicitiis cura ut confirmatas habeas'.[2] In English public life political differences and personal relationships are usually regarded as separate departments of life; politicians who violently attack one another in the House of Commons may yet retain cordial personal friendships. At Rome it was often otherwise.

It is this far-reaching nexus of personal and family relationships and obligations that underlies the basis of Roman public life, a fact which the nobles themselves may have sought to obscure. Its form naturally will have varied at different periods of Rome's history. Thus in early days the tie of the clan was probably the predominant factor: the head of a patrician *gens* wielded immense authority and various families would group themselves around such leading patrician clans as the Fabii, Aemilii, and Claudii. During the last century of the Republic when personal ambitions rocked the State to its foundations, political organization became more complex and blatant, and *principes* in pursuit of power and glory were able to build up 'parties' of followers, devoted to a personal leader, on a hitherto unprecedented scale. Between these extremes of the solidarity of the *gens* and the career-making of individuals one might expect to find during the mid-Republic groups which were still based upon a *gens* and associated *gentes* but which at times might be more influenced by the personality of a leader whose *auctoritas* prevailed beyond his *gens*.

However that may be, no fundamental change in the very nature of political life should be postulated as between the late and mid-Republic. The deterioration of public morals and political stability betokened no chemical metathesis in the body politic: wealth and its misuse merely provided a sharper weapon in the political armoury of the nobility. In the century before the Gracchi the steadiness and prestige of the Senate, a more widespread sense of responsibility to

---

[1] R. Syme, *RR*, 12. Cf. W. Kroll (*Die Kultur der Ciceronischen Zeit*, i, ch. 2, esp. pp. 55 ff.), who shows that *amicitia* in Cicero's writings virtually meant political co-operation. On the conventional obligations arising from *amicitia*, based on *fides*, see F. Schulz, *Principles of Roman Law*, 233 ff.

[2] *De pet. cons.* 25, 29. Later (§ 53) he warns Marcus against proclaiming a programme: 'nec tamen in petendo res publica capessenda est neque in senatu neque in contione.'

the State, and a tendency of successful generals to seek to outshine their peers rather than to challenge the government, all combined to limit the scale on which factional strife could flourish. But although lack of contemporary documents precludes so clear a vision of political life in this period as can be gained for the later Republic, the bitter personal and factional struggles which are recorded by Livy and other writers show that it was dominated by keen contests within the aristocracy whose members built up their power on the basis of family, friendship, and obligation.

These factional quarrels caused dissensions primarily within the nobility rather than within the State as a whole, and deeper cleavages were long prevented by the stolid common sense of the Roman from developing into the bitter extremes of factional warfare from which Greek cities so often suffered. But the People were not unaffected. True, the Roman plebs, unlike the ordinary Greek commonalty, was not politically-minded since normally it preferred to leave the responsibility of public affairs to relatively few leaders;[1] and because of this lack of keen personal participation Rome never became a democracy, although in theory the constitution was democratic. But this does not mean that ordinary Romans took no interest in the factional struggles of the nobles, to whom most of them were bound by ties of patronage or self-interest. Meeting in their Assembly, many ordinary citizens, who had neither desire nor opportunity to seek office themselves, will have participated with keenness in the election of the noble lords over whom they were constitutionally Sovereign, but to whose interests they were, in fact, subservient.

Since in the course of Rome's history groups tended to form around individuals and families, the main problem is to attempt to determine the extent of such groupings and the effect they had on public life.[2] The evidence, which shows that certain families worked together at different periods, is partly direct, such as Livy's descriptions of the political struggles which accompanied elections, and partly indirect. When it is found that certain groups of names tend to recur in the lists of magistrates, this is unlikely always to be due to chance. The magistrate who presided at elections could often exert considerable influence upon them. It must not of course be assumed that if *A* was

---

[1] Private citizens had no right of political initiative; the People could meet and act constitutionally only with magisterial co-operation. Before 186 B.C. there may have been few restrictions on the right of association (see P. W. Duff, *Personality in Roman Private Law*, 106), but private clubs with political aims are not known before the last century of the Republic; had they appeared, they could have been disbanded by magistrates or Senate.

[2] In his pioneer work F. Münzer has analysed the interrelationships of the chief families throughout the Republican period, but he has discussed general historical events only when they throw light on family relationships. See *Römische Adelsparteien und Adelsfamilien* (1920) and his numerous prosopographical articles in *PW*.

elected under the presidency of *B*, the latter was necessarily favourably disposed to the former on personal or political grounds. But when it is found that on many occasions members of *A*'s *gens* were elected under the presidency of members of *B*'s *gens*, a presumption is created that there may have been some understanding between the two *gentes* and that all the private machinery of family connexion, friendship, and obligation was put into motion. By supplementing the literary records with evidence of this type it is possible to discern something of the political co-operation of various families at different periods.

Where the evidence is slender, varying estimates of the importance of 'family politics' naturally have been reached, and some contradictory conclusions have led some critics to dismiss their influence as nugatory. Two examples may illustrate the point. Flamininus, for instance, has been recognized as both the political supporter and opponent of the Scipios.[1] Through this chink in the armour of the champions of family politics an attempt has been made to deliver a mortal blow at the whole theory.[2] But such criticism may be misdirected, since in the example quoted one of the two conclusions or the presupposition of a static relationship between Flamininus and Scipio may be wrong. Again, the same critic holds up to doubt a theory of which the implication is that Roman nobles could care more for group rivalries than for the safety of the State: while Hannibal was at the gates of Rome, the Fabii could endanger the city's existence by their quarrel with the Fulvians and Claudians, while Scipio availed himself of the discord to climb to power with the help of a middle group.[3] This theory may be correct or false, but its rejection demands more detailed criticism than the general assumption that external danger must inevitably promote internal unity and that the Roman nobility was immune from selfish policies. The fact that the Senate and People could remain at variance in the critical days after the disaster at Lake Trasimene should suggest a more cautious approach: if Rome was a house divided against itself even in time of national crisis, was the Senate never similarly divided?

The effect of factional interests on public policy on occasion may have been exaggerated,[4] but it is noteworthy that the warnings which have been issued against this danger implicitly emphasize the existence of group politics. For instance, it has been said that 'the Senate, not the consuls, was the head of the State, so that the group to which the consuls belonged was not by virtue of that fact in a position to dictate

[1] See p. 97.   [2] See G. De Sanctis, *Riv. Fil.* 1936, 193 ff.

[3] For this thesis see W. Schur, *Scipio Africanus und die Begründung der römischen Weltherrschaft.*

[4] For instance by W. Schur, op. cit. Building on the foundations laid by Münzer, he has erected an elaborate structure of relationships and rivalries in the light of which he interprets the main political history during the lifetime of Scipio Africanus.

the policy of the State. Sometimes . . . a group would not have strong men eligible for election to office; it does not follow that during that period the group would have no influence.'[1] This is a wise reminder that senatorial policy could not be shaped by the annual executive alone and that groups without leaders in office might still be powerful, but it emphasizes rather than denies the existence of such groups. Again, 'allegiance to the family party was subordinate to allegiance to the State'. This, no doubt, was often true, but it is well to remember how difficult it is for individuals or groups to take a purely objective view of the needs of the State which they would normally regard as best served by the advancement of the policies and interests which they themselves represented. Another critic who minimizes the importance of party politics during the Hannibalic War and believes that 'the demand for competent leadership which the war created' offers a better explanation of the political scene, is nevertheless forced to the conclusion that, despite certain alleged fallacies in Schur's method, 'factional politics in some form undoubtedly existed at Rome during the Second Punic War' and 'from 218 to 201 the Fabii, Claudii and Cornelii dominated the political scene at Rome and other leading families seem to have aligned themselves with them as occasion arose'.[2]

These divergent view-points indicate the thorniness of the question, but even a critic of family politics like De Sanctis, who regards Schur's views as a *reductio ad absurdum* of Münzer's evidence, freely admits that family relationships could affect elections and that they have been studied accurately by Münzer. He may write, 'there is need to guard against considering these parties, or rather factions or coteries, in too rigid and mechanical a fashion: we are dealing with groups which constantly formed and dissolved, only to reappear in different forms',[3] but this warning is at the same time a candid recognition of the existence of these groups.

Thus we are faced with the unavoidable fact that groups did form. The problem is to supply answers to such questions as: what families can be shown to have supported others? how long in each case did this support endure? did such groups tend to become traditional or were they continually forming and dissolving? what effect did each group exercise on public life? did certain policies for either home or foreign affairs tend to be associated with certain groups? was the bond that held them together mainly personal or due to a common political outlook? how far did these groups really divide the Senate? was there a steady middle bloc in the Senate which made the interplay of group rivalries relatively superficial, or did the cleavages go deep and threaten the unity of the oligarchy—in a word, were the Senate and

[1] R. M. Haywood, *Scipio*, 45.   [2] Miss M. L. Patterson, *TAPA*, 1942, 320, 340.
[3] *Riv. Fil.* 1937, 84.

the elections controlled by an inner ring of families, and if so, who were they and what were their mutual relations?

It is not intended here to pass under review the nobility during the period of Rome's early growth, but rather to consider the evidence from the time of the Hannibalic War onwards and by keeping the general nature of the problem in mind to try to discover whether answers to any of these questions suggest themselves. First, however, it will be well to glance at the composition of the Roman nobility and to examine the methods by which it was able to exercise its power.

I

THE DOMINATION OF THE NOBLES

1. *The* Gentes *and* Nobles

THE *gens*, with its subdivision into *familiae*, was essentially a social group outside the constitutional machinery of the State, but nevertheless it formed the basis on which political life was organized. The *gentes* did not establish political gatherings whose resolutions were designed to bind the whole community, but they did meet to take corporate action in connexion with guardianships, property, and inheritance, and for common worship and sacrifice. Since their activities were private rather than public, they appointed no formal leaders, but the *paterfamilias* of the most powerful family would be the natural leader of his *gens*. Within his own family the *paterfamilias* exercised complete *potestas*, including even the *ius vitae necisque*,[1] but he was obliged by the *mos maiorum* to consult a council of relatives and friends (*consilium domesticum*) before taking any drastic action.[2] Thus representatives of *familiae* and *gentes* met together on occasion to transact their private business, and they would certainly also meet less formally to discuss the political advancement of their members; much of the electioneering tactics of the nobility must have been planned in family or gentile conclaves.[3]

When a *paterfamilias* died, each hitherto dependent son, freed from the *patria potestas*, established a family of his own, and none of these resultant families was theoretically more important than the others, since rights of primogeniture were not known, but it may be suspected that, in practice, elder sons had slightly more *auctoritas* if only because in normal circumstances they would have held higher magistracies than their younger brothers. Thus if a man gained recognition as the outstanding leader of his *gens*, this authority would tend to pass from eldest son to eldest son. If the incapacity, early death, or lack of age of an eldest son caused a break in the succession, a younger son or

---

[1] This early power was circumscribed by no legal limitation throughout Republican history. As late as *c.* 220 B.C. M. Fabius Buteo put his son to death for theft, while in 63 B.C. A. Fulvius Nobilior killed his son for a public crime, participation in the Catilinarian conspiracy (Oros. iv. 13; Sall. *Cat.* 39).

[2] For instance, in 307 B.C. the censors degraded a senator who had divorced his wife 'nullo amicorum in consilio adhibito' (Val. Max. ii. 9. 2).

[3] The famous family council of Brutus, Cassius, Cicero, Porcia, Servilia, and Tertulla (Cic. *Ad Att.* xv. 11) had its counterpart in earlier centuries. The relations of L. Scipio, an unworthy son of Africanus and praetor in 174, tried to hinder his public career (Val. Max. iii. 5. 1); cf. below, p. 192.

elder cousin might fill the breach, but the leadership would tend to revert to the descendants of the original house.[1]

The patrician *gentes* formed two groups (*maiores* and *minores*), the former consisting of the Aemilii, Claudii, Cornelii, Fabii, Valerii, and possibly the Manlii.[2] While the fortunes of other *gentes* rose and fell, these five or six patrician clans, often working closely with plebeian *gentes*, exercised a predominating influence until well into the second century, and at the same time struggled among themselves for outstanding power and position.

During the fifth century patrician control was unshaken and some families wielded almost regal power. Later generations believed that the Fabii held seven successive consulships (485–479 B.C.) and thus gained a position in the State which was a pale reflection of the recent rule of the Tarquins. Further, a relatively small number of the patrician *gentes* managed to secure for themselves a large proportion of the curule magistracies.[3] This exclusive patrician government, however, gradually weakened under plebeian pressure, and a decline in the number of patrician families as well as in their political influence can be traced in the fourth century, together with a corresponding increase in the number of plebeian families which gained curule magistracies.[4] In the third century the process was accelerated;[5] and by the second the plebeian element predominated and acquired a majority not only in the magistracies as a whole but even in the curule offices.[6] Thus

---

[1] On leadership within the Fabian *gens* see below, ch. ii.

[2] Mommsen (*Röm. Forsch.* i. 258; *Staatsr.* iii. 31, 868; *Dr. publ.* VI. i. 33, VII. 41) includes the Manlii, but Münzer (*RA*, 99) argues that the Manlii came nearest in rank, but were not equal to the five chief houses. Other *gentes*, as the Sulpicii, stood a little below them.

[3] During the fifth century the 195 or so known curule magistrates came from 53 *gentes*, some 61 other *gentes* being represented among the non-curule magistrates. But of these 195 curule magistrates 79 were members of only 7 *gentes* (the Valerii, Verginii, Servilii, Fabii, Cornelii, Furii, and Iulii). See Willems, *Sénat.* i. 69 ff. The figures derive from the Fasti which, although notoriously unreliable for the fifth century, undoubtedly contain a genuine nucleus.

[4] About 110 patrician curule magistrates were drawn from 29 *gentes*; in other words, some 24 *gentes* ceased to have curule members in the Senate. Ten of these 29 *gentes* each supplied 5 or more magistrates, the other 19 *gentes* being represented by only 1 to 3 each. The plebeian families in this century gained some 43 curule magistrates drawn from 28 *gentes*.

[5] From 312 to 216 B.C. the number of patrician *gentes* supplying curule magistrates dropped from 29 to 14; these furnished 73 such officers, one *gens* alone (the Cornelian) supplying 16, while 3 other *gentes* (Fabii, Valerii, and Aemilii) each supplied 9. The plebeians who reached curule office numbered 75 and were drawn from 36 *gentes*. In this period, therefore, of the 148 known curule senators 73 patricians belonged to 15 *gentes* and 75 plebeians to 36 *gentes*.

[6] It is estimated that in 179 B.C. the Senate contained 88 patricians (63 being of curule rank) and 216 plebeians (110 of curule status). The 88 patrician senators derived from 17 *gentes*, the Cornelian alone furnishing 23 senators (16 of these held curule office); of the other patrician *gentes* the Claudii supplied 8 curule magistrates, the Aemilii, Fabii, Manlii, and Valerii 6 each.

a gradual transformation took place in the composition of the Senate and higher magistracies, and the old patrician aristocracy was replaced by a newer patricio-plebeian governing caste. At the same time, although the People had gained such constitutional power by 287 B.C. that the development of a full democracy might seem to be imminent, the government nevertheless remained in the hands of an oligarchy.

The successful blending of these two elements was due in some cases to the sharing of a similar social background, in others to an increasing identity of political and economic interest. In early days members of the aristocracies of neighbouring towns had swelled the ranks of the governing class at Rome. Apart from the Etruscan Tarquinii, the Iulii and Servilii are said to have come to Rome from Alba Longa; the Claudii, probably the Valerii and Veturii, and perhaps the Fabii were of Sabine origin. Later many other families from Latium and central Italy, some perhaps from Etruria and Campania also, came to Rome where their interests were often guarded and promoted by patrician families who wished to strengthen their own political influence and the State as a whole.[1] Some of these immigrant plebeians, helped by patrician patronage or by their own achievements in war, established families which gradually gained an influence and dignity second only to that of the great patrician houses. Other families of newcomers exerted their greatest influence in the first generation: men like Ti. Coruncanius from Tusculum (the first plebeian Pontifex Maximus and consul in 280) and M'. Curius Dentatus (perhaps a Sabine, who defeated Pyrrhus and was four times consul) were not succeeded in the consulship by their sons; they were received by the Roman nobility for their individual worth and a similar patronage was not extended to any descendants.

Although the older and newer elements soon blended into a fresh caste, the resultant aristocracy was not a homogeneous body with equal privilege for all: within was an inner circle of *nobiles*. In the Ciceronian age *nobilitas* connoted men or their descendants who had reached the consulship,[2] but in the third and early second centuries the nobility may have comprised the descendants of all curule magis-

---

[1] Willems, *Sénat*. i. 179 ff. The Fulvii and Iuventii came from Tusculum, which according to Cicero (*Pro Plancio*, 19) supplied more consular families than any other *municipium*. Q. Anicius (aedile of 304 B.C.) came from Praeneste. The Licinii (or Lecne) and perhaps the Calpurnii were of Etruscan origin. The Marcii may have come from S. Latium, the Otacilii from Beneventum, the Plautii perhaps from Tibur, the Atilii from Campania. Münzer (*RA*, 44 ff., 56 ff.) argues for these last two cases, which are, however, questioned by K. J. Beloch (*Röm. Gesch.* 338 f.), followed by H. Stuart Jones (*CAH*, vii. 548–9).

[2] This is the view of M. Gelzer (*Die Nobilität der römischen Republik*, 21 ff.) which is accepted by R. Syme (*RR*, 10) and by A. Afzelius (*Class. et Med.* 1938, 40 ff.). Thus L. Licinius Murena (*cos.* 62) could be charged with *novitas generis* though members of his family had been praetors for three generations.

trates; the distinction between consular and praetorian families arose slowly, and it is doubtful whether before 227 B.C. any praetor came from a non-consular family.[1] Once the patricio-plebeian aristocracy had established its ascendancy, members of unennobled families seldom climbed to highest office. Outstanding personal qualities might carry an outsider as far as the quaestorship or sometimes to the praetorship, but without the support of one or more of the noble families the intruder seldom reached the consulship; when he succeeded, or perhaps at first in looser terminology, when he gained any curule office, he was known as a *novus homo* and became the *auctor* or *princeps nobilitatis*, ennobling his house for ever.

Between 284 and 254 B.C. nine new families won the consulship, though it is not known how many of them, if any, had never held a praetorship; in the next thirty years only six succeeded and from 223 to 195 B.C., five. Sixteen of the 108 consuls between 200 and 146 B.C. were members of *gentes* whose names had not previously appeared in the Fasti, but only four of these are known to have been from families which had never held curule office.[2] Further, while the 200 consulships from 232 to 133 B.C. were shared by 58 families, 159 of these consuls came from only 26 of the families, and 99, nearly half the total, came from only 10.[3]

The same families predominated in the tenure of the praetorship, although this office was not guarded quite so closely against newcomers; 151 of the 262 praetors known between 218 and 167 B.C. came from 20 families.[4] Although a greater number of unennobled families would naturally be represented in the lower magistracies, any member of the Cornelian, Claudian, or Fulvian *gens* who was not incapacitated by health or outstanding inefficiency, could reasonably

---

[1] See A. Afzelius, 'Zur Definition der römischen Nobilität vor der Zeit Ciceros', *Class. et Med.* 1945, 150, esp. 184 ff. He argues that in early times the *nobiles* were those who had the *ius imaginum* (on this see below, p. 252) by which they became 'known' (*nobilis* or *gnobilis* is derived from the same root as *noscere*) to a wider public. He would date the change by which descendants of consuls began to rank as *nobiles* and those of praetors did not to the time of Ti. Gracchus, when the Optimate party was taking shape under pressure from the Populares and the parties within the nobility played a lesser role (op. cit. 198 ff.).

[2] Cato (195), Acilius Glabrio (191), Cn. Octavius (165), and L. Mummius (146).

[3] De Sanctis, IV. i. 487. The consulships were divided among the following *gentes*: Patrician: Cornelii, 23; Aemilii, 11; Fabii, 9; Postumii, 9; Valerii, 7; Claudii, 7; Manlii, 6; Servilii, 5; Sulpicii, 4; Quinctii, 4; i.e. 10 *gentes* holding 85 consulships out of 92. Plebeian: Fulvii, 10; Claudii Marcelli, 9; Sempronii, 8; Iunii, Atilii, Marcii, Calpurnii, Popillii, Livii, Licinii, Aelii, 4 each; Flaminii, Hostilii, Minucii, Caecilii, Aurelii, 3 each; i.e. 16 *gentes* holding 74 consulships out of 108 (on 8 occasions both consuls were plebeians). A. Afzelius (*Class. et Med.* 1945, 188 f.) reckons that in 227 B.C. the nobility comprised some 20 patrician and 26 plebeian families, or if the families from which the curule aediles derived are included, some 52 families in all.

[4] Patrician: Cornelii, 24; Claudii, 15; Manlii, 11; Valerii, 9; Fabii, 8; Aemilii, 7; Postumii, 6; Furii, 6; Quinctii, 4; Sulpicii, 4. Plebeian: Fulvii, 11; Sempronii, 7; Atilii, 7; Licinii, 6; Terentii, 5; Iunii, 5; Claudii Marcelli, 4; Hostilii, 4; Porcii, 4; and Baebii, 4.

anticipate reaching at least the praetorship in the second century. Outsiders could only exceptionally attain to a magistracy such as would enable them to exercise much influence on public policy. Effective control rested in the hands of some twenty or less families, who commanded armies, governed the provinces, and by guiding senatorial policy shaped the destiny of Rome and the world. Of them Sallust wrote 'omnis gratia, potentia, honos, divitiae apud illos sunt aut ubi illi volunt', and of their era, 'regna, provinciae, leges, iura, iudicia, bella atque paces, postremo divina et humana omnia penes paucos erant'.[1]

11. *Patronage and Clientship*

A wide basis for the political influence of the nobility was provided by their clients, a fundamental element in Roman life.[2] In Rome's early days the man who lacked the protection of his own family could not safeguard his life or property without the legal assistance of a patron. Thus, the manumitted slave, the son who broke away from his family, the stranger whom trade had attracted,[3] or even the poor citizen who had fallen under the domination of an oppressive noble might turn to an aristocratic patron who would grant protection and perhaps land for occupation. In return the client, who stood in a filial relationship towards his patron, rendered certain services, which were customary but not enforceable at law.

Although with the creation of the tribunate constitutional protection against ill-usage developed, the institution of patronage survived in various ways. Freedmen, for instance, were bound to their former masters by both specific obligations and a general *obsequium*, while freemen could still voluntarily become clients (*se commendare in fidem alicuius*). Though religious or legal ties were lacking, patron and client remained bound by strong reciprocal duties which might become

---

[1] Sall. *Cat.* 20. 8; *Iug.* 31. 20. True, Sallust dates the period when 'coepere nobilitas dignitatem, populus libertatem in lubidinem vortere', to the Gracchan revolution and its consequences, and he can write 'ante Carthaginem deletam populus et senatus Romanus placide modesteque inter se rem publicam tractabant' (*Iug.* 41. 2); but he has idealized the past in contrast with the mob-politics of his own lifetime. He rightly stresses the lack of serious friction between Senate and People, but if he had attended meetings of the Senate *c.* 170 B.C., he might not have laid such emphasis on *modestia* and have glossed over the internal disputes so lightly. His observations on the power of the oligarchy can well be applied to the earlier part of the second century.

[2] 'Le patronage explique qu'au milieu des lois d'égalité, les grandes familles aient toujours gardé le pouvoir. . . . La clientèle n'était pas dans les lois . . . mais elle régnait dans la société' (Fustel de Coulanges, *Hist. des instit. pol. de l'anc. France: les origines du système féodal*[5], 224).

[3] On the large-scale immigration to Rome of Italian and foreign workers during the sixth century and the political problems which their settlement created see H. Last, *JRS*, 1945, 33 ff. If the primary result of the Servian reforms was to extend Roman citizenship to these settlers, a large body of humble citizens was thereby created who would look to various influential patrons for the furtherance of their interests.

hereditary. *Patrocinium* and *clientela* are words closely bound up with the conception of *fides, praesidium, amicitia,* and *hospitium.*[1] Cato stressed the high duty that a man owed to his clients, a duty which Aulus Gellius placed second only to that owing to *parentes* and *pupilli.*[2] The forms which this relationship assumed would depend largely upon the social and economic status of the client: the poor client might need help in cash or land, others would seek protection in the law courts, and the more successful and ambitious might look for assistance in seeking a political career at Rome. These three main forms of patronage, in return for which the votes of the client would be given for his patron, may be briefly considered.

First, economic help. The senatorial nobility formed a landed aristocracy and must have had some free men working on their estates as tenants at will, whose interests would be bound up with their own. The size of their estates at different periods and consequently the amount of free labour they employed are unfortunately obscure. The nature of land-tenure in early Rome is a notoriously vexed question, but it can hardly be doubted that, while the holding of the average citizen was meagre, some of the leading families had secured sizeable estates; the necessity for a limiting clause in the section of the Licinian-Sextian Rogations which deals with land-tenure suggests that these estates were increasing in the mid-fourth century. But the legends which glorify Rome's early farmer-heroes, such as Cincinnatus, Curius Dentatus, and C. Fabricius, represent them as owners of small plots, and these men, while not members of the *gentes maiores,* were no doubt typical of a large class. In the days of the First Punic War M. Atilius Regulus owned a farm of seven *iugera* of poor soil in an unhealthy district, but against him may be placed L. Postumius Megillus (*cos.* III in 291) who scandalously forced 2,000 of his soldiers to work on his own estate.[3] Thus even in the third century many nobles must have had large and increasing estates which enabled them to extend the range of their patronage by offers of employment, or even perhaps by grants of land. As the *latifundia* increased in number and size early in the second century, so more labour would be required and a greater number of clients could be aided, although against this must be set the partial supersession of tillage by grazing and the gradual ousting of free by slave labour. Cato's *De Agri Cultura,* however, well illustrates the opportunities and need for contract-work and extra labour on a mixed farm.

---

[1] See the examples quoted by M. Gelzer, *Nobilität,* p. 52, n. 7 (e.g. Aul. Gell. v. 13. 3; Cic. *Ad fam.* vii. 17. 2; *Pro Rosc. Am.* 106).

[2] Frg. 190 M, see p. 272. Gellius (v. 13. 2) advances this decreasing scale: *parentes, pupilli, clientes, hospites, cognati,* and *adfines.*

[3] See Columella, 1. 4. 2, Pliny, *NH,* xvii. 27–8, Val. Max. iv. 4. 6 for Regulus; Dion. Hal. xvii (xviii) 4. 3 for Postumius.

Despite the paucity of direct evidence, it is extremely probable that the Roman nobles on occasion also helped the small townsfolk and that many artisans and shopkeepers became their clients; the need to dispose of the agricultural produce of their estates would bring them into contact with at least one class of small trader. Such help, if it ever took the form of financial aid, involves the question of the sources of wealth. Apart from the main source of income from their lands, the nobles in theory had little opportunity for enriching themselves, since they were debarred from industry by tradition and from overseas trade by law (*lex Claudia* of 218). But a senator could get round this law by allowing his freedmen to trade for him or by making loans on bottomry, so that his commercial interests, though not advertised, may not always have been negligible,[1] a fact suggested by the need to pass the *lex Claudia*; nor may he have disdained indirect interest in the small industry of his day. Then there was war, which added to the financial resources of the patron and at the same time formed a more open way of winning favour and gaining help. Even before the Second Punic War windfalls from war-booty had been large.[2] The bulk of these funds would be paid into the Roman Treasury, but generals had considerable discretionary powers to distribute the movable part of the booty to their men; officers received their share and although generals were expected to use their portion for religious dedications or public Games, doubtless some of it found its way into their own pockets.[3] A further form of enrichment developed in the second century when States made honorary gifts of golden crowns to Roman generals in an attempt to win their pity and patronage. Thus, by augmenting from war the incomes which they derived from their landed estates, noble patrons might well be able to help needy clients and extend the range of their patronage.

If, therefore, economic factors played a not unimportant, though unadvertised, role in the working of patronage, it may be asked what direct influence the nobles could exert upon the commercial classes, both upon the rich Equites and through them upon the votes of many humbler men bound to them by economic ties. This question gains increasing importance, since after the Second Punic War, in proportion as opportunities for economic exploitation of an expanding em-

---

[1] For Cato's maritime loans, which he negotiated through a freedman named Quintio, see Plut. *Cato*, 21. 6. As a *novus homo* Cato had less scruples about maritime insurance than many of the older nobility. His properties near Campania may have stimulated this interest. [2] See Tenney Frank, *Econ. Surv.* i. 67.

[3] e.g. Scipio Africanus at his triumph in 201 distributed to each of his soldiers 400 *asses ex praeda* (L. xxx. 45. 3). For a list of booty gained between 200 and 157 B.C. see T. Frank, *Econ. Surv.* i. 127 ff. The unashamed avowal of the benefits of war is illustrated in the terms of the treaty of Rome and Aetolia against Philip (212 or 211): all conquered territory was left to the Aetolians ('bare ground, roofs, and walls'!), but the Romans were to have all the booty ('omnis praeda populi Romani esset'): L. xxvi. 24. 11.

pire were created, the business men grew in number and influence. The commercial classes had first become conscious of their unity and influence during the Hannibalic War when in 215 the government was forced to exempt from military service three companies of nineteen men who supplied materials for the army in Spain on credit. From this time onward Rome counterbalanced her failure to build up an adequate professional Civil Service by increasingly enlisting the help of private business men, as individuals or in small joint-stock companies, to contract for public works, to exploit her real estate by allowing them to collect certain taxes and customs, and to operate some mines in Spain and Macedonia. By such undertakings and by trading, banking, and money-lending the Equites gradually consolidated their power.[1]

The censors, who were responsible for the equestrian census as well as for letting out public contracts, obviously could exert considerable influence upon the Equites. Since the censorship was the crown of a political career the censors would not be concerned to win for themselves the political support of their business associates, but they might wish to engage their votes on behalf of the kinsmen or friends whom they sought to advance to office. Besides the censors, the regular magistrates also could exercise pressure through their responsibility for securing military supplies, equipment, and transport. Since the State was slow to use the services of the Equites on a large scale, the magistrates continued to conduct such business during the Eastern wars of the early second century: as late as 167 B.C. a praetor and consul seem to have managed a contract for horses and military clothing, although they may possibly have used knights as intermediaries.[2] Thus Roman magistrates often had recourse to the cooperation of traders. Through these middlemen and the industrial classes themselves they could exert political pressure: the small shopkeepers, if citizens, who supplied equipment for a praetor's army,

---

[1] Polybius (vi. 17. 2–4) gives a classic description of the functions of the Equites about 150 B.C., but it must not be applied to an earlier period (cf. T. Frank, *Econ. Surv.* i. 148 ff.). Their rise was slow. For instance, they received the contracts for public buildings, but these were not large before *c.* 184 (the Hannibalic War was not a time for building, while the censors of 199, 194, and 189 let very few contracts, and such contracts did not include buildings outside Rome until 174).

The Equites were socially a class below the senators. During the third century censors in their *lectio* had added to the *equites equo publico* men whose incomes permitted them to serve in the cavalry *equo privato* (when the requisite income was fixed by law is uncertain). Thus an equestrian order of 'new rich' developed, some of whom might hope to gain office as *novi homines*, but the senators generally managed to exclude them, partly by trying to monopolize for their own sons the 18 equestrian centuries *equo publico*, which developed into a body of rich young cadets; from these the military tribunes and prefects were generally chosen, and it was from such beginnings that political advancement usually started.

[2] L. xxxvi. 2. 12; xxxvii. 2. 50; xlii. 31. 8; xliv. 16. 1–4. Cf. T. Frank, *Econ. Surv.* i. 149.

would hardly fail to vote in his favour when he stood for the consulship. In theory the landed gentry was remote from the small trader:
in practice the links between them probably were closer than is often
suspected and may at times have developed into formal patronage.

A second important factor which led to the rise of clients was the
need to seek legal help and protection against the nobles. In early days
when knowledge of the law was confined to the governing class a
humble man would be powerless against patrician oppression unless
he could enlist the support of one of them. With the growth of the
tribunate the weak found other champions, but many continued to
seek the voluntary help of a noble patron in the law courts. This could
more easily be obtained because at Rome jurists (*iuris consulti* or *iuris
prudentes*) were professional lawyers only in a limited sense; they were
generally nobles who regarded jurisprudence as part of the art of
government and who gave advice (*responsa*) to individuals or to
magistrates. Thus nobles with technical legal knowledge could often
help clients who would thereafter be in their debt. Later, under the
economic strain of the Hannibalic War patrons began to disregard
the principle that they should accept no honorarium for legal aid,[1] so
that in 204 a *lex Cincia* was passed which forbade gifts and fees for
legal service,[2] while previously the poor had been forbidden by a *lex
Publicia* (? 209) to give the rich any gifts at the Saturnalia except wax
candles.[3] Thus patrons were reminded that their duty should spring
from *praesidium* pure and undefiled.

Further, oratory played a great part in public life. Indeed, distinction in oratory or law ranked with nobility of birth and military service
as one of the three claims to the consulship.[4] Cato's rough but incisive
speech in Senate House and law court paved the way for a *novus homo*
to the consulship more than a century before Cicero's more rotund
periods advanced him to an even greater fame. Besides smoothing his
own pathway a noble might increase the number of his friends and
clients, not only by his knowledge of law but also by his skilful advocacy
of their claims or innocence in the law courts. To have avoided such
an obligation would have seemed unnatural to a Roman; thus young
Scipio Aemilianus complained to Polybius that he was considered to
be far removed from the true Roman character and ways, because he
did not care for pleading in the law courts.[5] Further, Polybius was

---

[1] L. xxxiv. 4. 9: 'vectigalis iam et stipendiaria plebs esse senatui coeperat.'

[2] L. xxix. 20. 11; xxxiv. 4. 9; Cic. *De sen.* 10.

[3] Macrobius, *Sat.* i. 7. 33; cf. L. xxvii. 20. 11.

[4] Cic. *Brut.* 84, 239, 256; *Pro Mur.* 24; *De orat.* i. 131; *Pro Plancio*, 62.

[5] xxxi. 23. 11 (Incidentally Polybius' sympathy on this occasion was the origin of their
friendship.) On patronage exercised through advocacy compare the example of Crassus,
who often gained popularity by undertaking cases when Pompey, Caesar, and Cicero
refused (Plut. *Crassus*, 3. 3).

well aware of the political control which the nobles exercised through the courts in his day: 'the judges are taken from members of the Senate in the majority of trials, whether public or private, in which the charges are heavy; consequently, all citizens are much at its mercy, and being alarmed at the uncertainty as to when they may need its aid, are cautious about resisting or actively opposing its will.'[1]

Thirdly, political patronage was a potent weapon. Aspirants to office in Rome, both members of minor *gentes* living in the capital and influential citizens in the Italian municipalities, often sought help from one of the great noble families. This humble approach to office was not despised by men of such independent spirit as Cato who was helped by Valerius Flaccus, and Marius who sought the patronage of the Caecilii Metelli. Scipio Africanus started on their careers many 'new men', such as his friend Laelius (*cos.* 190), Acilius Glabrio (*cos.* 191), and Sex. Digitius (*pr.* 194), while his family secured a praetorship for his secretary, C. Cicereius, ten years after his master's death. The number of such men to reach high office as clients of the nobility may have been small, but many nobles must have exerted sufficient influence to help their clients at least as far as the quaestorship or tribunate. These men would, in turn, put their own clients' votes at the disposal of their patron whose political influence would thus grow deeper.

A fourth form of patronage, important during the last century of the Republic but less operative earlier, is that of an outstanding Roman towards a municipality, colony, or province.[2] Roman municipalities or provincials might choose distinguished Romans to defend or represent their interests in the capital;[3] a magistrate who served in a district might be selected as its patron,[4] while patronage of a district often became hereditary in the family of the general who first reduced it.[5] The *principes* of the late Republic fully exploited these ties of personal allegiance in their struggle for individual power,[6] but this theme need not be pursued farther here, since, although it would add to the fame of a candidate to have many provincial clients, the direct effect

---

[1] vi. 17.   [2] See M. Gelzer, *Nobilität*, 70 ff.

[3] Cicero was particularly proud of the fact that the Roman citizens of Capua chose him as patron (*Pro Sest.* 9; *In Pis.* 25). The Spanish envoys who complained at Rome in 171 about the rapacity of Roman governors chose as patrons three ex-governors of their country (see p. 201). An example of an individual in a province seeking a patron at Rome is Sthenius of Thermae who fled before Verres' persecution and had already enjoyed the *hospitium* of Marius.

[4] Thus the people of Cyprus and Cappadocia were named the clients of Cato Uticensis (Cic. *Ad fam.* xv. 4. 15; *De fin.* iv. 56). Caesar as praetor undertook the patronage of Further Spain, and in the East a Roman magistrate was often called πάτρων as well as εὐεργέτης and σωτήρ.

[5] C. Fabricius 'universos (Samnites) in clientela habebat' (Val. Max. iv. 3. 6). The Marcelli were patrons of Sicily as descendants of M. Claudius Marcellus who stormed Syracuse (Cic. *In Verr.* ii. 2. 122; 4. 90).

[6] Cf. R. Syme, *RR*, 261.

on the elections in Rome would be small because few provincials would be citizens or present in Rome. But it has some relevance in so far as Roman nobles became patrons of towns which might receive full franchise and some of whose citizens might be present in Rome on occasion to record a vote.

Thus patronage in its various forms, economic, legal, or political, formed one of the main bases of the power of the Roman nobility and provided a means by which one family could outbid another.

III. *Influence over the Elections*

The methods by which rival groups of nobles gained and held power were threefold: control of the elections, of the Senate, and of the religious machinery of the State. Since the first of these was the most important, electoral procedure may be briefly described.[1]

Prospective candidates first announced their intention to stand, but as the magistrate who presided at the elections had considerable discretionary powers to accept or reject any candidature, common sense would lead a candidate to sound the magistrate beforehand. Thus he customarily made a preliminary notification of his intention (*professio*) to the presiding officer who would announce his acceptance or rejection.[2] Next followed canvassing (*petitio*). Accompanied by a large escort of friends and dependants, a candidate visited the Forum wearing a specially whitened toga (*candidatus*) and greeted the voters he met. Special meetings designed to put the claims of individuals before the public were not held, but candidates could probably advance their own views and criticize their rivals at meetings (*contiones*) summoned by friendly magistrates to discuss public business. Greater detail is known about the more elaborate procedure of the later Republic when the electorate embraced all Italy. Then men might start canvassing a year in advance and used election agents (*divisores*), each of whom was responsible for soliciting the votes of part of a tribe; political clubs became more influential and bribery increased.[3]

Magistrates were elected directly by the People: consuls, praetors, and censors by the Comitia Centuriata under the normal presidency of a consul; curule aediles and quaestors by the Comitia Tributa under a consul, praetor, or dictator; the plebeian aediles and tribunes by the Concilium Plebis under a tribune. For proceedings to be valid favourable auspices had to be obtained: here lay open a wide field for abuse (see pp. 26 ff.). After completing the *auspicatio* the presiding

---

[1] In general see Mommsen, *Staatsr.*; A. H. J. Greenidge, *Roman Public Life*; G. W. Botsford, *The Roman Assemblies*.

[2] This preliminary *professio* was not legally obligatory until *c.* 98 B.C. when a candidate was required to give 17 days' notice before the day of the elections.

[3] On the efforts made by politicians to cultivate their fellow tribesmen (*tribules*) and to use their friends to solicit the support of other tribes see L. R. Taylor, *Party Politics*, 62 f.

magistrate summoned the citizens to a preliminary *contio*, where after sacrifice and prayer the business which was to come before the Comitia was stated and possibly discussed; discussion always preceded acts of legislation and jurisdiction, but not certainly election. After the withdrawal of any non-voters the People divided into centuries or tribes, and a Comitia was held in an enclosure (*ovile* or *saepta*) divided by ropes or wooden fences into small sections for members of each century or tribe. Votes in each compartment were registered singly as voters left the enclosures through narrow passages (*pontes*). Before the introduction of vote by ballot in 139 B.C., votes were given verbally and recorded by tellers (*rogatores*) on tablets by means of points (*puncta*). This open voting, although carried out under the eye of the magistrate on his tribunal, offered obvious opportunities for intimidation or future reprisals.

A system of group-voting prevailed: each century or tribe recorded one vote which had been determined by a majority vote of its individual members. In the Comitia Centuriata votes were recorded in order of precedence, based on a timocratic system. The eighteen centuries of Equites, which included most of the patricians, were asked first,[1] then the eighty centuries of the first class, next those of the four other classes in succession, and finally the five centuries of supernumeraries. Voting, however, continued only until a majority of the centuries had voted in favour of any candidate. If the Equites and first class voted alike, a majority was obtained (98 centuries out of 193) and voting was discontinued, but after the reform of the Comitia Centuriata (in 241 B.C. or later) the voting power of the higher classes was modified. The number of centuries in the first class was reduced from eighty to seventy and they were brought into relation with the thirty-five tribes by the assignment of two centuries (one of *seniores* and one of *iuniores*) to each tribe. The nature of the changes carried out in the other four classes is uncertain,[2] but in any case the reform made the Comitia more democratic,[3] and by depriving the combined Equites and first class of a clear majority brought the effective voting lower down the scale. Thus the middle-class people would ordinarily be enabled to register their votes and exercise a predominant influence; if

[1] Hence the equestrian centuries were called *praerogativae*, unless it is that one of their centuries was chosen by lot to record its vote before all the others (*centuria praerogativa*).

[2] It is unnecessary here to enter into this notoriously vexed question beyond noting that there are two main views: first, that the total number of centuries remained at 193, and ten centuries of the first class were transferred to the lower classes by some method unknown, or secondly, that the total number of centuries was raised from 193 to 373 by fixing the number in each of the five classes at 70 (i.e. $5 \times 70 = 350 + 18$ centuries of Equites and 5 supernumerary centuries = 373). On the evidence afforded by the new Tabula Hebena, which supports the former view, see G. Tibiletti, *Athenaeum*, 1949, 223 ff.

[3] Dionys. Hal. iv. 21. 3: μεταβέβληκεν εἰς τὸ δημοτικώτερον.

they combined with the rich, the poor would have no voice, but if they sided with the lower classes the rich could be checked.

At some date, probably when the Comitia Centuriata was reformed, the equestrian centuries lost the privilege of recording the first vote, which fell to a *centuria praerogativa* chosen by lot from the first class.[1] This was important because the Romans readily followed a lead, and the announcement of the prerogative vote had great influence on the subsequent voters, partly perhaps for superstitious reasons.[2] It might even be possible on occasion to 'work' the lot so that it fell upon a century containing men who were known to support, or who could be persuaded to support, a given candidate.[3]

Finally, when a majority of votes had been recorded for any candidate, his election was still not legally valid until the presiding officer made a formal announcement of the result (*renuntiatio*); this in exceptional circumstances he could refuse to make.[4] Thus from *professio* to *renuntiatio* a candidate's chances could be furthered or retarded by the presiding magistrate, who as a representative of the nobility as a whole could help to exclude undesirable candidates or as a supporter of a noble family or coterie could advance the claims of its adherents to the detriment of its rivals.[5]

It is difficult to assess the size of the electorate which the nobles sought to control. There may have been between 40,000 and 90,000 potential voters in Rome at election time during the period from the Second Punic to the Third Macedonian War, but only a small proportion is likely to have attended the Comitia: Cicero suggests that the Assemblies were normally ill-attended in his day.[6] At public-spirited Athens the annual meeting of the Ecclesia for ostracism required a quorum of 6,000 members out of at least 35,000 men, while an attendance of 5,000 at a regular meeting was considered a record in difficult war-time conditions.[7] At Rome elections occurred only

---

[1] Possibly from the *iuniores*, the fighting men. After the reform 12 centuries of Equites either retained the right of voting first or else voted with the first class (L. xliii. 16. 14), but their other 6 centuries (*sex suffragia*) voted after the first class. If 'prima classis vocatur, renuntiatur' is to be read in Cic. *Phil.* ii. 82, then the votes of the first class were announced before the other classes voted, but in the Oxford text A. C. Clark follows Madvig in rejecting this repetition of 'renuntiatur'.

[2] Cic. *Pro Plancio*, 49; *Ad Q. fr.* ii. 14. 4; *De div.* i. 103; Festus, 249. 7.

[3] For an example of tampering with the lot (*sortitio*) for the allocation of provinces see Cic. *Ad fam.* v. 2. 3 (62 B.C.).

[4] e.g. Piso (*cos.* 67) refused to recognize the election of Palicanus (Val. Max. iii. 8. 3).

[5] An extreme example of magisterial interference occurred in 215, when Q. Fabius Maximus, the presiding officer, objected to the election of two men for whom the *centuria praerogativa* had already voted, and managed to secure his own re-election in place of one of them! See below, p. 59.

[6] Cic. *Pro Sest.* 109. On the size of the electorate see p. 273.

[7] Thuc. viii. 72. On ostracism the above is the more probable view; the alternative, that 6,000 votes were required to effect the ostracism of any one individual, would of course involve the assumption of a larger attendance.

once a year, but a maximum attendance of 4,000 to 10,000 would seem a likely guess, and in practice the number probably was considerably less. But the nobles did not need to win all these votes. Only a bare majority of the centuries or tribes had to be secured, and further, thanks to the system of group-voting, only a bare majority of votes within each century or tribe was needed; thus theoretically a large proportion of the electorate could be disregarded.

A distinction must be made between the Comitia Centuriata, which elected the higher magistrates, and the tribal assemblies, which elected the lesser magistrates and enacted most of the legislation. In the former, if the nobles themselves voted solidly and could influence the middle classes they could gain their will, whereas if they knew that the middle classes were hostile they could tilt the balance by appealing to the lowest classes. Thus the number of centuries to be won over was limited and the nobles by voting solid generally could impose their will on the community in matters which affected their class interests. But in elections the situation was more complicated, since the various cliques of the nobility wished to see their own men elected; thus the voting might involve a greater number of centuries before a decision was reached. Further, in the Comitia Centuriata the classification of the citizens depended on wealth, on age (after the division into *seniores* and *iuniores*), and only to a limited extent, after the reform which subordinated the centuries to the tribes, on residence.

In the Tribal Assemblies the position was different: the basis was the tribe, a territorial division.[1] After 241 B.C. there were 35, of which 4 were in the city (*urbanae*), 16 relatively near Rome, and the remaining 15 in other parts of Italy. The difference between the number of urban and rural tribes did not correspond proportionately with the numbers of citizens enrolled in each. On the face of it the citizens who lived in Rome, perhaps one-third of the electorate, were apparently confined to 4 tribes, while the other two-thirds comprised 31 tribes. In an actual election the disproportion would seem even greater, since only a small fraction of the members of the rural tribes would be present in Rome; if, for instance, one hundred farmers from a rural tribe were present, while a thousand members of an urban tribe voted, then each farmer would exert ten times as much influence on the result as each city-dweller. Thus the citizens resident in Rome were far from swamping the votes of the farmers of Italy.[2]

The clue to the secret by which the nobility controlled the assemblies has been sought in this fact.[3] Since the rural tribes numbered 31 out

---

[1] No distinction need be drawn here between the Comitia Tributa and the Concilium Plebis, since the diminishing number of patricians rendered their exclusion from the Concilium Plebis of little practical importance.

[2] Cf. F. B. Marsh, *History of the Roman World 146–30 B.C.*, p. 19.

[3] Marsh, op. cit. 21 ff.

of 35 (and their centuries perhaps 310 out of 373), the nobility could disregard the numerous residents in Rome and concentrate on winning a majority of the rural tribes; this would not be difficult, since the attendance from these tribes would usually be small. Further, the nobles themselves, who were large landowners, would be enrolled in the rural tribes where their influence would be greater, since a land-owner had the right to be registered in any tribe where he owned land, irrespective of his place of residence.[1] They would also secure the registration of their freedmen in the rural tribes, while many of their clients would derive from country districts. This view, however, is based on the assumption that the *plebs urbana* continued to be con-fined to the four urban tribes, whereas in fact it comprised many men whose ancestors, or who themselves, had moved to Rome and retained their registration in their original rural tribe.[2] The number of these town-dwellers registered in rural tribes, which was increased by the reform of 179 B.C. (see below, pp. 182 f.) and by the general drift from countryside to town in the second century, may not have been very great at the time of the Hannibalic War, but was continually growing. Thus although the influence of the residents of Rome *vis-à-vis* that of the country-dwellers was greater than has sometimes been sup-posed, nevertheless the control of the tribes by the nobles might be no less, since the votes of members of rural tribes resident in Rome might be obtained as easily as those of the country members.[3]

The attempt of the nobles to control the elections was thus made easier by the willingness of many voters to follow a strong lead from the *centuria praerogativa*, and by the system of group-voting and tribal organization. A further source of influence was the military origin of the Comitia Centuriata, once a mustering of the citizens in arms, which had only gradually developed into a political meeting. Doubt-less some sense of military discipline still survived and the wish of the presiding officer, made clear in the preceding *contio*, seemed like a distant echo of a commanding officer's order. Also the bonds of war service must have counted when veterans, mustering in their separate

[1] There is, however, some evidence (cf. Dessau, *ILS*, 949 and perhaps 4942) that some families remained in an urban tribe in order to gain distinction by emphasizing their claim to be descended from the earlier inhabitants of Rome. See H. Last, *AJP*, 1937, 469. Cf. L. R. Taylor, *Party Politics*, 53, 201 n. 14.

[2] Mommsen, *Staatsr.* 113, 402 ff., detected the first signs of the breakdown of the system whereby the *plebs urbana* was confined to the four urban tribes as early as 312 B.C. It had certainly begun in the middle of the third century. Ultimately the urban plebs so controlled the other 31 tribes that by A.D. 200 *tribus XXXV* meant little more than the urban proletariat. For this and a full criticism of F. B. Marsh's view see H. Last, *AJP*, 1937, 469 ff.

[3] L. R. Taylor (*Party Politics*, 57 ff.) has shown that in Cicero's day the voters in Italy, living outside Rome, were of decisive importance in the elections held by the centuries, while the urban plebs had greater influence in the legislative assemblies of the tribes.

centuries to vote, found their war comrades and the centurion who had led them to victory. Further, each century was divided into *iuniores* (men of military age) and *seniores*; now in the course of nature the latter would be outnumbered by the former (thus incidentally the Comitia was biased slightly in favour of age), but these *seniores* would be particularly prone to vote in favour of their old commanders, while a sense of military discipline and tradition would often cause a century of *iuniores* to follow the lead of its corresponding century of *seniores*. Nor should the influence of the centurion, the ancient sergeant-major, be overlooked; many members of his century would follow his lead as readily at the hustings as on the field of battle, while others, mindful of future campaigns, might believe that imitation was the sincerest form of flattery. Here, then, in the military origin and organization of the Comitia and in the loyalty of men to ex-officers was a powerful source of support for rival political candidates.

A more direct method of winning votes was bribery. *Ambitus*, which originally meant canvassing proper,[1] was later applied to corrupt canvassing. The first laws *de ambitu* in this sense were passed in 181 (lex Cornelia Baebia) and in 159, while the elections in 166 were conducted *ambitiosissime*.[2] The evil only became widespread later, but the need for legislation early in the second century demonstrates its existence then:[3] its growth was a symptom of the moral decline which accompanied the influx of wealth and changing standards of life.

But bribery could take the more subtle form of *panem et circenses*. The efforts of Roman emperors to buy the loyalty of the army by donations and to secure the subservience of the people by gifts and Games have a long prehistory in the Republic. Significantly one of the earliest references to such calculated generosity concerns Scipio Africanus, the first individual who might have sought to challenge the rule of the Senate: as aedile in 213 he celebrated the Roman Games for two days and distributed a *congius* (*c.* 3 quarts) of oil in each street.[4] However little the average Roman may have thought about the implication of this, Scipio himself will have known that Hellenistic monarchs were accustomed to distribute oil at Games. The evil grew: the *congiaria* given by Glabrio when seeking the censorship of 189 were so scandalously large that they ruined his chances (p. 137). Further, public banquets (*epulae*), originally religious ceremonies,

---

[1] L. vii. 15. 12.   [2] Obsequens, 12.

[3] For a contemporary reference (before 184 B.C.) see Plautus, *Amphit.* 74: 'quasi magistratum sibi alterive ambiverit'. Polybius, contrasting Roman rectitude with Carthaginian avarice, remarks that 'the Carthaginians obtain office by open bribery, but among the Romans the penalty for it is death' (vi. 56). In fact a Roman could anticipate the execution of a capital sentence by voluntary exile.

[4] See ch. vi, § iii. L. xxv. 2. In connexion with his election to the aedileship Polybius (x. 5. 6) calls Scipio μεγαλόδωρος.

were given under the conduct of *septemviri epulones* at public Games, or by private individuals at the triumphs or funerals of famous men.[1] But like direct bribery these evils probably began to flourish only in the second century.

More serious was the manner in which the Senate used the national resources, gained in war, to win popular support by increasing the number of public Games. Thereby the influence of the aediles, to whom the *cura ludorum* belonged, was greatly enhanced, and this magistracy became an important rung in the ladder to highest office. To the Ludi Romani were added the Ludi Plebeii in 220, the Apollinares in 212, the Megalenses in 204, the Ceriales before 202, and the Florenses in 173. This great increase was prompted partly by the desire to distract civilian attention from the Hannibalic War and to strengthen morale, but the expectation of being entertained by the State survived the war. The length of the Games, originally one day, was gradually increased to 5, 7, or even 14 days, and at times they were prolonged by the trick of finding a technical flaw in the accompanying ritual which necessitated a repetition (*instauratio*) of the whole festival. The Games themselves, originally circus races and dramatic performances, were enhanced by beast hunts and gladiatorial contests.[2] The State provided the main funds,[3] and by liberality or parsimony the Senate could help or hinder the magistrates responsible, but individual aediles could augment the State allowance out of their own pockets. Other magistrates also courted popularity by giving Games: for instance, at those given for ten days by M. Fulvius Nobilior in 186 'many actors from Greece came to do him honour, and athletic contests were introduced for the first time in Rome. The hunting of lions and panthers formed a novel feature, and the whole spectacle presented almost as much splendour and variety as those of the present day', wrote Livy.[4]

This form of bribery was a paying investment. Of the curule aediles, who had charge of the Ludi Romani (and, after their institution, of the Megalenses), all those known between 217 and 187 B.C. reached the consulship or praetorship. Of the plebeian aediles, responsible for the Ludi Plebeii and Ceriales, we have an almost complete list

[1] Tables were set in the Forum and each guest, who at first had brought food in a basket (*sportula*) as at a picnic, was later given some instead. Finally, the *sportula* became a gift in cash in place of, or in addition to, a gift in kind. Whether the Roman nobility indulged in this form of patronage and bribery as early as the first half of the second century can hardly be determined. When in 129 B.C. Q. Fabius Maximus Allobrogicus gave the Roman people a banquet in honour of the death of Scipio Aemilianus he entrusted the arrangements to his relative Q. Tubero whose meanness cost him the praetorship (Cic. *Pro Mur.* 75-6; Val. Max. vii. 5. 81).   [2] L. xliv. 18: increased lavishness of aediles of 169.
[3] For instance the Ludi Romani at the end of the First Punic War appear to have cost 200,000 sesterces (Dion. Hal. vii. 71) and those of 217 B.C. 333,333 sesterces (L. xxii. 10. 7).
[4] L. xxxix. 22. 1-2.

between 210 and 197; the names of 27 out of the 28 are recorded and
all but two of these reached the praetorship; further, not less than 17,
including Cato, stood for the praetorship while actually holding the
aedileship and gained office thanks to the direct impression which
their Games had made on the people, while 7 others became praetors
only a little later.[1] An attempt to remedy this last abuse was made in
196 when the rule that a magistrate in office could not stand for
another magistracy was applied to the plebeian aedileship.[2] Further,
a *senatusconsultum* was passed at the time of the Games given by Ti.
Sempronius Gracchus as aedile in 182, and renewed in 179, fixing
a limit for expenditure on the Games because the cost incurred by
Gracchus had burdened not only Italy and the Latin allies, but the
provinces as well.[3] But the evil remained and the aedileship was a good
road to popular favour and a form of corruption that was tolerated by
public opinion.[4] These, then, were some of the ways in which the
nobility could bribe the electorate, but such abuses were perhaps not
serious before the early decades of the second century.

IV. *Control of Politics, Religion, and Public Opinion*

By such means the nobility controlled the elections, and thus, with
the Roman method of voting, a syndicate of nobles on occasion might
sweep the polls. But control of the elections, especially of the curule
magistrates, would to a large extent give control of the Senate, where
the influence of the higher magistrates was out of proportion to their
numbers. This may be seen from a brief consideration of senatorial
procedure. It was the consuls, praetors, and tribunes (exceptionally
dictators, *interreges*, or *magistri equitum*) who had the right to convoke
and preside over the Senate (*ius agendi cum patribus*). The consuls
usually took the lead, and, if need be, by their *maior potestas* they
could hinder a praetor from summoning a meeting, while custom
prevented a tribune from doing so when a consul was in Rome. When,
however, a meeting had been summoned, and the business which the
convoking and presiding consul laid before it had been discussed, then
other magistrates with the *ius referendi* (praetors or tribunes) could lay
questions before the House. But the presiding officer exercised great
influence on the debate: he determined the order of business and

---

[1] Mommsen, *Staatsr.* i. 533 (*Dr. pub.* ii. 187), and A. Aymard, *Rev. Ét. Anc.* 1943,
222 n. 5. The 24 aediles who reached the praetorship are known; the 25th did not become
praetor because he had already held the office (on the assumption that Ti. Claudius
Asellus, the aedile of 205, is to be identified with the praetor of 206: cf. Aymard, but
contrast Münzer, *PW*, s.v. Claudius nos. 61, 62); the two who failed to reach the
praetorship were Q. Catius (aedile 210) and L. Laetorius (202); the 28th was probably
Q. Caecilius Metellus who became consul without having been praetor.

[2] This can be deduced from the fact that after 196 there is no example of a man holding
the praetorship without an interval after the plebeian aedileship. See Mommsen, loc. cit.

[3] L. xl. 44. 12.

[4] Cf. De Sanctis, IV. i. 493.

submitted to the judgement of the House whichever he liked of the opinions which had emerged in the course of debate. He asked senators for their advice (*quid censes?*) in the order of their official rank: first the *princeps senatus*, then the *censorii, consulares, praetorii, aedilicii, tribunicii*, and *quaestorii*, magistrates-elect generally being consulted before ex-magistrates of similar rank. As debates could not be allowed to drag on indefinitely, in practice the turn of non-curule members (*pedarii*) to speak would seldom be reached. Further, these junior members would tend to follow a strong lead for various reasons: the personal *auctoritas* of outstanding senior statesmen; the almost filial relationship between a quaestor and the consul to whom he was attached; a cautious desire to promote their own careers; and above all the fact that the *censorii* and *consulares* exercised a kind of *praerogativa*, the expression of their opinion often being regarded with almost superstitious reverence. The formal method of voting by a division (*discessio*) was often rendered unnecessary when senators, without rising, added a few words of agreement to a speech[1] or left their seats and stood near the man whose views they supported.[2] Thus the general feeling of the House often could be gauged without spending time on a formal count, while from the point of view of family politics the act of supporters standing around their spokesman would emphasize the division of personal loyalties more vividly than a recorded vote.

If a group of nobles could control the Senate, they would direct policy in general, since the Senate's influence on finance and foreign affairs was virtually unquestioned until the time of Tiberius Gracchus, while it gained increasing competence in judicial matters. Further, it regulated the chief military appointments, prorogued magistrates' commands, and occasionally dispensed with the use of sortition in assigning duties to magistrates. Control of the military appointments would in turn help to provide more spoils of war and so to replenish the funds available for patronage. The men who ruled the Senate ruled the State.

Thus the nobles exercised power by controlling the elections and Senate: their control of the State religion remains to be considered.[3] Strictly religious matters were the concern of various priesthoods, but those which had political implications were left to magistrates, who could consult the priests, or not, as they liked. In general the Roman attitude was to consult the gods by seeking a sign of encouragement or warning in order to test the rightness of a preconceived plan. This

---

[1] *Verbo adsentiri*: Sall. *Cat.* 52. 1; cf. Cic. *Ad fam.* v. 2. 9, *sedens iis adsensi*.

[2] *In alienam sententiam pedibus ire*: Gell. iii. 18. 1.

[3] See in general, Mommsen, *Staatsr.* i. 76; A. H. J. Greenidge, *Roman Public Life*; L. R. Taylor, *Party Politics*, ch. iv.

simple demand for 'yea' or 'nay' obviated the need for an elaborate priesthood: the gods did not reveal their will through the medium of a sacerdotal order which alone could interpret it. In theory, therefore, any Roman citizen could invoke auspices without help from priest or magistrate, but naturally any action which affected the State concerned the magistrates, and *auspicia publica* were distinguished from *auspicia privata*. Custom demanded that the gods should be consulted before most public actions (such as the election of a magistrate), and the taking of *auspicia publica* became part of a magistrate's duty. 'The imperium and the auspicia are indissolubly connected; they are the divine and human side of the same power.'[1]

Auspices were of two kinds: *auspicia oblativa* and *impetrativa*. The former came unsought, as a flash of lightning before a meeting of the Comitia or a sudden noise.[2] The magistrate, however, could turn a blind eye or a deaf ear, unless the omen was announced by another magistrate (*obnuntiatio*) or by an augur. *Auspicia impetrativa*, on the other hand, were deliberately sought and took various forms, as signs from the flight of birds, the movements or sounds of quadrupeds, thunder or lightning, or the behaviour of special chickens during feeding. These auspices had to be taken on the same day and spot as the proposed action (e.g. on the president's platform in the Campus Martius for meetings of the Comitia Centuriata), and magistrates often started soon after midnight and sometimes even carried through the action itself before daybreak in order to prevent any flaw (*vitium*). If a magistrate failed to get a favourable omen, he had to repeat the process the next day (*repetere auspicia*). If he proceeded despite unfavourable omens, or if later it was shown that a flaw had occurred in the ceremony (e.g. of election or legislation), the action was invalidated through this *vitium*, which necessitated the resignation of the elected magistrate, or the re-enactment of the law. If such a flaw was detected only after the consuls had actually entered office, an interregnum became necessary for a renewal of the auspices (*renovatio auspiciorum*).

Augurs and pontiffs were primarily priests, not prophets or magistrates, but since the Roman nobles coveted these priesthoods both colleges in practice consisted of statesmen. It was of great value to a magistrate to have the support of the augurs. When the validity of any ceremony was in doubt, the question could be referred to the augural college by the magistrate concerned or by the Senate. Here was room for scandal. If the augurs could be persuaded to allege that a defect had occurred in the auspication at an election, the magistrate so elected must either resign or else, like C. Flaminius, challenge the

---

[1] A. H. J. Greenidge, op. cit. 162.
[2] Even the squeak of a mouse: 'occentusque soricis auditus Fabio Maximo dictaturam . . . deponendi causam praebuit' (Val. Max. i. 1. 5). See below, p. 274.

authority of the Senate and the religious feeling of the whole people. Another form of abuse arose from the *obnuntiatio* of *auspicia oblativa*. Bibulus' attempt to hinder Caesar in 59 B.C. by scanning the heavens (*de caelo servare*) is a classic example of one consul obnuntiating against his colleague. An instance of an augur falsely reporting unfavourable omens is Antony's scandalous adjournment of an election meeting when a majority of votes had been nearly recorded in favour of Dolabella. This abuse had increased in the later Republic (the more easily after the *leges Aelia et Fufia* of *c*. 150 B.C. had recognized the right of tribunes and curule magistrates to obstruct assemblies by *obnuntiatio*), but it goes back to the Hannibalic War, if not to the Samnite Wars.[1]

Without further elaboration many possibilities of political wire-pulling are apparent, especially in connexion with the elections, and it can be said that 'membership of the augural college was the highest ambition of the Roman statesman, when its decree could upset a law, stave off a capital charge, or force a consul to abdicate . . . the decision as to the future of the state often rested wholly with the college of augurs.'[2] Further, the pontiffs, whose duty was to preserve the body of religious tradition, were the final authority on all matters relating to maintaining satisfactory relations with the old Roman gods; they had wide sacerdotal functions, and acted on occasion as advisers to magistrates. Their control of the calendar afforded particular opportunities for manipulation in the interest of individuals.[3] Since both colleges were filled by co-optation, the nobles had a powerful weapon in their armoury to be used against the People and in the battles of their own rival families.

In short, by gaining control of the elections, the Senate, and the priesthoods noble families could sway the State, and their chief means were birth and family tradition, patronage, and alliance: 'vetus nobilitas, maiorum fortia facta, cognatorum et adfinum opes, multae clientelae'.[4]

---

[1] L. viii. 23. 17.

[2] A. H. J. Greenidge, *Roman Public Life*, 166. Cf. Cic. *De div.* i. 89.

[3] In 191 the consul Acilius Glabrio carried a measure (lex Acilia) which had important bearing on the control which the nobility could exercise upon the State through religion: as Glabrio was a *novus homo*, he was presumably acting for the Scipionic group. This measure empowered the pontiffs to intercalate the calendar at their discretion (Censorinus, *De die nat.* xx. 6), the calendar being notoriously out of gear with the solar year (see De Sanctis, IV. i. 386 ff.). The immediate result of the lex Acilia, however, was, according to Censorinus, to make matters worse: 'most of the pontiffs, either from hatred or favour, in order to cut short or extend the tenure of office, or in order that a farmer of the public revenue might gain or lose by the length of a year, by intercalating more or less at their pleasure, deliberately made worse what had been entrusted to them to set right.' This is perhaps not quite accurate, because by 168 B.C. the maladjustment had been reduced from 4 to 2½ months, but no doubt it well reflects the political results of the measure. Macrobius (*Sat.* i. 13. 21) derived his knowledge of the lex Acilia from a certain Fulvius, who will have been M. Fulvius Nobilior who set up Fasti with notes in his temple to Hercules Musarum (see p. 253). [4] Sall. *Iug.* 85. 4.

The influence of these cliques of nobles was very great but not unchecked. Considerations of patriotism on occasion might force them to subordinate coterie to State, while action by the People might impose some effective limitation. This was possible because there were still many independent small landowners within reach of the city who could come in on important occasions, and thus a sturdy independent country opinion could still make itself felt. Further, the People's representatives, the tribunes, were always in the city. Although at this period they may have used their powers of veto or impeachment sparingly, they would presumably prevent any very flagrant attempt to 'work' the elections, for instance if a presiding magistrate refused to accept the name of a properly qualified candidate. The extent of the influence of the People and their tribunes is summarized in a few sentences of Polybius:

the People are the sole source of honours and of punishment . . . they are the only court to try capital charges . . . they bestow offices on the deserving; they have the absolute power of passing or rejecting laws . . . they deliberate on the question of peace or war . . . even in matters which directly affect senators (e.g. if any one introduces a law meant to diminish the Senate's traditional authority, or to deprive senators of certain dignities and offices, or even to cut down their private property), the People have the sole power of passing or rejecting any such law. But most important of all is the fact that, if a single one of the tribunes interposes his veto, the Senate not only are unable to pass a decree, but cannot even hold a meeting at all, whether formal or informal. Now the tribunes are always bound to carry out the decree of the People, and above all things to have regard to their wishes; therefore for all these reasons the Senate stands in awe of the masses and cannot neglect the feelings of the People.[1]

The sphere in which the People expressed their views to the nobility most strongly was warfare, where their ideas were often based on personal experience and in general were progressive. They had learned from experience of warfare in the fourth and third centuries that it was profitable to themselves, even more perhaps than to the nobles. Success in war would help their leaders to a political career, and provide spoils for the rank and file. In campaigns overseas they might not get, nor perhaps did they want, more land, but they could expect good prize-money. When the Senate procrastinated about declaring war against Carthage in 264 B.C., the democratic leaders of the new nobility urged the People to accept the Mamertine alliance, which meant war, and in expectation of ὠφελεῖαι they agreed. At the end of the war, which brought a large haul of spoils and slaves, the People insisted on stiffening the peace-terms imposed by Lutatius on Carthage by adding 1,000 talents to the indemnity. Thereafter in 232 through their champion C. Flaminius they defied the Senate and

[1] P. vi. 14. 16.

forced through a law to parcel out some land in north Italy confiscated from the Senones. During the Hannibalic War, as will be seen, they supported an aggressive policy. In Italy they would press for a decisive battle at Cannae which might result in a large haul of slaves, and they would favour overseas campaigns which would bring in spoils: hence their support of the more progressive nobles, especially Scipio Africanus, and perhaps Marcellus. True, the People at first voted against renewing the war with Philip of Macedon in 200, but that was due less to a reversal of their forward policy than to sheer exhaustion after the Hannibalic War. In brief, popular action might limit or constrain the influence of the nobility on occasion, but in the main the nobles skilfully controlled the People; the chief domestic struggles were waged between rival groups of nobles rather than between nobles and commons.

Such general political conditions have often been compared with those of eighteenth-century England,[1] and in fact a Roman noble of the time of Cato might not have felt much out of his element in England during the period of the Whig oligarchy under the first two Georges when 'about seventy great families, in alliance or in rivalry among themselves, exercised the power and patronage of the State'.[2] Comparison with the government of Walpole and the Pelhams is helpful if not pushed too far. For instance, when Walpole and his brother-in-law, Townshend, ousted the Stanhope–Sunderland cabinet (1721), when Walpole succumbed to a coalition of the Whig factions led by Lord Wilmington but energized by Lord Carteret and the two Pelhams (1742), when the brothers undermined Carteret two years later, or when the Grenville–Bedford ministry (the 'Bloomsbury Gang') collapsed before Grafton and Rockingham, such manœuvres of the cliques would have been understood by the Romans. The Roman nobles had their equivalents to 'pocket', 'rotten', and 'crown' boroughs, and they resembled the 'big landowners, who, if united, were the deciding influence in 39 out of 40 English counties'.[3] *Mutatis mutandis*, two observations could well be applied to Rome: 'About 1750 there were no parties in our sense of the term . . . eighteenth century Administrations, not being able to control individual Members through a party machine and a party-trained electorate, had to bind their following by posts of honour, places of benefit, contracts and pensions', and 'the number of men in the Parliament of 1761 who were unsupported by family, "party", or local connexions, but sat merely because they had money and were prepared to spend it on elections, was exceedingly small.'[4]

---

[1] e.g. Mommsen, *History of Rome*, ii. 340. [2] G. M. Trevelyan, *History of England*, 512.
[3] L. B. Namier, *The Structure of Politics at the Accession of George III*, 86.
[4] Ibid. 264, 208.

II

EARLY FAMILY GROUPINGS

1. *The Fabian Group*

THE early history of some of the chief *gentes* may now be sketched in brief outline in order to indicate their relationships at the time of the outbreak of the Hannibalic War. First the Fabii, who had outstanding power during the early centuries of the Republic. For three generations they held the position of *princeps senatus* for three consecutive periods.[1] M. Fabius Ambustus, consul three times and a conservative in his attitude towards the plebeians, was a leading figure in Roman life from 360 to 322. His son, Q. Fabius Maximus Rullianus, who rallied the nobility against the censor Appius Claudius Caecus, was consul five times (between 322 and 295), dictator twice, and censor. His career began in the lifetime of his father (he was curule aedile in 331) and overlapped with that of his son, Q. Fabius Gurges, who was politically active from his aedileship in 295 until at least 276 or perhaps until 265.[2] Thereafter, as Gurges' son was either dead or had not advanced far on a political career and his grandson was only about thirteen years old, a gap occurred in the main line of the house which was partly bridged by other Fabii (Num. Fabius Buteo, *cos.* 247; M. Fabius Buteo, *cos.* 245, censor and *princeps senatus*). When, however, Gurges' grandson, Q. Fabius Maximus Verrucosus (later Cunctator), was grown up, he soon overshadowed the collateral branches of the family and started a career which was marked by five consulships (between 233 and 209). So great was his influence that he was able to secure a consulship for his ineffective son even in the critical days of the Hannibalic War (213).

The Fabii formed alliances with leading men and families of other Italian towns and probably attracted fresh blood to Rome from Etruria and Campania where they had important interests.[3] For example, the first mixed marriage recorded in this old patrician family was between a daughter of M. Fabius Ambustus (consular tribune in 381) and a plebeian Licinius.[4] As Licinius is an Etruscan name and the Fabii had influence in Etruria, it has been plausibly suggested that

---

[1] 'In omni aevo . . . reperitur . . . (familia) una Fabiorum, in qua tres continui principes senatus, M. Fabius Ambustus, Fabius Rullianus filius, Q. Fabius Gurges nepos' (Pliny, *NH*, vii. 133).

[2] He was *cos.* II in 276 and possibly *cos.* III in 265, but more probably the Gurges who was consul in 265 was his son; the consul of 265 was killed during his consulship. See K. J. Beloch, *Röm. Gesch.* 458 n. 1.   [3] Münzer, *RA*, 55 ff.

[4] L. ix. 13. 25.

the Fabii first attracted the Licinii to Rome. Other immigrants may include the Ogulnii and Laetorii from Etruria, the Fulvii and Mamilii from Tusculum, and the Atilii and Otacilii from Campania.[1] Whether or not the Fabii instigated all these migrations and whether or not the origin of these families has in each case been accurately defined, the Fabii clearly had close political connexions with many of them.

Thus many *gentes* linked their fortunes with those of the Fabii.[2] First, the Atilii. The marriage of a daughter of Fabius Rullianus to A. Atilius Calatinus[3] is the second known example of a union between the Fabii and a plebeian house. M. Atilius Regulus, the second member of his *gens* to attain the consulship, was elected for 294 in the Comitia presided over by Fabius Rullianus who was then at the height of his fame, enjoying his fifth consulship and the glory derived from his victory at Sentinum. During the First Punic War, besides the Atilii Reguli, two other Atilii reached the consulship: A. Atilius Calatinus (son of the above-mentioned Calatinus and grandson of Fabius Rullianus) and C. Atilius Bulbus. Both men were twice consul and once censor, each within a space of eleven years (258–247; 245–234). Although at this time the main house of the Fabii was eclipsed, the collateral families were in prominence with the Atilii. Numerius Fabius Buteo was consul in 247 and under his presidency Atilius Calatinus was elected censor, an office which no other member of his family reached. In 246, with M. Fabius Licinus as consul, M. Fabius Buteo (brother of the consul of 247) and C. Atilius Bulbus (the only member of his *gens* with this cognomen to reach the consulship) were elected for 245. Thus a close connexion between the Fabii and the Atilii from the time of the Samnite Wars to the First Punic War may reasonably be assumed.

The patrician Manlii were also linked with the Fabii. In the fourth century there had been a *bloc* for five years when the patrician consuls were: M. Fabius Ambustus (360), Cn. Manlius (359), C. Fabius (358), Cn. Manlius II (357), and M. Fabius II (356). A century later in the years 247–245 the patrician consuls were Num. Fabius Buteo, M. Fabius Licinus, and M. Fabius Buteo; the patrician censor was A. Manlius Torquatus, whose father may well have owed his consulship in 299 to Fabius Rullianus. He himself was the only man in a

---

[1] Cf. p. 10 n. 1.

[2] F. Münzer, *RA*, 55 ff. F. Cornelius (*Untersuchungen zur frühen römischen Geschichte*, 113 ff.) has tried to trace the political groupings during the fifth century. Since many of the families involved had lapsed into obscurity by the third century, the matter need not be pursued here, except to note that he distinguishes one group comprising the Fabii, Cornelii, and Aemilii in 485–479. This need not be questioned on the ground that the Fabii and the Cornelii later were bitter rivals, since such political alliances may not have endured three hundred years, but the early juxtaposition of the names might mean that these two families shared the chief offices as rivals, not as allies.

[3] Val. Max. viii. 1.

century to be censor without having held the consulship,[1] and his election was surely backed by the Fabii. Of the four plebeian magistrates during this triennium the censor was A. Atilius Calatinus, nephew of Fabius Gurges, and the consuls were L. Caecilius Metellus, M'. Otacilius Crassus, and C. Atilius Bulbus. Of these the Atilii and Otacilius probably belonged to the Fabian group; the position of Caecilius Metellus is more doubtful.[2]

The Fasti of 265–261, which include two Marcii, two Fulvii, two Mamilii, and two Otacilii, suggest further groupings.[3] Marcius Rutilus Censorinus, the only man to hold the office of censor twice, must obviously have been influential and may well have overshadowed his patrician colleague. In fact, when the priestly colleges were opened to the plebeians in 300, he became both augur and pontiff, a combination of offices which was repeated perhaps only once before the time of Caesar, by Fabius Cunctator. Further, he was elected to the signal honour of a second censorship when Fabius Gurges was consul, while he had been a colleague of Fabius Rullianus in the consulship of 310. Philippus, the other Marcius in this list, must also have been a man of weight. As consul in 281 he had celebrated a triumph over the Etruscans and in 263 was appointed by Fulvius Maximus as his second-in-command for the ceremony of driving a nail into the temple of Jupiter, a magic procedure intended to avert pestilence;[4] doubtless, like Marcius Rutilus, he was also a priest.

L. Fulvius Curvus, the first Fulvius recorded in the Fasti, was consul with Fabius Rullianus in 322, but in the next century the

---

[1] His predecessor in this position was Appius Claudius Caecus in 312, his successor P. Crassus Dives in 210.

[2] The main connexion of the Caecilii seems to have been with the Aemilian-Scipionic-Servilian group. Lucius' father had been consul in 284 with a Servilius, while he himself had followed P. Servilius Geminus in both his consulships (251 and 247); his son Quintus was a loyal follower of Scipio Africanus. He himself, however, in 249 had been named *magister equitum* by the dictator A. Atilius Calatinus (the only dictator to hold a command outside Italy), while Caecilius when himself *dictator comitiorum habendorum causa* in 224 took Num. Fabius Buteo his old colleague in the consulship as his *magister equitum* and thus was one of the few plebeian dictators to choose a patrician *magister equitum*. Thus the political loyalties of the Caecilii apparently varied at different periods, and in the second part of his career L. Caecilius Metellus was friendly with the Fabian group. In a later day the Caecilii Metelli were among the chief supporters of L. Cornelius Sulla.

[3] 265 Q. Fabius Maximus Gurges   L. Mamilius Vitulus
     Cens. Cn. Cornelius Blasio   C. Marcius Rutilus II
   264 Ap. Claudius Caudex   M. Fulvius Flaccus
   263 M'. Valerius Maximus   M'. Otacilius Crassus
     Dict. clavi fig. causa.   Cn. Fulvius Maximus Centumalus
     Mag. equit.   Q. Marcius Philippus
   262 L. Postumius Megellus   Q. Mamilius Vitulus
   261 L. Valerius Flaccus   T. Otacilius Crassus

[4] On this ceremony, which Mommsen (*Röm. Chronol.*[2] 176 ff.) wrongly thought occurred every hundred years, see K. J. Beloch, *Röm. Gesch.* 36, and A. Momigliano, *Bull. Com. Arch.* 1930, 29 ff.

Fulvii were alienated from the Fabii (see pp. 37 f.). The Mamilii, who like the Fulvii came from Tusculum, had been living in Rome for three generations before they reached the consulship, which the fourth generation attained when, doubtless with the help of Fabius Gurges and N. Fabius Pictor (*cos.* 266), L. Mamilius Vitulus became consul in 265 with Fabius Gurges. The connexion of the Otacilii with the Fabii is recorded in the tradition that the only Fabius to survive the disaster to the Fabian *gens* at the Cremera in 477 married a daughter of Otacilius of Malventum (later Beneventum).[1] Of the two Otacilii who reached the consulship early in the First Punic War, T. Otacilius Crassus was again consul in 246 when the Fabii were holding consulships 247–245 (see p. 32); the connexion of the families in the Second Punic War is discussed below (p. 59). Thus, as Münzer has argued, besides the Atilii, Manlii, and Marcii, the Fulvii and Mamilii from Tusculum and the Otacilii from Beneventum probably were linked by personal and political ties to the Fabii.

The Ogulnii, probably an Etruscan family, also had many contacts with the Fabii. Q. and Cn. Ogulnius were elected curule aediles for 296 during the fourth consulship of Fabius Rullianus, while a century later M. Ogulnius was elected praetor for 182 during the consulship of Q. Fabius Labeo. Interest centres mainly on Q. Ogulnius who with his brother Gnaeus was tribune in 300 and carried a measure to increase the number of pontiffs and augurs and to fill the new places with plebeians.[2] As aediles in 296 the brothers took measures to safeguard the welfare of the plebeians and to maintain the cult of Jupiter Capitolinus, while they set up a statue of the wolf suckling Romulus and Remus. Q. Ogulnius headed an embassy sent to Epidaurus to bring the cult of Aesculapius to Rome, in conformity with a resolution of the Senate carried in 292, when Fabius Gurges was holding his first consulship; then in 273 he went with N. Fabius Pictor to the Ptolemaic court at Alexandria on an embassy led by Fabius Gurges, who had by this time held a second consulship and the censorship. He was consul with C. Fabius Pictor (doubtless the brother of N. Fabius Pictor) in 269, the year when silver coins were first issued by Rome, and was later dictator (257). Thus Ogulnius, whose contribution to the religious, political, and economic life of the period appears considerable, was closely associated with the Fabii,[3] and his career is a good example of that type of co-operation between a major patrician and a lesser plebeian family which must have so often existed even

---

[1] Auct. *De praen.* 6; Fest. 170.

[2] Beloch (*Röm. Gesch.* 350 ff.), however, dates this lex Ogulnia to 296.

[3] This link is symbolized in the didrachma portraying (*obv.*) Hercules and (*rev.*) she-wolf and twins, if the view of H. Mattingly (*JRS*, 1945, 67 n. 14) is correct, that Hercules, the founder of the Fabian *gens*, refers to C. Fabius, and the twins to Q. Ogulnius. On the date see Pliny, *NH.* xxxiii. 44, and H. Mattingly, op. cit. See Frontispiece nos. 11, 12.

when the surviving evidence does not permit us to establish such a link as a fact.

11. *The Aemilian Group*

Another grouping of families has been traced around the Aemilii, comprising the Livii, Veturii, Servilii, Papirii, and Pomponii.[1] The first member of the Livian *gens* to reach the consulship, Livius Denter, held office in 302 with Aemilius Paullus. Thereafter the Livii lapse into obscurity until 219 when M. Livius Salinator was consul with L. Aemilius Paullus, except that in 236 M'. Aemilius (Lepidus) and M. Livius Salinator, doubtless the leaders of the patrician and plebeian halves of the decemviral college, were responsible for the Ludi Saeculares.[2] Later the sons of the consuls of 219 were long connected in their careers. The Servilii, in alliance with the Aemilii in the years 366 to 362, enjoyed a flourishing period which ended with the plebeian victory and the Licinian reforms.[3] Then after a century of obscurity they struggled to the front again in the First Punic War, when Cn. Servilius Caepio was consul in 253 (with C. Sempronius Blaesus) and P. Servilius Geminus (probably his cousin) in 252 (with C. Aurelius Cotta) and again in 248. Later this patrician *gens* became plebeian, the *transitio ad plebem* probably being accomplished by C. Servilius Geminus (son of the consul of 252) before he was taken prisoner in 218. The Veturii, who had influence in the fourth century, like the Servilii suffered eclipse for a century and then re-emerged before the Hannibalic War, probably with the help of other families: L. Veturius Philo (*cos.* 220) probably belonged to the Aemilian-Livian group, a connexion which can also be seen in the course of the war.

The Aemilii themselves had seen ups and downs. Well to the fore in the period of the Pyrrhic War (285–278), thereafter they failed for forty years to reach high office, apart from one consulship in 255. At this point another grouping has been discerned.[4] The eight consuls of 233–230 included two Aemilii, one Papirius, two Pomponii, and one Iunius. The Papirii had not held even one consulship for forty years, and were linked with the Aemilii not only by a similar decline but by marriage when Papiria (daughter of the consul of 231) married the son of Aemilius Paullus who fell at Cannae. The four plebeian consuls of this group (Pomponii, Publicius, and Iunius) probably stood in the same camp. The Iunii had been connected with the Aemilii at the end of the fourth century, while Iunius Pera (*cos.* 230)

[1] Münzer, *RA*, 155 ff. (Aemilii), 225 ff. (Livii), 123 ff. (Veturii), 132 ff. (Servilii), 160 ff. (Papirii), 161 ff. (Pomponii).
[2] *CIL*, i, p. 29: 'Ludi Saeculares tert(ii) M'. Aemilio M'. f., M. Livio M. f. M. n. Salinatore mag(istris) xvir(um).' [3] Münzer, *RA*, 23.
[4] Ibid. 160 ff.

reached the censorship under the consul of 225, Aemilius Papus, and was in fact the last of his house to become consul. After 230 the Aemilii also declined: Aemilius Barbula (*cos.* 230) and Aemilius Papus (*cos.* 225) were the last consular representatives of their houses. Paullus, the next Aemilius to reach the consulship, was killed at Cannae; thereafter there was no Aemilian consul for nearly thirty years.

With this group were linked, as will be seen later, the Cornelii Scipiones, the Licinii (whose earlier connexions may have been with the Fabii), and the Caecilii. The career of Scipio Africanus, whose mother was a Pomponia and whose wife an Aemilia, ran closely parallel to that of P. Licinius Crassus, while Q. Caecilius Metellus was his staunch supporter. There appears to have been a *bloc* of these groups in office during the First Punic War.[1] In 284 C. Servilius Tucca had been a colleague of L. Caecilius Metellus and successor to M. Aemilius Lepidus. His nephews were probably the cousins Cn. Servilius Caepio (*cos.* 253) and P. Servilius Geminus (*cos.* 252). The former followed in office Cn. Cornelius Scipio (*cos.* II in 254); the latter had C. Aurelius Cotta as colleague in both his consulships (252 and 248), while he was followed in both consulships by L. Caecilius Metellus, the later Pontifex Maximus whose support may have weakened (p. 33 n. 2) but whose son Quintus later co-operated with Scipio Africanus. Cn. Cornelius Scipio (*cos.* 254) stood between an Aemilius (M. Paullus 255) and a Servilius (Cn. Caepio 253), just as his nephew P. Cornelius Scipio did in 218 (L. Aemilius Paullus 219, Cn. Servilius Geminus 217).

III. *The Claudian Group*

The Claudii were characterized by Livy as a 'familia superbissima ac crudelissima in plebem Romanam', a charge echoed by many Roman writers. Mommsen, however, has long since shown that this patrician house should be regarded not as supporters of an unbending aristocracy, but rather as producing men who have some title to be called the predecessors of the Gracchi,[2] and whose interests were more often civilian than military. Demagogic tendencies, however, did not quench their pride (*vetus atque insita Claudiae familiae superbia*), even though the plebs might not be the chief sufferers from it. It has been said that 'there was no epoch of Rome's history but could show a Claudius intolerably arrogant towards the *nobiles* his rivals, or grasping personal power under cover of liberal politics'.[3] 'Patricia gens Claudia ... duodetriginta consulatus, dictaturas quinque, censuras septem, triumphos sex, duas ovationes adepta est.'[4]

[1] Schur, *Scipio*, 122 ff.   [2] Mommsen, *Hist. of Rome*, Eng. trans. Vol. I, Appendix.
[3] R. Syme, *RR*, 19. Cf. Tac. *Ann*. i. 4.   [4] Sueton. *Tib*. 1. 1–2.

The political predominance of the Claudii owed much to Appius Claudius Caecus at the time of the great Samnite War: 'quattuor robustos filios, quinque filias, tantam domum, tantas clientelas Appius regebat et caecus et senex.'[1] If the names of the men whom his five daughters married were known, the means by which he exerted his political influence would be clearer. An attempt has been made to show that at this period Claudius co-operated with the Valerii Maximi, Sulpicii Saverriones, Volumnii, Iunii Bruti, Marcii Philippi, and Sempronii Sophi and that in the period 298–294 the Claudii and Fabii formed a coalition.[2] However that may be, three of Claudius' sons reached the consulship: Appius Claudius Caecus in 268 (he apparently died without an heir) and P. Claudius Pulcher in 249; the third brother C. Claudius Centho, consul with M. Sempronius Tuditanus in 240, had little support from the families which on Schur's supposition had been friendly with his father, since some had died out and others had sunk into insignificance.

The Sempronii, however, seem to have been linked with the Claudii, though not without exceptions, from the days of Ap. Claudius Caecus to those of the Gracchi. The first noteworthy Sempronius was P. Sophus (*cos.* 304, censor 299) whose son was consul with the eldest son of Ap. Claudius Caecus in 268. Then in 240 a new branch was represented in M. Sempronius Tuditanus, consul with C. Claudius Centho, the third son of Caecus; his son, M. Sempronius Tuditanus, was consul in 185 with Ap. Claudius Pulcher, a grandson of Caecus. The first Sempronius Gracchus to reach the consulship was Tiberius in 238. His son (*cos.* I in 215), as will be seen, was closely connected with Ap. Claudius Pulcher in the Hannibalic War, while his grandson was consul in 177 with C. Claudius Pulcher, a brother of the Appius with whom Sempronius Tuditanus was consul in 185. This long succession of joint consulships between the two families culminated in the marriage of the two tribunes Tiberius and C. Gracchus with two cousins, Claudia and Licinia, the granddaughters of C. Claudius Pulcher (*cos.* 177).[3] The support which Ti. Gracchus received in his agrarian reforms from his father-in-law, Appius Claudius Pulcher, the Princeps Senatus, is well known.

The Claudii gained a further ally in Q. Fulvius Flaccus who was driven into their camp by the political manœuvres of 231 when he and T. Manlius Torquatus, declared *vitio creati* by the augurs, were deprived of their censorship. As it was Fabius who stepped into the vacant censorship, Fabius who was one of the most influential members of the augural college which he had entered thirty-four years

[1] Cic. De sen. 37.
[2] Schur, *Hermes*, 1924, 463 ff.
[3] See Münzer, *RA*, 270 ff.; Schur, *Hermes*, 1924, 470 f.

before, and Fabius who similarly pulled the wires in 215 to annul the consular election of Marcellus in order to make room for himself, he may be presumed responsible for losing the support of Fulvius and for presenting the Claudii with a new supporter. The story of how Fulvius with the Claudian group later undermined Fabius' position belongs to the period after Cannae.

III

LIBERAL POLITICS AND POPULAR
LEADERS

(218–216 B.C.)

1. *The Aemilian-Scipionic Group*

A GLANCE at the Fasti of 222–216 B.C.[1] suggests that the Aemilian-Scipionic group, supported by the Livii, Servilii, and Minucii,[2] held a predominating position in the Senate which was responsible for the declaration of the Second Punic War and for the direction of its opening campaigns. During these years they gained the seven patrician consulships, one censorship, and two or three plebeian consulships, while a senior member of the group, L. Cornelius Lentulus Caudinus (*cos.* 237 and censor 236) became Pontifex Maximus in 221, and possibly *princeps senatus* in 220.[3] The conduct of the war by these men and by the Senate in general did not pass unchallenged by the People, who put forward their own leaders to command armies with disastrous results. But although the extant tradition, which is essentially aristocratic in outlook, naturally emphasizes the clash between Senate and People, traces of rivalry and differences within the Senate itself can still be discerned, while there is sufficient evidence to discount some of the censure which the popular leaders have suffered.

As the Hannibalic War broke out when the Aemilian-Scipionic group was holding the chief magistracies, two questions arise: whether any particular responsibility for the war rests upon them, and the wider issue of Rome's general liability. War guilt should not be

[1] 222 Cn. Cornelius Scipio   M. Claudius Marcellus
221 P. Cornelius Scipio Asina   M. Minucius Rufus
220 L. Veturius Philo   C. Lutatius Catulus
     Censors: L. Aemilius Papus   C. Flaminius
219 L. Aemilius Paullus   M. Livius Salinator
218 P. Cornelius Scipio   Ti. Sempronius Longus
217 Cn. Servilius Geminus   C. Flaminius II
216 L. Aemilius Paullus II   C. Terentius Varro

On the Fasti of 221–219 see p. 273.

[2] See p. 35. For the Minucii see p. 46 n. 2. Lutatius' political outlook is not known.

[3] Dio Cassius (frg. 55) and Zonaras (viii. 22) may imply that Lentulus was *princeps senatus* in 219; if so, he must have been elected in the *lectio senatus* of 220. This implication is accepted by Münzer (*PW*, s.v. Cornelius, n. 211), but it conflicts with the view that M. Fabius Buteo, who was the oldest living *censorius* in 216, remained *princeps senatus*. If Lentulus was in fact chosen to succeed Buteo in 220, the Fabii suffered a serious political reverse, since the honour had been almost a hereditary one in the family (cf. Pliny, *NH*, vii. 41, 133). See also p. 70.

assigned solely to either Rome or Carthage on the hypothesis of ambitious desires for revenge by the house of Barca or the adoption of an aggressive Weltpolitik by a large part of the Roman Senate. Rome's interference in the internal affairs of her ally Saguntum, where an anti-Punic faction was installed by force after a clash with the neighbouring Torboletae who were subject to Carthage, may justify the view that 'the balance of aggression must incline against Rome',[1] but it is equally clear that by his subsequent attack on Saguntum Hannibal deliberately precipitated war with Rome. Foreseeing that he was about to throw down the gauntlet, Rome warned him to respect Saguntum (winter 220–219) and lodged a similar *caveat* at Carthage,[2] but when he laid siege to the town (spring 219), the Senate took no precipitate action. Some members may have hesitated on moral grounds, believing that the dispatch of military help would infringe the Ebro treaty of 226. However that may be, the Senate clearly decided that risk of war on two fronts must be avoided by first clearing up the Adriatic where Demetrius of Pharos was pillaging Illyrian cities which were under Roman protection.[3] Thus Saguntum was allowed to face Hannibal's assault unaided, and the two consuls, L. Aemilius Paullus and M. Livius Salinator, were sent to Illyricum.[4] On their return to Rome by the autumn they were granted triumphs,[5] but the government instead of pressing on with urgent military preparations did nothing even when Saguntum fell after an eight months' siege and Roman prestige was badly shaken (c. Nov. 219). Not until the spring of 218 was action taken and an ultimatum, which really involved a declaration of war, was sent to Carthage.[6]

At what point the Senate decided that war with Carthage was inevitable cannot be determined. Dio Cassius records that on the fall of Saguntum there was a senatorial debate in which L. Cornelius Lentulus proposed an immediate declaration of war, Q. Fabius Maximus the sending of an embassy. This tradition was ridiculed by Polybius: 'there was no debate on the question of war, as some historians assert, who even add the speeches delivered on either side. . . . I need not waste any more words upon such compositions as those of

[1] CAH, viii. 31.

[2] Rome sent two embassies to Carthage, one before the siege of Saguntum (P. iii. 15), the other after its fall (iii. 20). Livy's account (xxi. 6; 9. 3–11. 2) is confused because apologetic.

[3] P. iii. 16. 1.

[4] Polybius (iii. 16. 7; 18–19) refers to Aemilius only, but the annalistic tradition (Dio Cass. frg. 51; Zon. viii. 20) mentions both consuls. Aemilius probably conducted the main campaign by land, while Livius was in command at sea.

[5] In order to honour the Aemilii, Polybius (iii. 19. 12) does not record the triumph of Livius, which is, however, attested in *De vir. ill.* 50. 1.

[6] Polybius (iii. 20) wrongly says that when the Romans heard of the disaster at Saguntum they at once (παραχρῆμα) elected envoys whom they sent in all haste (κατὰ σπουδήν) to Carthage. Cf. De Sanctis, III. i. 424 n. 86.

Chaereas and Sosylus which in my judgment are more like the gossip of the barber's shop and the pavement than history.'[1]

But this version of events should not be rejected so hastily, especially as Polybius' own account of the outbreak of the war is not beyond criticism. If there was no debate, the Senate during the summer or autumn of 219 must have decided to declare war on Carthage as soon as Saguntum fell;[2] but if such a decision had been taken, more urgent preparations should have been set on foot. To suggest that the Senate hoped Saguntum would succeed in holding out until the campaigning season of 218 and that in consequence it remained inactive through the previous summer and winter involves an unwarranted assumption of short-sightedness in a body which apparently did not include many 'appeasers'. Dio Cassius' reference to a senatorial debate may therefore represent more than mere gossip. Further, an indication of political opinion emerges. The Cornelii were eager to start the war as soon as it was inevitable (as they were eager to press on with its prosecution later), while the Fabii counselled caution; if the advice of the former had been taken, the war might have been fought in Spain or Gaul rather than in Italy.[3]

Besides the question of war and peace the further problem of the ultimate object of Roman policy was probably thrashed out; was this to be limited to crushing Hannibal and Carthaginian power in Spain or was it to aim at the destruction of Carthage as a great Power? Roman military dispositions in 218 suggest the latter decision.[4] Such a policy was probably consistently upheld by the Scipionic group throughout the war despite the fact that Hannibal temporarily forced on Rome a defensive strategy which the Fabians later wished to maintain although it would have resulted in a negotiated peace and the survival of Carthage as an independent power. But when at last

---

[1] P. iii. 20. The tradition recorded by Dio (Zon. viii. 22) probably derives from an early reliable source and may not have been limited to Chaereas and Sosylus, the latter of whom accompanied Hannibal on his campaign. It probably reached Dio through a Latin writer (? Coelius). Livy omitted it either because he patriotically rejected the idea that the Romans hesitated when once Saguntum had fallen or because he respected Polybius' criticism. Cf. De Sanctis, III. ii. 197.

[2] Polybius (iii. 20. 2) says that a year before the fall of Saguntum the Romans had announced that they would declare war on the Carthaginians if they entered Saguntine territory, but this statement cannot be accepted. Cf. De Sanctis, III. i. 424 n. 86.

[3] It may be objected that a Cornelius and a Fabius were invented by Dio's source as prototypes of P. Cornelius Scipio and Fabius Cunctator who later in the war urged an offensive and defensive strategy respectively. But if that were so, why should a relatively obscure L. Cornelius Lentulus (probably the consul of 237) be chosen? Would not Africanus' father, P. Cornelius Scipio, who was consul-elect in 219, have made a better prototype? In fact the reference to Lentulus, who though prominent at the time (possibly being *princeps senatus*; cf. p. 39 n. 3) was not likely to be well remembered by later generations, creates confidence in the tradition. For the possibility of a decision in Spain see *CAH*, vii. 815; P. iii. 15. 13.

[4] Cf. F. E. Adcock, *The Roman Art of War*, 79–82.

conditions allowed, Scipio Africanus secured a reversion to the policy which his father had doubtless advocated at the outbreak of the war.[1]

Late in March 218, after the Senate and People had conditionally decided on war, five senatorial *legati* went to Carthage to demand the surrender of Hannibal and his staff (*rerum repetitio* or *clarigatio*); when their demands were refused, they conveyed the decision of war (*indictio belli*).[2] The composition of the embassy points again to the predominance of the Aemilian group. The commissioners were C. Licinius (probably the consul of 236), Q. Baebius Tamphilus (one of the commissioners sent to Hannibal in 220), M. Livius Salinator and L. Aemilius Paullus (*coss.* 219), the leader being a Fabius, probably not the famous Q. Fabius Maximus Cunctator but M. Fabius Buteo who had been consul more than twenty-five years before.[3] Since he was the only member out of sympathy with the Aemilian group,[4] he may have been included to give dignity to the proceedings and also to ensure that no reasonable offer of restitution by Carthage was rejected out of hand by any of his more impetuous colleagues.

Other aspects of foreign affairs must have been debated in the Senate during the winter of 219/18. Policy towards Philip V, the new king of Macedon, with whom Demetrius of Pharos had taken refuge, needed definition, while the northern frontier required safeguarding against further Gallic threats. To this end Latin colonies were planned at Placentia and Cremona,[5] but the Boian Gauls, encouraged by news of Hannibal's movements and supported by the Insubres, swept over the Po valley, drove the new colonists into Mutina, and treacherously captured the three land commissioners.

This Gallic rising had repercussions on Rome's wider strategy. The Senate, doubtless persuaded by the driving force and wide outlook of the Scipios, had decided that P. Cornelius Scipio should strike at Spain from Massilia, while the other consul, Ti. Sempronius Longus, planned to invade Africa from Sicily. But the trouble in north Italy

[1] F. R. Kramer ('Massilian Diplomacy before the Second Punic War', *AJP*, 1948, pp. 1 ff.) argues that the Aemilian faction, stimulated by Massilian propaganda, had advocated a policy of wider commitments in the interest of national security in order to forestall the possibility of a Gallic-Carthaginian coalition in 231 and 226, urging that Rome's self-interest was involved in checking Punic aggrandizement in Spain.

[2] On the transference of the duties of the *fetiales* to senatorial *legati* and the modification of Rome's formal procedure in the declaration of war when she had to deal with overseas powers see F. W. Walbank, *JRS*, 1937, 192 ff., and *CP*, 1949, 15 ff.

[3] See p. 274.

[4] The consuls of 219 were prominent leaders in the Aemilian-Scipionic group; the Licinii were friendly (cf. Münzer, *RA*, 183 ff.), as also Baebius must have been to judge from the political relations of his sons, who owed their consulships largely to Aemilius Paullus (see below, p. 170). A certain L. Baebius (perhaps the praetor of 189: L. xxxvii. 40; 50; 57) was a legate of Scipio Africanus in Africa (L. xxx. 25).

[5] The colonial commissioners were C. Lutatius Catulus (*cos.* 220) and probably C. Servilius Geminus and M. Annius, whose families seem to have belonged to the Aemilian-Scipionic group. See pp. 273 f.

side-tracked the force destined for Spain, so that owing to the delay entailed in raising a new army Scipio failed to hold the Rhône against Hannibal, who had taken the initiative with masterly speed and now turned north to cross the Alps. Scipio himself hastened back to north Italy, probably in order 'to guide the Senate's policy rather than to be guided by it',[1] but he wisely sent his army on to Spain under his brother Gnaeus. This decision to try to deny the resources of Spain to Hannibal, combined with Scipio's ultimate objective of driving the Carthaginians completely out of the peninsula, was a main factor in achieving final victory.

To meet the emergency of Hannibal's arrival in north Italy, Sempronius, who had captured Malta, was recalled from Sicily, where a praetor, M. Aemilius Lepidus, remained on guard, while south Italy was covered by a smaller naval squadron under Sextus Pomponius, whose family also adhered to the Aemilian group.[2] After a clash with Hannibal at the Ticinus Scipio, who had been wounded, wisely awaited his colleague in a strong position on the Trebia. Sempronius Longus on arrival was eager to re-engage the enemy, but Scipio refused. Their subsequent quarrel probably arose from military rather than personal or political considerations. True, the two commanders may have belonged to different political groups, since the majority of the Sempronii supported the Claudii (p. 37); but, on the other hand, as their sons co-operated as colleagues in the consulship of 194, the Longi may have been more friendly than other Sempronian families to the Cornelii. However that may be, Sempronius, having failed to convince Scipio, decided to act, as he could owing to Scipio's illness: after a successful skirmish he put all to the test with disastrous results. Both Polybius, in his comparatively sober account, and Livy, more dramatically, emphasize that Sempronius acted from ambition, blind confidence, and the desire to win the credit of a decisive action before Scipio was well or the consuls of the next year took over the command.[3] Polybius' connexion with the Scipios may have led him to follow a tradition which stressed Sempronius' errors in an attempt to minimize Scipio's responsibility, and after all Sempronius may have judged that the legions which had not yet been tested against Hannibal in the field would prove invincible, yet the verdict of the Roman People must stand. Sempronius, who escaped to Rome to hold the elections, did not have his command renewed, while Scipio was rewarded by being sent to Spain with prolonged *imperium* and his far-

---

[1] *CAH*, viii. 39.

[2] Cf. Münzer, *RA*, 160 ff. In the north before Hannibal arrived two praetors, whose families supported the Fabii, had been operating: L. Manlius Vulso, who had been surprised by the Boii, was rescued by his colleague C. Atilius Serranus.

[3] P. iii. 68 ff.; L. xxi. 52 ff. Polybius (70. 7) implies that the elections had taken place, but Livy (53. 6; 57. 4) shows that they had not (cf. L. xxi. 15. 6).

seeing policy was thus confirmed. Sempronius, somewhat chastened, would be less likely to try to block the candidature of a member of the Aemilian-Scipionic group.

II. *Flaminius and Minucius*

At the elections for 217 B.C. members of the Aemilian-Scipionic group gained the patrician consulship for Cn. Servilius Geminus and three praetorships,[1] but the second consul was the People's favourite, C. Flaminius who had championed their cause against the nobility. As tribune in 232 he had carried an agrarian law in the plebeian Assembly without consulting the Senate. His governorship of Sicily as praetor in 227 was long remembered with gratitude by the provincials. Consul in 223, he had advanced boldly against the Insubres, disregarding an order from the Senate to return to Rome on the ground that a fault had been found in the form of his election. After this successful challenge to the religious control of the nobility, he had campaigned not without credit and then was voted a triumph by the People in the teeth of the Senate's refusal. As censor in 220 he began the construction of the great road to Ariminum towards his land settlements in the north, and a year or so later he was the only senator to support the lex Claudia which limited the maritime trade of senators.[2] Thus his brilliant career had demonstrated the theoretical sovereignty of the Roman People, which had been finally vindicated by the Hortensian law of 287, and now his election to a second consulship in 217 reflected popular discontent with senatorial conduct of the war. The choice, however, was unfortunate. Although a skilled political leader and a courageous fighter, Flaminius lacked the qualities of generalship most needed at the moment.

Livy, who followed a tradition hostile to the People and their leaders, describes how Flaminius, neglecting to perform the proper religious ceremonies before he left Rome, slunk off to Ariminum to enter his consulship there, for fear he should be stopped by the Senate. In vain the Senate ordered him to return to discharge his religious duties, and when his colleague, Cn. Servilius, duly entered upon his consulship in Rome and outlined to the Senate his intended policy, the indignation against Flaminius burst out afresh. This tradition, which rightly reflects the animus of the Senate towards Flaminius, is clearly biased against him.[3]

[1] M. Pomponius Matho, M. Aemilius, and A. Cornelius Mammula; the fourth praetor, T. Otacilius Crassus, was a Fabian. As it will not be necessary to record the names of all the praetors each year, reference may be made here, once and for all, to the list of praetors on pp. 306 ff.

[2] For another possible anti-senatorial measure of this period see p. 48 n. 3.

[3] L. xxi. 63; xxii. 1. It is in part demonstrably false, since it is contradicted by Polybius' statement (iii. 77. 1) that Flaminius went to Arretium, not Ariminum. Some confusion in

The plan of campaign was to abandon the plains of north Italy, where Hannibal's cavalry and Gallic allies were most useful, and to defend central Italy, with Flaminius guarding the west, Servilius the east. Hannibal, after crossing the Apennines, failed to draw Flaminius into battle near Arretium, but then lured him to death and disaster at Lake Trasimene; subsequently he defeated a cavalry detachment on its way from Servilius to help Flaminius. Again the main tradition is prejudiced against Flaminius, who 'would not seek counsel from God or man'.[1] But if the motives attributed to him are disregarded (and little can have been known about them, since most of his staff died with him in battle), the facts of the campaign go far to rehabilitate his reputation. He is alleged to have fought because he was ashamed to let Hannibal advance towards Rome unopposed, but if this had been his main motive, he probably would have attacked when Hannibal deliberately exposed his flank on his way to Cortona. When Hannibal swung off from the main route to Rome and took the road from Cortona to Perusia via Trasimene, Flaminius' intention in following was probably not to force an action but to save his colleague from having to face Hannibal alone. Further, the tradition that Servilius and Flaminius refused to co-operate is contradicted by Servilius' dispatch of cavalry to Flaminius, while he himself was hastening along the Via Flaminia to his colleague's aid.[2] Thus, the facts that Flaminius avoided battle when Hannibal tried to lure him to attack and that he attempted to co-operate with his colleague show that much of the hostile tradition against him must be discounted. He was, however, outwitted and he probably acted impetuously, although it is not certain that any other contemporary general would have risen superior to Hannibal's genius.[3]

The disaster at Trasimene, which exposed the road to Rome, caused such a crisis that after prolonged senatorial debates the traditional remedy of nominating a dictator was applied, although there had been no dictator with full military *imperium* for over thirty years. But a dictator could be constitutionally appointed only by the consuls, of whom one was dead and the other cut off from Rome by Hannibal, So

Livy's source between Arretium and Ariminum may have suggested the incident of Flaminius' premature departure to his province, which would form an artistic counterpart to his refusal to leave his province in 223: both times he neglected his religious obligations.

[1] L. xxii. 3. 5 (cf. P. iii. 80. 3: Φλαμίνιον ὀχλοκόπον καὶ δημαγωγόν). Traces of a more favourable tradition, however, survive (? from Coelius). Polybius (iii. 84. 6) says that in the battle Flaminius was δυσχρηστούμενον καὶ περικακοῦντα, but Livy (xxii. 5. 1) admits a different view: 'consul perculsis omnibus ipse satis in re trepida inpavidus'.

[2] P. iii. 86. 3 (cf. 82. 4).

[3] According to Livy (xxii. 9) Fabius Maximus attributed Flaminius' defeat more to neglect of his religious duties than to bad generalship, but this remark hardly derives from a tradition more favourable to Flaminius. If true, it would suggest that Fabius chose the easier way to restore public morale: it would be easier in future to avoid mistakes in ritual than in generalship.

the choice was left to the Comitia Centuriata which elected Q. Fabius Maximus by whose experience and caution it was hoped the fortunes of the day might be retrieved.[1] In harmony with this extraordinary procedure the choice of the Master of the Horse was transferred from the dictator to the Comitia which appointed M. Minucius Rufus, who had seen military service against the Istrians as consul in 221, and was the first member of his family, though not of his *gens*, to reach the consulship. The essence of the dictatorship was absolute power, but Fabius was now supported by one whose authority, though subordinate, derived from the People, not from himself.

The explanation of this procedure is complicated. First, the full dictatorship had been so long in abeyance that some qualms may have been felt about entrusting supreme control to one man without any check. Again, the nobility may have secured the election of so staunch a conservative as Fabius by acquiescing in the People's choice of someone in whom they trusted as Magister Equitum. Or the cause may have been popular demand rather than conservative concession: the People, who had lost Flaminius, may have asserted their power to nominate another leader. But behind all this the factions within the nobility played their part, the more easily as the appointment had been left to the Comitia Centuriata rather than to the more democratic assemblies. The Aemilian-Scipionic faction was beginning to suffer eclipse. Although the Scipios were doing good work in Spain, Trebia had been followed by Trasimene, for which Servilius was indirectly responsible, since the general plan of campaign was the work of both consuls and of the Senate in which the Aemilian-Scipionic group predominated. Thus the rival Fabians were able to advance their leader to a responsible position, but not unhampered, since the Minucii belonged to the circle of the Cornelii.[2] Minucius' appointment represents not only the will of the People but also an attempt by the dominant group in the Senate to check the rising power of the Fabii.[3] Yet it was a dangerous precedent to seek to hamper the absolute power of the dictator.

[1] Fabius had been consul in 233 and again in 228. On his dictatorships see pp. 274 f.

[2] M. Minucius Rufus (*cos.* 221) was preceded in the consulship by Cn. Cornelius Scipio and had P. Scipio as colleague; Q. Minucius Thermus (*cos.* 193) was preceded by Scipio Africanus and was colleague of L. Cornelius Merula. Q. Minucius Rufus (*cos.* 197) was colleague of C. Cornelius Cethegus, while M. Minucius Rufus (*cos.* 110) was preceded by P. Scipio Nasica, and Ti. Minucius (*cos.* 305) by P. Cornelius Arvina. These facts are striking because no other Minucii held the consulship between 305 and 110.

[3] M. L. Patterson (*TAPA*, 1942, 321) explains the appointments as the result of the desire to place two experienced soldiers in command. She writes: 'Both Schur and Münzer consider the appointment of Fabius and his Master of Horse, M. Minucius Rufus, politically significant. The unusual form of their election was, however, directly due to the uncertainty of communications with the surviving consul.' But this cannot be the whole explanation: it fails entirely to show why Fabius was robbed of the normal right to nominate his own Magister Equitum.

Fabius' first act was to placate the gods whom Flaminius had slighted; reference was made to the Sibylline books, and Games were held in order to restore public morale. He then consulted the Senate about military policy and doubtless outlined his strategy of dogging Hannibal's heels and avoiding a pitched battle. Taking over Servilius' army he marched with two new legions into Apulia, but when Hannibal, failing to entice him to battle, struck across the Apennines into fertile Campania, Fabius could only follow and watch him devastating the land of Rome's allies. This purely defensive strategy was justified only as a temporary expedient. The Romans still had reason to trust their legions; Trebia had not been an overwhelming defeat nor Trasimene a pitched battle, while their fatal lack of tactical flexibility was not clearly demonstrated until Cannae. Fabius must use his breathing-space to out-manœuvre Hannibal and thus force him to fight on ground favourable to the Romans: only thus could he justify the severe moral and economic loss in which he involved the Roman cause. At last the chance came which might have vindicated his strategy.[1] He held the pass through which Hannibal wished to return to winter quarters in Apulia; here Hannibal's cavalry might be checked and the Roman legions might hope to defeat the enemy in close fighting. But the over-cautious Fabius, like the impetuous Flaminius, was outwitted: Hannibal's ruse of the oxen with blazing faggots tied to their horns won for his army an unhindered passage through the mountains.

At length the opposition to Fabius which all this time had been increasing in his own army, among the allies and in Rome, was too loud to be disregarded: he was recalled to Rome, nominally on religious business but actually to consult the Senate. He left his army in command of Minucius Rufus, who throughout the campaign had actively criticized the dictator's defensive policy. Hardly was Fabius' back turned when Minucius disobeyed his orders and attacked Hannibal with some success. That Hannibal regarded this revival of activity as more than a mere pin-prick is shown by the fact that he left his camp and brought all his forces into Geruneum. Minucius' action, when reported in Rome, would be exaggerated into a great Roman victory by those who were dissatisfied with Fabius and now made their influence felt.

Fabius tried to stem the tide of popular discontent by getting a consul elected in place of Flaminius. This presumably would lead to the restoration of normal consular authority and his own resignation. But if he could get a friendly consul in office and the hostile Minucius

---

[1] Polybius (iii. 93. 1) admits that Fabius contemplated the possibility of a general engagement: 'Fabius thought that at least he would be able to carry off their booty . . . and possibly even put an end to the whole campaign owing to the great advantage his position gave him.'

out of office and at the same time stifle popular criticism, his own political position might be strengthened.[1] But his choice of M. Atilius Regulus, son of the famous Regulus and already consul in 227, was unfortunate.[2] It pleased neither the People nor many senators. The new consul was too old to give fresh life and vigour to the war, as the People desired, and the Aemilian faction was still strong enough, particularly after Minucius' slight success, to object to the appointment of a Fabian nominee. The People therefore passed a measure to co-ordinate the power of the Master of the Horse with that of the dictator: that is, they were to be co-dictators, almost a contradiction in terms, since the essence of the dictatorship lay in the delegation of absolute power to one man in contrast to the divided commands of the consuls. This extraordinary curtailment of the power of the dictatorship struck at its very roots so that hereafter it gradually fell into disuse.[3]

When after this political upheaval Fabius returned to Minucius, the two generals divided the army and encamped apart. Hannibal, counting on their discord and on Minucius' desire for battle, soon drew him into an engagement which would, it is said, have proved disastrous had not Fabius brought immediate help. But the tradition is pro-Fabian and has clearly exaggerated both Minucius' danger and the value of Fabius' aid;[4] Livy's delight at Fabius' success culminates in an almost ludicrous scene where the humbled Minucius sees the

---

[1] In any case, even if Fabius did not resign before the end of his six-months period of office, he would be strengthening his political control between the end of his dictatorship (c. Dec. 217, since Trasimene had been fought in June: cf. De Sanctis, III. ii. 120) and the entry of the new consuls into office in Mar. 216.

[2] On the friendly relations of the Fabii and Atilii see p. 32. During this critical period a plebiscite removed the ban on holding the consulship twice within ten years during the period of the war in Italy (L. xxvii. 6. 7). The purpose was no doubt partly to ensure that 'ability as a commander was to be a factor of major importance in the election of consuls' (M. L. Patterson, TAPA, 1942, 321), but it also had a political aspect. Atilius could not technically be consul again until 216 unless the ban were removed. Fabius probably suggested this measure in order to get his friend into office and also perhaps with an eye to his own future: at any rate he gained more from it than Atilius did. The ban had already been disregarded in the election of C. Flaminius to a second consulship in 217 after his first in 223, but doubtless the nobility wished to have a legal basis for such procedure by which the People had arbitrarily re-elected their champion. Despite Livy's silence, this bill apparently applied to other magistracies besides the consulship, at any rate to the praetorship (M. Pomponius Matho was praetor in 217 and 216, Q. Fulvius Flaccus in 215 and 214).

[3] See p. 275. The text of Livy (xxii. 25) names the proposer of the measure M. Metellus, but Plutarch (Fab. 7) gives M. Metilius. He is probably the author of the lex Metilia de fullonibus, which Pliny (NH, xxxv, 197) places in 220–219; there is no need to conjecture the existence of a second tribune of the same name, since the tribune of 217 may have carried in the form of a plebiscite a censorial edict of 220 (cf. Münzer, PW, s.v. Metilius n. 9). He was probably connected with C. Flaminius, since he secured popular approval for an enactment of Flaminius' censorship in 220 and held the tribunate during Flaminius' second consulship. Livy adds that the measure to appoint Minucius was supported by Terentius Varro.   [4] Cf. De Sanctis, III. ii. 54.

folly of his ways and seeks pardon and a reconciliation with his erstwhile foe. After the battle the command was taken over by the two
consuls, Servilius and Regulus.[1]

III. *Terentius Varro*

The elections for 216 provoked sharp political intrigue. The consuls, who were too busy to come to Rome, proposed the appointment
of an interrex, but the Senate decided on the nomination of a dictator
to hold the elections. The consuls named L. Veturius Philo (*cos.* 220),
who appointed M. Pomponius Matho (probably the consul of 231) as
his Master of the Horse, but their nomination was declared invalid
and they had to resign. The Senate then appointed C. Claudius
Centho (*cos.* 240, censor 225) as interrex, and he in turn nominated
P. Cornelius Asina (*cos.* 221) to conduct the elections.[2] According to
Livy a bitter struggle ensued between the nobles, who had five candidates,[3] and the People, who put forward the demagogue C. Terentius
Varro (*pr.* 218). This resulted in the sole election of Varro, who then
conducted a second election to appoint a colleague. The nobles,
realizing that their candidates were not strong enough, successfully
put forward the reluctant L. Aemilius Paullus (*cos.* 219): the State
had need of tried men. The new praetors also had all held office
before, and three if not four of them were ex-consuls.

Thus Livy's account emphasizes the contest between the nobility
and the People's candidate Varro, but some difficulties in the narrative
suggest that the nobles themselves were far from united.[4] Q. Baebius
Herennius, a tribune and relative of Varro, 'accused not only the
Senate but also the augurs because they had prevented the dictator
from carrying through the elections'.[5] He alleged that the consuls had
deliberately stayed away from Rome in order to bring about an interregnum; they were first thwarted by the appointment of a dictator,
but then gained their way after his appointment had been annulled by the augurs. This implies that Varro hoped to win the election
with the help of the dictator, but was checked when the augurs intervened. But the head of the college of augurs was Fabius,[6] whom Livy

---

[1] During Fabius' dictatorship and under the strain of war the bronze coinage was
reduced from an *as* of 10 oz. to one of 6 oz.: see H. Mattingly, *JRS*, 1945, 73.

[2] An interrex was elected probably by the patrician senators; he had to nominate a
successor. A minimum of two interreges was essential, since the one elected first was not
qualified to hold consular elections, perhaps because he was considered to have received
the *auspicia* irregularly. Each succeeding interrex held office for five days: the highest
number of interreges recorded is fourteen (L. viii. 2. 3).

[3] The patricians were P. Cornelius Merenda, L. Manlius Vulso (probably the praetor
of 218), and M. Aemilius Lepidus (*pr.* 218), and the plebeians C. Atilius Serranus (*pr.* 218)
and Q. Aelius Paetus. Merenda and Paetus had presumably been praetors shortly before
218.   [4] L. xxii. 33–5; Münzer, *RA*, 124 ff.   [5] L. xxii. 34. 3.

[6] Münzer, *RA*, 54; 83. At the end of his life (203) Fabius had been augur for 62 years
(L. xxx. 26. 7; cf. Pliny, *NH*, vii. 156); he probably replaced his grandfather Gurges who

mentions as Varro's opponent without making clear how he was involved.[1] These cryptic references to Fabius imply something more
than an attempt by the aristocracy to postpone the elections and to fob
off the popular candidate.

Further, the interregnum is puzzling, since an interrex normally
was appointed only when the consulship was empty; absence of the
consuls on military service usually led to the appointment of a dictator
comitiorum habendorum causa.[2] It is possible that Livy has misunder-
stood the situation and that in fact the elections had been postponed
until the consuls' year of office was at an end; but this is improbable,
since in that case the appointment of an interrex would have been
automatic because the 'auspices would have returned to the *patres*'
and no dictatorship would have been considered. Further, the establishment of an interregnum probably involved reviving a dying custom, like the revival of the full dictatorship earlier in the year (pp. 45 f.).[3]
However that may be, the attempt to establish one in 217 with both
consuls alive and well suggests considerable political intrigue.

The key to the situation is probably the annulment of the dictatorship by the augurs under the influence of Fabius, which shows that
it was he who wanted the interregnum. When the consuls originally
suggested an interregnum, the proposal presumably came from Fabius'
supporter Atilius Regulus, rather than from Servilius. The Senate,
under the leadership of the Aemilian group, rejected the idea and
through Servilius appointed their man Veturius dictator.[4] Under his
presidency the Fabian candidates for the consulship, the patrician
L. Manlius Vulso (whose father was allied with the Atilii and Fabii
in the First Punic War) and the plebeian C. Atilius Serranus would
have little hope of success. Fabius therefore set in motion the religious
machinery of the augural college to annul Veturius' appointment in

---

died in 265. Other members of the augural college in 217 were C. Atilius Serranus (*pr.* 218),
M. Claudius Marcellus (*cos.* I, 222), Sp. Carvilius Maximus (*cos.* 234), M. Aemilius
Lepidus (*cos.* 232), P. Furius Philus (*cos.* 223), M. Pomponius Matho (? = the Pomponius
sent to Delphi in 205: L. xxviii. 45. 12), and probably T. Otacilius Crassus (*pr.* 217) and
Cn. Cornelius Lentulus (? = *cos.* 201). Fabius could presumably count on the support
of Atilius, Marcellus, and Otacilius; perhaps Pomponius and Lentulus were junior members who could be discounted. Lepidus and Furius are likely to have been his opponents,
as also Carvilius who, unlike Fabius, had not opposed Flaminius' land bill in 232. As
Münzer points out, Fabius had a masterly ability to use spiritual weapons in secular
contests.   [1] xxii. 34. 2; 5–7.

[2] The only recorded case of absence on military service resulting in an interregnum
which could be cited as a precedent was in 355 (L. vii. 17), but this is hardly a parallel
because the episode was intimately bound up with the Struggle of the Orders.

[3] No interreges were appointed between 216 and 166, except Q. Fabius Maximus, perhaps in 208 (*CIL*, i, p. 194), and while 19 are known between 509 and 291 B.C., none is
recorded between 291 and 217. This lacuna might be due entirely to the loss of the second
decade of Livy, but the cessation during the next fifty years suggests that interregna may
have been less common in the third than in the fourth century. For a list of interreges see
Williams, *Sénat*, ii. 10 ff.   [4] On the Veturii see above, p. 35.

order to help his own party candidates; a further motive may have been to prevent Varro's election, if it may be assumed that he had more chance of success under the presidency of Veturius than under a pro-Fabian interrex. But Fabius' attempt miscarried, since the interrex appointed to conduct the election was P. Cornelius Asina who was not a member of his group.

Only the fact of these political moves is known; what lay behind them must be conjecture. But there is another relevant fact: at some point the Senate decided to abandon Fabius' cautious policy and to risk all in a pitched battle. Fabius' position during the elections was precarious. His strategy had involved him in great unpopularity which his success at Gerunium had but partially counteracted. It is probable, then, that on the strength of this he was enabled to assert his influence in politics up to a point, that the balance hung evenly for a moment, and that then the Senate, under the influence of the spirited Aemilian group and popular demands, determined to abandon Fabius' strategy. Cornelius Asina held the elections; Varro alone was successful and he then conducted the election of his colleague. L. Aemilius Paullus, a reluctant candidate, was not particularly well disposed towards the plebs whose tribunes had accused him of appropriating spoil after the Illyrian War. He was presumably put forward by the Aemilian group not so much as a representative of the nobility to counteract the popular demands—for these had been met by the appointment of Varro—as to ensure the election of one of their members rather than a Fabian candidate.[1] The result of the first election had shown that neither of the Aemilian-Scipionic candidates (M. Aemilius Lepidus and P. Cornelius Merenda) was strong enough (in fact neither of them ever reached the consulship, although Lepidus gained a second praetorship in 213), so a better candidate had to be found. If Livy's statement that 'all who had been Varro's rivals withdrew their candidature' can be accepted, the collapse of the Fabii will have been complete. To sum up: the Fabian party tried to win control in opposition to the same Aemilian-Scipionic group which had been working together in recent years,[2] but it failed because under pressure from the People, whose candidate was elected without difficulty, the Senate as a whole decided to adopt a more active policy against Hannibal.

The attitude of the Senate to Varro and of Varro to his colleague Aemilius have been distorted in the main tradition, which represents the consuls of 216 as bitter rivals and blames Varro for the campaign which ended so disastrously at Cannae. Polybius, the intimate friend

[1] See p. 275.
[2] P. Scipio Asina, consul in 221 and interrex in 217, helped L. Veturius Philo to the consulship of 220 and a dictatorship in 217; L. Aemilius Paullus followed Veturius' magistracies in his consulships for 219 and 216.

of Aemilius' grandson, Scipio Aemilianus, naturally followed the Aemilian family tradition which made Varro the scapegoat. The Livian tradition goes farther: not content with merely blaming Varro, it paints his portrait in lurid colours as a vulgar demagogue and the son of a butcher.[1] But an examination of his career suggests a different conclusion. He had been quaestor, plebeian and curule aedile, and praetor, and there is no record that he was ever tribune. Further, even after Cannae he held many civil and military offices: his magistracy was prolonged until 213; he commanded a legion in Etruria in 208 and 207; he led a deputation sent to Philip in 203 and another to Africa in 200. Thus while tradition makes him a radical demagogue opposed to the Senate, his career suggests that he enjoyed the Senate's confidence despite his joint responsibility for Cannae.[2] Since Livy records his origin merely as a tradition, his real background must remain obscure. The father doubtless had some connexion with meat. If he had been a grazier, the son's interest in stock-farming would have made him less of an outsider to the landed aristocracy. Or perhaps the father supplied meat and leather to the armies; some two centuries later P. Ventidius, who was in fact an army contractor, was derided as a muleteer. Only sterling worth would have gained the consulship for a *novus homo*, but Varro's qualities may have been better suited to the popular leader than to the opponent of Hannibal.

Varro's attitude to his colleague also has probably been distorted. If there was ill-feeling between them, it probably arose from personal reasons, but Polybius does not suggest any differences until they were within sight of the enemy. Further, the decision to give battle rested on the will of the Senate,[3] backed no doubt by popular demand, and both commanders were equally responsible for the strategic movements of the Roman army. Even though tactical decisions may have been due to Varro, references to Aemilius' disagreement are probably exaggerated or fictitious.[4]

When news came that Hannibal had moved to Cannae, Aemilius and Varro took over from Servilius and Regulus whose commands

---

[1] L. xxii. 25. 18–26. 4.

[2] Servius' explanation (*ad Aen.* xi. 743) of the origin of Varro's *cognomen* may suggest that he served in Illyricum at some time. Traces of a more favourable tradition are found in Florus, i. 22. 17 ('ducum fugit alter, alter occisus est; dubium uter maiore animo'), and in Frontinus, *Strat.* iv. 5. 6.

[3] ἡ τῆς συγκλήτου γνώμη (P. iii. 108. 2. Cf. 107. 7: οἱ δ' ἐβουλεύσαντο μάχεσθαι καὶ συμβάλλειν τοῖς πολεμίοις. Cf. Appian, *Han.* 17. This point is not given by Livy (cf. xxii. 32. 2; 43). The Senate, though responsible for the decision to fight, naturally allowed its generals discretion to choose the moment (P. iii. 108. 1: σὺν καιρῷ).

[4] Cf. De Sanctis, iii. ii. 56 n. 89. When Livy (xxii. 39–40) depicts Aemilius as a disciple of Fabian strategy, this is no doubt due to a late annalist who wished to exculpate the grandfather of Scipio Aemilianus. Polybius' attempt (iii. 110. 8) to excuse Aemilius, on the ground that after the preliminary cavalry attack he could not withdraw and was thus forced to camp by the river, is not convincing.

had been prolonged. Regulus was relieved of his command because of his age, according to Livy, or possibly for political reasons—he was the one Fabian in a group comprising Aemilius, Servilius, Minucius, and Varro.[1] The Roman forces then advanced to Cannae where in that dark hour Aemilius, Minucius, and Servilius perished with the flower of their troops. The policy of the Aemilian-Scipionic group had indeed been put to the test, and its leaders killed. The political result of Cannae was the victory of Fabius the Cunctator and the termination of control by the Aemilian-Scipionic group and of interference by the People.

The People, desirous of a quick decision and a final battle which would bring spoils and a good haul of slaves, had put forward leaders who failed. Hereafter, in the main, they wisely left the control of the war to the Senate, whose power was elevated by the need for swifter decisions and action than could be taken by a cumbrous popular assembly. Their leaders, however, have not received fair treatment in the ancient tradition, which is essentially aristocratic. This pro-senatorial and anti-popular interpretation of history, originating in Polybius' sources, was elaborated farther by writers who saw in past history precedents for the Gracchan revolution against the senatorial monopoly of government: thus Flaminius might appear as a prototype of the two Gracchi, combining the faults of both, Tiberius' agrarian socialism and Gaius' disregard of religious form. Finally Livy, who himself lived through the civil wars and saw both the dangers of popular control and the restoration of dignity, if not authority, to the Senate by Augustus, regarded the Senate as the hero of the Hannibalic War and in glorifying it has done injustice to the representatives of the People.

The fact that the rise and fall of these popular leaders roughly coincided with that of the Aemilian-Scipionic faction suggests the possibility that this faction was more tolerant of the People than were the other noble families. There is some evidence to support such a view. It has been said that 'the democratic fervour which had made possible the reform of the centuries was still at work. That reform is perhaps to be credited with the elevation of a new group of plebeians to the consulship, for instance the two Pomponii (in 233 and 231), Poplicius Malleolus (232), L. Apustius (226), and in bringing back to prominence the families of Papirius (231) and Aemilius Lepidus (232), for a long time in obscurity.'[2] The political co-operation of the Aemilii, Papirii, Pomponii, and Publicius in 233–230 has already been

---

[1] Polybius (iii. 114. 6; 116. 11) says that Regulus stopped and was killed in battle. This is probably due to a confusion of his name Marcus with M. Minucius Rufus who was killed. Regulus was censor in 214.

[2] Tenney Frank, *CAH*, vii. 806.

mentioned.[1] It was in 232 when Aemilius and Publicius were consuls that Flaminius as tribune carried his agrarian law in opposition to a large group of senators who included Q. Fabius Maximus.[2] This measure, though open to criticism at many points, certainly did not begin 'the demoralization of the people'; it was bitterly opposed chiefly because Flaminius disregarded the Senate and brought it directly before the People. The group of plebeians who had just won their way to the consulship might not look on this conduct with such disfavour as the conservative Fabii. Later Flaminius was consul in 223 with a member of the Aemilian group, P. Furius Philus, and after their campaign he was voted a triumph by the People, together with his colleague, in spite of the Senate. Three years later he was censor with L. Aemilius Papus. In 217 he held the consulship a second time at the People's wish, and notwithstanding the distortions of the tradition co-operated loyally with his colleague Servilius. Thus his career was closely linked with the Aemilii and his opponents were their opponents.[3] Further, his son started his career as quaestor to Scipio Africanus in Spain in 210 and held the consulship in 187 with M. Aemilius Lepidus.

M. Minucius Rufus, who enjoyed popular support, was also closely linked with the Aemilian-Scipionic faction: he was consul with P. Cornelius Scipio Asina, was elected *magister equitum* and then co-dictator in the consulship of Servilius, and proved a doughty adversary to Fabius. He can scarcely be regarded as an upstart demagogue, since whatever may be thought of the claims of the Minucii to consulships in the fifth century, one had undoubtedly been consul in 305, but both Polybius and Livy emphasize his reliance upon the support of the People.[4] Again, Varro was consul with Aemilius Paullus, and their rivalry was exaggerated, if not invented, by tradition. Further, it is significant that the outstanding occasion after Cannae when the People expressed its wish in any matter of vital concern was their election of young P. Cornelius Scipio to his Spanish command at a moment when after an eclipse of several years the Aemilian-Scipionic faction began to reassert its power. Finally, the Scipios were far from conservative; if they were not champions of the People, they at least brought much fresh blood into the Senate. Africanus sponsored and

---

[1] Cf. pp. 35 f. See Münzer, *RA*, 160 ff.

[2] Cicero, *De sen.* 4. 11. He wrongly dates this in 228. Concerning the passage De Sanctis (III. i. 333 n. 181) says 'the only certain thing is that the party which opposed the measure is the one to which Fabius belonged'.

[3] F. R. Kramer recently has argued (*AJP*, 1948, pp. 1 ff.) that Flaminius' agrarian measure 'which must be considered in its wider context as a step to stabilize the northern frontier as well as a move in the arena of domestic politics to strengthen the plebeians' (p. 10), was mutually supplementary to, and integrally connected with, the concern of the Aemilii to meet the threat of a Gallic-Punic coalition (see above, p. 42). The two groups co-operated to establish a strong frontier against the Gauls.

[4] P. iii. 90. 6; 103. 5; L. xxii. 27. 1.

set on their careers many 'new men', as C. Laelius, M'. Acilius Glabrio, and Sex. Digitius.

Thus the evidence points in one direction and suggests that the Aemilian-Scipionic group was a liberal progressive section of the Senate which was more ready than the conservatives under Fabius to listen to the demands of the People, and that it was more tolerant of, or even co-operated with, the leaders whom the People put forward. These leaders, so far from being mere demagogues and braggarts, were men of energy and ability, lacking only that level-headed caution and poise which perhaps could only be gained from long personal experience and long family tradition.

IV

CONSERVATIVE STRATEGY AND POLITICS

(216–207 B.C.)

1. *Fabius Cunctator*

CANNAE proved that the strategy advocated by Fabius must now be adopted, but he did not win political control immediately or without opposition. After the disaster Varro, who had rallied the survivors, was summoned to Rome and was thanked for not despairing of the Republic; his legionary command was prolonged. Then on senatorial authority a dictator was appointed, probably nominated by Varro or possibly elected by the Comitia Centuriata as in 217. M. Iunius Pera (*cos.* 230; censor 225), whose political career had been linked with the Aemilii, was chosen, becoming the last dictator to receive full military *imperium* in Rome.[1]

An immediate task was to revise the list of senators so sadly depleted by war. Many ex-consuls, praetors, and aediles had fought and fallen as military tribunes at Cannae, and senators of all grades had voluntarily served in the ranks; Trebia and Trasimene had previously taken their toll. Unusual methods were adopted. Instead of the election of censors, a second dictator was appointed 'sine magistro equitum senatus legendi caussa',[2] and this task of fundamental importance was entrusted to a single magistrate, no doubt by vote of the People. The oldest living ex-censor, M. Fabius Buteo (censor 241), was chosen, and the Senate summoned Varro to Rome to name him. Buteo expressed disapproval of the procedure, removed no one from the senatorial roll, appointed all those who had held curule or other office and then those who had distinguished themselves in war, 177 new members in all; his task completed, he promptly laid down his dictatorship.[3] Thus a striking change came about in the composition of the Senate, and many men were admitted less for their family connexions than as a reward for military service, though no doubt the dictator kept in mind the antecedents of his nominees, especially in

---

[1] L. xxii. 57. 9. The statement of Valerius Maximus (iii. 4. 4; iv. 5. 2) that Varro himself was offered and refused the dictatorship may be rejected, although it shows traces of a tradition more favourable to the 'butcher's son'. On Iunius Pera see Münzer, *RA*, 163. His *magister equitum* was Ti. Sempronius Gracchus, who was curule aedile in 216.

[2] Fasti Cap. *ad an. 216*. Cf. Mommsen, *Staatsr.* ii. 159 n. 2 (*Dr. publ.* iii. 181 n. 2).

[3] L. xxiii. 22–3.

view of the recent activities of the People's leaders. The immediate political result of the change may have been to strengthen the grip of the nobility, because policy must normally have been shaped by the senior members, who, though few in number, now doubtless gained in prestige.[1]

The military position after Cannae remained gloomy: many cities, including Capua, revolted from Rome. Hannibal, though thwarted by Marcellus at Nola,[2] ultimately captured Casilinum despite brilliant attempts by Sempronius Gracchus to revictual it. Gracchus' effort was rewarded by election to the consulship of 215, his colleague being L. Postumius, who was campaigning against the Gauls, but when news came of Postumius' defeat and death, Gracchus had to preside over another election. M. Claudius Marcellus (cos. I in 222) was the favoured candidate; he was now holding a second praetorship, but his *imperium* for 215 had recently been renewed as proconsular by a special decree of the People.[3] He was unanimously elected in place of Postumius, but thunder was conveniently heard and the augurs declared that he was *vitio creatus*. The patricians spread a rumour that the gods were displeased at the election of two plebeian consuls. Marcellus thereupon resigned and in his place Q. Fabius Maximus was elected as consul for the third time.[4]

A glimpse of the strength of the various groups can now be gained. The dictator Iunius Pera, even if he had the influence, could hardly have helped the Aemilian-Scipionic group, because it had few leaders left except the Scipios in Spain. Instead, he appointed a *magister equitum* from the Claudian group (Ti. Sempronius Gracchus) as being a lesser evil perhaps than one of the Fabii, who secured for Buteo the important task of filling the Senate. The consulships of 215 were divided between the Claudii (Sempronius) and the Fabii (Postumius), but all four praetors were Claudians, among them Fabius' bitter enemy, Q. Fulvius Flaccus.[5] After Marcellus had replaced Postumius,

---

[1] E. Cavaignac in a demographic study ('Le sénat de 220', *Rev. Étud. Lat.* 1932, 458 ff.) has emphasized the increased influence of the tribunician element in the revised senate, but no doubt Fabius attempted to counterbalance this by choosing where possible as the military 'outsiders' younger members of the old noble families or their clients. Cavaignac reckons that the Senate of 220 B.C. contained 120 members of aedilician or higher rank (10 *dictatorii* and *censorii*, 30 *consulares*, 30 *praetorii*, and 50 *aedilicii*) and 180 *quaestorii*, *tribunicii*, and *tribunicii non quaestorii*; in 215 it had 60 *aedilicii* and higher magistrates, 90 old *tribunicii* and *quaestorii* including a not negligible number of *tribunicii non quaestorii*, 90 other *tribunicii non quaestorii*, and 60 'outsiders'.

[2] Livy patriotically omits a set-back inflicted on the dictator Iunius. See Front. *Strat.* ii. 5. 25; Polyaenus, vi. 38. 6; Zon. ix. 3.

[3] Livy (xxiii. 30. 19) implies that the grant was made before the second consular election; may it not have been after it, as a consolation prize?

[4] Ibid. 24; 31. See pp. 275 f.

[5] It is noteworthy that the sons of these four praetors co-operated in the next century. See p. 186.

his position was challenged by the augurs presumably under the influence of Fabius, who had successfully opposed the dictatorship of Veturius in 217 by similar means and now himself obtained Marcellus' consulship without apparently embittering Marcellus. When Fabius had secured the dismissal of his friends Manlius Torquatus and Fulvius Flaccus from the censorship in 231 as *vitio creati* in order to step into their shoes, he had driven the outraged Flaccus into the arms of the rival Claudii. But now Marcellus, himself a Claudian, allowed Fabius to elbow him out of office. The best explanation is that Marcellus, whose family was plebeian, was an adherent of the Fabii, not of the patrician Claudii, and that there was some private understanding between the two men. This supposition becomes more intelligible when it is seen how Fabius later repaid Marcellus by intriguing and securing for him a consulship at the next elections.

The election and withdrawal of Marcellus may even have been staged by him and Fabius in order to moderate the ambitions of the People, and the unprecedented election of two plebeian consuls have been encouraged merely in order that the patricians could publicly voice disapproval and by augural procedure force a plebeian consul to abdicate in order to make room, with an appearance of reluctance, for a patrician. If Fabius carried through such a farce with Marcellus' co-operation, the impression made upon the plebeians would have been considerable because Marcellus was not an aspiring young magistrate, but an ex-consul who had won the *spolia opima* and received a triumph. If the Aemilian-Cornelian group had been more favourable to the People, Fabius may have used his growing influence to score off it, while at the same time administering a reproof to the People, who were already discouraged after the failure of Flaminius and Varro. Further, Fabius, already long an augur, gained a fresh channel of influence when he was chosen as a pontiff.[1]

In order to counter Fabius' strategy of exhaustion, Carthage aimed at embarrassing Rome by prosecuting the war more vigorously in Spain, Sardinia, and Sicily, and making an alliance with Philip of Macedon. But under Fabius' guidance, and with many commands in the hands of his friends, Rome at first made good headway against this new Carthaginian strategy. The Fabian T. Manlius Torquatus (*cos.* I, 235) took command in Sardinia and defeated the enemy.

---

[1] Fabius, Q. Caecilius Metellus (*cos.* 206), and Q. Fulvius Flaccus (*cos.* I, 237) replaced the pontiffs L. Aemilius Paullus, Q. Aelius Paetus, and P. Scantinius who had died (L. xxiii. 21. 7). The members of the college, arranged in seniority as *consulares* (since the date of the election to the pontificate of some is not known), were now: the patricians L. Cornelius Lentulus (*cos.* 237), Pontifex Maximus, T. Manlius Torquatus (*cos.* 235), Q. Fabius Maximus (*cos.* I, 233), and C. Papirius Maso (*cos.* 231); and the plebeians Q. Fulvius Flaccus (*cos.* I, 237), M. Pomponius Matho (*cos.* 231), T. Otacilius Crassus (*pr.* 217), Q. Caecilius Metellus (*cos.* 206), and P. Licinius Crassus (*cos.* 205).

Another Fabian, T. Otacilius Crassus, the half-brother of Marcellus, was successful in Sicily, which he had governed since 217, having had family connexions with the island since his father and uncle had served there in the First Punic War. Despite some Carthaginian progress in southern Italy Sempronius, Fabius, and Marcellus managed to thwart Hannibal's attacks on Cumae and Nola.

Fabius then held the elections for 214.[1] When the junior century of the tribe Aniensis was voting for T. Otacilius (*pr.* 217) and M. Aemilius Regillus (probably the praetor of 217), Fabius suddenly objected: to Aemilius because, as a *flamen*, he was needed in Rome, to Otacilius because he lacked experience. Fabius, who next year thrust his own son into the consulship, scorned nepotism with a lofty gesture: 'Otacilius married my sister's daughter . . . but I cannot place private relationship before the welfare of the State.' Voting was recommenced, and Fabius himself was elected consul for the fourth time, Marcellus *in absentia* for the third. Thus Fabius, presiding at his own election, gained a second consecutive consulship and also secured a praetorship for his son, Quintus, who was then curule aedile; Marcellus received repayment for his exclusion from the consulship the previous year, while Otacilius gained a second praetorship as a consolation prize. True, Livy naturally records that opposition to the re-voting had come from Otacilius, rather than from the Aemilii as might be expected, but he may well have missed the inner meaning. The whole affair may have been prearranged and the different roles assigned beforehand merely to deceive the People, just as in the previous year Fabius' apparently cavalier treatment of Marcellus had not broken their political *amicitia*.[2]

Fabius gained a further political success when presiding over the election of censors for 214, since one successful candidate was M. Atilius Regulus (*cos.* I, 227; II, 217). Regulus, with his colleague P. Furius Philus (*cos.* 223), punished all the men who were reported to have planned to abandon Italy after the defeat at Cannae,[3] the ringleader being M. Caecilius Metellus, who was then quaestor.[4] Nevertheless, Metellus was elected tribune, and on entering office (10 Dec.

[1] A. Cornelius Mammula (*pr.* 217), a possible candidate, may have considered that his performance in Sardinia did not justify hopes of election; he did not win further office. Otacilius had asked to be sent home from Sicily in 216, but had been refused (L. xxiii. 21. 3); had he been hoping to stand for the consulship a year earlier? On the elections see L. xxiv. 7. 11–9. 5.

[2] Cf. Münzer, *RA*, 74. His view is accepted by J. H. Thiel, *The History of Roman Sea-Power*, 71 n. 7, who shows that Otacilius' failure was not due to any alleged naval incompetence, since he retained his command.

[3] Those 'qui publicum equum habebant' were deprived of their horses and all 'tribu moti, aerarii facti'. P. Fraccaro (*Athenaeum*, 1933, 150 ff.) has shown that this involved removal from a rural to an urban tribe and subjection to higher *tributum*.

[4] See L. xxii. 53, where Caecilius is named Lucius (unless the text is to be emended).

214) he turned on the censors and was only prevented by his colleagues from demanding their trial before the People, presumably on the ground that their condemnation of him had been unduly harsh, if not unjust, a supposition which seems reasonable in view of the continued faith of the People in him and the fact that he had not been removed from the Senate by Fabius Buteo in 216. Atilius, rather than Furius, probably will have instigated the original charge, first because the Caecilii, like the Furii, were friendly to the Cornelii, and he might be glad to try to discredit a rival family (though the Cornelii could retort by showing that it was young P. Scipio who had prevented the desertion after Cannae), and secondly because Furius' own son, Publius, had been among the faint-hearts at the council at Canusium and may now have been punished by the censors. However that may be, the censors thus tried to discourage and punish any shirking of military duty, but the death of Furius prevented the completion of the lustrum and involved the abdication of Atilius.[1]

Military operations, carried out by Fabius, Marcellus, and the proconsul Sempronius, were unspectacular but not unsuccessful,[2] and popular satisfaction with the conduct of the war was reflected in the uneventful elections for 213.[3] With Fabius presiding, his son Quintus was elected consul together with Ti. Sempronius Gracchus (consul for the second time). The success of young Fabius, who thus held three curule offices consecutively (aedile 215, praetor 214, and consul 213), was a remarkable testimony to his father's political influence. He had served under his father in 217 and then as military tribune at Cannae, but little is heard of him after his consulship.[4] Most of the commands in 213 remained in the same hands, but the year was not very prosperous: the siege of Capua was not yet undertaken, while that of Syracuse caused considerable strain. The elections for 212 would reveal the discontent of the People.

The popularity of the Fabii began to wane, but under the Cunctator's skilful direction they had enjoyed a spell of great political in-

---

[1] L. xxiv. 11; 18; 43. Cf. the new fragment of Fasti Cap. (*Inscr. Ital.* XIII. i, p. 46): 'Cens. M. Atilius M. f. M. n. Regulus abd. P. Furius Sp. f. M. n. Philus in mag. m(ortuus) est.' Two other senior senators died in 213: L. Cornelius Lentulus (*cos.* 237) and C. Papirius Maso (*cos.* 231): L. xxv. 2. Their deaths did not greatly affect the balance of family influence in the college of pontiffs, since they were replaced by M. Cornelius Cethegus and Cn. Servilius Caepio, while the office of Pontifex Maximus, held by Lentulus, was gained by P. Licinius Crassus in the following year (p. 67).

[2] The biggest set-back was the revolt of Syracuse whither Marcellus was dispatched during the winter. M. Valerius Laevinus (*pr.* II, 215) crossed to Illyricum in 214 to check Philip of Macedon, now Hannibal's ally.

[3] L. xxiv. 43. 5–6.

[4] L. xxii. 23; Front. *Strat.* iv. 6. 1; Dio, frg. 56. 11 (two anecdotes of 213). Livy (xxv. 3. 3; xxvii. 8. 13) refers to his activities in 212 and 209, but references in 208 (xxvii. 29. 4) and 207 (xxviii. 9. 1) may be to another Fabius, possibly the Cunctator's grandson who died in 196. The consul of 213 died before his father, between 207 and 203, if not earlier.

fluence. What manner of man, then, was their leader? There is no good reason to question the essential truth of Plutarch's portrait of his personal character, although to some extent this may have been built up around his strategic *cunctatio*.[1] Nicknamed Verrucosus from a wart on his upper lip, as a child he was also called Ovicula ('the Lamb') on account of his mild temper. Slowness of speech and deliberation gave an impression of stupidity which was belied by his prudence and constancy in time of action. As a member of the two priestly colleges whose resources he exploited to the full in his own political interests, he is not likely to have been swayed by religious or superstitious fears. Perhaps an impressive figure, he at any rate took care to impose his personality on the People; for instance, he obtained the Senate's permission to serve on horseback, and as dictator in 217 was accompanied by his full escort of 24 lictors, while an anecdote records that after Trasimene he ordered the surviving consul Servilius to dismiss his lictors with their *fasces* and visit him as a private person. After the capture of Tarentum he set up on the Capitol an equestrian statue of himself, together with a colossal statue of Hercules, the mythical ancestor of the Fabii, brought from Tarentum. His attitude to the cultural life of Rome is largely unknown, but that he may have been among the anti-Hellenists could be deduced from such facts as that, unlike Marcellus at Syracuse, he did not, with one exception, touch the pictures and statues at Tarentum ('let the Tarentines keep their angry gods'), that young Cato followed his habit and manner of life, and that he was among those who later criticized Scipio's Greek way of life in Sicily.[2] As the head of one of Rome's oldest patrician families with large landed estates, by nature conservative and an admirer of old-fashioned discipline, he probably thought on traditional lines.[3] But if he was slow to move with the times, he was alert enough to control the hidden machinery of patronage and *amicitia* with an astuteness that baffled his rivals. And it was perhaps well for Rome that he succeeded, since however low a view is taken of his military ability, his steadying lead in days of disaster was invaluable: *bellum Punicum secundum enervavit.*

11. *The Fulvian-Claudian Group*

To save recalling the consuls, a dictator was appointed to hold the elections for 212.[4] The consul Sempronius Gracchus, whose influence apparently outweighed that of his young colleague Fabius, opened a way for the Claudian-Fulvian group by nominating C. Claudius

---

[1] On Plutarch's *Fabius* and its sources see De Sanctis, III. ii. 206 ff.

[2] L. xxvii. 16 and Plut. *Fab.* 22 (statues); Plut. *Cato*, 3; L. xxix. 19 (Scipio).

[3] See also below, p. 76. Cf. the anecdote of how he gladly respected the order of his son, then consul, to dismount (L. xxiv. 44; Plut. *Fab.* 24).   [4] L. xxv. 2.

Centho (*cos.* 240; interrex 217); he in turn appointed Q. Fulvius Flaccus as Master of the Horse. Under Centho's presidency his *magister equitum* and his nephew Ap. Claudius Pulcher were elected, while two of the new praetors, Cn. Fulvius Flaccus and C. Claudius Nero, belonged to the same group.[1] The Fabii were conspicuous by their absence. Evidently the People were restless and wanted a new direction to be given to the war. Neither consul had previously held that office during the war; Flaccus had been consul as far back as 237 and 222, while Appius Claudius, who had been praetor in Sicily in 215, had taken part with Marcellus in the campaign of 213. All but one of the commands in Italy were changed, Sempronius alone having his prolonged. C. Claudius Nero took over from Varro, Cn. Fulvius Flaccus from M. Aemilius Lepidus, and the two consuls from Fabius and Cn. Fulvius Centumalus. Outside Italy, however, arrangements remained unaltered: the Fabii retained Marcellus and Otacilius in Sicily, the Claudii had Mucius Scaevola in Sardinia and Valerius Laevinus in Macedon, and the two Scipio brothers remained in Spain.

The Fulvian-Claudian commanders fared well with one exception: Sempronius Gracchus was defeated and killed in Lucania, a serious loss which deprived the Claudian group of a prominent supporter and Rome of an outstanding general. Q. Fulvius Flaccus, however, won a success at Beneventum[2] and in the autumn, with his colleague and the praetor C. Claudius Nero, he at last started the regular siege and circumvallation of Capua. In this or the following autumn the Claudians gained further popularity when it was known that their supporter Valerius Laevinus had negotiated a very satisfactory treaty with the Aetolians, whereby the brunt of the land warfare against Philip was transferred to them, while the Romans were specifically granted all the movable booty. The fact that the agreement was not ratified by the Senate for two years suggests that it was mainly Laevinus' own work and possibly that some senators had doubts about its moral implications (and perhaps about Laevinus' ruthless enslavement of Anticyra). Such a naked avowal that Roman intervention in Greece would enrich Roman armies at the expense of Rome's allies might not

---

[1] Dictators appointed to conduct elections appear normally to have commended to the electorate the claims of their *magistri equitum*. At any rate, of eight such dictators during the Hannibalic War five proclaimed their *magistri equitum* as consuls (in 216, 213, 207, 203, 202: L. xxiii. 24; xxv. 2; xxviii. 10; xxx. 26; 39). The dictator of 210 proclaimed himself consul (xxvii. 5); the other two were dictators in 208 and 205 (xxvii. 33–4; xxix. 11). Cf. Mommsen, *Staatsr.* ii. 174 (*Dr. publ.* iii. 109).

[2] There is little reason to suppose with Kahrstedt (*Gesch. d. Karth.* iii. 475, n. 1) that Flaccus' success is a reduplication of that of Gracchus in 215. The tradition obscures the fact of Sempronius' defeat, but it cannot deny his death, which is confirmed by the subsequent disbanding of his surviving troops, the *volones*, the slaves who had been enrolled after Cannae. Cf. De Sanctis, iii. ii. 291.

please some, but it would enhance the popularity of the Claudian group with the People.[1]

An outstanding domestic event of 212 was the exposure of some fraudulent contractors of whom the chief was a M. Postumius. When the Senate took no action in order to avoid offending the *publicani* at a critical period in the war, two tribunes, Sp. and L. Carvilius, demanded that Postumius should be fined. The *publicani* hoped that another tribune, C. Servilius Casca, a relative of Postumius, would veto proceedings, but, in fact, amid considerable public disturbances Servilius did little; thereupon the Carvilii indicted Postumius for treason and drove him into exile.[2] The episode is significant because it illustrates the tension between the Senate and People and the growing importance of the Equites. It also illuminates the methods by which Roman noble families tried to hush up domestic scandals, since the tribune Servilius, whose role was not very creditable, was probably not a Casca but none other than C. Servilius Geminus (*cos.* 203); the annalistic tradition while recounting the incident has suppressed the part played in it by Geminus by substituting another *cognomen* (rare at this period) to the greater glory of the Servilii Gemini.[3]

The elections for 211, conducted by Claudius Pulcher, and the distribution of commands reflect continuing general satisfaction with the Claudii-Fulvii.[4] Two other members of the group were successful: P. Sulpicius Galba and Cn. Fulvius Centumalus, both less experienced than their predecessors. Centumalus had only been praetor in 213, while Galba had held no curule office. The victory of two such untried men indicates the strength and popularity of their group.[5] The commands of the two consuls of 212 and of C. Claudius Nero

---

[1] Since the Claudian-Fulvian group was powerful in both 212 and 211, the precise date of the treaty is less important from the point of view of party politics. For arguments in favour of autumn 211 see F. W. Walbank, *Philip V*, 83; 301 ff.; a strong case, however, can be made for autumn 212. The treaty contained some unusual clauses, which are only paralleled in Greek international law: see E. Taubler, *Imperium Romanum*, i. 430 ff.

[2] L. xxv. 3. 8–4. 11. Cf. E. G. Hardy, *JRS*, 1913, 32 ff.

[3] This is the ingenious view of Münzer (*RA*, 140–1), who suggests (cf. *PW*, s.v. Servilius, n. 60) that C. Servilius, a legate who got corn through to the beleaguered Roman garrison at Tarentum (L. xxv. 15. 4), is also to be identified with the consul of 203. It is no objection that he was a tribune (in 204 two tribunes even left Italy: L. xxix. 20. 11, cf. Mommsen, *Staatsr.* ii. 292), but other possibilities are open (e.g. he might be a son of the consul of 217).

[4] L. xxv. 41. 8–13.

[5] It has been urged by M. L. Patterson (*TAPA*, 1942, 329) that these appointments indicate the lack of available men of experience rather than factional interests, but even if the shortage of tried men was acute (though Fabius Cunctator was still fit for active campaigning and another consulship, even if a man like T. Manlius Torquatus was considered past his fighting days), there still remains the question why Sulpicius and Fulvius were chosen out of the less experienced candidates rather than men of similar status from other families.

G

were prolonged, and most of the rest remained unchanged.[1] In Italy the year was crowned with success: Capua surrendered after the failure of Hannibal's dash on Rome. Meantime came news of the defeat and death of the two Scipios in Spain, but this enabled the Claudii to win another important command: the propraetor C. Claudius Nero, who was at Capua in the place of his wounded cousin Ap. Claudius Pulcher, was appointed to Spain.

But war was thinning the ranks of the Claudii: Sempronius Gracchus had been killed in 212, Ap. Claudius Pulcher lay dying at Capua, and the prosecution of Cn. Fulvius Flaccus would damage the reputation of his brother Quintus, whose political position was becoming isolated, especially in view of Nero's short tenure of the Spanish command and the revival of Fabius, whose friend Marcellus had captured Syracuse and was on his way back to Italy. Marcellus' supporters, however, were not strong enough to obtain a triumph for him: he had to be content with an ovation and a private triumph on the Alban Mount.[2]

The election results for 210 showed the Claudii and Fabii equally balanced, but Livy's account[3] raises difficulties. Under Fulvius' presidency the century of juniors, who voted first, declared for T. Manlius Torquatus (*cos.* 235 and 224; censor 231) and for T. Otacilius *in absentia*. But Manlius objected because of his defective eye-sight and asked the century to re-vote. After consulting its century of seniors, who said that the choice really lay between Q. Fabius and M. Marcellus, or, if fresh blood was wanted, M. Valerius Laevinus, it then re-voted, the other centuries followed its lead, and Marcellus and Laevinus were elected. Thereafter news came of the death in Sicily of Otacilius, who would have been elected with Manlius if the proceedings had not been interrupted.

Difficulties arise: for instance, why should the withdrawal of Manlius have affected the election of the absent Otacilius? Possibly Livy has confused the order of events, and news of Otacilius' death reached Rome before the actual election; in that case votes would not have been actually cast for him, but he might have been known to be a likely winner. Or perhaps there was some wish to elect the two generals from Sicily, Marcellus and Otacilius, and Manlius was put

---

[1] Cn. Fulvius Flaccus (the younger brother of the consul of 212, Q. Fulvius Flaccus) returned from Apulia to Rome, was prosecuted, and went into exile (L. xxvi. 2. 7–3. 12). The charge was probably not a supposed defeat at Herdonea, which is a doublet of that of Cn. Fulvius Centumalus there in 210, but perhaps *perduellio*. Cf. De Sanctis, III. ii. 459 n. 28. It is somewhat surprising to find that C. Sempronius Blaesus, the tribune who initiated the prosecution, served as a legate to Q. Fulvius Flaccus in 210 (L. xxvii. 6).

[2] Two other senior *consulares* died in 211, Sp. Carvilius Maximus Ruga (*cos.* I, 234, II, 228: the first Roman known to have divorced his wife for barrenness: Aul. Gell. iv. 3. 2) and M. Pomponius Matho who as consul in 231 had pacified Sardinia; they were respectively augur and pontiff.

[3] xxvi. 22.

forward to prevent the possibility of two plebeian consuls.[1] But the whole account resembles that of the elections for 214 when Fabius forced through his own and Marcellus' election despite the preliminary voting in favour of Otacilius and Aemilius Regillus. Probably therefore Livy's account of Otacilius' part in 211 is merely a duplication, which was due to Valerius Antias who worked up the episode in accordance with the traditional austerity of the Manlii and placed it in 211 to honour a Valerius, M. Valerius Laevinus, whom the People preferred to Otacilius (perhaps because of his Aetolian treaty). But even if Otacilius is eliminated from the account, Manlius' part remains obscure. Clearly his physical infirmity is introduced merely to emphasize his patriotism and to explain his withdrawal; in fact the objection would doubtless have occurred to him before submitting his name as a candidate. It is possible that the Fabian candidates were Fabius himself, Manlius, and Marcellus, that Manlius withdrew to avoid splitting the vote since he and Fabius were patricians and could not both be elected, and that the Claudians were strong enough to prevent the election of two Fabian candidates. This at any rate was the result: the Fabii were represented by Marcellus (*cos.* IV), the Claudii by Laevinus (*cos.* II),[2] and both consuls were the men who were responsible for the successes of the year outside Italy.[3]

III. *Balance of the Claudian, Fabian, and Scipionic Groups*

The deaths of P. and Cn. Scipio in Spain in 211 robbed their group of its most active leaders; only the old L. Veturius Philo (*cos.* 220) and the useless Scipio Asina[4] remained. M. Livius Salinator was still in exile, and the next generation seemed yet too young: Gnaeus' son,

---

[1] Cf. Münzer, *RA*, 75 f.

[2] The new fragments of the Capitoline Fasti make Laevinus consul II, thus agreeing with L. xxix. 11. 3 ('M. Valerium Laevinum, qui bis consul fuerat'). See p. 273.

[3] On the elections for 210 see De Sanctis, III. ii. 256 n. 111; 376; Münzer, *RA*, 75; Schur, *Scipio*, 123. The key is found by R. M. Haywood (*Scipio*, 50) in the shortage of outstanding men: the People turned to Manlius because they 'did not want to select men who had held the consulship within ten years but had difficulty in finding any able man who had not. The sudden elevation of P. Sulpicius Galba to the consulship for 211 in spite of his not having held a curule office, and the happenings at the next election (L. xxvii. 6. 2–12) seem to point the same way.' It is difficult, however, to believe that constitutional scruples formed the chief reason in a critical period when Marcellus was consul four times within ten years, Fabius three times, Sempronius Gracchus and Q. Fulvius Flaccus twice. The People apparently had no objection to investing Scipio, a mere *privatus*, with proconsular imperium, a precedent which might prove as dangerous to the constitution as iteration of the consulship within ten years.

[4] Scipio Asina (*cos.* 221) had been successful against the Histri. He can hardly have been one of the three land-commissioners captured in 218 (L. xxi. 25. 4; cf. below, p. 274), because he was interrex in 217 (L. xxii. 34. 1: the Livian tradition may represent a doublet of the capture of his father Cn. Scipio Asina). He was still alive in 211 (L. xxvi. 8. 2), but as he had not been employed in any major command his military abilities presumably were not rated high.

P. Cornelius Scipio Nasica, was a lad of 12 or 14, while Publius' son, who now became head of his family and had strengthened the connexion with the Aemilii by marrying a daughter of Aemilius Paullus, was only about 24. But although the Claudii held the main commands and the Fabii began to revive with Marcellus' success at Syracuse, the balance between these two groups, exemplified in the consulship of 210, was soon to be altered by the Scipionic group which again flashed into prominence by gaining an extraordinary new military command and two censorships.

Although he had only been aedile (in 213), young Publius Scipio was suddenly invested by the People with a proconsular command to supersede Claudius Nero in Spain, an appointment which marks an important step in Rome's constitutional development.[1] Livy's naïve account that no one else had dared to seek this responsible post may be rejected,[2] and Mommsen might be right in supposing that the Senate had arranged that Scipio should be the only candidate. But why was Scipio chosen? Probably because the People, backed by the approval of many senators and seeing the opportunity for more spoils in overseas campaigns, wanted an offensive to be renewed in Spain. Nor was their choice wild: though young, Scipio had gained military experience during the past eight years in Italy (and, for all that is known, in Spain also), while his extraordinary and almost mystical confidence in himself and his abilities marked him out as a potential leader among the average Roman commanders of his day.

The view that 'the Senate recalled Nero and sent Scipio to replace him because a sudden shortage of men made Nero's presence at home necessary'[3] has little to commend it. The war in Italy had reached something like a stalemate, and if Nero was so urgently needed at home, why was he not elected to high office until 207? Even if he arrived back too late for the elections for 209, he could have been elected consul for 208 instead of the less-known T. Quinctius Crispinus.[4] True, he served as legate under Marcellus in 209, but that in itself would scarcely justify his recall from Spain. Doubtless there was a shortage of first-class men,[5] and an examination of the younger men

[1] With him, though with *imperium minus*, was appointed the propraetor M. Iunius Silanus (*pr.* 212), whose family was friendly with the Scipios (L. xxvi. 18–19).

[2] Dislike of serving in Spain, 'ut nemo audeat in Hispaniam imperium accipere', reflects conditions of *c.* 150 B.C. Cf. p. 234.

[3] R. M. Haywood, *Scipio*, 48.

[4] R. M. Haywood does not strengthen his case by remarking (p. 50) that Nero was probably eliminated from the elections for 208 'by popular enthusiasm for Marcellus, another patrician'. Marcellus was in fact a plebeian, and his patrician colleague was Quinctius Crispinus.

[5] Ti. Sempronius Gracchus had died in 212, Ap. Claudius Pulcher, Otacilius Crassus, and the two Scipios in 211, and Cn. Fulvius Centumalus in 210. Ti. Sempronius Longus (*cos.* 218) also died in 210, but his political and military career had apparently ended at Trebia.

available may show that none was so promising as Scipio.[1] This might help to explain the choice of Scipio for the Spanish command, but it does not adequately account for the prior decision to supersede Nero; that is best explained by the desire for renewed offensive action for which Scipio with the tradition of his father and uncle might seem better suited than Nero whose military experience at Syracuse and Capua had been more static.

The Scipionic group received support from another remarkable young man, P. Licinius Crassus, who was a close contemporary of Scipio Africanus, since both were born about 235, held the consulship in 205, and died in 183.[2] Licinius flashed into sudden prominence by defeating two much more experienced rivals for the post of Pontifex Maximus.[3] He had become a pontiff at an early age (some time before 216) and through the circumstances of war found himself by 213 one of the senior members of the College. Of the four patrician pontiffs when he entered the College only one survived, of the plebeian only two.[4] When Lentulus, the Pontifex Maximus, died in 213, the candidates for the post were young Licinius, together with T. Manlius Torquatus and Q. Fulvius Flaccus who had been joint censors in 231 and consuls in 224. But Manlius may have been handicapped by his patrician pride and severity,[5] while Fulvius had little to recommend him: from the point of view of the priests he was the youngest plebeian member, to the patricians his combination of a third consulship with the office of Pontifex Maximus might suggest excessive influence, while his election would mean withdrawing a competent general from action against Hannibal.[6] Thus age and experience gave place to youth: Licinius Crassus having paved the way with his aedilician Games in 212 was elected: 'nobilis idem ac dives'. He was indeed, in Livy's view, one of the most cultured men of his day: exceptionally strong and handsome, a good soldier, a versatile orator, and deeply versed in pontifical law.[7]

Licinius' next victory was to step straight into the censorship of 210 without having been consul, his colleague being the old L. Veturius Philo (*cos.* 220), another supporter of the Aemilian-Scipionic group. The new censors achieved little because the death of Veturius prevented the completion of the *lustrum*, and Licinius had to resign, but first they had reinstated M. Livius Salinator in public life.[8] Prosecuted after his consulship in 219, Livius had gone into exile, bitterly incensed against C. Claudius Nero who had probably served under him as

---

[1] Cf. Haywood, op. cit. 51–2.   [2] See p. 276.
[3] Pliny, *NH*, xxi. 6; L. xxv. 5. 2–4.
[4] On the pontiffs in 216 see p. 58 n. 1. In 213 L. Cornelius Lentulus and C. Papirius Maso were replaced by M. Cornelius Cethegus and Cn. Servilius Caepio (L. xxv. 2. 1).
[5] L. xxii. 60. 5; xxvi. 22. 9.   [6] Cf. Münzer, *RA*, 186 f.
[7] L. xxx. 1. 4–5. Cf. Cic. *De or.* iii. 134; *De sen.* 27; 50; 61.   [8] L. xxvii. 6, 34.

military tribune and had appeared as a witness for the prosecution. He had remained inactive during the first part of the war through bitterness and because his father-in-law, Pacuvius of Capua, had gone over to the enemy, but when Capua became Roman again, Livius could return more easily. His reinstatement was a triumph for the Aemilian-Scipionic group: they had won the command in Spain, two of their supporters had reached the censorship, and now once more they had a leader of consular rank in Rome. Other offices fell to their friends: one curule aedileship was held by the young L. Veturius in 211[1] and another by P. Licinius Varus in 210; in 211 C. Livius Salinator (son of the reinstated consular) became a pontiff, M. Servilius Geminus an augur, M. Aemilius Lepidus a Keeper of the Sacred Books,[2] and in 210 C. Servilius Geminus became a pontiff.

Early in 210 the new consul Marcellus came under fire: the Sicilians complained about his conduct in Sicily and he was criticized in the Senate by Manlius Torquatus, who may have been antagonized by Marcellus' success and his own failure at the consular elections. A majority in the Senate, however, supported Marcellus, confirmed his actions, and secured for him the command against Hannibal, while Laevinus was sent to Sicily.[3] In the distribution of the other commands the Claudii-Fulvii were still predominant: P. Sulpicius succeeded Laevinus in Macedonia,[4] Cn. Fulvius Centumalus remained as proconsul in Apulia until his defeat and death later in the year, and Q. Fulvius Flaccus continued in Campania. Marcellus, the one Fabian general of the year in Italy, remained true to the Cunctator's strategy, although a slightly bolder move, such as an advance against Tarentum, might have been worth risking.[5] Thus, as often before, the advantages gained were disproportionate to the sacrifices involved, and so through war-weariness twelve Latin colonies in central Italy refused to contribute their annual contingents. The political influence of the Fulvii and Fabii might be fairly evenly balanced, but it was fortunate for Rome that the Aemilian-Scipionic faction was reasserting itself, for it was this group that produced the architect of final victory.

This equipoise between the Fabian and Claudian-Fulvian groups was seen in the elections for 209 which provoked considerable intrigue.[6] The Senate, reluctant to disengage Marcellus from Hannibal, summoned Laevinus from Sicily to conduct them; this decision may have been reached on purely military grounds or it may represent a political success for the Claudian-Fulvians. On arrival, however, Laevinus

---

[1] On the date see Münzer, *RA*, 126 f.   [2] L. xxvi. 23.
[3] Ibid. 29–32.
[4] Holleaux, *CAH*, viii. 127, places this in 211, a year earlier, but see Walbank, *Philip V*, 301. The change of command probably does not represent a change of policy.
[5] Cf. De Sanctis, iii. ii. 475 f.   [6] L. xxvii. 5–6.

startled the Senate by communicating information about a Carthaginian plan to recover Sicily which he had received from M. Valerius Messalla, probably his cousin, after a raid on north Africa. The Senate thereupon ordered him to name a dictator to hold the elections and then hasten back to his province, but Laevinus said that when he reached Sicily he would nominate Messalla. This raised a storm of protest, since a dictator could be nominated only if he were on Italian soil. In this difficulty the Senate, doubtless remembering how the People had elected a dictator after Trasimene, ordered Laevinus to consult the People and nominate the man of their choice. When he refused, the tribunes intervened and consulted the People, who decided upon Q. Fulvius, the conqueror of Capua. Laevinus promptly left for Sicily, so that Marcellus had to be recalled to nominate Fulvius, who then as dictator on the recommendation of the People named Crassus, the Pontifex Maximus, as his *magister equitum*.[1]

But even so all was not plain sailing: the first century had voted for Fulvius and Fabius when two tribunes, C. and L. Arrenius (voicing the views of the Aemilian-Scipionic group?), objected to a presiding officer himself seeking election. But Fulvius quoted the precedent of Fabius in 215, the tribunes finally gave way, and Q. Fabius Maximus became consul for the fifth time, Q. Fulvius Flaccus for the fourth. The Aemilii had not yet sufficient strength to wrest control, which was still swinging between the Fabii and Fulvii.[2]

But the political scene was changing. War casualties, old age, and iteration of the consulship had combined to thin the ranks of the *consulares* to an astonishing extent: not more than a dozen survived and of these some were probably useless through incapacity or old age.[3]

---

[1] Livy (xxvii. 6. 17) mentions Crassus' censorship after his nomination as Master of the Horse (5. 19) but implies that the censorship was held first (6. 17). This is confirmed by the new fragment of the Capitoline Fasti: 'posteaquam censura abiit, mag. eq.' M. L. Patterson (*TAPA*, 1942, 332) raises an objection: 'though supposedly a Fulvio-Claudian, he (Laevinus) refused to make or sanction any legal appointment. Therefore it was Marcellus, considered a supporter of Fabius, who confirmed the nomination of Q. Fulvius Flaccus.' But it looks as if Laevinus sulked when he failed to get Messalla appointed, and after that the matter was taken out of his hands: he was ordered to nominate the man chosen by the People. That nominee presumably would have to be named in any case, so that Laevinus could still indulge his personal pique, and leave Rome knowing that Q. Fulvius would be named by his colleague Marcellus, a situation that might well appeal to his ill-humour.

[2] Of all the praetors of 213–211 only one had yet reached the consulship: Cn. Fulvius Centumalus.

The Scipionic group gained three of the four aedileships of 209 for Cornelius Lentulus Caudinus, C. Servilius Geminus (on the difficulties of his legal position see p. 276), and Q. Caecilius Metellus. Livy (xxvii. 21. 9) gives L. Cornelius Caudinus, perhaps a son of P. Cornelius Lentulus Caudinus (*cos.* 236) and a brother of P. Cornelius Caudinus (*pr.* 203). But since the aedile Lucius does not appear again and his *praenomen* is missing in the Puteanus MS., Münzer (*PW*, s.v. Cornelius n. 212) has conjectured that the consul of 236 may have had only one son, Publius, aedile in 209 and praetor in 203.

[3] Those known to survive are: Q. Fulvius Flaccus, T. Manlius Torquatus, Q. Fabius

This shortage is demonstrated by the censorial elections for 209: neither of the new censors, M. Cornelius Cethegus (*pr.* 211) and P. Sempronius Tuditanus (*pr.* 213, *propr.* 212–211), had held the consulship, though Cethegus' success doubtless owed something to his powers of persuasive oratory: 'flos delibatus populi suadaeque medulla'.[1] The censors disagreed about nominating a new *princeps senatus*, a position vacant since the death of the last occupant, either L. Cornelius Lentulus in 213 or M. Fabius Buteo (p. 39 n. 3). The choice had fallen to the lot of Sempronius who proposed to nominate Fabius Cunctator (censor 230), but Cethegus wished to follow the custom of choosing the oldest surviving patrician *censorius*, now Manlius Torquatus (censor 231);[2] Cethegus finally gave way and Fabius was chosen. Since both candidates belonged to the same group, the discussion must have turned more upon personal qualifications or constitutional propriety than family interests, especially as no other men could have been seriously considered; the only other really senior *censorius*, Q. Fulvius Flaccus (censor 231), was excluded as a plebeian. Thereafter the censors struck off from the senatorial list eight names, which included M. Caecilius Metellus, thus upholding the decision of their predecessors and vindicating censorial authority (pp. 59 f.).

The year 209, which opened with the gloomy prospect of slow advance gained at great sacrifice amid serious allied dissatisfaction, ended more successfully. Fulvius with Marcellus, whose command had been prolonged, held Hannibal at bay, while the cautious Fabius assailed Tarentum, which soon fell through internal treachery. Meanwhile in Spain the whole complexion of the war was altered by Scipio's capture of New Carthage: he could now plan an offensive farther south with the prospect of driving the Carthaginians completely out of Spain instead of merely trying to hold them in check. The political situation is summed up by Livy: 'Romae fama Scipionis in dies crescere, Fabio Tarentum captum astu magis quam virtute gloriae tamen esse, Fulvi senescere fama.'[3]

An attack on Marcellus, led by a tribune C. Publicius Bibulus who proceeded to criticize the whole nobility, heralded the elections for

---

Maximus, M. Claudius Marcellus, C. Lutatius Catulus (*cos.* 220, but a prisoner of war until 203), M. Livius Salinator, C. Terentius Varro, young Q. Fabius Maximus, P. Sulpicius Galba, and M. Valerius Laevinus. The 'doubtfuls', with the dates of the last references to them, are M. Iunius Pera (216), M. Atilius Regulus (214), L. Aemilius Papus (216), and P. Cornelius Scipio Asina (211).   [1] Ennius *apud* Cic. *Brut.* 58.

[2] If this custom had been rigidly applied, Cornelius Lentulus cannot have been *princeps senatus*, since Buteo was a senior *censorius*; but if it was set aside in 209, it may have been set aside in 220. Willems (*Sénat,* i. 112 n. 4) argues that Cethegus' appeal to this custom suggests that at least the last *princeps senatus* must have conformed to tradition, i.e. must therefore have been Buteo. But it could be argued that if the tradition had once been disregarded, there would be more point in Cethegus urging that it should be retained. The question must remain undecided.   [3] L. xxvii. 20. 9.

208.[1] This move points either to general discontent with senatorial conduct of the war or to an intrigue against Marcellus by his political opponents. In any case the attack misfired, since Marcellus brilliantly vindicated himself and was elected to his fifth consulship. His success was doubtless due to the desire to finish the war before the restlessness and sacrifices of the allies became too severe, since he seemed to be the only man able to face, if not to conquer, Hannibal. His colleague T. Quinctius Crispinus stepped straight from his praetorship (209) into the consulship, thus beating all the praetors of 212–210. He had served with Marcellus at Syracuse in 213, had fought at Capua in 212, and had been elected praetor during Marcellus' fourth consulship. Thus the year had re-established Fabius' position. With the capture of Tarentum to his credit, as *princeps senatus* and proconsul, supported by the two new consuls, he had eclipsed Fulvius, but Scipio's victory in the west showed where he would have to face a new rival.

The two consuls joined forces near Venusia perhaps with the intention of giving battle to Hannibal if they could win a favourable position, but while reconnoitring, Marcellus was killed, and Crispinus was wounded and died later. With the loss of 'the Sword of Rome', hope of ever defeating Hannibal grew yet more remote, since Marcellus had been the one general whose energy had prevented the complete failure of Fabius' strategy. Further, Scipio's momentous decision after his engagement at Baecula not to abandon Spain in a wild goose chase after Hasdrubal meant that a fresh Carthaginian army might soon appear in north Italy and Rome would have to brace herself to withstand the shock.

Before he died Crispinus named the aged Manlius Torquatus dictator to conduct the elections, but owing to the death of the two consuls the dictator had in effect, if not *de iure*, supreme control.[2] The elections were held under the shadow of Hasdrubal's threatened invasion. A consul endowed with initiative and caution was needed, and C. Claudius Nero, who had fought at Capua and had then faced Hasdrubal in Spain, appeared the outstanding candidate. The difficulty was to find a colleague for him: Fabius, Valerius Laevinus, and Manlius were excluded because it was illegal to have two patrician consuls, so men turned to M. Livius Salinator, despite his well-known personal animosity towards Nero, dating from his exile in 218. Livius, who had been reinstated in 210, had not spoken in the Senate until 208 when the conduct of his kinsman, M. Livius Macatus, the commander of the garrison of Tarentum, was criticized; in the debate he

---

[1] Ibid. 20. 9–21. 5.

[2] Ibid. 33. 6–35. 1. See note, p. 277. Manlius' *magister equitum* was C. Servilius Geminus, then curule aedile.

probably crossed swords with Fabius who supported the suggestion that the censors should deal with Macatus.[1] Reluctant and embittered, he finally came forward and was elected to his second consulship as Nero's colleague. At the praetorian elections four plebeians were elected for the first time in Rome's history.

Fabius was becoming isolated: his friends Marcellus and Crispinus were dead, and his son was unfitted to take a leading position. It has been suggested that Fabius therefore had turned to Livius and his friends:[2] believing that the Claudian-Fulvian group would win one consulship for Nero (whose election could scarcely be avoided in view of the threat of Hasdrubal's invasion, because Nero had faced him in Spain) and having no candidate of his own group to put forward, Fabius was forced to co-operate with Livius; in line with this the dying Crispinus had nominated Manlius dictator, Manlius had named C. Servilius as *magister equitum*, and Fabius himself had given his son as legate to Livius. But this coalition, which involves the incidental anomaly that, while the main reason of Nero's appointment was his previous contact with Hasdrubal, he was given the command in the south against Hannibal, need not be postulated. It is sufficient explanation that after the failure of his friends Fabius was temporarily eclipsed and his age militated against a further command for himself. With the Fabians overshadowed, the Claudians could put forward a candidate; Q. Fulvius Flaccus was perhaps, like Fabius, too old, so their choice fell on the younger Claudius Nero. The reviving Aemilian-Scipionic group seized the opportunity and had in Livius Salinator a suitable candidate.[3] He was under 50, his campaign in Illyria in 219 with Aemilius Paullus had secured him a triumph, and he might prove a welcome change from the none too successful commanders of the last few years.

Livius probably had considerable support from the People,[4] whose leaders in the early years of the war had been less antagonistic to the more liberal Aemilian-Scipionic group (pp. 53 ff.); they may well have wished to make redress for the summary treatment which he had received ten years before. They had insisted on Scipio's appointment to Spain in 210, had exerted some unusual, if obscure, influence on the conduct of the elections for 209 (p. 69), and had been restless at the subsequent election (pp. 70 f.); further, the election of four plebeian praetors for 207 suggests popular pressure. The People therefore may have shown more enthusiasm than some senators for Livius'

---

[1] L. xxvii. 25, 34. On Macatus see *PW*, s.v. Livius, n. 24, and Münzer, *RA*, 231.

[2] Schur, *Scipio*, 127.

[3] 'Some authorities assert that P. Scipio sent M. Livius reinforcements from Spain' before Metaurus (L. xxvii. 38. 11). This may not be historically true, but it indicates a tradition which tells of the friendly co-operation of these two men.

[4] Ibid. 34. 11.

appointment. In any case he probably did not receive help from Fabius; if he did, it is curious that he twice rebuffed him when, as *princeps senatus*, Fabius tried to reconcile him with his colleague Nero.[1] Yet despite Fabius' failure the Senate succeeded in forcing the consuls to co-operate. This is proved by the facts of the subsequent campaign, although their later quarrels during their joint censorship in 204 suggest an official rather than a personal reconciliation.

The famous story of the year 207 need not be repeated in detail. Nero and Q. Fulvius Flaccus successfully held Hannibal south of Canusium, while Livius awaited Hasdrubal in north Italy. Then after intercepting Hasdrubal's dispatches to his brother, Nero boldly marched to join Livius at the Metaurus, where the two consuls defeated Hasdrubal in the first real victory in the field in Italy during the war. Metaurus was Rome's crowning mercy: it forced Hannibal on to the defensive and restored confidence in the armies of Rome and the loyalty of her allies.[2] Later the two consuls returned to Rome and were granted triumphs, which they agreed to celebrate as one, but since the battle had been fought in Livius' province and under his *auspicia*, and as he had his army with him while Nero's was still in south Italy, Livius drove at the head of the troops, while Nero rode alone on horseback. Nero's self-effacing acceptance of the second place is said to have increased his reputation still further, even at the expense of Livius.[3]

The electoral procedure for 206 was unusual.[4] Although both consuls were apparently in Rome, the elections were conducted by a dictator; Livius was appointed by his colleague Nero and then nominated Q. Caecilius Metellus as Master of the Horse. Two officers who had rendered good service in the Metaurus campaign, L. Veturius and Q. Caecilius, were suggested as consular candidates by the equestrian order; backed by the consuls they were duly elected. Thereafter the dictator laid down his office and went to Etruria where he had been commissioned by the Senate to hold an inquiry on the loyalty of some cantons. This peculiar electoral procedure has provoked the suggestion that Livius may have received dictatorial power in order to

---

[1] Ibid. 35. 6–8; 40. 8.

[2] The good news was brought to Rome by three envoys from Livius, all members of the Aemilian-Scipionic group: L. Veturius Philo, P. Licinius Varus, and Q. Caecilius Metellus.

[3] This tradition which Livy follows (xxviii. 9) perhaps derives from the annalist Claudius Quadrigarius; at any rate it is more favourable to Claudius Nero than to Livy's own namesake, and has emphasized his superior service, though technically his contribution to victory, great though it was, warranted only an *ovatio*. It represented Nero as the real victor, although in fact both in his preparations for the campaign (xxvii. 38. 7–10; 45. 3) and at his triumph Livius predominated over his colleague and the Senate; it may even have exaggerated the degree of co-operation between the two consuls in an attempt to minimize traces of party strife. Cf. Münzer, *PW*, s.v. Livius n. 33, and *RA*, 124–6, 418.

[4] L. xxviii. 10. For a precedent, in 339 B.C., see Münzer, *RA*, 34 f.

carry out this commission rather than merely to conduct the elections.[1] However that may be, Nero's action in appointing his rival to the dictatorship presupposes that the working agreement reached between them during their campaign had not yet broken down. Seeing the influence of his family and friends was giving place to the Aemilian-Scipionic group, Nero may even have made a virtue of necessity and co-operated with Livius to check the Fabii.

A turning-point in the war was at hand. Hannibal was now at bay in Italy with little prospect of reinforcement from abroad, while in the following year the Carthaginians were to be driven neck and crop out of Spain and thus a way would be opened for a blow at Carthage itself. In Rome, too, the triangular contest between the groups was reaching its climax: soon Scipio was to flash past his rivals in a blaze of glory which led to the defeat of Hannibal and final victory over the national enemy.

[1] Bandel, *Die röm. Diktaturen*, 140.

V

THE FIRST PREDOMINANCE AND DECLINE OF SCIPIO AFRICANUS

(206–201 B.C.)

1. *The Scipionic Group*

IN Italy the year 206 was comparatively uneventful. The centre of operations had shifted to the west, where after his victory at Ilipa Scipio swept the Carthaginians completely out of Spain, thus altering the complexion of the whole war. He returned to Rome just in time to stand for the consular elections at which the friendly L. Veturius Philo presided.[1] Doubtless through Fabius' opposition, he failed to secure the grant of a triumph, which as a mere *privatus cum imperio* he could not claim,[2] but his plan to invade Africa was well known and a record number of voters flocked to Rome to see the conqueror of Spain; their enthusiasm and confidence was heightened when he sacrificed a hecatomb of oxen, vowed in Spain, to Iuppiter Capitolinus, in whose temple he had often communed. The god would reward their hero with further victories, the People give him the consulship. Scipio was elected with the Pontifex Maximus, Licinius Crassus, as his colleague. Two at least of the new praetors, Cn. Servilius Caepio and L. Aemilius Papus, belonged to friendly families, and both curule aediles were Cornelii, Cn. and L. Cornelius Lentulus.

When the allocation of provinces was discussed and Scipio asked for Africa, Fabius renewed his attack and fought Scipio's African project tooth and nail. Finally, a nominal compromise was reached by which one consul should command in Sicily with the right to sail to Africa if he thought fit; since Scipio's colleague Crassus, as Pontifex Maximus, was debarred from leaving Italy, Scipio had clearly triumphed.[3] But he was further checked when given the command of

---

[1] L. xxviii. 38. 6–11.

[2] Ibid. 4 (cf. xxxi. 20. 3); Dio (frg. 57. 56). Appian (*Iber*. 38. 154) and Polybius (xi. 33. 7: κάλλιστον θρίαμβον) say that he did celebrate a triumph. He may have held a private one on the Alban Mount. Cf. Degrassi, *Inscr. Ital.* XIII. i, p. 551.

[3] Details of the discussion in the Senate (L. xxviii. 45) are somewhat doubtful. When asked by Q. Fulvius whether he would abide by the Senate's decision on the allocation of provinces or would appeal to the People, Scipio replied that he would act as he thought best in the interests of the State. The tribunes then intervened and said that if Scipio entrusted the decision to the Senate its decision should be final and there should be no appeal to the People, but if he did not entrust it, the tribunes would support any senator who refused to vote on Scipio's motion. Scipio could thus drop his motion and appeal to

only the two legions in Sicily, comprising the disgraced survivors of Cannaé; by an appeal for volunteers, however, he forged a weapon to strike at Carthage and circumvented the opposition. This was based upon both political and military differences. Politically, Fabius represented those who did not look beyond Italy for Rome's future. Such men wished to stem the tide of Hellenism which was flooding Rome, to finish the war with all speed, to heal the wounds which it had inflicted on the Italian country-side, and perhaps to develop northern Italy.[1] Some may even have been ready by 205 to attempt a compromise peace with Carthage by which she would be allowed to retain her African possessions.[2] The other view, represented by Scipio, whose horizon had been broadened by family tradition and personal experience in Spain, was that a purely Italian policy was outdated and that Rome must become a Mediterranean power. The military objectives of the two parties varied correspondingly. The Fabians wished merely to drive Hannibal from Italy, Scipio to crush Hannibal and Carthage. Fabius' strategy was not designed to conquer Carthage. Scipio, however, by skilful, and now tested, tactical reforms had forged an army which could face Hannibal in the open field. To defeat Hannibal in Italy, at length a possibility, might terminate the war, but Carthage would remain a danger, since enthusiasm for an African expedition could scarcely be kindled once fighting had ceased in Italy. Scipio therefore determined to disregard the enemy's main forces, strike at the base, and so force Hannibal to return to Africa to fight the decisive battle. After a hard political struggle, in which if need be he was apparently prepared to refer the matter over the head of the Senate to the People, Scipio won the day.[3]

The Scipionic group maintained its predominance in the elections for 204.[4] As Crassus was ill, he proposed with senatorial sanction that

the People, but after a day's delay he decided to leave the question to the Senate. R. M. Haywood (*Scipio*, 54) accepts the tribunician decree as genuine, but De Sanctis (III. ii. 645) is more probably correct in regarding it as a forgery (by Valerius Antias ?). The one fact which emerges is that Scipio clearly was prepared to appeal to the People if he failed to gain his own way in the Senate, and that he could not be overawed by the prestige of senior senators. When he gave in, he presumably must have concluded or have been assured privately that the Senate would prefer compromise to an appeal to the People.

[1] See above, p. 61. Perhaps Fabius' authority was behind the Senate's instruction to the consuls to commence the re-settlement of the country-side before they started for the war. The consuls ordered as many men as possible to return to their ravaged farms in Latium, and the colonists at Cremona and Placentia, who had fled under Gallic pressure, to return home (L. xxviii. 11. 8–11).

[2] Ed. Meyer, *Meister der Politik*, i. 101, 131 ff.; *Kl. Schr.* ii. 353 n. 2. For a striking description of the narrow peasant outlook of the Senate before the Hannibalic War see M. Holleaux, *Rome, la Grèce*, etc., 169 ff. ('la répugnance aux nouveautés, la timidité devant l'inconnu, naturelle aux âmes paysannes'). This view is regarded as an underestimate of the spirit of the *Patres* by J. Carcopino, *Points de vue sur l'impérialisme romaine*, 58 ff.   [3] On the political activities of the poet Naevius at this period see pp. 253 f.
[4] L. xxix. 10–11.

Scipio's friend Q. Caecilius Metellus should be appointed dictator to conduct the elections; Metellus then named his former colleague L. Veturius Philo as *magister equitum*. The consuls elected were the two censors of 209, M. Cornelius Cethegus and P. Sempronius Tuditanus. The latter, who had served in Gaul as praetor and propraetor (213–211) and had been censor without having held the consulship, had been sent earlier in the year with proconsular *imperium* to Greece.[1] Failing to kindle any enthusiasm among the disillusioned Aetolians, who, neglected by Rome, had made peace with Philip, Sempronius also concluded a peace with Philip. It is tempting to see here a move instigated by Scipio who wished to eliminate any possibility that Philip might attempt to interfere in Italy or Africa while he himself was busy planning his invasion of Africa. Sempronius now received his reward for this satisfactory settlement of Macedonian affairs. The new praetors of 204 included Scipio's cousin, M. Pomponius Matho, and M. Marcius Ralla, who later served as Scipio's legate in Africa in 202 and accompanied the Carthaginian peace embassy to Rome.[2] All four aediles were from families friendly to the Scipionic group: C. Livius and M. Servilius Geminus (curule), P. Aelius and P. Villius (plebeian). The commands of the leaders of the Scipionic party were prolonged: Scipio in Africa, Crassus in Bruttium, M. Livius in Gaul. Another honour fell to the house when Nasica, Scipio's cousin and the son of Cn. Scipio who had been killed in Spain, was chosen, as the best and noblest man in the State, to receive the Mater Idaea who was being brought from Asia Minor to Rome.[3]

At the beginning of 204 the Opposition under Fabius seized a chance to attack the absent Scipio. The misconduct of Scipio's lieutenant Pleminius, who had been left at Locri after its capture by Scipio, gave rise to a grave scandal. Q. Metellus, who championed Scipio's cause in the Senate against Fabius' wild proposal to recall him, advocated the dispatch of a commission of inquiry. This, however, was led by M. Pomponius, the new praetor of Sicily and Scipio's own cousin, and if it went to criticize it stayed to bless: Pleminius was brought to book, but Scipio remained unscathed. The year passed uneventfully in the field in Italy, while Scipio established a foothold in Africa.[4] In Rome the new censors, Livius Salinator and Claudius

---

[1] The precise date of Sulpicius Galba's recall is not stated, although the prolongation of his *imperium* is not mentioned after 208; possibly he returned in 207 (L. xxvii. 22. 10; xxix. 12. 2). Cf. De Sanctis, III. ii. 429 n. 83.

[2] Schur (*Scipio*, 41) arbitrarily identifies Marcius with L. Marcius (? Septimus), who in 211 rallied the defeated Roman armies in Spain where he continued to serve under P. Scipio; his *cognomen* is uncertain (cf. L. xxxii. 2; xxv. 37; xxviii. 28).

[3] On this honour for Nasica see E. Schmähling, *Die Sittenaufsicht der Censoren*, 6 f. For the commissioners, who were sent to fetch the sacred stone and received a friendly welcome from Attalus, see L. xxix. 11. 3.

[4] This may have been slightly precarious. J. H. Thiel (*Roman Sea-Power*, 160)

Nero, reappointed Fabius as Leader of the House, but their old rivalry soon flared up so bitterly that each declared the other disfranchized. Details of their quarrel may not be trustworthy[1] but behind it may lie the political manœuvring of the Claudian group to reassert itself. In the elections for 203, however, the Scipionic party still seemed supreme: under the presidency of Cornelius Cethegus, Cn. Servilius Caepio (*pr.* 205) and C. Servilius Geminus (*pr.* 206) were elected consuls.[2] The rise of the Servilii had been unspectacular but steady; no year since 213 had passed without one of the three men, C. and M. Servilius Geminus and Cn. Servilius Caepio, gaining some political or religious office: *Servilia familia inlustris in fastis.*[3] Having won power, however, they deserted their former friends.

11. *Servilian Opposition*

Military and political developments in 203 were critical. A diversionary landing by Mago in Liguria was smashed by the consul C. Servilius, supported by M. Cornelius Cethegus and P. Quinctilius Varus. In Africa victory followed victory: Scipio surprised the encamped forces of Hasdrubal and his Numidian ally Syphax, defeated the enemy in open battle at Campi Magni, and occupied Cirta. In the autumn Carthage sought an armistice and Scipio discussed terms of peace, while Hannibal had been forced to leave Italy and return to his native land. Thus Scipio's strategy was gloriously vindicated. When his friend Laelius reached Rome with the captured Syphax, the Senate decreed four days' thanksgiving amid scenes of great popular rejoicing.

But when the Senate began to discuss the proposed peace terms, the debate showed that Scipio's victories were stirring up jealousy and hostility even among some of his former friends. M. Livius demonstrated his sympathy with the Servilii by proposing an adjournment until at least one of the consuls should return. When Metellus, Scipio's loyal supporter, advocated the acceptance of his proposals on the ground that the man on the spot knew best, the Claudii rallied to the attack. They had advanced again in the previous year with the censorship of Claudius Nero, and now M. Valerius Laevinus urged that the Carthaginian overtures should be rejected and the war carried on. Whether Fabius, who died some time during the year, lived long

suggests that in his report to the Senate Scipio may have exaggerated his early cavalry victory in order to prevent his political opponents profiting by his difficult situation and trying to replace him by another commander.   [1] L. xxix. 37.

[2] Ibid. 38. Of the praetors at least P. Cornelius Lentulus and P. Villius Tappulus were friendly to the Scipionic group.

[3] Cf. Münzer, *RA*, 142. 213 B.C. Cn. pontifex; 212 C. *trib. pleb.*; 211 M. augur; 210 C. pontifex; 209 C. *aed. pleb.*; 208 C. *aed. cur.* and *mag. equit.*; 207 Cn. *aed. cur.*; 206 C. praetor; 205 Cn. praetor; 204 M. *aed. cur.*; 203 Cn. and C. consuls. Pliny, *NH*, xxxiv. 137.

enough to take part in the debate is uncertain. Notwithstanding Livy's statement that Valerius' proposal was passed, Scipio's terms were ultimately ratified.[1] The attack had miscarried, but it was ominous.[2]

The events leading to the elections for 202 tell the same story. Livy's account is confused, since he found his authorities divided.[3] One version suggests that the consul Cn. Servilius Caepio had determined to make a direct assault on Scipio's position by crossing to Sicily with the intention of sailing to Africa. The Senate instructed a praetor to stop him, but he disregarded orders from a subordinate; a dictator, P. Sulpicius Galba, was therefore appointed (*creatus*, presumably by the People) who recalled Caepio *pro iure maioris imperi*. Thereafter the dictator spent the rest of the year with his *magister equitum*, M. Servilius Geminus, visiting cities which had revolted from Rome during the war, and the elections were held by the consul, C. Servilius Geminus. According to the other version, the consul C. Servilius stepped out of his province Etruria into that of the proconsul M. Cornelius Cethegus in order to rescue his father, who had been captured by the Boii sixteen years before. After bringing him to Rome, where he secured the passage of a bill of indemnity for an unwitting infringement of the law (cf. pp. 276 f.), he returned to his province where he was so busy that his *imperium* was prolonged for another year; since he was unable to come to Rome, he named Sulpicius Galba dictator (*dictus*) to hold the elections.[4] Details of the tradition of Caepio's wild act may be false, but it at least suggests growing rivalry of the Servilii towards Scipio. The elections point the same way. When the Claudian dictator Galba appointed as his Master of Horse the consul's brother, M. Servilius Geminus, the result was foreshadowed: M. Servilius Geminus and Ti. Claudius Nero were elected. The secession of the Servilii to the Claudii was clear.[5]

Livy narrates that when the new consuls entered office in March 202 they convened the Senate to allocate the provinces. Both wanted Africa, but through the intervention of Q. Metellus they were instructed to act with the tribunes of the plebs who were to ask the People whom they wished to conduct the war in Africa: the unanimous vote was for Scipio. Nevertheless the consuls ballotted for their provinces, and Africa fell to Ti. Claudius, who was granted *imperium* co-ordinate with Scipio's, and fifty ships; M. Servilius received Etruria.[6] Later, when the Carthaginians had broken the truce and hostilities

---

[1] This is established beyond doubt by Polybius' definite assertion (xv. 1. 3).

[2] L. xxx. 23. On the ratification of the terms and the political history during Scipio's absence see De Sanctis, III. ii. 652, 544; Schur, *Scipio*, 62 ff., 129 ff.; Münzer, *RA*, 143 ff.; Scullard, *Scipio*, 222 ff.   [3] xxx. 26. 12.

[4] Ibid. 19. 6; 24. 1–4; 26. 12; 27. 6. Cf. Fasti Capit. where Galba is named *dict. comit. habend. caussa*.   [5] See further, appendix, p. 277.

[6] L. xxx. 27. See further, 38.

had recommenced in Africa, Claudius was ordered to take the fleet to Africa, but he delayed his preparations because the Senate had decided that Scipio rather than he should fix the terms of the peace; when ultimately the fleet was ready, it was wrecked by a storm.

This account is very doubtful. The Senate had not the right to disregard the People's vote; the question of Scipio's command did not require discussion by the People if his *imperium* had been prolonged in 203 for the duration of the war[1] although a colleague could be sent to him; also the discussion was futile if peace had just been concluded. The truth behind Livy's account probably is that, while the consuls wanted some share in the final victory, there was no serious question of recalling Scipio, but that when news came that the armistice had been broken, Claudius was ordered to prepare a fleet. When ready, this was wrecked, and before it could be repaired Claudius' year of office expired and his command was not prolonged.[2]

In Africa the year 202 was marked by the renewal of the war after the Carthaginians had broken the armistice, followed by Scipio's final campaign against Hannibal which ended at Zama. In Rome political intrigues continued. The consul M. Servilius and his brother Gaius tried to control events by one or other of them remaining there all the year. Although Etruria had been assigned to Marcus, he stopped in Rome for part of the year, while Gaius remained in Etruria as proconsul. Then Marcus named Gaius dictator to hold the elections, probably with the object of enabling him to stop in Rome while he himself went off to his province; P. Aelius Paetus was made *magister equitum*. Livy adds that although various dates were fixed for the elections the weather prevented them from being held, so that after 14 March 201 the Republic was without curule magistrates.[3]

Clearly the religious machinery by which augurs could postpone elections had been set in motion. Either therefore the pro-Scipionic opposition had tried to delay them until the end of the consular year when the dictator's period of office perhaps should end,[4] or else the augurs had co-operated with Servilius in order to allow him to exercise power longer; in view of the composition of the augural college the latter alternative seems more probable.[5] In any case he remained in

---

[1] L. xxx. 1. 10.   [2] Cf. De Sanctis, III. ii. 545 n. 157, and see further, p. 278.

[3] If the dictator, whose office was curule, remained in office legally or illegally (see n. 4), Livy's statement is inaccurate, but it should not be pressed too closely. He clearly means to imply that the normal curule magistrates (consuls, praetors, &c.) had not been elected. The passage should not be used as evidence to show that the dictator's office had ended.

[4] From this passage (L. xxx. 39) Mommsen (*Staatsr.* ii. 160 n. 4) deduced that it was necessary for a dictator to resign when the consul who had nominated him retired from office. A. Aymard (*Rev. Ét. Anc.* 1944, 242 ff.) rejects this and argues that the dictator was bound only by the six months' limit.

[5] Of the seven known augurs four may be accounted among the opponents of Scipio and members of the Claudian-Servilian clique: M. Servilius Geminus, Cn. Cornelius

office at least until 19 April when he celebrated the Cerialia.[1] Thus for more than a month the State was without the normal curule magistrates and was administered by the dictator, his *magister equitum*, and the tribunes of the plebs if these last had been elected. At length the elections were held, possibly by an interrex or more probably by the dictator, and two men of his choice were elected: his Master of Horse, P. Aelius Paetus, and Cn. Cornelius Lentulus.[2] The reader of Livy's account of all these disturbances must be very conscious that the historian wrote after the period of the dictatorship of Julius Caesar and the dislocation of magistracies at that time, but there may yet be a basic element of truth in his narrative. At any rate this misuse of the dictatorship led to its desuetude.[3]

Lentulus made one last unavailing attempt against Scipio, if any belief is to be accorded to Livy's annalistic tradition, by trying to prevent the Senate from transacting any business until Africa had been assigned to him. Two tribunes, Q. Minucius Thermus and M'. Acilius Glabrio, both Scipio's staunch supporters later, intervened by putting the matter before the People, who voted unanimously for Scipio. The Senate compromised to the extent that Lentulus was assigned a fleet and was to sail to Sicily; if peace negotiations failed, he was to sail to Africa, but only with power at sea, for Scipio was to retain full command by land. But the negotiations did not fail. The Senate followed the People's wish and decreed that Scipio, together with ten commissioners, was to make peace with Carthage on such terms as he thought fit.[4] Thus the conqueror of Hannibal, having vindicated his military strategy, triumphed also in the political field; he negotiated a wise peace such as could never have been made if Hannibal had been defeated in Italy, and he had withstood the attacks of his political opponents, now joined by many of his erstwhile allies. His success owed much to the enthusiastic and loyal support of the People of Rome.

Lentulus (the augur is probably to be identified with the consul of 201), P. Aelius Paetus and Ti. Sempronius Gracchus. Young Q. Fabius Maximus, recently elected augur and probably a grandson of Cunctator, would presumably not oppose any measure hostile to Scipio. The two other augurs were L. Quinctius Flamininus and Ti. Sempronius Longus.

[1] The plebeian aediles of 202, P. Aelius Tubero and L. Laetorius, had held the Plebeian Games including the *epulum Iovis* (on 13 Nov.), but were then, very belatedly, found to have been irregularly appointed (*vitio creati*) and had to resign. As presumably the aedilician elections for 201 had not been held, Servilius gained the honour of celebrating the Cerialia (see L. xxx. 39. 8). Very few examples are known of plebeian, as opposed to curule, magistrates being forced to resign through faulty election (cf. Mommsen, *Staatsr.* iii. 364; *Dr. pub.* VI. i. 418). On a speech by Cato which may apply to this matter see p. 256.

[2] L. xxx. 39, 40 (esp. 39. 8; 40. 4–5). Cf. Münzer, *RA*, 144–5; Schur, *Scipio*, 66.

[3] See p. 279.

[4] On the question of a senatorial debate see p. 279.

III. *Scipio after Zama*

When Scipio returned from Africa he found Rome at the cross-roads: the formulation of her foreign policy was at a critical stage and the handful of nobles in the Senate, on whom in the last analysis the responsibility for the decision lay, held in their hands the future destiny of Rome and the world. A new generation was at the helm: Q. Fulvius Flaccus had died about 205, Fabius Maximus in 203, Manlius Torquatus in 202. In fact no man who had held the consulship before 211, except Varro the scapegoat of Cannae, was still in harness, while a surprisingly small number of the men who had been praetors since 212 had reached the consulship: of the 36 praetors of 212–204 B.C. only 7 succeeded instead of the 18 who might normally have aspired to it.[1] While members of the older generation had survived, they had tended to monopolize office even into the second half of the war; the result was that a crop of newer men sprang suddenly to the fore towards the end, when more openings occurred, and Rome was short of older men of wide experience. These leaders were faced not only by broader international problems but also by a domestic question: would the conqueror of Hannibal raise any constitutional issues or seek to challenge the hostile faction in the Senate?

The Servilii had forsaken their traditional loyalty to the Scipionic group; joining the Claudians and strengthened by the adhesion of Cn. Cornelius Lentulus, they had held the chief offices from 203 to 201 and had persistently attacked Scipio in his absence. In the Senate their attacks had been countered by Q. Caecilius Metellus, while Scipio had received still stronger support from the People whose tribunes, Q. Minucius Thermus and M'. Acilius Glabrio, had intervened on his behalf. This opposition, unlike that of Fabius and his group earlier, was based not on questions of policy but on personal ambition. The Servilii and Claudii, jealous of Scipio's increasing success, had tried to snatch victory from his grasp, or failing that at least the fruits of victory. Unable to undermine the People's faith in its hero, they had built up a powerful clique in the Senate, the more easily because many senators would view with misgiving the possibility that Scipio might tend to rely on popular support, especially as he could not count on the backing of more than four or five of the senior senators.[2]

---

[1] It may be assumed that M. Iunius Pera (*cos.* 230; dict. 216), M. Atilius Regulus (*cos.* 227; censor 214), L. Aemilius Papus (censor 220), and P. Cornelius Scipio Asina (*cos.* 221) had died. L. Lutatius Catulus (*cos.* 220) was released from captivity in 203 but was not very useful. M. Livius Salinator (*cos.* I, 219) is not heard of after 203. C. Terentius Varro (*cos.* 216) served on a commission in 200, but presumably died soon afterwards. Young Fabius Maximus (*cos.* 213) had predeceased his father.

[2] Scipio could rely on only Q. Caecilius Metellus, P. Licinius Crassus, L. Veturius Philo, probably M. Cornelius Cethegus, and perhaps C. Terentius Varro. For the senior senators in 201 see pp. 280 f.

The unconstitutional tenure of the dictatorship by C. Servilius, lasting into 201, may have caused the internal balance within the Servilian-Claudian coalition to swing towards the Claudii, but the Servilii were not immediately eclipsed, and the coalition, although unsuccessful in its attempts to hinder Scipio in Africa, was still powerful. The consuls of 201 had shown their hands, Cn. Cornelius Lentulus by attempting to secure the African command and to block the peace, P. Aelius Paetus by having served as *magister equitum* to C. Servilius.[1] Nor did the praetors of 201 belong to families friendly to Scipio. Indeed the political views of the praetor urbanus, M. Iunius Pennus, appear to have been decidedly unfavourable. When instructed to appoint a commission of ten to allocate some *ager publicus* in Samnium and Apulia for the settlement of Scipio's African veterans, he nominated only one man who was known to have supported Scipio's interests: this, however, was Q. Caecilius Metellus (*cos.* 206), who was the senior member, if priority in holding the consulship gave seniority.[2] This commission is interesting from several aspects. The provision of land for long-service soldiers was undertaken as an obligation by the State and not left to the initiative of their general, as often happened later with disastrous consequences to the Republic. Further, Scipio's political opponents were able to steal some of his thunder by gaining considerable control over the composition of the commission, and while the measure would temporarily increase Scipio's popularity, it involved removing far from Rome and the Comitia many of his loyal veterans.

Scipio's popularity reached its zenith when he celebrated his triumph in 201 amid scenes of great enthusiasm, but although he was honoured by the title of Africanus and was recognized two years later as the first citizen of Rome by his appointment as *princeps senatus* and censor, his exact influence is difficult to gauge. It has been said that 'the victory of Zama made Cornelius Scipio the most powerful man at Rome. It would seem that any member of his family could then have any office which he desired. Seven Cornelii are recorded as consuls during the ten years after Zama.'[3] But his position was not so absolute. True, Livy has recorded that the People wished to make

[1] Paetus was later reconciled with Scipio (pp. 96 f.).

[2] The nine other commissioners were: the brothers C. and M. Servilius Geminus (*coss.* 203 and 202); an otherwise unknown P. Servilius, probably their brother or cousin (cf. Münzer, *RA*, 146); P. Aelius Paetus (*cos.* 201); P. Villius Tappulus, plebeian aedile with Paetus in 204 and elected praetor with him at the same elections in which the Servilii gained the consulship; M. Fulvius Flaccus, perhaps the tribune who opposed the election of Flamininus in 199; then three men who later represented the old Fabian group, L. and A. Hostilius Cato (praetors in 207) and T. Quinctius Flamininus, curule aedile in 201 (L. xxxi. 4. 1–3). The attempt by R. M. Haywood (*Scipio*, 71) to suggest that the majority of the commissioners was friendly to Scipio is not convincing.

[3] *CAH*, viii. 368.

him a monarch, but his testimony is hardly credible. He tells how Tiberius Gracchus charged Scipio towards the end of his life with disregarding the tribunate and contrasts this with Scipio's earlier magnanimity: 'Gracchus reminded his hearers how severely Scipio rebuked the People for wishing to make him perpetual consul and dictator; how he had prevented them from raising statues to him in the Comitium, the Rostra, the Senate House, and in the shrine of Iuppiter on the Capitol, and how he had prevented a decree from being passed authorizing his image decked in triumphal garb to be borne in procession from the temple of Iuppiter Optimus Maximus.' There can be little doubt that this account derives from a political pamphlet masquerading as a speech of Ti. Gracchus and that it is a reflection on the conduct of a later dictator, either Sulla or Julius Caesar.[1] A serious suggestion that the Republic should be converted into a monarchy would surely have left other traces in the extant tradition. Such a revolution might conceivably have come two generations after Scipio, of whose adopted grandson it has been written: 'if he had been bolder or less scrupulous the monarchy might have come from Spain in 133 instead of from Gaul in 49, for, when Scipio Aemilianus returned to Rome as her deliverer, no element was lacking but his own resolve to be monarch.'[2] Many, however, will feel that even here the problem has been antedated; still less can the threat of monarchy have been an actual danger in 200 B.C.

True, Scipio's position and nature were kingly,[3] but there is little beyond Livy's worthless statement to suggest that Scipio could have effected a *coup d'état*. If such a thought ever crossed his mind—and according to Polybius he often thought of monarchy, in some part of the world if not in Rome itself—it was only to be rejected. Though naturally regal and desirous of rule, Scipio was too clear-sighted and great-minded to play the demagogue. Nor perhaps did he deliberately court the People; his popularity rested partly on admiration for his dazzling personality, but more on the prospect of booty which his overseas campaigns opened up and on the psychological release from feelings of frustration which his aggressive policy must have occasioned when the war was dragging on so slowly in Italy. He certainly would not and probably could not have broken the power of the Senate. A member of one of the most aristocratic Roman families, he was too class-conscious and loyal, as well as too wise, to pit his strength against the Senate which had won undying prestige by its conduct of the war. Instead, he sank back into the life of a private citizen, a noble among nobles, soon to be forced to enter the arena of

---

[1] L. xxxviii. 56. See below, p. 282.   [2] A. Schulten, *CAH*, viii. 323.
[3] Cf. some of his enemies' alleged remarks: L. xxviii. 42. 22; xxxviii. 51. 4; 54. 6; Seneca, *Epist*. xiii. 1 (86). 3.

party politics in order to maintain the pre-eminence of his family and friends, and only accepting a further military command when his country had need of him.

But if there was little fear of dictatorship, the rapidity and irregularity of Scipio's extraordinary career at least gave good grounds for suspicion and envy. When only 22 and under the legal age he became aedile. Without having been praetor or consul he had been elected on a wave of popular enthusiasm to a proconsular command which lasted not one year but five. Contrary to custom, when only 29 he had been elected consul and had set at naught the policy of the aged and experienced *princeps senatus* and of his following in the Senate. During the next four years he had fought successfully in Africa as proconsul and had virtually dictated the peace terms to the defeated enemy. Thus for ten years (210–201) he had held supreme command successively in Spain, Italy, and Africa, the inspired hero of a devoted army and of a grateful people, respected alike by Spaniard, Greek, and Carthaginian. It is true that other men had overstepped the boundaries normally laid down by the constitution, which had perforce been adapted to the rigours of war. By legal dispensation from the ten years' interval, Fabius had been consul three times (215, 214, 209), Marcellus four times (215, 214, 210, 208), and Fulvius Flaccus twice (212, 209), while their promagistracies had kept them in office for even longer periods (e.g. Marcellus in Sicily from 214 to 211 and in Italy from 210 to 209). But there was a vital difference. War took its toll, and neither Fabius, Marcellus, nor Fulvius survived. And what was necessary in war became intolerable in peace.

Scipio's position was unique and the nobility began to realize the meaning of the advice given to Periander of Corinth by Thrasybulus of Miletus who took Periander's messenger into a cornfield and struck the heads off all the taller stalks—a policy which Aristotle justified as 'not only expedient for tyrants or in practice confined to them, but equally necessary in oligarchies and democracies'. Athens had recourse to ostracism, Rome to factional politics within the Senate. If there is about Scipio something reminiscent of the captive lion who, his freedom lost, is forced through the tricks of the circus, it was because he preferred to play, none too successfully, the game of politics rather than allow the Roman mob to acclaim him 'King' even in thought, a title which he had heard and refused from his devoted Spanish allies some years before. Polybius takes that occasion to remark upon his exceptional greatness of mind; for after his conquests of Africa and Asia 'he had made the greatest and richest part of the world subject to Rome and in doing so had numerous opportunities of acquiring regal sway (δυναστείαν βασιλικήν) in whatever parts of the world suited his purpose or wish. For such achievements were enough to kindle pride, not merely in any human breast but even, if I may say so without irreverence, in that of a god. But Scipio's greatness of soul (μεγαλοψυχία) was so superior to the common standard of mankind that he again and again rejected what Fortune had put within his grasp, the prize beyond which men's boldest prayers do not go—the power of a king (βασιλεία); and he valued more highly his country and his loyalty to her than that royalty which men gaze at with such admiration and envy.'[1] True, Polybius was a Greek, to whom the supreme political temptation was tyranny, and matters may have appeared slightly different in Roman eyes. But Scipio was well acquainted with the history of Greek tyranny and monarchy;[2] and this noteworthy judgement by Polybius, made long before the military dictatorships of Marius, Sulla, or Caesar, should be accorded full weight in any estimate of Scipio's influence even though the precise offer of a permanent dictatorship, as recorded by Livy, must be regarded as unhistorical.

Scipio thus had to face his fellow-senators as an equal. He seems to have accepted quietly the predominance of the Claudian-Servilian group and not to have made any immediate effort to win important positions for his family or friends. The explanation may well be that he wanted a period of rest. He had seen ten years' active service, training armies, organizing, campaigning, and fighting. During a winter in Syracuse he had snatched the opportunities of culture and relaxation which the Greek city offered to him, thereby incurring the hostile contempt of the more rigidly Roman Fabius. Men of a past age are not lay figures, but flesh and blood. Scipio might well be eager to devote some time to that Greek culture which he so admired, to renew old friendships, and to seek society in Rome rather than to attempt to establish the power of his family in the Senate where his own personal position at least was supreme.

A further explanation of his apparent inactivity after his return may be found in his attitude to foreign affairs. Owing to the inadequacy of the sources no clear indication of the part which he played in shaping foreign policy at this time can be given, but in view of the liberality of his policy towards the East in general it has been suggested that he did not support the Senate's decision to send a harsh ultimatum to

---

[1] P. x. 40.

[2] When asked whom he thought the greatest statesmen combining boldness and wisdom, Scipio is alleged to have named Agathocles and Dionysius (P. xv. 35. 6). This might be taken to prove his admiration for tyranny (though obviously it is not evidence for Scipio's attitude to the Roman constitution), but on the other hand the context of the remark might have been connected with the strenuousness of the efforts of these two Syracusan tyrants against Carthage. On the remark of the Catilinarian P. Lentulus 'se esse tertium illum Cornelium, ad quem regnum huius urbis atque imperium pervenire esset necesse; Cinnam ante se et Sullam fuisse' (Cic. In Cat. iii. 9; cf. Quint. v. 10. 30) and its possible background see Münzer, RA, 100.

Philip, King of Macedon, and to precipitate immediate war in 200, when the way of diplomacy was still open.[1] This suggestion deserves further consideration. The Senate as a whole clearly approved of immediate action and the sources do not refer to any division of opinion within its ranks; the opposition came from the People. Now in so far as Scipio had popular support, he would have his finger more closely on the pulse of popular feeling, while at the same time he would know the temper of his troops, and to what extent they looked forward to demobilization. If he had been eager for an immediate declaration of war on Philip, his immense popularity would surely have weighed with the People; in other words, the fact that they at first refused to declare war may suggest that he did not urge it. In view of his successful personal diplomacy with native princes in Spain and Africa, he may well have thought that a less brusque approach should be made to Philip, whose confidence he did in fact quickly win when they met later. His previous experience may also have turned his thoughts to development of the West rather than to an immediate and irrevocable interference in Eastern affairs. The supposition, then, that he opposed senatorial policy and perhaps even urged the People to avoid war would help to explain his sinking into the background at a moment when it would be reasonable to suppose that his country would have sought to employ his outstanding military gifts.

Such a view of his attitude in 201 is based mainly on its congruence with his ideas of foreign policy in general, which will be discussed later, rather than on any definite indication in the ancient sources. But there are two pieces of confirmatory evidence, slight indeed but not valueless when no scrap of evidence should be neglected. First, the tribune who urged the People to reject the Senate's proposal of war was Q. Baebius; nothing else is known about this man, but the Baebii seem to have been friendly to the Aemilian-Scipionic group.[2] Secondly, Scipio's friend, Licinius Crassus, the Pontifex Maximus, tried on a point of religious procedure to obstruct the consul Galba before he sailed to Greece in 200. When Galba was authorized to vow Games to Iuppiter, Licinius objected on the score that by precedent a definite sum had to be named and set aside or else the vow could not be duly discharged. Galba, however, was instructed to refer the question to the whole pontifical college, and it decided in his favour.[3]

[1] See A. H. McDonald, *JRS*, 1938, 154; 160. On the situation in Greece and the motives of senatorial policy see the following chapter.

[2] L. xxxi. 6. See above, p. 42 n. 4.

[3] L. xxxi. 9. This striking rejection of the authority of the Pontifex Maximus appears less puzzling when the composition of the College of Pontiffs is analysed. Licinius Crassus could, on family grounds, count only on Caecilius Metellus (*cos.* 206) and M. Cornelius Cethegus (*cos.* 204). The claim of P. Sulpicius Galba would probably be supported by Q. Fulvius Flaccus (*cos.* I, 233) if he was still alive (he is not heard of after 205), by the

Thus Licinius' attack proved abortive, but although a mere pin-prick, it may indicate his objection to senatorial policy towards Philip. Thus Scipio's temporary eclipse may perhaps be partly attributed to his disapproval of the Senate's hasty action, as well as to his desire for rest, to the predominance of a rival faction in the Senate, and to his exceptional, but from the point of view of his peers potentially dangerous, popularity.

two Servilii (Cn. Caepio and C. Geminus, *coss.* 203), by Livius Salinator who like his father may have deserted Scipio (see p. 78), and by two recently chosen pontiffs, Ser. Sulpicius Galba (aedile of 209 and probably brother of P. Sulpicius Galba the consul) and C. Sulpicius Galba (or Galus, probably the praetor of 211). The religious point at issue was probably that if the vow was indefinite the corresponding response of the gods might be indefinite. Incidentally, despite this rebuff the chief Pontiff's authority was unshaken, because when a hymn had to be sung throughout the city to counteract certain ill-omened portents, P. Licinius Tegula, doubtless his client, was chosen to compose the hymn.

VI

SENATORIAL GROUPS AND FLAMININUS

(201–196 B.C.)

1. *Senatorial Policy in West and East*[1]

ALTHOUGH the menace of Carthage at long last was removed, immense tasks of reconstruction and consolidation awaited Roman statesmanship. There was financial exhaustion at Rome. Large parts of Italy, especially in the south, were devastated and depopulated, and few cities from Capua to Tarentum had escaped looting, destruction, or enslavement by either Carthaginian armies or Roman punitive expeditions. Cisalpine Gaul, conquered just before the war, had been lost and the Gauls were planning a concerted attack upon Italy. Ligurian tribes needed curbing, and access to Genoa must be recovered. With Spain now on her hands Rome must safeguard communications with the West and reach an understanding with the hill tribes which could threaten the land route. Spain itself must be organized. Desire for its possession had not been among the motives which had driven Rome to war with Carthage, but it remained one of the chief prizes of victory. Apart from any wish to exploit its natural resources, serious problems of administration were involved, since the peninsula contained many peoples of diverse grades of civilization; if the southern and more settled districts were to be held and protected, the menace of the wilder tribes of the centre must be faced. And overshadowing these urgent problems at home and in the West was the crucial task of determining a policy towards the whole Hellenistic world, now in a ferment since the balance of power had been rudely upset by the aggression of Macedon and Syria against a weakened Egypt.

Apart from her handling of the Eastern question, Rome acted with a strange lack of decision due in part to sheer war-weariness. No comprehensive attempt was made to stabilize the financial situation until 187. Much of the ravaged land in Italy was confiscated by the Senate and declared *ager publicus*, but little immediate attempt was made to improve conditions, apart from settling some of Scipio's veterans in Samnium and Apulia; for the rest the censors rented land to any who would undertake the venture. Poverty and lack of manpower hindered large-scale schemes of reclamation or colonization. It was Gallic threats rather than Roman initiative which forced Rome

---

[1] In general see De Sanctis, IV. i; M. Holleaux, *CAH*, viii, chs. 6–7; T. Frank, *CAH*, viii, chs. 11–12, and *Econ. Survey*, i, chs. 3–4; G. Colin, *Rome et la Grèce*; A. H. McDonald, *CHJ*, 1939, 124 ff.

to a speedy and enduring settlement of the northern frontier. Liguria could wait, and even in Spain reorganization was postponed for a few years.

Rome's fundamental problem, the solution of which would affect the whole future history of Europe, was whether to deal with East or West, with the civilized or the barbarian world. If she undertook responsibilities in the West she would have to meet the barbarians on the fringe. This would not impose undue difficulties, granted determination and an aggressive spirit: Hamilcar and Hannibal had overrun central Spain in a few years, while the conquest of the whole of Gaul was accomplished by Caesar within a decade. The legions which had defeated Hannibal and were soon to crush Philip and Antiochus would scarcely have failed against the less disciplined peoples of northern and western Europe. But Rome's intentions were not aggressive. She determined to hold and secure what she had got, to meet problems as they arose, and to tackle the barbarians piecemeal as the threat developed at this or that point.

Whether it would have been less painful for the barbarian world and indeed for Rome herself if she had undertaken a more systematic plan of conquest in the West is a question which admits of no certain answer. Clearly it was here that her mission lay and her chief contribution to world history was the romanization of western Europe. If the establishment of her power there had been sharp and short, at least she would have avoided some of the evil effects which the prolonged struggles had upon the honour of her generals; she might also have forestalled those barbarian attacks which later allowed the first of her great military dictators to leap into the saddle. Be that as it may, Cisalpine Gaul was the only section of the barbarian world that was firmly handled: there conquest was relatively quick and was soon followed by settlement, colonization, romanization, and peace.

Instead of facing the West as a unit Rome turned eastwards. Believing, perhaps mistakenly, that Syria and Macedon might soon threaten Roman security, the Senate goaded an unwilling People into war. Thus, far from dealing comprehensively with the more backward West where her mission could have been, and ultimately was, both political and civilizing, Rome addressed herself to the more difficult problem of facing civilized peoples, who might profit by her lessons in political statecraft but who did not need her culture and could be less easily assimilated into her body politic. If Rome had been the leader of a western empire when she first came into closer relations with the Hellenistic world, her eastern contacts might have been more fruitful and less harmful.[1]

[1] Cf. A. H. McDonald, *The Rise of Roman Imperialism* (Sydney, 1940), 6, and M. Holleaux, *CAH*, viii. 239.

Attempts have been made to define the elusive point when Rome developed from a purely Italian power into a city-state with imperial interests which finally embraced both the eastern and western parts of the Mediterranean world. This, for example, has been dated to the end of the Hannibalic War: a spirit of militarism and imperialism was born when the war changed from a defensive struggle to one for supremacy. After her victory Rome would tolerate no Power as an equal. Her ambition could have been tempered by respect for her opponents, but she saw only the weakness of the East which offered her riches, glory, and dominion.[1] Further, Scipio Africanus has been made the villain of the piece: as his military genius was a main factor in winning the war, as thereafter, with Fabius dead, he was the first man in Rome, and as an outburst of militarism followed the war, therefore he was responsible and an ardent militarist.[2] Many objections to this characterization of Scipio at once occur (what is the evidence for it? did the death of Fabius remove all serious opposition to Scipio, so that he could mould Roman policy? if so, why was he not appointed to command in the war which he is alleged to have inspired?), but more fundamental than the personal aspect is the doubtful assumption that Rome's policy was aggressive. She was slow to launch upon systematic conquest in the West; what, then, was her Eastern policy?

The dominant motive which led the Senate to advocate a declaration of war on Philip of Macedon and thus to gain a decisive influence in Greek affairs has been interpreted in widely different ways: as aggressive militarism, commercial interests, philhellenic sentiments and an altruistic desire to protect Greece against Macedonian aggression, political obligation incurred under the Treaty of Phoenice, or defensive imperialism designed to anticipate the danger of an attack by Philip, Rome's old opponent in the First Macedonian War. This last view may here be accepted in the form so brilliantly expounded by M. Holleaux and amplified in detail by more recent writers.[3] The

---

[1] See De Sanctis, IV. i. 21 ff. Such a view can be based on Polybius' explicit statement that Zama was a battle 'on which everything depended, and which assigned universal dominion to the Romans': ἡ μὲν οὖν ἐπὶ πᾶσι γενομένη μάχη καὶ τὰ ὅλα κρίνασα Ῥωμαίοις (xv. 15. 1). So Shuckburgh, but W. R. Paton translates 'decided the war' (based on iii. 70. 7; but cf. xv. 9. 2; 10. 2). Polybius also (xxxi. 25. 6) offers a slightly later date: it was generally believed that when the kingdom of Macedon was overthrown universal dominion was obtained beyond dispute.

[2] De Sanctis (op. cit.), followed by J. Carcopino (*Points de vue sur l'impérialisme romain*, 10; 67 ff.).

[3] For a brief summary of the more important views put forward before 1935 see H. H. Scullard, *Roman World*, 257 ff. See further G. T. Griffith, *CHJ*, 1935, A. H. McDonald and F. W. Walbank, *JRS*, 1937, and F. W. Walbank, *Philip V*. The view of E. Bickermann (*Rev. Phil.* 1935), that the Peace of Phoenice was a κοινὴ εἰρήνη which included Athens and that Rome was under legal obligation to aid Athens when attacked by Philip has been rejected by J. A. O. Larsen (*CP*, 1937, 15 ff.). M. Rostovtzeff (*Soc. Econ. Hist. Hellen.*

essential factor is that the Senate decided to interfere in Greek affairs quite suddenly (towards the end of 201), thus completely reversing its previous policy. That the Senate would be unlikely to intervene again in the East immediately after the Hannibalic War is clear on general grounds, such as war-weariness, the need for economic recovery in Italy and for military precautions in Cisalpine Gaul and Liguria, and the possibility of exploitation in the West. That the Senate intended to avoid intervention is proved by the complete Roman withdrawal from Greece after the Peace of Phoenice in 205 and by the harsh rejection of an Aetolian appeal for help against Philip's aggression in 202 when the Senate slammed the door in the face of the embassy.[1] This was not the diplomacy which would pave the way for a policy of future intervention in Greece; rather, it clearly demonstrated the Senate's indifference to Philip and Greece. Yet in the autumn of 201 P. Sulpicius Galba, a soldier well versed in Greek affairs, was elected consul for 200 and then given Macedonia as his province; soon afterwards he invited the Roman People to declare war on Philip, presumably on the ground of the king's aggression against Attalus of Pergamum. When the People refused, the Senate sent a commission to Greece to explain the ultimatum which they intended to present to Philip, and finally succeeded in persuading the People to declare war in July, when news had come that Athens, supported by Rhodes and Pergamum, had been goaded into declaring war on Philip who was storming various cities in Thrace, while his general Philocles was ravaging Attica.[2]

The Senate had thus turned from a clear intention not to become

World, i. 52) has emphasized the background of Roman fears: 'Alexander—such was the firm belief of the leading historians of the time—had been determined to add the West to his world empire, and since his day Pyrrhus had shown that there were men in Greece willing and able to make the attempt and to unite against Rome all who disliked her supremacy in Italian affairs. Rome was suspicious of the Hellenistic East, with its great inventions in the field of strategy, tactics, and war machinery. Rome felt herself in this respect a pupil of Greece and was afraid of her teacher.' A. Afzelius (_Die römische Kriegsmacht_, 14 f.) has drawn attention to the impact of the events of the Hannibalic War on Roman thought: Philip's pact with Hannibal in 215 revealed the potential range of the policy of one of the Hellenistic powers which might become dangerous if Philip ever achieved full control over Greece, while the confidence with which Rome had started the war must have been soon shaken by its unexpected course, and she would become mistrustful of any shiftings of power in the surrounding world.

[1] On the date of the Aetolian embassy see F. W. Walbank, _Philip V_, 310 f. A. H. McDonald (_JRS_, 1937, 185) has well emphasized the significance of the bitterness of the rebuff.

[2] The appeal of Athens for help during the summer of 200 did not affect the legal aspect of Roman diplomacy, but it may well have influenced Roman sentiment. A. H. McDonald and F. W. Walbank (op. cit.) believe that the Athenian ambassador Cephisodorus reached Rome in July _after_ the Comitia had declared war. The exact timing, however, has scarcely been proved, and Cephisodorus might have arrived just before the second meeting of the Comitia; if so, his appeal may well have helped the Senate in its difficult task of pushing the People over the brink of formal war.

entangled in Greek affairs to a feverish desire to precipitate war. The explanation of this remarkable change is to be found in the revelation made to the Senate by Rhodian and Pergamene ambassadors in the autumn of 201 about a secret pact formed by Philip and Antiochus in the winter of 203/2 under which they purposed to partition the overseas possessions of Egypt.[1] This pact was represented by the ambassadors as a direct threat to Rome: Antiochus, the conqueror of the East and a second Alexander the Great, in alliance with Philip, whose reviving naval power was not unimposing, might well alarm the Senate. It was the sudden realization of the breakdown of the balance of power in the Hellenistic world, of the weakness of Egypt, and of the growing threat which the piratical conduct of Philip and Antiochus offered to Roman security that provoked the Senate's sudden decision that Philip's power must immediately be curbed. The fact that the Senate probably overestimated the danger and that the two kings were not an imminent menace suggests that Roman policy may have been too hasty, not that it was essentially aggressive.

11. *Servilian-Claudian and Scipionic Rivalry*

A defeat in Cisalpine Gaul apparently did not affect the electoral influence of the consul Aelius Paetus under whose presidency P. Sulpicius Galba, for the second time, and C. Aurelius Cotta were elected consuls for 200.[2] If the latter, whose family connexions were with the Servilii, had joined their secession from Scipio, both consuls will have been supporters of the Claudian-Servilian group. The choice of Galba revealed the Senate's intention: he was again posted to Macedonia where he had served from 210 to c. 206. Apart from Terentius Varro, Galba was the senior *consularis* and the only patrician eligible for re-election without infringement of the necessary ten-year interval, which became obligatory again with the end of the Hannibalic War.[3] The Claudii gained another command in the propraetorship of M. Valerius Falto in Sardinia, but they lost by death a senior supporter who had great experience of Greek affairs, M. Valerius Laevinus.[4] Other appointments suggest that Scipio did not wish to leave the entire conduct of affairs to the Claudian group. Three praetors, Q. Minucius Rufus, L. Furius Purpureo, and C. Sergius Plancus,[5] were probably his supporters, while M'. Acilius Glabrio, one of the 'new men' whom Scipio helped on their careers, became a keeper of the Sacred Books.[6]

[1] The attempt of D. Magie (*JRS*, 1939, 32 ff.) to dismiss the pact as a fabrication of Rhodian propaganda, designed to frighten Rome, which deceived both Rome and Polybius, is not completely convincing (cf. Walbank, *Philip V*, 113 n. 4), but true or false, it had the same effect on the Senate.   [2] L. xxxi. 4. 4.   [3] See p. 48 n. 2.
[4] L. xxxi. 8. 9; 50. 4.   [5] On the Sergii see p. 282.
[6] 'Control by the Scipios over the college of pontiffs, which they much needed (p. 87

During the summer of 200, after their earlier refusal in January, the People were persuaded to declare war on Philip. A triumviral commission, which had already been dispatched to Greece to publish abroad the terms of Rome's ultimatum to Philip, contained two members of the Claudian group, C. Claudius Nero (the victor of Metaurus) and P. Sempronius Tuditanus, who had served in Greece in 205 and would be included for his knowledge of Greek affairs. The third commissioner was M. Aemilius Lepidus, whose later history shows that he was loyal to the tradition of his family. His appointment, perhaps due to Scipio's influence, was a great honour, since he was young, had held no high office, and possibly was not yet a senator,[1] but it was justified by his subsequent brilliant career and by his skilful diplomacy when he was chosen by his colleagues to convey the actual ultimatum to Philip.[2] To this the king replied by rejecting Rome's demands and sticking to the legally sound argument that he had committed no act of aggression against any signatory of the Peace of Phoenice which he had made with Rome in 205. Rome thus declared war nominally in defence of Greek autonomy, but her underlying motive was an attempt to maintain the *status quo* in the East: 'Greece must be maintained independent as a neutral zone guaranteed against Macedonian or Syrian occupation'.[3]

The far-reaching fears, however, which had driven the Senate into this hasty action, were soon somewhat relieved, because the commissioners who proceeded to Syria found that the Syro-Macedonian pact had virtually broken down. Antiochus, worried at the extent of Philip's aggressions, had withdrawn his help in the Aegean, but had himself been exploiting the situation by defeating an Egyptian army and occupying Coele Syria. The Roman commissioners had to accept this *fait accompli*, and in return were probably assured of the king's neutrality in the Macedonian War.[4] When they went on to Alexandria they received a good welcome, because the Egyptians either were ignorant that Rome had betrayed their cause to Antiochus or were willing to accept the situation in view of Rome's measures to defend their interests against Philip in the Aegean.[5]

n. 3), was increased the following year by the appointment of Cn. Cornelius Scipio Hispallus (son of the *cos.* of 222 and himself *cos.* in 176) and M. Aemilius Lepidus to replace Servius and Gaius Sulpicius who had died.

[1] L. xxxi. 2. 3; 8. 4. Cf. A. H. McDonald and F. W. Walbank, *JRS*, 1937, 195–6.

[2] P. xvi. 34.

[3] A. H. McDonald, *JRS*, 1937, 207.

[4] For the view that this was the objective of the Roman mission in Syria see M. Holleaux, *Rev. Ét. Anc.* 1913, pp. 1 ff.; F. W. Walbank, *Philip V*, 316; A. H. McDonald, *JRS*, 1937, 204. According to Polybius (xvi. 27. 5) it was to arbitrate between Syria and Egypt.

[5] On the legend that Aemilius stayed on in Egypt as guardian of the young king see below, p. 237 n. 3. Behind it lies the fact that hereafter he had particularly close and friendly relations with the Ptolemaic dynasty.

Although Eastern affairs and the dispatch of an expeditionary force to Greece under Sulpicius Galba claimed most attention, the Senate did not neglect the west and north. The legions in Spain were reduced to one, and in 200 L. Cornelius Lentulus was replaced by C. Cornelius Cethegus, another *privatus* with proconsular *imperium*; this may be accounted a success for Scipio, if Lucius had followed his brother Gnaeus (*cos.* 201) into the Claudian-Servilian camp. In the north, Gallic tribes stormed Placentia in 200, but the praetor L. Furius Purpureo managed to save Cremona and defeat the Insubres.[1] These events had domestic repercussions. A tribune Ti. Sempronius Longus, a partisan of Scipio who later held the consulship with him, successfully opposed a request for a triumph by L. Cornelius Lentulus, who had to be content with an ovation.[2] Greater disturbance was caused when the praetor Furius, who had won his victory before the consul Cotta had reached his province, hurried back to Rome and asked for a triumph in Cotta's absence. This was granted, but only after considerable opposition.[3] Since Furius' family tradition and career suggest that he was an adherent of the Scipios, while the opposition would come mainly from the Claudian party to which Cotta belonged, these intrigues resulted in a victory for the Scipionic group, which secured a triumph for Furius and denied one to Lentulus. Other domestic events which kept members of the Scipionic group before the public included a clash between Licinius and Galba (above, p. 87); the celebration of the Games which Scipio had vowed in Africa; and a decree that his veterans should receive two *iugera* of land for every year served in Spain or Africa.[4]

Under Cotta's presidency the Claudian group secured both consulships for 199: L. Cornelius Lentulus and P. Villius Tappulus. Lentulus' success is noteworthy because he had probably not held the praetorship.[5] After serving in Spain under Scipio, he had remained there in 206 as a *privatus* with proconsular *imperium*. Though elected curule aedile for 205 with his brother Gnaeus (*cos.* 201), his provincial command was prolonged until his return to Rome in 200, when he

[1] Much of Livy's account of this campaign (xxxi. 10; 21) is probably a doublet of the victory of C. Cornelius Cethegus in 197, but Furius' triumph is not invented (as suggested by Münzer, *PW*, s.v. Furius n. 86), and the victory is assured by the reference to the temple vowed by Furius to Veiovis (L. xxxi. 21. 12) and dedicated in 194 (L. xxxiv. 53. 7; Ovid, *Fasti*, i. 293; *Cal. Praen. CIL*, i², 305; *Not. Scav.* 1921, 84). Furius vowed a second temple as consul in 196 and dedicated it 'in Capitolio' in 192.

[2] L. xxxi. 20.   [3] L. xxxi. 47. 4–49. 3.

[4] A colonial commission to Venusia consisted of C. Terentius Varro (*cos.* 216), T. Quinctius Flamininus, and P. Cornelius Scipio Nasica. Varro also led a commission to N. Africa; with him were two *praetorii* who had been aediles together in 206, Sp. Lucretius, general in Cisalpine Gaul 205–202, and Cn. Octavius who after commanding a fleet (204–203) had been Scipio's legate in Africa (L. xxxi. 11. 4–18).

[5] Ibid. 49. 8–12. He is distinguished by Münzer from L. Cornelius Lentulus, the praetor of 211 (*PW*, s.v. Cornelius n. 187).

had failed to obtain a triumph (p. 95). His election, which was doubtless promoted by his brother and the Claudian-Servilian group, was
facilitated by a paucity of rival candidates.[1] His group, however, met
with a set-back at the subsequent censorial elections when Scipio
Africanus himself was elected together with P. Aelius Paetus.[2]

The military appointments for 199 are instructive. Lentulus received Italy, and Villius Macedonia, but Villius' predecessor in Macedonia, Galba, had only arrived there late in 200, so that if Villius went
out early in 199 Galba would lose the opportunity of a campaign.
A compromise must have been reached, by which Villius received
Macedonia on the tacit understanding that he would not hurry to his
province. The political implication is to confirm the view that Villius
and Galba belonged to the same group and to suggest that Flamininus,
who succeeded Villius in Greece, belonged to a rival section; he went
out early and thus prevented Villius conducting a serious campaign.
The constitutional implication is that the Claudian group maintained,
by choice or through pressure, the principle of annual commands now
that the overriding needs of the Hannibalic War were over. Judging
it unwise or being unable to prolong Galba's command legally, they
met the situation by his remaining in Macedonia until his successor
arrived. Villius delayed out of deference to Galba on political and
military grounds, hoping for like treatment from his own successor.

Galba's campaign in 199 was not inspiring: he invaded Macedon,
inflicted a slight defeat on Philip, which swung over the Aetolians to
support Rome, and then retired to his base.[3] Meantime, at home L.
Manlius Acidinus after six years' service in Spain was granted an
ovation by the Senate, but was prevented from holding it by a tribune,
P. Porcius Laeca,[4] perhaps on the ground that as governor of Hispania
Ulterior he had fought against Indibilis in Citerior under the auspices
of his colleague. A more important domestic event was the censorship
of Scipio Africanus and P. Aelius Paetus, who worked together har-
moniously, so that Aelius probably weakened in his loyalty to the

---

[1] See appendix, pp. 282 f.

[2] There cannot have been a large field of patrician candidates. Scipio's chief rivals must
have been Cn. Servilius Caepio (*cos.* 203), Cn. Cornelius Lentulus (*cos.* 201), and, if still
living, Ti. Claudius Nero (*cos.* 202): none of them was senior to him as a consular.
P. Sulpicius Galba (*cos.* I, 211) was absent, campaigning in Greece. The other patrician
consular was L. Veturius Philo (*cos.* 206), a supporter of Scipio; if still alive in 199, he
would not be likely to stand as a rival to Africanus.

[3] In Spain Cn. Cornelius Blasio and L. Stertinius succeeded C. Cornelius Cethegus
(who returned to hold the aedileship) and L. Manlius Acidinus. In Cisalpine Gaul the
praetor Cn. Baebius Tamphilus, whose command had been prolonged, suffered a reverse
at the hands of the Insubres before the consul Lentulus arrived.

[4] It was probably during his tribunate rather than as praetor (195) that Laeca carried
a measure which extended the *ius provocationis* to Roman citizens in Italy and the provinces, a measure celebrated on the coinage of two of his descendants (see Frontispiece
No. 14 and *BM. Cat. Coins Rn. Rep.* i. 151). Cf. A. H. McDonald, *JRS*, 1944, 19.

Claudian group when he came under the spell of Scipio's personality; the Aelii may long have been supporters of the Cornelii and only temporarily deserted them when Publius held office under the seceding Servilius. Scipio was nominated by Aelius as *princeps senatus*, a post vacant since the death of Q. Fabius Maximus; he was appointed over the heads of two or three patrician ex-censors senior to him,[1] and thus became officially the leader of the senatorial oligarchy. The censors acted with great moderation and did not remove a single name from the senatorial roll, but they achieved little. Thus Scipio's censorship, like his second consulship, was disappointing: despite the need for reconstruction in many spheres, he formed no general policy: 'vir memorabilis, bellicis tamen quam pacis artibus memorabilior'.[2]

III. *Flamininus*

The elections for 198 were marked by the emergence of T. Quinctius Flamininus, the future liberator of Greece. As he had only been quaestor, two tribunes, M. Fulvius and Manius Curius, at first opposed his candidature, but then deferred to the Senate's wish to allow the People a free choice. Flamininus, whose prospects must have been helped by the marked absence of outstanding *praetorii* already noted (pp. 96, 282 f.), was then elected with Sex. Aelius Paetus, who like him had not been praetor although he had held the curule aedileship in 200. Flamininus received Macedonia as his province, Paetus Italy, while L. Lentulus (*cos.* 199) had his command prolonged.[3]

Flamininus, a young man of scarcely 30, had vaulted from the quaestorship straight into the consulship. What does this event mean when viewed from the angle of factional politics? Contradictory answers have been given. Münzer, followed by Schur, believes that owing to the close connexion of the Quinctian and Fabian *gentes* Flamininus became the head of the leaderless Fabian faction, which he was able to raise to fresh power; Scipio's opponents thus found a long-sought counterbalance to the influence of the victor of Zama. A very different view is that of T. Frank, followed by R. M. Haywood; the former writes:[4] 'A letter written by the Scipios to the Greek city of Heraclea in 190 displays the same philhellenic sentiments as the pronouncements of Flamininus, who was responsible for the adoption by the Senate of the policy these pronouncements represent. To insist in the face of such agreement that Flamininus must have been an opponent of Scipio because his wife's sister was the wife of a distant

---

[1] Two were from friendly families: P. Licinius Crassus (*cens.* 210) and M. Cornelius Cethegus (*cens.* 209); the only other possible claimant was C. Claudius Nero (*cens.* 204), but he is not heard of after 201 and may have been dead.

[2] L. xxxviii. 53. 9. On the censorship see L. xxxii. 7.   [3] Ibid. 7. 8–9. 5.

[4] *CAH*, viii. 368.

relative of Fabius Maximus is to misunderstand the political-minded-ness of Roman nobles.' While the first part of this statement may be roughly true, the irony of the second is scarcely justified; the case for a connexion of the Quinctii with the Fabii is not so tenuous. Nor does this view explain whence Scipio derived sufficient influence to win the command for Flamininus; if he was so dominant, he might be expected to have secured, if not his own appointment, at least that of a member of his own *gens*. The fact, however, that Flamininus has been claimed as both a rival and a protégé of Scipio has led some critics to despair (cf. pp. 5 f.), but this is unnecessary, since both views have a weakness: Münzer's disregards the common philhellenic outlook of Scipio and Flamininus, Frank's disregards the traditional family connexions and politics of the Quinctii. Further, both presuppose a static relationship, whereas the mutual attitude of the two men may well have changed in the course of a few years.

The connexion of the Quinctii with the Fabii and Marcellus, which was strengthened by marriage if Flamininus married a Fabia,[1] is seen in the association of the two *gentes* in the common cult of the Luper-calia.[2] Both branches of the Quinctii, the Crispini and the Flaminini, had supported the Fabii and Marcellus in the Hannibalic War; for instance, T. Quinctius Crispinus had served under Marcellus in 213, was elected praetor in his fourth consulship, and became consul with him in 208. Further, his son (*pr.* 186) was connected with the son of Marcellus, while a certain D. Quinctius was entrusted with a naval command by Marcellus in 210. Titus Quinctius Flamininus, who had begun his career as military tribune under the consul Marcellus in 208, had been rewarded at the age of 23 by being appointed propraetor *extra ordinem* to command the garrison at Tarentum (205–204), although he had held no curule office. His brother Lucius, the elder perhaps by only a year, had been appointed an augur at the early age of 16 in 213 when Fabius Cunctator and M. Marcellus were at the head respectively of the patrician and plebeian halves of the augural college.[3] Philhellenism would form a further link between Flamininus and Marcellus. Thus it is difficult to reject the view that Flamininus was connected with the old Fabian party. But it is equally difficult to reject the supposition that a philhellenic policy actuated both Scipio and Flamininus, the evidence for which will be considered later.

---

[1] Flamininus had on his staff in Greece in 197 a certain Q. Fabius whom Polybius (xviii. 10. 8) describes as his wife's nephew. If the nephew was the son of his wife's brother and not of his wife's sister, his wife must have been a Fabia. Livy (xxxii. 36) says that Q. Fabius 'uxoris Quincti sororis filius erat', but his interpretation of Polybius' ἀδελφιδοῦς may not be accurate.

[2] See Münzer, *RA*, 115 ff.

[3] Lucius' early start was not maintained: although aedile in 201 and praetor in 199 he was then overtaken by his brother.

To meet this difficulty a compromise may be suggested. Scipio may have wished to avoid precipitate action against Philip and to try a diplomatic approach first (cf. pp. 86 f.), but once the war was launched, as a philhellenist and a soldier he may have acquiesced in a policy based on the principle of autonomy for Greece which was to be guaranteed by Roman power. Further, although the Senate as a whole approved the war, views about its prosecution may have varied; the grim Claudian house and the more liberal Scipios would differ about means, if not ends. After the somewhat unspectacular performances of Galba and Villius, Scipio could advocate the adoption of more energetic military and diplomatic action against Philip and of a more generous policy towards the Greeks, who remembered with bitterness Galba's earlier stay in their country. But Scipio apparently lacked sufficient support to win the command for himself. The nobility as a whole feared to entrust him with a first-class military command which would give him the chance of placing the Roman people once again deeply in his debt. If at the head of a devoted army he were to humble Philip and earn the gratitude of Greece, would he again retire quietly into private life? But if there were obstacles to his own appointment, he saw an opportunity for checking the Claudian group through the advancement of one who shared his own views of Greek culture and was well suited to pose as the champion of Hellenism. Scipio therefore probably encouraged the election of Flamininus.[1] True, this meant compromising with the Fabian group, but with its support he could withstand the claims of the Claudii.

If such a coalition helps to account for the election of Flamininus, the rivalry which undoubtedly existed later between him and his erstwhile patron has still to be explained. This will have arisen partly from natural jealousy aroused by Flamininus' extraordinary success, but more, as will be seen, from his determination to go farther in his policy of freeing Greece than Scipio deemed wise when Antiochus

---

[1] Flamininus took nearly 9,000 reinforcements to Greece of whom 3,000 were drawn from Scipio's veterans of the Spanish and African campaigns (Plut. *Flam.* 3; L. xxxii. 8. 2; 9. 1, 6). The men were recruited at the very time that his predecessor in Macedonia, P. Villius, was faced with a mutiny among his troops, 2,000 of whom had been transferred after Zama to Sicily and then to Macedonia; their complaint was that, though regarded as volunteers, they had in fact been conscripted and in any case they wished to be discharged (L. xxxii. 3). Thus some of Scipio's veterans were tired of fighting (and Livy does not suggest that Villius' men had necessarily served longer than the African campaign), while others who had fought even in Spain (210–206) were ready to fight again under Flamininus. It would seem improbable that Flamininus could have recruited these men so easily if it was known that Scipio was his political rival; rather, it would not be unreasonable to suppose that Scipio himself appealed to his veterans on Flamininus' behalf and to find here confirmation that Scipio supported Flamininus. On the other hand, it might be said that some of Scipio's veterans who had been discharged after Zama may have been ready to volunteer for fresh service after a breathing-space merely because war, with its prospects of spoils, was becoming a more congenial way of life to them, whereas Villius' men were merely wanting to see their homes again.

was threatening and because the *rapprochement* between Scipio and the Fabii involved the revival of a party which was traditionally hostile to him and which, being strengthened by Flamininus' success, brought into prominence other men who were opposed to Scipio.[1]

But since the evidence for such a view is slight, it may be that Flamininus derived his main support from that average senatorial opinion which was later to crystallize in the formation of a middle bloc. The majority of senators were probably not anti-Hellenists, but combined Greek cultural interests with a traditional Roman foreign policy. Flamininus differed from them in that he was ready to carry his philhellenism into politics. In this, it is true, he was closer to Scipio, but with a difference: while Flamininus championed the old Hellenic idea of the autonomy of the Greek city-state against the Hellenistic kingdoms, Scipio was more ready to attempt to deal with the Hellenistic world as a whole and maintain its balance of monarchies, leagues, and cities. Scipio's policy would not be attractive to the main body of senators, because it could be implemented only by Scipio himself with his outstanding personal and diplomatic gifts. On the other hand, they might be ready to support Flamininus because his policy would provide splendid propaganda and at the same time permit more traditional methods: Greece could be established as a neutral zone under Roman protection against all possible aggression.[2] On this view, therefore, Flamininus will have won his command by agreement with a large body of senators (including the old Fabian group, but not the Claudians), and not specifically as a protégé of Scipio. Yet even so, Scipio, having failed to achieve what he considered to be the best policy, may not have withheld support from this second-best plan: Flamininus might well seem preferable to his Claudian predecessors in Greece.

When the Senate had originally decided that Macedon should be checked, common sense would dictate that Rome should aim at win-

---

[1] If this hypothesis be accepted, namely, that a coalition was formed between the Scipionic party and the supporters of the old Fabian group headed by Flamininus with the object of breaking the predominance of the Claudii, its development would be as follows. It secured nearly all the high offices in 197, which were shared by supporters of the two groups (see p. 104), but as the Scipionic group had two consuls in office they tried, in vain, to check Flamininus (p. 105). In 196 the two groups again shared many of the chief magistracies (p. 106), but in 195 the Fabian group gained both consulships and was now well able to stand on its own feet (p. 110); if it had been willing for the moment to compromise to regain its position, it now showed its real intentions by attacking Scipio's African policy (p. 114). The emergence of Cato involved a complete rift between the Scipios and the more conservative section of the Fabian group, while the more progressive section under Flamininus would be alienated by Scipio's objection to the immediate fulfilment of Flamininus' policy of the evacuation of Greece in 194 (p. 116).

[2] This view derives from the published ideas of A. H. McDonald (*JRS*, 1938, 153 ff.; 1944, 24 f., &c.) and personal discussion with him, but naturally I do not wish to attribute to him any point which he might prefer to disclaim nor at the same time to fail to acknowledge any part of my debt to him.

ning the support of the Greeks against Philip: hence the basis of her policy was to champion their autonomy against the king's aggression.[1] While the philhellenic nobles may not have been devoid of all altruistic motives, the main reason for the adoption of this policy was its likely promotion of Roman security and interests; if it coincided with the sentiments of some of them, so much the better. But the application of such a policy, which aimed at winning Greek support and friendship, needed rare diplomatic address, which Galba probably lacked. Flamininus, however, was 'exceedingly acute, if ever a Roman was. The skill with which he conducted public business and private negotiations could not be surpassed', wrote Polybius.[2] In some respects he resembled Scipio Africanus. His magnetic personality, his enthusiasm, his Hellenic culture, the tact and adaptability which he displayed instead of the blunt and often brutal self-assertiveness of the Roman, all these found their counterpart in Scipio. But shallow and vain, ambitious and domineering, he lacked that soundness of character and loftiness of soul which were felt by all who came into personal contact with Africanus. Yet if Rome's object was to break the power of Macedon and to free Greece, few men could have carried out this programme with less loss of blood and without robbing the Greeks of their remaining self-respect. Here was a Roman consul who sought their friendship and promised their freedom instead of spurning their ideals and exposing their weakness.[3]

The aims of Flamininus and the Senate were soon made clear. He landed in Greece in 198, earlier in the year than his predecessors had done, and thus displaced Villius: he would not wait upon a Claudian commander.[4] He then met Philip at the Aous, and demanded that the king should abandon all the Greek states he held, whether captured or inherited: Rome was going to protect Greek freedom and drive Philip out of Greece. Philip's counter-terms were rejected and negotiations broke down. Had they been accepted, Macedon would have

---

[1] When the Romans based their policy of intervention in Greece upon a proclamation of 'freedom', they were using a word with a long and ambiguous history; it was the Hellenistic, rather than the older Hellenic, conception that they adopted. This theoretically meant complete sovereignty, but in practice often involved a privileged status granted by kings to cities rather than complete independence (see e.g. A. H. M. Jones, *Anatolian Studies presented to W. H. Buckler*, 103 ff.).

[2] xviii. 12. 3–4. Cf. Plut. *Flam.* 1–2.

[3] Flamininus spoke Greek with a good accent: he was no barbarian, as some of the Greeks had been led to expect (cf. ibid. 5). Naturally he wrote in Greek the inscriptions for his dedications at Delphi, but it is more surprising to find that the inscription on his statue in Rome was also in Greek (ibid. 12 and 1). If his appearance was slightly unkempt (as in his portrait on the famous gold *stater*), his manners were civilized and charming (see e.g. the anecdote of how he captivated some Theban dignitaries: ibid. 6). Polybius emphasizes his pleasantries and smiles in his interview with Philip at Nicaea (xviii. 6), a welcome change from the pompous dignity of many a Roman.

[4] Villius' naval legate, C. Livius, was similarly displaced by the consul's brother and legate, Lucius Flamininus, after he had just put to sea (L. xxxii. 16).

remained an autonomous Great Power, though humbled.[1] But future peace and security necessitated breaking the power of Macedon. As Scipio had realized that lasting peace could not be secured merely by driving Hannibal from Italy, so now Flamininus wished to deprive Macedon, like Carthage, of an essentially independent foreign policy. His terms reflected official senatorial policy, since their insistence upon the liberation of all Greek states went beyond those offered in 200 and are unlikely to have been due to his initiative alone.[2]

News soon reached Flamininus that his brother Lucius, who commanded the Roman fleet, with the support of Attalus and Rhodes, had won over the Achaean League.[3] Some have seen in this success merely the natural result of Roman military pressure,[4] others have hailed it as a great diplomatic victory for Flamininus.[5] At any rate he had moulded the circumstances which produced the result and the continuance of Achaean support is proof of his success. Thus strengthened, Flamininus turned again to negotiation at the request of Philip whom he agreed to meet at Nicaea. With his eye on the elections in Rome, he wanted to play for time; if his command was prolonged, he would wish to crush Philip on the field of battle, but if a successor was to be sent to harvest where he had sown, he might rather suggest terms.[6] As little was achieved on the first day of the conference, Philip urged that Flamininus should meet him in private, without Rome's Greek allies; they agreed to this procedure, thereby delegating to Flamininus authority to treat with Philip in their name, and at last officially recognizing Rome as their leader.[7] By this astute move Flamininus gained unity of command while he prepared to trick Philip, who assumed that he was well-disposed. When no agreement was reached, it was decided to refer the question to the Senate. Philip and the allies dispatched embassies to Rome, while Flamininus sent Amynander, king of Athamania, 'knowing that he was a man of pliable character and would easily be persuaded by his own friends in the city to take any course they might propose'. He also sent as personal envoys his wife's nephew, Q. Fabius, together with Appius Claudius Nero and Q. Fulvius.[8] The Claudian tradition of service in Greece

[1] Cf. De Sanctis, IV. i. 62. For the terms see L. xxxii. 10; Diod. xxviii. 11; App. *Maced.* 5.

[2] Cf. T. Frank, *Roman Imperialism*, 161 n. 29.   [3] On the negotiations see A. Aymard, *Les Premiers rapports de Rome et de la confédération achaïenne*, 1 ff., 83 ff.

[4] Cf. M. Holleaux, *CAH*, viii. 170: 'the Achaeans had to choose between Rome as ally or as enemy: the knife was at their throat. Refusal meant immediate attack by three fleets.'

[5] Cf. F. M. Wood, *AJP*, 1941, 285 f.

[6] Cf. M. Holleaux, *Rev. Ét. Gr.* 1923, 115 ff., and *CAH*, viii. 172; F. W. Walbank, *Philip V*, 159.

[7] On the conference see P. xviii. 1–10. Cf. A. Aymard, *Premiers rapports*, 114; F. M. Wood, *AJP*, 1941, 277 ff.

[8] Probably to be identified with Q. Fulvius Flaccus, *consul suffectus* in 180 (see *PW*, s.v. Fulvius n. 60). Willems (*Sénat*, i. 319), however, would identify the consul of 180 with Q. Fulvius, a tribune in 193; see below. Appius Claudius Nero was praetor in 195.

had apparently led to the staff appointments of Fulvius and Claudius; possibly Flamininus had won over these two young men and hoped to use them to influence the Claudian element in Rome on his behalf.

The envoys arrived before the Senate had decided whether both consuls of 197 should be sent to Gaul or one should supersede Flamininus. But when once his 'friends had assured themselves that both consuls would remain in Italy owing to fear of the Gauls',[1] the allied ambassadors were allowed to appear; they bluntly stated their grievances against Philip, and raised the question of his evacuation of the 'Fetters of Greece' (Chalcis, Acrocorinth, and Demetrias). When Philip's envoys had to admit that they had no instructions about these towns they were dismissed by the Senate and the war was renewed. Since at his private meeting with Philip Flamininus must have discussed the future of these towns, and since it must have been in reliance on Flamininus' guidance that Philip had been induced to refer the whole question to the Senate, Flamininus apparently had been ready to betray the Greeks and urge the acceptance of peace with Philip on these terms if his command had not been prolonged.[2] But such a sacrifice of principle proved unnecessary. Once his own future was secure, Flamininus deliberately allowed a diplomatic rupture.

Flamininus' policy clearly was based on trickery: the only doubt is whether the dupes were to be the Greeks or Philip. Although the ancient tradition implies that one or other was to be sacrificed in accordance with the result of the intrigue for the prolongation of his command, a recent attempt has been made to 'whitewash' Flamininus.[3] His diplomatic victory at Nicaea was so resounding that 'he could hope for very little personal gain by . . . preparing a peace the administration of which would fall to a successor as surely as the command of a continued war'. This view seems to imply that Flamininus, if superseded, would not have advocated peace (and betraying the Greeks) because the glory of enforcing such a peace would fall to another. But surely if he had successfully urged the acceptance of terms, he would have spiked the guns of his political opponents, since the peace would have been recognized as that of the negotiator rather than that of the man who actually enforced its terms.

If an attempt is to be made to save Flamininus' reputation, it would rest better first on the inherent improbability that if he had been superseded he would have had sufficient political influence to persuade

---

[1] On the political situation in Rome see below, p. 105.

[2] P. xviii. 10–12; L. xxxii. 32. See M. Holleaux, *Rev. Ét. Gr.* 1925, 115 ff.

[3] See F. M. Wood (*TAPA*, 1939, 93 ff.), who believes that the tradition hostile to Flamininus was started by Polybius who would not allow any contemporary to outshine his hero Philopoemen; knowing the intensity of the rivalry between Philopoemen and Flamininus, Polybius uttered the slander of Flamininus' 'selfish ambition'.

the Senate to accept his terms, and secondly on the general hypothesis that in view of his later insistence on the evacuation of the
Fetters he would have been reluctant to concede them to Philip now.
But such assumptions can hardly outweigh the Polybian tradition.[1]
Flamininus doubtless hoped that it would be unnecessary to betray
the Greeks, but in the last resort he was probably prepared to urge the
Senate to accept Philip's terms rather than to see a rival win that
military glory which was almost within his grasp. But his honour was
saved! By successful political wire-pulling and careful timing[2] he had
skilfully secured his own position, tricked and neutralized Philip until
nearer the campaigning season, and was enabled to make good his
promises to his Greek allies and to win personal military glory.

The elections for 197 had been conducted by Sex. Aelius Paetus,
who since his brother's friendly tenure of the censorship with Scipio
probably transferred his support to the Scipionic group, to which the
new consuls, C. Cornelius Cethegus and Q. Minucius Rufus, belonged.
Cethegus, like Flamininus and Sextus Aelius in the previous year, had
reached the consulship without having been praetor; he had held proconsular *imperium* as a *privatus* in Spain and then became aedile (199).
Scipio himself had set the example of overleaping the lower grades of
office and now his friends followed suit; that they could do so is proof
of his reviving influence. Other supporters among the officials of the
year included two praetors (whose number was now raised to six),
M. Minucius Rufus and M. Sergius Silus; one curule aedile, his
cousin Nasica; and both plebeian aediles, M'. Acilius Glabrio and
C. Laelius.[3] But Flamininus' success had helped the revival of the
old Fabian party, which now secured two or three praetorships (L.
Manlius Vulso, L. Atilius, and (?) M. Helvius) and the second curule
aedileship (Cn. Manlius Vulso).[4] The group's recovery had been
gradual but steady.[5]

[1] Further, Flamininus was quite willing, if necessary, to sacrifice the Asiatic Greeks
in 193 in order to reach a compromise with Antiochus. See p. 120.

[2] The conference at Nicaea was held in November. The Ides of March fell in Dec.
or Jan. of the Julian calendar (see F. W. Walbank, *Philip V*, 321 n. 5, and the literature
cited there).

[3] L. xxxii. 27. 5–8. Glabrio had been tribune of the plebs in 201 and *decemvir sacrorum*
in 200. On his close connexion with Scipio, under whose patronage he may first have
come to Rome from Greek southern Italy, see Münzer, *RA*, 91 f. Laelius was Scipio's
personal and intimate friend; he had been prefect of the fleet in the brilliant attack on
Carthago Nova in 209, had fought under Scipio at Baecula and Ilipa, and had taken a
leading part in the African campaign, when he defeated Syphax. He may only have received
citizenship about this time and was elected quaestor in 202, but was back in Africa in
time to command the left wing at Zama.

[4] If the hypothesis mentioned above (p. 99) is accepted, namely that a coalition was
formed between the Scipionic party and the supporters of the old Fabian section headed
by Flamininus with the object of breaking the predominance of the Claudii, then it was
so successful that it secured nearly all the higher offices in 197.

[5] In 201 they had one praetor (M. Fabius Buteo) and two curule aediles (T. Quinctius

When the new consuls were about to ballot for Italy and Macedonia, two tribunes intervened on behalf of Flamininus on the pretext
that annual commands were bad,[1] and, as has been said, the Senate
decided to prolong Flamininus' command and to allot Italy to the two
consuls. This abortive attempt to supersede Flamininus may have
been supported by the Claudian group, which earlier had adopted
the principle of annual commands in Greece, though as they had won
neither of the new consulships they had no man of their own to send
out; they scored a notable success, however, when Sulpicius Galba
and Villius Tappulus, Flamininus' two predecessors in Greece, were
appointed as his *legati*. But the prime movers are more likely to have
been the Scipionic group. Now that they had two consuls who were
more closely associated with their own *gens*, they may have felt disposed to limit the career of Flamininus, the more so if they had wind
of his private scheming; his diplomacy might seem designed to
advance his own interest rather than Rome's, and Scipio Africanus
perhaps felt that the issue was being unnecessarily complicated by
Flamininus' personal ambition. But on military grounds, in view of
the increasing unrest in north Italy, the decision to leave Flamininus
in Greece may have been wise.

The year 197 was critical on all fronts. A vast insurrection swept
over Spain; Cornelius Cethegus defeated the Insubres and Cenomani[2]
in north Italy, while his colleague Minucius Rufus operated farther
west; and in Greece Flamininus brought the war to an end by defeating Philip at Cynoscephalae. Despite protests from his Aetolian allies,
who wished to invade and destroy Macedon, Flamininus announced
his intention of treating with Philip on the terms laid down at Nicaea,
namely, that the king should abandon all his possessions outside
Macedon. To crush Macedon completely would expose Greece to
attack from the northern barbarians, and might encourage the ambitions of Antiochus, who having asserted his power in Coele Syria
against Ptolemy was free to attempt to regain his hereditary possessions in Asia Minor and Thrace. Apart, therefore, from any desire to
make peace before he might be superseded, Flamininus had solid

Flamininus and L. Valerius Flaccus: the Valerii Flacci, unlike most of the Valerii, seem
to have sided with the Fabii; see Schur, *Scipio*, 108); in 200 they had one curule aedile
(M. Claudius Marcellus); in 199 two praetors (L. Quinctius Flamininus and L. Valerius
Flaccus), one curule aedile (C. Valerius Flaccus), and one or two plebeian aediles (M. Porcius Cato and (?) C. Helvius); in 198 one consul (T. Quinctius Flamininus), two or three
praetors (M. Claudius Marcellus, M. Porcius Cato, and (?) C. Helvius), and perhaps a
plebeian aedile (M. Helvius); and then in 197 three praetors and a curule aedile.

[1] L. xxxii. 28. It is somewhat surprising to find that one of the tribunes was a Q. Fulvius
(otherwise unknown); perhaps Q. Fulvius Flaccus, whom Flamininus had sent to Rome,
secured his services. The other tribune was L. Oppius Salinator (*pr.* 191).

[2] A fragmentary inscription may form part of an *elogium* to Cethegus: 'et Cenom[anos
. . . d]ucem eo[rum . . .' (*Inscr. Ital.* XIII. iii, p. 40). Cf. L. xxxiii. 23. 4.

reasons for concluding an armistice with Philip and referring details to the Senate.

On their return from north Italy both consuls asked for a triumph, but two tribunes, who admitted Cethegus' claim, insisted that his influence should not be allowed to win this honour for Minucius. Cethegus was granted his triumph which he celebrated while still in office; Minucius, denied an official triumph, celebrated a private one on the Alban Mount. Other public entertainments included the Roman Games, staged by the curule aediles, Scipio Nasica and Cn. Manlius Vulso, which were more magnificent than usual and were repeated three times, and the Plebeian Games, the responsibility of Acilius Glabrio and Laelius, which were repeated seven times.[1] Members of the Scipionic group were thus well to the front, and the elections for 196 reflected the continuing revival of Scipios and Fabians: the new consuls were L. Furius Purpureo, who adhered to the Scipios, and the Fabian M. Claudius Marcellus, son of the victor of Syracuse.[2] Of the praetors at least four were supporters of Scipio: M'. Acilius Glabrio, C. Laelius, Q. Minucius Thermus, and Ti. Sempronius Longus. Thus nearly all the chief offices were again held by supporters of Scipio and the Fabian party. The Fabii also secured two religious appointments when in 196 the consul Marcellus and L. Valerius Flaccus were made pontiffs, while the Scipios gained further lustre when Cn. Cornelius Blasio was granted an ovation for victories gained in Spain in 199 and 198. Further, Marcellus was granted a triumph for finishing the war in Transpadane Gaul, though his colleague Furius, who had triumphed over the Insubres as praetor in 200, failed to obtain a second triumph now; and Q. Minucius Thermus received one for a success in southern Spain.[3]

When the peace delegations arrived from Greece, the Senate had to decide upon the terms. Anxiety about the insurrections in Cisalpine Gaul and Spain and still more about Antiochus' intentions resulted in the formulation of moderate, or even generous, terms; it can hardly be doubted that Scipio Africanus, who had arranged humane terms for the defeated Hannibal and who later tried to negotiate a more generous settlement for Antiochus than the Senate would allow, argued strongly in favour of moderation towards Philip and generosity towards Greece. Philip was to be deprived of his external conquests and his fleet, to surrender to the Romans all the Greek cities and fortresses which he held, but to retain his kingdom. Further, it was laid down that 'all the rest of the Greeks in Asia and Europe were to be free and governed by their own laws': a resounding declaration of Rome's philhellenic policy, which was both a manifesto to Greece and

[1] L. xxxiii. 25. [2] Ibid. 24. 1–2.
[3] On Minucius see ibid. 26, 43, 44; *Inscr. Ital.* XIII. i, pp. 78, 338, 552.

a warning to Antiochus. To enforce this decision ten senatorial commissioners were appointed to consult with Flamininus on details of the settlement; they were given discretionary powers to deal with the question of the Three Fetters in the light of their assessment of the growing threat of Antiochus.[1]

It is noteworthy that the Claudian-Servilian group was fairly strongly represented among the *consulares* on the commission (with Galba, Tappulus, Cn. Lentulus, and Caepio), partly perhaps because of the long Claudian tradition of service in Greece, and partly because they had a considerable number of consulars available, whereas the Fabii probably had none except Flamininus himself. The Scipionic group, however, had such men available (e.g. Caecilius Metellus (*cos.* 206), Licinius Crassus (*cos.* 205), or Africanus himself), but won fewer places.

The view that the Senate, fearing Antiochus, disapproved of Flamininus' intention to evacuate the Fetters of Greece (an intention based on the assumption that Antiochus did not constitute a menace) and appointed this commission to check him, has little to commend it; if there had been strong disapproval the Senate would hardly have adopted such a roundabout method of expressing it, while Polybius states clearly that Flamininus was in fact conscious of the threat from Antiochus.[2] As in general the majority of the Senate accepted the views of Flamininus, there is little reason to suppose that it deliberately chose commissioners hostile to him in order to enforce a different policy.[3] But the Claudian members of the board, especially Sulpicius Galba and Villius Tappulus who must have envied Flamininus the victory which they had been unable to achieve, acted as a check on his rigid philhellenism, and differences did arise between them. The most serious was the question of the immediate evacuation of Greece and the withdrawal of garrisons from the Fetters: Flamininus at length persuaded them to free Corinth at once, while still holding Acrocorinth, Demetrias, and Chalcis. Here the dispute arose not because Flamininus was indifferent to Antiochus, but perhaps because he

---

[1] The board included P. Sulpicius Galba (*cos.* I, 211) and P. Villius Tappulus (*cos.* 199), both of whom had fought in Greece, Cn. Cornelius Lentulus (*cos.* 201), P. Cornelius Lentulus Caudinus (*pr.* 203), L. Stertinius (proconsul in Spain, 199), and L. Terentius Massiliota (aedile 200); other members probably were P. Aelius Paetus (*cos.* 201; cf. L. xxxiv. 59. 8), Cn. Octavius (*pr.* 205), and Cn. Servilius Caepio (*cos.* 203; cf. L. xxxv. 23. 5); the number may perhaps be completed by including the proconsul's brother, L. Quinctius Flamininus.

[2] The view is that of L. Homo (*Rev. hist.* 1916, p. 6) and A. Passerini (*Athenaeum*, 1932, 110 ff., 326 ff.). But see P. xviii. 39. 3 and 43. 2. Nor, it may be noted, was Flamininus indifferent to his personal interests; his desire for a speedy settlement was dictated by the fear that Antiochus' advance might encourage Philip to continue the war by holding out in Macedon and that in consequence Flamininus himself would be superseded and lose the credit for ending the war.

[3] A. Aymard, *Premiers rapports*, 173 n. 31.

argued that the best barrier against him was the creation of goodwill, not military occupation, in Greece;[1] the Claudian commissioners, with their grimmer military record in Greece, may well have been less susceptible to Greek sentiment. A more serious threat to Flamininus' control arose at Rome, where a rift appeared within the Fabian group. When the Senate was about to allot Italy to both consuls, Marcellus, who was doubtless actuated by personal jealousy, urged that peace should not be made with Philip. The Senate hesitated until two tribunes insisted on consulting the People. They unanimously voted for peace, Flamininus' command was prolonged, and Marcellus failed to win Macedonia.

The arrival of the Roman commissioners with the senatorial decree in Greece was followed by the famous scene at the Isthmian Games where Flamininus at the height of his career theatrically proclaimed to the assembled Greeks their freedom. But the moment of exhilaration soon passed. Although no tribute, garrisons, or law were imposed, Rome swept aside the Greeks and proceeded to 'settle Hellenic affairs'. It became clear that Rome was to be the sole interpreter of what she meant by her pledge of freedom: in accordance with her own will she disposed of the Greek cities ceded by Philip, assigning some to the Achaean or Aetolian Leagues and forming others into new leagues of their own. The commissioners even proposed to hand over Eretria and Oreus to Eumenes of Pergamum, but Flamininus insisted upon their independence and his decision was later supported by the Senate.[2] But he interpreted the pledge that the cities should 'be under their ancestral laws' somewhat curiously in Thessaly; there he himself chose 'the members of the council and the jurors mainly on a property qualification and put power into the hands of those whose interest it was that everything should be tranquil and quiet'.[3] By the end of the year the Ten Commissioners returned to Rome, leaving Flamininus to complete the settlement; they could report that, through the good offices of Cn. Cornelius, Philip was seeking an alliance with Rome: he might now be used against Antiochus, who must have appeared irritatingly successful to Philip in his hour of defeat. Secondly the Aetolians, who were on the point of revolt, had been persuaded to refer their troubles to the Senate. But the commissioners could not advise the immediate evacuation of Greece. However suspicious this must have seemed to the Greeks themselves, who began to doubt the

[1] A. Aymard, *Premiers rapports*, 179 n. 50.
[2] P. xviii. 47; L. xxxiii. 34. They had been occupied by Attalus, Eumenes' father; their continued occupation by Pergamum would be a reward for past, and a claim to future, services, but the subjection of Greek territory to a king clashed with the complete liberation which Rome had promised Greece.
[3] L. xxxiv. 51; Dittenberger, *Syll.*[3], 674. On the settlement see *CAH*, viii. 183-4; F. W. Walbank, *Philip V*, 181-2.

integrity of Rome's intentions, it was absolutely necessary. Friendship with Philip, the pacification of Aetolia, the continued military occupation of Greece, all pointed in one direction—Antiochus.

The Senate's proclamation of freedom for all the Greeks in Europe and Asia, made perhaps with greater moral than legal justification, was a challenge to Antiochus who advanced through Asia Minor to the Hellespont; whatever may have been his legal title to intervene in the affairs of the autonomous Greek cities, he was prepared to use either force or promises of freedom to gain his way. Threatened by his advance and encouraged by Eumenes of Pergamum, Lampsacus, the first Asiatic city to do so, appealed to Rome[1] whose policy towards Antiochus, which had remained cautious until peace was finally made with Philip, now gradually hardened. Undeterred, Antiochus entered the Thracian Chersonese, which he claimed as ancestral territory, but his envoys, sent on a mission of conciliation and explanation, received a curt reply from Flamininus. Flamininus' diplomacy, however, which had been so successful against Philip, received a rude shock when four commissioners (P. Lentulus, L. Terentius, P. Villius, and L. Cornelius Lentulus) were sent to the king. He denounced Roman interference in Asia in contrast with his own non-intervention in Italian affairs, explained his legal rights in Thrace, neatly parried Rome's sudden solicitude for Egypt by announcing that he was arranging a marriage-alliance with Ptolemy, and agreed to admit Rhodian but not Roman arbitration about Lampsacus. The conference thus ended in a deadlock. This was a pity, because if Rome had made an attempt to define the king's sphere of interest in Thrace and could have convinced herself that his intentions towards her were not hostile, an amicable arrangement might have been reached. But distrustful and somewhat alarmed, she refused to tolerate in the East a Great Power which one day might turn to open hostility.

[1] The Lampsacene envoys, who happened to meet L. Flamininus in the Aegean, received an encouraging message: Dittenberger, *Syll.*[3] 591.

VII

THE SCIPIONIC RECOVERY

(196–191 B.C.)

1. *M. Porcius Cato*

U NDER the shadow of these hardening relations with Antiochus
the elections for 195 were held by the consul Marcellus: the
reviving Fabian group obtained both consulships, for L. Valerius Flaccus and M. Porcius Cato, and at least three praetorships;[1]
Valerius received the Gallic command and Cato was posted to Hither
Spain. The spread of revolt in Spain required the dispatch of a consular army, which could be spared more easily after Marcellus' victory
in Cisalpine Gaul. Before Cato left for his province, however, news
came that Q. Minucius Thermus had gained a success in south
Spain. This may well have sharpened the rivalry between the political
groups, since Minucius had with smaller forces gained a victory which
laid the foundations for Cato's more spectacular campaign.

On reaching Spain Cato found that communications between the
two provinces, which had been cut by the rebellion, had been successfully reopened by M. Helvius, a praetor of 197, who had been delayed
there by illness.[2] After subduing Hispania Citerior Cato marched south
where he failed to make decisive use of his military strength in the
field and tried to buy off some Celtiberian mercenaries who had gone
to help the rebel Turdetani. Returning from this inglorious episode,
he attacked Segontia and Numantia without success, although Rome
was not technically at war with the Celtiberians. After stamping out
some resurgent resistance in Catalonia and exploiting the mines, he
returned to Rome. His achievement has been somewhat overrated,
partly through the interest which attaches to his personality; in fact
he owed his success less to his generalship than to the number of his
troops, which exceeded that allocated to his predecessors. He had
checked, but failed to break, the spirit of revolt, and he had inflamed
the hatred of the Celtiberians towards Rome.

Cato, who had been born at Tusculum about 234 B.C.[3] and later

---

[1] Cn. Manlius Vulso, P. Porcius Laeca, and P. Manlius.

[2] Helvius was granted an ovation. That his command was consular is shown by a combination of Fasti Triumphales and Fasti Urbisalvenses; in the latter a magistrate who is
to be identified with Helvius is described as 'pro consule o⟨vans de Celtiberis⟩': see *Inscr.
Ital.* xiii. i, p. 552. On this *imperium* see Mommsen, *Staatsr.* ii. 647 (*Dr. publ.* iv. 361).

[3] Cic. *De sen.* 10. The tradition (e.g. L. xxxix. 40. 12; Plut. *Cato,* 15. 5) which makes
Cato ninety when he prosecuted Galba in 149 B.C. is wrong.

lived on a farm in Sabine country, came of good yeoman stock, though
as no member of his family had held curule office at Rome, he was
a *novus homo*. Proud of his ancestors' bravery in the field, he used to
praise his father as a bold soldier and recorded that his great-grand-
father had five horses killed under him in battle.[1] He himself fought
in Campania after Cannae, served as military tribune under Marcellus
in Sicily from 214 until perhaps 210, and took part in the battle of
Metaurus.[2] When not on military service he spent much time working
with his own hands on his Sabine estate and practising as an advocate
in the surrounding villages where he quickly gained a reputation as a
good lawyer and a capable orator.[3] His incisive speech, combined with
his rugged honesty, his simple living, and his dogged perseverance,
attracted the attention of Valerius Flaccus whose estates bordered
upon his own. Under Valerius' patronage he went to Rome, where he
soon made his mark as an orator and perhaps was influenced by the
aged Fabius, though his reputation may not yet have been sufficient to
lead to intimate personal contacts.[4]

[1] Plut. *Cato*, 1. 1. In the Fasti Capitolini at Cato's consulship the *praenomen* of his grandfather is missing; though given at his censorship, it has been erased (*Inscr. Ital.* XIII.
i, p. 121). Cato himself (*apud* Plut.) speaks of 'his father Marcus and Cato his great-
grandfather'. Thus the latter lacked a *praenomen* and was probably not a full Roman
citizen. For a defence of Plutarch's remark (*Cato*, 1. 3) that Cato's original *cognomen* was
Priscus, not Cato, see E. V. Marmorale, *Cato Maior*, 26 f.; F. della Corte, *Catone Censore*,
152 f.; *per contra* see P. Fraccaro, *Atti R. Ac. Mant.* 1910, 11 n. 3.

[2] It is possible, though not very probable, that before Cato went to Sicily he was with
Fabius at Capua in 214 (so Cic. *De sen.* 10). Rejected by Fraccaro (op. cit. 117), this
view has been defended by Marmorale (*Cato*, 30) and Della Corte (*Catone*, 112) who
believe that Cato held two military tribunates: he held the first at the personal choice of
the proconsul Marcellus in 214 (Nepos, *Cato*, i. 2); he was elected by the People to the
second (probably in 207) after he had settled in Rome on the advice of Valerius Flaccus
(Plut. *Cato*, 3. 3). Della Corte even suggests that a line might have dropped out of Nepos
(*Cato*, i. 2) and the passage might read 'Q. Fabio ⟨M. Claudio consulibus miles ad Capuam
profectus est, Cn. Fulvio⟩ M. Claudio consulibus tribunus militum in Sicilia fuit'. However that may be, the view of Plutarch (*Cato*, 2. 3) that Cato was with Fabius at the sack
of Tarentum in 209 is almost certainly to be rejected: see Fraccaro (op. cit. 17 f.);
R. E. Smith (*CQ*, 1940, 105 ff.). The story will have been invented by those writers who
wished to emphasize the connexion of the two men, and will have been used and elaborated
by an author who wanted to get Cato to meet a Pythagorean named Nearchus, who
preached to him the gospel that the simple life was the best; this tradition showed that,
despite his hostility to Greece, Cato still owed something to Greek influences.

[3] On his early oratory see p. 256.

[4] De Sanctis (III. ii. 507 n. 107) believes that Cato was not a disciple of Fabius: there
would be little sympathy between the rough impetuous farmer and the proud moderate
patrician; and even if Cato did serve under Fabius, this would not prove the existence of
friendly relations between them. But Valerius was also a patrician and he did not hesitate
to extend his friendship to Cato. If Valerius belonged to the Fabian circle, it is probable
that Cato would come under its influence. But the anecdote that Cato as Scipio's quaestor
in Sicily, disgusted with Scipio's lavish expenditure, returned to Rome and joined Fabius
in his attack on Scipio may be rejected. It involves placing Cato's quaestorship in 205
(cf. the error of Nepos, *Cato*, 1. 3: quaestor obtigit P. Africano consuli), while it was
in fact in 204 (Cic. *Brutus*, 60). See P. Fraccaro (op. cit. 22 ff.) and De Sanctis (III.
ii. 517 n. 113) *contra* Münzer (*Hermes*, 1905, 68 ff.). The error perhaps derives from a

In 204 he obtained the quaestorship and served under Scipio, perhaps commanding with Laelius the left wing of the expeditionary force to Africa. It was at this time that his hatred of Scipio was engendered. He may well have envied the spectacular rise to fame of a man about his own age, but apart from jealousy or any personal cause, which tradition has failed to record, tension must have arisen from difference of temperament. Plutarch tells how Cato, as Scipio's financial assistant, blamed him for his liberality to his troops in Sicily, and how he complained in the Senate that Scipio was wasting enormous sums and loitering about in palaestras and theatres like the master of a festival rather than an army commander. Although this anecdote falsely asserts that Cato joined Fabius in his attack on Scipio, it probably reflects the cause of his hostility: Cato could not understand Scipio's culture and love of the Greek way of life; lack of understanding led to distrust, and soon to hatred.[1]

In Sardinia, whither he was driven by storm or went to secure supplies for Scipio's troops, Cato met Ennius and took him back to Rome in 203 or 202. The influence which the poet, who hellenized Roman literature without destroying its national spirit, exercised on Cato must have been considerable, and the tradition that he taught Cato Greek may well be true.[2] Cato then won the plebeian aedileship for 199 with C. Helvius, and while still holding office gained the praetorship for 198, aided by the impression created by the Games for which he had been responsible shortly before the elections: his aristocratic friends knew how to advance their favourites. His province was Sardinia; here he harshly suppressed usury which he did not regard as *honestum*,[3] and checked the sums levied on the provincials for the upkeep of governors.[4] Austere in his own demands

biography which presented Cato as Scipio's opponent and was used by Cicero, Nepos, and Plutarch: see R. E. Smith, op. cit. 105.

[1] Plut. *Cato*, 3. 5–7. There is little reason to suppose that the whole story of Cato's hatred of Scipio at this time is false and is a mere ante-dating of his later hatred (*c.* 187).

[2] *De vir. ill.* 47 (probably from Nepos, see R. E. Smith, op. cit. 107 n. 2). The tradition in Cicero and Plutarch that Cato learnt Greek only in his old age is improbable and is contradicted by such statements of Plutarch as that he thought that Cato's writings showed Greek influence (2. 4) and that Cato could have addressed the Athenians in Greek in 190 but preferred Latin (12. 4). For possible Greek influences in a speech which Cato delivered in Spain in 195 see p. 257.

[3] L. xxxii. 27. 3–4. On Cato's hatred of usury see Cic. *De offic.* ii. 89; Cato, *De agr.* 1. For a speech by Cato about a usury law see p. 257. See also p. 222.

[4] A *lex Porcia de sumptu provinciali* (mentioned in the *lex Antonia de Termessibus*, Dessau, *ILS*, 38) perhaps should be assigned to this period, as also a *lex Porcia de provocatione* which extended the *ius provocationis* from capital offences to those punishable by scourging (Festus, p. 234; Livy, *Per.* lvii; Pliny, *NH*, xiv. 14; Plut. *C. Gr.* 9. See also Bloch–Carcopino, *La Rep. rom.* ii. 146; De Sanctis, IV. i. 530; A. H. McDonald, *JRS*, 1944, 19). Both these laws might date from the time of Cato's consulship, but more probably belong to his praetorship (as P. Fraccaro, *Encicl. Ital.* s.v. Cato). Cato himself said 'pro re publica, pro scapulis atque aerario, rei publicae profui' (frg. 127 M.), if 'profui' is read for 'profuit' as McDonald, loc. cit.

(he made his circuit of the cities on foot with a single public officer), he was inexorable in the administration of justice, so that Roman power never inspired greater fear or affection;[1] protection of the rights of provincials remained a mark of his policy. Three years later his oratorical abilities, his stern uprightness, and the support of the agricultural classes won for him the consulship, his victory representing the revival of the conservative element of the old Fabian group which flourished alongside the more liberal section represented earlier by men like Marcellus, now by Flamininus.

Before he went to his province two tribunes, M. Fundanius and L. Valerius, raised an issue 'which though unimportant in itself resulted in a violent party conflict'.[2] They proposed the repeal of the Oppian law, a sumptuary measure passed in 215 during the strain of the Punic War, whereby no woman might own more than half an ounce of gold, wear a multi-coloured dress, or ride in a two-horsed vehicle within a mile of Rome except for religious purposes. The law was defended by two other tribunes, M. and P. Iunius Brutus, and when feeling ran high Cato delivered a speech in its defence.[3] The theme was congenial, since he was eager to revive Rome's earlier simplicities and moderation, and he believed in the power of legislation to effect this. His puritanical life bore out his principles. He boasted on a later occasion that his clothing never cost more than 100 *denarii*, nor his meat or fish more than 30 *asses*; that even when praetor and consul he drank the same wine as his slaves; that he immediately sold a piece of embroidered Babylonian tapestry which he inherited; that none of his farm-houses had plastered walls.[4] His attack was directed against the group of nobles whose sympathy with Greek culture was in his estimation undermining the old Roman character. He had disapproved of Scipio's way of life in Sicily,[5] and doubtless equally disliked the conduct of his wife Aemilia of whom Polybius wrote: 'This lady used to display great magnificence whenever she took part in women's religious ceremonies. For apart from the richness of her own dress and of the decorations of her carriage, all the baskets, cups, and other utensils of the sacrifice were of gold or silver and were borne in her train on such solemn occasions, while the number of her maids and servants in attendance was correspondingly large.' But such pictures and the invectives of Cato should not suggest that Roman society was luxurious if judged even by later Roman standards. Scipio himself died a poor man, while the Romans of the Empire could regard his country house at Liternum as a model

[1] Plut. *Cato*, 6. 3.   [2] L. xxxiv. 1. 1.   [3] On Cato's speech see p. 257.
[4] Plut. *Cato*, 4. 3. See below, p. 270.
[5] It is interesting to compare the reaction of the Jew to Hellenism (2 Maccabees, 4); cf. Fabius' disapproval of the time Scipio spent in the gymnasium in his Greek cloak and slippers.

of ancient simplicity.[1] But to Cato, Scipio and his circle seemed to encourage all those foreign elements which he feared would undermine Roman morality. He was, however, unable to withstand the tide of popular feeling and the Oppian law was repealed. The incident must have stirred up much ill-feeling and increased the enmity between these two men, whose relations were further strained by an attack on Scipio's African policy.

At Carthage Hannibal had been summoned from retirement and appointed Sufete (196). He promptly introduced some revolutionary democratic and financial reforms, long overdue, and thus antagonized the ruling oligarchs, who replied by appealing to Rome, where they precipitated a political crisis and provided ammunition for Scipio's opponents. It would be argued that Scipio's generous peace-terms after Zama had allowed Hannibal to win control at Carthage, which he might raise to greatness once again; with the East so unsettled this might be serious, especially as Hannibal's enemies alleged that he was intriguing with Antiochus. Scipio himself maintained that it was beneath the dignity of Rome to meddle in the party politics of Carthage or to treat Hannibal, their defeated foe, as a common criminal. This more generous attitude was also the wiser, since apart from the accusations of his political opponents there is no evidence that Hannibal was plotting with Antiochus. But Scipio's rivals won the day: Cn. Servilius Caepio, M. Claudius Marcellus, and Q. Terentius Culleo were sent to Carthage, nominally about a frontier dispute, but actually to accuse Hannibal who at once fled secretly and ultimately reached the court of Antiochus; that he sought asylum beyond the reach of Rome does not prove that he had previously intrigued with the king. The attack on Scipio had thus misfired, unless his opponents could believe that a Hannibal at the court of Antiochus was less dangerous than a Hannibal at Carthage where, though a popular leader, he was checked by the disgruntled oligarchs. But the fact of the attack shows the strength of Scipio's political rivals, and there can be little doubt that the move was directed by Cato.[2]

In Greece also there were troubles, arising from the ambitious designs of Nabis, tyrant of Sparta. If he was allowed free play, he might threaten the whole Peloponnese, and Greece find herself overshadowed by Nabis instead of Philip; he might even look towards Antiochus. To check him would increase stability in Greece and also afford a legitimate reason for maintaining Roman troops there for another year, which some considered desirable on account of Antiochus, without at the same time giving colour to the anti-Roman propaganda of the Aetolians who had questioned the sincerity of Rome's

---

[1] Seneca, *Epist.* xiii. 1 (86).
[2] On the date of Hannibal's flight see p. 284.

pledge to evacuate Greece completely.[1] The Senate favoured war against Nabis, but decided to leave details to the discretion of Flamininus on the spot and to prolong his command.[2]

On receiving the Senate's instructions about Nabis,[3] in the spring of 195 Flamininus held a conference of representatives of all the Greeks—the first such assembly since the days of Alexander the Great —which after a strong lead by Flamininus voted for war. An allied army then defeated Nabis who was allowed to retain control at Sparta only by accepting Rome's terms. These were crippling but not mortal to Nabis, and, like those reached with Philip, were not so severe as many of Rome's Greek allies wished. Flamininus' work in Greece was now drawing to a close.[4] But any relief felt at Rome at the re-establishment of peace in Greece must have been somewhat modified when it was known that Antiochus had spent the summer consolidating his position in Thrace and that on his return to Ephesus he had been joined by Hannibal.[5]

11. *Scipio's Second Consulship*

The time had come for Scipio to rouse himself. He could now stand for the consulship of 194 since the necessary ten-year interval after his first consulship had elapsed; he had made no attempt to set aside constitutional procedure. But his position was shaken and the influence of the conservatives had been growing; he must now become a party leader and try to get men into office who would owe their position and allegiance to him. Although some of the old allies of his family had deserted him, the majority of the Cornelii remained loyal, as well as the Licinii, Furii, and Minucii; he had also the support of the new men whom he had brought into political life. At the polls his group won a sweeping success. He himself was elected consul together with the young Ti. Sempronius Longus,[6] whose father had been consul

---

[1] See A. Aymard, *Premiers rapports*, 194 f.

[2] On Livy's account of the senatorial debate (xxxiii. 45. 3; his annalistic account is for once preferable to that derived from Polybius; xxxiv. 32. 5; see De Sanctis, IV. i. 105) and on the absence of a legal reason for a *bellum iustum* (perhaps it was argued that Nabis' tyrannical conduct had placed him outside the law, or that he had violated Greek autonomy) see A. Aymard, *Premiers rapports*, 198 f., who also refutes the theory of A. Passerini (*Athenaeum*, 1932, 326 ff.) that the war was willed by the Ten Commissioners and not by Flamininus: on this point they seem to have been in agreement.

[3] These were perhaps brought by Villius Tappulus and Sulpicius Galba, if they had returned to Rome with the rest of the Ten Commissioners the previous winter. The former was in Greece in 195 (L. xxxiv. 33. 12), the latter may have been (cf. 35. 1).

[4] Ibid. 33. 14. The basis of the charge that Flamininus was eager to finish the war lest it should drag on until the provinces for 194 were allocated and he might be superseded, is not new and wears a little thin by repetition.

[5] In north Italy Valerius Flaccus was credited with a victory over the Boii, but little weight can be given to this annalistic account (ibid. 22. 1–3).

[6] Sempronius' career had been: 210, augur and *decemvir sacrorum*; 200, tribune of the

with his father in 218. Three praetors were Cornelii (Scipio Nasica, Cn. Cornelius Merenda, and Cn. Cornelius Blasio) and two others were his old officer Sex. Digitius[1] and the friendly Cn. Domitius Ahenobarbus. The censors were C. Cornelius Cethegus (*cos.* 197) and Sex. Aelius Paetus (*cos.* 198).

One reason for Scipio's striking victory at the elections must have been fear of Hannibal. Criticism of his African policy had resulted in Hannibal's flight to Antiochus. When the elections were held soon after the news had reached Rome the pendulum of popularity naturally swung back in his favour; Hannibal's conqueror must be elected consul to face the danger of a Hannibal who could now inflame Antiochus' hostility to Rome. Fear of the future and mistrust of the policy being pursued in Greece must also have contributed to Scipio's decision to seek office. He knew the measure of Hannibal's hatred of Rome, which would again be fanned into a flame by Rome's ungenerous treatment of him.

The Senate in general took the view that as the wars in Spain and Macedonia had ended, Italy should be assigned to both consuls. But Scipio urged that one consul was enough; the other ought to have Macedonia because war was pending against Antiochus, who had crossed into Europe and would soon be driven by double pressure from the Aetolians and Hannibal to commence hostilities. This proposal was a direct criticism of Flamininus' policy, but it concerned the interpretation and application of that policy rather than its principles. Scipio would urge that to evacuate Greece completely would create a vacuum into which Antiochus inevitably would be drawn; in the interests of the Greeks themselves Rome should maintain an army there for a little longer and hold the main fortresses. Rumours were no doubt current that Hannibal was urging Antiochus to invade Italy; Carthage might be stimulated to co-operate, and trouble could easily be stirred up in Spain and north Italy which were scarcely yet settled. Greece, therefore, must be held as a barrier against the Syrian king. To this Flamininus could object that Greece was now pacified; continued occupation would strain Greek patience to the breaking-point. Many Greeks had been sceptical about Rome's promise of freedom, while the Aetolians had openly asserted that the Romans would never withdraw. It would not do for Antiochus to find a discontented Greece which he could turn against Rome. Let Roman deeds match Roman words. Flamininus had consistently advocated this policy, and in 196 had differed on this very point from the Ten

plebs, opposed the triumph of L. Cornelius Lentulus; 198, curule aedile; 197, *triumvir col. ded.*; 196, praetor in Sardinia; 195, propraetor in Sardinia. L. xxxiv. 42. 3.

[1] On Digitius, who may have come from Paestum to Rome under Scipio's patronage, see Münzer, *RA*, 92 f. He had served as *socius navalis* with Scipio's fleet at New Carthage (209) where he won a *corona muralis*. He probably then received Roman citizenship.

Commissioners who had insisted upon the immediate retention of the Fetters. Thus his application of the principle of autonomy in Greece was somewhat narrowly conceived and 'worked exclusively in favour of the cities, at the expense of the monarchies and federations. In this his conception may be called Hellenic rather than Hellenistic . . . he insisted that the Roman declaration of policy should be fulfilled to the letter.'[1] In the end his policy prevailed over that of Scipio: the Senate decided to recall the army from Greece and assigned Italy to both consuls.

That Scipio's policy was dictated by more than personal ambition and that he sincerely believed in the threat from Antiochus and Hannibal is suggested by the measures which he took to guard the unprotected seaports in southern Italy: maritime colonies were founded at Puteoli, Volturnum, Liternum, Salernum, Buxentum, Sipontum, Tempsa, and Croton. If Hannibal were to provoke an invasion of Italy, he should find it prepared. But was Scipio misled by a will-o'-the-wisp? True, Antiochus did not invade Greece as soon as the Romans withdrew nor did Hannibal persuade him to invade Italy, even if he ever suggested it; and in the event matters were allowed to drift on both sides. But Scipio preferred to try to force the issue and not allow Antiochus time to mature his plans with Hannibal's help; and there was always the chance that he might yield if Rome showed a mixture of determination and conciliation. Scipio may even have pressed for a command in Greece in order to try to avert war by his personal diplomacy and 'his object at this stage was diplomatic rather than military',[2] as earlier he may have deprecated the harsh ultimatum sent to Philip in 200. If his advice had been followed, it would probably either have averted the war, although causing discontent, if not open fighting, to blaze up again in Greece, or have precipitated war with Antiochus and led to his defeat a few years earlier. The risk was perhaps worth incurring, but the Senate refused to attempt to reach a *modus vivendi* with Antiochus and to believe his denial of hostility towards Rome. This nervous attitude, arising from suspicion and fear, was strengthened when Hannibal's support of Antiochus and the activities of Rome's enemies in Greece were considered. Scipio's policy was based on a deeper appreciation of the conditions of the Hellenistic world as a whole, monarchies as well as cities, and on a different conception of Roman foreign politics from that of many senators, who preferred, if not appeasement, at least to let matters drift. If need be Rome could fight; at any rate she would not consent to deal with Antiochus on terms of complete equality.

However different the aims of Cato and Flamininus were, Cato also would disapprove of Scipio's policy and would follow Flamininus'

[1] See A. H. McDonald, *JRS*, 1938, 155.   [2] Ibid. 156.

lead, less on principle than on practical grounds. He would welcome the evacuation of Greece, not for the sake of the Greeks whose influence he disliked but from a narrowly nationalistic outlook and a desire to have nothing to do with Greece. Further, he was eager not to give Scipio a chance of putting Rome more deeply in his debt. Thus the two very different sections of the old Fabian party, represented by Cato and Flamininus, were held together a little longer by their common desire that Greece should be evacuated and that Scipio should not hold a command there.

Scipio's second consulship was peaceful but disappointing. Though he was again named *princeps senatus* and many magistracies were held by his friends, he achieved little. If he was not to protect Roman interests in Greece, where he thought the point of danger lay, he was not going to busy himself with minor disturbances. His friends could finish Cato's work in Spain, where the number of legions was again reduced to two; although Digitius was defeated in Hither Spain, Scipio's cousin Nasica curbed the Turdetani and defeated the Lusitani.[1] In north Italy Scipio might have anticipated the successes of 192/1, but he left the conduct of the campaign to his colleague Sempronius, who fought indecisively against the Boii.[2] His main concern was the foundation of coastal colonies to protect Italy against possible invasion;[3] the supervising commissioners comprised many members of the Scipionic group.[4] In addition, Scipio's consulship is marked by a petty victory over his rivals. When his friend Licinius Crassus, the Pontifex Maximus, declared that the observation of the Ver Sacrum had not been properly carried out by Cato and Flaccus the previous year, it had to be observed again: such was the political triumph of the conqueror of Hannibal.[5]

[1] Livy (xxxiv. 43. 6) rightly records that in 194 Hispania Citerior fell to Sex. Digitius and Ulterior to P. Cornelius (Scipio Nasica). Plutarch (*Cato*, 11) records a false tradition that P. Scipio Africanus went there. Nepos (*Cato*, 2) gives a compromise, that Africanus tried but failed to succeed Cato; in fact, however, Africanus had nothing to do with Spain this year. For Nasica's campaign see L. xxxv. 1–2.

[2] Livy (xxxiv. 48. 1) records two traditions: one that Scipio joined his colleague and marched through the territory of the Boii and Ligurians, plundering as he went; the other that he did nothing memorable; the latter is the true tradition.

[3] The primary object of their foundation was military and defensive. Cf. E. T. Salmon, *JRS*, 1936, 51 ff.　　　　[4] See L. xxxiv. 45.

[5] It was probably at Scipio's instigation that the censors reserved special places for senators at the Roman Games. This would please the nobility but annoy the People, and Scipio himself is said later to have regretted the change (ibid. 54). It is probably to his second consulship that an anecdote recording his haughty temper belongs: he threatened to open the Treasury himself, if he was not given access (see e.g. P. xxiii. 14. 5. Cf. Mommsen, *Staatsr*. ii. 124 n. 3).

The poverty of Scipio's second consulship has provoked the criticism that he formulated no programme of conquest, civilization, and colonization in the barbarous regions of the West, but was misled by the Eastern mirage and by his desire, shared by others, to show the superiority of Roman arms over the civilized Powers (De Sanctis, iv. i. 578 f.). But this criticism is hardly just, even if it be assumed that the initial conquest could somehow

During his consulship Scipio was forced to witness the triumphs of his two rivals, Cato and Flamininus, in the spring and autumn. Cato, the *novus homo*, made the most of his opportunity to show up the generals of the nobility: he had granted a large amount of booty to his men already in Spain because 'it was better that many Romans should go home with silver in their pockets than a few with gold'; he himself had taken no part of the booty except what he ate and drank. After his triumph he regaled the people with a speech *in contione*, expounding his exploits in phrases which show that he did not disdain rhetorical devices.[1] Flamininus' three-day triumph was even more spectacular.

Flamininus, whose personal success must have been very galling to Scipio, had gained his way and returned from Greece, leaving not a Roman soldier behind and having created a solid body of goodwill there: Scipio had won the support of half-civilized chieftains in Spain and Africa, but Flamininus counted the bourgeoisie of Greece in his *clientela*.[2] Scipio, as successor to the vanquished Barcid viceroys, had perhaps allowed his own portrait to appear on silver coinage issued in Spain, but Flamininus in Greece had ordered the issue of gold coins bearing his portrait and on the reverse a Victory.[3] Scipio had been hailed as a king by impetuous Spanish tribes and had inspired his troops with a strong faith in the divine inspiration of their general, but in Greece Flamininus, whose offerings had enriched many a temple, was hailed as Saviour and received homage alongside the gods. He shared dedications with Heracles and Apollo, and was granted a priesthood which survived until Plutarch's day; after sacrifice and libation a paean was sung which celebrated him along with Zeus and Roma and Roman Faith: 'Hail, Paean Apollo, hail, Titus our Saviour.'[4] In Scipio Greek and Roman elements were blended. Although in the legend which grew up around him he became the spiritual descendant

be justified! First, Scipio might have tried to spread civilization (he left a colony of veterans at Italica in Spain, who would tend to romanize the Baetis valley), but the civilizing influence which he admired was Roman life tempered by Greek culture, and this was only slowly spreading in Italy; the barbarian West must wait. Large-scale colonization in the West was impracticable; Italy needed all the man-power that could be found to help repair the ravages of war. And if Scipio was misled by the Eastern situation, this can hardly have seemed a 'mirage' in 194.   [1] On his speech see pp. 257 f.

[2] Cf. A. Aymard, *Premiers rapports*, 287.

[3] See p. 255. Both issues are extremely significant and must have offended the Roman nobility. It was little more than a hundred years since the first Greek monarch had placed his own portrait, wearing the royal diadem, on his coins (Ptolemy Soter), and another century and a half was to pass before a Roman coin bore the likeness of a living man. Further, the right of portraiture here may be connected with the deification of the person; see G. MacDonald, *Coin Types*, 153 ff. See the Frontispiece.

[4] Plut. *Flam.* 16. He was hailed as Saviour also at Gythium in the Peloponnese and had a festival which was still celebrated under Tiberius (Dittenberger, *Syll.*[3] 592). When dedicating an offering at Delphi he described himself as godlike (θεῖος) and suggested divine descent by the use of the title 'son of Aeneas' (Αἰνεάδας: Plut. *Flam.* 12).

of Achilles and Alexander, and his frequent communing with Iuppiter in the Capitoline temple must have seemed somewhat unusual, yet he combined with this mystical religious conviction the common sense of a Roman soldier and man of action; some contemporaries may have been annoyed by his conscious superiority, but most recognized his magnanimity and strength of character.[1] Flamininus was more vain, shallow, and pretentious, seeking applause and intriguing for power, consumed by ambition; his eager acceptance of semi-divine honours in Greece must have offended many, but he had won considerable success in war and by diplomacy: his triumph was not undeserved.

Despite the rival displays the predominance of the Scipionic group was maintained at the elections for 193 which Africanus conducted. Both new consuls, L. Cornelius Merula and Q. Minucius Thermus, belonged to his group, he could count on his brother L. Cornelius Scipio and C. Flaminius among the praetors, and the curule aediles, M. Aemilius Lepidus and L. Aemilius Paullus, were members of a friendly *gens* which had been eclipsed for some time. Early in the year the Senate authorized Flamininus and the Ten Commissioners to negotiate with representatives whom Antiochus had sent to propose a treaty of friendship in an attempt to clarify or force the issue. When Flamininus proposed that Antiochus should abandon his claim either to Thrace or to the autonomous Greek cities of Asia, his offer involved a compromise of principle and a change of policy: Rome was willing to forgo her claim to protect Greek freedom if she could get Antiochus out of Europe. That this was her main concern is implied in a promise by Flamininus to the delegates of some Asiatic cities then in Rome that Rome would uphold their claims unless Antiochus withdrew from Europe.[2] While Rome's previous interference on behalf of these towns need not be interpreted as a mere diplomatic manœuvre,[3] Roman policy clearly was becoming less idealistic under the shadow of Antiochus' advance.[4] Although the suggestion had formally come from Flamininus, the influence of Africanus, who had urged the adoption of a more realistic policy in Greece itself, may have been at work. Further, Rome's offer shows that at length she was ready to adopt from the Greeks the theory of 'spheres of influence'.[5] But it was too late. Antiochus may have been short-sighted, but he could hardly be expected to renounce his claims either in Europe or Asia at the mere

[1] On the Scipionic legend and his character see H. H. Scullard, *Scipio*, 13 ff., 275 ff.

[2] The Senate declared Teos 'exempt from payments of money as far as the Roman people was concerned', and thus reaffirmed its policy towards the Greek cities: Roman goodwill is emphasized, but it must be reciprocal. See Dittenberger, *Syll.*[3] 601: a letter of M. Valerius Messalla (*pr.* 193) comprising the Senate's statement.

[3] As suggested by M. Holleaux, *CAH*, viii. 200.

[4] Cf. A. H. McDonald, *JRS*, 1938, 157–8.

[5] Cf. T. Frank, *Roman Imperialism*, 171.

dictate of Rome, while no compromise would endure unless Rome could finally overcome her mistrust of the king.

When no decision was reached in Rome, Sulpicius led an embassy to the East in an effort at least to postpone a final rupture, but little came of it.[1] Negotiations were protracted and on one occasion, during Antiochus' absence, the Romans conferred with Hannibal at Ephesus, perhaps with the intention of arousing Antiochus' suspicions against him,[2] but later Eumenes of Pergamum, who wanted war, succeeded in wrecking the subsequent conference with Antiochus.

Meantime, news arrived that an agent of Hannibal named Aristo was stirring up trouble at Carthage, although in the event little came of his agitation. At the same time Masinissa availed himself of this commotion to seize some land which he claimed under the treaty of 201.[3] The Senate therefore sent a commission to Africa, comprising Scipio Africanus and his two friends, C. Cornelius Cethegus (the censor of 194) and M. Minucius Rufus, who either decided in Masinissa's favour (so Appian) or left the question open on grounds of expediency: any action which might antagonize Masinissa and complicate the situation in north Africa must be avoided.[4] The primary purpose of the embassy, however, must have been to obtain first-hand information about the situation in Carthage and the designs of Hannibal and Antiochus. During the previous year Scipio had emphasized the necessity for watching the East, by opposing the complete evacuation of Greece and by founding maritime colonies to protect Italy. After the report of Aristo's activities, his fears must have appeared less ill-founded and uneasiness would increase while the long-delayed return of the commission under Sulpicius was awaited. So Scipio was allowed to go to Carthage, but his inquiries did not end there: when his colleagues returned to Rome he went on to the Eastern Mediterranean. His precise movements are uncertain, but three points are clear. The journey was short, because he was back in Rome for the elections for 192; he visited Delos, where he dedicated a golden crown to Apollo; and it was this visit to the East that gave rise to the fiction that he was a member of Sulpicius' delegation and it formed a background to the story of his meeting with Hannibal at Ephesus.[5] He

---

[1] The ambassadors were P. Sulpicius, P. Villius, and P. Aelius, but not Scipio Africanus, despite a contrary tradition.   [2] Cf. P. iii. 11.

[3] Appian, *Pun.* 67. According to Livy (xxxiv. 62), Masinissa had attacked Emporia; but this should be dated thirty years later (P. xxxi. 21). Livy's mistake, however, probably arose from the record of a frontier dispute (that mentioned by Appian) to which the attack on Emporia was falsely referred. See A. H. McDonald, *JRS*, 1938, 157.

[4] L. xxxiv. 60–2; Justin, xxxi. 3–4; Appian, *Syr.* 7–8.

[5] That Scipio made a voyage to the Eastern Mediterranean in 193 is the brilliant hypothesis of M. Holleaux (*Hermes*, 1913, 75 ff.). Though it is attested by only one text (Dio, Zon. ix. 18. 12–13, which is followed by some unreliable statements), it is supported by some epigraphical evidence (a visit by Scipio to Delos in 193 would help to explain his

may possibly have had unofficial talks with Hannibal, but if, on the other hand, the episode of their interview is dismissed, together with the pleasant anecdote that adorns it, then he will have had to assess Hannibal's intentions by less direct means.

What, then, were Hannibal's intentions? He had already proposed that Antiochus should invade Greece while he himself organized a diversion in Carthage. It is improbable that he envisaged an immediate attempt on Italy itself, although that was doubtless his ultimate objective. If, as tradition records, he did, in fact, urge Antiochus to provide him with a force for an attack on Italy, the king refused because he had not yet decided to break with Rome. If, however, war was to be forced on him, Antiochus might well look to a reviving Carthage to help him to compel Rome to accept a compromise peace, and he would welcome the resurgence of Carthage as a counterbalance to Rome in the Western Mediterranean.

III. *Successes of the Scipionic Group*

A small political skirmish arose from the request of the consul Cornelius Merula for a triumph. He had defeated the Boii and returned to Rome to conduct the elections, having handed over his army to one of his staff-officers, M. Claudius Marcellus (*cos.* 196). But Marcellus had written privately to many senators alleging that Merula's generalship had not justified a triumph. When the Senate discussed the matter, Q. Caecilius Metellus suggested an adjournment until Marcellus arrived to substantiate his charges, but added that Merula should have handed over his army to Sempronius Longus (*cos.* 194), another staff-officer, and brought Marcellus with him. Merula, however, persisted until checked by two tribunes, but his case appears weak, since he was criticized by Metellus, who belonged to the Cornelian group. Further, the fact that he handed over his army to his hostile legate Marcellus rather than to Sempronius, a member of his own party, suggests that he was trying to keep Marcellus out of the way and probably alienated the sympathy of the other Cornelii. Marcellus may have been aflame with righteous indignation, but he had also skilfully discredited a member of a rival political coterie who was about to conduct the elections.

These developed into a tug-of-war between Africanus and Flamininus, and canvassing was keener than usual. The patrician candidates were Africanus' cousin Nasica, lately back from Spain with a brilliant

---

dedication of a golden laurel crown; cf. p. 131 n. 1). Further, Scipio's presence in Asia when Hannibal and Roman ambassadors were also there would explain the origin of the story of the meeting of Scipio and Hannibal, whether or not the meeting itself is accepted as an historic fact.

record; Titus' brother, L. Quinctius Flamininus, who had commanded the fleet off Greece, and Cn. Manlius Vulso (*pr.* 195). Three of the plebeian candidates were Africanus' supporters: C. Laelius (*pr.* 196), his intimate friend who had shared all his campaigns, C. Livius Salinator (*pr.* 202), and M'. Acilius Glabrio (*pr.* 196); the fourth, Cn. Domitius (*pr.* 194), was also perhaps friendly. On personal, and perhaps on military, grounds, Nasica had stronger claims than L. Flamininus; in his youth he had been chosen to welcome the Great Mother Goddess from Asia in 204, while Lucius Flamininus was later expelled from the Senate for immoral conduct. But Lucius was elected with Domitius as his colleague.

Flamininus' victory probably owed much to the desire to maintain a policy of non-intervention in Greece. Although the Roman ambassadors had not returned from Antiochus before the elections, they may have sent preliminary reports that relations, though strained, were still unbroken. Scipio, who was back in Rome, could report his personal impressions and current rumours but could give little hard fact concerning the intentions of Hannibal or Antiochus. Another reassuring sign was that when in the early summer the Aetolians appealed to Antiochus, Philip, and Nabis, in an attempt to combine them against Rome, Philip and Antiochus had made no move. True, Nabis acted, but too quickly; the Achaeans under Philopoemen, ready to check him, at once lodged a protest at Rome. How much of this news reached Rome in time to influence the elections is uncertain, but it was probably thought best to try to settle Greece with as little disturbance as possible, while Philip still remained loyal and Antiochus aloof. Flamininus was therefore sent there together with Cn. Octavius, Cn. Servilius, and P. Villius Tappulus.

But Rome was nervous and military precautions were not neglected. While L. Flamininus received Gaul as his province, Domitius was to lead the legions wherever the Senate decided. One praetor, M. Baebius Tamphilus, concentrated troops in south Italy, while another, A. Atilius Serranus, led a small squadron to the East 'to defend the allies'.[1] More colonies were planned in accordance with Africanus' policy, a Latin one near Thurii in 193 and a military one in Bruttium the next year.

In the spring of 192 Antiochus acted. His envoy told the Aetolians that the king was ready to join them in restoring Greek freedom, and in Flamininus' very presence the Aetolians reached a decision to ask Antiochus to free Greece and arbitrate between them and Rome: the king could thus play the same role of liberator in Greece as Rome had to the cities of Asia, not yet by open war but by armed mediation.[2] The Aetolians secured Demetrias and thus while sacrificing any

---

[1] L. xxxv. 20. 8–12 is confused, but 22. 2 corrects this.   [2] P. xx. 8. 1.

lingering hope of obtaining help from Philip they could offer Antiochus a good base. In late October he arrived in Greece, hoping that if the Romans insisted on war the campaign might be fought in Greece; he sought recognition as an equal Power, not the destruction of Rome. Soon afterwards Baebius crossed to Epirus with an advance guard.[1] But Rome had cause for anxiety in another quarter also. Both consuls had been sent against the Boii in an attempt to finish off the war in north Italy before a new conflict started in the East, but the inefficiency of L. Flamininus did not help the Roman cause, although Minucius Thermus was more successful against the Ligurians.[2]

The imminence of war led to early elections for 191 (Sept.–Oct.), at which Nasica and Manlius Vulso stood again; the third patrician candidate was L. Cornelius, brother of Africanus. Nasica was elected with the plebeian M'. Acilius Glabrio, a *novus homo* and protégé of the Scipios, and four at least of the praetors belonged to families friendly to Scipio: L. Aemilius Paullus, M. Aemilius Lepidus, C. Livius Salinator II, and A. Cornelius Mammula. The Scipios thus recovered some ground: Flamininus' diplomacy was good in its place, and he must be allowed to carry on in Greece, but Africanus' warnings now seemed to be coming true: hence the election result.

In Greece disturbances in many cities in favour of Antiochus were soon checked. Cato, who was serving as a military tribune,[3] advanced the Roman cause in Patrae, Aegium, Corinth, and probably also at Athens, where he insisted on speaking in Latin. The Athenians were impressed by the pungency of his remarks, although they may have disliked this brusque display of national temper.[4] By November Flamininus had persuaded the Achaeans to declare war on Antiochus and the Aetolians. When one of Antiochus' generals almost annihilated

---

[1] Reject L. xxxv. 20. 11; 23. 5; 24. 7 that Baebius had two legions: see De Sanctis, IV. i. 156 n. 75.

[2] In Spain Nobilior advanced into the central highlands and captured Toledo; he was granted an *ovatio*, the first obtained for success in Spain since Cato's governorship.

[3] Livy (xxxvi. 17. 1) names Cato and L. Valerius Flaccus as legates serving under Acilius; Cicero (*De sen.* 32), Plutarch (*Cato*, 12. 1), and Appian (*Syr.* 18) call them military tribunes. The Livian tradition has perhaps changed tribunes into legates *ad maiorem Catonis gloriam*. Mommsen (*Rom. Forsch.* ii. 64) and Schur (*Scipio*, 83) suppose that Cato went to Greece only to keep an eye on the commanders. This would explain his willingness to accept a subordinate position, but he also may have been genuinely alarmed at the military situation. Examples of consulars who served as military tribunes are C. Claudius Pulcher (*cos.* 177) in 171 and C. Cassius Longinus (*cos.* 171) in 170.

[4] Plut. *Cato*, 12. The incident probably belongs to this time. Less probable alternatives are either when Cato was returning to Rome after Thermopylae or when he was sent to join Fulvius Nobilior at Ambracia. Cf. De Sanctis, IV. i. 150 n. 68 and 213 n. 155. One of Cato's points was that the Roman sword was mightier than Antiochus' pen (frg. 60): 'Antiochus epistulis bellum gerit, calamo et atramento militat'. Doubtless Antiochus had followed the Greek custom of circulating an open letter to the Greeks as propaganda (cf. B. Janzer, *Cato*, pp. 5–6). This point may tell against the argument of F. Della Corte (*Catone*, 160 ff.) for 189, since Antiochus would hardly try to stir up trouble in Greece after Magnesia.

a small detachment of Roman troops he provided the Romans with a justification for declaring war, and destroyed his master's claim that he had come to liberate Greece without fighting Rome. Soon afterwards the new consuls entered office, and the People declared war on Antiochus and the Aetolians; Greece was allotted to Acilius, Italy to Nasica.[1] L. Scipio, who had failed to win the consulship, accompanied Acilius to Greece, doubtless to gain experience in a theatre of war in which he might hope later to have command.

Antiochus suffered an initial set-back when he learnt that Philip had decided to give Rome active support; he thus reaped the harvest of his disregard of the warnings of Hannibal who had clearly perceived the need to win over or neutralize Philip.[2] Now that Philip's support of the Roman cause rendered an attack on Italy less probable, the Romans could with safety fling their main strength into Greece; to have done this earlier would have been both unwise and needlessly provocative. In February their expeditionary force landed in Epirus; by April Acilius had wrested Thessaly from Antiochus and then faced him at Thermopylae. When the pass was turned by the skill of Cato, who, like his friend and patron Valerius Flaccus, was serving on Acilius' staff, Antiochus fled, thrust out of Greece with a single blow.[3]

News of Thermopylae was brought to Rome by Cato, who had been sent by Acilius and wished no political rival to steal his thunder. He travelled at great speed, entered the city by night, and got a praetor to summon the Senate at daybreak. While he was making his report L. Scipio, who had been sent by Acilius some days before Cato, entered the Senate House and found that Cato had outstripped him; the Senate then instructed both commanders to report to the People.[4] Behind this episode lay some petty intrigue: each group wished to make political capital by announcing the victory. Acilius had sent the friendly L. Scipio first, perhaps secretly, and then in view of Cato's contribution to the victory had perhaps been unable to refuse his request to be allowed to report at Rome. While L. Scipio, unaware of this development, was taking his time, Cato, either suspecting a trick or knowing that he had a rival to outstrip, hastened to Rome first.[5]

---

[1] On the consultation of the Fetiales by Acilius see F. W. Walbank, *JRS*, 1937, 195; L. xxxvi. 3. On the *lex Acilia de intercalando* see p. 28 n. 3.

[2] Cf. L. xxxvi. 7. 17–20 (probably Polybian).

[3] Two traditions of the battle survive: the Polybian (in ibid. 17. 1 f., and Appian, *Syr.* 18) and that of Cato preserved in Plut. *Cato*, 13–14. In the former the consul holds the centre of the picture, although Cato's contribution to the victory is fully recognized; in the latter the victory is naturally attributed to Cato's outflanking movement. See also p. 259.

[4] L. xxxvi. 21. 4–8.

[5] It is conceivable that the two messengers derive from two separate annalistic accounts which have been combined.

In his report Cato gave the Senate no understatement of his own contribution to victory: he said that those who saw him pursuing the enemy and hewing them down were convinced that Cato owed less to Rome than Rome to Cato.[1] Doubtless the victory caused much relief in Rome, but thoughtful senators would remember that although Antiochus had fled from Greece his main forces in Syria were still intact.

In Greece the Aetolians determined to fight on, since Acilius demanded unconditional surrender. This harsh Roman policy was unwise, since it benefited Philip and destroyed the ideal of a free Greece, while a war of sieges would give Antiochus a breathing-space. Flamininus, with greater insight, induced Acilius to grant the Aetolians a truce during which they appealed to the Senate. As he had already pacified the Peloponnese, Flamininus thus neutralized Greece while the score was settled with Antiochus, who in the meantime had already suffered a naval defeat at the hands of C. Livius Salinator (son of the victor of Metaurus) and Eumenes.[2]

Other Roman successes followed. Nasica won a resounding victory over the Boii, who were driven from one half of their territory and gradually retired from the other half, thus leaving the district available for colonization and romanization. For this he was granted a triumph by the Senate, despite delaying tactics by a tribune, P. Sempronius Blaesus; if the Scipios' political opponents were trying to test their popularity, they received a clear answer.[3] Minucius Thermus, however, failed to gain a triumph for his successes against the Ligurians.[4]

This year of unbroken success (191), together with the succeeding one, signalized the high-water mark of the Scipionic group. Rome must have resounded with their fame: Acilius had driven Antiochus from Greece; Livius had defeated the king's navy; Nasica had crushed the Boii who had been a constant reminder of the Gallic sack of Rome some 200 years before; Minucius was successful against the Ligurians; Flaminius and Aemilius were campaigning in Spain; and all were political supporters of Africanus. In addition, visible proof of their glory was displayed in the magnificent triumph of Nasica, who earlier in the year also had celebrated for ten days Games which he had vowed during battle as praetor in Spain; the temple of Mater Magna, whom as a youth he had conducted to Rome, was dedicated and

---

[1] Plutarch (*Cato*, 14) says, with reference to Cato's spoken or written word, that his account was boastful and pompous.

[2] J. H. Thiel (*Roman Sea-Power*, 294 ff.), who takes a high view of Livius' naval achievements, supposes that he acted independently in boldly deciding to transfer the war immediately to Asiatic waters. More probably, however, Livius' strategy will have formed part of that designed by the Scipionic group.

[3] L. xxxvi. 39–40.

[4] See the confused references to Minucius: L. xxxv. 3; 11 (193); 21 (192); xxxvi. 38 (191); xxxvii. 46 (the triumph denied). On Cato's attack on Minucius see pp. 133 f.

Games were exhibited. Further, a temple to Iuventas, which M. Livius had vowed at Metaurus, was dedicated with the usual Games, and when news came of the victory of Livius' son over Antiochus' fleet, the Senate declared a public *supplicatio* for nine days. Throughout the year the Scipionic group kept its standard flying for all men to see.

VIII

THE SECOND PREDOMINANCE AND DECLINE OF SCIPIO AFRICANUS

(190–184 B.C.)

1. *Scipio and the Greek East*

THE Senate next reached the important decision that the ejection of Antiochus from Greece was not an adequate guarantee of future security. He must be defeated in his own country and forced well back from the Greek cities of Asia Minor, while his kingdom must be reduced from the rank of a Great Power. As Africanus was now politically successful and had urged a similar policy in regard to Hannibal and Carthage in 205, he presumably advocated this policy —on this occasion without the opposition of a Fabius: no dissentient voice is heard.[1] The motive behind this decision should not be attributed to aggressive imperialism, militarism, or even primarily the desire for personal glory; once the war had started, drastic action was needed to secure the future peace of Rome and the Eastern Mediterranean. The commander best fitted to face the Great King and Hannibal was obviously Africanus, but constitutionally he could not now be re-elected consul. The difficulty was met when his brother Lucius and his old friend and officer, C. Laelius, were elected consuls for 190, 'Africanum intuentibus cunctis'.

Livy says that as both consuls wanted Greece Laelius, who had great influence in the Senate,[2] proposed that it should allocate the provinces *extra sortem*: Lucius agreed, and when Africanus declared that if the Senate assigned Greece to his brother, he would serve as his *legatus*, Lucius was given Greece. But Cicero records a different version: when Asia had fallen by lot to Lucius, the Senate was about to transfer the command to Laelius, because Lucius was not considered to have sufficient energy of body or mind, when Africanus protested and said he would serve on Lucius' staff; no change was therefore made.[3] Laelius was a competent soldier, but as a *novus homo* he can scarcely have had much independent influence in the Senate; he had failed to win the consulship in 193 and perhaps again in 192

---

[1] Flamininus was back in Rome; he had been out of Greece only 18 months during the previous 7½ years (cf. A. Aymard, *Premiers rapports*, 387 n. 2). He presumably concurred.

[2] L. xxxvii. 1. 7: 'multum Laelius in senatu poterat'.

[3] Cic. *Phil.* xi. 7. See further, p. 284.

when another Scipionic candidate, Acilius, won the plebeian place. The Scipios therefore had probably supported his election now on the understanding that he would co-operate loyally and not claim Greece,[1] but would allow Lucius to obtain the command against Antiochus. Thus Africanus gained effective command and the Scipionic group was at the height of its influence.

When the Scipios reached Greece they found that Acilius had recommenced siege-warfare against the Aetolians, who had failed to obtain more lenient terms from the Senate and were fighting on. Unwilling to spend time crushing the country piecemeal or to leave an unbeaten Aetolia in their rear, they welcomed an Athenian offer of mediation. Africanus used his personal diplomacy with such success that he persuaded the Aetolians to agree to a six months' armistice during which they sent envoys to Rome to seek milder terms, but he was evidently handicapped by the Senate's harsh decision which he had no authority to moderate. In the circumstances the Aetolian acceptance of the truce was a lucky contribution to the security of the armies marching to Asia, and was achieved only through the good atmosphere created by Africanus. Precautions were also taken against Philip to whom the Scipios sent an able and energetic young man, Ti. Sempronius Gracchus, later the son-in-law of Africanus and father of the Gracchi. The Senate had recently sent home Philip's son Demetrius, a hostage in Rome, and had conditionally promised to remit his tribute; Philip thus knew where his interests lay and informed Gracchus of his preparations to facilitate the passage of the Roman army. His desire to co-operate with Rome was strengthened by the personal friendship which he formed with Africanus when they met soon afterwards, and thus the security of the Roman army on its march through Macedonia and Thrace owed something to the *comitas* and *dexteritas* of Africanus who, when safely through Macedonia, announced to Philip the Senate's decision to cancel the rest of his indemnity.[2] Soon afterwards the way to Asia was opened by the victory of L. Aemilius Regillus, Livius' successor, over Antiochus' fleet.

The Scipios next diplomatically detached Prusias of Bithynia from Antiochus' cause and secured his neutrality by sending him a letter, which was reinforced by a special visit from C. Livius, explaining that it was not Rome's policy to overthrow all kings:

so far from depriving any of the existing kings of their sovereignties, the Romans had even themselves created some new kingdoms and increased the power of other princes . . . as Andobales and Colichas in Spain, Masinissa in Africa, and Pleuratus in Illyria, all of whom they had raised from petty and insignificant princes to the position of undisputed royalty. They further mentioned Philip

[1] Münzer, *PW*, s.v. Laelius n. 2.   [2] L. xxxvii. 7. 15. Cf. xxviii. 18. 6.

and Nabis in Greece. They had conquered Philip in war . . . yet, after receiving a slight proof of his goodwill, they had restored his son and hostages, had remitted the tribute and restored many of the cities taken in the course of the war. As for Nabis, though they might have utterly destroyed him, they had spared him, although a tyrant, on receiving the usual pledges. In view of this they urged Prusias not to be afraid about his kingdom.'[1]

With the way thus paved by their diplomacy the Scipios crossed the Hellespont: for the first time a Roman army entered Asia.[2]

Despite the need to face Antiochus before his army grew to formidable proportions, Africanus waited a month: he was a Salian priest and during the holy days when the *ancilia* were carried in procession no Salian priest who was absent from Rome might move. Antiochus seized the chance to negotiate: he would abandon his claims in Thrace and Asia Minor and pay half the cost of the war. As these terms would leave the power of Syria substantially intact and would not remove the possibility of future wars with Rome, the Scipios demanded his withdrawal beyond the Taurus Mountains and the whole cost of the war. This Antiochus would not consider, but he privately informed Africanus that he would return his son, who had fallen into his hands, without ransom, and he further offered Africanus an immense bribe if he would support the terms which Antiochus had suggested. Scipio refused, but rumours of this incident later gave his political enemies a good weapon.[3] Negotiations had failed: war remained.

The Roman army advanced, but Africanus fell ill and had to be left behind. Learning of this, Antiochus at once returned his son without ransom. Scipio is said to have shown his gratitude by advising Antiochus not to fight until he himself had rejoined the Roman army. This cryptic advice naturally later gave colour to the accusations of Africanus' opponents. What did he mean? Treachery to his country can be ruled out. Did he still hope by his personal influence even at the eleventh hour to bring about a peaceful settlement?[4] Or if it was to be war, did he wish to win the battle in person either from private ambition or from a belief that thus victory would be more certain and complete? Or did he wish to repay Antiochus' kindness by ensuring the king's personal safety in defeat? His motives may have been mixed. He probably desired the defeat, but not the annihilation, of the Syrian monarchy, and the re-establishment of a balance of powers,

---

[1] P. xxi. 11.

[2] For possible contemporary references in the poets see p. 254.

[3] The version of Polybius (deriving from the Greek history written by Africanus' son— as Mommsen?) and of Livy who follows Polybius, derives from a pro-Scipionic source and does not hint at any dishonourable act on his part. Less favourable versions doubtless circulated. Cf. Dio (Zon. ix. 20. 9) who suggests that Scipio arranged the armistice after Magnesia because he was well disposed towards Antiochus for his son's sake and because he did not wish to leave the settlement to a successor.

[4] Cf. A. H. McDonald, *JRS*, 1938, 159.

now subordinated to Rome; to crush Antiochus completely would be no less dangerous for the future peace of the East than acceptance of his earlier terms. Philip had been confirmed on his throne: Antiochus should not lose his. Rome's mission, as Scipio probably conceived it, was not to destroy other political units but to dominate them in order to ensure their protection and to secure peace. But whatever Scipio's motives were, it is clear how they would be interpreted by his enemies at home. In fact his advice had little effect on the king, who withdrew eastwards to seek ground where his cavalry, chariots, and superior numbers would have full scope.

At Magnesia the fate of the Seleucid Empire was decided, much credit for the Roman victory falling to Cn. Domitius Ahenobarbus, who in the absence of Africanus and in view of the mediocre abilities of L. Scipio was the effective commander. Africanus, who was well enough to meet the king's envoys at Sardes, imposed preliminary terms roughly similar to those proposed before the battle. He thus wished to leave Syria humbled but alive, and to give Rome no further occasion for interference and dispute. Additional terms, however, were later imposed by the Senate, where a reaction had taken place against the Scipios: Antiochus must surrender most of his fleet and his elephants, and must not war in Europe or the Aegean; if attacked, he could resist, but must not thereafter have sovereignty over or ally himself with the aggressor. Scipio's terms would have allowed Syria to maintain a prosperous national life under a Roman protectorate, but the Senate's, by weakening the central authority, would hasten the breaking up of the State and inevitably result in Rome being drawn into the East.

By defeating Antiochus the Scipios had delivered the Greek cities of Asia Minor. That this task was congenial is clear on both cultural and political grounds. Their life and habits show them to have been among the foremost supporters of the wave of Hellenism which was sweeping over Rome, while they were conspicuous among those Romans who now began to honour the shrines of Greece.[1] Their policy is illustrated by two inscriptions containing letters written to Asiatic cities. That to Colophon Nova, which had supported Rome by revolting from Antiochus and had to stand siege by him in consequence, granted the city *asylia*. That to Heraclea-by-Latmos, which

[1] A gift to Delphi from the spoils of Hasdrubal's camp after Ilipa (L. xxviii. 45. 12). A personal dedication to Apollo at Delphi by Africanus (spring 190), in return for which he probably received proxeny: see *Klio*, 1921, 153; *SEG*, i. 144. His friends Glabrio and Livius played a considerable part in establishing the autonomy of Delphi after the battle of Thermopylae: see Glabrio's letter, *BCH*, 1932, 3, and that of Livius Salinator (early 188), *BCH*, 1930, 40; Glabrio's decisions were confirmed by the Senate: see letters of the praetor Sp. Postumius, *BCH*, 1930, 39. The two Scipio brothers also dedicated three crowns at Delos (Dittenberger, *Syll.* ii.³ 617), probably in 193 and 189 (the complicated chronology cannot be discussed here), and received reciprocal honours.

had hastened to submit to Rome directly after Magnesia, recognized and guaranteed the liberty and autonomy of the inhabitants, promised Rome's goodwill and favour and similar treatment to all cities which surrendered, and emphasized the Scipios' philhellenic policy: 'for our part we are well disposed to all Greeks'. The sincerity of the pledge is seen in the dispatch of a Roman officer to protect the interests of Heraclea in the disturbed period of resettlement and in the fact that in the next few years Heraclea was allowed to carry on a war with Miletus without Roman interference. Although in the final settlement, when the claims of some cities conflicted with those of Rome's allies, Pergamum and Rhodes, the former were sometimes sacrificed to the latter, these inscriptions show that Scipionic policy was to liberate all Greeks who had supported the Roman cause or who surrendered at once; the Senate was less eager to continue this liberal treatment.[1]

Apart from any interest in Greek political theory arising from his reading of Greek literature, Scipio must have been led by his personal experiences to formulate some conception of what Rome's attitude to conquered nations should be. Having spent the first ten years of his active life fighting in Spain and Africa, he could hardly have retained a narrow continental outlook like some of his contemporaries. Despite the lack of precise evidence, the clues provided by his dealings with the Greeks and other foreign powers, together with the character of the settlements he sought to impose on Rome's conquered foes, suggest that he championed Rome's protectorate mission in the world. Hannibal and Antiochus could both testify that the policy of their conqueror foreshadowed something of Virgil's later thought, 'parcere subiectis et debellare superbos'. The Greeks were to be free; the barbarians to be won over to alliance or else crushed; the monarchs of the Hellenistic world were to be humbled but not dethroned or enslaved; client princes were to check their movements and prevent the danger of their revival; the existing units, whether autonomous cities, federations, kings, native princes, or backward tribes, were thus to be maintained; a balance of power was to be created, all dependent on Rome. With this established, Rome could largely withdraw and allow

---

[1] See M. Holleaux, *Riv. Fil.* 1924, 29 (Colophon); De Sanctis, IV. i. 226 n. and 576 n. (Heraclea); Dittenberger, *Syll.* ii.³ 633 (Heraclea and Miletus). An inscription, found in 1928 at Aptera in west Crete, records honours offered by the city to L. and P. Scipio, to Cn. Cornelius (more probably Scipio Hispallus, *cos.* 176, than Cn. Cornelius Merenda, *pr.* 194) and L. Aemilius (Regillus): see *Riv. Fil.* 1929, 60 ff. The date of the Scipios' visit to Crete must have been the summer of 189; its object is less certain. It may have been planned as a break in the homeward journey after Africanus' recent illness, but was probably connected with the visit of the praetor, Q. Fabius Labeo, who tried to check internal disturbances in Crete and to rescue some Roman prisoners, the victims of piracy, though without much success. Since many Cretan cities had helped Philip at the end of the Hannibalic War, a small reminder of Roman power by the conquerors of Antiochus might seem good policy, while the Scipios may also have wished to follow up a report that Hannibal had fled to Crete after Magnesia and was seeking help from Gortyna.

free life to flourish under her protecting aegis. Greek culture was doubtless to be fostered and, tempered with Roman steadiness and common sense, might well be encouraged to spread westwards.

To initiate such a policy Scipio was well suited. In the Hellenistic world diplomacy was an old art, which ill suited the blunt forcefulness of many an early Roman. But Rome produced a new type to meet her new need. Flamininus possessed the finesse necessary to deal with the intricate political needs of the Greek city-states, while Scipio's sympathetic approach and personal magnetism allowed him to win the confidence of kings and princes as well as the devotion of his troops. But his ideals perhaps had little prospect of realization. The weakness and servility of many of the peoples with whom Rome dealt; the increase of militarism; the decay of the old national character which was accelerated by the assimilation of some of the worse aspects of Greek life and by the influx of wealth; the refusal to re-order a constitution which had been framed for a city-state to meet the demands of an empire—these were some of the obstacles. Above all, the liberal politics of the Scipios were challenged by Cato, who fearing the corrupting influences of the Greek world preached a doctrine of isolationism and narrow nationalism, which in turn had to give way to the needs of the time and was replaced by a far more aggressive attitude than the one he had combated.

11. *Attacks on the Scipionic Group*

Victory had been gained in the East, but the Scipios were recalled before their task was completed. Their supersession had been preceded by attacks upon their friends. The first to come under fire was Q. Minucius Thermus, who had served as military tribune under Scipio in Africa (202); then as plebeian tribune, acting with Glabrio, he had upheld Scipio's interests against Cn. Lentulus (201). Curule aedile in 198 with Sempronius Longus, another supporter of Scipio, he was appointed one of the commissioners for the maritime colonies of 194. For successes during his praetorship in Spain (196) he was accorded a triumph and, with Africanus conducting the elections, he obtained the consulship of 193 with Cornelius Merula. Thereafter this 'fortis ac strenuus vir' campaigned against the Ligurians with varying success until he returned to Rome as proconsul in 190 when he sought a second triumph. Cato rallied to the attack and denounced him in the Senate.[1]

To gain a triumph it was necessary to have killed 5,000 of the enemy;[2] Minucius' claim to have destroyed 9,000 was stigmatized by

---

[1] Appian, *Pun.* 36 and 44; L. xxx. 40. 9–10; 43. 2–3; xxxii. 27. 8; 29. 4; xxxiii. 44; xxxiv. 10, 45, 54; xxxviii. 41. 3; xxxvii. 46. On Cato's speech see appendix, p. 258.
[2] Val. Max. ii. 8. 1.

Cato as a lie, which it may have been in view of the renewed activity of the Ligurians.[1] Cato next charged him with a *nefarium facinus*, perhaps extortion, and then widened his accusation to include a whole series of crimes: he had killed ten men and 'cut them up like bacon'; he was guilty of unnatural vice; he valued neither 'fidem neque ius-iurandum neque pudicitiam'; he had had ten other men scourged, evidently the officials of an allied community, because they had not provided adequate supplies.[2] Such treatment must have shocked Cato who in his own administration in Sardinia had been careful to uphold Rome's good name. There may have been some truth behind his charges, because the Senate denied Minucius a triumph, but the fact that he was apparently not brought to trial and was one of the *decem-viri* sent to Asia in the following year suggests that he did not fail to rebut at least some of the accusations. But while Cato was probably genuinely concerned about Minucius' alleged breach of the *fides maiorum*, he also welcomed the chance to discredit a member of the Scipionic group and incidentally to contrast Minucius' alleged military inefficiency with his own military record in Spain and Greece, which had won for him in the eyes of the people something of the glory which surrounded the generals of the aristocracy, thus smoothing the path of his political advancement.[3]

The Scipionic party counter-attacked: Cato was brought into the law-courts, probably by a tribunician prosecution, on some charge relating to his conduct during his consulship in Spain. He would scarcely have laid himself open to any charge of peculation or extravagance, but his extremely individualistic behaviour may have afforded his opponents some excuse to attack his methods of administration. After remarking bitterly that his care for his country had become dangerous for him, he contrasted his way of life and policy with those of his accusers and then dealt in detail with his Spanish campaign, restrained by no undue modesty. Finally he had a gibe at the mildness of the censors, probably those of 194 (Aelius and Cethegus), the implication being that if he himself were successful at the next censorial elections he would not imitate this insipid conduct. The success of his speech and the result of the trial are not known; presumably he was acquitted or else proceedings were dropped before the end.[4]

During the next few months opposition to the Scipios gradually hardened and although the consul Laelius would try to protect their interests he was in Cisalpine Gaul part of the time as well as being a *novus homo*. The manner in which Africanus had handled the question of the allocation of provinces in the Senate in March 190 had demonstrated his power but it helped to unite the nobles against him.[5]

---

[1] L. xxxv. 21; xl. 38. 1.   [2] See p. 258.
[3] Cf. his later boast: frg. 70 M. See p. 264.   [4] See p. 258.   [5] Schur, *Scipio*, 88.

Gradually a coalition, comprising many old supporters of the Fabian and Claudian-Fulvian groups, formed as a middle bloc representative of average senatorial opinion, with the Scipionic group under Africanus' outstanding personal leadership on the one side and the reactionaries like Cato and Valerius Flaccus on the other.[1] As will be seen in more detail later, the coalition included old followers of the Claudians and Fulvians (as the Sempronii and Sulpicii) and of the Fabians (as the Manlii, Postumii, Quinctilii, Atilii, and Marcii).

The new grouping is seen in the consular elections for 189 which were held 'magna contentione'.[2] Since Laelius was presiding and news of the naval victory of Aemilius Regillus and the safe arrival of the army in Asia had reached Rome (and for each event a *supplicatio* had been voted), the Scipionic group had reason to hope for success, but they were thwarted. The patrician candidates were their supporter M. Aemilius Lepidus, Cn. Manlius Vulso (aedile 197; *pr.* 195; he had failed at the consular elections for 192 and 191), and M. Valerius Messalla (*pr.* 193); the only plebeian was M. Fulvius Nobilior (aedile 196, *pr.* and *propr.* in Spain 193–192). Aemilius, who had shown considerable ability during his mission to Ptolemy and Philip in 200, gained popularity by his public buildings as aedile in 193 with L. Aemilius Paullus,[3] and thus had won a praetorship for 191 when the fortunes of the Scipionic group were rising. His command in Sicily was prolonged, but he left his province without senatorial permission in order to stand for the consulship in 190. His political opponents apparently were trying to keep him out of the way or to ensure his failure: if he returned he would incur the Senate's displeasure, while if he remained he could not make his *professio* or canvass in person.

The plebeian candidate, Fulvius, was alone elected, because the patricians had split the voting and none had gained the necessary absolute majority of votes. On the following day he named Manlius as his colleague, presumably either on the strength of the previous day's voting or after conducting another election, the result of which he would be in a strong position to influence. In any case he secured the rejection of Aemilius by obtaining Manlius as his colleague; Valerius Messalla apparently was at the bottom of the poll.[4] Thus the

---

[1] Cf. A. H. McDonald, *JRS*, 1938, 162. [2] L. xxxvii. 47. 6–8.

[3] L. xxxv. 10. 11–12 (*aedilitas insignis*).

[4] L. xxxvii. 47. 7: 'Fulvius consul unus creatur, cum ceteri centurias non explessent, isque postero die Cn. Manlium Lepido deiecto—nam Messalla iacuit—collegam dixit.' Mommsen (*Staatsr.* i. 217 f.; *Dr. publ.* i. 246 f.) rejects the view that 'collegam dixit' means that Fulvius co-opted his colleague and believes that the passage means an election by the People. In that case why did Livy use *dicere* rather than *renuntiare*, the usual word for a presiding magistrate's declaration of the result of an election? Fulvius did not co-opt Manlius without the People's authority, but he may have named him because he knew that he had received more votes than Aemilius or Valerius on the previous day. In any case, from the point of view of party affairs, the important aspect is that Fulvius, the

representatives of the Claudian-Fulvian group engineered the defeat of the Scipionic candidate and aided Manlius whose family links had been with the Fabii. Possibly Fulvius would rather have helped Valerius Messalla whose family had been connected with the Claudii, and could not because Valerius polled so few votes, but more likely he deliberately chose to help Manlius and so to establish the new coalition; he compensated Valerius by promoting his candidature the following year (p. 138). At any rate the closer co-operation of the Claudii and Fabii as a middle bloc was foreshadowed, an arrangement which was further demonstrated by the fact that four praetors for 189 were probably Fabians (Q. Fabius Labeo, Q. Fabius Pictor, Sp. Postumius Albinus, and L. Plautius Hypsaeus), and a fifth, M. Sempronius Tuditanus, supported the Claudii, while L. Baebius Dives was the only follower of the Scipios in the college.[1]

The new consuls pressed home their success and persuaded the Senate to revert to the system of annual commands. L. Scipio was superseded; Asia fell to Manlius and Aetolia to Fulvius, while Q. Fabius Labeo succeeded Aemilius Regillus in the eastern naval command. Laelius was retained as proconsul on colonial work in Cisalpine Gaul; his opponents would wish to keep him out of Rome.[2] Before the praetors went to their provinces Licinius Crassus, the Pontifex Maximus, forbade Q. Fabius Pictor, who was Flamen Quirinalis, to leave Rome for Sardinia.[3] According to Livy's dramatic account a considerable dispute ensued: debates in the Senate and Assembly, orders issued on both sides, sureties taken, fines imposed, tribunes invoked, and appeals to the People. *Religio ad postremum vicit*: Fabius had to bow to the Pontiff's authority, and received the peregrine jurisdiction. Thus a friend of the Scipios robbed a Fabius of a provincial command. Soon afterwards the victory at Magnesia was announced in a dispatch from L. Scipio, who must have hoped that the Senate would extend to him such permission to complete his work in Asia as Africanus had received in Spain and Africa; but although Livy implies that the matter was debated, no change was made and Manlius was sent to the East as arranged.[4] When, however, ten commissioners

consul-elect, and not Laelius, the consul, was the man responsible for the appointment of the second consul.

[1] The Plautii were probably friendly towards the Fabii: Münzer, *RA*, 36 ff., has argued for a connexion between the Plautii and the pro-Fabian Manlii in the fourth century. A colonial commission for Placentia and Cremona (190) and Bononia (189) was dominated by the Valerii, but contained as junior member one whose family had supported the Fabii: the members were L. Valerius Flaccus (*cos.* 195), L. Valerius Tappo (*pr.* 192), and M. Atilius Serranus (*pr.* 174). See L. xxxvii. 46. 11; 57. 7.   [2] Ibid. 50.

[3] The incident was not forgotten: a coin of the moneyer N. Fabius Pictor (*c.* 93 B.C., or more probably *c.* 110) depicts Q. Fabius Pictor with the military attributes of a praetor and the priestly ornaments of a Flamen Quirinalis. See Frontispiece No. 21.

[4] L. xxxvii. 51.

were appointed to assist Manlius in the settlement, the Scipionic group was more successful and was well represented.[1] Manlius probably had a difficult team to drive and there are traces of lack of unanimity.

A fierce struggle for the censorship followed.[2] The candidates were Scipio Nasica and Acilius Glabrio, T. Flamininus and M. Claudius Marcellus, Valerius Flaccus and Cato; the first pair were Scipio's supporters, the second represented the more liberal section of the old Fabian party, the third were the reactionaries. Glabrio, who not only had defeated Antiochus and the Aetolians at Thermopylae but had distributed much oil and wine ('quibus magnam partem hominum obligerat'), was the most popular candidate, but a *novus homo*. Two tribunes[3] impeached him on a charge of having failed to carry in his triumph or deposit in the Treasury some of the spoil from the camp of Antiochus, and demanded a fine of 100,000 *asses*. The evidence given by his staff officers and military tribunes was conflicting. One of these was Cato. Although he was a rival candidate for the censorship and despite the almost filial bonds of loyalty that linked *legati* and *imperator*,[4] Cato so far from showing any reluctance 'ante alios testis conspiciebatur'. He declared that he had not seen in the triumphal procession some gold and silver vases which he had noticed among the booty in Antiochus' camp.[5] Glabrio then withdrew his candidature, whereupon the tribunes dropped further proceedings.[6]

Glabrio's guilt or innocence cannot be established, especially as generals had considerable discretionary powers in the disposal of booty (cf. pp. 292 f.), but it can hardly be doubted that Cato was behind the prosecution and that his object was primarily political, since the inquiry was abandoned when Glabrio had withdrawn.[7] Although he introduced the weapon of scandal into political life with initial success, he soon found that it was a boomerang: Glabrio, when retiring, gave

[1] L. xxxviii. 45–6. They included Q. Minucius Rufus (*cos.* 197), L. Furius Purpureo (*cos.* 196), Q. Minucius Thermus (*cos.* 193), Cn. Cornelius Merenda (*pr.* 194), L. Aemilius Paullus (*pr.* 191), and perhaps P. Aelius Tubero (*pr.* 201) and P. Cornelius Lentulus (*pr.* 203). The other commissioners were Ap. Claudius Nero (*pr.* 195), M. Iunius Brutus (*pr.* 191), and L. Aurunculeius (*pr.* 190). L. Aemilius Paullus is probably to be identified with the future victor at Pydna and the brother-in-law of Africanus; Willems (*Sénat*, i. 348) suggests that the commissioner was a different person because the praetor of 191 had not yet returned from Spain when the commission was nominated, but he may have got back before it started (he had been defeated by the Lusitani in 190, but reversed matters in spring 189). Aemilius and Furius pressed for greater moderation to be shown to Antiochus than Manlius wished.   [2] L. xxxvii. 57. 9–58. 2.

[3] P. Sempronius Gracchus (probably the elder brother of Tiberius, the father of the Gracchi) and C. Sempronius Rutilus.

[4] Cic. *De orat.* ii. 200.   [5] On Cato's speech see Appendix, p. 259.

[6] Livy's remark that the People refused to vote on the fine (xxxvii. 58. 1) is rejected by Bloch, *Rev. Ét. Anc.* 1906, 89, and Fraccaro, *Processi*, 382.

[7] At this time or in 184 (p. 150) Cato prosecuted Ti. Sempronius Longus, who had served as Glabrio's legate: on this and his speech *De re A. Atili* see below, pp. 259 f.

as his reason that his competitor was defaming him with perjured evidence and was as much a *novus homo* as himself. Nasica was probably compromised by the charge against Glabrio, Cato was hoisted with his own petard, while the reputation of his patron Valerius Flaccus would not be improved. Thus with Fulvius Nobilior presiding, the victory of Flamininus and Marcellus was assured.[1] On entering office the new censors acted with moderation; they dared not issue a direct political challenge to Africanus, but reappointed him *princeps senatus* for a third period.[2]

Fulvius Nobilior finally crushed the Aetolians after they had again been rebuffed by the Senate and had renewed war on Philip; he then paid a hurried visit to Rome to conduct the elections for 188 before returning to capture Cephallenia, which had been excluded from the Aetolian settlement.[3] At the elections he took a strong line with his enemy, Aemilius Lepidus, and blocked his candidature.[4] The only other candidates known are the two successful men, M. Valerius Messalla and C. Livius Salinator. In view of Messalla's unspectacular career (*pr.* 193), Fulvius' arrogant influence at the elections, and the general drift of the Claudian-Fulvian and Fabian groups away from the Scipios, it may be supposed that Messalla's success had been promoted by Fulvius. C. Livius Salinator (son of the consul of 219) had become a pontiff in 211 and praetor in 202; he commanded a fleet in the Macedonian war (199–198) and served under Cornelius Merula against the Boii (193); after failing to win the consulship for 192 he had held a second praetorship and defeated Antiochus' navy (191); he prepared for the Scipios' crossing into Asia and went on a successful diplomatic mission to Prusias (190); for these services he now was rewarded.[5] But if the Scipios could count on his support, they would find little help among the praetors of 188.[6]

In the course of 188 the Scipios returned to Rome with Aemilius

---

[1] See further, p. 285.   [2] L. xxxviii. 28. 1–2.

[3] See F. W. Walbank, *Philip V*, 333, for the chronology of Fulvius' movements.

[4] L. xxxviii. 35: 'petentem deiecisset'. The procedure is not clear. Did Fulvius refuse to accept Lepidus' candidature or should the force of the present participle suggest that he permitted Lepidus to start canvassing and then blocked him?

[5] It is uncertain whether Livius received a triumph for his naval victory. De Sanctis (IV. i. 185 n. 120) thinks it probable in view of Livius' later career. He certainly deserved it far more than his successors, Regillus and Fabius, who did receive triumphs.

[6] They were Q. Marcius Philippus, M. Claudius Marcellus, C. Stertinius, C. Atinius, P. Claudius Pulcher, and L. Manlius Acidinus. Livy names P. Claudius Pulcher praetor in 188 (xxxviii. 35. 2) and Ap. Claudius Pulcher, his brother, praetor in 187 (42. 3). He also makes Publius curule aedile in 189 (35. 5). As it is improbable that Publius would have held the aedileship and praetorship in consecutive years without a year's interval, it is likely that Livy has inverted the praetorships of the two brothers (cf. Mommsen, *Staatsr.* i. 525. 1) or has made Publius instead of Appius the aedile of 189 (cf. Willems, *Sénat*, i. 373). Perhaps the latter is the more probable, as it would involve a slip in one passage only of Livy, whereas the former view would mean that Livy made the mistake twice.

Regillus, whose request for a triumph for his naval victory was granted. The claim of L. Scipio, however, was challenged on the ground that Thermopylae had been the decisive victory: Magnesia was a mere epilogue. This suggestion, for·which Cato must have been responsible, was palpably false since Antiochus' main forces had not been engaged in Greece. Scipio gained his triumph which he celebrated on a grand scale; and not to be outdone by his brother, he took the *cognomen* Asiagenus.[1] But the Scipios must now rouse themselves: Nasica and Glabrio had been defeated at the censorial elections, Lepidus had failed to win the consulship, Laelius had not proved a great political success, Aemilius Paullus and other supporters of consular and praetorian rank were absent on the Asiatic commission. So Africanus must build up his position in Rome once again in order to influence the elections for 187.[2]

The year 188 witnessed the Eastern settlement. The commands of both Fulvius and Manlius were prolonged; they thus scored a political victory since the Senate allowed them what it had denied to the Scipios. The consuls, Valerius and Livius, were fobbed off with Liguria and Gaul.[3] Manlius, meanwhile, had reduced to submission the Galatians who were a constant menace to the Greek and native communities of Asia Minor, but he marred this necessary piece of police work by his cruelty and avarice. He then held a peace conference at Apamea and the terms imposed on Antiochus were executed. The king was confined to Syria and much of the territory he ceded was assigned to Pergamum and Rhodes. The status of some of the Greek towns of the western seaboard provoked controversy, since Eumenes of Pergamum, who had previously championed their liberty, now claimed sovereignty over them, while the Rhodians in jealousy urged their liberation, which the Scipios had already promised to those that had surrendered. It was decided that cities which had been subject to Antiochus should be *liberae et immunes*, but those which had been tributary to Attalus or had opposed Rome during the war should pay tribute to Eumenes. Thus of Rome's two allies in Asia Pergamum received the lion's share of the spoils. Rhodes was granted

---

[1] Triumph of Regillus: L. xxxvii. 58. 3–4; L. Scipio: ibid. 59. Livy dates the triumph of Lucius to the end of the intercalary month before March, by implication of 189, but this must be corrected to 188, since Scipio did not return to Rome until after March 189, while Livy himself says 'triumphavit anno fere post quam consulatu abiit' (59. 6). Regillus' triumph on 1 Feb. must also be referred to 188 since he returned to Italy with Scipio (P. xxi. 24. 17). The new fragment of the Fasti Triumphales (*Inscr. Ital.* XIII. i, pp. 80, 553) unfortunately throws no light on the year since the right-hand side of the stone, where the year of the triumph was entered, is missing. For an inscription commemorating Regillus' exploits see L. xl. 52. The oldest document to record the *cognomen* of Lucius (Dessau, *ILS*, 8) gives the hybrid form Asiagenus; Diodorus (xxxiv. 33. 1) and Livy (xxxix. 44. 1, &c.) give Asiagenes; while Fasti Capit., his *elogium* (*Inscr. Ital.* XIII. iii, p. 21 n. 15), and imperial writers give Asiaticus.   [2] Cf. Schur, *Scipio*, 90 ff.

[3] L. xxxviii. 35–6.

adequate recompense for her invaluable help, but the independent
Republic fared worse than the subservient client-king. Rome deliberately built up the power of Eumenes, partly in order that his kingdom
might form a wedge between Syria and Macedonia, partly to check
the ambitions of the border states of Bithynia, Pontus, Cappadocia,
and Galatia. Thus the three major Hellenistic monarchies were held
apart and the lesser states of Asia Minor were left in a precarious
balance, which Eumenes could control as long as he obeyed Roman
wishes. The settlement was a far cry from the proclamation of liberation with which Rome had entered the war, but it involved at least
a partial fulfilment and showed that Rome herself wished for no direct
administration of Asiatic affairs.

In the autumn Manlius evacuated Asia, leaving Eumenes instead
of a Roman army as a bulwark against future disturbances. On his
return journey he was attacked by some Thracian tribes and lost much
booty and many men, including the commissioner, Minucius Thermus. Unlike Scipio, he had failed to secure the co-operation of Philip,
who was annoyed at a recent hardening of the Senate's policy towards
him, especially his exclusion from Aenus and Maronea and the sub-
stitution of Eumenes for Antiochus as master of the Thracian Chersonese.[1] On the whole he may have felt that co-operation with Rome
had not brought adequate recognition. His friend Scipio had been
superseded: he looked on grimly when Manlius was attacked.

Manlius, however, was outstripped by his admiral, Q. Fabius
Labeo, who reached Rome first and despite some tribunician opposition was granted an undeserved triumph 'de rege Antiocho'. The consular elections for 187 were conducted by Valerius Messalla whose
record in Liguria was undistinguished. Aemilius Lepidus, whose
candidature in 190 and 189 had been blocked by Fulvius Nobilior,
was elected, together with C. Flaminius. The elections had been postponed until 18 February. Since neither consul seems to have been
kept from Rome by critical military operations, the delay was possibly
due to political intrigues designed to block Aemilius Ledipus once
again, either in the interests of one of the praetorian members of the
decemviri in Asia who might hope to get back in time to stand, or
possibly in the expectation that Fulvius Nobilior might return in time
to throw the full weight of his influence into the balance against
Lepidus, an intrigue in which Valerius might co-operate the more
readily as he owed his own election to Fulvius' help.

Of the new consuls Aemilius would support the Scipios, but Flaminius' position is not so clear. His father, the consul who fell at Trasimene in 217, had probably stood closer to the Aemilian-Scipionic
group than to the rest of the nobility. The son had been quaestor to

[1] On Philip's legitimate grievances see F. W. Walbank, *Philip V*, 216–18.

Africanus in Spain in 210 and had been elected praetor for 193 in the year of Africanus' second consulship; he served in Spain where his command was successively prolonged until 190, a fact which suggests that he was a competent soldier. His colleague in Hispania Ulterior was Fulvius Nobilior and his later conduct suggests that he was attracted to Fulvius away from the Scipios. It cannot be decided whether he reached the consulship with the help of Africanus and then showed his friendship for Fulvius, or whether he abandoned Africanus' patronage before standing for the consulship which he would then have gained with the support of Fulvius mediated through Valerius Messalla. At any rate the Scipios had begun to reassert their political influence in elections which produced at least one friendly consul and perhaps three praetors (Q. Terentius Culleo, L. Terentius Massaliota, and M. Furius Crassipes).[1]

The Scipionic group then took the offensive. When the Senate proposed to assign Liguria to both consuls, Aemilius Lepidus urged that, if the Senate decided that forces should be retained in Greece and Asia, he and his colleague should supersede Fulvius and Manlius; if not, these commanders and their armies should be recalled. As a loyal supporter of the Scipios, who had been robbed of the fruits of their victory over Antiochus by senatorial insistence upon annual commands, Lepidus emphasized that Manlius and Fulvius had already been abroad for two years 'acting as kings'. As the campaigns in the East were over and Manlius was in fact already half-way home, Lepidus could scarcely have expected to succeed to a command in the East, but he may well have drawn the Senate's attention to the undesirability of prorogation and so stopped the supporters of Manlius or Fulvius seeking any extension for them. In the event both consuls did useful work in north Italy: Lepidus constructed the Via Aemilia through Bononia to Placentia, and Flaminius the Via Flaminia from Arretium over the mountains to Bononia.

Aemilius Lepidus next launched a direct attack upon the absent Fulvius Nobilior, who had previously kept him out of the consulship, by introducing some Ambraciotes into the Senate to complain about Fulvius' unprovoked attack upon their city and his brutal plundering. He was opposed by his colleague Flaminius, but he returned to the

---

[1] The three other praetors, Ap. Claudius Pulcher, Ser. Sulpicius Galba, and Q. Fulvius Flaccus would belong to the Claudian-Fulvian group. Terentius Culleo had been freed from Carthaginian captivity by Africanus in 201 (L. xxx. 43. 11; 45. 5). Perhaps L. Terentius Massaliota was of the same political complexion: he had been plebeian aedile with Cn. Baebius Tamphilus in 200 and one of the *decemviri* with Flamininus in 196. The Furii probably adhered to the Scipios: see p. 106. M. Furius Crassipes had been one of the colonial commissioners appointed in 194 (L. xxxiv. 53); it is uncertain whether he is to be identified with (a) M. Furius who was sent to the Senate from Macedonia in 201 (L. xxx. 42), (b) M. Furius who served under L. Furius Purpureo in Cisalpine Gaul in 200 (L. xxxi. 21), or (c) M. Fourios, who dedicated offerings to Mars and Fortuna at Tusculum (*CIL*, i. 2. 48).

attack later when Fulvius arrived back in Rome. Meanwhile Manlius came under fire. On his return to Rome (spring 187) he asked for a triumph, but was opposed by the majority of the Ten Commissioners, led by the two pro-Scipionic members Furius Purpureo and Aemilius Paullus. They denied his right to have made war on the Galatians and criticized his method of waging it together with his disastrous return march through Thrace: the death of Minucius in Thrace gave point to their argument. According to Livy the feeling of the House when it adjourned was against Manlius, but next day, thanks largely to the exertions of his friends and relatives, the triumph was granted.[1]

Next, if Livy's order of events is to be trusted, the first direct assault was made upon the Scipios: Cato, seeing the revival of Africanus' influence and the activity of Lepidus and Paullus, decided to strike.[2] He instigated two tribunes, named Petillius, to demand in the Senate that L. Scipio should give an account of 500 talents which he had received from Antiochus after Magnesia as a condition of the armistice and as pay for his troops. The legal issue turned upon the question whether this sum should be classified as war-indemnity, of which a strict account should be rendered, or booty, over the administration of which generals had wide discretionary powers. It is not likely that Lucius was charged with peculation. Africanus intervened, knowing that the attack was really directed against himself; he tore up the account books before the eyes of the whole Senate, telling Petillius to look in the fragments for what he wanted to know. He indignantly asked the senators how they could quibble about 500 talents and not ask by whose agency 15,000 talents from Antiochus had come into the Treasury or how they had become masters of Asia, Africa, and Spain. The matter was allowed to drop, because the Senate, jealous though some of its members might be of the Scipios, remained loyal to its Princeps and disliked tribunician interference in financial affairs.

Nothing daunted, Cato took steps to enforce his demand elsewhere. Another tribune, C. Minucius Augurinus, was found to bring the question before the People. At the preliminary examination (*anquisitio*) in an informal *contio*, Minucius urged that L. Scipio should render his accounts. At this stage probably Cato delivered his speech *De pecunia regis Antiochi* in which he would argue that the 500 talents in question fell into a category for which account should be rendered to the Senate and People. Anticipating perhaps that another tribune would be found to veto proceedings at this or a later stage, Lucius

---

[1] L. xxxviii. 42–50. Not all the details may be accurate, but the opposition of Aemilius Paullus to Manlius both in Asia and in Rome need not be questioned. De Sanctis (IV. i. 225 n. 182) accepts the opposition towards Manlius' conduct, but thinks that the opposition to his triumph is perhaps an annalistic invention.

[2] Further details of the 'trials' of the Scipios are discussed in Appendix IV, pp. 290 ff.

refused to show more respect for the People than he had for the Senate. To have acceded now would have involved admitting that he had been wrong in the Senate; also the account books had been destroyed. His refusal, however, would provoke suspicion and rumours of peculation. Minucius therefore imposed a fine on Lucius because he refused to account for this money.

The normal procedure would then have been for Lucius to appeal to the verdict of the People (*iudicium populi*). But Minucius added further insult by demanding surety with the threat of imprisonment if Lucius refused: this (strictly legal) demand was exceptionally harsh. Africanus then appealed on behalf of his brother to the tribunes, but eight refused to help. Lucius remained obdurate and Minucius ordered his arrest, but the tenth tribune, Ti. Sempronius Gracchus, intervened and protected Lucius from imprisonment. The demand for surety was thus quashed, but what of Minucius' fine? No certain answer can be given: probably Gracchus' intervention caused Minucius to drop his accusation and the whole question was allowed to fall into abeyance. Cato had gained his political objective of discrediting the Scipios; he may not have wished to push the matter to a vote of the People which might even have had an embarrassing result. Similarly two years before, the attack on Glabrio had been called off when once its political purpose had been achieved. It is less likely that the fine was exacted, while Valerius Antias' pathetic account should be rejected: he described how Lucius' property was sold but was insufficient to meet the fine, how his relatives supplied the balance, and how he went to the East to retrieve his lost fortunes by arbitrating between Antiochus and Eumenes.[1]

A minor episode occurred which did not redound to the credit of the Scipionic group, though the scandal was small enough if compared with the charges that had been laid at the doors of Manlius and Fulvius. The praetor, M. Furius Crassipes, presumably a supporter of the Scipios, had sought fame by disarming the Cenomani, who had been unoffending or even friendly towards Rome. When they complained at Rome, the Senate instructed Aemilius Lepidus, who was in north Italy, to investigate. He ordered Furius to restore their arms to the Cenomani and leave his province; Furius may even have been fined for this gratuitous attempt to create new enemies for the Republic.[2] The credit of the Scipios was perhaps restored somewhat by Aemilius' decisive action.

More striking was the attempt to thwart Fulvius Nobilior, who returned from Aetolia and asked for a triumph while the consuls were

---

[1] The presence of a Minucius in Cato's service is surprising, as the links of this *gens* had been with the Scipios. On the relations of Gracchus and the Scipios see pp. 295 f.

[2] L. xxxix. 3; Diodorus, xxix. 14.

in north Italy. Aemilius Lepidus used a tribune, M. Aburius, to veto proceedings until he could return to Rome, but the Senate supported Fulvius, while Tiberius Gracchus, a fellow-tribune, denounced Aburius in a speech which in Livy's version reflects the political atmosphere of the late Republic: Aburius was acting as the tool of an angry consul instead of as a protector of the people. On the proposal of the urban praetor, Ser. Sulpicius Galba, whose family had supported the Claudii-Fulvii, the Senate decreed a triumph to Fulvius, who then said that on the day he captured Ambracia he had vowed Games to Iuppiter for which the cities had 'contributed' 100 pounds of gold. He asked that this sum after being carried in his triumph should be set apart. After consulting the pontiffs, who ruled that not so much need be spent, the Senate allowed him to use only one-fifth of the gold, and thus limited the scale of his Games. He found a further fly in the ointment: news came that Aemilius Lepidus was hurrying back to Rome. As, however, Aemilius was providentially delayed by illness, Fulvius decided to make hay while the sun shone and hurriedly celebrated in lavish style on 23 December the triumph which he had fixed for the following January.[1] As the tribunes of 187 would have just gone out of office, Fulvius may have hoped that, with Aburius removed, Aemilius would not have had time to persuade any of the new tribunes to try obstructive tactics.

Aemilius, to whom the task of presiding at the elections for 186 had been assigned, was unable to act, so Flaminius presided: Sp. Postumius Albinus and Q. Marcius Philippus were elected consuls. Before they entered office Manlius at last celebrated his triumph. He had delayed because he feared that he might have been involved in the attack upon the Scipios. Polybius records that in the discussion in the Senate Africanus had referred to 3,000 talents. Since his brother was strictly responsible only for 500, while the additional 2,500 which were to be paid on ratification of the peace-terms would be the responsibility of his successor Manlius, Manlius' financial activities presumably had also been discussed by the Senate. Further, according to Livy, Manlius feared that he might be charged with maintaining lax discipline and helping to introduce Eastern luxuries into the Roman army and Roman life. Clearly he expected that Cato might turn his fire away from the Scipios upon him.[2] In his triumph he overshadowed Fulvius' effort in his display of spoil, despite the fact

---

[1] L. xxxix. 4–5.

[2] Livy (ibid. 6. 4) gives as the reason for Manlius' delay his desire to avoid prosecution under the Petillian law while Q. Terentius Culleo was praetor and lest he should be caught in the flames of the verdict which had condemned L. Scipio. As this is bound up with Antias' false account of the procedure adopted against L. Scipio, the details cannot be accepted, but Polybius' remark alone is sufficient to suggest that Manlius had good cause to fear an attack by Cato, while his conscience may not have been as clear as Scipio's.

that he had lost part of his booty in Thrace. If his indulgence gained him more popularity with his troops than with the people, his friends redressed the balance by persuading the Senate to use the spoils from the East to repay $25\frac{1}{2}$ imposts of *tributum*, a most important step in restoring public confidence and financial stability.

III. *The Final Attack on the Scipios*

After the defeat of Carthage, Macedonia, and Syria, Roman security seemed no longer threatened and military action could be focused on the barbarian fringe where defence was necessary, but no vital challenge to Roman safety developed for many years. After a period of comparative peace the Lusitani and Celtiberians attacked again in 187, but Rome, freed from Eastern commitments, could intensify her effort, and maintained an increased force of four legions in Spain until 179. During the same decade the northern frontier also received the attention of both consuls each year. The Ligurians were defeated in the field, weakened by deportation, and cordoned off by a ring of colonies (Bononia, 189; Mutina, Parma, 183; Luca, c. 178; Luna, 177);[1] thus they gradually ceased to threaten Cisalpine Gaul and Roman communications with Spain.

With foreign affairs less pressing, the Senate had an opportunity to consider its policy towards the Latin and Italian allies. Since some members of the Scipionic group were involved and Cato has been blamed for an increasing interference in the internal affairs of the allies, the question may be briefly considered. Although Rome failed to rise to the occasion by planning a wider federation and making generous grants of her franchise such as the past services and cultural affinities of many of the allies would have justified,[2] three measures in line with the more liberal traditions of the past were carried. The Capuans, who by a law of 210 had forfeited their Roman citizenship for ever as punishment for their revolt, were placed on the register at Rome in 189, probably without voting rights, and in 188 they received *ius conubi*.[3] In 189 the tribune Terentius Culleo carried a measure which granted full citizenship to sons of freedmen and allowed them to be enrolled in the rural tribes,[4] while in 188 the municipalities of Arpinum, Formiae, and Fundi received full citizenship in place of *civitas sine suffragio* by a plebiscite.[5]

The Senate is sometimes charged with having adopted a policy

---

[1] On Luca see E. T. Salmon, *CQ*, 1933, 30–5, and A. H. McDonald, *CHJ*, 1939, 128 n. 24.

[2] e.g. in 180 Cumae asked the Roman Senate for permission to adopt Latin in place of Oscan as its official language (L. xl. 42. 13).   [3] L. xxxviii. 28. 4; 36. 5–6.

[4] Plut. *Flam.* 18. 1. For another view see *JRS*, 1962, 207.

[5] L. xxxviii. 36. 7–9. It is noteworthy that the Senate recognized the right of the People to grant citizenship.

which aimed increasingly at interference in Latin and Italian affairs. For instance, a measure of 193, which provided that debts contracted between Roman citizens and Latins or Italians should come under Roman laws of usury, has been regarded as disclosing a 'tendency on the part of the Senate to disregard the provisions of old treaties without asking for a revision of them'.[1] The equity of this measure cannot fairly be questioned, nor did it strictly involve interference with allied internal affairs since it did not apply to contracts between allies. Further, it may not have been a unilateral act but have been agreed upon by the allied cities, or at any rate not enforced until the opinion of some of them had been canvassed. Its effect, however, was unfortunate in that it emphasized the difference in political status between Romans and allies at a time when their business differences were disappearing.[2]

Further trouble arose when many Latins, attracted by economic or other causes, migrated to Rome, where they could become citizens if they settled down.[3] This movement upset the system of allied mobilization: if Latin towns were depleted, they might not be able to fulfil their military obligations. The difficulty was realized in 193 when the consul Minucius Thermus raised the levy of allied troops not in accordance with the old *formula sociorum* but in proportion to the *iuniores* fit for service available in each town.[4] As this procedure was apparently not continued and as extended campaigns increased their difficulties, the Latins in 187 asked for the repatriation of those who had migrated to Rome. Terentius Culleo, now praetor, was ordered to repatriate all Latins who either themselves or whose fathers had been registered in a Latin city in 204 or after; he sent home no less than 12,000 men.[5] This was not an exclusive and selfish alien-act by which Rome discriminated against the Latins, as is sometimes said,[6] but rather a liberal, if short-sighted, move. Rome would lose men who were useful from both military and economic points of view, and made this sacrifice at the request of the Latin authorities themselves. But the constitutional implications of Rome's action were serious, since it infringed the *ius migrandi* and thus violated the constitution of the Confederacy and the personal rights of the lower classes of Latin citizens. Soon afterwards, as the conditions in 177 suggest, the Senate restricted the *ius migrandi* of *all* Latin colonies: henceforth every

[1] T. Frank, *CAH*, viii. 353.

[2] Cf. A. H. McDonald, *CHJ*, 1939, 126–7.

[3] For the view that Latin colonies founded before 265 (including the 12 which defaulted in 209) had the full *ius migrandi*, while those founded after 265 could claim citizenship in Rome only if they had left a son behind in their colonies, see E. T. Salmon, *JRS*, 1936, 55 ff., and A. H. McDonald, *JRS*, 1944, 12.

[4] L. xxxiv. 56. 5–6.

[5] Cf. A. H. McDonald, *JRS*, 1944, 20 ff. for this interpretation of L. xxxix. 3. 5–6.

[6] De Sanctis, IV. i. 560 ff.; Bloch–Carcopino, *Hist. rom.* 139–40.

Latin who came to Rome to gain citizenship must leave a son behind him.[1]

Another action which has been claimed as an example of Roman interference in allied affairs is the suppression of the Bacchic cult throughout Italy in 186.[2] The spread of these rites had produced a wave of crime and licence, which the Senate determined to suppress in the interests of public law and order, not from a desire to persecute a religion. Treating the movement as a conspiracy (*coniuratio*) which threatened public security in Rome and Italy, the Senate instituted an inquiry, forbade cult meetings throughout Italy, and ordered the arrest of all cult officials in Roman territory and the execution of all those found guilty of crime; thereafter it ordered the destruction of all Bacchic shrines throughout Italy, and circumscribed and legalized the future celebration of the cult.

Though action was taken first in Rome and Roman territory, it had to be extended to allied territory if the evil was to be stamped out. The wording of the inscription (*SC. de Bacchanalibus*) which records the Senate's decision and the consuls' communication of it to the allied local authorities shows that the consuls felt considerable embarrassment in their task and that they suggested rather than insisted upon the death penalty for the violation of the decree and were careful to avoid giving the impression of magisterial interference in allied territory by emphasizing the Senate's responsibility. The constitutional implications of the Senate's action were grave for both Rome and the Confederacy: in a matter which it regarded as subversive of public security as well as public morality it did not consult the People but assumed dictatorial powers, while it acted as a central executive authority which exerted moral pressure upon the allies to accept its will.[3] This interference in the internal concerns of the allies has been attributed to the reaction led by Cato against the Scipionic group which was blamed for having opened the door to Greek cults and influence.[4] But while there is little doubt that Cato was heart and soul in the attempt to suppress the evil, his motive will have been moral and social rather than the desire to interfere in allied affairs.[5] Indeed the countermeasures probably had the consent of the allied leaders, who would be ready to co-operate with the Roman nobility in an effort to suppress any movement which might threaten their social or political security.

Thus the Senate may be acquitted of the charge of malicious intervention in allied affairs. The degree of tact displayed by the Senate

[1] Cf. A. H. McDonald, *JRS*, 1944, 22 f.
[2] On this see Ed. Fraenkel, *Hermes*, 1932, 369 ff.; Krause, ibid., 1936, 214 ff.; M. Gelzer, ibid., 275 ff.; S. Accame, *Riv. Fil.* 1938, 225 ff.; A. H. McDonald, *JRS*, 1944, 26 ff.
[3] Cf. A. H. McDonald, ibid.   [4] De Sanctis, iv. i. 598 ff.; T. Frank, *CAH*, viii. 352.
[5] On Cato's speech see p. 259.

or Roman magistrates no doubt varied on occasion,[1] but unless Rome inaugurated a totally new policy towards her allies and spread her citizenship more widely, it was inevitable that her growing centralized power would gradually tilt the balance against the allies; Roman control would overshadow the local authorities until at length they became part of the machinery worked by the central government, and thereby a real municipal system would be created.[2] Nevertheless at this period Roman policy remained liberal, if judged by traditional standards, and it probably had the support of Scipio Africanus: at any rate it was his friend Minucius Thermus who first tackled the Latin conscription problem, and another friend, Terentius Culleo, who co-operated with the Latin leaders in 187 and brought in a generous bill enfranchising sons of freedmen.

The Bacchanalian Conspiracy was symptomatic of a decline in social standards; it emphasized that Eastern conquest brought moral evils as well as gold and silver in its train, and gave point to Cato's demands for a return to a more austere manner of life. But both consuls of 186 gained credit for the way in which they conducted the inquiry, although Marcius Philippus spoilt his record later by suffering a defeat in Liguria. He wisely did not hasten back to Rome where Sp. Postumius conducted uneventful elections: the new consuls were Appius Claudius Pulcher and M. Sempronius Tuditanus.

After an unsensational year[3] some wire-pulling lay behind the elections for 184, which fell by lot to Sempronius' presidency. His colleague, Ap. Claudius Pulcher, hastened to Rome to canvass for his own brother Publius, the only candidate who was standing for the first time. The others were the patricians L. Aemilius Paullus (*pr.* 191), Q. Fabius Labeo (*pr.* 189), and Ser. Sulpicius Galba (*pr.* 187), and the plebeians L. Porcius Licinus (*pr.* 193), Q. Terentius Culleo (*pr.* 187), and Cn. Baebius Tamphilus (*pr.* 197). The three patricians thought that their previous candidatures gave them a stronger claim than P. Claudius, and Livy implies that they would tend to co-operate to block him. Fabius Labeo and Porcius Licinus were regarded as the probable winners, but owing to the fiery canvassing of the consul Appius, his brother Publius gained the patrician place. His success

---

[1] See, for example, L. xxxii. 26. 18; xxxix. 19. 2; xl. 19. 5; xlv. 43. 9. Cf. A. N. Sherwin-White, *Roman Citizenship*, 100.

[2] See Sherwin-White, ibid. On P. vi. 13. 4–5, see A. H. McDonald, *JRS*, 1944, 13.

[3] Suspicion of Philip led to the dispatch of Caecilius Metellus (*cos.* 206), M. Baebius Tamphilus (*pr.* 192; he had had previous contacts with Philip), and Ti. Sempronius Gracchus (tribune 187) to Greece (L. xxxix. 24. 13). Polybius (xxii. 6. 6) gives Tiberius Claudius in place of Ti. Sempronius, but this is probably a slip (by the epitomator?), as Livy repeats the name Sempronius in another passage (xxxix. 33. 1) which derives from Polybius. If Ti. Claudius were correct, he could be Ti. Claudius Nero, praetor of 181. R. M. Geer (*TAPA*, 1939, 385 n. 10) supports the claims of Tiberius Nero, because he believes that Gracchus was not yet a senator; on this, certainty cannot be reached.

doubtless owed much to the co-operation of the presiding magistrate, Sempronius, with Appius Claudius; Livy, who makes the latter the chief villain, blames the 'vis Claudiana' for what was partly due to a working agreement between the Sempronii and the Claudii, families which had co-operated in the past.[1] The successful plebeian candidate was Porcius Licinus in whose support the whole middle group and the reactionary right wing (Cato and Valerius) will have worked against the Scipionic candidates, Terentius and Baebius. The Claudii gained a further success when Appius Claudius was appointed early in 184 to head another commission to Greece, where he had already served under Flamininus in 195 and again in 191.

Two disputes arose. First the praetors Calpurnius and Quinctius alleged that Spain was pacified through their successes and asked for permission to bring their legions home, that is, presumably to reduce the garrison to the normal number of two, but the praetors of 184 designated for Spain, P. Sempronius Longus and A. Terentius Varro, objected. In the resultant clash of opinion 'each side was supported by some tribunes and one of the consuls'. P. Claudius Pulcher probably would support the new praetors, of whom one was a Sempronius (thus he could help to repay M. Sempronius Tuditanus for assisting him to the consulship), while L. Porcius Licinus (in view of the old connexion of the Fabii with the Quinctii, and of the Porcii with the Fabii) might support the claims of the old praetors, Quinctius and Calpurnius. On balance the decision went in favour of the new praetors who were instructed to take out reinforcements, organize them into four legions in Spain, and then discharge the surplus there, but this arrangement was partly a compromise, since the old praetors were thus enabled to bring some of their troops home with them.

The second dispute resulted from the death of the praetor C. Decimius. Candidates for the vacancy were Cn. Sicinius and L. Pupius (aediles of 185), C. Valerius Flaccus (flamen Dialis and brother of Cato's patron), and Q. Fulvius Flaccus (curule aedile[2] and eldest son of that Q. Fulvius Flaccus who was four times consul between 237 and 209). The real struggle was between Valerius and Fulvius, but some of the tribunes objected to Fulvius because he was aedile; the

---

[1] L. xxxix. 32. Cf. Münzer, RA, 192, who points out that the four patrician candidates had held the praetorship within a short time of each other (191–187), whereas there was a much wider gap between the praetorships of the plebeian candidates (197–187). The candidates included three of the praetors of 187: P. Claudius, Galba, and Terentius (so Münzer, who dates the praetorship of P. Claudius to 187, not 188; but see above, p. 138 n. 6). Despite the fact that all but Publius had stood before and might therefore hope for preferential treatment, of the patricians, Sulpicius Galba, Publius' colleague in aedileship and praetorship, would have no advantage over him, nor would the plebeian Terentius in respect of precedence or origin.

[2] Livy (xxxix. 39) wrongly states that he was curule aedile designate. See Mommsen, Staatsr. i. 513, and Münzer, RA, 194.

consul L. Porcius, who also opposed Fulvius, was instructed by the Senate to ask him to stand down. Fulvius replied evasively that he would do nothing unworthy of himself, but on the day of the election stood firm. Porcius suspended the election, and the Senate moved that Porcius refer the matter to the People. There Fulvius kindled such enthusiasm that amid disputes between the tribunes themselves and between them and the consul the Senate finally decided that owing to Fulvius' obstinacy and the 'prava studia hominum' five praetors were sufficient. Thus Porcius had supported Valerius, whose office as flamen Dialis should have made a secular office unnecessary, against Fulvius and the People. As appears from the censorial elections which followed, the Porcii and Valerii were in sharp rivalry with the Fulvii. Both Porcii and Fulvii came originally from Tusculum and their enmity may have had deep roots: the Fulvii, who had long enjoyed citizenship and high office in Rome, may have despised the Porcii as parvenus, since not even Cato's grandfather appears to have been a full Roman citizen.[1]

A struggle for the censorship followed. Nine candidates presented themselves: the patricians L. Valerius Flaccus, L. Cornelius Scipio, P. Cornelius Scipio Nasica, Cn. Manlius Vulso, and L. Furius Purpureo; the plebeians M. Porcius Cato, M. Fulvius Nobilior, Ti. Sempronius Longus, and M. Sempronius Tuditanus. Valerius and Cato worked together, while according to Livy all the other candidates opposed Cato not so much to keep out a *novus homo* as because they feared that his censorship would be strict and aggressive. The Scipios were represented in strength: they probably counted on Sempronius Longus among the plebeian candidates, while Nasica's character and competent career might appeal to many who would hesitate to vote for Lucius Scipio; Furius Purpureo may have insisted on standing mainly in order to keep up his old feud against Manlius Vulso. Nasica shared with Valerius and Cato the advantage, if such it was, of having stood at the previous censorial elections. With four supporters in the field the Scipios may thus have tried to impress the public with their strength, but concentration of effort might have paid better. The effect upon the elections of Cato's direct attack upon Africanus this year must remain doubtful, since it cannot be dated accurately; if it was delivered just before the elections, it would obviously explain the failure of the Scipionic candidates. Cato may also have attempted to discredit the candidature of Sempronius Longus by prosecuting him, as on a previous occasion he had witnessed against Glabrio (p. 137).[2] The candidate whose chance must have seemed least promising was Sempronius Tuditanus. He had been consul as recently as 185, whereas all the others were much his seniors, having been consuls

[1] Cf. p. 111 n. 1.   [2] See p. 259.

between 196 and 189; further, his achievements had been modest. His candidature is to be explained by Claudian support: as presiding consul he had helped Claudius Pulcher to the consulship for 184, and now no doubt he expected his *quid pro quo*. He was unlucky, however, because the censorial elections probably were conducted by the other consul, Porcius Licinus, who certainly presided at the election for the extra praetor.[1] The assumption of Porcius' presidency accords well with the fact that the successful candidates were his kinsman Cato and Valerius Flaccus, who thus won a notable victory.

Sometime during 184[2] Cato was emboldened to make a final assault upon Africanus. If he acted before the censorial elections, his primary purpose was obviously to discredit the candidature of L. Scipio; less probably he was encouraged by his own successful election to try to end the political influence of his rivals once and for all.[3] The details of his manœuvre are very obscure.[4] He apparently put forward a tribune, M. Naevius, to accuse Africanus before the Tribes with the proposed sentence of a fine; the charge will have been Africanus' relations with Antiochus and may even have been bluntly defined as treason, to which colour would be lent by Africanus' private dealings with the king, his alleged advice to him before Magnesia, his relatively easy peace-terms, and the fact that the king had returned his son without a ransom. Cato might have little evidence to substantiate such a charge, but it would be plausible enough as a weapon to discredit Scipio. As before, during the attack upon his brother, Africanus diverted the enemy's fire by an appeal to his past services to his country. He merely said that it ill became the Roman People to listen to accusations against himself, when his accusers owed their very power of speech to him. He left the Assembly, and the People dispersed. By sheer force of personality he won a great temporary triumph, but the charge was unanswered; so knowing that his enemies would press home their advantage, now old and ill and always averse to the game of politics, he decided to withdraw. Cato, his object achieved, took no further action. At Liternum in the following year the conqueror of Hannibal and the founder of Roman power in three continents, in Africa, Asia, and Spain, died, a king uncrowned because his loyalty to his fellow nobles and the constitution had stayed his hand when unbounded popularity and military power seemed to

---

[1] On this and Tuditanus' candidacy see Münzer, *RA*, 193. On the elections, L. xxxix. 40–1.

[2] The occasion of the prosecution of C. Piso, who was granted a triumph, by Cato is not known: cf. p. 272.

[3] If the attack did coincide with the anniversary of Zama and if that battle was fought towards the end of 202, then Cato must have acted after the censorial elections, but both these hypotheses are too uncertain to warrant any such conclusion.

[4] See pp. 298 ff.

be placing a crown within his reach. Wisely he cast away ambition:
to have grasped the shadow would have caused his own downfall
amid dishonour and civil war. Instead he died in exile, and it was his
ungrateful country that was dishonoured.[1]

[1] Polybius almost certainly recorded Scipio's death under the year 183 (xxiii. 14), but
Cicero (*De sen.* 19) and Livy (xxxix. 52) place it in the year preceding Cato's censorship (184). The date 187, given by Valerius Antias, must be rejected. Livy, who specifically
rejected Polybius, based his argument on the fact that, while censor, Valerius Flaccus was
appointed *princeps senatus* in place of Scipio; unless, therefore, Scipio's name had been
removed from the senatorial list (an idea which Livy rejects), he must have died before
the censorship of Flaccus and Cato (184). But this argument is based on the assumption
that a new *princeps senatus* was chosen at the beginning of the censorship. This is unnecessary; the censors remained in office during the first part of 183, and it is probably then
that Scipio died and the new *princeps senatus* was appointed. The fact that Livy does not
refer to the appointment of Valerius as *princeps senatus* in his general account of Cato's
censorship (xxxix. 42–4) supports the view that this appointment was not among the early
acts of the censorship. See further, De Sanctis, IV. i. 597 n. 277.

IX

CATO'S CENSORSHIP AND THE MIDDLE GROUP

(184–181 B.C.)

1. *Cato's Censorship*

CATO'S censorship is remarkable less for any positive reforms than for the spirit in which it was conducted and the impression which it made upon Roman tradition. Censors had more arbitrary and personal influence than other regular magistrates, because they did not have to account for their acts;[1] since they were not appointed strictly to administer the law,[2] they had far greater latitude than, for instance, praetors, who were limited by the *edictum perpetuum*. On entering office immediately after the elections, normally held in April, they held a *contio* in the Campus Martius preparatory to the *census* proper, or registration of the citizens. Here they announced the moral principles by which they proposed to exercise their *censoria potestas*, explained any novelties which they intended to introduce into their edict, and remarked on any new evils which they thought might be endangering the State.[3] They then published in the form of a written edict the chief arrangements for the census.

Their main administrative duties were the assessment of the property of citizens and the assignment of them to their proper tribes, classes, and centuries; the revision of the lists of senators and knights, which involved an estimation of the moral fitness of individuals to exercise their functions in the State (*regimen morum*); leasing the public revenues and maintaining public property; and a final purification (*lustrum*) of the People. It is not generally possible to trace the precise order in which they performed their tasks, many of which might be tackled concurrently, but after their preliminary proclamation of policy the *lectio Senatus* would be among their first duties.

From one aspect Cato's censorship was a landmark in Rome's history: it epitomized the clash between the old and the new. Cato stands forth as the representative of the older type of Roman, of that

---

[1] Dion. Hal. xix. 16: ἀρχὴ ἀνυπεύθυνος. Cf. Varro, *LL*, v. 81. This immunity from control is attested in a senatorial decree of 204 B.C. (L. xxix. 37. 17; Val. Max. vii. 2. 6).

[2] Cf. Varro, *LL*, vi. 71: 'quod tum et praetorium ius ad legem et censorium iudicium ad aequum existimabatur.'

[3] On this aspect of their activity see E. Schmähling, *Die Sittenaufsicht der Censoren* (1938).

solid core of countrymen who had defeated Hannibal. Cautious, shrewd, hard-headed and hard-hearted, unimaginative and unadaptable, endowed with excessive respect for the more rigid ancestral qualities of the Roman People, distrustful of Greek influences although not so ignorant of them as tradition sometimes suggests, Cato championed the last real attempt of the old-fashioned Romans to re-establish a more austere manner of life in face of the social and moral decline which was resulting from Rome's expansion in the Mediterranean world and her contacts with the East. He wished his censorship to accomplish a real purification of the people, not merely a ritual *lustrum*. Hence, unlike his predecessors, he acted harshly, and the natural result was much bitterness: 'nobilis censura fuit simultatiumque plena'.[1]

Cato wished to restrain all elements in Roman life, the Senate, Equites, and People, the Latins and Italians, and to keep them within the traditional mould which history had hitherto prescribed for them. His ideal was not ignoble and the example which he set in his private life might appeal to some, but the result was bound to be failure: he could neither stop, still less put back, the clock, nor by a few legislative measures and personal example induce widespread moral regeneration. True, he was no fool, although in face of the suave Hellenized nobles the *novus homo* aggressively played the part of a countryman, thereby gaining self-confidence and at the same time partly hiding his wide knowledge and interests, but he was more concerned with symptoms than causes and failed to get to grips with the vital problems of the day. Only by a thoroughgoing programme of reform, based on a keen appreciation of the fundamental needs of Rome and Italy, could the senatorial government and the Republic itself be saved from ultimate destruction. Rome was entering upon a new epoch; much hard thinking and unselfish action were required to effect a healthy union between the institutions and traditions of the past and the wider demands of the present. Cato might point to some of the needs, but his reactionary attitude towards others involved his ultimate failure to redeem Roman society.

Grounds there certainly were for his severity, to which point was given by the recent Bacchanalian Conspiracy. Although Livy has drawn a lurid picture of the crime, immorality, and disorder which attended it, he has merely heightened the colours; in sober fact, the public conscience was severely shocked and the Senate regarded the movement as a challenge to law and order which threatened the government. The realization that the worshippers were organized in secret societies, that the movement arose among slaves and freedmen and spread among the plantations and ranches that were springing up

[1] L. xxxix. 44. 9.

in Etruria, Campania, and Apulia, that the cult itself derived from Greece, and that its mystical rites were highly suspect—such factors even apart from the public disorders which the conspiracy evoked would be sufficient to render it a public menace in the estimation of many Romans besides Cato. But despite the prompt and sensible counter-measures, which avoided persecuting the cult as such and the consequent risk of creating a body of religious martyrs, the evil was not eradicated in 186, since renewed inquiries had to be undertaken until 181.

Other symptoms of public unrest were a widespread conspiracy of slave herdsmen in Apulia, where they took to brigandage on a considerable scale in 185, and cases of poisoning in 184 and 180 which demanded investigation.[1] Even the army had on occasion shown discontent at its terms of service, and lack of discipline resulted. There had been a mutiny in Greece in 198 and insubordination in 190, while even Cato had difficulty with his cavalry in Spain in 195; the complaints of the soldiers were supported by the tribunes in 193; Vulso had to bribe his troops by granting donations and relaxing discipline in 189; there was discontent in the Spanish army in 184.[2] Even more urgent, because it was ever flaunting itself in the capital, was the problem of luxury and personal display which increased rapidly as a result of the Eastern wars.

To such questions Cato devoted his attention, doubtless hoping that if he could restore a more austere manner of life other problems would settle themselves. But the need to adjust the constitution to new claims, to infuse fresh blood and ideals in the Senate, to define the political activities of the business classes, to awaken the People to their political responsibilities, to modify relations with the Latins and Italians, to face the economic upheavals caused by the influx of capital and slave labour, to shape a comprehensive foreign policy which should balance the claims of East and West, of Rome and the provinces, such problems were either neglected or tackled half-heartedly. The senatorial nobility was entering upon an era of tolerably efficient government, but was blind to the needs of the future or too selfish to try to envisage them. Some sought reform by reaction, others by greater liberalism, but a political genius who could analyse all the needs of his day, formulate practical solutions, and win sufficient moral backing to carry them through did not arise until the body of

---

[1] L. xxxix. 29. 9; 38. 3; 41. 5–7; xl. 19. 9; 37. 1–7.

[2] L. xxxii. 3. 2–7; xxxvii. 32. 11–14; Cato, frg. 20–1 M; L. xxxiv. 56. 9; xxxviii. 23. 4; 44. 9–50; xxxix. 6. 3–7. 5; 38. 6–12. Cf. A. H. McDonald, *CHJ*, 1939, 129, 132. Such conditions may have helped to extort the concession which a lex Porcia granted: that citizens on military service should have the right of appeal against punishment in the field. This law, however, can only be dated between 198 and 134 and may have been carried during the Spanish Wars of 150–135: cf. A. H. McDonald, *JRS*, 1944, 19 f.

the Roman Republic had become too rotten to be revivified. Cato, like his great rival Scipio, could not justly claim the title of statesman, but at least he tried to re-establish that widespread sense of duty and moral responsibility which was the prerequisite of any far-reaching reforms. Unfortunately for Rome he looked backwards rather than forwards.

The new measures which Cato proposed to take against luxury were outlined at the preliminary *contio*. As consul he had vainly opposed the repeal of the lex Oppia; as censor he intended to answer this repeal by edict. He imposed a tax, equivalent to at least 3 per cent., on ornaments, women's clothing, certain vehicles, and luxury slaves,[1] and he indignantly told the People, perhaps on this occasion, that no better proof could be shown of the degeneracy of the State than that good-looking slaves should cost more than a farm, or a jar of pickled fish more than a carter.[2] Statues and other *objets d'art*, a by-product of Rome's Eastern conquests, were also made liable to a luxury tax.[3] In denouncing these Cato probably took the opportunity to condemn the increasing practice of erecting public statues to famous men, and even to Roman ladies in the provinces, presumably that is to the wives of provincial governors.[4] His denunciation was doubtless sharpened by his hatred of the increasing importance of women in public life; and the man who suppressed the names of outstanding generals in his *Origines* would hardly welcome the individual glory which men sought by the erection of statues. He used to boast that 'his own image was borne about in the hearts of his fellow-citizens', and that he would prefer that men should ask why he had no statue, rather than why he had one. He changed his tune, however, when the people erected a statue in honour of his censorship in the temple of Health, with an inscription which recorded, not his military commands or his triumph, but that when the Roman State was tottering he was made censor and by helpful guidance, wise restraints, and sound teachings restored it once again.[5]

---

[1] L. xxxix. 44; Plut. *Cato*, 18; Nepos, *Cato*, 2. 3; cf. p. 260. On the question of the taxation see Mommsen, *Staatsr.* ii. 395 n. 7; Fraccaro, *St. Stor.* 1911, 91–7; De Sanctis, III. ii. 624. The tax applied to slaves worth more than 10,000 *asses*; since the normal price of a slave was some 5,000 *asses*, the purpose of the tax will have been to limit the influx into Roman homes of highly trained Greeks whose morals and views might be harmful, rather than to help the small farmer by trying to check the spread of slave labour.

[2] P. xxxi. 25.　　　　　　　　　[3] Cato delivered a speech *De signis et tabulis*: see p. 260.

[4] Pliny, *NH*, xxxiv. 6. 31. This custom must have been increasing, because a law of 215 had forbidden the erection of women's statues in open places. For the base of a statue to Cornelia, daughter of Scipio Africanus, to which Pliny refers in this passage, see *Inscr. Ital.* XIII, *fasc.* iii (*Elogia*), p. 53. Statues to two Greek cooks aroused Cato's wrath in a speech against a certain Lepidus: see p. 260. A gilded statue of Acilius Glabrio, the friend of Scipio Africanus, the first of its kind in Rome, was placed in the temple to Pietas which he had vowed at the battle of Thermopylae in 191 and which his son had dedicated in 181 (L. xl. 34. 4; Val. Max. ii. 5. 1).　　　　　　　　[5] Plut. *Cato*, 19.

Another form of self-display was for soldiers to place their war-spoils in the most conspicuous places in their houses.[1] Some might go farther and exhibit trophies which they had obtained by other less honest means, since the possession of such spoils, genuine or fictitious, had a certain political as well as social value: Buteo in 216 had added to the Senate some 'qui spolia ex hoste fixa domi haberent'.[2] In a speech *Ne spolia figerentur nisi de hoste capta* Cato probably denounced the abuse of this practice and may have suggested that some generals did not stop despoiling their opponents as soon as peace was made.[3]

In revising the list of the Senate Cato did not at first have to appoint a new *princeps senatus*: Scipio Africanus did not suffer the final indignity of having his name struck off the list. After his death, however, early in 183, Cato placed his friend and colleague, Valerius Flaccus, at the head of the list. It had been customary to appoint the senior surviving patrician ex-censor, but this procedure had been set aside in 209 in favour of Fabius (p. 70) and Scipio himself had become *princeps senatus* when still well under 40; seniority had yielded to outstanding merit and service to the State. Now Cato disregarded the claims of Cornelius Cethegus, censor of 194 (if, as is probable, he was still living: the latest reference to him is in 193), and of T. Flamininus, the patrician censor of 189, who had both seniority and service to commend him, in order to honour Flaccus.

Before this, however, in 184 Cato had conducted the ordinary *lectio senatus* with exceptional severity: he expelled seven men including a consular and at least one praetorian. This action appeared unduly harsh partly by contrast with his predecessors' greater leniency, but more because only junior members normally were expelled.[4] The consular was L. Quinctius Flamininus, brother of the victor of Cynoscephalae, who during his campaign against the Boii in 192 had got drunk at a banquet and, in order to please a favourite Carthaginian boy, with his own hand had cut down a Boian noble who had come with his children to seek Roman protection.[5] Hitherto he had avoided punishment because the crime had been committed within the sphere of his military authority (*militiae*) and against an enemy (*hostis*), but he did not escape the moral condemnation of Cato who was often

---

[1] P. vi. 39. 10.   [2] L. xxiii. 23. 6.
[3] See p. 261.
[4] The censors of 199, 194, and 189 had expelled none, three, and four respectively. But in 252 B.C. 16 senators had been expelled, 8 in 209, 7 in 204, 9 in 174, 7 in 169 (32 in 115 and 64 in 70 B.C.). But even in the severe year 174, when a praetor, a praetorian, and the brother of the censor were expelled, the consulars remained immune. Cf. P. Fraccaro, *Stud. Stor.* 1911, 99–100.
[5] Livy's account (xxxix. 42–3) was based (not necessarily directly, but possibly through Nepos) on a speech by Cato (see p. 261). Versions of the episode by Valerius Antias and Plutarch (*Cato*, 17; *Flam.* 16) tone down some details of the crime. See further, Fraccaro, *Stud. Stor.* 1911, 9 ff., 14 ff.

aroused by acts of cruelty or oppression against Rome's allies or subjects.

Censorial procedure was to place a mark (*nota*) in the register against the name of anyone considered unworthy. The reason need not be communicated to the man himself or be given when the revised list of the Senate was read aloud to the People from the Rostrum, although it was usually stated in the document which the censors deposited in the archives (*subscriptio censoria*). Thus a censor could act solely on the basis of his arbitrary power, and the first knowledge that Flamininus may have received of his disgrace would be when he heard the revised list being read aloud (*recitatio*). But men as influential as the Flaminini could seek an explanation in the *contio* by appealing to public opinion; this they did.[1] Cato replied by delivering a damning speech in which he must have castigated Flamininus' neglect of the *mos maiorum* and the *fides populi Romani*, and pointed to the demoralizing effects of Greek standards of sexual morality and to the conditions prevailing in the military quarters of the generals of the nobility. Cato then challenged him, if he denied the charges, to a formal trial with monetary securities (*sponsio*), but Flamininus remained silent and Cato won a striking moral and political victory. Titus Flamininus, whose relations with his brother were very close,[2] would be involved in the disgrace. Thus Cato avenged his defeat by Titus at the censorial elections of 189, exposed the moral weakness of some of the Hellenizing nobles, and later was able to pass over the superior claims of Titus and appoint his own colleague, Valerius Flaccus, as *princeps senatus*.

Cato also expelled from the Senate a certain Manilius (or Manlius) who had good prospects for the consulship, because, it is said, he kissed his own wife in the presence of his daughter![3] If this anecdote,

---

[1] Plut. *Flam.* 19. 1 is more correct than Plut. *Cato*, 17. 5 where it is stated that T. Flamininus appealed to the People. There could be no question of a *provocatio* against the censor's authority. Fraccaro, *Stud. Stor.* 1911, 22, rejects the view of Mommsen, *Staatsr.* ii³. 386 (based on Cic. *Pro Cluent.* 120), that the question was referred to the People in another form.

[2] L. xl. 12. 17. According to Plut. *Cato*, 17. 6, Lucius soon regained popular favour.

[3] Ibid. 17. 7. The name Manilius is doubtful. If he had good hopes of the consulship he must presumably have been of praetorian standing, but no Manilius is contained in the praetorian fasti of 218–179. The name may be a corruption of Mamilius or Manlius. No Mamilius figures among the praetors, but there are several Manlii. Of these A. Manlius Vulso (*cos.* 178) is possible; true, his name is not among the praetors, but it is very improbable that he reached the consulship without having been praetor and Willem's suggestion (*Sénat*, i. 324) that he was *praetor suffectus* of 189 may be accepted. If ejected from the Senate by Cato, he will have been restored by the censors of 179 (who, as will be seen, were friendly to the Manlii); he gained the consulship of 178 with the help of the consuls of 179, L. Manlius Acidinus and Q. Fulvius Flaccus (see below, p. 184). An alternative is P. Manlius, praetor in Spain with Cato in 195; it may have been there that he incurred Cato's hatred. He held a second praetorship in 182, by which he would regain entry into the Senate.

Cato's care for the proprieties of married life is seen in his punishment of a certain

which at any rate illustrates Cato's rigidly doctrinaire outlook, is to be regarded with any seriousness, the offence must have lain in so acting in front of a child. Cato had high ideals of a father's duties: he himself taught his son to read because he thought that the child should not be indebted to a slave for such a priceless thing as education, while he declared that his son's presence put him on guard against indecencies of speech.[1]

The censors then had to review the knights.[2] The nucleus of the equestrian order comprised 1,800 cavalrymen aged 18 to 45 (*equites equo publico*), enrolled in 18 centuries; men over 45 with the necessary property qualifications could remain knights though not for active service, while another group consisted of men under 45 who provided their own horses. Before the time of the Gracchi senators appear to have retained their public horse and their privileged position in the 18 centuries; even after this period sons of senators continued to be enrolled among the junior *equites* until they became magistrates and senators or until they reached the age of 45. The censors reviewed the *equites equo publico* in the Forum, where the whole corps filed past, each man leading his horse by the bridle when his name was called by a herald. The censor then either passed ('traduc equum') or discharged him ('vende equum'). Discharge was either *sine ignominia* or an act of censure. In the former case the reason would be the completion of the normal period of service, in the latter some moral weakness in the knight's character or failure to look after his horse properly. As a penalty the censors could impose a further period of service on the knight at his own expense.[3] They also had to fill up any gaps in the centuries.

Cato began with an astonishing example: he expelled L. Cornelius Scipio Asiaticus.[4] Lucius may have been over 45 and perhaps not fit for cavalry service, and Cato may have wished to abolish the practice of allowing ageing senators to retain their horses, but the fact that Cato started with his old political rival was scandalous. True, the discharge was not marked by *ignominia*, as Asiaticus was not expelled from the Senate also, but this was a public insult, which would not strengthen the idea that Cato's reforming zeal in the interests of a

Nasica for an untimely jest about his wife (Aul. Gell. iv. 20. 3–6; Cic. *De orat.* ii. 260). This Nasica can scarcely have been a man of note, but Cato's hatred of the Scipios was not apparently confined to the famous.

Another of the seven expelled senators was probably a Claudius Nero, but his identity is uncertain: see p. 261.

[1] Cato, however, retained the services of an accomplished slave named Chilo, a γραμματιστής, who 'taught many boys' (Plut. *Cato*, 20. 3). Cato apparently was less concerned with the corrupting influence of a Greek slave upon his neighbours' children, since he allowed Chilo to teach others and presumably himself took the profit.

[2] See A. H. J. Greenidge, *Roman Public Life*, 224 ff.; P. Fraccaro, *Stud. Stor.* 1911, 106 ff.

[3] L. xxvii. 11. 14 (209 B.C.).   [4] L. xxxix. 44. 1; Plut. *Cato*, 18. 1.

sound body of cavalry was entirely disinterested. Cato's second victim, expelled with *ignominia*, was a certain L. Veturius, perhaps the son of the consul of 206 and a member of a family which was friendly with the Scipionic group. Two reasons were given: first, that Veturius had neglected some private religious rites of his *gens*, and secondly, that he was too fat for cavalry service.[1]

Cato, however, was genuinely concerned about the cavalry. He had seen how in the Hannibalic War Rome had suffered defeats through its inefficiency and insufficiency and how this defect had been remedied less by using Roman resources than by reliance upon allied cavalry; then as consul in Spain he had to face a panic among his own cavalry.[2] He probably wished to see the *equites* become an effective body of cavalrymen instead of a privileged aristocratic corps of young noblemen: hence his attempt to weed out the physically and morally unfit. Further, he proposed to raise the number of equestrian centuries and in a speech to the Senate urged an increase from 1,800 to 2,200 men.[3] But here he challenged the vested interests of the nobility, who for voting purposes were mainly enrolled in the 18 centuries. They were unwilling to share their privileges with others and no doubt thought that if the number of *equites* attached to the legions needed to be increased this could be done by drawing on the men who possessed the equestrian census but not the *equus publicus*; by this means they would safeguard their class interests and save the State from the burden of providing horses and upkeep for a greater number. Thus Cato failed in his attempt to increase the number and fighting efficiency of the Roman cavalry—and to increase his own political influence, since as censor he would have been responsible for selecting and enrolling the new *equites* who would then have been in his debt.

The censors performed some other tasks which in origin were not an integral part of the census and in the exercise of which they were more subject to supervision by the Senate or People. These comprised financial duties, such as leasing taxes and contracts for *opera publica*, the upkeep of public property, and the administrative jurisdiction which these tasks involved.[4] In arranging State-contracts the censors had wide discretionary powers, but when once the contracts had been

---

[1] On this second point Cato made merry: see p. 261.   [2] See p. 257.

[3] One hundred of the 400 additional *equites equo publico* would presumably have been attached to each of the four consular legions (at Cannae the number of cavalry attached to each legion had been raised by 100: see L. xxii. 36. 3), but it is not clear how they would have been arranged in the electoral centuries. Mommsen supposed that Cato would have raised the number in each of the 18 centuries from 100 to 120, thus making a total of 2,160 men (*Staatsr.* iii. 260); but it is difficult to believe that the figure 2,200 given in Cato's speech is only a round number. More probably Cato envisaged an increase of the equestrian centuries from 18 to 22. See p. 262.

[4] Private individuals also who neglected their lands and crops were apparently subjected to Cato's censorial *nota* and relegated to the *aerarii*: see Gellius, iv. 12. 1.

fixed any revision could be granted only by the Senate. Although these more material activities were supplementary to the moral work of the censors, Cato carried them out.in the same rigid spirit.

Finding evidence of abuse and speculation in connexion with the public water-supply, Cato cut off the pipes by which people drew water from the State aqueducts for use in their private houses, gardens, or fields.[1] Tapping the public supply presumably was illegal or at any rate subject to payment.[2] To drive home the lesson Cato delivered a public speech in which he apparently charged a certain L. Furius with having bought up badly irrigated fields cheaply and using the public water-supply to increase their fertility and value; Cato further explained his views on the *regimen aquarum* and the responsibility of the officials involved.[3] This Furius may have been Purpureo, the consul of 196 and Cato's competitor for the censorship, but even if he was only a lesser member of his *gens*, Cato would be glad to find a victim in the ranks of a family associated with the Scipios.[4]

Another abuse which stimulated Cato's reforming zeal was the erection of private buildings up against public buildings or on public ground: these had to be demolished within thirty days.[5] Public opinion must normally have tolerated this misuse of public land, since men would hardly have invested capital in such buildings unless they had a sanguine hope that they would remain undisturbed. He also perhaps cleared away some private buildings that were encroaching on some shrines,[6] and removed some statues from public ground.

The victims of Cato's measures probably were offered help by a tribune M. Caelius who threatened to use his veto. This was legally possible because in the exercise of their duties relating to *opera publica* (which could in fact have been carried out by any of the higher magistrates) censors were subject to possible supervision; consuls, whose *potestas* was less than the censors', could not intervene, but tribunes could. Cato replied to this threat by delivering a speech against Caelius in which he soundly trounced him as a babbling clown and a corrupt tribune.[7] Caelius did not press his point, but probably returned to the attack later.

---

[1] L. xxxix. 44. 4; Plut. *Cato*, 19. 1.　　　　　　[2] Frontinus, *De aqu.* 94.

[3] See p. 262.

[4] The argument of P. Fraccaro (*Stud. Stor.* 1911, 39, 51) against the identification with Purpureo does not seem very cogent. Cato would doubtless choose as eminent an offender as he could find. The imposition of a fine would not necessarily involve expulsion from the Senate, especially if the *lectio Senatus* had already been completed, i.e. there is no reason (with Fraccaro) to reject Purpureo because he still remained a member of the Senate. Q. Minucius Thermus, who had incurred far more serious accusations in 190, had served on an official commission immediately afterwards (see p. 134).

[5] L. xxxix. 44. 4.

[6] See p. 262. On similar activity by the censors of 179 see L. xl. 51. 8.

[7] See pp. 262 f.

Cato's handling of the public contracts (*censorum locationes*) provoked further discontent. The censors may have started by issuing an
edict which excluded some unreliable contractors from undertaking
any new contracts.[1] This is suggested by the fragment of a speech of
Cato against a certain Oppius, who had undertaken to supply wine
for the public sacrifices, presumably under a contract granted by the
censors of the previous *lustrum*.[2] Oppius had put down only a small
guarantee, and perhaps as the result of a bad harvest and high prices
he preferred to forfeit his deposit rather than to continue to supply
wine at a loss. Cato appears to have excluded him from seeking any
further contracts and probably developed his own views on the responsibilities of private contractors towards the State. After this
warning the censors farmed the taxes to the highest bidders, and let
out the contracts to those offering the lowest tenders.[3] The capitalists
were annoyed and began to agitate. This was feasible because although
the censors allocated the contracts, the Senate had considerable control over their subsequent working.[4] Censors imbued with a good
senatorial outlook doubtless had some regard for vested interests, and
Cato's neglect of these in an effort to strike a hard bargain for the
benefit of the State caused much dissatisfaction. This was voiced in
the Senate by Titus Flamininus, who seized the chance to attack the
man who had expelled his brother from the Senate.[5] The violent discussion which followed was probably the occasion of Cato's delivering
a speech in which besides defending his action he explained his ideas
of duty in a State where prosperity had led to laxity of administration.[6]
He was, however, overruled by the Senate which, yielding to financial
interests, annulled his arrangements and ordered the contracts to be
re-let.[7] Cato answered the Senate's decree with an edict which forbade
those contractors who had treated the earlier contracts with contempt
to make new bids.[8] With his colleague he then signed fresh contracts
for everything on slightly easier terms. The Senate had asserted its
authority, but Cato yielded more in the letter than spirit.

Flamininus and his supporters pressed home their advantage by
inciting some tribunes to call Cato to account before the People and
fine him two talents.[9] The precise ground of accusation is unknown,

---

[1] L. xliii. 16. 2. Cf. P. Fraccaro, *Stud. Stor.* 1911, 121 ff.

[2] On this censorial function see Mommsen, *Staatsr.* ii. 62 f. Oppius is otherwise
unknown; as he was a *publicanus* or *eques* he cannot be identified with Q. Oppius, the
tribune of 191. On Cato's speech see p. 263.

[3] L. xxxix. 44. 7. Cf. Plut. *Cato*, 19. 1.   [4] P. vi. 17.

[5] Plut. *Cato*, 19. 2.   [6] On the speech *ad litis censorias* see pp. 263 f.

[7] De Sanctis, IV. i. 602, suggests that the Senate's action may have been unconstitutional and Cato could have disregarded it: in any case he was unwilling to provoke a
constitutional crisis.

[8] Alternatively to the view expressed above, this might have been the occasion of Cato's
speech against Oppius.   [9] Plut. *Cato*, 19. 2.

but it probably arose from his previous quarrel with the tribune Caelius, who may now have joined in the attack. The trial must have been stopped by the veto of another tribune, since it is unlikely that the Senate intervened, as it did in 204; Cato at any rate was not condemned.[1]

The building programme of Cato and Valerius Flaccus was conceived on generous lines. Censors received a fixed grant from the Senate for the preservation and construction of public buildings; the amount would be determined after their plans had been discussed by the Senate. Cato's proposal to construct a basilica in the Forum provoked some opposition, but he got his way, and the Basilica Porcia was built, perhaps the first basilica to be constructed in Rome.[2] That Cato, the anti-Hellenist, should instigate the erection of a building that was Greek in name and form may seem strange, but he must have seen in south Italy and Greece how much more useful a covered building was than an open forum for the transaction of business. While the Hellenized Roman nobility might indulge their individual and self-advertising tastes by constructing luxurious private buildings in Hellenistic style, Cato followed a good Roman tradition by erecting a building for public utility. Further, it was probably built not in the new Hellenistic manner with stone architraves and ornamental stucco friezes but in the old Tuscan style with timber architraves covered with terra-cotta revetments like most of Rome's ancient and venerated temples.

But the censors' greatest constructional work was even more useful and at the same time more typically Roman: the overhauling of Rome's sewage system.[3] The details were probably keenly debated in the Senate where Cato justified his policy.[4] The scale of this work has not perhaps been adequately emphasized by Livy, who regarded the Tarquins as the chief architects of Rome's drainage system, but it becomes clear, if we accept the almost contemporary evidence of the annalist Acilius, that the censors spent 1,000 talents (6,000,000 *denarii*) upon it.[5] This is a staggering sum (the annual war indemnity from Carthage was only 200 talents, that from Antiochus 1,000) and is seen in its right proportion when contrasted either with the expenditure of the censors in a more normal year (e.g. in 179 B.C. the total building programme was probably under 500,000 *denarii*) or with the

[1] On Cato's speech *Pro se contra C. Cassium* see p. 270.

[2] Opposition: Plut. *Cato*, 19. 2. On Cato's speech see p. 264. There was no basilica in 210 (L. xxvi. 27. 3). To obtain the site, Cato had to buy up some property (L. xxxix. 44. 7).

[3] L. xxxix. 44. 5.

[4] This may be inferred from two unassigned fragments of Cato's speeches: see p. 264.

[5] *Apud* Dion. Hal. iii. 67. 5. This stupendous sum is accepted, apparently without qualms, by Tenney Frank (*Econ. Survey*, i. 144, 184), although neither expensive material nor much skilled labour would be needed.

cost of the Basilica Porcia (a single item among the censors' contracts) which may be put at some 25,000 *denarii*.[1] If the figure of six million *denarii* is correct, Cato's scheme must have been much more thorough than is elsewhere suggested. No doubt most of Rome's open drainage channels, some of which dated from the regal period, were covered in and the whole system was widely extended. Well might the Roman People erect a statue in Cato's honour in the temple of Health: while attempting to restore their moral health, he promoted their physical well-being by his insistence upon sanitation.[2]

The completion of a censorship was marked by a formal purification of the people (*lustratio*), more probably when the censors went out of office than when the strict *census* had been completed. An ox, sheep, and pig (*suovetaurilia*) were led around and then sacrificed on behalf of the whole assembled army in the Campus Martius. Although there is no evidence that censors made a formal speech on such occasions, Cato delivered a speech *De lustri sui felicitate*.[3] This fact and the discontent that his censorship had aroused render it probable that someone challenged the *felicitas* and validity of his *lustrum*, and that he vindicated his actions in this speech.[4] The attack may well have been launched by L. Minucius Thermus, who was probably a son of the consul of 193 who had been one of Cato's victims in 190 (pp. 133 f.); he will have welcomed the chance to criticize the administration of his father's opponent.[5] In his defence Cato enlarged upon his Spartan youth, military service, diplomatic activity, perseverance, and self-abnegation.[6] Such a catalogue of the more austere Roman virtues might well come from a speech in which he expatiated on the *felicitas* of his censorship.

Such, then, was the range of Cato's activities.[7] A censor who spent more than six million *denarii* on public works cannot be said to have accomplished nothing, but in relation to the problems of the day

---

[1] For these estimates see T. Frank, *Econ. Survey*, i. 153. The cost of the Basilica Aemilia is reckoned at 25,000 *denarii*: the Porcia would be about the same.

[2] Plut. *Cato*, 19. 3. Pliny's statement (*NH*, 19. 23) that Cato wished to pave the Forum with sharp stones in order to discourage loungers need not be taken seriously. On the loiterers see Plautus, *Curc.* 476 ff. On further building activity see L. xxxix. 44. 6.

[3] So Eumenius (a rhetorician of the Constantinian period), *Gratiarum act. Const. Aug.* 13. See p. 264.

[4] Unpropitious acts which could mar the *felicitas* of a *census* include a censor's seeing a corpse or the changing of the appointed day without augural permission. A later example of such a challenge is when Claudius Asellus in 139 challenged the *felicitas* of the *lustrum* of Scipio Aemilianus.

[5] Thermus will have been the tribune of 183 and may be identified with the legate of Fulvius Flaccus in Spain in 181–180 and the legate of the consul Manlius Vulso in Istria in 176. He is probably the same man as he whom Cato accused in 154.

[6] These points come from a speech *De suis virtutibus contra Thermum* which is probably to be identified with *In Thermum post censuram* and *De lustri sui felicitate*; see p. 264.

[7] References to two other speeches, which were probably censorial, attest but do not illuminate other activities of Cato; see pp. 264 f.

Cato's work was disappointing. His attempt to enforce a programme of moral rearmament by legislation and personal example was too rigidly conceived and too narrowly based. The Romans of his day were not the Romans of the Pyrrhic War, nor were their problems identical: not all Cato's moral forcefulness and wishful thinking could bring back the past. Although he may have deliberately exaggerated his anti-Hellenic attitude, partly as the shield of a *novus homo* against the darts of a proud nobility in an attempt to show that the outsider was a truer Roman than the nobles themselves, yet it must be admitted that the general trend of his policy was too reactionary and that the real value of his censorship lay less in what he accomplished than in the impression which it made upon later generations: in Cato they saw the true nature of the Roman censorship, *sanctissimus magistratus*.

11. *The Middle Bloc*

Amid the quarrels of the Scipionic group and Cato, the Claudian-Fulvians and many old supporters of the Fabii had gradually formed a central coalition whose earlier struggles may be summarized. It had gained its first success at the elections for 189 by obtaining both consulships (Manlius Vulso and Fulvius Nobilior) with the defeat of the Scipionic candidate Aemilius Lepidus, both censorships (T. Flamininus and Claudius Marcellus) with the defeat of the Scipionic candidates (Nasica and Glabrio) and of the reactionaries (Cato and Valerius), and five praetorships (p. 136). Then it secured the supersession of L. Scipio by Manlius in Asia, and in the elections for 188 gained one consulship (for Valerius Messalla) by blocking the candidature of Aemilius Lepidus, and at least four praetorships (p. 138), while the commands of Manlius and Fulvius were prolonged for 188.

Against this set-back the Scipios made an effort to rally: they secured a large proportion of the places on the decemviral commission sent to Asia and got one friendly consul (Livius Salinator) for 188, in which year Aemilius Regillus and L. Scipio obtained triumphs. The return of L. Scipio and Africanus to Rome may have reminded the people that the victors of Magnesia had been treated somewhat shabbily; at any rate the Scipios rallied sufficient support to win at least one consulship for 187 (Aemilius Lepidus) and three praetorships, though the Claudian-Fulvian group gained the other three (p. 141). After securing the termination of the commands of Manlius and Nobilior, the Scipionic group challenged, though ultimately in vain, the request of these two generals for triumphs. But the most impressive event of 187 was Cato's double attack on L. Scipio: although not entirely successful, it emphasized the autocratic behaviour of the Scipios and cast suspicion on their honour.

During the next two or three years the middle group held its ground. Under the presidency of the friendly Flaminius they gained both consulships for 186 (Sp. Postumius and Q. Marcius); and in that year Fulvius Nobilior advertised the achievements of his group by magnificent Games, to which L. Scipio replied with a counter-exhibition, designed to obliterate memories of recent scandals.[1] With Postumius presiding, friendly consuls were installed for 185 (Ap. Claudius Pulcher and Sempronius Tuditanus) together with four praetors (two Postumii, Atilius, and M. Claudius Marcellinus). After an ovation granted to Manlius Acidinus, the two consuls co-operated to get P. Claudius Pulcher, the brother of one, elected consul for 184 together with Porcius Licinus as his plebeian colleague. This meant passing over two friendly patrician candidates (Fabius Labeo and Sulpicius Galba) and helping Porcius who tended to the right wing under his kinsman, Porcius Cato, but it also involved the defeat of three Scipionic candidates (Aemilius Paullus, Terentius Culleo, and Baebius Tamphilus). Political struggles of the year included the dispute about appointing a *praetor suffectus* (in which L. Porcius supported C. Valerius Flaccus against Q. Fulvius Flaccus) and the censorial elections, probably conducted by L. Porcius, in which Porcius Cato and Valerius Flaccus defeated aspirants of both the middle group (Vulso, Nobilior, and Sempronius Tuditanus) and the Scipionic party (L. Scipio, Nasica, Furius Purpureo, and Sempronius Longus). Thus the reactionaries won a great victory which led to the final overthrow of the Scipios in 184. The middle group, however, was not hit so hard: after two Fulvii and Fabius Labeo had gained commissionerships,[2] and L. Quinctius Crispinus had celebrated a triumph, they won both consulships for 183 (Fabius Labeo and M. Claudius Marcellus). Meantime Cato, at the height of his authority, was striving to improve the administration by pillorying all offenders, whether supporters of the Scipios (as L. Scipio, L. Veturius, Minucius Thermus, and a Furius) or of the middle group (as L. Flamininus, Claudius Nero, and a Manlius).

In the religious sphere the middle group made good headway.[3] At the end of 184 their supporter Sp. Postumius Albinus (*pr.* 183 and *cos.* 174) replaced the deceased Cn. Cornelius Lentulus (*cos.* 201) as augur. Early in 183 the Pontifex Maximus, Licinius Crassus, died after holding office for thirty years, a longer period than anyone else until the triumvir Lepidus. He was succeeded by C. Servilius Gemi-

[1] L. xxxix. 22. Antias' statement that Lucius went to the East, where he collected money and actors for the Games, may be rejected.

[2] M. Fulvius Flaccus (a brother of the aedile Quintus? see Münzer, *PW*, s.v. Fulvius n. 57), Q. Fulvius Nobilior (a younger son of the conqueror of Aetolia), and Labeo: commissioners for Potentia and Pisaurum.

[3] L. xxxix. 45. 8–46. 4.

nus (*cos.* 203) who like Cn. Cornelius Lentulus had abandoned the traditional loyalty of his family towards Scipio, while M. Sempronius (*cos.* 185), who had failed at the recent censorial elections, was co-opted as a pontiff to fill the vacancy. Thus Sempronius and Postumius would strengthen the grip of the middle group on the religious machinery of the State. The funeral of Licinius Crassus was made the occasion for a public feast and funeral Games; proceedings were interrupted by a violent storm, but the Licinii had done their best to honour their dead and impress the electorate.

Several members of the middle group were represented on diplomatic and colonial missions (e.g. Q. Marcius Philippus went to Greece, and T. Flamininus to Prusias, who betrayed Hannibal to the Romans), but the Scipionic group secured many places on others. A strong board, sent to check a migration of the Gauls, comprised Furius Purpureo (*cos.* 196), Q. Minucius (probably the consul of 197), and a Claudian-Fulvian as junior member, L. Manlius Acidinus (*pr.* 188); since they came back *cum donis*, their mission was both successful and lucrative.[1] The commissioners for the important Latin colony at Aquileia were Scipio Nasica (*cos.* 191) and two Claudian-Fulvians: C. Flaminius (probably the consul of 187) and L. Manlius Acidinus.[2] For the Roman colonies of Mutina and Parma honours were divided: the senior member Aemilius Lepidus (*cos.* 187) had as colleagues the Fabian L. Quinctius Crispinus (*pr.* 186) and T. Aebutius Carus.[3]

Discussion of the colonial policy of this period has provoked some deductions about the attitude of Rome and Cato towards the Latins, which now seem in need of modification. After the sudden burst of colonizing in 194 when nine Roman colonies, followed by two Latin ones (Copia, 193, and Vibo, 192), were founded on the coast, primarily for defence, there was a lull (apart from the Latin settlement of Bononia in 189, designed against the Ligurian menace) until another series of Roman colonies was planned: Pisaurum and Potentia in 184, and Mutina, Parma, and Saturnia in 183. In this latter year, after discussion whether the settlement should be Roman or Latin, a Latin colony was planned at Aquileia which was finally settled by 181; a Roman colony also was planted at Graviscae, to be followed by another at Luna (177) and a Latin colony at Luca (*c.* 178).

It is now generally agreed that the purpose of these new colonies was military and defensive,[4] Aquileia being founded to protect the

---

[1] Ibid. 54. 13–55. 4.

[2] Manlius' name is recorded in an inscription from Aquileia (*CIL*, I. ii. 538).

[3] The commissioners for Saturnia were Q. Fabius Labeo (presumably the consul of 183), C. Afranius Stellio (*pr.* 185), and Ti. Sempronius Gracchus, the tribune of 187; Afranius' political alignment is unknown, while Gracchus had saved L. Scipio though without much enthusiasm.

[4] Cf. p. 145. E. T. Salmon (*JRS*, 1936, 51 ff.) has stressed their military function in

north-east frontier against the Istri, a people of Illyrian origin who had recently established greater internal unity under one king. Roman attention was directed to the district when as a by-product of the great Celtic migrations a group of the Carni tried to settle in Italy between the Veneti and Istri. Warned off by the Romans (186), they were disarmed in 183 by the consul, Claudius Marcellus, under threat of war; when they complained, the Senate sent commissioners who ordered Marcellus to restore their arms provided they withdrew from Italy. The two senior commissioners, Furius Purpureo and Q. Minucius, were supporters of the Scipionic group and may have welcomed a chance to rap Marcellus over the knuckles. Marcellus then planned an Istrian war, but he received a discouraging reply when he consulted the Senate, which at this time was discussing the foundation of Aquileia.[1] Whether its settlement first provoked the Istri to hostilities or whether prior raiding by the Istri was one of the causes of its foundation,[2] the district obviously needed policing.

More controversial than the purpose is the question of the composition of the colonies. Before the Hannibalic War Latin colonies had been more in favour than Roman. The primary function of both was military, and as Latins could join citizen colonies (just as they had the right to acquire citizenship by settling in Rome itself), the latter theoretically differed very little in composition. The main difference, apart from the retention of citizen rights by Romans in Roman colonies and their sacrifice of them if they joined Latin colonies, was size: Roman colonies, limited to 300 members, were settled on coastal districts which did not offer much prospect of development. In the early second century procedure remained at first traditional: the numerous small defensive settlements in 194 were Roman, the large inland colony at Bononia in 189 was Latin, and Pisaurum and Potentia on the Adriatic coast in 184 were Roman. But in 183 Mutina and Parma, settled as large inland colonies of 2,000

contrast with other views, e.g. that of Reid (economic; to settle veterans), or Karlowa and F. F. Abbott (romanizing agents), or Mommsen (punitive against rebellious tribes). Cf. A. H. McDonald, *CHJ*, 1939, 128, who emphasizes that the small grants of land (5 *iugera* at Mutina, 8 at Parma, 6½ at Luna) point to their specifically military functions, while the large number of colonists (2,000 at these three colonies) only proves the scale of operations against the Ligurians.

[1] L. xxxix. 55. 5, reading 'id senatui non placuit'. Cf. the annalist L. Piso (*apud* Pliny, *NH*, iii. 131): 'et ab Aquileia ad XII lapidem deletum oppidum etiam invito senatu a M. Claudio Marcello L. Piso auctor est.' De Sanctis, iv. i. 429 n. 79, thinks that *invito senatu* is an error. It may well be, as the Senate would probably wish to see the new settlement of the Gauls destroyed, but it may have arisen from a misunderstanding of the fact that Marcellus was obviously outrunning the Senate's wishes in general. On the Gauls and Istri see L. xxxix. 22. 6-7; 45. 6-7; 54-5.

[2] Mommsen, followed by Frank (*CAH*, viii. 328). Salmon, *JRS*, 1936, 55, however, thinks that L. xxxix. 55. 4 proves that the Istri were restless before 181, but the passage only states that Marcellus planned to attack the Istri, an intention which may have been preventative rather than punitive. L. xl. 18. 4, however, refers to Istrian piracy in 181.

citizens each, were Roman, not Latin, while Aquileia with exceptionally large allotments was only made a Latin colony after debate.

This innovation has been interpreted as the beginning of a selfish anti-Latin policy which excluded the Latins from the fruits of conquest, and as the work of Cato who forced it through despite the more liberal policies of the Scipionic group.[1] But the first part of this view breaks down because there is no evidence that Parma and Mutina were exclusively inhabited by Romans: there were non-Romans in Pisaurum and Potentia in 184.[2] Cato's part also has been rejected, because, it is said, evidence is lacking that he initiated the new policy of inland citizen-colonization, and even if he was responsible, he would scarcely have excluded the Latins, since he seems to have encouraged the Latins to become Roman citizens.[3] But though he may be acquitted from the charge of an anti-Latin policy, it is not certain that he was not interested in the development of northern Italy. It is, however, almost impossible to attempt to assign a definite colonial policy to any group at this time, since they were so evenly balanced: the Claudian-Fulvians had been successful recently at the polls, the Scipionic group, as will be seen, made an unexpected recovery in 183, while in the background was Cato whose moral authority must have been great in the year in which he vacated the censorship. Nor is much light thrown upon which groups favoured Latin or Roman colonies by the composition of the commissions, since for both Aquileia and Mutina the senior member was a supporter of the Scipios (Nasica and Aemilius Lepidus), while the middle group gained the other places. But the question is of less importance, if it is admitted that the choice of a Roman or Latin colony did not involve a policy of serious discrimination against the Latins.

What, then, was the reason for the choice of Roman colonies at Mutina and Parma? One motive was to check a decline in the number of Roman citizens. When as a result of Latin protests it became difficult to maintain citizen numbers by means of Latin migration to Rome, the Romans decided that they could not afford to lose more citizens by settlement in Latin colonies: hence Latin colonization soon ceased (Aquileia, the last big one, was followed only by Luca in 178)

---

[1] T. Frank, *CAH*, viii. 332, 353, 374; F. F. Abbott, *CP*, 1915, 366; De Sanctis, IV. i. 589–90.

[2] Cic. *Brut.* 79. Cf. E. T. Salmon, *JRS*, 1936, 66. It is true that in 195 Rome had excluded the Ferentines from the new citizen colonies (L. xxxiv. 42. 5), but that may have been as a result of allied requests.

[3] Salmon, loc. cit. The last suggestion is based on T. Frank's view (*CAH*, viii. 356) that as Latins had succeeded in settling in Rome in the decade after the alien act of 187 (as is proved by the request of their cities in 177 that they should again be sent home), Cato must have favoured their settling in Rome. But it is hazardous to suppose that Cato's influence was so paramount and that this slacker policy represents his views alone.

and Roman colonies were sent instead.[1] Or the dominating motive may have been strategic: the decision whether Aquileia should be Latin or Roman 'turned upon the degree of military action which might be necessary'.[2] If the military need was paramount, Roman colonies with small allotments would be established, although the number of settlers now greatly exceeded the traditional 300; where there was expectation of greater economic or commercial development Latin colonies with larger allotments were established, but if these proved inadequate for defensive purposes, their numbers would be increased (e.g. in 169 an additional 1,500 families were sent to Aquileia). Thus the citizen colony was gradually assimilated to the Latin; its size and distance from Rome encouraged interest in municipal affairs, and the suggestion that the duovirate or dual *praetura*, on the model of the Latin colonies, was first introduced into Roman colonies at this time is attractive.[3] With the subsequent decline of military need all colonization practically ceased until the time of the Gracchi.

The Scipionic group made a surprising recovery at the elections for 182, partly perhaps through a revulsion of feeling when news came of the death of Africanus at Liternum; many of his old supporters, shocked at the realization that he had been hounded into virtual exile and death by Cato, may have recorded their votes in favour of families which could claim to have been his allies. Another cause may be found in the record of the Claudian-Fabian consuls of 183. Fabius Labeo had achieved little in Liguria, while the desire of Claudius for an Istrian campaign outran senatorial policy. He was recalled to hold the elections, perhaps because the Senate thought that he would be safer in Rome than left to his own devices in the north. However that may be, two supporters of the Scipionic group, L. Aemilius Paullus, the brother-in-law of Africanus, and Cn. Baebius Tamphilus, gained the consulship for 182, while the middle group obtained four praetorships.[4] The new consuls were the two senior men among the unsuccessful candidates for 184 and both had waited long after holding praetorships, Aemilius in 191 and Baebius as far back as 199; Livy[5] implicitly comments on this long interval by remarking that Aemilius Paullus had been curule aedile with Aemilius Lepidus (in 193), who reached the consulship five years before Paullus. Baebius must have owed his election to Aemilius and the old Scipionic group: a *novus homo*,[6] he had been defeated by the Insubres when praetor in 199,

[1] Salmon, *JRS*, 1936, 66.
[2] A. H. McDonald, *CHJ*, 1939, 128.
[3] A. N. Sherwin-White, *Roman Citizenship*, 81.
[4] Q. Fulvius Flaccus, M. Valerius Laevinus, P. Manlius II, and M. Ogulnius Gallus.
[5] L. xxxix. 56. 4.
[6] It is uncertain whether his father Q. Baebius had been praetor; he may well have been since he was one of the commissioners sent to Saguntum and Carthage at the out-

and then passed over for the next sixteen years. With such a record, his success presupposes powerful backing. The Fabii and Claudii, however, managed to prolong the commands of the consuls of 183 on the northern frontier, where neither they nor the consuls of 182 achieved anything memorable. In Spain their representatives Q. Fulvius Flaccus and P. Manlius won no striking success, though Fulvius prepared the way for an attack on Celtiberia.[1]

After an uneventful year the electoral arrangements for 181 were remarkable. In view of the threat of the Transalpine Gauls, the consuls agreed that Aemilius should remain in the north, while Cn. Baebius should hold the elections 'quia M. Baebius frater eius consulatum petebat'.[2] Here was family politics indeed, open and unashamed! Three years before, a scandal had been caused when the patrician consul Claudius, while in office, had canvassed for his own brother, with his colleague and friend Sempronius conducting the elections. Now a plebeian consul from a comparatively obscure family openly conducted the elections when his brother was a candidate. M. Baebius Tamphilus and P. Cornelius Cethegus were elected, and another proof was given of the co-operation of the Aemilii, Cornelii, and Baebii.[3] The middle group, however, gained at least three praetorships (Q. Fabius Maximus,[4] Q. Fabius Buteo,[5] and Ti. Claudius Nero).

Some military successes were gained this year. Some disaffection was stamped out in Corsica and checked in Sardinia; in Liguria Aemilius Paullus at last decisively defeated the Ingauni, while in Spain Fulvius Flaccus overran Celtiberia Citerior. Eastern affairs, though quiet, caused some anxiety. At home the year was marked by the well-earned triumph of Aemilius Paullus, by plague and drought, by further Bacchanalian trouble in Apulia, and by an attempt to check the spread of Pythagorean and Orphic beliefs. Forged writings, discovered in the tomb of Numa, were declared by the *praetor urbanus*, Q. Petillius, to be subversive of the national religion and with senatorial approval the books were publicly burned. Here surely may be

break of the Hannibalic War (L. xxi. 6. 8; 18. 1); there is no record that the *gens* had been ennobled through the consulship (cf. above, p. 42 n. 4).

[1] L. xl. 16. 4–11 (Liguria and Spain). A. Terentius, Fulvius' predecessor, received an ovation. Many diplomatic deputations were received (ibid. 2. 6–8) and a commission was sent to north Africa (ibid. 17. 1–6).   [2] Ibid. 17. 8.

[3] Livy (xl. 18. 1) wrongly names the consul P. Cornelius Lentulus.

[4] Probably a grandson of the Cunctator, whose son Quintus had died before him between 207 and 203. Quintus had a son, also Q. Fabius Maximus, who was elected augur in 203, but died in 196 before holding any magistracy. The Q. Fabius elected praetor for 181, however, cannot have been the brother of the young augur (because of the same *praenomen*), but will have been a grandson of Cunctator by a son other than the Quintus mentioned above.

[5] Probably the son of either M. Fabius Buteo (*pr.* 201) or Q. Fabius Buteo (*pr.* 196); these two men were either brothers or cousins and were probably grandsons of M. Fabius Buteo, the censor of 241.

seen the hand of Cato, the foe of foreign cults: the fact that the ground where the writings were 'discovered' belonged to a L. Petillius and that the inquiry was conducted by Q. Petillius, Cato's agent in his attack on the Scipios, suggests that Cato staged the episode as a demonstration against foreign cults.[1]

III. *Domestic and Foreign Policy*

The political influence of Cato at this time is difficult to assess. As a *novus homo* he was less caught up in that network of political obligation and intermarriage which bound together in groups the leading noble families. His noble patron and colleague, Valerius Flaccus, had pulled the strings for him in the past, but Flaccus died about this time and Cato himself was a senior statesman. Though no doubt he exerted his influence to help into office men whose political and moral views he approved, yet he hardly stood at the head of a group in quite the same way as a Fabius or Scipio had in the past or as the Fulvii were now seeking to do; he probably made his influence felt less by direct political wire-pulling than by the *auctoritas* with which his life and censorship had invested him. Less of a party leader than the average Roman noble, he was able to display his natural independence of spirit in Senate House and law court. His attitude to many problems of the day unfortunately is unknown, but an echo of his voice occasionally survives to reveal his views on some of the legislation of these years.

A tribunician *lex Orchia* of 182, which limited the number of guests that might be entertained at a single party, would receive Cato's full approval and may even have been his handiwork; soon afterwards he opposed an attempt to abrogate it.[2] Nor will he have been silent in the debate in 182 when the Senate, appalled that the cost of the Games given by Sempronius Gracchus as aedile should have burdened the Italian allies and provincials, passed a resolution, which was renewed in 179, to limit such expenditure.[3] Then in 181 the consuls Baebius and Cornelius carried a *lex de ambitu*, which apparently established the death penalty for electoral corruption.[4] This measure was probably a *lex satura* and also enacted that in alternate years there

---

[1] L. xl. 19. 6–7; 34. 12–13 (Corsica and Sardinia); 25–8 (Liguria); 30–3 (Spain); 20. 1–4 (deputations); 20. 5–24 (Macedonian affairs); 34. 7–9 (Aemilius' triumph); 19. 3–8 (plague); 29. 2 (drought); 19. 9–10 (Bacchanalia); 29. 3–14 (books of Numa); 34. 2–3 (settlement of Aquileia); 29. 1–2 (colony at Graviscae).

[2] On this speech see p. 265.   [3] L. xl. 44. 11–12. Cf. above, p. 25.

[4] L. xl. 19. 11: 'leges (? legem) de ambitu consules ex auctoritate senatus ad populum tulerunt.' The reading 'leges' of the codex Moguntinus should be retained, if the law is considered to form part of the *lex Baebia de praetoribus*. It is easier to suppose that 'leges' was corrupted into 'legem' than vice versa. On the penalty see P. vi. 56. 4. Nothing else is known about this law, since the *lex Cornelia de ambitu* recorded by Schol. Bob. p. 361 Or. (*ad* Cic. *Pro Sulla*, 17), probably refers to a measure of Sulla.

should be four instead of six praetors.[1] This would allow praetors in Spain a two years' command and obviate the waste of time caused by the long journeys thither, but by decreasing the number of praetorships it restricted the number of men who could hope for the consulship. This would not please the nobility as a whole, since the younger men would dislike any attempt to limit their prospects, and in fact this part of the law was soon abolished.[2] Cato apparently commended the bill to the People in a speech *De ambitu*, and later, when that part of the bill which dealt with the praetorship was threatened with repeal, he again rallied, though unsuccessfully, to its support.[3]

More important was the *lex Villia annalis*, carried in 180 by a tribune, L. Villius, who thereby gained the *cognomen* Annalis. It fixed the minimum age at which men could become candidates for or hold magistracies, and it may also have prescribed a two-year interval between offices and the order in which they must be held (i.e. quaestorship, curule aedileship, praetorship, and consulship; the aedileship, though popular, was not essential, nor could it be made so, since there were only two curule aediles and six praetors). As ten years' military service, which from 212 B.C. commenced at the age of 17, was a necessary qualification for political office, no one could reach the consulship before the age of 37 (or 34, if he omitted the aedileship).[4] This fixing

---

[1] This is more probable than the assumption that a separate *lex Baebia de praetoribus* was carried. L. xl. 44. 2: 'praetores quattuor post multos annos lege Baebia creati, quae alternis quaternos iubebat creari'. This does not mean that in 180 for the first time four praetors were elected in accordance with a Baebian law which had been carried years before (by the praetor M. Baebius Tamphilus in 192), but that four praetors were elected many years after the normal number of six had been established in 198. Mommsen (*Staatsr.* ii. 198) suspected that this was the same law as the *lex de ambitu*, and Fraccaro (*Stud. Stor.* 1910, 245) seems to have proved it, despite the view of Klebs (*PW*, ii. 2728). The number of praetors was not reduced until 179, but this does not prove that the law was not carried until 180: it could have been passed in 181 after the six praetors had already been elected for 180.

[2] The praetors were limited to four in 179 and 177 but not thereafter, so that the law must have been cancelled in 176, when the praetor P. Licinius Crassus declined an overseas province because of his religious duties and the People were thus made to realize that a greater number of praetors was necessary. See Münzer, *RA*, 198 n. 1. Fraccaro (op. cit. 243) and Malcovati (*ORF*, 54–5) think that it was abrogated in 179/8 because there were again six praetors elected for 177 (L. xli. 8), but two of their names (Cn. Cornelius Scipio and C. Valerius Laevinus) appear among the praetors of 179 and so must have been interpoated in the list of 177, when there will have been only four. Cf. p. 187 n. 2. A. Afzelius (*Class. et Med.* 1945, 198) suggests that the primary object of the measure was to limit the increase in the number of praetorian families. But against this is the fact that Cato supported it: he would hardly approve a proposal which would work in favour of the more exclusive consular families and would make it harder for outsiders like himself to gain high office—unless the *nobilis* in him was trying to forget the *novus homo*.

[3] *Ne lex Baebia derogaretur dissuasio* (probably delivered *in contione*). The use of *derogare*, which means to abolish part of a law (Ulpian, *Lib. regul.* 3) supports the view that the lex Baebia was a double measure. See p. 266.

[4] 'Eo anno rogatio primum lata est ab L. Villio tribuno plebis, quot annos nati quemque magistratum peterent caperentque' (L. xl. 44. 1). See Mommsen, *Staatsr.* i. 527; De Sanctis, IV. i. 509–11. A. Afzelius (*Class. et Med.* 1946, 263 ff.) has argued against

of minimum age-limits for office would check the speedy advance of ambitious young nobles and preclude the repetition of such scandals as when 'superior Africanus et T. Flamininus admodum adulescentes consules facti'.[1] In so far as the measure protected the Senate against the risk of magisterial dictatorship by subordinating the individual to the class and by consolidating the ranks of the oligarchy, it would receive senatorial approval. But it would also enable *novi homines* to climb higher up the ladder of office by preventing ambitious nobles from seizing all the plums while they were yet young.

It is noteworthy that these measures to curb electoral corruption and limit the number and influence of the magistrates were carried during three years in which the plebeian consuls were *novi homines*, at least in the general sense of the term, and during the *lustrum* of the greatest *novus homo* of all before Marius.[2] Their purpose in part will have been to check the political influence of the noble families and to open the highest offices to a wider circle of citizens. Further, they were enacted at a time when the old Scipionic group, which had displayed a liberal attitude in helping 'new men' to office, was enjoying a slight resurgence of influence, and they will have been welcomed by the Fulvii, who after securing the highest offices for themselves then tried to put forward, as will be seen, other lesser families like the Mucii and Hostilii.

While the Scipios and the middle group had been struggling for the chief magistracies in the years 189–186, policy towards Philip and the Achaeans had been restrained despite considerable provocation. This was primarily due, no doubt, to the overriding needs of the Syrian war and settlement, but after 185 a noticeable hardening of attitude took place and in this factional interests may have had some part. Philip, who had been irritated by Rome's less generous policy after the recall of the Scipios in 189 (p. 140), made matters worse by occupying the two cities of Maronea and Aeneus (187 or 186), but the fact that the Senate in 185 sent out two supporters of Scipio (Caecilius Metellus and Baebius Tamphilus) to investigate suggests that Scipio may have made a final attempt to revert to a more generous

---

Mommsen's view that a biennium was prescribed by this law, although he admits that such an interval was customary; he believes that the age-limits for each office were specifically stated in the law, based on the ten years' military service which was prescribed as a legal qualification for the quaestorship. Cicero (*De orat.* ii. 261) refers to another *lex annalis*: 'ut olim Rusca cum ferret legem annalem, dissuasor M. Servilius: "dic mihi," inquit, "Pinari, num …".' A certain M. Pinarius Rusca was praetor in 181 and may have proposed such a measure in this year, or earlier if he had ever been a tribune (it is not known whether this branch of the Pinarii was plebeian). If so, he failed to carry the measure because Livy expressly states that Villius' law was the first passed (*primum lata*). Alternatively the Pinarius might be a son or descendant of the praetor of 181; cf. Mommsen, *Staatsr.* i. 511 n. 1 (*Dr. publ.* ii. 183 n. 2).

[1] Cic. *Phil.* v. 47.　　　　　　　　　　　　　　[2] Cf. Münzer, *RA*, 198.

policy during the period between his decline and fall. This conciliatory attempt, however, was unfortunately thwarted by the king's stubbornness.[1] The Senate therefore decided to favour the Greeks at Philip's expense and in 184 sent out another commission under Ap. Claudius Pulcher (*cos.* 185), who had served in 195 and 191 under Flamininus, the champion of Greek independence against Philip's aggression. Relations steadily deteriorated: Philip was further antagonized by the arrival of another commission under Q. Marcius Philippus in 183 and he began to suspect that Flamininus was trying to undermine the loyalty of his son Demetrius who had spent some time in Rome as a token of his father's good faith. Amid increasing Roman suspicions of his attempts to strengthen his kingdom and increasing domestic anguish at the quarrels of his sons, Philip finally died in 179. His son Perseus, who had been responsible for his brother's death, succeeded to the throne and received the 'friendship' of Rome.

Rome's alliance with Achaea, no less than that with Philip, involved her unwillingly in the internal quarrels of Greece. When fighting broke out between Sparta and Achaea (188), the Senate refused to become entangled even at the price of having to swallow some insults. In 185, after his conference with Philip, Metellus visited the Peloponnese, presumably with conciliatory intention, but his diplomacy failed and he received a personal affront from the Achaean League. His failure will have strengthened the policy and grip of the rival middle group, who defeated three Scipionic consular candidates for 184 and decided upon a stiffer policy against Achaea as against Philip; Appius Claudius was therefore sent to threaten the Achaeans. In the following year (183) T. Flamininus, Caecilius Metellus, and Appius Claudius, three experts on Peloponnesian affairs (there can be no question of party differences here), were sent out to draft a settlement. But when it appeared that trouble with Philip was less likely to develop (Marcius Philippus had enforced the evacuation of Maronea without provoking Philip to open hostility), the Senate reverted to its earlier attitude of barking rather than biting, and the Achaeans were permitted to disregard part of the triumviral settlement with impunity. They even insulted Flamininus later: he broke a journey to Bithynia at Naupactus and summoned the Achaean Assembly, but the magistrates refused to convene a meeting and the Liberator of Greece had to resume his journey. But soon afterwards, with the death of Philopoemen,

---

[1] F. W. Walbank (*Philip V*, 231) suggests that Philip's attitude was due to his belief that the Romans were already committed to the hostile Thessalian interpretation of his compact with Baebius in 191 and that Baebius' demeanour will have given him a clue. But Baebius' presence can be interpreted as a Roman guarantee of fair play, and Philip may have been goaded into his hasty outburst by a realization that he had wrongly anticipated from the composition of the commission that he would be favourably treated, and that the Romans were going to insist on acting as genuine arbitrators.

Achaean policy changed under the guidance of the pro-Roman Callicrates, who advised the Roman Senate to take a stronger line. Thus Callicrates succeeded in bringing the long Achaeo-Spartan imbroglio to an end, and if he subordinated his country to Rome, he at least re-established peace in the Peloponnese for thirty years. But a new era in the relations of Greece and Rome was inaugurated, according to Polybius, whereby Rome tended to support those who appealed to her authority, whether right or wrong.[1]

The sudden stiffening of Roman policy to Achaea and Philip in 185 has been attributed to Cato's political defeat of the Scipios.[2] But although the hardening of policy does coincide with the period of Cato's censorship and the subsequent slackening with his retirement from office, too little is certain about his political position in Rome or about his precise views on foreign policy to justify the assertion that he was the leader of the new policy. He probably supported, but may not have initiated, the changes; these may have had a wider basis and should be attributed to the middle group in general.

Finally, it is during this period that Flamininus made his last appearance in history. Since his censorship (189) he had played a minor role and must have been affected by his brother's expulsion from the Senate (184), but he emerged again into the limelight when his knowledge of Greek affairs was needed (183). But apart from this he cuts a very mean figure. When on a diplomatic mission to Prusias of Bithynia, either on his own initiative or acting on senatorial orders,[3] he forced Prusias to surrender Hannibal who took his life to avoid capture. Again, it was his friendship with a dissolute Messenian named Deinocrates that had led to his humiliation by the Achaeans,[4] and by playing upon the ambition and vanity of an inexperienced youth Flamininus had used Demetrius as a tool to check Philip; but in the process he undermined the father's belief in the son's loyalty and thereby he indirectly contributed to the tragedy which ended in the murder of Demetrius. It would almost seem that the middle group was using Flamininus to do their dirty work: at any rate the Saviour of the Greeks, whose votaries had sung paeans 'To Zeus and Titus and Rome's Good Faith', had set fame before honour and sullied the record of his earlier achievements. After these inglorious episodes he remains unnoticed until his death in 174.

---

[1] P. xxiv. 8–10.   [2] T. Frank, *Roman Imperialism*, 199–200.

[3] L. xxxix. 51; Plut. *Flam.* 20; Nepos, *Han.* 12; Justin, xxxii. 4. 18; Appian, *Syr.* 11; Dio Cass. frg. 64, &c. Nepos and Justin say, and Livy suggests, that Flamininus was acting for the Senate; Plutarch and Appian (? Polybius) blame Flamininus.

[4] An anecdote records that even Flamininus was disgusted with his friend's behaviour in Rome (P. xxiii. 5).

X

THE FULVIAN PREDOMINANCE

(180–175 B.C.)

1. *Fulvian Leadership*

THE next few years witnessed a great strengthening of the middle group under the leadership of the Fulvii. Although the elections for 180 were conducted by M. Baebius, he failed to secure the success of any candidates of the Scipionic group, if such there were. The new consuls were A. Postumius Albinus Luscus (*pr.* 185; probably a cousin of Sp. Postumius Albinus, the consul of 186)[1] and C. Calpurnius Piso, who was thus rewarded for his striking victory as propraetor in Spain in 185 and was the first of his family to reach the consulship.[2]

But Piso died, murdered, it was said, by his wife Quarta Hostilia. When many other distinguished men, including members of the priestly colleges, also died, suspicion of poisoning became widespread. The Senate therefore ordered two praetors, C. Claudius and C. Maenius, to conduct inquiries in and outside Rome respectively, and Maenius later reported that he had sentenced 3,000 offenders. Apparently a crime wave had swept over Italy as an aftermath of the Bacchanalian disturbances, although some of the alleged murders may have been due to the plague which was still raging. The Senate may have conducted an ostentatious inquiry in order to allay panic by attributing to criminal activity, which could be checked, that which was due to less controllable Nature, but in any case pestilence and crime probably walked hand in hand.[3] Hostilia may be given the benefit of the doubt and Piso's death be attributed to the plague, but suspicions increased when her son Q. Fulvius Flaccus was declared *consul suffectus* in place

---

[1] The *cognomen* Luscus is given by Livy (xl. 35. 1; xlv. 17. 2), but not in the Capitoline Fasti. Münzer (*RA*, 213 n. 1) believes that it is supported by a corrupt passage of Festus (p. 360 L.) where he would read 'morbum ocularem'.

[2] Three praetors of 180, Ti. Sempronius Gracchus (Scipio's rescuer, but probably a middle-group man), L. Postumius Albinus (probably brother of the new consul), and A. Hostilius Mancinus (perhaps a nephew of the other consul, Piso), may be reckoned supporters of the Fulvii, who gained a fourth praetor when C. Claudius Pulcher replaced Ti. Minucius Molliculus who died. A. Hostilius Mancinus L. f. was probably the son of L. Hostilius Mancinus who served under Fabius in 217 (L. xxii. 15). C. Calpurnius Piso married a Hostilia (widow of Cn. Fulvius Flaccus, *pr.* 212) who might belong to the Hostilii Mancini and have been the sister of L. Hostilius. If she was, the praetor of 180 will have been her nephew and have probably owed his election partly to her influence, which soon afterwards was used to help her son to the consulship.

[3] For a possible connexion of a speech by Cato with this episode see p. 265.

of his stepfather; she is even rumoured to have said, after Albinus and Piso had been elected, that she was preparing to canvass for Fulvius and would secure his election within two months.

The new *consul suffectus* was son of Cn. Fulvius Flaccus (*pr.* 212) and cousin of his namesake Q. Fulvius Flaccus (Q. f.) who was campaigning in Celtiberia. After his praetorship in 187 he had been defeated three times in the consular elections (probably in 183, 182, and 181) and though a member of an old plebeian family he had been beaten by three men who were the first of their name to reach the consulship, Cn. and M. Baebius and his own stepfather Calpurnius Piso. Of these the two Baebii had held the praetorship long before him (199 and 192), Piso a year after him (186). Since a successful attempt to gain the consulship after three failures was unusual,[1] Fulvius' mother probably believed that her son had little further hope, when the opportune death of Piso gave her a chance to push Quintus forward in one final attempt.[2] The political influence of Roman matrons was obviously considerable, although unfortunately their activity is seldom recorded. Fulvius managed to maintain the influence of his family despite the scandal that hung over his mother and despite further trouble on account of a relative, M. Fulvius (probably his cousin), who as military tribune tried to disband a legion on his own responsibility; A. Postumius took prompt action to counter this folly and reported the matter to the Senate which relegated Marcus to Further Spain.[3]

Roman arms met with success in 180. In Spain, Q. Fulvius Flaccus Q. f. snatched a victory over the Celtiberians before being called off by his successor Ti. Sempronius Gracchus,[4] who in turn by a successful battle and tactful diplomacy terminated the first Celtiberian War and gave Spain comparative peace for twenty-five years. In Liguria also peace was brought nearer.[5]

[1] Of the seven candidates who stood for the consulship in 185 five obtained it within three years (Claudius Pulcher and Porcius Licinus in 184, Fabius Labeo in 183, Aemilius Paullus and Cn. Baebius in 182), while the other two (Sulpicius Galba and Terentius Culleo, praetors 187) either abandoned the attempt or continued to fail.

[2] L. xl. 37. 6. Cf. Münzer, *RA*, 196–7.

[3] L. xl. 41. 7–11. Livy names him M. Fulvius Nobilior, a brother of Q. Fulvius who was, however, a Flaccus. The problem is complicated. Münzer (*PW*, s.v. Fulvius n. 57) is probably right in supposing that Livy has mistaken Nobilior for Flaccus; the military tribune will then have been M. Fulvius Flaccus, a brother of Q. Fulvius Flaccus (*cos.* 179) and a cousin of Q. Fulvius Flaccus (*cos. suff.* 180).

[4] See further, p. 265.

[5] After the victory of Aemilius Paullus over the Ingauni (181), the Apuani were reduced by the proconsuls Cornelius Cethegus and M. Baebius and by the consuls Postumius and Fulvius Flaccus; many were deported to Samnium. Livy hesitates about assigning the credit. First he attributes it to Cornelius and Baebius who were granted a triumph for their decisive victory, but he then says that they were the first men to enjoy a triumph without having waged a war, implying that the effective work had been done by their predecessor Aemilius. Finally he assigns a successful campaign against the Apuani to

These successes served the Fulvian cause in the elections for 179, which were perhaps conducted by Q. Fulvius Flaccus Cn. f., since his operational base in Liguria was nearer to Rome than that of his colleague Postumius.[1] Q. Fulvius Flaccus Q. f., while waiting outside the city for a triumph, was elected consul. His colleague was L. Manlius Acidinus, who had been praetor in 188 in Hispania Citerior where he had remained until a victory in 186 for which he had received an ovation; thereafter he had served on an embassy to the Gauls and as commissioner for Aquileia (183–181). Livy, who baldly records the election of Fulvius and Manlius, fails to mention that they were brothers: *hei fratres germani fuerunt* (Fast. Cap.). They were in fact sons of Q. Fulvius Flaccus, the victor of Capua, but Lucius had been adopted by L. Manlius Acidinus (*pr.* 210; he had administered Spain with proconsular authority from 206 until 199 but had failed to gain the consulship); this is the first recorded case of a plebeian being adopted by a patrician family.[2] Thus both consuls were of plebeian birth, although two plebeian consuls did not hold office together until 172. Their election was also noteworthy because while Manlius had been praetor as far back as 188, Fulvius had been praetor in 182 and only returned to Rome in 180 when he stood for office at the very first opportunity sanctioned by custom and perhaps specified in the new lex Annalis. Thus two Fulvian brothers gained the consulship, probably under the presidency of their cousin, while three of the four praetorships (reduced by the lex Baebia to four this year) were won by members of friendly families, C. Valerius Laevinus and Q. and P. Mucius Scaevola.[3]

The Fulvii gained further influence in the priesthoods,[4] while the

Postumius and Flaccus (L. xl. 37. 8–38. 9; 41. 1–6). His confusion derives from his use of two annalistic sources (? Valerius and Claudius). As the deported Apuani were known later as Ligures Baebiani et Corneliani (Pliny, *NH*, iii. 105) the consuls of 181 probably were the main conquerors; the claim that their triumph was undeserved will have come from the propaganda of their Fulvian successors whom they robbed of the chance of outstanding military victory. To watch over Liguria a Latin colony was founded at Luca; the commissioners were Q. Fabius Buteo (propraetor, who had been dealing with an Istrian attack on Aquileia) and M. and P. Popillius Laenas, members of a family which was soon to make its weight felt (L. xl. 43. 1).

[1] Cf. Münzer, *RA*, 199.   [2] L. xl. 43. 4; Velleius, ii. 8. 2.

[3] The fourth, Cn. Cornelius Scipio Hispallus, was a brother of Nasica (*cos.* 191) and a cousin of Africanus. An anecdote (Cic. *De orat.* ii. 260) records the displeasure of the Scipionic group at Manlius' election to the consulship.

[4] Q. Fulvius Flaccus Q. f. was co-opted as a pontiff, and a certain Q. Fulvius M. f. (possibly his nephew) became a member of the college of Epulones in place of P. Manlius who died soon after his return from Spain. Q. Fulvius M. f. cannot be certainly identified. He was too young (L. xl. 42. 7) to be Q. Fulvius M. f. Nobilior (colonial commissioner for Potentia in 184, later consul in 153, and the younger son of the consul of 189). He might be the son of the somewhat mysterious M. Fulvius (Flaccus), military tribune in 180 and brother of the two consuls of 179, whose nephew he will then have been.

Fabius Labeo (*cos.* 183) became a pontiff in place of Valerius Flaccus, Cato's patron, another victim of the plague. Trouble arose in filling the vacancy caused by the death of

election of a new Pontifex Maximus to succeed C. Servilius Geminus led to a far-reaching political intrigue and to the re-orientation of some family loyalties. The facts, as recorded by Livy, are briefly that Aemilius Lepidus (*cos.* 187) was elected Pontifex Maximus, that he and his old enemy M. Fulvius Nobilior were elected censors for 179, that the two censors were reconciled, and finally that Lepidus was named *princeps senatus*. But a suggestion that the reconciliation took place before, not after, the two enemies had become censors explains much that is otherwise obscure.[1] Lepidus, who wanted to become both Pontifex Maximus and censor, was faced with a problem: among the pontiffs he had considerable influence, but the censorial elections would be conducted by a Fulvius and the influence of the Fulvii in the Comitia would be strong, since they had one consul and two consuls-elect at the end of 180. Lepidus therefore reached an understanding with them on their terms, namely, that he should become Pontifex Maximus and at the same time help to get one of them co-opted as a pontiff, to wit, the consul-elect (Q. Fulvius Flaccus Q. f.), and that then they would co-operate in Lepidus' election as censor together with one of themselves (Nobilior). After the censors had entered office a public reconciliation could be staged and the alliance be further strengthened owing to the death of the *princeps senatus*, Valerius Flaccus; as this position was the preserve of the patrician *gentes maiores*, the plebeian Fulvii could support Lepidus' claim without any loss to themselves.

This scheme was put into operation. The election of a Pontifex Maximus was made by 17 tribes (chosen by lot from the 35) under the presidency of the youngest pontiff, i.e. the one who had the least chance of being elected, in this case Q. Fabius Labeo;[2] the consuls,

the *rex sacrificulus*, Cn. Cornelius Dolabella (priest since 208 and thereby debarred from a political career). The Pontifex Maximus, C. Servilius Geminus, ordered L. Cornelius Dolabella to resign his post of *duumvir navalis* in order to be inaugurated as *rex*, but Lucius refused. Servilius imposed a fine, but when the matter was being discussed by the Assembly on appeal, a thunderstorm interrupted proceedings and the pontiffs were prevented from appointing him; in his stead they inaugurated a certain P. Cloelius Siculus. Dolabella apparently had good friends among the augurs, who welcomed the storm as an excuse to break up the Assembly; he preferred a life on the ocean wave (he was operating off Ancona in 178) to the restrictions imposed upon the *rex sacrorum*. The augurs co-opted P. Scipio, the eldest son of Africanus whom ill-health kept from an active political life, to replace Sp. Postumius Albinus (*cos.* 186). The augural college will now have comprised the patricians L. Quinctius Flamininus (*cos.* 192; augur since 213), L. Aemilius Paullus (*cos.* 182; aug. 193/1), C. Claudius Pulcher (*cos.* 177; aug. 195), and P. Scipio, and the plebeians P. Aelius Paetus (censor 199), M. Servilus Geminus (*cos.* 202; aug. 211), Ti. Sempronius Longus (*cos.* 194; aug. 210), and probably Ti. Sempronius Gracchus (*cos.*177).

[1] See Münzer, *RA*, 200 ff.

[2] At the end of 180, after the death of C. Servilius Geminus, the college consisted of the patricians Cn. Servilius Caepio (*cos.* 203; pontiff 213), Aemilius Lepidus (*cos.* 187; pont. 199), Cn. Cornelius Scipio Hispallus (*cos.* 176; pont. 199), and Q. Fabius Labeo (*cos.* 183; pont. 180), and the plebeians Q. Caecilius Metellus (dictator 205; pont. 216),

who had something to do with arranging the elections, never presided.[1]
According to Livy[2] Lepidus had to face 'multi clari viri' as rival
candidates, but in fact there were only two: Caecilius Metellus, the
oldest member of the whole college and of the plebeian half, and
Cn. Servilius Caepio, the senior member of the patrician half and
kinsman of the deceased Pontifex Maximus. Of the rest Scipio Hispallus had been a pontiff as long as Lepidus but had not yet reached
the consulship, while M. Claudius Marcellus, though censor in 189,
was Lepidus' junior as a pontiff: neither perhaps would have much
chance. Caepio was the most dangerous of Lepidus' competitors, since
Metellus, whose prospects were weaker, perhaps threw in his hand
and co-operated with Lepidus in line with the support which his
family in the past had given to the Aemilii: at any rate he later played
the role of peace-maker between Lepidus and Nobilior in their public
reconciliation. Against his chief rival, Caepio, Lepidus therefore rallied
the support of his own family and the Fulvian group and thus won
the office for himself.

Lepidus and the Fulvii co-operated again in the election of the
censors. The majority of the seven candidates defeated by Cato and
Valerius in 184 were still living, but only one, Fulvius Nobilior, was
now successful. All four of the unsuccessful patrician candidates of
184 (Scipio Asiaticus, Scipio Nasica, Manlius Vulso, and Furius Purpureo) may have been alive, although only Nasica's survival is attested,
but presumably the two Scipios and Furius would have little chance
of election in 179. Perhaps none of them stood again, so that Lepidus
would have no rivals of superior status. The three unsuccessful plebeian candidates of 184, Fulvius Nobilior, Sempronius Longus, and
Sempronius Tuditanus, all survived. If the two Sempronii stood
against Nobilior in 179, the struggle for the plebeian place may have
been keener than for the patrician, but the association of Longus with
Africanus would not improve his chances, while the Claudii-Fulvii
may have been able to persuade Tuditanus to stand down for Nobilior.
Lepidus and Nobilior therefore could go to the poll with few, if any,
rivals of equal status, knowing that their candidature was backed by
the influence of both their families and that the elections were conducted by a friendly consul. Further, the People were humoured by
Q. Fulvius Flaccus, who, after celebrating his triumph, exhibited for
ten days magnificent Games which he had vowed in Spain.[3] All went

---

M. Claudius Marcellus (cens. 189; pont. 196), C. Livius Salinator (*cos.* 188), and M. Sempronius Tuditanus (*cos.* 185; pont. 183).   [1] Cic. *Ad Brut.* 1. 5. 4.

[2] xl. 42. 12.

[3] The building of a temple to Fortuna Equestris, which Flaccus had also vowed in
return for the splendid work done by his cavalry against the Celtiberians, was commenced.
He had 'collected' money from the Spaniards for this purpose, but the Senate limited
the amount that he was to spend.

well, and the Fulvii, a plebeian family from Tusculum, now reached
the height of their power; two brothers were consuls, another Fulvius
was censor, and they had the support of Lepidus, censor, *princeps
senatus*, and Pontifex Maximus.

11. *The Censorship of 179 B.C.*

The censorship of Lepidus and Nobilior in 179 was considerably
milder than that of Cato: only three members were ejected from the
Senate. Although 'censores fideli concordia senatum legerunt', their
reconciliation did not produce complete identity of views, since Lepidus was more lenient than his colleague: he retained on the senatorial
roll some names, unfortunately not recorded, which Nobilior had
omitted. The censors' building activities were considerable, but more
moderate than those of their predecessors.[1] Towards the Latins they
must have been lenient, because two years later there was a renewed
demand that those who had settled in Rome since 187 should be
returned to their native cities.[2] Their most important work was a
reform of the Comitia Centuriata of which the details must remain
obscure. 'They changed the arrangement for voting and drew up the
tribal lists by districts according to the birth, conditions, and callings
of the men.'[3] Presumably 'birth' refers chiefly to the possession or
absence of free birth, 'condition' applies to the possession or absence
of children, which would qualify a freedman father for enrolment in
a rural tribe, and 'calling' means in effect a man's financial position
(his *census* status), which would depend mainly on his occupation and
property.

Two main groups of people seem to have been affected: the middle-
class and freedmen. It has been supposed that by this measure free-
born citizens, according to their status, might be enrolled in rural
tribes even if they did not hold property in the tribal district to which
they were assigned.[4] This would represent an attempt to extend over
a wider area the voting power of some of those who had previously
been confined to the four urban tribes and to give greater political
influence to the increasing number of business men who swelled the
ranks of the middle-class in the city. The men who were thus transferred to the rural tribes would tend to swamp, or at any rate modify,
the votes of the small country farmers enrolled in the same tribes,

---

[1] L. xl. 51.   [2] This was enforced by a lex Claudia of 177.
[3] L. xl. 51. 9: 'mutarunt suffragia regionatimque generibus hominum causisque et
quaestibus tribus descripserunt.' Unfortunately no other source throws any light on this
obscure sentence. See De Sanctis, IV. i. 606; McDonald, *CHJ*, 1939, 134. The attempt
by F. Smith (*Die römische Timokratie*) to prove that the five classes were first established
by the censors of 179 has not met with much support. L. xl. 51. 9, on which it is based,
makes no mention of classes. Cf. Botsford, *Roman Assemblies*, 85 n. 3.
[4] De Sanctis, IV. i. 606.

who would seldom have the leisure to come in large numbers to the city to record their votes. Thus, while the tribal system became still less territorial in basis and less representative of local or sectional interests, the middle-class in the city received greater political influence at the expense of the farmers. The measure would thus represent a move by the middle party in the State, headed by Lepidus and Nobilior and directed both against the old nobility who relied upon the votes of the rural classes outside Rome and their poorer clients in the city, and perhaps against Cato so far as he was the champion of country interests.

The second group of people affected by the new procedure were freedmen, whose political importance needs no emphasis: they adopted their patron's gentile name and naturally would tend to follow the wishes of the family they had served. By a liberal measure carried in 189 by a supporter of Scipio Africanus, Terentius Culleo, sons of freedmen (*libertini*) had been enrolled in the rural tribes. Either by this same plebiscite, or more probably by the action of the censors of 179, freedmen themselves who possessed land valued above 30,000 sesterces (*c.* £300, i.e. those whose census was equal to that of the first or second class of the centuries) were no longer confined to the four urban tribes, but could be registered in the rural tribes. The censors granted this privilege also to all freedmen who had a son and possessed any landed property in a rural tribe.[1] By this generous measure the censors injected into the rural tribes yet another element in addition to some middle-class representatives. Their action was well conceived and timely; it would also help to win further electoral support for the group which they themselves represented. Cato will hardly have approved of this procedure in so far as it benefited the middle-class traders at the expense of the farmers: he will certainly have disapproved granting greater influence to freedmen of Greek or Eastern origin: it was bad enough to have ex-slaves in the urban tribes without exposing the thirty-one rural tribes to this alien taint.

Cato's dislike of the relative mildness of the censors and some of their specific measures found expression in a speech in which he assailed Fulvius Nobilior probably at the close of the lustration, just as he himself had been attacked after his censorship (p. 164). The nominal object of the criticism, which may have first been voiced by a tribune, will have been one of Fulvius' administrative acts, probably in connexion with the *regimen aquarum*.[2] Cato then reinforced the charge with a general attack on the censorship and Fulvius' whole career which in Cato's eyes had helped to corrupt the stern simplicity of the *mos maiorum*. He may have punned on Nobilior's name, calling

---

[1] L. xlv. 15, 1–2. Cf. De Sanctis, IV. i. 557–8; McDonald, *CHJ*, 1939, 134, 138.
[2] Cf. frg. 153 M. See p. 266.

him Mobilior,[1] and criticized the fact that he had awarded military decorations (*coronae*) to men merely for making ramparts or digging wells, and that he had taken Ennius to Aetolia, presumably in order that the warrior might not lack a bard to record his Aristeia. In his dislike of self-advertisement by soldiers, Cato forgot his own account of his exploits at Thermopylae. The medicine was particularly bitter, since he himself had brought Ennius to Rome, only to see him attracted by the hellenizing Scipios and Fulvii. No doubt Cato also criticized Fulvius' removal of statues and pictures from Ambracia to Rome.[2] If the attack took the form of a trial, the result is not known. Hereafter Fulvius disappears from history; he perhaps died soon.

III. *Fulvian Relations with other Families*

The Fulvii, now at the height of their influence in alliance with the Aemilii, had little difficulty in getting friendly consuls elected for 178. The consul Q. Fulvius Flaccus Q. f., who had already triumphed over the Celtiberians in 180, was granted a second triumph in 179 over the Ligurians, more because of his political influence than his achievements.[3] He then fixed the date of, and presumably conducted, the consular elections, at which A. Manlius Vulso and M. Iunius Brutus were returned. The latter, who was the first Iunius to reach the consulship for half a century and the first Brutus for a whole century, had lived obscurely since his praetorship twelve years before: his success clearly owed much to his friends. As the Iunii had been linked with the Aemilii, M. Iunius presumably was brought into the Fulvian fold by the censor Aemilius Lepidus with whom he had held the praetorship in 191. The success of Manlius Vulso merely emphasized the link between the Manlii and Fulvii: not only had the Manlii Acidini saved their house from extinction by adopting a plebeian Fulvius (*cos.* 179), but Cn. Manlius Vulso had owed his consulship in 189 to Fulvius Nobilior (p. 135). A. Manlius Vulso, the brother of Gnaeus, had served on a colonial commission in 193 and had probably been *praetor suffectus* in 189 during the consulship of his brother and Fulvius Nobilior; for the next ten years he remained in the background, like Iunius Brutus, but at length reached the consulship when the Fulvii were strong enough to help him.[4]

[1] Cic. *De orat.* ii. 63. 256. Alternatively this jest might refer to Fulvius' son Quintus (*cos.* 153) whom Cato attacked in the Senate (Livy, *Per.* xlix).

[2] L. xxxviii. 9. 13. [3] L. xl. 59. 1.

[4] On these elections cf. Münzer, *RA*, 203, who refers to another link between the Fulvii and Manlii in the person of a certain P. Manlius. He was probably a plebeian and became one of the first *triumviri epulones*, when this priesthood was instituted in 196. He was praetor with a fellow-priest, P. Porcius Laeca, and his kinsman Cn. Manlius Vulso in 195 when Porcius Cato was consul. His successor as priest in 180 was a certain Q. Fulvius (see p. 179 n. 4). For the praetors of 178, some of whom may have been Fulvian nominees, see pp. 283 f.

As neither of the two Fulvian brothers, Q. Flaccus and L. Manlius, nor their cousin Q. Flaccus, could hold another consulship for at least ten years, while the censorship of Fulvius Nobilior was the coping-stone of his career, the Fulvii sought to prolong their influence by helping friends to office. Their success is shown by the fact that the consulship was obtained by relatively few of the men who had held the praetorship immediately before the peak-point of their political influence, while the praetors of 180 and the next few years were much more successful.[1] Of the thirty praetors of 185–181, three died early and one was precluded from a further political career by becoming a priest. The majority of the remaining twenty-six probably lived at least another decade, since praetors were men in their prime, but only five reached the consulship, although most belonged to old families; that is, although one-third could and should have been consuls, only one-fifth were successful.[2]

But the prospects of the praetors of 180 and 179 were much brighter. Four of the six praetors of 180 became consuls,[3] as did all four praetors of 179.[4] As two of the praetors of 180 were consuls in 177 and and two praetors of 179 consuls in 176, their promotion was astonishingly quick and came immediately after the customary two years' interval. The speedy advancement of P. Mucius, whose consulship in 175 ennobled the Mucii Scaevolae, and of Q. Mucius in 174 was promoted by the Fulvii. It is noteworthy that P. Mucius had as his patrician colleague Lepidus, the *princeps senatus*, who held a second consulship, and that Q. Mucius reached the consulship in the year of the censorship of Q. Fulvius Flaccus.[5] With the election of Q. Mucius, the last of the praetors of 179 had reached the consulship, so that the way was cleared for two more praetors of 180, Postumius Albinus (173) and the new man Hostilius Mancinus (170). But before this in 174 Sp. Postumius Albinus reached the consulship, being the last successful representative of those who had been praetors before 180. Thereafter many younger men who had been praetors since 179 became consuls after short intervals, and the way was blocked for the old brigade of 185–181, none of whom now had any chance, not because the *lex Villia Annalis* had upset their prospects but because

[1] This has been demonstrated by Münzer, *RA*, 204 ff.
[2] For the later careers of the praetors of 185–181 see p. 283.
[3] Ti. Sempronius Gracchus and Claudius Pulcher as soon as 177 (the latter was a surprising appointment because Claudius had only been *praetor suffectus*, and that through the influence of the consul Q. Fulvius Flaccus, himself *suffectus*), Postumius Albinus in 173, and Hostilius Mancinus in 170.
[4] Scipio Hispallus (176), Valerius Laevinus (*suffectus* 176), P. Mucius Scaevola (175), and Q. Mucius Scaevola (174).
[5] The rise of the Mucii was even more spectacular than that of the Baebii (Cn. Baebius *cos.* 182, M. Baebius 181) because they reached the consulship only four and five years after their praetorships, whereas the Baebii had waited seventeen and eleven years.

the elections were worked in the interests of a group of younger men.[1]

Thus the Fulvii strengthened their influence by alliances with old patrician *gentes*, like the Sabine Claudii Pulchri and Valerii, and with newer plebeian families, as the Mucii and Hostilii, thereby reproducing the pattern of the past since the fathers of four of these men had been praetors together in 215.[2] The coalition was consolidated by, and partly arose from, intermarriage. For instance, Q. Fulvius Flaccus (*cos. suff.* 180) was the son of a Hostilia; she in turn was probably the aunt of A. Hostilius Mancinus who gained the praetorship in 180 and the consulship ten years later (p. 177 n. 2). C. Valerius Laevinus (*pr.* 179 and *cos. suff.* 176) was related to the Fulvii, being the younger half-brother of the Aetolian conqueror, Fulvius Nobilior.[3] Their mother's name is not recorded. Her first husband, M. Fulvius Nobilior Serv. f., is unknown to history; presumably he died early and certainly did not climb higher than the praetorship. She then married M. Valerius (*cos.* 210) and bore Gaius, the future consul of 176.[4] Further links are obscure, but it is striking that in the year 179 six of the eight highest offices were held by three pairs of brothers: the two sons of Q. Fulvius Flaccus were consuls, two Mucii Scaevolae were praetors, and the two half-brothers Nobilior and Laevinus were respectively censor and praetor. As the other censor Lepidus was an ally, the fourth praetor Scipio was in a minority of one.

The main event of 178 B.C. was the Istrian campaign of the consul Manlius Vulso, who had been assigned to Gaul, but rushed into war without consulting the Senate. Some senators, however, may not have been entirely displeased, since they may have judged the war necessary without being certain whether the People would vote for it.[5] When Manlius advanced over the Timavus, the Istrians stormed one of his camps, driving the men in panic to the coast.[6] News of this set-back caused such alarm in Rome that a levy was held throughout Italy, and Manlius' colleague was sent with reinforcements, but on arrival Iunius found that Manlius, after steadying his troops, had successfully counter-attacked. Manlius' conduct was sharply criticized in Rome where two tribunes, A. Licinius Nerva and C. Papirius

[1] Cf. Münzer, *RA*, 206–7.

[2] M. Valerius Laevinus, father of Gaius (*cos.* 176), Ap. Claudius Pulcher, father of Gaius (*cos.* 177), Q. Fulvius Flaccus, father of the consuls of 179, and Q. Mucius Scaevola, father of the consuls of 175 and 174 (cf. p. 57 n. 5).   [3] L. xxxviii. 9. 8.

[4] The consul of 176 had an elder brother, M. Valerius Laevinus, who was praetor in 182 but did not obtain the consulship. Presumably these two men were full brothers, although Marcus might have been the son of a previous wife of the consul of 210.

[5] Cf. De Sanctis, IV. i. 430.

[6] Livy's account (xli. 1–5) of the campaign is interesting as one of the few, before the Gracchan age, which derives from a Latin source unspoilt by gross exaggeration or imitation of Greek rhetorical writing; it shows the Roman soldiers as men who could conquer fear, not as robot heroes. Cf. De Sanctis, IV. i. 432.

Turdus (members of families which had supported the Scipios in the past and now opposed the Claudian-Fulvian group), introduced a motion that his command, which had been prorogued, should terminate in March 177 in order that he might be court-martialled, but the measure was vetoed by another tribune, Q. Aelius. When Iunius returned to conduct the elections, the tribunes renewed their attack on Manlius, arguing that he should have come in place of Iunius in order to have justified his conduct. Cato delivered a speech *De re Histriae militari* at some point during these discussions, probably in the senatorial debate after news had come of Manlius' disaster; his object may have been to allay public panic as well as to criticize Manlius.[1]

At the consular elections for 177 Ti. Sempronius Gracchus was rewarded for his successful handling of the Celtiberian war. Already in 178 he and his colleague in Spain, L. Postumius, had been granted triumphs over the Celtiberians and Lusitanians respectively. Gracchus' fellow-consul was C. Claudius Pulcher, who won this office in the shortest legal time after his praetorship of 180; he was the third son of the consul of 212. His elder brother Publius had owed his consulship in 184 largely to the help of their eldest brother Appius (*cos.* 185) and his colleague Sempronius Tuditanus; now Gaius received Fulvian backing, while Sempronius Gracchus, who was somewhat more independent than Tuditanus of the Claudian-Fulvian group, may have worked in with them at this election.[2]

Foreign affairs in 177 centred around Istria and Sardinia. Because of serious disturbances a consul was sent to Sardinia for the first time for fifty years. The appointment of Sempronius Gracchus is interesting, because he was a descendant of the Gracchus who had first occupied the island in 238, and he may have preserved relations of patronage there.[3] The campaign, which he continued as proconsul in

---

[1] See p. 267.

[2] Münzer (*RA*, 207–8) is inclined to reckon Gracchus as a rival of the Fulvii, but if this were so it is difficult to see whence he derived his support, unless he had the backing of the Scipionic group, which is unlikely. On his connivance at his colleague's secret departure from Rome, which suggests friendship, see L. xli. 10. 5, and below, p. 188. The praetors for 177 were P. Aelius Tubero (? II), C. Quinctius Flamininus, C. Numisius, and L. Mummius. Livy (xli. 8. 1) adds Cn. Cornelius Scipio and C. Valerius Laevinus, but he also names them as praetors in 179 (xl. 44. 2); probably the lex Baebia was operative in 177 and there were only four praetors (p. 173 n. 2). Aelius Tubero may be identical with the praetor of 201. The identification of C. Flamininus is uncertain; he seems too young to be a brother and too old to be a son of T. or L. Flamininus, though he could be a brother perhaps by a second marriage of the father. Or, as Livy's list is unreliable, the original entry may have been C. Quinctius, to which the cognomen Flamininus has been added falsely instead of Crispinus. If a Crispinus, he could be a brother of L. Crispinus (*pr.* 186): see Münzer, *RA*, 120–1. L. Mummius, *tribunus plebis* with his brother or cousin Quintus in 187, was father of the more famous consul of 146. In 177 the pontiff M. Claudius Marcellus (*cos.* 196; cens. 189) died, but the priesthood was retained in the family by the appointment of his son Marcus, later three times consul (166, 155, 152).

[3] Cf. De Sanctis, IV. i. 440; L. xli. 6. 5–7; 9. 1–2; 12. 4–6; 17. 1–4.

176, was completely successful. Meantime Claudius Pulcher, to whom Istria was assigned, was impatient to be off when he learned that early in 177 Manlius and Iunius had renewed their attack on the Istri. He left Rome at dead of night without offering the usual prayers, without his lictors, and without informing anyone except his colleague Gracchus. On reaching his province he publicly taunted Manlius with the initial failure of his campaign and ordered him and Brutus to leave; they retorted that they would obey his order when he had left Rome after the due formalities. Claudius returned to Rome and three days later rushed back to his province, where he found Manlius and Brutus besieging Nesactium. He took over and completed the operation; after the death of their king all the Istrian tribes soon submitted. Further opportunities for glory awaited Claudius: hearing through the Senate from Ti. Claudius Nero (*pr.* 178 and acting proconsul at Pisa) that the Ligurians had attacked Mutina, he hastened to the scene and won a victory. On his return to Rome he celebrated a double triumph over the Istrians and Ligurians, but the glory of this exceptional honour was somewhat overshadowed by his meanness: he gave the allied troops under his command only half as much as the Romans, thereby unwisely exacerbating relations between Romans and Italians.[1]

No account of the elections for 176 has been preserved, but the new consuls were an ill-assorted pair: Cn. Cornelius Scipio Hispallus (*pr.* 179), Nasica's brother and Africanus' cousin, and Q. Petillius Spurinus, who as tribune had attacked the Scipios and was the only praetor of 181 to reach the consulship. Scipio's success may have owed something to a reaction against the unedifying quarrel in the Fulvian group, who in turn may have backed Petillius as a counterweight to reviving Scipionic hopes. Of the praetors three may be reckoned supporters of Scipio and opponents of the Claudian-Fulvians: M. Cornelius Scipio Maluginensis, L. Papirius Maso, and P. Licinius Crassus: apart from the support given by their families in the past a Licinius and a Papirius had criticized Manlius in 178 (p. 186). The other three, M. Popillius Laenas, L. Aquilius Gallus, and M. Aburius, were representatives of the new families which were elbowing their way to the front.

Scipio was not destined to see his province, but died soon after a fall from his horse. This was lucky for the Fulvian group: with Petillius presiding they secured the election of C. Valerius Laevinus (*pr.* 179) as *consul suffectus*. Meantime two praetors had asked to be

[1] L. xli. 12; 14. 1–3. In 16. 7–9 (176 B.C.) Livy repeats his account of Claudius' victory. The triumph is referred by the Fasti Triumphales to the year of his consulship (177). The cause of Livy's doublet might be that Ti. Claudius Nero remained in Liguria until the consul of 176 arrived (14. 11); Livy may have come across another reference to him in his source and confused him with C. Claudius (16. 7). The doublet, however, may well have been in Livy's source already.

excused from going to their provinces. Popillius' excuse for not going to Sardinia was that Gracchus and the praetor T. Aebutius were doing well (this was true enough) and that it was unwise to change horses in mid-stream. When the Senate had excused him, Licinius Crassus alleged on oath that his religious duties prevented him from going to Hispania Citerior, and Scipio Maluginensis pleaded for a similar indulgence; both were excused, and M. Titinius and T. Fonteius were ordered to remain in Spain with proconsular authority. This unprecedented movement presumably reflects the growing independence of some of the younger men against the Senate which found further expression later.

The *consul suffectus* Valerius reached Liguria just after Petillius had taken over from C. Claudius;[1] they attacked the Ligurians separately and successfully, but Petillius was killed. Thereupon those 'periti religionum iurisque publici' ruled that the *consul suffectus*, Valerius, could not rightly conduct the elections for 175. Apparently an attempt was being made to check the Fulvians by the augurs, among whom Fulvian influence was weak; they could only rely upon C. Claudius Pulcher (*cos.* 177). What followed is obscure, because a gap occurs in Livy's text. Presumably an interrex was appointed or else Valerius disregarded the ruling of the augurs. At any rate the Fulvians successfully reasserted their influence and obtained the consulship for one of their most eminent supporters, the *princeps senatus* Aemilius Lepidus who thus gained his second consulship, together with P. Mucius Scaevola, whose speedy rise to high office has already been noted (p. 185). In their year of office both consuls fought successfully against the Ligurians and gained triumphs.[2]

[1] So Livy (xli. 18. 5). If Livy's date for C. Claudius' triumph (177) is retained, either he must have gone back to north Italy or Livy has confused him with Ti. Claudius Nero (p. 188 n. 1).

[2] For the triumphs see *Inscr. Ital.* XIII. i, p. 555.

XI

FULVIAN DECLINE AND NEW GROUPS

(174–169 B.C.)

1. *The Postumian Group*

THE Fulvii had to share the plums of the elections for 174 with another *gens*, the Postumii. They secured the appointment of the younger Mucian brother, Q. Mucius Scaevola, as consul, and of Q. Fulvius Flaccus Q. f. (*cos.* 179 and now head of the family) as censor: thus Flaccus, following Fulvius Nobilior (censor 179), kept one censorship within the *gens*. But the second consulship was gained by Sp. Postumius Albinus Paullulus and the second censorship by A. Postumius Albinus Luscus, while L. Postumius Albinus won the consulship for the next year (173). The success of these three brothers was remarkable. The eldest, Aulus, had been elected praetor for 185, together with L. Postumius Tempsanus, with the help of his cousin Sp. Postumius Albinus L. f. (*cos.* 186). The second brother, Spurius, was praetor in 183.[1] Then in 180 Aulus reached the consulship (as successor to P. Cornelius Cethegus who had been his colleague as aedile in 187) and the third brother became praetor.

But at this point, when the Fulvii gained greater control, the careers of the Postumii were checked for the next five years: Spurius did not reach the consulship although he was qualified by 180, nor did Lucius though he returned from Spain in triumph in 178 and was ready by 177. Lucius' failure must have been all the more galling to him when he remembered how Q. Fulvius Flaccus, who had come back from Spain in 180, was immediately elected to the consulship of 179. Thus the Postumii apparently had been shouldered aside by the Fulvian group and tension may have existed between them from 180 when the consul A. Postumius had occasion to reprimand a Fulvius for disbanding a legion (p. 178). When, however, the Fulvii became less prominent and were putting forward men like the Mucii, the Postumii came to the fore again with a censorship and two consulships in 174 and 173, while Aulus succeeded L. Cornelius Lentulus on the decemviral college (173).

Nor did the Fulvians get many praetorships for 174. L. Claudius

---

[1] There were three Spurii Postumii at this period: (*a*) the consul of 186, L. f., who was probably an augur and died in 180; (*b*) the consul of 174, A. f.; and (*c*) a Spurius Sp. f. Magnus, whose existence is deduced from Sp. Albinus Magnus, consul of 148, who was Sp. f. Sp. n. (Dessau, *ILS*, 5806). On the Postumii see Münzer, *RA*, 212 ff.

and perhaps M. Atilius Serranus may be reckoned among their supporters, but the old Scipionic group was represented by L. Cornelius Scipio, P. Furius Philus, and perhaps Cn. Servilius Caepio (later *cos.* in 169).[1] The success of L. Scipio, Africanus' son who had been captured by Antiochus and released unransomed before Magnesia (p. 130), is striking, and is said to have been promoted by Africanus' secretary Cicereius, who abandoned his own candidature in order to support Lucius. The value of this alleged aid cannot be estimated, but L. Scipio repaid the debt by helping to secure the election of Cicereius to the praetorship for the following year.[2] Other friends of Africanus emerged from the shadows: C. Laelius, of whom nothing is recorded since his proconsulship in 189, led a commission to Perseus in 174, on which Sex. Digitius, last heard of as legate of L. Scipio Asiaticus in 190, also served;[3] and Q. Minucius Rufus (*cos.* 197) was sent to settle civil strife in Crete.[4] On the other hand, the Fulvians cornered the most influential places on a commission sent to arbitrate in an internal dispute of the Aetolians.[5]

The growing influence of the Postumii was demonstrated in the censorship of 174: A. Postumius Albinus, so far from being overruled by his colleague Q. Fulvius Flaccus, may even have been the stronger.

---

[1] The sixth praetor, whose name is missing in Livy, almost certainly was C. Cassius Longinus, a representative of the newer men, who became consul in 171. Cf. Münzer, *RA*, 219.

[2] According to Valerius Maximus (iv. 5. 3.) a son of Africanus named Gnaeus gained the praetorship with Cicereius' help. According to Mommsen this will have been Cn. Scipio (*pr.* 177 and governor of Gaul), and since Livy gives L. Scipio as *praetor peregrinus* of 174, Africanus must have had two sons, Cn. and L., as well as the invalid Publius. But Weissenborn (on L. xli. 8. 1) has shown that the account of Valerius Maximus would apply only to a *praetor peregrinus*, not to a provincial governor, while it has been seen above (p. 187 n. 2) that Livy's statement that Cn. Scipio was a praetor in 177 should be dismissed as a doublet of Cn. Scipio Hispallus (cousin of Africanus) who was praetor in 179. Münzer (cf. *PW*, s.v. Cornelius n. 325) is thus to be followed in his rejection of a son named Gnaeus, and the reference in Valerius Maximus is to be applied to Lucius.

[3] The third member, M. Valerius Messalla (*cos.* 188), presumably owed his election to the Fulvians. Livy (xli. 22. 3) has just described the return of a commission sent to north Africa to investigate rumours that Perseus was intriguing at Carthage; the personnel are not known (presumably Livy mentioned it in the missing portion of this book). Possibly Laelius and Digitius with their intimate knowledge of African affairs, gained when serving under Africanus, may have been sent to Africa as well as to Greece; or Livy might have confused the members of the two commissions.

[4] Livy (xli. 25. 7) names Q. Minucius. Mommsen (*CIL*, 1. 72) thought that this man must be the son of the consul of 197, but the mission is likely to have been entrusted to a senator of fairly high rank and Livy does not give the son of Minucius among the curule magistrates before 167. Cf. Willems, *Sénat*, i. 316 n. 6. If this argument is rejected, Minucius could be identified with a military tribune who served at Mutina under L. Cornelius Merula in 193 (L. xxxv. 5. 3). Cf. Münzer, *PW*, s.v. Minucius n. 23.

[5] The members were C. Valerius Laevinus (half-brother of M. Fulvius Nobilior and *consul suffectus* of 176), Ap. Claudius Pulcher (*cos.* 185), C. Memmius (*pr.* 172), M. Popillius Laenas (*cos.* 173), and L. Canuleius Dives (probably the praetor of 171): L. xli. 25. 5. The idea that Memmius was praetor twice, in 175 and 172, lacks support. See Münzer, *RA*, 218, and *PW*, s.v. Memmius n. 4.

P

He asserted his right as patrician censor to close the *lustrum*, a privilege which the plebeian M. Fulvius Nobilior apparently had usurped in 179.[1] His predominance was more marked when he expelled from the Senate his colleague's younger brother, M. Fulvius Flaccus.[2] His reason may have been the conduct of Marcus when military tribune in 180; the friendship of the Fulvian censors had saved Marcus in 179, but now Postumius was able, despite his colleague, to punish him. The revision of the senatorial and equestrian lists was exceptionally severe. No less than nine senators were expelled and, although the consulars remained immune, a praetorian and a praetor suffered, namely M. Cornelius Scipio Maluginensis (*pr.* 176) and L. Cornelius Scipio (*pr.* 174). The ground for these expulsions is not known. The objection to Maluginensis, who may at some time have been prosecuted by Cato,[3] can hardly have been that he was one of the praetors who did not go to their provinces, since the other two so far from being disgraced soon obtained the consulship—unless it was thought that, while they had valid reasons, he was merely malingering and had made a false declaration on oath (p. 189). The offence of L. Scipio must have been serious, since he was ejected while in office, but apparently even his relations regarded him as a degenerate son of Africanus.[4] The censors thus struck especially hard at the reviving Scipionic group. Aemilius Lepidus was retained as *princeps senatus*, thanks partly to his alliance with the Fulvii. The building programme was considerable and for the first time the censors began to direct operations outside Rome in citizen colonies and municipalities with money supplied by the cities in question. Postumius apparently began to doubt the wisdom of this policy and declared that he would not go on without express orders from the Roman Senate and People, but Fulvius Flaccus continued on his own responsibility to arrange for public works at Pisaurum, Potentia, Fundi, and Sinuessa. It is noteworthy that the Fulvii had a special interest in Pisaurum and Potentia, since two of the family had been commissioners for their foundation.[5] Thus, although Livy records that the censorship was harmonious, Postumius' treatment of Fulvius' brother and Fulvius' insistence upon making contracts in Italian cities suggest some discord.

After a year in which the Claudian-Fulvians could claim the only military success,[6] the consuls elected for 173 were the youngest of the

---

[1] This may be deduced from the fact that only Nobilior is named in the title of the speech in which Cato attacked the censorship of 179. See above, pp. 183 f.

[2] L. xli. 27. 2. See further p. 286.   [3] See p. 268.

[4] Val. Max. iii. 5. 1.

[5] L. xxxix. 44. 11.

[6] Ap. Claudius Centho (*pr.* 175) was granted an *ovatio* for checking a Celtiberian outbreak, while M. Aemilius Lepidus crushed a civil disturbance at Patavium (L. xli. 26; 27. 3–4). Livy refers to Aemilius as consul, but he should be proconsul unless the episode belongs to 175. The Fasti Urbisalvenses, which supplement Fasti Triumph. Capit., con-

three Postumian brothers, L. Postumius Albinus (*pr.* 180), and M. Popillius Laenas (*pr.* 176).[1] Thus the Postumii, who had succeeded in thrusting past the Fulvii, now had to share office with another plebeian family, the Popillii, who obtained a second consulship in 172 for Gaius, younger brother of Marcus. The first Popillius Laenas had appeared in the consular Fasti as early as 359 and his son in 316, but thereafter little is heard of the family. Now the two brothers became consuls with spectacular suddenness, since both probably won office at the earliest opportunity: Marcus was certainly praetor in 176 and Gaius almost certainly in 175. Their success, like that of the two other groups of brothers, the Mucii (175–174) and the Postumii (174–173), illustrates the influence of presiding magistrates. The college of praetors elected for 173 was remarkable because no less than three members had held the office before.[2] This re-election may suggest that the need for experienced men was felt in view of the deteriorating Eastern situation, especially since two praetors (Matienus and Cicereius) came from untried families. Of these Cicereius at any rate proved successful: he suppressed a revolt in Corsica and received a triumph.

The period of Fulvian domination was coming to an end. M. Fulvius Nobilior had died, probably a victim of the plague of 174, and his two sons were as yet too young for high office; the elder, Marcus, became tribune of the plebs in 171 and consul in 159, the younger, Quintus, was consul in 153. The censor Fulvius Flaccus, who had failed to save his brother Marcus from expulsion from the Senate, was himself involved in a scandal in 173. In order to adorn a temple of Fortuna Equestris, which he had vowed as praetor in Spain and was now building, he pillaged some marble tiles from the famous temple of Iuno Lacinia in Bruttium, a temple which neither Pyrrhus nor Hannibal had violated. Though this might be in line with the tradition of his *gens*, since his relative Fulvius Nobilior had returned from Greece laden with works of art, the action was the more obnoxious since it was a censor's duty to conserve temples. It was an offence against constitutional procedure, against Rome's allies, and against heaven. Fulvius' action was bitterly criticized in the Senate, where Cato will not have been silent, and he was ordered to return the tiles and offer expiatory sacrifices to Iuno. The Senate, however, seems to have been more concerned with blaming Fulvius and appeasing the

firm Livy's statement that Appius Claudius had proconsular authority (*Inscr. Ital.* XIII. i, p. 556). A further outbreak of plague in 174 resulted in some changes in the priestly colleges (see pp. 285 f.), while T. Quinctius Flamininus died at the age of fifty-five amid the twilight shadows of his former glories.

[1] L. xli. 28. 3: 'quibus (sc. comitiis) magna contentione habitis propter multitudinem petentium'.

[2] M. Furius Crassipes (187), A. Atilius Serranus (192), and C. Cluvius Saxula (178). A fourth praetor N. Fabius Buteo, who died soon, was not replaced, but his province was assigned to P. Furius Philus who had administered it the previous year.

goddess than with restoring the temple, since the tiles, when returned, were allowed to remain in the temple precinct, because 'there was no one who understood how to replace them'. After the dedication of the temple of Fortuna, Fulvius exhibited scenic Games, but in the next year he came to a tragic end: on learning that one of his sons who was serving in Illyricum had died and that the other was seriously ill, he hanged himself, driven mad, the superstitious proclaimed, by Iuno Lacinia.[1]

11. *The Popillian Group*

The scandal which darkened the last days of Fulvius Flaccus was mild compared with the increasing violence and rapacity displayed by many of the newer men who were gaining power. The conduct of Postumius and Popillius, the consuls of 173, who were posted to Liguria, illustrates this tendency. The former was first sent to Campania to deal with some private landowners who had been encroaching upon public land. His journey was marked by an unpleasant incident at Praeneste, against which he had a grudge because when he had once made a personal visit to the city in order to sacrifice in the temple of Fortune he had not received any mark of honour. He now ordered the chief magistrates to welcome him and prepare accommodation, and the Praenestines, through modesty or fear, accepted the burden of their unwelcome guest.[2] 'Before this consul', wrote Livy, 'no one had ever been a burden or expense to the allies.' Magistrates had been provided with mules, tents, and other equipment in order to obviate any need to requisition such things from the allies, and had enjoyed the hospitality of private citizens. Postumius' action represents a magistrate's abuse of his *imperium* rather than an attempt by the Senate to humiliate an allied city, but it set a dangerous precedent which led to a steady deterioration of Rome's friendly relations with her allies.[3]

The behaviour of Popillius Laenas was even more arbitrary. After defeating the Ligurian Statielli and accepting their unconditional surrender, he sacked their town, disarmed and sold them into slavery, and disposed of their property. On receiving his dispatch the Senate censured him for his cruelty and for attacking without a just cause a tribe which had not been at war with Rome since 179: he was ordered to restore liberty and arms to the Ligurians and to return the purchase-money and as much of their property as could be recovered,

---

[1] L. xlii. 3; 10. 5; 28. 10–12.

[2] Münzer (*RA*, 212 n. 1) compares the reaction of the Praenestines with that of the allies in Bruttium to Fulvius' conduct: see L. xlii. 1. 12 and 3. 3–5.

[3] Discrimination was shown against the allies when some land in north Italy was distributed to settlers: Latins received three *iugera*, Romans ten. For the supervising commission, led by Lepidus, see ibid. 4. 4.

nor was he to leave his province until he had completed the settlement. Popillius refused to obey: he sent his army to winter quarters at Pisa, returned to Rome, and fined the praetor A. Atilius who had originally read his dispatch to the Senate and criticized his conduct. He asked the Senate to rescind its resolution and to decree a thanksgiving for his victory, but failing to carry off the occasion by bluff, he returned to his province and the dispute continued to smoulder until the following year.[1]

After a year in which diplomatic precautions were taken against trouble in Greece and Rome's friendship and alliance were renewed with Antiochus IV, the new king of Syria,[2] the result of the elections for 172 must have electrified the older nobility. The new consuls were C. Popillius Laenas and P. Aelius Ligus, the former being the brother of the consul of 173 who was flouting the Senate at this very time. His success demonstrates the immense popular support which the Popillii were enjoying and it was achieved during his brother's absence, since the elections were conducted by L. Postumius. Even more revolutionary is a fact which Livy glosses over: for the first time in Roman history both consuls were plebeians: *ambo primi de plebe* (Fasti Capitol.). Further, all six praetors and the curule aediles were plebeians; thus all ten curule magistracies were held by plebeians.[3] Nay more, in the next two years (171 and 170) all the consuls were again plebeians. Not only did the plebeians thus sweep the board, but their rise to power had been remarkably quick. M. Popillius (*cos.* 173) had been praetor in 176, both consuls of 172 were praetors in 175, and though P. Licinius Crassus had to wait five years for the consulship in 171, his colleague, C. Cassius Longinus, had been praetor in 174.[4] Clearly a new group of men had shouldered their way to office. The Popillii emerged after more than a century of obscurity (p. 193); Aelius Ligus came from a good *gens*, but his family was hitherto unknown; Cassius Longinus was the first member of his family to reach the consulship, apart from Spurius Cassius in the early fifth century. Thus the patrician *gentes* and the older plebeian *gentes*, who had worked with them, suffered a considerable set-back before the attack of these newer men, who with popular support forced them out of all the curule offices in 172. The cause of the quarrels which developed between some of these men and the Senate thus becomes more plain.

This tension found expression in the continuation of the dispute between the Senate and M. Popillius. When the new consul, Aelius Ligus, reopened the question of Popillius' conduct in Liguria, his

---

[1] Ibid. 7–9.

[2] See ibid. 5. 8–10; 6. 4–6 (Roman embassies to Greece); 6. 10 (Antiochus).

[3] The only doubt concerns Sp. Lucretius, but he probably was a plebeian. As the year was an odd one by the Varronian era, the curule aediles must have been plebeians.

[4] Cf. Münzer, *RA*, 218–19.

colleague, C. Popillius, persuaded him to drop the matter. As war with Perseus seemed threatening, both consuls hoped for Macedonia, but the Senate posted them to Liguria and refused to make Macedonia a province unless the question of M. Popillius was discussed. It apparently thought that the consuls were not steady enough to be entrusted with so delicate a sphere and would not make good commanders if war should break out; it was better to work for a postponement of war. The consuls, whose request for fresh troops was refused, replied by announcing that they would transact no public business other than provincial administration.

The Senate was still more angered when later M. Popillius reported that he had killed a further 6,000 Statielli. Two tribunes, M. Marcius Sermo and Q. Marcius Scylla, carried a bill to establish a judicial inquiry, which was entrusted to the praetor C. Licinius Crassus, and the consuls, who had played into Popillius' hands by refusing to go to their province, were compelled to take over by the threat of a tribunician fine. But Popillius still delayed returning to Rome until forced by a threat that his case would be judged in his absence. After severely criticizing him the Senate instructed two praetors (Licinius and Cn. Sicinius) to free all Ligurians who had not been in arms against Rome since 179, while the consul C. Popillius was to assign them some land beyond the Po. M. Popillius appeared twice before Licinius, but on the third day of the trial the praetor, 'gratia consulis absentis et Popilliae familiae precibus victus', postponed the hearing until 15 March 171 when the case would come before the new magistrates. Thus Popillius escaped and demonstrated the influence of his family, but many Ligurian slaves recovered their freedom and were settled where they were less dangerous. Justice had not been vindicated, but a practical solution was reached, which was all the more necessary as the war with Perseus approached. Later C. Popillius was criticized for failure to liberate some Ligurians and for his delay in coming to Rome to hold the elections. When they were held on 18 February (= Nov. 172, Julian), he again showed his power: the new consuls were P. Licinius Crassus, elder brother of the praetor of 172 who had just saved Popillius' brother, and C. Cassius Longinus. Clearly there was a working alliance between the Popillii and the Licinii Crassi, and once again two plebeian consuls were elected.[1]

Nevertheless the Senate decided that war with Perseus could no longer be postponed, dispatched Sicinius with a holding force to Epirus, and made Italy and Macedonia the consular provinces. As both consuls wanted Macedonia, Cassius tried to filch it from his colleague by arguing that as Licinius had refused on religious grounds to go to his praetorian province in 176, so now he could not leave

[1] The patricians obtained two of the praetorships. L. xlii. 10. 9–15; 21 and 22; 28. 1–5.

Italy. The Senate, however, insisted that the consuls should ballot, and as a result Licinius obtained Macedonia. Apparently Licinius had more friends than Cassius had in the Senate, but neither consul can have been very popular there, since Licinius will have lost favour through his brother's support of the Popillii.

These two Licinii were probably nephews of P. Licinius Crassus Dives (cos. 205),[1] and like Aemilius Lepidus will have transferred their support from the Scipios to the Claudian-Fulvian group and then tended towards the extremists. Apart from the fact that Licinius' family had been more prominent in recent years than that of Cassius, a connexion with the Claudian-Fulvians would help to explain why the Senate favoured Licinius against Cassius for the Macedonian command. The connexion is further illustrated by Licinius' staff appointments; on senatorial advice the Assembly this year delegated to the consuls and praetors the selection of the military tribunes, and thus Licinius secured the appointment of C. Claudius Pulcher (cos. 177) and Q. Mucius Scaevola (cos. 174) as military tribunes, and also took on his staff M. Valerius Laevinus (pr. 182) and two young Manlii Acidini.[2] This novel procedure evoked a speech from Cato De tribunis militum, delivered in the Senate or Comitia, in which he must have spoken against the measure probably on the ground that it would give undue influence to a clique.[3]

Licinius thus won a political victory over his colleague, but Cassius refused to admit defeat. Later in the year the Senate was startled to learn that he had left his province and was trying to advance through Illyricum to Macedonia thereby leaving northern Italy exposed and imperilling his army in difficult country. A crowded Senate ordered the praetor C. Sulpicius to select three men to overtake and warn him not to attack any tribe without senatorial authorization: there must be no second M. Popillius to dishonour Rome's international relations and to flout the wishes of the Senate, especially now that war with Perseus had started. The three commissioners were M. Cornelius Cethegus (cos. 160), M. Fulvius (presumably not the expelled senator, brother of the censor of 174), and P. Marcius Rex, a curiously

---

[1] They were probably sons of Gaius, one of the two unknown brothers of Dives. Cf. Münzer, RA, 220.

[2] L. xlii. 49. 9. L. Manlius was perhaps the son of the cos. of 179 and perhaps quaestor in 168 (L. xlv. 13. 12). Marcus is not found elsewhere among the praenomina of the patrician Manlii and his existence may be questioned (cf. Münzer, PW, s.v. Manlius n. 45). The consul Licinius also had as his legate his brother Gaius who as praetor in 172 had helped to prepare the fleet as well as to extricate M. Popillius from a difficulty (L. xlii. 27).

[3] Ibid. 31. 4–5; 49. 9. On Cato's speech see p. 268. It is noteworthy that later Cato delivered speeches against Cassius, the consul of 171 (in 153), against one of the praetors, C. Sulpicius Galba, and against P. Furius Philus, the brother of another, Lucius (see below). He will scarcely have approved of Licinius Crassus or other praetors of the year, such as the rapacious C. Lucretius.

undistinguished body to carry the Senate's order to a defaulting consul. Their welcome is not recorded, as a lacuna occurs in the text of Livy, but Cassius remained intransigent: in the following year (170) a deputation arrived in Rome from a Gallic chief charging Cassius, who was now serving as military tribune in Macedonia under A. Hostilius, with plundering and enslaving pro-Roman Alpine tribes. Further complaints followed from the Carni, Istri, and Iapydes. The Senate pleaded ignorance but refused to investigate the charges in Cassius' absence, though promising to do so later if requested. Meantime an attempt was made to buy off the plaintiffs by distributing presents and by sending Roman commissioners to proclaim the Senate's decision to the tribes. Such was the humiliation of a Senate which had become involved in a major war while unable to control some of the leaders whom the People had put forward.[1]

III. *Scandals and Reforms*

From the day in 179 when Perseus ascended the throne, the war clouds had been gathering, but although during the period of Fulvian influence little was done to try to scatter them, it remained for the more violent plebeian clique to precipitate the cloud-burst. Neither side was at first anxious for a war which nevertheless gradually came to be regarded as inevitable. Perseus had renewed his father's agreements with Rome, but at the same time he accepted Philip's policy of strengthening Macedonia, and thus many of his actions, however innocent, could be interpreted as threatening Roman interests. Yet the Senate showed no disposition to force the issue: the number of embassies which went to Greece demonstrates the continuing desire for explanations rather than war. Matters, however, were brought to a head when Eumenes of Pergamum visited Rome in 172; his accusations against Perseus convinced a majority of senators that the time for action was imminent. Cato, however, was more cautious and looked with disgust and alarm at the favours which some senators showered upon Eumenes; when assured that Eumenes was an excellent man and a friend of Rome, he replied, 'Granted, but the animal known as king is by nature carnivorous'.[2] Nevertheless the new clique of plebeian magistrates, who looked for glory in war, gradually overbore the more cautious elements in the Senate.

Before open warfare, a successful diplomatic offensive was launched against Perseus. Q. Marcius Philippus (*cos.* 186) led a commission to

---

[1] L. xlii. 31. 1; 32. 1–5; xliii. 1. 4–12; 5.

[2] Plut. *Cato*, 8. The anecdote might, however, be referred to Eumenes' previous visit to Rome in 189 when he advanced his claims in Asia Minor against those of Rhodes (P. xxi. 18 ff.).

Greece,[1] and in October 172 (Julian) he met Perseus and tricked him into sending a further embassy to Rome although he knew that the Senate had decided upon war.[2] The Romans sought to immobilize Perseus, not in order to avoid an embarrassing interval between the delivery of an ultimatum and the voting of war by the Comitia,[3] but to tie his hands until the beginning of the next campaigning season.[4]

This piece of sharp practice was followed in November by the dispatch of a force under Cn. Sicinius (*pr.* I, 183, II, 172) to Epirus to check any counter-move by Perseus and to hold a bridgehead for the consular army which was to follow.[5] Then after the entry of the consuls of 171 into office (Dec. 172, Julian) the Comitia met and agreed that as Perseus had broken his treaty by attacking Rome's allies and was planning war against Rome, war should be declared upon him unless he gave satisfaction.[6] Soon afterwards Marcius and his colleagues returned and reported to the Senate how they had hoodwinked Perseus. The Senate was divided, as before the First Punic War. The elder senators ('veteres et moris antiqui memores'), who surely included Cato, denounced this un-Roman deceit, but the majority preferred expediency to honour: 'cui potior utilis quam honesti cura erat'.[7] At last Perseus' ambassadors, who had been deliberately kept waiting for some four months, were granted an audience by the Senate and warned to leave Italy within a month. The campaigning season was at hand, Perseus had been held at arm's length long enough, and now in Rome's good time all pretence could be dropped.

Some of the elder senators may sincerely have believed that the declaration of war on Perseus did not involve a war of aggression,

[1] The other members were A. Atilius Serranus (*pr.* I in 192, when he commanded a squadron in Greek waters; *pr.* II in 173, when he renewed treaty relations with Syria); P. (*cos.* 162) and Ser. (*pr.* 169) Cornelius Lentulus; and L. Decimius.

[2] T. Frank (*CP*, 1910, 358–61) dismissed the story of a 'truce' granted to Perseus (cf. H. H. Scullard, *Roman World*, 292, which I now reject), but without sufficient reason: cf. Münzer, *PW*, s.v. Marcius n. 79; Otto, *Gesch. Zeit VI Ptol.* 64 n. 1; F. W. Walbank, *JRS*, 1941, 86 ff.

[3] As De Sanctis, IV. i. 275. Walbank (op. cit.) has shown that the fetial procedure had been adapted for use in the declaration of overseas wars, by the Senate and People giving a conditional sanction to a war, so that the rejection of the *rerum repetitio* implied the start of a war (this incidentally increased the influence of the Senate over the People and of the magistrate abroad who was on the spot).

[4] It was necessary to bridge the period between the entry of the new consuls into office (i.e. the time when wars were usually declared; this fell on the Ides of March, which by the Julian calendar was Nov.–Dec. of the previous year) and the next campaigning season (i.e. the awkward gap between November and the following spring when the enemy, anticipating a subsequent attack by Rome, might take the initiative). See Walbank, op. cit.

[5] On the chronology see U. Kahrstedt, *Klio*, 1911, 415, who followed and reinforced by Walbank (op. cit. 82) has demonstrated that the embassy of Marcius preceded Sicinius' landing, which occurred about the Ides of Feb. 171, i.e. Nov. 172 by the Julian calendar (Livy's 'paucis post diebus' cannot be accepted: xlii. 37. 1).

[6] Ibid. 30. 10–11.

[7] Ibid. 47. 9 (following Polybius).

which was forbidden by Rome's fetial law, and that their action was in spirit defensive. The validity of such a belief cannot be established without a deeper insight into their genuine anxieties and into Perseus' motives and intentions than the sources provide. The deliberate manner, however, in which Perseus had been tricked was repugnant to their moral scruples, which had already been offended by Popillius' attacks on unoffending Ligurians and by Cassius' enslavement of innocent Alpine tribes. These new men were not merely flouting the will of the elder senators, but were imperilling the *mos maiorum*.

The methods employed in the rest of Rome's diplomatic offensive were less open to question; various commissions were sent to Greece and Asia Minor to encourage Rome's friends and overawe the waverers.[1] Thus there could be little real anxiety about the issue of the war, but many besides his political enemies may have had misgivings when they remembered that the commander-in-chief, P. Licinius Crassus, had never commanded an army (p. 189); he had, however, on his staff two consulars and other men with some military experience (see p. 197). His performance when he reached Greece was mediocre: he was severely trounced by Perseus near Larissa and then fought another slight engagement, which Roman annalists magnified into a great victory. Meantime the praetor Lucretius Gallus, the commander of the fleet, had spent his time plundering Boeotia by land.

At the consular elections for 170 two plebeians were chosen, for the third time running, but they were not quite so inexperienced as the recent consuls who had gained office so soon after their praetorships. One, A. Atilius Serranus, had served in Greece as praetor in 192 and operated at sea against Antiochus (191); he had held a second praetorship in 173 and came from an old and distinguished family. His colleague, A. Hostilius Mancinus, came from a new family but had been backed by the Fulvii; he had waited for the consulship for ten years since his praetorship. Evidently the electorate was still under the influence of the newer plebeian movement, but some perhaps were beginning to hesitate to entrust the conduct of the war to men as raw as the consuls of 171. Yet it was Hostilius, the consul who lacked

---

[1] Genthius of Illyricum was warned (L. xlii. 26. 2–7; 37. 2). Marcius' commission confirmed the adherence of the Achaean League and won over part of Boeotia. An embassy to the East found the pro-Roman party uppermost at Rhodes; Eumenes, the Greek cities, and Ariarathes of Cappadocia were friendly; Prusias of Bithynia, Perseus' brother-in-law, merely wished to be neutral; Syria and Egypt, though mutually hostile, were united in their profession of loyalty to Rome. Rumours of Perseus' intrigues at Carthage proved to have little substance. Commissions to get allied military help included visits to Africa and Crete, led respectively by L. and A. Postumius (ibid. 35. 7). Livy's references to some other embassies should be rejected, e.g. xlii. 25. 1 (172 to Greece; annalistic invention, deriving from the Roman propaganda of justification); 19. 7–8 (accept 45. 1–2, cf. P. xxvii. 3. 1; this will have started *c*. Oct. 172, Julian); 26. 7–8 (return of embassy from East).

military experience, that was sent to Macedonia. He had the doubtful
advantage of receiving on his strength as military tribune C. Cassius
Longinus (cos. 171), while the latter's colleague, P. Licinius Crassus,
served as proconsul and cruelly plundered many Greek cities.[1] Hostilius achieved little: he was more concerned with curbing his own
marauding troops than with pursuing the war against Perseus, who
during the following winter advanced into Illyricum, hoping that if he
opened up communications he might persuade Genthius to abandon
his alliance with Rome.[2]

The behaviour of Rome's commanders in the field provoked a storm
of criticism at home. Apart from the scandal caused when C. Cassius
left his province and attacked the Alpine tribes (p. 197), the ruthless
and rapacious spirit in which the consul Licinius and the praetor
Lucretius had conducted the war was sharply censured. While Lucretius was enjoying the fruits of his spoils at his estate at Antium, the
Abderites charged his successor Hortensius with storming their town
and enslaving the population. The Senate, which had already condemned the sack of Coronea by Lucretius, sent commissioners to
restore freedom to the Abderites, and to reprimand Hostilius and
Hortensius for waging a *bellum iniustum*. Soon afterwards ambassadors
came from Chalcis to accuse Lucretius and Hortensius with plundering
their city. Their case was taken up by two tribunes, M. Iuventius
Thalna (cos. 163) and Cn. Aufidius, who demanded a fine of a million
asses; the 35 tribes unanimously found Lucretius guilty.[3]

Finally, a scandal, which arose in the West and came to a head in
171, may be mentioned. When both Spanish provinces complained of
the rapacity and oppression of the Roman magistrates, the first court
to try claims for redress (*repetundae*) was established, a landmark in
the history of Roman provincial administration. The praetor L. Canuleius, to whom Spain had been assigned, was instructed to appoint
five senatorial *recuperatores* to try the individuals from whom the
Spaniards demanded redress. The plaintiffs from Hither Spain chose
Cato and Scipio Nasica as patrons, those from Further Spain chose
Aemilius Paullus (cos. I, 182) and C. Sulpicius Gallus, all of whom,
except Sulpicius, had served in Spain. The selection of these senior
ex-governors of Spain demonstrates that the Spaniards regarded some
of their rulers as men of principle and throws into relief the corruption
of the younger generation. The *recuperatores* at the third sitting
acquitted M. Titinius who had governed Spain 178–176, but P. Furius
Philus (governor 174–173) and M. Matienus (praetor in Further Spain

---

[1] Livy, *Per.* xliii.
[2] Perseus defeated Roman counter-attacks by L. Coelius and Ap. Claudius: L. xliii.
21. 1 (Polybius). A doublet of this attack is given by L. xliii. 9. 6–10. 8 (annalistic), where
the Roman commander is given as Ap. Claudius (Centho), the praetor of 175.
[3] L. xliii. 4. 5–13; 7. 5–8. 10.

in 173) anticipated condemnation by voluntary exile.[1] As this was a
civil action, the defendants presumably left Rome to avoid a subsequent prosecution before the Assembly and to avoid restoring their
spoil which they could then enjoy at Praeneste and Tibur instead of
at Rome. A rumour that the plaintiffs had been prevented by their
patrons from summoning to court some members of the nobility may
be partly pure scandal, since it is unlikely that Cato would be backward
in unearthing abuses, but these suspicions increased when Canuleius
dropped the case and went off to his province. Lip-service had been
paid to the cause of justice, enough dirty linen had been washed in
public, and even Cato may have felt that Roman dignity now demanded silence.

To prevent a recurrence of these evils Roman magistrates were
deprived of the right to value corn which was requisitioned for the
governor's household (*frumentum aestimatum*) and the produce on
which a 5 per cent. tax was levied for the support of the troops; nor
were they to send *praefecti* around the towns to collect the tribute in
money, which the Spaniards preferred to gather and hand over to the
Roman officials. These measures throw a lurid light upon the abuses
to which the provincials had been subjected. Particularly bitter pills
to swallow will have been such acts as the collection of money by
Q. Fulvius for the erection of a temple to Fortuna which he vowed
when fighting the Celtiberians: the Spaniards were forced to pay for
a memorial of their own defeat.[2] Thus with this series of scandals
coming to light at Rome, with reports of disorders in the Roman army,
and with little success being achieved in the field against Perseus,
Roman administration cannot have seemed very healthy in 170.

It was against this gloomy background that the consul Atilius
returned from Liguria to conduct the elections for 169. The nobility
determined to reassert itself. Partly to bring its full weight to bear
upon the electorate, partly to stress the gravity of the hour, all senators
in Italy, except those engaged on public business, were recalled to
Rome, and those in the city were forbidden to leave. The result was
not unsatisfactory: the new consuls were Q. Marcius Philippus (*cos.* I
in 186 with Sp. Postumius Albinus) and the patrician Cn. Servilius
Caepio. Since Livy gives the names in this order, the plebeian Marcius
may have topped the poll, but at any rate the run of exclusively
plebeian colleges had been broken.[3] It is noteworthy that the presiding
magistrate had been a fellow-commissioner with Marcius on his
notorious visit to Perseus (172/171). The more conservative senators,

---

[1] Cf. Ps. Ascon. *In divin.* 66, p. 203: 'Cato accusavit . . . P. Furium pro iisdem (sc.
Lusitanis) propter iniquissimam aestimationem frumenti.' See p. 268. The fact that the
Furii had been supporters of the Scipios would give a keener edge to Cato's indignation.
[2] L. xl. 44.   [3] L. xliii. 11. 6. Cf. Münzer, *RA*, 152.

who had disapproved of the Machiavellian diplomacy of Marcius and Atilius, may now have been willing to support them on the understanding that Marcius, unlike Atilius, should not have a plebeian colleague; at any rate, whatever his past record, Marcius had enjoyed considerably more experience than some of his immediate predecessors. His colleague, Servilius Caepio, the eldest son of the consul of 203, may in the circumstances have appealed to both patricians and plebeians as a suitable candidate. His career had been steady and unspectacular; curule aedile in 179, praetor in 174 in Spain, he had waited four years before his consulship in 169. This average performance would make him appear a safe candidate from the patrician side, while the fact that one branch of his *gens*, the Servilii Gemini, had gone over to the plebs just before the Hannibalic War (p. 35) might help to commend him to the plebeians.[1]

Most of the praetors of 169 belonged to patrician or noble plebeian families[2] and the same conservative tendency is observable at the censorial elections: the candidates were not the ex-consuls of the last few years, but *principes civitatis*, men of the Fulvian circle and its supporters.[3] Claudius Pulcher (*cos.* 177) defeated his two patrician competitors, C. Valerius Laevinus (*cos. suff.* 176) and L. Postumius Albinus (*cos.* 173);[4] Ti. Sempronius Gracchus (*cos.* 177) defeated the plebeians M. Iunius Brutus (*cos.* 178) and P. Mucius Scaevola (*cos.* 175). With foreign affairs so unsettled, the need for experienced men at home was the greater.

Marcius Philippus gained Macedonia as his province, and his cousin, Figulus, was given the naval command against Perseus. His military record, which included a sharp reverse at the hands of the Ligurians during his first consulship, might not inspire great confidence, but then his colleague Caepio may not have enjoyed even that amount of military experience: the record of his activity as praetor in Spain has been lost. Difficulties were encountered in raising new troops, because the consuls, with an eye on their own popularity, failed to exert adequate pressure. The Senate therefore allowed two praetors, C. Sulpicius and M. Claudius, to take over the business from the

---

[1] Cf. ibid., 152–3. His embassy to Macedonia in 172 (L. xlii. 25. 1) must be rejected as an annalistic fiction.

[2] They included a cousin of the new consul, C. Marcius Figulus. Both men were elderly and were grandsons of Q. Philippus (*cos.* 281); their father Gaius is unknown. Figulus was consul in 162 and 156. T. Marcius Figulus (L. xliii. 13. 6) was probably his brother. See Münzer, *RA*, 153 n. 1.

[3] L. xliii. 14. 1. Cf. Münzer, *RA*, 222. One possible candidate was removed by death this year, C. Livius Salinator (*cos.* 188). His place as pontiff was filled by M. Servilius, probably a son of Geminus (*cos.* 202). T. Manlius Torquatus (*pr.* 170 and *cos.* 165) replaced L. Furius Philus (*pr.* 171). Lucius Flamininus also died this year: L. xliii. 11. 13.

[4] Of the three Postumii brothers, Aulus had been censor in 174, while the youngest, Lucius, stood now. Presumably the second brother, Spurius (*cos.* 174), had died.

consuls; this task they carried through with some help from the censors, who had to face a further problem. The readiness with which the commanders in Macedonia had granted leave necessitated a comb-out in Italy: the censors ordered all men who had been conscripted in or after 172 to return to Macedonia within a month. When the second consul, Servilius Caepio, who received north Italy, asked the Senate which two of the four newly raised legions he should take to Gaul, the matter was referred to the praetors. Servilius, indignant at being subjected to the will of the praetors, dismissed the Senate; the praetors gave him freedom of choice.[1] Two explanations of this extraordinary procedure are possible: either the plebeian element in the Senate got the upper hand and showed its annoyance at the election of a patrician consul by trying to humiliate him, or, more probably, in view of the independence recently shown by so many plebeian magistrates, the Senate decided to demonstrate that the consuls as well as the praetors were subject to its control.

An attempt to improve Rome's recent bad name in Greece was made by sending Gaius Popillius, whose record was far from clean, together with Cn. Octavius (aedile 172) to proclaim that no one should make any contribution to the Roman commanders except that fixed by the Senate. Further, Hostilius had re-established better discipline in the Roman army. It was to this somewhat reassured Greece that Marcius came in 169. His achievement, when compared with that of his predecessors or even with his own past military record, was not inconsiderable, since he succeeded in turning the Olympus range. But this success was nullified by Perseus' subsequent capture of Dium: consequently Rome's allies began to waver. At Rhodes the anti-Roman party received envoys from Perseus; mysterious, but ineffective, negotiations took place between Eumenes and Perseus (pp. 286 f.); help offered by the Achaean League was distrusted by Marcius; the Macedonian navy began to operate off Asia Minor; and in the autumn Perseus gained the help of the Illyrian chief Genthius.

Meantime the censors were acting with a severity that reflected the restlessness of recent years. After choosing M. Aemilius Lepidus once more as *princeps senatus*, they degraded seven senators and many *equites*, and announced that they would not accept tenders from contractors who had worked for the last censors, presumably because they regarded the recent contracts as too favourable or the work as inefficient. This led to open conflict. Unable to get redress from the Senate, the capitalists enlisted the help of a tribune, P. Rutilius, an *eques* who was already annoyed with the censors because they had fined a client of his who had objected when ordered to pull down a wall that faced a public building. Rutilius announced that he would

[1] L. xliii. 14. 1–15. 5.

propose the cancellation and re-letting of all contracts made by the censors. When Claudius Pulcher called for silence at a preliminary *contio*, Rutilius charged him with impugning the tribunician authority by virtue of which he had summoned the meeting. Then he accused both censors of *perduellio*. They decided to face the charge while in office, although under no obligation to do so, and refrained from any public business until the trial was finished. A majority of the first class, which included most of the rich *equites*, naturally voted against Claudius, who would, it is said, have been condemned but for the entreaties of the leading nobles and the support of Gracchus, who was personally popular. He escaped by the vote of eight centuries only and the case against Gracchus was then dropped. Even if some of the details of this episode are suspect, the quarrel demonstrates the strength of the *equites* and the seriousness of a growing breach between them and the senators. Yet clearly the Senate was still predominant and, though the People had the last word, the censors backed by the Senate were able to withstand tribunician attack and even dared to strike Rutilius from the list of *equites* immediately after the expiration of his tribunate in December.

In another sphere also the censors showed a retrograde harshness. In 174 the Senate had apparently withdrawn the privilege of voting in a rural tribe from one of the two classes which received it in 179, namely all freedmen who had a son and owned land in a rural tribe. Now in 169–8 the censors, while not changing existing arrangements as they affected freedmen already registered, provided that in future all freedmen, except those with a property qualification of 30,000 sesterces, should be confined to one urban tribe.[1] Thus the liberal measures of 179 were cancelled except where they affected the rich freedmen. When the censors, whose building programme was moderate, asked that they might extend their 18 months' period of office in order to complete the repair of some buildings, their request was vetoed, either in the Senate or Assembly, by a tribune named Cn. Tremellius, who was annoyed that he had not been placed by them on the senatorial list.[2]

In line with this severe censorship a tribune Q. Voconius Saxa in 169 carried a law which forbade a testator of the highest property class to make a woman his heir and limited other legacies to a sum less than that received by the heir.[3] Its purpose was to ensure a male

---

[1] L. xlv. 15. 1–7, a corrupt and difficult passage. See A. H. McDonald, *CHJ*, 1939, 135, 138.

[2] L. xliii. 15. 6–16. 16; xliv. 16. 9. These two accounts of the censorship perhaps derive from two different annalistic sources (Claudius and Valerius).

[3] Cic. *De sen.* 14, attributes this measure to 169 and is to be preferred to the *Periocha* of Livy xli which assigns it to an earlier date (probably 175). The confusion may have arisen from the fact that there were two different chronological traditions about Cato's life

succession, to keep the bulk of the senatorial estates in the hands of the younger men, to prevent women gaining control of large amounts of capital, and thus to check the emancipation of women, who were gaining much greater freedom as 'free' marriage (*sine in manu conventione*) became more common. Cato spoke in its support 'magna voce et bonis lateribus'; he would disapprove of the power to live in greater luxury which the right to inherit property gave to those women who were no longer subject to their husbands' *manus*, and also the greater political freedom which they were winning.[1] Thus in several directions some attempt was made to tighten up discipline on the home front, while the war in Greece was prosecuted with greater efficiency.

(cf. above, p. 110 n. 3; and H. Nissen, *Kritische Untersuchungen über die Quellen der 4 und 5 Dekade des Livius*, 225). Augustine (*De civ. Dei*, iii. 21) who denounced the law ('qua lege quid iniquius dici aut cogitari, ignoro'), throws no light upon its date. Cf. Cic. *Pro Balbo*, 8. 21; *In Verr.* i. 107.

[1] Cf. Plut. *Cato*, 8. 2. See also p. 268.

XII

THE ACHIEVEMENT OF AEMILIUS PAULLUS

(168–167 B.C.)

1. *Aemilius Paullus and the East*

THE situation in Macedonia, although improving, demanded more drastic military action. The desire for this was expressed in the consular elections for 168 which were conducted by the patrician Servilius Caepio. The plebeians again acquiesced in the election of one patrician, and as in the recent censorial elections the need was felt for men of the older tradition to ensure a stiffening of the home front, so now the conduct of the war was entrusted to L. Aemilius Paullus, who had gained military experience as praetor in Spain (191–190) and as consul (182) in Liguria where he defeated the Ingauni (181). He also had first-hand experience of Hellenistic affairs through his service on the decemviral commission of 188 which had settled the East after Magnesia, and, although over sixty, he was still strong enough to lead his men into battle and to retain their respect for his physical prowess as well as for his generalship.[1]

Recalled to the consulship of 168, Paullus had as his plebeian colleague C. Licinius Crassus, the praetor urbanus of 172, who after saving M. Popillius Laenas from condemnation had served in Greece under his elder brother Publius whose election to the consulship had been promoted by the Popillii. The Licinii Crassi had probably followed Aemilius Lepidus into the Claudian-Fulvian camp and had then supported the emerging group of plebeian extremists (p. 197). Their co-operation with the Popillii is beyond doubt, but they may have been more popular in the Senate than newer men like Cassius. The fact that P. Crassus had been compelled to wait five years after his praetorship for his consulship, while his political allies had reached the consulship more quickly, may suggest that he was not fully acceptable to the plebeian set; he had, however, followed their tradition in plundering Greece when proconsul in 170. His election therefore would please the plebeians and might appear slightly less distasteful to the older nobility than that of some of his recent predecessors.

Aemilius Paullus, who received the Macedonian command while Licinius had to be content with Italy,[2] was the son of L. Aemilius

---

[1] L. xliv. 41. 1.

[2] According to Livy (xliv. 17. 7) the provinces were, as usual, assigned by lot, but the

who had fallen at Cannae and had been associated with the Scipios. His sister Aemilia had married Scipio Africanus, who was only some eight years his senior in age but whose rise to the consulship had been as quick as Aemilius' had been slow. It is noteworthy that men belonging to several families which had supported the Aemilian-Scipionic group in the past now began to emerge. Although Aemilius' colleague, Licinius Crassus, may have received no electioneering help from him, at any rate his family had been closely associated with Africanus. Also three or four of the praetors of 168 belonged to pro-Scipionic families: Cn. Baebius Tamphilus (his relationship to the consuls of 182 and 181 is uncertain), C. Papirius Carbo (Aemilius Paullus had married a Papiria, daughter of C. Papirius Maso, *cos.* 231), Cn. Octavius (son of Cn. Octavius who served as legate of Africanus in Africa), and perhaps P. Fonteius Balbus.[1] Further, when Paullus obtained the Senate's permission to send a commission to Greece to collect last-minute information on the political and military situation, he chose Cn. Domitius Ahenobarbus, A. Licinius Nerva, and L. Baebius.[2]

The scene was now set for the final overthrow of Perseus: the home front was somewhat chastened, adequate armies were in the field, and the troops were disciplined under the command of an upright and capable general who did not lack sympathy for Greek life. The praetor Anicius brought Genthius to his knees in Illyricum, a second praetor, Cn. Octavius, assumed command of the fleet, and Aemilius Paullus advanced to deliver the *coup de grâce* to Perseus on the field of Pydna, whither the king had been forced to retire as a result of a turning movement executed by two young nobles, P. Scipio Nasica Corculum and Paullus' own son, Q. Fabius Maximus Aemilianus.[3] Victory was complete and Perseus was soon in Roman hands.

Meantime, the other two great Hellenistic monarchies had been

elogium of Paullus states 'iterum cos. ut cum rege ⟨Per⟩se bellum gereret ap⟨. . . f⟩actus est' (*CIL*, i, p. 194). Cf. Plut. *Aemil.* 10; Justin, xxxiii. 1. 6. The interpretation of *ap . . :* is difficult: *apsens* is contradicted by Plutarch's statement that Paullus was present, while Degrassi (*Inscr. Ital.* XIII. iii, p. 63) dislikes both Mommsen's suggestion of *a populo* and his own *apnuens* on epigraphical grounds.

[1] Not much is known about the Fonteii, but Ti. Fonteius had played an important part in the Spanish campaign of 212/11 as legate to P. Scipio, and perhaps the family was attached to the Scipios. T. Fonteius Capito was praetor in 178, P. Fonteius Capito in 169, M. Fonteius in 166. Like the Iuventii, the Fonteii came from Tusculum. Both families are seen in the praetorian Fasti at this time (the Fonteii in 169, 168, and 166; M. Iuventius Thalna in 167), while Iuventius Thalna reached the consulship in 163. There is no evidence to suggest that their success was promoted by either of the two greater families from Tusculum, the Porcii Catones or the Fulvii. On the Fonteii and Iuventii see Münzer, *RA*, 48 n. 1 (cf. Cic. *Pro Font.* 41, *Pro Plancio*, 12, 19, &c.).

[2] Domitius, presumably the son of the general who had fought with the Scipios at Magnesia, rather than the man himself, was later *cos. suffectus* in 162. Licinius was perhaps the tribune of 178 who tried to stop the prorogation of the command of A. Manlius Vulso; he became praetor in 166.

[3] Nasica was the son of the consul of 191 who had recently died; he was the son-in-law

checked. Syria, which had retained its independence after Magnesia, became, with the loss of its satrapies in Asia Minor, more isolated from the Greek world and more interested in the East; and Antiochus Epiphanes began to nurture hopes of asserting some form of control over Egypt itself. Although loyal to his agreement with Rome, he also determined to 'be strong enough to resist any infringement by the Romans of the treaty of Apamea, that is to say, any attempt by Rome to intervene in the domestic affairs of Syria and Egypt'.[1] But with the Macedonian war on her hands Rome would be very sensitive to any changes in the East, where trouble soon developed. Whether secretly encouraged by Rome in an attempt to check Antiochus or merely desiring to make hay while the sun shone, the guardians of Ptolemy VI Philometor planned to recover Coele Syria from Antiochus, who was not reluctant for a struggle which might result in his occupation of Egypt while Rome's attention was diverted elsewhere.

While a Syrian embassy protested in Rome against Ptolemy's attack, Egyptian envoys were asserting their loyalty to Rome. The Egyptians were even ready to offer to mediate between Rome and Perseus. This was pure folly and implied that Egypt was among those peoples who did not wish for a complete Roman victory. Fortunately for Egypt her envoys wisely listened to the advice of the *princeps senatus*, Aemilius Lepidus, whose interest in Egypt went back to 200 B.C. (p. 94 n. 5), and did not raise the matter. But Rome had to tread warily: to have driven either Ptolemy or Antiochus into alliance with Perseus would have created a serious situation. The Senate therefore avoided committing itself to Antiochus' envoys and told the Egyptians that Marcius Philippus 'would be commissioned to write to Ptolemy on the subject, as he should think it most to the interest of Rome and his own honour'.[2] In view of Philippus' past record the Senate could be confident that, if need arose, he would place his *fides* towards his country before honourable dealing with other powers. What direct action, if any, he took is unknown, but later, when visited by some Rhodian envoys in Greece, he secretly tried to persuade one of them to mediate between

---

of Scipio Africanus, whose elder daughter Cornelia was his wife. Q. Fabius was the eldest son of Aemilius Paullus himself, but after his mother Papiria had been divorced and his father had married another woman whose name is not recorded, he was adopted by Q. Fabius Maximus (a grandson of the Cunctator). His younger brother, known later as P. Cornelius Scipio Aemilianus, was adopted by their cousin P. Scipio, the son of Africanus, and served at Pydna although only 17 years old. The joy which his father Paullus felt after the victory at Pydna was somewhat tempered until the boy, who had been carried off in the press to another part of the field, returned safely to camp late in the day (L. xliv. 44). Paullus had two sons by his second wife, but one boy, aged 12, died five days before his triumph over Perseus in 167, and the elder, aged 14, died three days after it (L. xlv. 40. 7).

[1] M. Rostovtzeff, *Soc. Econ. Hist. Hell. World*, 63. On Antiochus' policy see pp. 696 ff.

[2] P. xxviii. 1. Cf. Otto, *Gesch. Zeit VI. Ptol.* 45–6. The formula in the instructions sent to Marcius will have been 'ita ut ei e republica fidéque sua videretur'.

Egypt and Syria, apparently wishing to remain in the background himself (pp. 217 n. 1; 287).

For the moment, however, the Senate had played its cards with skill and had encouraged both powers without committing itself to either. Thus the Syro-Egyptian war could go on unhindered. Antiochus counter-attacked, captured Philometor, and championed his cause against that of his brother (later Ptolemy VII Euergetes Physcon) whom the Alexandrians installed upon the throne. But when Antiochus himself assumed the title of king of Egypt as protector of Philometor, the international implications of the situation became serious. The younger Ptolemy Euergetes appealed to the Senate which decided that diplomatic pressure from Marcius in Greece was not sufficient and sent out T. Numisius to try to mediate between Syria and Egypt or possibly between the two Ptolemies; a man of some experience, but not high rank, was chosen perhaps in order to save Roman prestige if the mission proved unsuccessful.[1] But Antiochus, who could argue that he was trying to restore the rightful king Philometor, against a rebel government in Alexandria, withdrew after an unsuccessful attack on the city, hoping in future to control Egypt through the rivalry of the two kings, Philometor in Memphis and Euergetes in Alexandria. His departure was hastened by news of trouble in Palestine, which, in view of Rome's later alliance with the Jews, may have been fomented by Rome in order to embarrass him.

The two Ptolemies, however, decided to patch up their quarrel. When Antiochus again threatened, they appealed to the Senate, which sent out C. Popillius Laenas (cos. 172), accompanied by C. Decimius (pr. 169) and C. Hostilius.[2] The envoys, who prudently delayed at Delos

[1] Numisius is mentioned in the SC. de Thisbaeis (see e.g. Fontes Iuris Romani Ante-Iustiniani, 1², p. 242), and was probably a quaestorius; later in 167 he was one of the decemviri sent to Macedonia (L. xlv. 17. 3). Cf. Otto, op. cit. 63. See below, p. 212 n. 1.

[2] On the Egyptian appeals to Rome see Otto (op. cit. 60–3) who shows that Livy (xliv. 19. 6 ff.) is wrong in connecting the dispatch of Popillius' commission with the appeal of Euergetes, as this must have been lodged before the two brothers patched up their quarrel, i.e. at least before the beginning of the consular year 168 (end of 169 Julian) if not earlier, while Popillius was sent out after that. Therefore the sending of an embassy to Rome by the two brothers, which Livy does not record, would in any case have to be postulated, but in fact such a one is quoted by Justin (xxxiv. 2. 7–8), while the commission of Numisius, which Polybius records (xxix. 25), can be identified with that sent in reply to Euergetes' request. Egypt also appealed to the Achaean League. Although Lycortas and Polybius urged that help should be sent, Callicrates' proposal to send ambassadors to mediate, which was supported by a dispatch from Marcius, gained the day: Marcius apparently judged that any renewal of Antiochus' threat to Alexandria would not be serious, and wished Rome alone to have the glory of protecting Egypt without any help from Achaea. P. xxix. 23–5. Cf. Otto, op. cit. 75–6.

Antiochus' invasion of Egypt has usually been placed in 169, but it and the subsequent reconciliation of the two Ptolemies now appear to have been completed by the end of 170, since a vineyard lease shows (if its dating is quite accurate) that the joint reign of Philometor with his sister-wife Cleopatra and his brother Euergetes was recognized in the Fayum by Nov. 170. See E. G. Turner, Bull. John Rylands Library, 1948, 148 ff.

until Pydna had been won, then proceeded to Egypt which Antiochus had again entered, after seizing Cyprus *en route*. At Eleusis, a suburb of Alexandria, Popillius handed the Senate's dispatch to Antiochus, who was ordered to reply before he stepped out of a circle drawn around him in the sand by Popillius. The king of Syria meekly obeyed and withdrew from Egypt at the command of a man whom even the older Roman nobility might regard as an upstart, but he knew that the order was backed by the full weight of the authority of Rome which had just toppled Perseus off his throne. The Roman commissioners then ordered the Syrian army to withdraw from Cyprus, which remained an Egyptian dependency. Thus Egypt, the weakest of the three great Hellenistic monarchies, was saved by Rome when Macedonia was overthrown and Syria humiliated.

The diplomatic victory of Popillius, combined with the military victory of Paullus, was a sign that the temporarily weakened leadership of the nobility at home was recovering and that the newer and older men were blending into a greater unity; with the home front more united, the State appeared more powerful than ever.[1] The victories at the same time demonstrated to the world at large that Greek predominance in the Hellenistic East had finally succumbed to Roman power.[2]

11. *The Aemilian-Scipionic Group*

The victory of Aemilius Paullus resulted in the emergence of more men from families associated with the old Aemilian-Scipionic group. He sent his own son Q. Fabius, together with L. Cornelius Lentulus and Q. Caecilius Metellus (the future conqueror of Perseus' would-be successor Andriscus), to announce the result of Pydna at Rome. The consuls of 167 came from the same circle, though once again they were both plebeians: Q. Aelius Paetus (probably the son of P. Aelius who had been censor with Africanus in 199) and M. Iunius Pennus (*pr.* 172 and son of the praetor of 202). Three praetors, however, were representatives of the middle Claudian-Fulvian bloc: Ti. Claudius Nero, Cn. Fulvius, and A. Manlius Torquatus. Aemilius Paullus and L. Anicius had their commands in Macedonia and Illyricum prolonged, the new consuls being posted to north Italy; and senatorial commissions were set up to help the commanders in their task of settlement. Of the five men sent to Illyricum four were representatives of the minor families associated with the Scipios;[3] the ten

---

[1] Cf. Münzer, *RA*, 223, who refers to the comment by Gelzer (*Nobilität*, 115) on this incident: the position of the Roman nobility both internally and externally 'immer mehr fürstlichen Charakter annahm'.

[2] The Jews were impressed (Daniel, 11. 30). But Antiochus' kingdom remained strong and his policy basically unchanged. Cf. Rostovtzeff, op. cit. 67 f.

[3] They were P. Aelius Ligus (*cos.* 172); C. Cicereius (Africanus' former secretary; *pr.* 173); Cn. Baebius Tamphilus (*pr.* 168); P. Terentius Tuscivicanus; P. Manlius.

commissioners sent to Paullus were drawn from a wider circle, although several of the junior members may have owed their appointments to his influence.[1]

The Senate discussed the principles of settlement and agreed that the Macedonian monarchy should be abolished and the Macedonians and Illyrians should be free; there would be no drastic change of policy or annexation of territory in Greece. This decision probably represented the policy of Aemilius Paullus and his friends, who may have regarded the older philhellenic policy of Scipio Africanus, though perhaps not the more doctrinaire form advocated by Flamininus, as wise in its day and generation, and now have tried to adapt it to the needs of their time. One change, however, must be made. Roman policy might remain without an anti-monarchic bias (p. 129), but it tended to harden as Roman power increased and the kings became weaker and more servile; the conclusion was now reached that peace in the Balkans would be more secure if the Macedonian monarchy was abolished. In consequence Paullus refused to treat with Perseus as long as he clung to the title of king, but after his unconditional surrender he showed him a kindly respect.[2] The policy of freedom for Macedonia and Greece received support in the Senate from another quarter: Cato argued that 'Macedonia must be set free, since we cannot guard her'.[3] His motive and arguments would differ from those of the philhellenic nobles; he wished to have nothing to do with Eastern conquest, fearing its demoralizing influences and the opportunities of wealth and power which it offered to Roman generals. It is not recorded whether any of the ambitious plebeian leaders, who in recent years had enriched themselves by provincial maladministration, argued for the annexation of Macedonia; if so, they were outvoted. The

[1] They were two ex-censors, Postumius Albinus (cens. 174) and Claudius Pulcher (cens. 169); probably three consulars, Fabius Labeo (cos. 183), Marcius Philippus (cos. II, 169), and Licinius Crassus (cos. 168 and colleague of Paullus), together with Cn. Domitius Ahenobarbus (an ambassador in Greece already in 169), Ser. Cornelius Sulla (pr. 175), L. Iunius (possibly a brother of the cos. of 178), T. Numisius Tarquiniensis, and A. Terentius Varro (pr. 184). See L. xlv. 17. 1–3. Of the consulars Livy's text gives only Licinius. The suggestion that one was Q. Fabius Labeo is based on the fact that a Labeo was sent to Lesbos (ibid. 31. 14). He had commanded a fleet in the Aegean as praetor in 189 and was cos. 183; as his death is not recorded in the extant books of Livy, he was probably alive in 167. The inclusion of Marcius Philippus (so Weissenborn) is based merely on his expert knowledge of Greek affairs.

[2] L. xlv. 4–8.

[3] 'Quare omnia trans Euphratem ac Tigrim (sc. Hadrianus) reliquit exemplo, ut dicebat, Catonis, qui Macedonas liberos pronuntiavit, quia tueri non poterant' (S.H.A. Hadr. 5. 3; Cato, frg. 161 M.). The reading 'teneri' forms a better contrast to 'liberos', and Janzer (Cato, 68 n. 214) aptly compares Fronto p. 206 N.: 'Hadrianus provincias manu Traiani captas omittere maluit quam exercitu retinere.' But Cato would scarcely have admitted Rome's inability to hold Macedonia, since she was clearly strong enough (as the event proved in 146); more probably he was arguing that Macedonia could not be adequately guarded without Roman commitments in the Balkans which he regarded as undesirable. See also p. 269.

greater internal unity, now established, found expression in a policy to which the philhellenists, the reactionaries, and the middle bloc could all subscribe.

After a goodwill tour through Greece, Paullus was joined by the *decemviri* and proclaimed the final terms of settlement: the Macedonians were to be free and pay to Rome annually half what they had paid to their king in direct tax, their country was to be divided into four Republics without political or economic intercourse with each other.[1] The economic terms were fair and even generous, but the boon of political liberty, though unexpected, was not much desired since the partition of the country violated the Macedonians' sense of nationhood. Thus a settlement which treated them as Greeks rather than barbarians and which its authors could regard as generous and conciliatory, largely failed to achieve its object. The treatment of Illyricum, which was divided into three districts, was based on similar principles.

In view of this moderation Rome's treatment of Epirus is the more difficult to understand. As Epirus had given Perseus some support, Anicius had already marched through the country which at once surrendered apart from four towns which he quickly reduced (168), but in the following year, acting upon direct orders from the Senate, Paullus invaded Epirus once more, took seventy towns, sent 150,000 Epirotes to the slave-market, and left the country desolate. The Epirotes apparently had committed no hostile act after their *deditio* to Anicius, and they might well have expected not to be treated more harshly than Macedonia, the protagonist, or even Illyricum; if so, they suffered a brutal disillusionment. Their fate probably reflects a change in Roman policy, which took a harsher turn in 167 when the more extreme plebeian leaders in the Senate forced through a severer settlement which Paullus dutifully executed though personally disapproving of it. In the formation of this harsher policy Charops, a pro-Roman Epirote, played an obscure but considerable part. In order to strengthen his own political position and to have a freer field in which to play the tyrant, he may well have urged the more brutal plebeian senators, who had themselves plundered Greece in recent years, to order the 'purging' of Epirus with fire and sword. The immediate consequence, however, of this change in Roman policy will have been to increase the distaste which Paullus felt towards the plebeian nobility, and to have weakened in the eyes of the world the moral authority which the more moderate treatment of Macedonia and Illyricum had gained for their conqueror.[2]

Rome's treatment of Greece, though somewhat less brutal, was

---

[1] See *CAH*, viii. 273, and J. A. O. Larsen, *CP*, 1949, 73 ff.

[2] On Charops see P. xxvii. 15; xxx. 12; 32. 12. On his influence on Roman policy see H. H. Scullard, *JRS*, 1945, 58 ff.

conceived in a similarly realistic and cynical spirit. Threats of future
disorders must be prevented by instilling a wholesome respect for the
might of Rome. This could most easily be achieved by rewarding the
loyal, punishing the rebellious, establishing local pro-Roman leaders
in control, and removing all suspect politicians so that no leaders
would be left to organize political opposition: Greece could remain
free as long as she was weak and disunited. How far these pro-Roman
'collaborators' may justly be regarded as traitors it is difficult to say:
some may have genuinely believed that in co-operation with Rome
lay the only hope for their countries' future, but the majority seem to
have been self-seeking time-servers. They readily supplied their
Roman masters with lists of political suspects, so that leaders from
Aetolia, Acarnania, Epirus, and Boeotia were deported to Rome for
trial. Achaea received similar treatment, but with less justice, since
her conduct had been correct. But the senatorial commissioners
listened to Callicrates' accusations against his fellow countrymen, and
1,000 Achaeans were deported to Italy for future trial. Polybius, one
of the men deported, expressly states that Paullus disapproved of the
charges brought by Callicrates and by the Aetolian Lyciscus, but he
did not disobey senatorial instructions.[1] His absence in Greece made
it easier for the extreme plebeian elements in the Senate to formulate
this harsher policy, against which he could not personally protest in
the Senate House. It may well have been supported also by Cato, who
with complete absence of sentiment would deprecate a more generous
policy which might involve Rome in further commitments in Greece.
Despite the prestige won at Pydna, Paullus did not dominate Roman
policy.

III. *The Senate and Pergamum and Rhodes*

With Greece overawed and purged, Macedonia prostrate, Syria
humiliated, and an enfeebled Egypt owing all to the strong arm of
Rome, the Senate had only to express its final dictate to the smaller
Hellenistic States of Pergamum and Rhodes. Here Roman policy was
shaped by previous intrigues and by a feeling that the great benefits
which these two States had received from Rome after the defeat of
Antiochus the Great had not been duly appreciated. Eumenes of
Pergamum, who had helped to precipitate the Third Macedonian War
and had rendered Rome loyal service during it, nevertheless had tried
to make the best of two worlds by entering into some negotiations
with Perseus.[2] Sufficient rumours of these proceedings leaked out
either genuinely to alarm the Senate or at any rate to give the extremist
elements an excuse to turn against Eumenes. When his brother Attalus
arrived in Rome in 167 to congratulate the Senate on the defeat of

---

[1] P. xxx. 13. 11. [2] P. xxix. 5–9. See below, p. 286.

Perseus and to complain about a recent attack by the Galatians upon Pergamum, 'some men of high rank', who unfortunately are not named by either Polybius or Livy, tried to corrupt Attalus' loyalty, and persuaded him to ask the Senate for part of his brother's kingdom. But before he committed himself in public he was recalled to a sense of duty by a councillor of his brother, and therefore merely congratulated the Senate and asked for help against the Galatians, suggesting also that he would like control of Aenus and Maronea. The Senate agreed; those senators who had negotiated with him thought that he would raise the question of Eumenes later, but they found themselves hoodwinked when Attalus promptly left Rome, and they could only vent their anger by cancelling the gift of Aenus and Maronea and sending P. Licinius Crassus (probably the consul of 171) to head a mission to the Galatians, whose aggressive behaviour might now appear slightly less heinous.

As earlier some senators had tried to play off Demetrius against Perseus, so now others sought to sow discord in the Attalid royal house, though with less tragic results.[1] These senators are probably to be identified with the less scrupulous plebeian group, including Marcius Philippus, whose diplomacy had previously shocked the more old-fashioned and upright: Antias has luckily preserved a reference to Philippus' friendly relations with Attalus and his hostility towards Eumenes. It was a man of the same kidney, Licinius Crassus, that was sent to the Galatians who were clearly promised a free hand by Rome, while Eumenes, whose military forces had been deployed alongside the Romans against Perseus instead of protecting their own country against the Galatians, had to fend for himself.

When Eumenes later arrived in Italy, seeking to improve his position, the Senate was somewhat embarrassed at the prospect of a personal meeting with the man whom they had proclaimed as 'their foremost and their greatest friend'.[2] Therefore, despite the fact that they had just given audience to King Prusias of Bithynia, whose help against Perseus had been much less and whose grovelling conduct excited the disgust of Polybius, they passed a decree that 'no king was to visit Rome'. Thus repulsed, Eumenes returned home to face renewed attacks from Galatia, a humbled and ill-rewarded client king.[3] In contrast Cotys, king of the Thracian Odrysae who had

---

[1] Livy (xlv. 19–20) in translating Polybius (xxx. 1–3) has cut down the last part of Polybius' narrative which is the most dishonourable to Rome.

[2] P. xxx. 19. 3.

[3] Polybius (xxxi. 6. 6) reports that this Roman insult to Eumenes increased the affection of the Greeks for him. The Ionian League hastened to show its sympathy by passing a decree in honour of the king who had shown himself 'a common benefactor of the Greeks'. Eumenes' letter in reply has been preserved: see C. B. Welles, *Royal Correspondence in the Hellenistic Period*, 209 ff.

supported Perseus, received magnanimous treatment from Rome: he was probably welcomed into alliance and his son, a Roman prisoner, was restored.[1] The king would prove a useful watchdog against Eumenes, whose control of the Thracian Chersonese, once Odrysian territory, he would regard with jealousy.

Rome's relations with Rhodes, which had received great advantages from the settlement of 188, had gradually deteriorated, so that a group of pro-Macedonian statesmen gradually gained influence there, but nothing was done to exasperate Rome until 168, when as the Third Macedonian War was still dragging on with its disruptive effect on their trade the Rhodians decided to attempt mediation. Unfortunately for them, however, their envoys had just arrived in Rome when news of Pydna came; this allowed Rome to take a stronger line and placed the envoys in an awkward position. After an unconvincing attempt to substitute a speech of congratulation for the one they had come to deliver, they were dismissed. Rhodes then appealed to the Roman commission which was on its way to Egypt; after a bullying speech from Popillius and a more conciliatory one from C. Decimius, the Rhodians condemned to death all who were convicted of having spoken or acted in favour of Perseus, and sent another embassy to Rome, which met with a frigid reception early in 167.

The issue was forced by a praetor, M'. Iuventius Thalna, who urged the People to declare war on Rhodes. He had an eye on a naval command for himself, and could hope for wide support from the People and trading classes: he would promise a quick victory, glory, spoils, and the elimination of the main commercial power in the eastern Mediterranean. His action, however, raised constitutional issues: though not illegal, it was certainly not customary to bring a question of declaring war before the People without prior discussion in the Senate. The Senate found two tribunes, M. Antonius and M. Pomponius, to check him, Antonius even dragging him down from the Rostra; but they also had acted precipitately because normally tribunes did not veto a proposal before the People had an opportunity to discuss it.

With its constitutional authority thus re-established the Senate proceeded to consider the Rhodian question at leisure.[2] The senators most bitterly opposed to Rhodes, according to Livy, were those who as consuls, praetors, or *legati* had recently fought in Macedonia; as Paullus was still in the Balkans, these men will have been the more extreme plebeian leaders of 171–169. Since there was no legal justification for declaring war, because the Rhodians had committed no

---

[1] P. xxx. 17; L. xlv. 42.
[2] The speech of the Rhodian Astymedes aroused the disgust of Polybius (xxx. 4–5. Cf. L. xlv. 21–5).

hostile act, their arguments will have been based in the last resort upon power-politics: though not emphasizing the material benefits which would fall to those who conducted and participated in such a war, they would stress the desirability of not missing such an opportunity to remove any possibility of future threats or danger.[1]

On the other side the Rhodian cause found its most impressive advocate in Cato, who strongly deprecated war. In one of his most famous speeches[2] he urged his fellow countrymen not to let success unbalance their judgement and perhaps suggested that the removal of potential rivalry was a moral danger. Besides emphasizing the past *beneficia* and *amicitia* of Rhodes towards Rome, he appears to have based his main argument upon the fact that as Rhodes had committed no act of hostility it would not be just (*aequum*) to punish her for hostile thoughts. This appeal to *aequitas* and the implication that a war against Rhodes would not be a *bellum iustum* is consonant with Cato's general traditional outlook, but in view of his later impassioned advocacy for a declaration of war on Carthage, where the legal issue was by no means clear, he may be supposed to have acted no less from motives of expediency than from moral scruples: any action that might increase Rome's permanent commitments in the East must be avoided. If justice and expediency coincided, so much the better. At any rate Cato's solicitude for the freedom of Greeks must have caused many a philhellenic senator to wonder whether Saul also was among the prophets. His arguments, which were probably supported by the friends of Aemilius Paullus,[3] won the day. Thus Rhodes escaped war, though not loss, and after a humiliating interval her request for an alliance was finally granted in 165. Thus the island was subjected to Rome's will almost as fully as by open war, and Cato and the patrician senators could congratulate themselves on attaining their objectives without having given the plebeian leaders a chance for further self-aggrandizement and gain.

On their return from the Macedonian War Aemilius Paullus, Anicius, and Octavius were decreed triumphs by the Senate, but trouble arose among Paullus' men: already irked by his strict discipline, they were dissatisfied with their booty and began to agitate against granting

---

[1] On the part that Q. Marcius Philippus may have played in these intrigues, see p. 287.

[2] Cato evidently regarded his speech *Pro Rhodiensibus* as one of his most important, because he included it in Book V of his *Origines*; excerpts seem to have been published separately later. See Aulus Gellius, vi. 3; Malcovati, *ORF*, 64–6 and frgs. 162–9; Janzer, *Cato*, 69–76. Cf. p. 269. The fact that Iuventius Thalna belonged to a noble family from Tusculum (Cic. *Pro Plancio*, 12, 19), Cato's own birthplace, may have increased Cato's hostility to the proposal.

[3] Besides Paullus' general moderation, it is noteworthy that the tribune Antonius, who had acted so effectively to avert a declaration of war, was his supporter: it was he who later summoned the Assembly in order that Paullus might address it immediately after his triumph (L. xlv. 40. 9).

their general his triumph. Their discontent was inflamed by Servius Sulpicius Galba, who had served as military tribune under Paullus and had a personal grievance against him. Among those who spoke in Paullus' favour was Servilius Geminus (*cos.* 202 and probably the oldest living consular), while Cato is not likely to have been silent when the question of a general's right to enforce strict discipline and economy was at stake.[1] Backed by such authority, the cause of Paullus prevailed, and while he received an honour that he richly deserved, the Senate had the satisfaction of seeing its control over the more unruly elements in the State re-established. For three days early in September 167 Paullus held a magnificent triumph with Perseus led in chains before his chariot; he then paid some 200 or 300 million sesterces into the Treasury, as a result of which the whole citizen body was relieved from the annual *tributum*.[2] On the following day Cn. Octavius celebrated his naval triumph over Perseus, and some $2\frac{1}{2}$ months later Anicius held his triumph over Genthius and the Illyrians, but the plebeian general could not equal the glory of the patrician Paullus, whose triumph symbolized the restored prestige and authority of the older senatorial families and traditions.

Rome appeared at the height of her power. The Hellenistic world lay in broken pieces at her feet and it owed any independence that it still enjoyed entirely to the patronage of a Power which fifty years before had appeared to Philip V as only 'a cloud in the West'. That cloud now filled the sky over the whole Mediterranean, bringing to some fertilizing showers, but to others destructive storms. Neither the drive of a Mithridates nor the genius of a Cleopatra could re-establish the absolute independence of any part of Alexander's empire, while the great days of Carthage also lay in the past. The barbarian world retained the will, but lacked the organized power, to strike a mortal blow. At home unity had been re-established, at least in appearance: rapacious provincial governors had been admonished and punished, impudent tribunes and magistrates had been overruled, restless veterans had been brought to heel, an older and higher standard of military discipline and public service had been reasserted, and many newer plebeian senators were less ready to challenge the older order.

But world predominance brought fresh problems and temptations:

---

[1] An anecdote is recorded from a speech by Cato *Contra Ser. Galbam ad milites* which probably should be dated to 167 (Gellius, i. 23. 1): see p. 269.

[2] 'per triduum IIII, III, prid. k. Decem.' (Fasti Cap. Pre-Julian calendar). Valerius Antias (*apud* L. xlv. 40. 1) gives 120 million sesterces, Velleius Paterculus (i. 9. 6) 210, and Pliny (*NH* xxxiii. 56) 300 million. Paullus apparently decided to let bygones be bygones, since he gave generously to his troops at his triumph, 100 *denarii* to each infantry-man. Flamininus in 194, Scipio Asiaticus in 188, and Fulvius Nobilior in 187 had given only 25 *denarii* (L. xxxiv. 52. 11; xxxvii. 59. 6; xxxix. 5. 17); Manlius Vulso in 186 and Q. Fulvius Flaccus in 180 had gone as high as 42 and 50 *den.* respectively (xxxix. 7; xl. 43. 5).

the generous philhellenism of the first decade of the century was out-moded, the attempt of Cato to reassert a rigid adherence to the *mos maiorum* was doomed to failure, and though men like Aemilianus might try to blend the better elements of Greek and Roman life into a larger unity, a cancer was gnawing at the body politic. True, the spirit might later shape another body for its dwelling-place, but the old form was doomed to gradual decline. The cleavage between Senate and People was now more serious than in the early years of the Hannibalic War, partly because the Senate was a less united and more self-seeking body. The scandals of recent years revealed an essential schism in the Senate, and demonstrated the strength of the popular backing which those senators could win who set personal gain before class loyalty. Such men as yet scarcely constituted a serious political danger as demagogues, but not many years were to pass before the Gracchi dis-closed that a greater danger to the senatorial government, which would not face the problems of the day, might come from popular leaders who aimed at the well-being of the people rather than at personal advantage. Such a moral challenge shook the government to its foundations, while the careers of the plebeian leaders of 171–169 pointed the way for later *populares* who like them set self before the Republic.

XIII

BALANCE OF POLICY AND GROUPS

(166–155 B.C.)

1. *Cato and a Changing World*

THE loss of the second half of Livy's fifth decade, with its record of election struggles and lists of praetors, renders impossible any detailed study of rivalries within the nobility during the period until Cato's death in 149. Nor can internal differences be brought into close relation with the conduct of foreign affairs; but this is less important at first because violent internal disagreement on external policy is not likely to have arisen for some time. Apart from episodes in Corsica, Liguria, and Dalmatia, peace was maintained and no major issues arose. The Senate had no mind for fighting the weakened Hellenistic world, which was rent with internal dissensions; these the Senate allayed or encouraged as it judged best in Rome's interest, while diplomatic pressure sufficed to keep the dissentients within bounds. Rivalry among senators for the chance to serve on foreign commissions, as well as for the home magistracies, must have continued, but the issues were generally petty in contrast with those of the previous fifty years. Cato, however, lived long enough to witness the emergence, though not the solution, of three greater problems: the insurrections in Spain, the treatment of Carthage, and the revolt in Macedonia. But before these are considered, the general complexion of home affairs in the years following Pydna may be noted, years which are badly chronicled but which are marked by a hardening of the heart and a weakening of the moral fibres of the governing class that gradually caused the mistress of the world to become the slave of her own desires.

The censorship of L. Aemilius Paullus and Q. Marcius Philippus in 164 illustrates the spirit of the times. Both were representatives of old Roman *gentes* (indeed Marcius could point to King Ancus Marcius and Coriolanus among the ancestors of the patrician branches of his *gens*), but while Paullus exemplified some of the more rigid aspects of the *mos maiorum* Philippus had moved with the times and displayed a 'slickness' ('nova et callida sapientia') that offended the old-fashioned. Their moderation in revising the list of senators and Equites illustrates the calmer waters that had been reached; they were more ready to drift with the tide than to attempt unpopular reforms; with the prestige and authority of the Senate restored, there was less need for severity and greater excuse for tolerance. A symbol of the new age was set before all men's eyes when Philippus dedicated a statue to Concordia.[1]

But such a gesture could not quell all private enmities, and this censorship was marked by a startling episode: Cato was charged with extravagance by his enemies before the censors. After delivering a speech *De sumptu suo*,[2] he presumably cleared himself, since not only does Pliny record that he was never condemned on any occasion that he was accused but it is also unlikely that Rome's greatest censor could have incurred the censors' reproof without some trace of this being left in the surviving tradition. Our knowledge of Cato's defence, scanty though it is, throws some light on the nature of the charge. He employed the trick of ordering the clerk of the court to read extracts from an earlier speech of his which recorded the uprightness of his administration;[3] at each fresh item, Cato would interrupt with some such phrase as 'They don't want to hear that now' (e.g. 'istud quoque dele; nolunt audire: recita porro'). There followed a series of denials: Cato had never distributed money when canvassing, had never set prefects in allied towns to rob them of their property, wives, or children, never deprived his troops of their due share of booty by distributing it among a few of his friends, never given his friends the chance to make money by assigning them official journeys, never distributed to his clerks or friends silver for the purchase of wine. But, concluded Cato, he dared not now recall these benefits to the State: one may do evil with impunity, but not good.[4]

The accusation, therefore, apparently was the extravagant misuse of public money, but since so far as is known Cato had not held any office recently and had been famed for the parsimony of his administration (he had even left in Spain the horse which had carried him through his consular campaign in order to save the State the cost of its transport), the formal charge may have related to his private expenditure; in this case he probably recalled his previous testimony to his carefulness in public expenditure merely to illustrate his general economy. Since in his old age he became fond of entertaining his neighbours, he may possibly on some occasion have infringed the lex Orchia of 182, which had limited the number of guests that might be entertained, and thus given his private enemies a heaven-sent chance to poke fun at him; the more so, since the law had perhaps been Cato's work; at any rate he had opposed its repeal, possibly with success (p. 172).

[1] Three junior senators were expelled (οὐ τῶν ἐπιφανῶν, Plut. *Aem. Paull.* 38. 9). On the censorship and statue see also Livy, *Per.* xlvi; Pliny, *NH*, vii. 214; xxvi. 5; Diod. xxxi. 25. 1; Val. Max. vii. 5. 3; Cic. *Pro dom.* 50; Censorin. *De die nat.* 23. 7; Festus 285 M.
[2] See p. 270.   [3] See p. 268.
[4] *Apud* Fronto p. 99 N.; Malcovati, frg. 171.

Cato concluded his speech with a startling remark: 'suum cuique per me uti atque frui licet'. This might suggest that he was beginning to realize the hopelessness of moral reform by legislation. If he was at length willing to live and let live, then indeed could Concordia flourish, but his future conduct suggests rather that this remark represents only a passing phase. When in 161 the consul C. Fannius carried a law to limit extravagant meals, Cato will not have withheld his support;[1] indeed he may well have instigated the measure in order to demonstrate the justice of his acquittal and the continued maintenance of his principles.

Yet Cato in 164 was a very different man from the youth who had worked on a Sabine farm or even the censor. Times were changing and, if he did not adapt himself to them, at any rate he did not remain quite the same. Now that his position in the State was assured and thirty years had passed since the consulship which had turned the *novus homo* into a *nobilis*, he may have moderated somewhat the rigidity of his manner of life: perhaps his great affection for his child (born *c.* 192) had helped to humanize him in some respects even though he still ruled his slaves with a rod of iron. But the change went deeper than greater liberality in his hospitality or the knocking off of some of his more awkward corners: it affected his whole life. He devoted himself to money-making, and the man who had worked on his own fields and had said that farming and frugality were the only two ways of getting money now became a capitalist and invested in business and commerce. He bought lakes, hot springs, districts for fullers, pitch factories, land with natural pasture, and forest; further, through a freedman, he lent money to shipping companies of fifty partners and cannily covered his own risks. The man who had denounced usury now lent money to his slaves who would buy, train, and then resell other young slaves, to his own profit. It would seem, however, that he tried to conceal these activities as far as possible and to discourage busybodies; if ever he had to send a slave to another man's house, he ordered him always to say, if asked, that he did not know what his master was doing.

When people gradually began to realize Cato's changing status and way of life, no doubt many of the small farmers of Italy, who had supported him in the past because he had been one of themselves and knew their life, began to cool off: but that would make little difference to him since, unless he wished to advance the prospects of some younger man, he no longer needed their votes at the elections. It was in this later part of his life that he wrote *De Agri Cultura*, perhaps partly to show his continued interest in the land, partly to recall his

---

[1] Pliny, *NH*, x. 139; Macrobius, *Sat.* iii. 17. 3 (wrongly assigns it to 159); Gell. ii. 24. 3; Tert. *Apol.* 6. 2; Athenaeus, vi. 108 (274).

earlier contacts. But although the work is full of practical knowledge, it reflects the interests of the man who could invest in an estate of 200 or 300 *iugera*, tended by a resident bailiff, rather than those of the really small farmer. Indeed much of Cato's later years was devoted to literary work, to composing the *Origines* and publishing his speeches. Though as distrustful as ever of philosophy, his literary interests widened. In short, while still keeping a shrewd eye on public affairs and ever ready to give battle in the Senate or law-courts, Cato seems to have developed his private life. If his slightly easier manners and less concealed culture pleased some of his fellow-senators, his some-what furtive money-making must have amused or shocked others. Despite the fact that his son married into a noble family, Cato never let the nobility forget that he was a *novus homo*.[1]

The death of Aemilius Paullus in 160 at the age of about 68 removed one of Cato's slightly younger contemporaries. He had been a stabi-lizing influence in Roman life, a patrician who was yet popular with the people, exemplifying many of the finer qualities of the earlier Roman character, but not unappreciative of the attraction of Greek influences. Politically, though not socially, he stood midway between Cato and the extreme plebeian nobility. Forced by a sense of duty to execute a harsh sentence in Epirus, he nevertheless died relatively poor although he had brought immense wealth into the State Treasury. At his funeral games the *Adelphi* of Terence was performed. The production of Terence's plays during the previous few years was a sign of the increasing hellenization of the Roman nobility, but Cato could have had little anxiety that this transportation of Athenian New Comedy with its lax morals to the Roman stage would seriously affect the Roman people, since they soon grew tired of the perfection of the poet's Attic grace and found rope-dancers and gladiators more attractive than the *Hecyra* (165), just as they had preferred that the Greek musicians whom Anicius had secured to enliven his triumph should split into groups to see which could make the most noise.

A more serious threat to traditional Roman ways of thought came from Greek philosophers. In 173 two Epicureans had been expelled from Rome, and in 161 a *senatusconsultum* enjoined the expulsion of philosophers and rhetoricians in general, but such measures achieved little. In 159, or possibly in 168, the Stoic Crates, an ambassador from Pergamum, happened to break his leg while in Rome and during his convalescence began to give lectures: Stoicism, with its emphasis on virtue, made a great impression on Roman society, an impression which was later deepened by the teaching of Panaetius.[2] Less good

---

[1] Plutarch (*Cato*, 21; 25) is the main source of information about the change in Cato's later years. Cf. F. della Corte, *Catone Censore*, 30 ff., 51 ff.

[2] Sueton. *De gramm.* 2: 'Crates . . . missus ad senatum ab Attalo rege inter secundum

resulted from the visit of three Greek philosophers, Critolaus the Peripatetic, Diogenes the Stoic, and Carneades the Academician, whom the Athenians sent to Rome in 155 to represent their point of view in a dispute which had arisen between Athens and Oropus. Not only did the ambassadors illustrate three styles of oratory, but the Scepticism of Carneades startled his audience at his lectures: he accepted principles one day which he refuted the next, he propounded the theory that justice is a convention, and suggested that Rome had conquered the world while pretending to defend everyone. This was too much for Cato who urged the dismissal of the embassy.[1] But not thus could Greek thought be stemmed.

With the disappearance of men of the type of Paullus, Cato must have felt increasingly isolated: an old man living amid new conditions, new ideas, and a new generation of men. Though, like most moralists, he may have exaggerated the decadence of the times, a real deterioration of standards, following the influx of wealth and ideas from the East, cannot be denied. It is attested by the contemporary evidence of Polybius, who contrasts the continence of young Aemilianus with the general extravagance and dissoluteness 'which had as it were burst into flame at this period'.[2] This decline may have been mainly confined to Rome itself and have affected the nobility in the first instance, but there lay the danger: if the governing class became rotten, there would be little hope for the Republic. Serious attempts were made to check this moral deterioration and Cato must have been backed by many responsible senators, but measures like the lex Fannia or the *senatusconsultum* of 161 which enjoined the expulsion of Greek philosophers and rhetoricians, or the law to check *ambitus* carried in 159, were merely palliative.[3]

The changing economic conditions, which formed the material background to this moral decline, are well known and require only

ac tertium bellum sub ipsam Enni mortem'. The difficulty is that Ennius died in 169 while Attalus II did not come to the throne until 160/59. Crates' visit therefore must be placed either in *c.* 159 and Suetonius' reference to Ennius' death be regarded as a loose one, or else in 168/7 when Eumenes sent his brother Attalus to Rome, 'cum Attalo' perhaps being read for 'ab Attalo'. It is one of the pleasant ironies of history that Crates broke his leg through stumbling into a drain: Cato as censor had spent a fortune in overhauling the sewage system and covering in open drains; had his work been a little more thorough, he might have spared Rome from the corrupting influence of Crates' lectures.

[1] See, for example, Plut. *Cato*, 22. C. Acilius, whose family had supported the Scipios and whose historical work had considerable influence upon later Roman annalists, had at his own request interpreted the first speeches of the ambassadors in the Senate. Cf. Cicero's remark (*De rep.* iii. 9) about Carneades, 'qui saepe optimas causas ingeni calumnia ludificari solet'. Cato's observation that philosophers were mere *mortualia* (winding sheets or funeral dirges: Gellius, xviii. 7. 3) might derive from a speech made on such an occasion.

[2] P. xxxi. 25. 6.

[3] Lex Fannia, see above, p. 222. Rhetoricians, Suet. *De rhet.* 1; 8. Gell. xv. 11. 1. *Lex de ambitu*, Livy, *Per.* xlvii; it is often called lex Cornelia Fulvia, though it is not certain that the consuls of 159 were responsible.

the briefest mention here.[1] First, the assured financial stability of the State was brought home to every citizen by the permanent suspension of *tributum* in 167. It was by this date that, according to the most recent view, the *denarius* after a period of competition with earlier *nummi* had finally established its mastery as the standard coin; amid the welter of Rome's older coinage of *quadrigati* and *victoriati* and the foreign coinage that poured into Italy (*argentum Oscense* from Spain, gold *Philippi* and silver tetradrachms from Greece, and *cistophori* from Asia) the new *denarius* had finally ousted the old, just as the plays of Terence had ousted those of Plautus.[2] This stability was well maintained, since there were coins and ore to the value of $25\frac{1}{2}$ million *denarii* in the Treasury-vaults in 157 B.C.[3] Wealth from the Eastern conquests accelerated the supersession of peasant husbandry by capitalist farming in many parts of Italy, land increasingly became an object of speculation, and *latifundia* spread because the wars had provided not only skilled and cultivated slaves but also a cruder type, such as Ligurians, Molossians from Epirus, or Sardinians and Corsicans after the final reduction of the latter island in 163, who worked the large estates, particularly in Etruria and south Italy. Slave labour also increased, though not to the same extent, in Latium and Campania, where fresh problems were created when after the Third Macedonian War provincial corn was no longer absorbed by the armies abroad, but was brought to Rome which thereby needed less corn from Latium.

It was in the light of these changing conditions that Cato wrote his *De Agri Cultura*. In it he illustrates the new type of mixed farming to which many Roman nobles were turning in Latium and Campania: men would invest in estates of 200 or 300 *iugera*, where the cultivation of the vine and olive took precedence over corn-growing, while grazing was even more profitable. The cities needed horses and wool, mutton and beef, as well as wine, oil, and vegetables. A resident bailiff and his wife could run an olive-plantation of 240 *iugera* with 11 slaves or a vineyard of 100 *iugera* with 14 slaves, since free labour could be drawn upon at harvest time; the capitalist owner could live the life of a gentleman in the city, while his richer neighbour might own far more extensive slave-plantations in Etruria. Those small farmers who failed to win a livelihood at home drifted off to seek their fortunes abroad or else to the cities, especially Rome itself, where they created an unemployment problem, which the Senate, uninterested in the promotion of industry, did nothing to solve. Indeed, if a measure which stopped mining in Italy belongs to this period, the Senate,

---

[1] See T. Frank, *Econ. Survey*, i, ch. 3; *CAH*, viii. 336 ff.; A. H. McDonald, *CHJ*, 1939, 136 ff. [2] See H. Mattingly, *JRS*, 1945, 76.
[3] Pliny, *NH*, xxxiii. 55.

actuated probably by a desire not to increase opportunities for the *publicani* and business class, publicly demonstrated its indifference to the possibilities of industrial expansion.[1] The task of draining the Pontine Marshes, which was entrusted to the consuls of 160, and a measure, of doubtful date, designed to protect Italian wine and oil against competition from Transalpine Gaul, were puny attempts to deal with a vast problem, and in any case were passed in the interest as much of the senatorial nobility as of the small farmer.[2]

11. *The Scipionic Revival*

Amid these economic and moral changes traditional Roman standards of life were carried on into the next generation by P. Cornelius Scipio Nasica Corculum, who though not a man after Cato's heart (after all he was a Scipio) nevertheless was a Roman of the older type. Son of the consul of 191, who had died *c.* 171, he had married Cornelia, the elder daughter of Africanus and sister of the mother of the Gracchi. He would be commended to Cato neither by his birth nor by the Games which he gave as aedile in 169, when he exhibited 63 African panthers and 40 bears and elephants, thereby availing himself of a plebiscite carried by Cn. Aufidius which raised a ban on the importation of such animals; the *senatusconsultum* which had originally imposed this restriction may well have been inspired by Cato.[3] In the following year Nasica had contributed substantially to the victory at Pydna by leading the turning movement around the Olympus range which had forced Perseus to retire to the final field of battle.

His election to the consulship for 162, together with C. Marcius Figulus, was accompanied by some political wire-pulling, of which the details and implications are obscure. In 163 the consul M'. Iuventius Thalna had dealt with an insurrection in Corsica, but died suddenly while reading a congratulatory dispatch from the Senate.[4] His colleague, Ti. Sempronius Gracchus, who was holding his second consulship, apparently took over command of Thalna's army and also conducted the elections for 162, at which Nasica was elected. After Nasica had reached his province of Corsica he was recalled by the news that Gracchus had discovered that he had vitiated the election by omitting to renew the auspices when after entering Rome to preside over the Senate he had again crossed the *pomerium* to conduct the

[1] Pliny, *NH*, iii. 138; xxxvii. 202. Cf. A. H. McDonald, *CHJ*, 1939, 139.

[2] Cic. *De Rep.* iii. 16. Cf. A. H. McDonald (loc. cit.), who avoids the exaggeration of Rostovtzeff and the depreciation of T. Frank in regard to the importance of this measure.

[3] L. xliv. 18. 8; Pliny, *NH*, viii. 64. Cf. De Sanctis, IV. i. 615 n. 319, who supports the view of Lange (*Rom. Alt.* ii³. 311) that the date was 170 when a certain Cn. Aufidius was tribune (L. xliii. 8. 2).

[4] Val. Max. ix. 12. 3; Pliny, *NH*, vii. 182. The *cognomen* Thalna appears to be Etruscan: see Schulze, *Zur Geschichte latein. Eigennamen*, 94.

elections in the Campus Martius. Thus Nasica and his colleague, *vitio creati*, were compelled to abdicate.[1] Gracchus' motives are not likely to have been purely disinterested, and he may well have tried to oust Nasica from an area which he may have considered his own preserve: apart from his activity there in the previous year he had served successfully in Sardinia during his first consulship (177). Personal ambition outweighed family ties (he and Nasica had married two Cornelias, the daughters of Africanus), and if there was any party significance in the move Gracchus failed to gain more than a personal success, since the consuls elected to replace Nasica and Marcius were P. Cornelius Lentulus and Cn. Domitius Ahenobarbus, whose family connexions had not been with the Claudian-Fulvians and the middle bloc.[2] Nasica's political career, however, was not disturbed; he became censor in 159 with M. Popillius Laenas,[3] and obtained a second consulship in 155 when he finished off a war in Dalmatia. It may be noted that his partner in the unfortunate consulship of 162, Marcius Figulus, had anticipated him by one year in gaining a second consulship, but Figulus' conduct of the war in Dalmatia, where he met with an initial set-back and only slowly regained the initiative, gave Nasica a chance to supersede his predecessor and gain a triumph.

In the years before this success the Cornelii had become more prominent in office. In 162 after the rejection of Nasica the consulship had been held by P. Cornelius Lentulus (son of the consul of 199) who had been aedile with Nasica in 169 and then taken part in the Macedonian War. In 161 L. Cornelius Merula was curule aedile, in 160 M. Cornelius Cethegus was consul, in 159 Cn. Cornelius Dolabella was consul and Nasica was censor. But after these four consulships in as many years the Cornelii gained only two more in the next eleven years: L. Cornelius Lentulus Lupus in 156 and Nasica again in 155, after which seven years elapsed until Scipio Aemilianus won his first consulship in 147. In contrast to this Cornelian revival around 160, and perhaps in an attempt to check it, the old Aemilian-Fulvian alliance, which went back to the censorship of Aemilius Lepidus and Fulvius Nobilior in 179, may have been renewed;[4] if so, Lepidus himself, who had been *princeps senatus* for twenty years, will have exerted his influence to achieve it. Nobilior's son, Marcus Fulvius, was consul in 159, while a relation of Lepidus, M. Aemilius Lepidus, became consul for 158; possibly the Popillii joined the group, since M. Popillius Laenas

---

[1] Cic. *De nat. deor.* ii. 11; *De div.* i. 33; *Ad Q. fr.* ii. 2. 1; Val. Max. i. 1. 3; Plut. *Marc.* 5. Cf. Mommsen, *Staatsr.* i. 103 n. 4 (*Dr. publ.* i. 118 n. 3).

[2] Descendants of the old Fabian group had recently won successes at the consular elections: M. Claudius Marcellus (son of the *cos.* of 196) for 166, and (perhaps under his presidency) T. Manlius Torquatus for 165, and A. Manlius Torquatus for 164.

[3] Little is recorded about this censorship: see Pliny, *NH*, vii. 215; xxxiv. 30; *De vir. ill.* 44. 3; Vell. Pat. ii. 3. 1; Gell. iv. 20. 11.   [4] Cf. Münzer, *RA*, 237–8.

gained the censorship for 159 and his younger brother, C. Popillius Laenas, obtained his second consulship for 158. With the loss of Livy's lists of praetors the speed with which these men reached the consulship cannot be determined, but all the praetors who held office in or before 167 and who finally obtained the consulship succeeded by 162, with the exception of Anicius Gallus; despite his Illyrian triumph eight years elapsed before he gained the consulship (160). It is unlikely that any of the Cornelian or Fulvian consuls had waited so long.

III. *The Senate and the East*

In the years that followed Pydna the conduct of foreign affairs became less controversial and offered the Roman nobles less opportunity for winning personal glory, although some military successes could be snatched from the barbarian fringe, where the security of the frontiers involved minor campaigning. One problem was to check the tribes of the Maritime Alps and thus safeguard the coast road to Massilia and Spain. Victories here secured triumphs for the consuls of 166 (C. Sulpicius Gallus and M. Claudius Marcellus) and some fighting seems to have continued until M. Fulvius Nobilior, as proconsul in 158, triumphed over the Ligures Veleiates (Eleates). A rebellion of the Apuani gave M. Claudius Marcellus, who held a second consulship in 155, a second triumph *de Liguribus et Apuanis*. Finally in 154 the Oxybian Ligures, who were harassing the trade routes of Massilia and had insulted a Roman ambassador, were crushed by Q. Opimius (*cos.* 154) who failed to obtain a triumph though his victory seems to have been decisive.[1] The successful crushing of trouble in Corsica by Iuventius Thalna (163) has already been mentioned; death robbed him of the chance of a triumph but afforded Gracchus an opportunity to intrigue against Nasica, who later found another field for military glory.

Piratical attacks by the Dalmatians against the island of Issa induced the Senate in 158 to send out a commission of inquiry, headed by C. Fannius (*cos.* 161), which received a rough welcome. The Senate used this excuse to declare war on the Dalmatians; the reasons, however, were, according to Polybius, the desire to settle a region which had been neglected ever since the expulsion of Demetrius of Pharos, and still more to prevent the Romans becoming enervated by a long-continued peace.[2] C. Marcius Figulus opened the campaign in 156, but met with an initial defeat which he later retrieved; meanwhile his colleague, L. Cornelius Lentulus Lupus, advanced in the North from Aquileia against the Pannonians, moving along the Drave as far as

---

[1] P. xxxiii. 8–10; Livy, *Per.* xlvii. The wounded commissioner was Flaminius, his colleagues being Popillius Laenas and L. Pupius.   [2] P. xxxii. 9; 13.

Segestia (Siscia), only to meet with disaster. This double defeat led to a demand for more experienced commanders so that Scipio Nasica and M. Claudius Marcellus were both elected to a second consulship for 155. While Marcellus secured the Ligurian frontier, Nasica brought the Dalmatian war to a successful conclusion, and both men were granted triumphs. This renewal of more energetic military measures marked the first step towards a new policy of overseas conquest.

In their contacts with the Hellenistic world, however, senators could achieve distinction in the field of diplomacy rather than of battle. An appeal from the Achaeans, asking for the trial or release of their fellow countrymen interned in Italy, was brusquely rejected; this uncompromising refusal to face the justice of the request crushed the spirit of the Greeks and encouraged 'collaborators' like Callicrates and Charops. Greece must be kept humble and have no political leaders except pro-Romans. Not much more consideration was shown to Eumenes after his humiliation in 167: the Senate listened to complaints from Prusias and from some Asiatic towns which accused Eumenes of intriguing with Antiochus Epiphanes. Eumenes then sent his brothers, Attalus and Athenaeus, to defend his cause before the Senate, but it remained suspicious; and C. Sulpicius Gallus who was sent to the East with M'. Sergius behaved outrageously: he openly sought evidence against Eumenes and welcomed informers at Sardis in the heart of his kingdom.

Asiatic affairs were further complicated when young Antiochus Eupator succeeded his father Epiphanes (early 163). His cousin Demetrius, who was a grandson of Antiochus the Great and the legitimate heir to the throne, was at Rome as a hostage and now asked the Senate to restore him to the Syrian throne. But the Senate, judging that young Antiochus would prove a more pliable instrument in the future, sent Cn. Octavius, Sp. Lucretius, and L. Aurelius to secure his succession and also to weaken Syria's military power by destroying some ships and elephants which were being held in excess of the limits fixed by the treaty of Apamea. The envoys were also to visit Galatia and Cappadocia. The Galatian Trocmi, having failed to annex any part of Cappadocia, had tried to undermine Rome's trust in Ariarathes, doubtless on the ground of his friendship with Eumenes, but the king had won the confidence of a mission headed by M. Iunius, and now welcomed Octavius' arrival. When he died soon afterwards (164/3), the Senate cordially extended Rome's friendship and alliance to his successor, Ariarathes V Eusebes Philopator, chiefly on the strength of a very favourable report by Ti. Gracchus on the late king and his kingdom.[1] In a subsequent struggle for the throne between Ariarathes,

[1] P. xxxi. 1–3; 6; 8–9.

supported by Attalus, and his brother Orophernes, supported by the Syrian Demetrius, Rome took little part, beyond showing a preference for Ariarathes. Thus the work of conciliation, which Gracchus had achieved in Spain some fifteen years earlier, was now matched by his championship of the cause of Cappadocia and of Rhodes, whose alliance he had successfully advocated, while his authority was recognized by election to a second consulship for 163.

Trouble soon flared up in Syria. A popular outburst resulted in the murder of Octavius, and Demetrius judged the time ripe for action; after a further vain appeal to the Senate, he escaped from Italy with the help of Polybius. The Senate took no drastic action, but merely sent Ti. Gracchus, L. Cornelius Lentulus, and Servilius Glaucia to watch the situation in the East.[1] Demetrius was welcomed in Syria, where he put to death young Antiochus, and he finally obtained official recognition from the Senate through the influence of Gracchus, the peace-maker.

Meanwhile Egypt was disturbed by the quarrels of the two brothers Ptolemy Philometor and Euergetes, which Rome turned to her own advantage if she did not actively promote them.[2] When Philometor was expelled from Egypt by Euergetes and sought help in Rome (164), the Senate probably only ordered the commission which was in the East under Octavius to try to settle the quarrel (163).[3] Euergetes' cruelty, however, led to a reaction in Egypt, and the brothers reached an understanding that Philometor should reign in Egypt and Cyprus, while Euergetes had Cyrene (163). This unity, however, was soon broken and in 162 Euergetes appeared in Rome to ask for the control of Cyprus. Despite a recommendation in favour of Philometor made by the commissioners Canuleius and Q. Marcius, and perhaps backed up by Cato and Scipio Aemilianus,[4] the Senate granted Euergetes' request. T. Manlius Torquatus and Cn. Cornelius Merula were sent to enforce this decision, which rested purely upon a consideration of

[1] P. xxxi. 11–15.

[2] Otto, *Gesch. Zeit VI. Ptol.* 91 ff., takes the latter view of Roman policy.

[3] E. R. Bevan, *History of Egypt*, 291, believes that the Senate at this point divided the Egyptian empire between the brothers, giving Philometor Egypt proper. But on the evidence of P. xxxi. 10, Otto (92 n. 5) has denied this. The Senate at some point sent out L. Canuleius Dives (= praetor of 171?) and the son of Marcius Philippus as observers; they may have had a hand in the arrangements, but, according to Otto, behind the scenes since Rome had not yet openly declared her support of Philometor. It is probable that the close connexions of M. Aemilius Lepidus with the Egyptian royal family will have led him to exercise some influence upon Roman policy, but nothing is known of any action by him.

[4] Cato supported Philometor later, calling him 'rex optimus atque beneficissimus'; see below, p. 271. For the low view that Scipio took of Euergetes see Athen. xii. 549c, 550a, and Plut. *Moral.* 201A, which ultimately derive from Panaetius, who accompanied Scipio on a journey to Egypt. This preference for Philometor over Euergetes will have affected Polybius' view.

Roman interests. Polybius comments: 'the Romans avail themselves with profound policy of the mistakes of others to augment and strengthen their own empire, under the guise of granting favours and benefiting those who commit the errors'.[1] But when the commissioners failed to enforce agreement between the brothers the Senate broke off diplomatic relations with Philometor and sent P. Apustius and C(n). Cornelius Lentulus to support Euergetes in his claim to Cyprus (161). And there the matter rested for a few years, except that with the support given to Euergetes may possibly be connected his decision to bequeath his kingdom to Rome in the event of his dying without legitimate heirs; if in fact he did draft such a will at this time, correspondence about it may have influenced senatorial opinion, but since it remained secret, little would be known about this in the world at large.[2]

Disturbances soon followed in Asia Minor. Attalus of Pergamum, who came to Rome in 160 to rebut further charges brought against his brother Eumenes by Prusias and the Galatians, was received favourably, and when in the following year Eumenes died, he succeeded to the throne and might have hoped that his popularity with Rome would secure the well-being of his country.[3] But trouble soon arose: in 156 Pergamum was invaded by Prusias of Bithynia. Attalus sent his brother Athenaeus to Rome, and the Senate dispatched a commission of inquiry. Then early in 155 other Roman envoys accompanied Athenaeus home with instructions to prevent Prusias waging war on Attalus. Prusias, however, replied by besieging the commissioners and Attalus in Pergamum, so that the Senate was forced to send ten more commissioners, headed by L. Anicius, C. Fannius, and Q. Fabius Maximus, to bring him to heel; this they did by helping to promote a combination against him, which included Cappadocia, Pontus, Rhodes, and Cyzicus. The war was finally brought to an end by yet another Roman commission, which forced Prusias to pay an indemnity and make restitution. Such an episode well illustrates how throughout the Hellenistic world numerous opportunities arose which Rome could have used as excuses for direct military intervention, but she preferred by diplomatic pressure to avoid decisive action and to keep all these precariously balanced powers subservient to her will.

[1] P. xxxi. 10. 7.

[2] The view of Otto (op. cit. 98 ff.) is that the famous Cyrene inscription, recording the 'Testament of Ptolemy the Younger', is not a reproduction of the will but a political document, and that the will itself should be assigned to 162/1. See below, p. 236.

[3] But Attalus had to act with prudence. For an interesting document which shows how carefully he had to weigh Roman reactions and suspicions see C. B. Welles, *Royal Correspondence in the Hellenistic Period*, 245 ff.

XIV

PROBLEMS AND POLICIES OF THE
SENATE

(155–150 B.C.)

1. *Senatorial Generals and Spain*

SENATORIAL policy during the decade after Pydna can be described
roughly as *laissez-faire*. A careful watch was kept on foreign
affairs, but little direct or violent action was taken, while at home
a series of slack censorships and indifference to the needs of the masses
of Rome and Italy did little to check the moral decline and economic
difficulties which were becoming apparent. Here and there a short
campaign was fought, diplomatic pressure stiffened, or a measure to
check extravagance, electoral corruption, or Greek influences was
passed, yet urgent problems in the main were neglected. But about
155 B.C. a change is noticeable: the chief reason for undertaking the
Dalmatian war was, according to Polybius, to check the increasing
enervation due to twelve years of peace. Other theatres of operations
were then opened up: in Spain war dragged on from 154 to 133, while
the smoking ruins of Carthage and Corinth testified to a new outburst
of Roman energy which culminated in 146 with the annexation of two
new provinces.

Further conquest involved the intensification rather than the alle-
viation of moral and economic problems at home, and according to
a contemporary witness the censorship of 154 marked a turning-point
in Roman life: the annalist Calpurnius Piso, who was himself later a
censor (probably 120; *cos.* 133), dates the overthrow of Roman
modesty from this year: 'a quo tempore pudicitiam subversam'.[1] The
censors themselves would inspire little confidence among the old-
fashioned: one, M. Valerius Messalla (*cos.* 161), had himself incurred
the censors' *nota*,[2] the other, C. Cassius Longinus, as consul in 171
had attacked Istria against senatorial orders. Little is known about
their censorship except that they tried to build a permanent theatre,
which the Senate, at the insistence of Scipio Nasica, ordered to be
destroyed: 'tamquam inutile et nociturum publicis moribus . . . popu-
lusque aliquamdiu stans ludos spectavit'.[3] Cassius also made a curious

---

[1] Pliny, *NH*, xvii. 245.   [2] Val. Max. ii. 9. 1 (9. 9).
[3] Livy, *Per.* xlviii; Vell. Pat. i. 15. 3; Val. Max. ii. 4. 2. Appian (*BC*, i. 28) wrongly
attributes the opposition to Nasica's grandson.

move, which may have been designed to hide from the People the serious lack of *concordia* among the senators on domestic issues: he transported to the Senate-house the statue of Concordia which Marcius Philippus had set up in a public place ten years before. When he asked the pontiffs whether he might not dedicate the statue and the Senate-house itself to Concordia, he was informed by the Pontifex Maximus, Aemilius Lepidus, that he could not unless he had been authorized by the People.[1] The older nobility had not forgiven his earlier intransigence. It is probable that Cassius also brought some charge against Cato who was forced to defend himself in the law-courts. From Cato's speech there survive only a contemptuous sigh of despair for the State and the observation that 'it is hard for one that has lived among men of one generation to make his defence before those of another'.[2]

In 154 there blazed up in Spain a series of wars which had serious repercussions on Roman conduct. For twenty-five years Spain had enjoyed peace, but at the price of continued Roman extortion. In 154 the Lusitanians raided Roman territory and defeated two praetors; in the next year they discomfited Mummius, the future destroyer of Corinth. As the revolt spread to the Celtiberians the Senate sent out the consul of 153, Q. Fulvius Nobilior; after an initial defeat and a fruitless attempt to storm Numantia, he was superseded by a competent soldier, M. Claudius Marcellus, who had governed both Spanish provinces (*pr.* 169) and had had experience of mountain warfare in Liguria (*cos.* 166). After the customary ten years' interval he had been given the unusual honour of a second consulship in 155 when he gained a second triumph over the Ligurians, and was now elected to a third consulship for 152 only three years later. He quickly reduced the tribes of the Jalon valley, induced the Arevacci to send ambassadors to Rome, and in a private dispatch urged the Senate to make peace, because, according to Appian, he wanted credit for ending the war.

But the Senate, now accustomed to the obsequious compliments of Greek kings, was in no mood to listen to barbarian tribesmen who spoke as free men conscious of their rights; it dismissed the Spaniards and ordered Marcellus to continue the war. Thus although the success of Roman arms, if followed by honest administration, would have sufficed to restore the peace which the Celtiberians had maintained for the last twenty-five years, the senatorial leaders preferred an opportunity for continued military successes and allowed the war to drag on.[3] Marcellus' motives may have been less base than those attributed to him by the Polybian tradition, which follows the point of view of Scipio Aemilianus; and if his advice had been taken by the

[1] Cic. *De dom.* 130; 136.   [2] Plut. *Cato*, 15. 4. See p. 270.
[3] Appian, *Iber.* 49; P. xxxv. 2–3.

Senate both Rome and Spain might have been spared much suffering. As it was, after some further operations he made peace with Numantia for the immense sum of 600 talents of silver, and apparently his authority saved him from any subsequent attack for having disregarded senatorial instructions.

Marcellus was then replaced by L. Licinius Lucullus (*cos.* 151) who met with difficulties both at home and abroad. A disinclination to serve in Spain after Nobilior's disaster, amounting almost to panic, affected all ranks, and when the consuls insisted on carrying through the levy they were even temporarily imprisoned by some tribunes who sought to get their friends exempted. At length, however, Scipio Aemilianus, who had been posted to Macedonia, by volunteering to serve in Spain, shamed others into following his example.[1] On reaching Spain Lucullus found peace established, but being eager for fame and wealth attacked the unoffending Vaccaei and treacherously massacred 20,000 men of Cauca; he then turned to Lusitania, leaving Celtiberia to enjoy seven years of uneasy peace. In Lusitania Sulpicius Galba had suffered a signal defeat (151), and though reinforced by Lucullus' arrival preferred treachery to arms; after making definite promises to the Lusitanians, he accepted their surrender, disarmed them, and then butchered a large number in cold blood. Among the survivors was Viriathus who lived to fight on: Rome's policy of fire and sword, enhanced by the treachery of her generals, led only to further wars and suffering.

The war raised many issues, including the question of re-election to the consulship. The law, which imposed a ten years' interval between two consulships, had been suspended during the Hannibalic War, but had been enforced thereafter: until 155 only seven men had gained a second, and none a third, consulship.[2] Now this signal honour was obtained for Marcellus, presumably by a special dispensation, but the precedent was not considered desirable and a measure was passed, probably in 151, which forbade even a second consulship. The majority of senators may have welcomed the bill because it would give any individual a slightly greater chance of reaching the consulship, while many may have been influenced by the example of Marcellus' independent attitude: there must be no successor to the man who counselled peace and tried to block the way to further victories and spoils. Cato, the *novus homo*, who would deprecate further honours for the older aristocracy, spoke in its favour.[3]

[1] P. xxxv. 4; Appian, *Iber.* 49; Livy, *Per.* xlviii.

[2] Scipio Africanus, *cos.* 205 and 194; M. Aemilius Lepidus, 187 and 175; Q. Marcius Philippus, 186 and 169; L. Aemilius Paullus, 182 and 168; Ti. Sempronius Gracchus, 177 and 163; C. Popillius Laenas, 172 and 158; M. Claudius Marcellus, 166 and 155. All but the last two had been censors.

[3] The measure cannot be dated with certainty, but it is probably to be connected with

Sulpicius Galba did not escape the consequences of his treachery without difficulty. On his return to Rome in 149 a tribune, L. Scribonius Libo, proposed that some surviving Lusitanians, whom Galba had sold into slavery in Gaul, should be set free. Cato, who had already attacked Galba in 167, supported the measure, while Q. Fulvius Nobilior, whom Cato had often handled roughly in the Senate, replied on Galba's behalf. In all Galba delivered three speeches, two against Libo and his proposal about the Lusitanians, and one against L. Cornelius Cethegus, who presumably supported the proposal. Galba's contention that the Lusitanians with a pretence of friendship had been about to attack his camp will have convinced few of his hearers. When he saw that he would be condemned he made a pitiful appeal, embracing his two children and his ward, the son of Sulpicius Gallus, innocent children who would suffer if he were punished: the proposal was quashed. Appian adds that Galba escaped punishment by means of his wealth, which was perhaps a more potent weapon than even the tears of the children.

The legal procedure involved is not very clear.[1] As the Lusitanians were still fighting on, they could not promote the prosecution of their betrayer. Presumably Galba was impeached by tribunes before the Tribal Assembly (as Lucretius in 170) or else the tribunes proposed the setting up of a special *quaestio*; if this second procedure was adopted,[2] Galba will have made his sentimental appeal against the establishment of a court where he knew he would have little chance of acquittal. Cato, despite his 85 years, rallied reluctantly to the attack in this the last year of his life. As he had recently secured a declaration of war upon Carthage which was carried through with great deceit, he might find it somewhat inconsistent to express fervid moral indignation at Galba's conduct, but he had good cause. For Galba had not merely massacred Spaniards, as his colleague Lucullus had done with impunity, but had shamelessly broken his formal pledge: the *fides* of Rome was mocked. A fragment of Cato's speech shows that he took the same line as in defending the Rhodians: the Lusitanians should be judged by their actions, not their wishes.[3] But despite Cato's

Marcellus' third consulship in 152; it will therefore have been carried in 152 or 151. Livy (*Per.* lvi) mentions it in connexion with the proposal to make an exception to it in electing Scipio Aemilianus to a second consulship in 134. Apart from that exception it remained in force until the time of Marius. On Cato's speech *Ne quis iterum consul fieret*, see pp. 270 f.

[1] Livy, *Per.* xlix; Appian, *Iber.* 60; Val. Max. viii. 1. 2; Cic. *De orat.* i. 227, *Brut.* 89, *Pro Mur.* 59; Quint. *Inst. Or.* ii. 15. 8; Fronto, *Ad M. Caes.* iii. 20 N. Cicero (*Brut.* 89) explains Cato's action as a *suasio*; other sources, probably wrongly, suggest a criminal trial: *accusare* (Gell. i. 12. 17; Ps.-Ascon. on Cic. *Div. in Caecil.* 66, p. 124 Or.); *ad populi iudicium adducere* (L. xxxix. 40. 12); *actioni tribuniciae subscribere* (Val. Max. viii. 1. 2). [2] The view of De Sanctis, IV. i. 482–3.

[3] Malcovati, 187. Cato published his speech in the seventh book of his *Origines* (Gell. xiii. 25. 15). See p. 271.

arguments Galba got off scot-free, and five years later became consul; the unfortunate Lusitanians remained in slavery. But to prevent such scandals in the future a tribune, L. Calpurnius Piso, carried a law which set up a permanent court, empanelled from senators and pre-sided over by a praetor, to deal with prosecutions for extortion (*quaestio de rebus repetundis*); its judgements were not subject to an appeal to the People or a tribune's veto. The influence of the Senate was thus immensely strengthened.

11. *Cato and Eastern Affairs*

The Egyptian question was reopened when in 154 Ptolemy Euer-getes appeared in Rome, alleging that his brother had tried to murder him, and as proof dramatically displayed in the Senate some knife-wounds on his body. Before leaving Cyrene he had tried to engage the sympathy of the Romans and to advertise the support that he had already received from them, by publishing his will, in which after mention of the alleged attempt upon his life it was proclaimed that should he die without legitimate heirs, his realm should be left to the Roman People (155). This calculated display of goodwill and pathos secured the continued support of the Senate which refused even to listen to a counter-embassy from his brother Philometor.[1] Five com-missioners, under Cn. Cornelius Merula and L. Minucius Thermus, were then sent to restore Euergetes to Cyprus, while Rome's allies in the East were invited to co-operate; but when this demonstration led to no concrete results the Romans apparently let the matter slide once again, perhaps because Spain and Carthage were to demand more attention.

Euergetes, left to his own devices, attempted to take Cyprus him-self, but was captured by his brother, who then generously restored him to Cyrene. This generosity may have owed something to the thought that a friendly gesture towards Rome's friend would be good policy. Philometor went farther and offered Euergetes the hand of his daughter, but Euergetes had other ideas. Some time after the death of Ti. Sempronius Gracchus (*c.* 152) he aspired to the hand of his widow, Cornelia, the daughter of Scipio Africanus, but this great lady, the mother of the Gracchi, declined the offer of Ptolemy the Pot-bellied (Physcon). Possibly the ambassador L. Minucius Thermus was used by Euergetes to try to arrange the marriage, since his family

---

[1] On the date of the publication of the will (cf. p. 231 for a possible earlier dating of its drafting) and its objects (which included the hint to Ptolemy's subjects in Cyrene that a revolt in his absence would lead to Roman annexation, not freedom or union with Egypt) see F. E. Adcock, *Cambr. Univ. Reporter*, 5 July 1932, who also suggests that 'the interval between the will and the visit to Rome may perhaps be explained by the possible need of procuring an invitation from the Senate in view of the restrictions on royal visits'.

was friendly with the Scipios; but if so, Minucius failed.[1] On his return from his mission he was attacked by Cato, who seized this chance of revenge against the man who some thirty years before had dared to challenge the *felicitas* of his censorial lustration (p. 164). If Cato suspected or knew that Minucius had been trying to arrange the marriage with Cornelia, his hatred will have been further stimulated: that a Roman aristocrat should marry a leading Hellenistic ruler would appal his narrow Roman mind. His precise accusation is unknown, but presumably it was corruption; Minucius might have received bribes in connexion with the proposed marriage. Cato suggested that he deserved capital punishment,[2] and referred in glowing terms to Philometor, 'rege optimo atque beneficissimo', whose cause he will have supported earlier, while the majority of the Senate, including some connected with the Scipios, had preferred to back Euergetes, though with a notable lack of persistence.

The Egyptian situation was complicated still further when Philometor's young son, Eupator, after being made joint ruler with his father, apparently became independent ruler of Cyprus (after spring 152), possibly as a result of Roman pressure, and very probably with the help of the *princeps senatus*, Aemilius Lepidus, who became his official or unofficial guardian.[3] The view has been taken that this marks the final stage of a deliberate attempt by Rome to weaken Egypt by splitting the Empire first into two, and then three, parts,[4] but it is not certain that the establishing of the independence of Eupator was entirely against his father's wish. Philometor might have arranged this in order to strengthen his son's hand against Euergetes, in the event of his own death, since Eupator's claim to Egypt would then be based on the fact that he was an independent king of Cyprus, as Euergetes was of Cyrene, while he had also been his father's co-ruler in Egypt itself. But even if Rome did wish to weaken Egypt in 152 because of dangers which loomed ahead elsewhere, that in itself does not necessarily mean that it was 'die Erfüllung des langgehegten römischen Wunsches'. In fact from the Roman point of view Egypt was probably too weak to cause much anxiety, and when Eupator died

---

[1] Cf. Otto, *Gesch. Zeit VI. Ptol.* 118 f.

[2] Frg. 76 M. This presumably refers to Minucius, since Cato would scarcely suggest that Ptolemy was worthy of the supreme punishment. See also p. 271.

[3] This is the view of Otto, op. cit. 119 ff., based upon three inscriptions from Cyprus which name Eupator βασιλεύς *simpliciter* (Dittenberger, *OGIS*, 125–7) and upon the well-known *denarius*, issued *c*. 66 B.C. probably by Lepidus who was later triumvir: *obv.* Head of Alexandria; *rev.* Lepidus placing a wreath on the head of a youth who holds a sceptre; M. LEPIDUS TUTOR REG. (See Frontispiece No. 19.) If this depicts an historical event, it cannot refer to 200 B.C. (p. 94 n. 5) but, as Otto argues, suits 152 admirably. The scene may, however, be symbolic, denoting the general interest of Lepidus in Egypt which began in 200.

[4] Cf. Otto, op. cit., *passim*, and esp. p. 123.

in 150 Rome, with other matters on hand, raised no objection to the reunion of Cyprus with Egypt.

Another incident in the Hellenistic world engaged Cato's attention. In 150 (or 151) Prusias of Bithynia asked Rome that his indemnity might be remitted (cf. p. 231), but after a senatorial debate, during which Cato upheld Attalus' claim, it was decided that Prusias must continue to pay.[1] Encouraged by Rome's support, Attalus next incited Prusias' son, Nicomedes, against his father. As Nicomedes had made influential friendships while living in Rome, the Senate was slow to act, but at last three commissioners were sent to check Attalus: M. Licinius, who was lame with gout, A. Mancinus, recently wounded by a tile falling on his head, and L. Malleolus, by repute the most stupid man in Rome. As the business was urgent Cato remarked sarcastically in the Senate: 'not only would Prusias perish before they got there, but Nicomedes would grow old in his kingdom. For how could a mission make haste, or if it did, how could it accomplish anything when it had neither feet, head, nor intelligence?' As Cato expected, Prusias was killed and Nicomedes succeeded, but Rome accepted the *fait accompli* as good relations were re-established between Bithynia and Pergamum.[2]

Thus despite his advancing years Cato was still able to take an active part in public debate and appears to have disapproved of the policy of encouraging dissension between or within kingdoms and to have championed the cause of Prusias against Nicomedes, and of Philopator against Physcon, as earlier he may have disapproved of the recognition of Demetrius and the previous attempt to play off Attalus against Eumenes. In any case the frequency with which the Senate accepted a compromise or even a reversal of its original decision instead of steadily forcing through its first plan will have irritated Cato's blunt and uncompromising spirit.

A perennial question was the release of the Achaeans interned in Italy. A renewed request for their return in 155 was refused by a very narrow margin, the balance being tilted against them by the praetor, A. Postumius, who was presiding in the Senate on that occasion: he ruled out a vote for postponement and insisted on a clear-cut decision for or against, which resulted in a rejection.[3] His attitude is curious since he was a philhellene; at any rate he wrote a poem and history in Greek, in the preface to which he asked pardon if, being a Roman, his command of Greek idiom was not perfect. For this Cato mocked him: he had undertaken the work voluntarily, not under orders from the Amphictyonic Council; he was like a boxer begging the spectators to pardon him if he could not stand the fatigue or the blows. Here is

---

[1] P. xxxiii. 13; Appian, *Mithr.* 3–4. On Cato's speech *De rege Attalo* see p. 271.
[2] P. xxxvi. 14; Plut. *Cato*, 9; Livy, *Per.* l.   [3] P. xxxiii. 1.

seen Cato's disapproval of the senatorial tradition of Roman historiography composed in Greek, against which he wrote his *Origines* as
a counterblast.[1]

The fate of the Achaeans was finally settled in 150, when at Polybius' request his friend Scipio Aemilianus gained the support of Cato.
This may have been easier to obtain because Cato's son Marcus, who
had died before his father in 152, had married Aemilia, daughter of
Paullus and sister of Scipio. Even so, Cato's support of the Achaeans'
cause in the senatorial debate was ungenerous and grudging: 'we sit
here all day, as though we had nothing else to do, debating whether
some old Greek dotards should be buried by Italian or Achaean
undertakers'. The man who had no concern for his old warhorse or
broken-down slaves was not going to bother much about a few elderly
Greeks, and when Polybius, elated at his success, wanted to go to the
Senate again to ask that the exiles on their return should enjoy the
same honours as before, Cato remarked that Polybius, like another
Odysseus, wanted to go 'a second time into the cave of the Cyclops,
because he had forgotten his cap and belt'.[2] The Senate tardily con-
sented to the release, now that it was too late to save Rome's honour,
partly because the 300 ageing survivors would not be likely to promote
trouble in their country, and partly because, with war against Carthage
looming near, a gesture of goodwill to Greece might not be amiss.
In the event, however, when the Achaeans found that Rome had
become involved in war in Africa, Spain, and Macedonia, their
extremists with suicidal folly forced a brief war on Rome, which
resulted in the destruction of Corinth and the dissolution of the
Achaean League (146).

From this brief sketch of Roman foreign policy since Pydna it is
clear that no statesman arose with the vision, decision, and driving-
power to shape a consistent policy. The Senate as a whole preferred
diplomacy to war, since wars gave ambitious generals opportunities
to win personal power, while individual senators, eager for their own
prestige, found satisfaction in defeating barbarians or humiliating
kings. But if the world at large interpreted Rome's procrastination
and indecision towards the Greek world as appeasement and weakness
rather than partial indifference, its eyes were soon opened. Cato's
policy perhaps did not amount to much more than an attempt to avoid

---

[1] Polybius, wounded by Postumius' attitude to the Achaeans, adds (xxxix. 1) that
Postumius was garrulous and ostentatious and was so affected and immoderate in his
leaning to Greek studies that he caused the Greek style to become offensive to older and
more respectable Romans. During a battle in the final Macedonian war he feigned illness
at Thebes, but nevertheless sent the Senate a lengthy dispatch describing the victory in
detail.

[2] P. xxxv. 6; Plut. *Cato*, 9. 2–3. Cf. F. W. Walbank, *Class. et Med.* 1948, 172 n. 2.
On Cato's speech see p. 271.

S

entangling commitments abroad, though he may have urged the Senate on occasion to remain loyal to the men whom it had first supported, and have stood for a kind of rough and ready justice to all. Nor, perhaps, can he be blamed for not having framed and executed a more thoroughgoing and consistent policy, since as a *novus homo* he lacked the continued support of the political caucuses which the old nobility had enjoyed. But towards the end of his life all his activity was focused on one end which he came to regard as crucial: the destruction of Carthage.

III. *Cato and the Scipios on Carthage*

After Hannibal's death Masinissa progressively encroached upon Carthaginian territory, and the boundary commissions, which Rome sent out in reply to appeals from Carthage, generally decided in his favour or left the question unsettled. Whether his raids received Rome's encouragement or, as is perhaps more likely, were the result of Rome's indifference, the situation became critical only when he occupied Tusca (? Thugga) and Rome sent out a commission of inquiry led by Cato, probably in 153.[1] The commissioners asked both Masinissa and Carthage to accept their decision in advance; the king, trusting his allies, agreed, but the Carthaginians, remembering the awards of previous commissions, stuck to the point that a violation of the treaty of 201 was the only real issue. No decision was reached, but the Roman envoys carefully noted the prosperity of the country-side and the reviving military and economic strength of Carthage itself.

On their return Cato described to the Senate the surprising resurgence of Rome's old enemy: the quarrel between Masinissa and Carthage could not be patched up, while Roman safety required nothing less than the destruction of Carthage—an observation with which he is said henceforth to have ended all his speeches.[2] It was perhaps on this occasion that he displayed in the Senate-house a ripe fig, which had been gathered in Carthage only three days before, in order to illustrate the proximity of the danger rather than to emphasize the recovery of an economic rival. He was probably right in supposing that Carthage had rearmed, since only by this means did she see any hope of checking Masinissa's advance in default of any support from Rome, but he was surely wrong in believing that this rearmament was directed against Rome.[3] His policy was opposed by Scipio Nasica, who apparently had sufficient backing in the Senate to achieve a temporary compromise.[4] At any rate he was sent out in charge of a mission of inquiry (probably in 152); he forced Masinissa to yield some of the

[1] See pp. 287 f.   [2] On Cato's speeches on this subject see p. 288.
[3] See pp. 288 f.
[4] On the result of the senatorial debate see p. 288.

ground he had seized, and perhaps warned Carthage against building up her naval and military strength.[1]

There perhaps the matter rested for a short time, unless Livy is to be followed when he records that after Masinissa's son Gulussa had reported continuing Carthaginian military preparations (in 152?), Cato again proposed war, Nasica urged caution, and a commission of ten senators was sent to Africa; when this returned (in 151?) with alarming reports, Cato and others urged the immediate declaration of war, but Nasica could find no case for a *bellum iustum*, so the Senate decided to refrain from war if Carthage disarmed, but otherwise the consuls of 150 should start the war.[2] However that may be, nothing decisive was done until 150 when Carthage, goaded beyond endurance by Masinissa, foolishly attacked him, thereby breaking her treaty of 201 with Rome and affording Cato and the war-party the excuse they needed. Further, her misjudgement of the military situation resulted in her having to capitulate to Masinissa: this both weakened Carthage and increased Masinissa's strength to a degree which Rome judged dangerous. Thus while Carthage humbly sought Rome's pardon, the Senate played for time until the campaigning season of 149; then war was finally declared.

There is no reason to doubt that Cato's motive was a sheer un-reasoning hatred of Carthage, which had become an *idée fixe* in the old man's mind. In trying to inflame his fellow countrymen with a similar hatred he harped upon the suffering and cruelty which Roman men, women, and children had endured in the Hannibalic War; on this he could speak with feeling since, unlike many senators, he him-self had lived through those grim days of half a century ago.[3] He also used an argument which was the direct opposite to that which he himself had employed twice, when speaking on behalf of Rhodes and against Sulpicius Galba: then he had urged that men must be judged by their actions, not their hostile intentions, but now he said: 'Cartha-ginienses nobis iam hostes sunt; nam qui omnia parat contra me, ut

---

[1] Livy, *Per.* xlviii. Zonaras (ix. 26) indicates that Nasica headed, as well as proposed, the mission.

[2] Livy is here probably guilty of duplication and one of the missions should be eliminated: cf. Kahrstedt, *Gesch. d. Karth.* iii. 621 ff. The circumstances of the first mission described in Livy, *Per.* xlviii, are highly suspicious: a grandson of Syphax, Arcobarzanes, had raised a large army on Carthaginian soil, nominally against Masinissa, actually against Rome, while Gisgo later so stirred the people against the Roman ambassadors that they had to flee to escape violence. The existence of Arcobarzanes is uncertain, the intention of his army to attack Rome may be rejected, and the threat to the Roman ambassadors is obviously an annalistic invention; the forcing of Masinissa to withdraw, which is recorded also by Zonaras, may be retained. There seems no ground to question the fact that Nasica led one mission to Africa, which is usually identified with this one of 152, but in view of the suspicious circumstances it could be equated with that of the *decemviri*; if so, the checking of Masinissa will have been placed a little too early. Kahrstedt's evaluation of the annalistic tradition is drastic: 'das ganze Plus an Tradition, das die römische Über-lieferung bietet ist unbenutzbar' (p. 624).   [3] See p. 271.

quo tempore velit, bellum possit inferre, hic iam mihi hostis est, tametsi nondum armis agat'. This from the lips of the man who but recently had denounced the intellectual and moral tergiversations of visiting Greek philosophers![1] With hatred went fear:[2] whether justified or not, it was probably very real to Cato who had convinced himself that Roman security required the elimination of Carthage. He is also said to have believed that this menace affected Rome internally no less than externally: only by the removal of the external threat would Rome be free to seek a cure for her domestic failings.[3]

The views of Scipio Nasica who had led the opposition, counselled moderation, ended every speech with the phrase δοκεῖ μοι Καρχηδόνα εἶναι, and prevented war for three years, appear equally unconvincing at first sight and equally dominated by concern for Rome's internal condition. According to Appian the motive of his policy was to secure that Roman discipline, which was already weakening, might be preserved through fear of Carthage.[4] Plutarch is more specific: only the continued threat of external pressure by a Power which was not strong enough to conquer Rome nor yet weak enough to be despised could check the excesses of the Roman People who by spurning the control of the Senate were threatening to destroy the State.[5] According to a passage of Diodorus which derives from Poseidonius[6] Scipio believed that fear of Carthage would not only promote discipline and peace at home, but would force Rome to act with greater moderation and clemency towards her subjects (ἐπιεικῶς καὶ ἐνδόξως ἄρχειν), while the destruction of Carthage would result in civil wars and stimulate the hatred of all subjects for the pride and covetousness of Roman magistrates: 'all of which accordingly happened to the Romans after the destruction of Carthage'.

This view of Poseidonius, with its stress on external consequences, may attribute more to Nasica than he really expressed at the time, while even Plutarch, deriving ultimately from Polybius, may represent a point of view which became more clear as the result of the tribunate of Tiberius Gracchus, but there is no reason to doubt that at bottom the theory that the Romans could only retain their virility by retaining external enemies represents Nasica's main argument. Neither the fact that this theory had been attributed to Q. Caecilius Metellus, the friend of Scipio Africanus, and to Africanus himself (as Cato recalled in his speech for the Rhodians in 167) nor its seeming jejuneness ('ces pensées semblent assez puériles', wrote Gsell) need mean that its attribution to Nasica is false; the doubt rather arises whether it should

---

[1] Frg. 184. He also doubtless harped upon *Punica fides*: in his *Origines* (iv, frg. 10 Jordan) he refers to six breaches of agreements by Carthage: 'Karthaginiensis sextum de foedere decessere.' [2] Pliny, *NH*, xv. 74. [3] Plut. *Cato*, 27. 3.
[4] Appian, *Lib*. 69: ἐς φόβον ἄρα καὶ τόνδε 'Ρωμαίων ἐκδιαιτωμένων ἤδη.
[5] Plut. *Cato*, 27. 1–2. [6] Diod. xxxiv. 33. 4–6. Cf. Jacoby, *FGH*, iiA n. 87, 112.

be assigned also to Africanus.[1] As applied specifically to Carthage it may well represent a slight distortion of a sound point of view: that Carthage must continue as a threat, not in the first instance to Rome, but to Masinissa, and that Roman security demanded a balance of power in north Africa. This may well have been the view of Africanus which Nasica took over and applied in 152 when he forced Masinissa to disgorge a small piece of his illicit gains. But the general view that Rome's internal strength was being undermined was gradually forcing itself upon thoughtful men, and Nasica was not alone in believing that the destruction of Carthage would fail to cure the ills of the Roman constitution and State.

What, then, was the chief reason for the declaration of war, since clearly the foolish infringement of the Zama treaty by Carthage merely provided the warmongers with a legal excuse for sweeping aside the opposition? While some senators doubtless genuinely echoed Cato's blind unreasoning hatred, the Senate as a whole was hard-headed and not to be rushed by mass emotion.[2] Could those whose minds were not clouded by passion believe that Carthage really constituted a danger to Rome? Most historians have felt that they could not, even when due allowance has been made for the fact that contemporary statesmen lacked the ability to foresee the future course of events; they have therefore sought some other explanation. Mommsen found it in the interests of Roman bankers and traders, but his view has been effectively rejected,[3] nor has much support been accorded to the theory of Rostovtzeff, who read into the fig incident an attempt by Cato to champion the interests of wealthy Roman landowners, whose vineyards and olive orchards were to be helped by the elimination of an economic rival.[4] There is little evidence in the ancient sources to justify the attempt to find in economic, rather than political, motives the mainspring of Roman policy.[5]

[1] Val. Max. viii. 2. 3; Appian, *Lib.* 65. Cf. Gsell, *Hist. anc. de l'Afrique du Nord*, iii. 331. The fact that this view was common in contemporary thought and something of a rhetorical commonplace does not prove that Nasica did not share it. Cf. M. Gelzer, *Philol.* 1931, 284–5, reprinted in *Vom römischen Staat*, i. 78 ff. See also p. 279.

[2] The attempt of Bilz (*Scipio Aemilianus* 21), to suggest that it was irrelevant whether Cato's facts were true or not because they were accepted blindly by a Senate which did not know the true situation ('niemand dachte daran, ihn zu kontrollieren') is not very convincing and implies a parochial outlook which can hardly have been that of the Senate of 150.

[3] See Kahrstedt, op. cit. 616 ff.; T. Frank, *Roman Imperialism*, 234; Gelzer, *Philol.* 1931, 295.

[4] Rostovtzeff, *History of the Ancient World*, ii. 81; *Soc. and Econ. History of the Roman Empire*, 21. M. Cary (*History of Rome*, 194) writes: 'if Cato had economic considerations in mind . . . he was probably thinking more of his shares in shipping companies'. Cf. L. Zancan, *Le cause della terza guerra punica*, 593–4, who prefers Mommsen to Rostovtzeff, though putting political before economic motives as the real cause.

[5] Cf. F. E. Adcock, *CHJ*, 1946, 117 f. In general see further T. Frank, *Roman Imperialism*, 277 ff.; M. Holleaux, *Rome, la Grèce et les monarchies hellénistiques*, 87 ff.

The view that it was fear of Masinissa that drove Rome to destroy Carthage is attractive. His new kingdom now encircled Carthage and might soon absorb it; the balance of power in Africa was upset and Rome must restore the equilibrium by occupying the territory of Carthage herself.[1] To this it may be objected that since Masinissa was nearly 90 years old and his successor was a man of peace, it is difficult to believe that any Roman could seriously have been frightened by the Numidian problem; in any case recourse might have been had to balancing off Carthage against Numidia, a policy which would have been probably safe and certainly inexpensive. This may indeed have been the intention of Nasica, but it involved checking Masinissa directly and encouraging Carthage, and such a reversal of Rome's policy of the last fifty years would not be popular.

Thus Cato was enabled to play upon old hatreds. How strong his political backing was, how widely based and how well organized the group behind Nasica was, and how soon Cato would have succeeded in persuading the Senate to act cannot be known, since by making the fatal mistake of suffering defeat at Masinissa's hands the Carthaginians sealed their doom at once: they had put their city within the king's grasp and they had broken their treaty with Rome; each act might have led to reprisals by Rome, combined they left Nasica and the peace-party at Rome no ground on which to stand. To that extent Carthage may be considered responsible for her own fate. A strong anti-Roman party in the city, whose existence gave some colour to Cato's fears, was ready to take hostile action if a good chance occurred, but it fatally misjudged the opportunity in acting when it did. True, there was a certain restlessness against Rome throughout the world which Polybius describes as ταραχὴ καὶ κίνησις and which manifested itself in the incredible folly of the resistance offered by the Achaean League and in the wild attempt of the pretender Andriscus to secure the Macedonian throne.[2] Carthage may have been affected by this feeling, especially as she had just paid the final instalment of her 50 years' war-indemnity to Rome. If she dreamed madly of successful revolt against Rome, she could justly be charged with major responsi-

---

[1] Kahrstedt, op. cit. 615–17, 642. For further remarks on this view see p. 289 below.

[2] P. iii. 4. 12. C. Seltman (*Num. Chron.* 1946, 89) suggests that this may be reflected in the puzzling coinage of Malta which takes on a strong Egyptian character (*obv.* head of Isis; *rev.* kneeling four-winged Being, wearing the double crown of Egypt). Although a Roman *municipium*, Malta may have published her pro-Egyptian sentiments, partly for commercial, but partly for political reasons, since Rome was so embarrassed in Africa, Macedonia, and Spain, and Ptolemy Philometor was so successful (he had prevented his brother, supported by Rome, from getting Cyprus and had intervened with great effect in Syria, where he helped to defeat the usurper Alexander Bala and had been hailed as king of Syria, an honour which he tactfully declined). Malta may well have hoped to make the best of two possible worlds.

bility for precipitating war,[1] but it must be remembered that for three years at least Cato had been threatening her existence and no attempt had been made to follow up the one check that had been imposed upon Masinissa. Carthage was desperate and her effort at self-preservation cannot fairly be construed as a mortal blow aimed at Rome. War guilt cannot be shifted on to her shoulders: she precipitated war, but Rome willed it.

The days of Punic Carthage were numbered. After Rome's declaration of war, she formally surrendered, gave hostages, and was disarmed. Then at last she heard Rome's terms: the city was to be destroyed. This decision, which allowed the Carthaginians to live ten miles from the sea and thus preserved their lives while destroying their commerce, may reflect a compromise between the harshness of Cato and the more lenient policy of Nasica, but if so it was ineffective, since it did not achieve its ends: the deceitful, though strictly legal, manner in which Rome enforced her will roused the passion of the Carthaginians who, though disarmed, resolved to resist. For three years they withstood the fury of a Roman siege until starvation led to final capitulation and destruction. Cato's will had triumphed, and though he did not live to see the day of victory, he at least foresaw success guaranteed by the military efficiency of Scipio Aemilianus, then serving as a military tribune.[2] But many must have felt that this display of power-politics contradicted his lifelong ambition to maintain the *mos maiorum*. Though many a Roman was still *vir fortis et strenuus*, other much-vaunted qualities had declined; the surviving Carthaginians, like the Epirotes, Corinthians, and Numantines, had little reason to believe in Roman *fides*, *simplicitas*, or *benevolentia*. Unable to adapt himself to the needs of the day Cato, through his last act of statesmanship, by a strange irony helped to undermine the moral authority of the Roman State: the destruction of Carthage aroused the disgust of a large part of the civilized world, and while some commended Rome's statecraft in removing a perpetual menace, and that without open injustice, others believed that she had been corrupted by lust for power and contrasted the earlier civilized methods of her policy with her present stratagems and deceits.[3]

---

[1] Zancan's main thesis, that in the last analysis Carthage was more responsible than Rome because she tried to follow a policy beyond her strength 'contro la realtà' (op. cit., p. 601) will not commend itself to all.

[2] P. xxxvi. 8: 'When he heard in Rome of the glorious achievements of Scipio he uttered a palinode to his criticisms about him: 'What have you heard? οἶος πέπνυται, τοὶ δε σκιαὶ ἀίσσουσιν.' Thus, it is said, shortly before his death Cato quoted Greek and praised a Scipio.

[3] For Polybius' summing up of contemporary feeling see xxxvi. 9. Scipio Nasica had withdrawn from Rome, or had conveniently been sent out of the way by his opponents, but he returned from Greece in time to lodge a final, but vain, protest in 146 against the enslavement of the Carthaginians (Zon. ix. 28. 4; 30. 7).

EPILOGUE

THE Rome of Cato's old age was very different from that of his youth. Even the city itself was assuming a fresh aspect, with basilicas, porticoes, and stoas, with new temples built in the Hellenistic manner with tufa walls covered with bright stucco, and private houses of increasing refinement for the rich, not to mention streets paved with stone and better drainage. In Cato's young days Roman literature had been rudimentary, with Livius Andronicus and Naevius pointing the way in poetry, but the second century saw the full flowering of the work of Ennius, Pacuvius, Plautus, Terence, Caecilius, and others, and while Roman historians began to write in Greek, Cato himself became the father of Latin prose with his historical works, speeches, and encyclopaedic treatises. In the spheres of art, philosophy, and religion also the onrush of Greek influences had swept aside Cato's puny attempts to stem them. And while Rome's cultural life was steadily being revolutionized by her hellenized nobility, her economic conditions were profoundly modified. Eastern conquest opened up the way for more than Greek ideas and Hellenistic luxury: capitalist farming replaced peasant husbandry in many parts of Italy and slave labour ousted free. Further, Rome's imperial responsibilities had immeasurably widened. In Cato's youth she was fighting for very life and independent existence. Then with dramatic suddenness the scene changed and within two or three decades she was recognized as the undisputed arbiter of the civilized world; soon she had a large overseas empire to administer directly, while her responsibilities and influence spread far beyond the confines of her provincial territory.

How the governing class responded to these changing political circumstances and how groups of nobles struggled for leadership among themselves it has been the chief purpose of this work to review. Despite the internal stresses and tensions the Senate as a body had maintained and increased its pre-eminence in the State, pursuing a steady and on the whole a traditional policy. Blind to many of the economic, social, and moral needs of the day, and somewhat shortsighted in its attitude towards the Italian confederacy, it had faced the problems of foreign policy with a large measure of skill and success. But even here it had been too hidebound by tradition. Rejecting instead of developing the personal diplomacy which Scipio Africanus had advocated, and unwilling to face the problems of the Hellenistic and barbarian worlds as units, let alone as one complete whole, the Senate had dealt with problems piecemeal. If it acted irrationally on occasion, its strategic aims remained fixed and traditional, dominated by a narrow military outlook. A defensive imperialism, based upon an anxiety to win control in order to eliminate threats from any quarter, combined with the methods of 'divide and rule', dictated a policy of subjugating disputed territory of strategic importance: hence, with the weakening of Pergamum, Rhodes, and all Hellenistic rulers, great and small, was linked the demolition of fortresses in Spain and Sardinia, the devastation of the whole country-side of Epirus, and finally the destruction of two great cities of the ancient world, Carthage and Corinth.[1] Such aims had so long dominated Roman policy that when the need for them became outmoded the senatorial nobility still acted on traditional lines and failed to face new problems with open minds or with greater humanity. At Cannae tactical rigidity had caused disaster: the Roman legions had broken because they could not bend. A similar stiffness of mind continued to direct Roman strategic policy, but here it was the rest of the world that broke: Rome stood unshaken.

Unshaken Rome may have been in the eyes of the whole Mediterranean world, but within her body politic all was not well. In 172 the first rumble had been heard of that storm which was to sweep away the existing constitution; in 133 the storm broke. Midway between these dates Scipio Nasica had urged that δυναστεία and ἐπιείκεια should not be regarded as mutually exclusive concepts, and the foreboding sense of danger, which took clearer shape when Corinth and Carthage went up in flames, was poignantly felt by Scipio Aemilianus when amid the ruins of Carthage he recalled Homer's lines ἔσσεται ἦμαρ ὅταν ποτ' ὀλώλῃ "Ιλιος ἱρή . . . .. Misuse of foreign conquest and empire inevitably involved retribution for the governing oligarchy; old standards of conduct were despised and the spectre of ochlocracy was not far off. So at least it soon appeared to Polybius who had stood beside Aemilianus watching the fall of Carthage. His old belief in the stability and relative permanence of the 'mixed' constitution of Rome was shaken as he began to perceive actual signs of its deterioration. Disturbed by these new ideas of change and mortality, he was finally driven to accept that doctrine of circular political development which the Stoics called *anacyclosis*.[2] Nasica's view was gradually vindicated: absence of external challenge led not, as Cato hoped, to internal peace, but to discord and finally to mob-rule.

The constitutional citadel, in which the might of the Roman People was entrenched under the leadership of their nobles, might appear impregnable, but the moral and economic foundations on which it

[1] See especially A. H. McDonald, *CHJ*, 1939, 141; *The Rise of Roman Imperialism*, 12. Cf. De Sanctis, IV. i. 473–4.

[2] See F. W. Walbank, *CQ*, 1943, 73 ff., for a striking demonstration of the effect of contemporary events on Polybius' conception of history, and how after 146 he was forced to add new chapters to his earlier account of the Roman constitution in the sixth book (4. 7–9. 14; 51. 4–8; 57, and perhaps 58).

rested were becoming insecure. After half a century, during which political and social stability had been maintained, the great days of senatorial government were waning, and the more clear-sighted senators became aware that all was not well with the State. True, Aemilianus made some attempt to check the decline, though he moved on traditional and too rigid lines, and Cicero at the price of forgetting its faults could look back to his age and circle as to a golden age of aristocratic government. But the Roman nobles of the period knew better. Once their internal weaknesses had been exposed by the Gracchi, all hope of lasting political and social security faded; the prospect of mob-rule or military dictatorship remained. An axe had been laid to the root of the tree. A century later the Republic crashed down. Julius Caesar on the field of Pharsalus, gazing on the Roman dead who had fallen in the Optimate cause, assigned a reason: 'This was their will.' The fault of the Roman nobles lay not in their stars.

SOURCES FOR SENATORIAL POLITICS

(a) Historians and Annalists

FOR the mid-Republic the works of only two great historians survive, and that not in their entirety: Polybius and Livy. On some aspects of Rome's internal history Polybius is not helpful, because he either was not interested in them or considered them alien to a universal history. With penetrating judgement and much inside information he sketched the working of those institutions which in his view helped to explain the gradual extension of Rome's unifying power, but he was more concerned with showing how the machinery worked than in examining how each part was constructed. The function of the Senate in relation to other bodies was more germane to his theme than an analysis of the political wire-pulling by which individuals or groups achieved office: *imperium*, not the *arcana imperii*, was his subject. An example of this limitation is shown in his handling of the downfall of Scipio Africanus. Despite his interest in the man and his family, he gives no satisfactory account of the political intrigues which led to the trials of the Scipios, but merely records a few anecdotes when briefly sketching the character of Africanus. He deliberately turned his back on the material in the archives of the Scipionic house, available to him through his friendship with Aemilianus if he had desired to record Rome's internal history.

Livy therefore remains the primary source of information about Rome's domestic concerns. He summed up and gave final shape to a tradition which had been developing for centuries. This derived ultimately from the Tabula Pontificum, a whitened tablet set up in the Regia each year by the Pontifex Maximus, who recorded the magistrates' names and daily events of religious significance such as festivals, dedications, prodigies, eclipses, and famines. At first national and political events probably were mentioned only if they had religious connexions (e.g. an election which had to be held again because of some fault in the auspication), but gradually an increasing number of events of general interest would be recorded. From Cato's well-known remark ('non lubet scribere, quod in tabula apud pontificem maximum est, quotiens annona cara, quotiens lunae aut solis lumine caligo aut quid obstiterit': Gellius ii. 28. 6) the political content might be judged extremely meagre, but Cato may have overstressed it because he probably was contrasting the bare annalistic and factual records of the Tabulae with the methods of a group of senatorial historians who wrote in Greek and whose tradition he himself followed in his Latin *Origines*. These writers include Q. Fabius Pictor (a senator during the Hannibalic War), L. Cincius Alimentus (*pr.* 210, and captured by Hannibal), and two men of the next generation, A. Postumius Albinus (*cos.* 151) and C. Acilius (see p. 224 n. 1). These men were experienced Roman statesmen, not armchair historians, who wrote in Greek to explain and justify Roman policy to the Greek world, but this primary purpose does not exclude the possibility that they also may have made some use of the Tabulae Pontificum.[1]

---

[1] On their reliability see T. Frank, *Life and Literature in the Roman Republic*, 171 ff. The view advanced by M. Gelzer (*Hermes*, 1933, 129 ff.; 1934, 46 ff.) that they were not

The first Roman historian to use Latin was Cato, whose *Origines* followed these models which in turn were influenced by Hellenistic episodic histories, particularly those dealing with the founding of cities.[1] With the hostility of the *novus homo* towards the older nobility and with his innate dislike of individual pre-eminence Cato probably had little to say about Rome's internal politics, since he even omitted the names of generals—though he did not hesitate to reproduce his own speech on behalf of the Rhodians in full in the fifth book.[2] The composition of Roman history was continued in Latin by L. Cassius Hemina, who wrote before the Third Punic War, and L. Calpurnius Piso (*cos.* 133), who were not uninfluenced by Cato's work, but probably utilized the Tabulae Pontificum to a greater extent for their factual information, maintained a strictly annalistic form, and devoted more attention to Rome's internal history.

An epoch in Roman historiography was the publication (*c.* 123 B.C.) by the Pontifex Maximus, Mucius Scaevola, of the Annales Maximi, based on the Tabulae Pontificum. Whether this represented the first publication of the material and whether it merely reproduced or considerably amplified the subject-matter, are vexed questions, but since senatorial writers presumably had access to the Tabulae Pontificum themselves, the existence of an earlier published edition would merely have made their work easier. In any case this publication provided a standard framework of Rome's history (including the official events of each year, the names of magistrates, the conduct of elections, and the distribution of commands, as well as religious and cult business), and formed the basis for the work of later annalists.

Further work was undertaken by Cn. Gellius of the Gracchan age, who wrote on a sober scale but somewhat more fully than his predecessors, and began to work up his material more in line with Hellenistic and rhetorical works. This tendency was followed by two writers of Sulla's time, by Q. Claudius Quadrigarius with moderation, and by Valerius Antias with more zeal than discretion. Claudius wrote at least 23 books in a simple style; Valerius chose a larger canvas and more flashy colours. Following Hellenistic models, he worked up his material to interest his readers often at the expense of truth; he invented or elaborated reports of speeches or debates in the Senate-house, Comitia, or law-courts, in a highly rhetorical style, and often distorted his material in the interests of family tradition or under the impulse of the political influences of his day. Thus the older and more sober annalistic tradition was overlaid by writers who through dramatic and sensational methods appealed to a wider public. Other annalists, as Licinius Macer and Aelius Tubero, continued to publish work, but it was Claudius and Valerius, who became the 'classical' annalists, whose work Livy chiefly followed.

---

annalists but political historians, following Hellenistic models, is valuable in emphasizing their purpose in writing, but perhaps needs some modification in its denial of their annalistic method: see F. W. Walbank, *CQ*, 1945, 1–18 (esp. 15–18). Gelzer's view clashes with Cicero's statement (*De orat.* ii. 52) that the early writers followed the same methods as that in the *annales maximi* and 'sine ullis ornamentis monumenta solum temporum, hominum, locorum gestarumque rerum reliquerunt', and establishes a false antithesis by its interpretation of Sempronius Asellio's distinction between *res gestae* and *annales* (Peter, *HRF*, frgs. 1 and 2 = Aul. Gell. v. 18. 8). In general see articles in *OCD* by A. H. McDonald on Annals, Historiography, and the individual annalists.

[1] Cf. P. x. 21. 3.   [2] Nepos, *Cato*, 3.

(b) *Archives and Documentary Material*

Besides the Tabulae Pontificum and the Annales Maximi other documents were available to historians in the archives and later in literary form. Permanent records were kept of the resolutions of the Senate,[1] expressed either as *senatus-consulta* or, if a resolution was vetoed, as a *senatus auctoritas*. These were drafted after the meeting by a committee chosen by the presiding magistrate, consisting usually of the proposer of the resolution together with some of his supporters; the names of the committee were recorded in the document,[2] and a copy of the motion was deposited in the aerarium. By Cicero's day a book embodying a list of the *senatusconsulta* of each year had been produced, probably as a private publication.[3] No record of senatorial debates was published until Caesar's day, but some private records must have been kept, at least of important matters, from earlier times. Magistrates, particularly those presiding, would take notes of outstanding points, and these *commentarii*, though kept privately, could later even be designated *tabulae publicae*.[4] Thus although, apart from any published speeches, little of the arguments used in senatorial debates might be available, official documents would provide the names of those who proposed, supported, or vetoed bills, while more detail might be gleaned from private memoranda in the archives of the nobility.

Some records of the legislative, elective, and judicial activities of the People also were available. Copies of laws, deposited in the aerarium,[5] contained the names of the *rogator*, of the century (*praerogativa*) or tribe (*principium*) which voted first, and of the man who cast the first vote for his group. When a magistrate was about to act with the People, his preliminary promulgation of business fixed the day of meeting and described his intention: in legislation it contained the text of the law, in prosecutions it named the accused, the charge, and the proposed penalty, in elections it stated the offices to be filled and at least in later times the list of candidates.[6] A law of 62 B.C. provided that a copy of the promulgated enactment should be filed in the aerarium in the presence of witnesses, to prevent the insertion of any amendments before the People was asked to accept it.[7] Further, records of the voting were deposited in the aerarium, both the list of the voters certified by the *rogatores* and, as a temporary check, the tablets themselves.[8] In judicial matters records not only of the trials but even of jury-lists

---

[1] See esp. Mommsen, *Staatsr.* iii. 1004–21 (*Dr. publ.* vii. 198–218).

[2] e.g. 'Sc(ribendo) arf(uerunt) M. Claud(ius) M. f., L. Valeri(us) P. f., Q. Minuci(us) C. f.' in the so-called *SC de Bacchanalibus* (*CIL*, i². 581). 'Scribendo adfuerunt M'. Acilius M'. f. Vol(tinia), T. Numisius T. f.' in the *SC de Thisbaeis* (Dittenberger, *Syll.*³ 646. 170 B.C.). Cf. Cic. *Ad fam.* viii. 8. 5 (*SC*), 6 (*senatus auctoritas*) of 51 B.C.

[3] Cic. *Ad Att.* xiii. 33. 3: 'eo libro in quo sunt senatus consulta Cn. Cornelio L. Mummio coss.' (i.e. 146 B.C.). Cf. *CIL*, viii. 270 (*Dr. publ.* vi. i. 494).

[4] Cic. *Pro Sulla*, 42; 40.

[5] First attested in a fragment of Sisenna (Peter, 117). In view of the general orderliness of the Romans it is surprising to find Cicero (*De leg.* iii. 46) complaining that laws in the aerarium were kept without method; but this complaint might be less relevant to conditions a century earlier when the bulk of the laws was less, and thus individual enactments might be found more easily.

[6] Mommsen, *Staatsr.* iii. 370 (*Dr. publ.* vi. i. 424).

[7] Schol. Bob. to Cic. *Pro Sest.* 135 (p. 130 Or.). Cf. Cic. *De leg.* iii. 11. Cf. Mommsen, *Staatsr.* ii. 546 (*Dr. publ.* iv. 246).

[8] Cic. *In Pis.* 36. For the tablets see Varro, *RR*, iii. 5. 18.

were kept in the aerarium in Cicero's day,[1] while fines imposed by the *iudicia populi* were collected by the urban quaestors who would keep accounts of these in the aerarium of which they were the guardians.[2] How much of this evidence can be applied to the early second century must remain uncertain, but sufficient official information must have been available to enable an inquirer to discover the main framework of the People's activities and the men responsible.

On the border-line between official and private documents were many papers which magistrates kept at home: nobles often preserved in their private archives (*tablinum*) the 'monumenta rerum in magistratu gestarum'.[3] In particular, censors on quitting office handed over part of their official documents to the urban quaestors for deposition in the aerarium, but they retained part in their private archives.[4] Thus all magistrates would accumulate a quantity of private papers which they might keep from interest or in order to initiate their sons into the mysteries of public life. Their *commentarii* might contain, besides memoranda of decisions taken by the Senate under their presidency, *sententiae* expressed in the course of debate and other points not strictly necessary for the formulation of the *senatusconsultum*.

More raw material for history was contained in *tituli, elogia, laudationes*, and family records. These domestic treasures were the outward expression of the deep family feeling which Cicero refers to in solemn words ('magnum est enim eadem habere monumenta maiorum, eisdem uti sacris, sepulchra habere communia') and which Horace ridiculed in the type of man who 'stupet in titulis et imaginibus'.[5] In the *atrium* of the house of every noble family were kept the waxen masks (*imagines*) of the dead members of the *gens* who had held curule office, accompanied by inscriptions (*tituli*) recording the magistracies held; the names of their descendants were added and all were linked up by lines along the walls to form genealogical trees, *stemmata*. Possession of the *ius imaginum* was a token of nobility, which was advertised to a wider public on the death of a curule magistrate. At the funeral hired actors impersonated the dead ancestors, wearing their *imagines* and robes of office, and sat on curule chairs in the Forum to hear the *laudatio funebris*, delivered by a son or relative of the dead man or by a magistrate, in which were celebrated not only his deeds but the exploits of the mighty dead.[6] Many of these funeral orations were not merely preserved in the family archives, but were published, as, for instance, those delivered over L. Caecilius Metellus (*died* 221), M. Claudius Marcellus, who died in 208, and Quintus, the son of Fabius Cunctator. With these orations were linked commentaries on individual families.[7] All such records were by their very nature biased, and uncritical or tendentious use of them by later writers has imported much falsehood into Roman history, as Cicero and Livy recognized,[8] but this distortion was less for later than for earlier times since the records were fuller.

[1] Cf. Cic. *Phil.* xv. 36.
[2] L. xxxviii. 58: 'Hostilius et Furius damnati (for *peculatus* in 187) praedes eodem die quaestoribus urbanis dederunt.'
[3] Pliny, *NH*, xxxv. 2. 7. Cf. Festus s.v. Tablinum, and Dionysius, i. 74. 5.
[4] L. xxix. 37. 7; Dionys. i. 74. 5.
[5] Cic. *De offic.* i. 55; Hor. *Sat.* i. 6. 17.
[6] See esp. P. vi. 53-4, and on the *ius imaginum* Mommsen, *Staatsr.* i. 442 (*Dr. publ.* ii. 84 ff.).
[7] e.g. on the Porcian *gens* (Gellius, xiii. 20. 17).
[8] Cic. *Brut.* 62; L. viii. 40. 4.

Other sources available to late annalists were the works of jurists and anti-
quaries which increased in number from Gracchan times. Further, the Tabulae
Pontificum and Annales Maximi could be supplemented by use of the *libri* (*commentarii*) of the *pontifices* and the *libri augurales* (*commentarii augurum*), which
contained regulations for the conduct of the colleges and quoted decisions taken
by them on doubtful points; here reference would often be made to the activities
of individual priests and magistrates. Special treatises also were written on the
various magistracies (e.g. by the annalist Cassius Hemina *De censoribus*), while
Sempronius Tuditanus (*cos.* 129) wrote *libri magistratuum*; here too might be
found allusions to the actions of individuals. Little need be said about the Fasti,
which were available in the Tabulae Pontificum and Annales Maximi, except
that Atticus, Cicero's friend, produced a *Liber Annalis*, a chronological table of
Roman history; this may have been one of the main sources of the surviving
Fasti which were set up in the Forum under Augustus.[1] Atticus also exemplifies
the increasing interest in family history, since he drew up pedigrees of the Claudii
Marcelli, the Fabii, and the Aemilii.

This brief catalogue of some of the public and private sources of information,
which were available to Roman historians before Livy, shows that there was a
considerable body of reliable material, which could be supplemented from less
trustworthy family traditions by annalists who preferred artistic effect to factual
truth. This elaboration was accomplished mainly by the annalists of Sulla's day,
and it was from writers like Valerius Antias that Livy received much of his
subject-matter and its arrangement. But though falsifications were often fabri-
cated in the interests of individual families and of the aristocracy as a whole, so
that popular leaders did not receive fair treatment (cf. Ch. III), it must be
remembered that the annalists themselves came from a variety of *gentes* and
would not be oblivious of their several traditions: the Fabii, Postumii, Acilii,
Cassii, Porcii, Calpurnii, Sempronii, Mucii, Valerii, Claudii, Aelii, Licinii, and
Livii are all represented. The traditions and interests of the Cornelii and Aemilii
were safeguarded by Polybius, while the son of Scipio Africanus himself wrote
a history in Greek. Thus many points of view went to the formation of the tradition found in Livy, but while he may have accepted its general form he was no
mere copyist: all his work is shot through with his own genius.

(c) Contemporary References: the Poets

The political activities of the poet Naevius. These belong to a lost chapter of
history. In 206 Naevius attacked the Caecilii Metelli in the ambiguous line 'Fato
Metelli Romae fiunt consules', to which Metellus replied in anger, 'Dabunt
malum Metelli Naevio poetae' (Ps.-Ascon. *ad* Cic. *In Verr.* i. 29). Because
Naevius constantly insulted the chief men (*principes*) of the State, the *triumviri*

---

[1] Fasti strictly comprised the old calendar of days when public business could and
could not legally be transacted (*dies fasti et nefasti*), but they came to include lists of
magistrates and priests and records of triumphs; they were thus closely linked with the
Tabulae Pontificum (see p. 249). A copy of the Fasti with notes was set up in the temple
of Hercules Musarum, erected by M. Fulvius Nobilior *c.* 187 (Macrobius, *Sat.* i. 12. 16).
The earliest surviving calendar, with consular Fasti, is that from Antium (*c.* 70 B.C.). The
so-called Fasti Capitolini were set up by Augustus in the Forum (not, as was usually
believed, on the walls of the new Regia, but on the triumphal arch of Augustus: see
A. Degrassi, *Inscr. Ital.* XIII. i).

capitales threw him into prison where he wrote two plays in which he apologized for his faults; he was therefore freed by the tribunes (Gellius, iii. 3. 15). For some reason (renewed insults or persecution by his enemies) he was exiled soon afterwards and withdrew to Utica where he died *c.* 201 (Jerome *ad ann.* 1816= 201 B.C.; Cic. *Brut.* 60). His verses about a youthful amatory escapade of Scipio Africanus (Gellius, vii. 8. 5) hardly suggest friendly relations with Scipio (W. Kroll, *Hermes*, 1931, 469–72, believes that Naevius was reconciled with Scipio after his imprisonment, accompanied him to Africa, and there wrote the verses, which contrasted Scipio's youthful humiliation by his father with his present glory, merely for camp-fire amusement. This view seems unnecessary, since while Naevius could not legally be banished to enemy territory, he could be banished and may have withdrawn to north Africa). As Scipio and Metellus were friends and both were attacked by Naevius, his gibes presumably had a political flavour. Tenney Frank may well be right in suggesting that Naevius supported Fabius' policy and that his continued criticism of the Scipionic group went beyond the limits which could be allowed to free speech in war-time (*AJP*, 1927, 105; *Life and Literature in the Roman Republic*, 34).

Naevius was incriminated under the clause of the Twelve Tables, 'si quis occentavisset', whether this was originally designed to cover slander and libel (cf. E. Fraenkel, *PW, Suppl.* VI, s.v. Naevius, and A. Momigliano, *JRS*, 1942, 120 ff.) or referred to magic and had to be stretched by some praetor of the Scipionic party to cover slander (T. Frank, op. cit., and Laura Robinson, *Freedom of Speech in the Roman Republic*, 3–6). Such action would not be difficult, because M. Caecilius Metellus (perhaps a brother of the consul Quintus: cf. *Eph. Arch.* 1910, 374) was praetor urbanus in 206 and also took over the functions of the praetor peregrinus (L. xxix. 13. 4; xxx. 1. 10).

Plautus and Scipio. Tenney Frank has suggested (*Anatolian Studies Presented to W. H. Buckler*, 85 f.) that Plautus, who supported Scipio's policy in 201 (*Cist.* 198–203; cf. *Miles Glor.* 219 ff., which favoured Scipio's African expedition: see A. West, *AJP*, 1887, 15), later feared that a philhellenic policy was being carried to dangerous lengths and so transferred his support to the Catonian group. Hence in 189 in the *Bacchides* he put into the mouth of Chrysalus a comparison of his successful tricks with those by which Troy was captured (926–74); he thus parodied Ennius, who had produced probably in 190 or 189 his Trojan play *Andromache* which indirectly honoured Scipio and emphasized the significance of his advance into Asia, and poked fun at Scipio's Eastern achievements. Frank supports this view by reference to the *Truculentus*, in which Plautus obliquely criticized the *Ambracia* of Ennius which celebrated the exploits of Fulvius Nobilior (l. 465), whom Frank believes on the basis of a common philhellenic policy to have been a supporter of Scipio. Further, he finds (*AJP*, 1932, 152 ff.) disparaging references to the Scipios in the *Trinummus* when they were being attacked by Cato. It would, however, be unwise to build too much on the *Bacchides* passage, which might be good fun without necessarily being critical of Scipio. Further, as Fulvius Nobilior probably did not in fact belong to Scipio's group, Plautus' criticism of him would not affect Scipio; and the criticism of Ennius might not be displeasing to Scipio, his former patron, now that the poet had celebrated the military exploits of a political rival.

(d) Inscriptions and Coins

Few inscriptions, especially those of a personal kind which are so useful for the history of imperial administration and imperial prosopography, illustrate the careers of individuals of this period. Fasti, Elogia, and some inscriptions from the Hellenistic East, which include some valuable letters and dedications, are the main items.

Roman Denarii. The view of H. Mattingly and E. S. G. Robinson that the *denarius* was introduced *c.* 187 B.C. is beyond reasonable doubt, but a margin of uncertainty remains about the *exact* dating of the early issues. This renders the identification of the earlier moneyers hypothetical, so that little can confidently be affirmed about this early stage in the careers of many Roman nobles for this period. Republican *denarii*, however, well illustrate the great part played by the *gens* in public life: the moneyers, who were appointed by the State and issued coins for the State, were allowed wide choice in the subject-matter of the types and freely drew upon the legendary and historical past of their families for material. Thus the coins which refer to this period, although adding little positive to our historical knowledge, provide fine illustrative material. See the indexes of *BM Coins of the Roman Republic.* [The *denarius* is now (1972) dated *c.* 211.]

Portraits of Scipio and Flamininus. The portrait head on the obverse of a *denarius* of Cn. Cornelius Blasio (see Frontispiece No. 4 and note) is usually identified as that of Scipio Africanus. Another view, however, has been advanced, though not fully developed, by E. S. G. Robinson, who in a note read to the Royal Numismatic Society (see *Proceedings of RNS*, 1930, p. 4, in *Num. Chron.* 1930) 'attempted to show that the Barcids inaugurated a silver coinage in Spain, which was continued by the Romans when Scipio captured New Carthage; that the Melcarth, bearded and unbearded, on the Carthaginian silver, may preserve the features of Hamilcar and Hannibal, and that a new obverse type, succeeding the unbearded Melcarth, is probably a portrait of Scipio Africanus. Confirmation of this view was sought in a rare copper coin of Canusium with the same portrait probably struck at the end of the Second Punic War and preserving the memory of Scipio's exploit at Canusium in 216 after Cannae, when he broke up a defeatist plot.' This attractive theory about Scipio's portrait appears convincing, provided that either or both of two assumptions can be accepted: that the portraits on the New Carthage and Canusium coins do represent the same man, or that the portrait on the New Carthage coin is felt to be a Roman head. See Frontispiece Nos. 1–3. This view involves dismissing the portrait on the Blasio *denarius*, but this could be explained as that of an ancestor of Blasio himself, e.g. Cn. Cornelius Blasio (*cos.* I, 270; II, 257; censor 265; triumphed 270); though little is known about him, he was obviously a man of importance in his day.

The Spanish issue is less likely to have been ordered by Scipio than a complimentary action by the captured Punic mint (cf. the offer of the title of king made to Scipio by a Spanish tribe: P. x. 40). Further discussion must await the fuller publication of the Barcid coinage of Spain.

The portrait of Flamininus appears on a rare gold coin issued in Greece: see Frontispiece Nos. 5, 6. The fact that it bears a legend in Latin (T. QUINCTI) suggests that it was issued by Flamininus himself; if it was a complimentary piece struck in his honour by the Greeks, the inscription probably would have been in Greek (cf. G. F. Hill, *Historical Greek Coins*, 136–7).

NOTES ON CATO'S SPEECHES[1]

CATO was one of the earliest Romans to publish his speeches. Cicero knew more than 150 of these (*Brut.* 65), which were either judicial or political. They display Cato's natural eloquence, dry humour, sarcasm, earnestness, self-confidence, and piety, and they contributed very considerably to the development of Roman oratory and prose.[2]

The following notes are intended merely to document and amplify some of the statements made in the body of this work. It may, however, be convenient to quote the fragments themselves fairly fully, because they are not easily accessible to all English readers since two of the collections are old and the third is not in print.

(a) The Early Speeches

Cato's youthful oratory. The remark of Nepos (*Cato*, 3. 3) that 'ab adulescentia confecit orationes' may not suggest but does not rule out the possibility that Cato published some of his early speeches, although none are known before 195 (cf. Fraccaro, *Atti R. Acc. Mant.* 1910, 21, *contra* Jordan, op. cit. lxii). A chronological difficulty arises from Plutarch's statement (cf. p. 111) that Valerius Flaccus was influenced by the reputation that young Cato had built up by his oratory in Sabine villages when he urged him to go to Rome where he was soon elected military tribune (Plut. *Cato*, 3. 2). As Cato was only 18 when he was serving in the army in 216 and went to Sicily as military tribune in 214, his oratorical achievements must have been antedated by Plutarch and other qualities in Cato must have attracted Valerius. Cato's early oratory may fall between 210, when he perhaps left Sicily, and 207, when he was again on military service (cf. Fraccaro, op. cit. 22).

De aedilibus vitio creatis. This speech has been connected (by Fraccaro, op. cit. 28 ff.) with the enforced resignation of the aediles of 202 B.C. (see p. 81 n. 1). This suggestion would be rendered more probable if Cato was an augur, but such a supposition, accepted as a fact by Malcovati (*ORF*, 83), depends upon the reading of Cicero, *De sen.* 64 ('in nostro collegio'; the Leyden MS. gives 'vestro'). Fragment 214 M. deals with the theme that there's many a slip 'twixt the cup and the lip: 'nunc ita aiunt, in segetibus, in herbis bona frumenta esse. nolite ibi nimiam spem habere. saepe audivi inter os atque offam multa intervenire posse; verumvero inter offam atque herbam, ibi vero longum intervallum est.'

Aediles plebis sacrosanctos esse. This cannot be dated (see Festus, p. 422. 17 L.; frg. 216 M.). Mommsen refers to it in connexion with the aedile who dealt with

---

[1] The fragments of the speeches have been collected by H. Meyer, *Oratorum Romanorum Fragmenta* (1842), H. Jordan, *Catonis praeter lib. de re rust. quae extant* (1860), and H. Malcovati, *Oratorum Romanorum Fragmenta*, vol. i (1930). For commentary see Malcovati, op. cit., B. Janzer, *Historische Untersuchungen zu den Redenfragmenten des M. Porcius Cato* (1937), and various articles by P. Fraccaro cited below.

[2] His style is summarized by Gellius (vi. 3. 53).

the Pleminius scandal of 204 (L. xxix. 20), but saw that it could not have been delivered then because Cato was not in Rome (*Staatsr.* ii. 472 n. 2; 486; *Dr. publ.* iv. 164 n. 1; 179 n. 1). Fraccaro (op. cit. 30) connects it with the year of Cato's own aedileship (199); this is possible, but quite uncertain.

De Laetorio. It is tempting to connect this speech with the dispossessed aedile of 202 (see p. 81 n. 1), but the one surviving fragment (204 M.: 'asinum aut musimonem aut arietem') affords no help for dating or identifying the Laetorius. There seems no good reason to question the reading 'De Laetorio' (*apud* Nonium, p. 200 L.): see Malcovati, *ORF*, p. 81.

Oratio quam habuit Numantiae apud equites. As consul in Spain (195) Cato had occasion to address the Roman knights serving in his army, perhaps in a spirit of encouragement rather than blame, in an attempt to improve their morale. Frg. 20 M.: 'cogitate cum animis vestris: si quid vos per laborem recte feceritis, labor ille a vobis cito recedet, bene factum a vobis, dum vivitis, non abscedet; sed si qua per voluptatem nequiter feceritis, voluptas cito abibit, nequiter factum illud apud vos semper manebit.' 21 M.: 'maiores seorsum atque divorsum pretium paravere bonis atque strenuis, decurionatus, optionatus, hastas donaticas, aliosque honores.' There are signs (e.g. Cato's contrast of *labor* and *voluptas*, which ultimately goes back to the sophist Prodicus) that he was influenced by Greek rhetoric (cf. Janzer, *Cato*, 2–4; Fraccaro, *Stud. Stor.* 1910, 135–8). This suggests that Cato had started his study of Greek early in his career (see p. 112 n. 2).

Dissuasio legis Iuniae de feneratione or *Dissuasio legis Iuniae. De feneratione.* If the former reading is adopted, Cato presumably objected to the lex Iunia on the ground that it was not sufficiently severe; if the latter, he used the occasion of an attack on a lex Iunia to speak on usury. On his attitude to usury see above, p. 112. The curule aediles of 192, M. Tuccius and P. Iunius Brutus, prosecuted many money-lenders (L. xxxv. 41. 10). This is probably the Iunius in question and the occasion was at this time or a few years earlier, possibly in Cato's consulship when Iunius may have been tribune (cf. Janzer, *Cato*, 17). Or, since aediles may have lacked the *ius agendi*, the proposer may have been M. Iunius Brutus (praetor 191): see Rotondi, *Leges Publicae*, 273. Frg. 58 M.: 'Camerini cives nostri oppidum pulchrum habuere, agrum optimum atque pulcherrimum, rem fortunatissimam. cum Romam veniebant, prorsus devertebantur pro hospitibus ad amicos suos.' 59 M.: 'tertio autem pedato item ex fenore discordia excrescebat.' The prosperity of Cameria apparently had been disturbed by the activities of usurers which provoked *discordia*.

Cato on the lex Oppia. No title or fragment of any speech by Cato on the lex Oppia (see p. 113) survives; it is uncertain whether he published one and, if so, whether Livy knew it. Having reached Cato's consulship Livy devotes twenty chapters to Cato and his policy (xxxiv. 1–20), and wishing to illustrate Cato's character he inserted a speech (2–4), either his own composition or based on one in his annalistic sources. It does not derive from Cato's original speech (if this ever existed) because it reveals no traces of Cato's style and contains some anachronisms, e.g. a reference to the Romans in Asia (4. 1). See Fraccaro, *Stud. Stor.* 1910, 132–4, and *Studi Liviani* (1934), *contra* E. Pais (*Atti d. R. Acc. d. Arch. Lett. e B. Arti di Napoli*, 1908, 123 ff.), who attempts to find traces of Cato's work in the Livian speech.

De triumpho ad populum. See p. 119. Only one alliterative phrase survives

(23 M.: 'asperrimo atque arduissimo aditu'), which may refer to Cato's capture of Bergium (cf. L. xxxiv. 21. 4).

In Q. Minucium Thermum. Cato is said to have delivered two speeches against Minucius Thermus, one *de falsis pugnis*, the other *de decem hominibus.* The surviving fragments may, however, derive from one speech, presumably delivered in the Senate, since there is no evidence that Cato also formally prosecuted Minucius in the courts. See Malcovati, *ORF,* frgs. 61–6, and cf. Drumann–Groebe, *Gesch. Roms,* v², 116 n. 2; Janzer, *Cato,* 18 ff.; and for the circumstances of the delivery pp. 133 f. above. The chief fragments are: 61 M.: 'tuum nefarium facinus peiore facinore operire postulas, succidias humanas facis, tantam trucidationem facis, decem funera facis, decem capita libera interficis, decem hominibus vitam eripis indicta causa, iniudicatis, incondemnatis.' 63 M.: 'neque fidem, neque iusiurandum, neque pudicitiam multifacit.' 66 M.: 'dixit a decemviris parum bene sibi cibaria curata esse. iussit vestimenta detrahi atque flagro caedi. decemviros Bruttiani verberavere, videre multi mortales. quis hanc contumeliam, quis hoc imperium, quis hanc servitutem ferre potest? nemo hoc rex ausus est facere; eane fieri bonis, bono genere gnatis, boni consultis? ubi societas? ubi fides maiorum? insignitas iniurias, plagas, verbera, vibices, eos dolores atque carnificinas per dedecus atque maximam contumeliam, inspectantibus popularibus suis atque multis mortalibus, te facere ausum esse? set quantum luctum, quantum gemitum, quid lacrimarum, quantum fletum factum audivi? servi iniurias nimis aegre ferunt: quid illos, bonos genere gnatos, magna virtute praeditos, opinamini animi habuisse atque habituros, dum vivent?' The reference to a *rex* is interesting. Was Cato thinking of Rome's early kings or the kings of the Hellenistic world? Fragment 82 M. might come from this speech and describe how Minucius dealt with his victims: 'nervo, carcere, moletrina'.

Dierum dictarum de consulatu suo. The variant titles of this speech (see above, p. 134) have been discussed by Fraccaro (*Stud. Stor.* 1910, 147 ff.), who argues that all the fragments derive from one and the same speech. A *terminus post quem* is fixed for the date by a reference to Thermopylae (frg. 51) as late 191; the view of Cima (*L'eloquenzia latina,* 31) that this reference was inserted later into the published speech is not tenable (cf. Fraccaro, op. cit.). The censors mentioned (frg. 52) must almost certainly be those of 194 or 189. Fraccaro (op. cit. 152–3) favours those of 189 (T. Flamininus and M. Claudius Marcellus) whose administration, like that of 194, was mild; he suggests that the trial was part of the attack of Cato's opponents when he was standing for the censorship of 184. The situation in the year 194, however, suits the facts even better, while the reference to the censors (Aelius and Cethegus) suggests that the prosecution originated from the Scipionic group: cf. Malcovati, *ORF,* pp. 25–6; A. H. McDonald, *JRS,* 1938, 162.

Livy drew on this speech and no doubt on Cato's *Origines* for his account of Cato's Spanish campaign (xxxiv. 8–21), either directly or more probably through an annalist; his description of the main battle (chs. 14 and 15) is notably clearer than the conventional battle-pieces of the annalists. On Livy's relation to Cato here see Fraccaro, *Stud. Stor.* 1910, 154 ff., and *Studi Liviani;* Janzer, *Cato,* 6 ff. Compare Cato, frg. 30, and L. xxxiv. 8. 5 and 16. 1; frg. 31 and L. 8. 6; 34 and 18. 2; 35 and 18. 2 and 11. 2; 37 and 13. 2; 38 and 39 and 14. 1 and 8; 42 and 19. 1; 44 and 19. 6.

Some 34 fragments survive; the following may be quoted: 23 M.: 'egoque iam pridem cognovi atque intellexi atque arbitror rem publicam curare industrie summum periculum esse.' 24 M.: 'atque quamquam multa nova miracula fecere inimici mei, tamen nequeo desinere mirari eorum audaciam atque confidentiam.' 25 M.: 'ei rei dant operam ut mihi falso maledicatur.' 27 M.: 'secus aetatem agerem quam illi egissent.' 28 M.: 'videtote quanto secus ego fecerim.' 29 M.: 'omnia ab integro paranda erant.' 30 M.: 'laudant me maximis laudibus, tantum navium, tantum exercitum, tantum commeatum non opinatum esse quemquam hominem comparare potuisse; id me tam maturrime comparavisse.' 33 M.: 'mihi atque classi obviam fiunt.' 50 M.: 'ego mihi haec monimenta sempiterno posui quae cepi.' 51 M.: 'item ubi ab Thermopulis atque ex Asia maximos tumultus maturis-sime disieci atque consedavi' (the similarity of the words *tumultus* and *consedavi* with ταραχή and κατεπράυνεν in Plutarch's account of Flamininus' activity before Thermopylae (*Cato*, 12. 3) leads Janzer (*Cato*, 13) to suggest that they derive from a common source, perhaps a *senatusconsultum* on their achievements, which Cato now referred to in his speech. The words *ex Asia* imply merely that the war had come from Asia, not that Cato had served there; nor is Cato's pre-sence in Asia to be deduced from Cic. *Pro Mur.* 14. 32). 52 M.: 'censores qui posthac fiunt, formidulosius atque segnius atque timidius pro re publica niten-tur.' Cf. also Plut. *Cato*, 5. 7; 10. 3.

In M'. Acilium Glabrionem. See p. 137. In the only fragment (84 M.: 'postquam navitas ex navibus eduxi, non ex militibus atque nautis piscatores penatores feci, sed arma dedi') Cato is probably contrasting his own careful conduct in Spain with some alleged neglect by Glabrio in Greece.

De praeda militibus dividenda. The occasion of the delivery of this speech is unknown, but Mommsen (*Röm. Forsch.* ii. 459) conjectured a connexion with the attack on Glabrio. It contained a pungent sentence, 221 M.: 'fures privatorum furtorum in nervo atque in compedibus aetatem agunt, fures publici in auro atque in purpura.' Two other fragments survive: 222 M.: 'tu dives fite'; 223 M.: 'fraudulenter atque avariter.'

Uti praeda in publicum referatur. In this speech (occasion unknown) Cato com-plained that Greek works of art, even statues of the gods, found their way into Roman private houses: 'miror audere atque religionem non tenere, statuas deo-rum, exempla earum facierum, signa domi pro supellectile statuere' (224 M.).

De re A. Atili. Nothing is known about the circumstances of this speech (frg. 208 M.), but since A. Atilius Serranus commanded the fleet in Greek waters against Antiochus in 191, it is tempting to connect the speech with him and with the general scandal of 189 (see p. 137), but there is no evidence to check the identification. The case probably was private and concerned the estate of an Atilius. Scaliger's attempt to emend the *index* (*apud* Fest., p. 464, 28 L.) to *De regis Attali vectigalibus* is not satisfactory (on that speech see pp. 238 and 271).

De coniuratione. This speech was probably concerned with the Bacchanalian conspiracy (see p. 147). Only one word survives: 'precem' (86 M.).

Contra Ti. Sempronium Longum. The date of this speech is not known, but it would fit 184 very well (see p. 150). Only one fragment is extant: 'si posset auctio fieri de artibus tuis, quasi supellectilis solet' (191 M.). Cato perhaps charged Longus with luxurious living. According to Plutarch (*Cato*, 12. 1) Cato had served as legate to Longus during his consulship in 194; this may well be, but since Plutarch alone records this it might be an error arising from the fact that both Cato and Longus had served under Acilius Glabrio in Greece in 191 (see p. 124, and L. xxxvi. 22; 24 for Longus). An alternative date for the speech is 189 (see p. 137) when Glabrio was prosecuted; Cato might well have sought to discredit Glabrio's legate Longus at the same time.

Contra Tiberium exulem. Not much can be made of this speech and its single fragment: 'quid si vadimonium capite obvoluto stitisses?' (192 M.). The Tiberius may be Longus; but the view of Jordan that Tiberius escaped condemnation by exile is not probable, since presumably the accused must have been in court for Cato to have addressed him (cf. Malcovati, *ORF*, i, p. 79). The MS. reading *exulem* (*apud* Gell. ii. 14. 1) is possibly corrupt.

(b) Speeches of Cato's Censorship

De vestitu et vehiculis. Cato assures the people that as censor he will not relax the severity which he had promised as a candidate, perhaps contrasting the behaviour of others who did not fulfil their election pledges: 'nam periniurium siet, cum mihi ob eos mores, quos prius habui, honos detur, ubi datus est, tum uti eos mutem atque alii modi sim' (107 M.). This remark may suggest that this was Cato's first speech as censor. See above, pp. 156 f.

De habitu. Two words alone survive: 'sanguen demittatur' (203 M.). Various suggestions have been advanced (see Malcovati, *ORF*, i, p. 80), e.g. that *habitus* = *vestitus* and that the speech should be connected with the *De vestitu*. Others believe that Habitus was a *cognomen* (cf., for example, A. Cluentius Habitus) or that the reading (*apud* Charis. p. 114. 17 B.) should be *De ambitu*.

De signis et tabulis. The sole fragment runs: 'honorem emptitavere, malefacta benefactis non redemptitavere' (109 M.). Fraccaro (*Stud. Stor.* 1911, 33 ff.) prefers to read 'honorem temptavere, benefacta benefactis non redemptitavere' (*apud* Fest., p. 364. 9 L.), though he admits that the manuscripts give '.1.efacta'. He interprets the meaning: 'I will not act as some magistrates who seek careers and do not repay the benefits which they have received from you by showing benefits to you.' Janzer connects the fragment with *De signis* and suggests that Cato is criticizing those who by wise spending and flattery have won the honour of a public statue, but who have failed to buy forgetfulness of their earlier lives. This explanation is scarcely needed; if the reading 'malefacta' is retained, Cato may merely have been contrasting the electoral practices of some of his contemporaries, which though corrupt did not necessarily result in beneficial officeholders, with his own incorruptibility and beneficial legislation.

Fraccaro believes that this fragment and that from *De vestitu* (107 M.) derive from one and the same speech of which the *index* would be: 'oratio de signis et tabulis, de vestitu et vehiculis (de mancipiis?)', and thinks it would be strange if Cato made two speeches on such kindred topics. But as Malcovati (p. 44 n.) points out, if the title was as Fraccaro suggests, it is difficult to see why Priscian (*GL*, ii, p. 226. 16 K.) should have referred to it as 'De vestitu et vehiculis'. One speech might have dealt with objects, another with persons.

In Lepidum. The erection of statues to two effeminate Greek cooks aroused Cato's wrath in a speech against a certain Lepidus (see p. 156 n. 4; Fronto, p. 223 N.; Cato, 196 M.). This Lepidus cannot be identified: he might be M. Aemilius

Lepidus (*cos.* I in 187) or his son (military tribune in 190: L. xxxvii. 43). Cato must have rejoiced to trounce a member of a pro-Scipionic family.

Ne spolia figerentur nisi de hoste capta. The only fragment is: 'sed tum, ubi ii dimissi sunt, revertantur resignatis vectigalibus' (110 M.). The speech was almost certainly delivered during Cato's censorship (see p. 157). Fraccaro (*Stud. Stor.* 1911, 37–8) rejects the view of Jordan (*Cato*, p. xcv) that the speech dealt with the spoils of Ambracia which Fulvius Nobilior wanted to display in his house, and that of Lange (*Röm. Alt.* ii³. 262) who connected the speech with legislation against the abuse of undeserved triumphs.

In L. Quinctium Flamininum. See pp. 157 f. Only one fragment of this speech, which has been utilized by Livy, survives: 'aliud est, Philippe, amor, longe aliud est cupido. accessit ilico alter, ubi alter recessit; alter bonus, alter malus' (89 M.). The fullness of Cato's information about Flamininus' *probrum* may have derived from friends in his camp: Cato and his supporters kept close watch on their political rivals.

De re Floria (i.e. *De re familiari Florii*). Cato, who had charged both L. Flamininus and Minucius Thermus with unnatural vice (above, p. 134), referred to the same topic in a private speech *De re Floria* (frgs. 205–7 M.; see Gellius, ix. 12. 7; x. 13. 1). For various conjectures about this speech see Malcovati, *ORF*, 81: e.g. that it refers to the Ludi Florales, or that the *index* should be emended to *De re Floriae* and concerned inheritance. The wildest suggestion comes from Meyer who tried to connect it with the Vestal Virgin Floronia who was condemned for unchastity in 216 (L. xxii. 57. 2); she will have been accused by Cato, aged 18, in one of his earliest appearances in the law-courts!

De moribus Claudi Neronis. The two fragments reveal little: 101 M.: 'pecunia mea rei publicae profuit quam isti modi uti tu es' (which at any rate illustrates Cato's good opinion of himself). 102 M.: 'haruspicem, fulguratorem si quis adducat.' Claudius' identity, his rank, whether senatorial or equestrian, and the cause of his offence are all uncertain, though the speech is probably correctly assigned to Cato's censorship (see p. 159 n.). Claudius may be identified with (i) Ti. Claudius Nero (son of the consul of 202) who was quaestor in 185 but does not seem to have reached higher office, or with (ii) Ap. Claudius Nero, legate of Flamininus in Greece (197–196), praetor in Spain (195), and one of the *decemviri* sent to Asia in 189 (see Münzer, *PW*, s.v. Claudius n. 245); he did not reach the consulship. Cato's enmity and knowledge of his mores might go back to his Spanish campaign of 195 (cf. Janzer, *Cato*, 35).

In L. Veturium de sacrificio commisso cum ei equum ademit. On this see above, p. 160; also Malcovati, *ORF*, pp. 37–8; Fraccaro, *Stud. Stor.* 1911, 41–6; Janzer, *Cato*, 33–6. Frg. 90 M.: 'quod tu, quod in te fuit, sacra stata, sollempnia, capite sancta deseruisti' (cf. Wissowa, *Religion und Kult. der Rom.* 65, 336). 91 M.: 'domi cum auspicamus, honorem me deum immortalium velim habuisse. servi, ancillae, si quis eorum sub centone crepuit, quod ego non sensi, nullum mihi vitium facit. si cui ibidem servo aut ancillae dormienti evenit, quod comitia prohibere solet, ne is quidem mihi vitium facit.' 95 M.: 'Graeco ritu fiebantur Saturnalia' (Cato is doubtless deprecating the introduction of Greek cults). 93 M.: 'qui illius impudentiam norat et duritudinem.' 98 M.: 'sedere non potest in equo trepidante.' 99 M.: 'hostem num unum icit?' 100 M.: 'propter tenuitatem et plebitatem.' Cf. also Gellius vi. 22. 1, and Plut. *Cato*, 9. 6.

Ut plura aera equestria fierent. See p. 160; Fraccaro, *Stud. Stor.* 1911, 47 ff., 106 ff.; Malcovati, *ORF*, p. 39; Janzer, *Cato*, 37–9. The speech is certainly to be assigned to Cato's censorship, and according to Priscian (*GL*, ii, p. 318. 21 K.) it was delivered in the Senate, which Cato would naturally consult even though possibly he himself had authority to act. Frg. 103 M.: 'nunc ergo arbitror oportere restitui, quin minus duobus milibus ducentis sit aerum equestrium.' 104 M.: 'de aeribus equestribus, de duobus milibus ac ducentis'. Janzer (*Cato*, 39) follows Lipsius in reading *institui* for *restitui* in frg. 103, because there is no reason to suppose that the number had ever previously been 2,200; the preceding *oporte-re* might explain the error. There seem three possible explanations of Cato's proposal: (1) an increase of the *aera equestria*, i.e. more allowance for the *equites*; (2) an increase in the number of those drawing *aera equestria*, i.e. an increase of the number of *equites equo publico*; or (3) that the *equites* should pay more *tributum*. The second is the probable meaning.

In L. Furium de aqua, qua multam ei dixit. See p. 161. This speech was more probably delivered *in contione* (cf. the censors of 169 who 'multam pro contione privato dixerunt': L. xliii. 16. 5) than in the Comitia as the result of an appeal by Furius to the People against the fine. Cf. Fraccaro, *Stud. Stor.* 1911, 51–4, 121; Janzer, *Cato*, 43–4. The following fragments may be quoted: 111 M.: 'domi meae saepe fuit'. 114 M.: 'o quanti ille agros emit, qua aquam duceret.' 115 M.: 'quod attinet ad salinatores aerarios, cui cura vectigalium resignat' (on the *salinatores aerarii* see Mommsen, *Staatsr.* ii. 436 n. 4). 116 M.: 'praetores secundum populum vindicias dicunt' (perhaps Cato had previously consulted the praetors on this matter).

De Indigitibus. See p. 161, and Fraccaro, *Stud. Stor.* 1911, 49 n. 2; Malcovati, *ORF*, p. 41. The only fragment is very corrupt: 106 M.: 'sinunt . . . ut bona rapiant; aut . . . sequestro dent.'

De agna musta pascenda. A fragment of a speech thus entitled might well apply to Cato's activity in clearing up the shrines (p. 161; cf. Janzer, *Cato*, 40), although Malcovati (p. 82) prefers to place it among Cato's private speeches. 211 M.: 'Citer ager alligatus ad sacra erit.'

Si se M. Caelius tribunus plebis appellasset. This speech against Caelius was more probably delivered when the misuse of public land was being discussed (see p. 161) than in connexion with Cato's leasing of public contracts. The title, which Gellius (i. 15. 8) quotes as 'si se M. Caelius trib. plebis appellasset', has provoked much controversy. Weber (*Comment. de M. Porcii Catonis vita*, 1831) took *trib. plebis* as an accusative and conjectured that Caelius falsely took the name of tribune. This cannot be correct, because (*a*) the Latin cannot mean this, and (*b*) that Caelius was a tribune is clear from frg. 121 ('cum convocari iubet'). Most scholars prefer to read *tribunus plebis*. The views of Meyer (*Orat. Rom. Frg.* 131) that *appellare = accusare*, and of Jordan that it refers to an *appellatio* of the tribune Caelius to the consul Cato may be rejected: why should a tribune, who had the *ius intercedendi*, need to appeal? Fraccaro (*Stud. Stor.* 1910, 257–72; 1911, 59 f., 120) believes that *appellare* is used in the technical sense of seeking *intercessio* from one magistrate against another. As most of Cato's magistracies had been exercised in the provinces (quaestorship, praetorship, and most of consulship) and it is unlikely that the speech would refer to his aedileship, Fraccaro is probably right in believing that Cato as censor delivered a speech against Caelius who had promised to help those whose interests Cato's severity had threatened. He assumes that the original title was 'oratio in M. Caelium tribunum plebis, cum auxilio fore pollicitus est, si se quis appellasset'. The chief difficulty here, as Malcovati (p. 49) feels, is the extent of the corruption of the *index*: no other title of Cato's speeches has been so contorted that the sense has been completely changed. The corruption is too much for Janzer (p. 46) who suggests that Cato did not wait until anyone had actually appealed for Caelius' help, but prepared to attack first; acting on a hypothesis ('si appellasset'), Cato composed a speech which could be used if Caelius did move in the matter; its title would have been 'si quis Caelium tribunum plebis appellasset'. Presumably Janzer believes that it was later published as personal invective or political propaganda. But it is difficult to believe that Cato would have composed a full-dress speech against a possible emergency, and Fraccaro's view seems preferable since the titles of many of Cato's speeches have been handed down in a variety of forms.

Jordan (p. lxx) attributed to this speech a remark of Cato (Plut. *Cato*, 9. 7): 'to a tribune of the plebs who had been accused of using poison and who was trying to force the passage of a useless bill Cato said: "Young man (ὦ μειρά-κιον), I do not know which is worse, to drink your mixtures or to enact your bills."' Fraccaro, who at first rejected the connexion (*Stud. Stor.* 1910, 262 n. 1) because Caelius was not introducing a *rogatio*, later inclined to accept it (*Stud. Stor.* 1911, 60 n. 3), though this difficulty remains unexplained. It may be, however, that Cato's reference to Caelius' useless legislation was general, and that Plutarch has erroneously particularized it: 'who was trying to force the passage of a bill'. The reference to Caelius as μειράκιον accords well with Cato's description of his clowning in frg. 125, while the mention of a *pharmocopola* in frg. 121 might contain an oblique reference to the poison used by Caelius.—The view of Jordan and Meyer that Fronto's remark (p. 68 N.) 'legi Catonis orationem . . . qua tribuno diem dixit' refers to this occasion must remain uncertain, because Cato clashed with tribunes more than once (cf. Malcovati, p. 50, and frg. 229).

121 M.: 'numquam tacet, quem morbus tenet loquendi tamquam veternosum bibendi atque dormiendi. quod si non conveniatis, cum convocari iubet, ita cupidus orationis conducat, qui auscultet. itaque auditis, non auscultatis, tamquam pharmacopolam. nam eius verba audiuntur; verum se nemo committit, si aeger est.' 122 M.: 'frusto panis conduci potest, vel uti taceat vel uti loquatur.' 123 M.: 'in coloniam, mehercules, scribere nolim, si trium virum sim, spatiatorem atque fescenninum.' 134 M.: 'descendit de cantherio, inde staticulos dare, ridicularia fundere.' 125 M.: 'praeterea cantat, ubi collibuit, interdum Graecos versus agit, iocos dicit, voces demutat, staticulos dat.' 126 M.: 'quid ego cum illo dissertem amplius, quem ego denique credo in pompa vectitatum ire ludis pro citeria, atque cum spectatoribus sermocinaturum.' 127 M.: 'si em percussi, saepe incolumis abii; praeterea pro re publica, pro scapulis atque aerario multum rei publicae profuit.'

Contra Oppium. See p. 162, and Fraccaro, *Stud. Stor.* 1911, 121 ff.; Malcovati, 46. Frg. 118 M.: 'vinum redemisti, praedia pro vini quadrantalibus sexaginta in publicum dedisti, vinum non dedisti.'

Ad litis censorias. See p. 162, and Fraccaro, *Stud. Stor.* 1911, 50, 125. Frg. 120 M.: 'scio fortunas secundas neglegentiam prendere solere quae uti prohibitum irem, quod in me esset, meo labori non parsi.' The sentence is somewhat obscure, but *neglegentiam*, not *fortunas*, should be taken as the subject of *prendere*.

Ut basilica aedificetur. See p. 163. The only fragment is 105 M.: 'antequam is vilicare coepit.'

Reliquiae incertae sedis (*on drainage works?*). Two unassigned fragments may well derive from a speech in which Cato justified his policy of reconstructing the sewage system (see p. 163). They are: 135 M.: 'cloacale flumen dixit Cato pro cloacarum omnium conluvie', and 136 M.: 'speca posita, quo aqua de via abiret.'

De lustri sui felicitate, In Thermum post censuram, and *De suis virtutibus contra Thermum*. These three titles may cover one and the same speech (see p. 164). Nothing, other than the fact of its delivery, is known about the *De lustri sui felicitate*, but Fraccaro has ingeniously identified it with *In Thermum post censuram* (see *Stud. Stor.* 1911, 63–7. Malcovati, *ORF*, p. 52 n. 7, regards the conjecture as acute, but not sufficiently certain to justify acceptance). There is a corrupt reference in Festus (p. 470.26 L.) to the *In Thermum*: 'sacrem porcum ... Cato adver⟨sus Q. Minucium The⟩rmum post ⟨censuram⟩: "... crem in sin ... quando pro ... me sacrem (porcum) ... primis fiet" ' (frg. 75 M.). The pig mentioned here might well be the victim in the lustral *suovetaurilia* after Cato's censorship, and the speech be identified with that on the *felicitas* of the *lustrum*, with an original title such as 'Adversus L. Minucium Thermum de lustri sui felicitate'.

In frg. 75 note the archaic 'sacrem' for 'sacrum'; 'post censuram' should mean 'censu peracto', not 'post notam censoriam'. One other fragment of this speech survives, 74 M.: 'qui ventrem suum non pro hoste habet, qui pro re publica, non pro sua, obsonat, qui stulte spondet, qui cupide aedificat.' The last phrase might refer to the ostentatious houses of the philhellenic nobility or to those people who had built on public land from which they had just been expelled by Cato's decision. Janzer (*Cato*, 50) finds in Cato's speech the first traces in Roman literature of Felicitas as a divine spirit; but it is not certain that Cato would regard this abstract conception in the same way as later Romans.

The speech *In Thermum* is very probably the same as that entitled *De suis virtutibus contra Thermum*, which was later than 189 and must refer to L. Minucius Thermus. The *terminus post quem* is fixed by Cato's statement: 'M. Fulvio consuli legatus sum in Aetoliam' (i.e. 189 B.C.; frg. 71 M.). Thermus cannot have been Q. Minucius Thermus who went to Asia in 190 and was killed on his way home. 69 M.: 'ego iam a principio in parsimonia atque in duritia atque industria omnem adulescentiam meam abstinui agro colendo, saxis Sabinis, silicibus repastinandis atque conserendis.' 70 M.: 'quid mihi fieret, si non ego stipendia omnia ordinarius meruissem semper?' 71 M.: 'M. Fulvio consuli legatus sum in Aetoliam, propterea quod ex Aetolia complures venerant: Aetolos pacem velle: de ea re oratores Romam profectos.' 72 M.: 'aliud est properare, aliud festinare. qui unum quid mature transigit, is properat, qui multa simul incipit neque perficit, is festinat.' 73 M.: 'quom essem in provincia legatus, quamplures ad praetores et consules vinum honorarium dabant: nunquam accepi, ne privatus quidem.'

Contra Annium. This speech probably belongs to Cato's censorship. 130 M.: 'nemo antea fecit super tali re cum hoc magistratu utique rem.' This may refer to the magistrates and others whom the censors were accustomed to consult (cf.

Varro, *LL*, vi. 87: 'ubi praetores tribunique plebei quique in consilium vocati sunt venerunt'). See Mommsen, *Staatsr.* i. 314, ii. 361; Malcovati, *ORF*, p. 50. Annius might be T. Annius Luscus, quaestor in 185, or less likely his son (*cos.* 153); more probably he is otherwise unknown.

In Q. Sulpicium. This also is probably censorial. 131 M.: 'quotiens vidi trulleos nassiternas pertusos; aqualis matellas sine ansis.' Cato, who attacked other members of the Sulpician *gens*, may be exposing the slovenliness of Sulpicius' household with its broken crockery, or else contrasting the luxuriousness of his household with the cheap and broken ware of early Roman households. If the *praenomen* Quintus is correct, this Sulpicius cannot be identified with any known Sulpicius.

(c) The Later Speeches

Pro L. Autronio. Nothing is known of the circumstances of the delivery, but the sole fragment suggests a possible connexion with the crime-wave of 180 B.C. (cf. p. 177): 199 M.: 'venefici postridie iussisti adesse in diem ex die; non ausi recusare.' See Priscian, *GL*, ii, p. 482. 9 K.: 'vetustissimi tamen et ausi pro ausus sum protulerunt.' The reading *venefici* for the MS. *beneficii* is Mommsen's conjecture. There is no need to read *Antonio* for *Autronio*.

Ne imperium sit veteri ubi novus venerit. There is not sufficient evidence to connect this speech with any known episode, nor does the one fragment help: 220 M: 'siticines et liticines et tubicines.' But the clash of authority between Q. Fulvius Flaccus and Ti. Sempronius Gracchus in Spain in 180 (see p. 178) is the kind of situation which might have given rise to subsequent dispute in Rome and the delivery of a speech by Cato on this topic.

Ne lex Orchia derogaretur dissuasio. See p. 172, and Fraccaro, *Stud. Stor.* 1910, 250 ff.; Malcovati, *ORF*, pp. 55–7; Janzer, *Cato*, 53–7. Macrobius (iii. 17. 2) refers to *speeches* of Cato ('lex Orchia, de qua Cato mox orationibus suis vociferebatur'), but the plural should not be pressed, despite two passages of Festus which suggest that Cato did deliver two speeches: one in which he spoke against the bill (p. 280. 31 L.: 'Cato in ea qua legem Orchiam dissuadet'), and a second in which he spoke against its abrogation (p. 220. 15 L.: 'Cato in suasione de lege Orchia derogaretur'). It is unlikely that Cato would speak against a sumptuary law. If it was not severe enough for his taste, he would probably have insisted on its being made more rigid; further, few would have approved of it, if Cato, the leader of the reform party, disapproved. Fraccaro therefore is probably correct in arguing for one speech by Cato and that the passage of Festus should read 'in dissuasione ne lex Orchia derogaretur'; the title of the speech will then have been '*Ne lex Orchia derogaretur dissuasio*', parallel with Cato's '*Ne lex Baebia derogaretur dissuasio*' of 181.

The date of its delivery is uncertain, but it was soon (*mox*) after the passage of the bill. Fraccaro, rejecting the force of Macrobius' *mox*, has argued that it was delivered after the *lex Fannia centussis* of 161 on the ground that the phrase 'qui antea . . . obsonitavere, postea centenis obsonitavere' (frg. 141 M.) refers to the lex Fannia. But this need not be so, as is shown by Malcovati and Janzer. If the lex Fannia fixed the maximum sum to be spent on banquets at 100 *asses*, the smallness of the sum would have made the lex Orchia unnecessary, since the more guests invited the less sumptuous would have been the fare for each. It is not certain how the text of this fragment should be completed. If the missing figure in the first phrase was less than 100, then Cato will have been explaining how expenses had increased since Hellenistic luxury had invaded Roman banquets; if the figure was over 100, Cato will have been explaining how effectively the lex Orchia was working.

That the bill was abrogated is generally assumed from a passage of Varro (*apud* Gell. xii. 11. 2), who in observing that the ideal number of guests was between the number of the Graces (three) and that of the Muses (nine) makes no reference to any legal limit to the maximum number. This *argumentum ex silentio*, however, is scarcely conclusive.

142 M.: 'percunctatum patris familiae nomen ne quis servum mitteret, lege sanctum fuisse ait Cato.' This presumably refers to the custom of having a slave (*nomenclator*) to remind his master of the names of people he met, but it is surprising to find this usage so early. Possibly Cato is referring to electoral procedure and methods of canvassing, a subject which he also dealt with in his *De ambitu*, delivered this same year. Cf. also Plutarch's remark (*Cato*, 21. 1) that none of Cato's slaves ever entered another man's house unless sent there by Cato or his wife. 143 M.: 'non aliter et M. Cato in legem Orchiam, conferens ea quae virtus . . ., ut summae gloriae sint a virtute proficiscentia, dedecoris vero praecipui existimentur, quae voluptas suadeat non sine labe vitiorum.' 145 M.: 'Cato enim sumptuarias leges cibarias appellat.' 146 M.: 'in atrio et duobus ferculis epulabantur antiqui' (perhaps he is contrasting the Greek custom of dining at a *triclinium* in a *cenaculum*). 149 M.: 'magna cura cibi, magna virtutis incuria.' Cf. Plut. *Cato*, 8. 1–2.

De ambitu. See p. 173. The only fragment is 138 M.: 'sed sunt partim, qui duarum rerum alterius utrius causa magistratum petunt.'

Ne lex Baebia derogaretur dissuasio. See pp. 172 f. Frg. 139 M.: 'hoc potius agam quod hic rogat' (this presumably attests Cato's approval of the proposal to retain the lesser number of praetors). 140 M.: 'pecuniam inlargibo tibi' (this might come from an illustration of the corruptibility of his contemporaries).

De M. Fulvi Nobilioris censura. See pp. 183 f. Frg. 151 M.: 'iam principio quis vidit corona donari quemquam, cum oppidum captum non esset aut castra hostium non incensa essent?' (Cato was thinking of the *corona muralis*, which was given to the man first over the enemy's town-wall, and the *corona castrensis* awarded to the first soldier to break into his camp, and is gibing at Fulvius' capture of Ambracia which was not stormed but surrendered. Cf. Gellius, v. 6. 24: 'Fulvius coronis donaverat milites, quia vallum curaverant aut quia putem strenue foderant'; this remark might come from Cato's speech). 152 M.: 'oratio Catonis, in qua obiecit ut probrum M. Nobiliori, quod is in provinciam poetas duxisset.' 153 M.: 'retricibus cum ait Cato in ea, quam scripsit, cum edissertavit Fulvi Nobilioris censuram, significat aquam eo nomine, quae est supra viam Ardeatinam inter lapidem secundum et tertium; qua inrigantur horti infra viam Ardeatinam et Asinariam usque ad Latinam.' On the ground that frgs. 151 and 152 deal with the period of Fulvius' consulship and frg. 153 with his censorship Meyer (pp. 52 and 95), Jordan (pp. lxxvi, lxxxiv), and Lange (ii. 237 and 263) argued that Cato delivered two speeches against Nobilior. The second obviously will have been after his censorship (179–178), but when was the first delivered? Meyer thinks in 187 during the senatorial debate on granting Fulvius a triumph.

Lange concurs, but suggests as an alternative the Senate meeting at which Ambracian envoys complained about Fulvius' conduct, when Cato will have supported M. Aemilius Lepidus. Jordan believes that Cato accused Fulvius after his return from Ambracia 'ob rem in provincia male gestam'. But Fraccaro (*Stud. Stor.* 1910, 272–80), followed by Malcovati (*ORF*, i, pp. 59 f.), has shown that (1) Cato could not have taken part in the Ambracian discussion in the Senate because he was in Greece serving under Fulvius, and (2) as Livy's description of the senatorial debate about Fulvius' triumph is full, Livy hardly would have omitted all reference to any full-dress speech by Cato. Fraccaro then seeks an alternative date: he rejects the winter of 187/6 because, as Manlius on his return to Rome was attacked for his bad discipline, Fulvius scarcely would have escaped a similar attack if he had given cause. The year 186, when attention was distracted by the Bacchanalian troubles and when Fulvius gave splendid Games, is improbable, while if Cato had accused Fulvius in 185, the latter would hardly have stood for the consulship of 184. Nor is it likely that, if the quarrel had already developed between Cato and Fulvius, Cato would have spared him during his censorship in 184: Cato reproached Fulvius with the *probrum* of having taken Ennius to Ambracia, which would have afforded him an excuse for removing Fulvius, like L. Flamininus or Scipio Asiaticus. If, therefore, no suitable occasion for this speech can be found between 187 and 184, it had better be dismissed and the frgs. 150 and 151 assigned to the same speech as frg. 152, i.e. after the censorship of 179. Such arguments cannot be conclusive, but they far outweigh the trifling objections raised by Janzer (*Cato*, 58) against this view: (1) an *argumentum ex silentio*, based on the fact that frgs. 151 and 152 do not mention the censorship— but there is no reason why they should, and (2) though Cato was in Greece during the Ambracian discussion, he could have attacked Fulvius when he had returned and was seeking a triumph; Fraccaro's objection that Livy does not mention his part in the debate is not serious, for Livy does not detail Cato's activity as legate of Fulvius in Ambracia (xxxviii. 1–11); therewith Fraccaro's other arguments against 186–184 fall to the ground (*sic*). But, apart from the fact that there was perhaps no particular reason for Livy to refer to Cato in Aetolia, Janzer has overlooked an important point: that Cato's criticism of Fulvius' lavish distribution of military honours (frg. 151) must have been made after the debate on the triumph because Livy expressly says that the gifts were made on the day of the triumph itself: 'multos eo die . . . in circo Flaminio tribunos praefectos equites centuriones, Romanos sociosque, donis militaribus donavit' (xxxix. 5. 17). Malcovati fails to mention this reference, which seems decisive against attributing a speech to 187.

De re Histriae militari. This speech, of which only one word ('punctatoriolas', 150 M.) survives, could have been delivered any time between 183 and 177. It is unlikely that the occasion was a senatorial debate on the wisdom of declaring war (as Meyer suggested), because the Senate probably did not debate the question. Most probably Cato spoke in connexion with Manlius' mismanagement of the campaign (178/7: see p. 187). An unassigned fragment (242 M.: 'te, C. Caecili, diem prodidisse militibus legionis III, cum proditionem non haberent') has been referred to this speech by M. E. Agnew (*AJP*, 1939, 214 ff.), who equates the unknown C. Caecilius with Livy's C. Aelius (L. xli. 1. 7; 4. 3) and with Ennius' Caelius (*apud* Macrob. *Sat.* vi. 3. 3).

Contra Cornelium ad populum. One fragment survives, 194 M.: 'ecquis incultior, religiosior, desertior, publicis negotis repulsior?' There is no evidence to identify the Cornelius, but at least Cato's second and fourth epithets (and perhaps the third: cf. Cic. *De orat.* ii. 260) would suit M. Cornelius Scipio Maluginensis (praetor, 176: see p. 192). If this Cornelius is the same as the one mentioned in the title of another speech by Cato (*Oratio de ea re quod sponsionem fecerat cum M. Cornelio*), his *praenomen* will be fixed as Marcus, but this is by no means certain. Since Maluginensis when praetor did not go to his province, no occasion is recorded when he might have been guilty of the extortion which Cato mentions in frg. 193 (see below); on the other hand, not many Cornelii with the *praenomen* Marcus are known in this period (M. Cornelius Cethegus, *cos.* 204, who died in 196, is perhaps too early; there are also M. Cethegus, *cos.* 160, and M. Mammula, an ambassador to Egypt in 173).

Oratio de ea re quod sponsionem fecerat cum M. Cornelio. See the previous speech and above, p. 221. Cato himself quoted extracts from this speech in a later speech *De sumptu suo* (p. 270). The sole fragment is 193 M.: 'numquam ego pecuniam neque meam neque sociorum per ambitionem dilargitus sum; numquam ego praefectos per sociorum vestrorum oppida imposivi, qui eorum bona coniuges liberos diriperent; numquam ego praedam neque quod de hostibus captum esset neque manubias inter pauculos amicos meos divisi, ut illis eriperem, qui cepissent; numquam ego evectionem datavi, quo amici mei per symbolos pecunias magnas caperent; numquam ego argentum pro vino congiario inter apparitores atque amicos meos disdidi, neque eos malo publico divites feci.'

De tribunis militum. For the occasion of the delivery of this speech in 172/1 see above, p. 197. The two fragments are: 154 M.: 'expedito pauperem plebeium atque proletarium', and 155 M.: 'loca ardua et cliva depressa'. It is hazardous to assume that in the first fragment Cato's social conscience was stirring and that he was pleading for greater electoral freedom for the poor, as Janzer (*Cato*, 62) suggests. The phrase might come from an idea which Cato was opposing, in an attempt to show the evil results of recent plebeian influence at the elections, or if it does represent Cato's own statement, he may have been suggesting that greater electoral freedom of the poor, who by ties of patronage would be more closely bound to the nobility, might result in strengthening the aristocracy at the expense of the newly emerging plebeian interests. Without the context further speculation is idle.

In legem Popilli. This speech might have some connexion with the scandals of 172–171 (see above, pp. 195 ff.), but in fact nothing is known about the occasion or law. The suggestion depends upon Mommsen's reading of Nonius (p. 124 L.), but other possible readings are 'legem populi' perhaps with reference to the *lex Porcia de provocatione*, or 'in legem Petilli' with reference to the trials of the Scipios (cf. Malcovati, *ORF*, p. 86). Frg. 225 M.: 'quod conpluriens usu venit omni tempore anteventum esse e re publica credimus.'

In P. Furium pro Hispanis. For the occasion in 171 see p. 201 above. Frg. 156 M.: 'utrubi bona, utrubi mala gratia capiatur, utrinde iram, utrinde factiones tibi pares.'

Suasio legis Voconiae. See pp. 205 f. Cato shows how a woman with property could flout her husband: 'principio vobis mulier magnam dotem adtulit; tum magnam pecuniam recipit, quam in viri potestatem non committit, eam pecuniam viro mutuam dat; postea ubi irata facta est, servum recepticium sectari atque flagitare virum iubet' (frg. 157 M.). Frg. 158 M.: 'agrum quem vir habet tollitur', may illustrate another result of a woman's independence. Cato's inquiry 'quid sit classicus, quid infra classem' (159 M.) may have envisaged the possibility of men trying to obviate the bill by pretending to belong to a lower class than the first. The lex Voconia was in fact thwarted by the invention of legal fictions. Cf. Cic. *In Verr.* i. 107; *De fin.* 2. 55.

De dote. The date is unknown (there is insufficient evidence to confirm the view of Meyer that it was delivered during Cato's censorship), but it may be mentioned here as it illustrates the arbitrary power which a husband could still exercise over his wife, if she was bound to him by the older forms of marriage. Frg. 218 M.: 'vir cum divortium fecit, mulieri iudex pro censore est; imperium, quod videtur, habet, si quid perverse taetreque factum est a muliere; multitatur, si vinum bibit; si cum alieno viro probri quid fecit, condemnatur.' 219 M.: 'in adulterio uxorem tuam si prehendisses, sine iudicio impune necares; illa te, si adulterares sive tu adulterarere, digito non auderet contingere, neque ius est.' The harshness of a more primitive age, which Cato was struggling to maintain, accorded ill with the feeling of the times.

De Macedonia liberanda. See p. 212 for frg. 161. The only other one is 160 M.: 'idque perpetuius atque firmius repsit.'

Pro Rhodiensibus. See p. 217. Since the fragments are accessible in Aulus Gellius, vi. 3, it is unnecessary to quote them *in extenso*, but a few sentences may be given. 162 M.: 'adversae res edomant et docent, quid opus siet facto; secundae res laetitia transvorsum trudere solent a recte consulendo atque intellegendo.' 163 M.: 'atque ego quidem arbitror, Rhodienses noluisse, nos ita depugnare, uti depugnatum est, neque regem Persen vinci. sed non Rhodienses modo id noluere, sed multos populos atque multas nationes idem noluisse arbitror atque haut scio an partim eorum fuerint, qui non nostrae contumeliae causa id noluerint evenire: sed enim id metuere, ne, si nemo esset homo, quem vereremur, quidquid luberet faceremus. ne sub solo imperio nostro in servitute nostra essent, libertatis suae causa in ea sententia fuisse arbitror.' 165 M.: 'qui acerrime advorsus eos dicit, ita dicit: hostes voluisse fieri. ecquis est tandem, qui vestrorum, quod ad sese attineat, aequum censeat poenas dare ob eam rem, quod arguatur male facere voluisse? nemo, opinor; nam ego, quod ad me attinet, nolim.'

Contra Ser. Galbam ad milites. See above, p. 218. Gellius, i. 23. 1: 'Historia de Papirio Praetextato dicta scriptaque est a M. Catone in oratione, qua usus est ad milites contra Galbam, cum multa quidem venustate atque luce atque munditia verborum. ea Catonis verba huic commentario indidissem, si libri copia fuisset id temporis, cum haec dictitavi.' Gellius then in his own words recounts the story how the boy Papirius gained the *cognomen* Praetextatus for his discretion. Cato's speech used to be assigned to 149, when in his old age he delivered a speech against this same Galba for his cruelty in Lusitania, but Cichorius (*Römische Studien*, 91–6), followed by Malcovati (*ORF*, pp. 66–9), has shown that it should be assigned to 167, since the pleasantness of the anecdote and the epithets applied by Gellius do not suit the occasion of this later speech which was delivered 'acerrime' (Livy, *Epit.* xlix) and 'summa contentione' (Cic. *Brut.* 80), while in 149 the troops would have been in Spain and not in Rome. Cichorius has further ingeniously suggested that as the *cognomen* Praetextatus is not found in the Papirian *gens* (Cicero in a letter to Papirius Paetus reviews the branches of the *gens* and does not give Praetextatus: *Ad fam.* ix. 21) and is found in the Sulpician *gens*, Gellius may have made a slip, since he was quoting the anecdote from memory, and have written Papirius in place of Sulpicius; he will then have been contrasting the wisdom of one of Sulpicius' young ancestors with the rashness of the military tribune.

De sumptu suo. This speech was attributed to the period of Cato's consulship until Fraccaro showed that it belonged to 164 (*Stud. Stor.* 1910, 378; cf. Malcovati, *ORF*, pp. 69–70). Gellius writes (xiii. 24. 1): 'M. Cato, consularis et censorius, . . . villas suas incultas et rudes, ne tectorio quidem praelitas fuisse dixit ad annum usque aetatis suae septuagesimum'; he then adds a few sentences of Cato's. It is extremely probable that these derive from the *De sumptu suo*; the reference to Cato's seventieth year, which was in 164 B.C., would then fix the date of the speech to that year. See above, pp. 221; 268.

A hint, which suggests a possible explanation of the charge, is found in Plutarch who records (*Cato*, 25) that the dinners that Cato gave in the country were more lavish. The comparison may be with those he gave in the town, or since Plutarch has just referred to Cato's composition of the *De Agri Cultura*, which was written in the later part of his life, he may mean that they were more lavish than in Cato's earlier days: hence a possible infringement of the lex Orchia.

Frg. 171 M.: 'vides in quo loco res publica siet, uti quod rei publicae bene fecissem, unde gratiam capiebam, nunc idem illud memorare non audeo, ne invidiae siet. ita inductum est male facere impoene, bene facere non impoene licere.' 173 M.: 'neque mihi aedificatio neque vasum neque vestimentum ullum est manupretiosum, neque pretiosus servus neque ancilla. si quid est quod utar, utor; si non est, egeo. suum cuique per me uti atque frui licet. vitio vertunt, quia multa egeo; at ego illis, quia nequeunt egere.' Cf. Plut. *Cato*, 4. 4.

Pro L. Caesetio. Nothing is known of the date and circumstances of its delivery, but it contains an austere sentiment similar to that expressed in the *De sumpto suo* (see above): 'audite, sultis, milites, si quis vestrum in bello superfuerit, si quis non invenerit pecuniam, egebit' (200 M.). The other fragment is 201 M.: 'quod ego me spero ostenturum.'

Pro se contra C. Cassium. See above, p. 233. Both the date of this speech and the identity of Cassius are doubtful. Fraccaro (*Stud. Stor.* 1911, 125 n. 1) suggests that it was delivered at the time when Cato was attacked for his handling of the censorial contracts (p. 162 f.); if this is so, the Cassius might be C. Cassius Longinus (*cos.* 171). Meyer and Malcovati, however, are perhaps more probably right in assigning it to 153. Livy (xxxix. 40. 11) and Plutarch (*Cato*, 15. 4), who wrongly place Cato's birth in 239 and make him 90 at his death, state that he was defendant in nearly fifty cases and in the last one was 86; this would fix the trial to 153 and Cassius would therefore be censor, acting during the last six months of his period of office or just afterwards. Frg. 174 M.: 'atque evenit ita, Quirites, uti in hac contumelia, quae mihi per huiusque petulantiam factum itur, rei quoque publicae medius fidius miserear, Quirites.'

Ne quis iterum consul fieret. See p. 234. Frg. 175 M.: 'dicere possum, quibus villae atque aedes aedificatae atque expolitae maximo opere citro atque ebore atque pavimentis Poenicis sient' (perhaps Cato is referring to consuls who used their provincial commands to enrich themselves and thus acquire luxurious houses). 176 M.: 'imperator laudem capit, exercitum meliorem industriiorem facit.' A dictum of Cato (Plut. *Cato*, 8. 5) may come from this speech: those who were eager to hold high office frequently were like men who did not know the road, but always sought to be attended by lictors, lest they lost their way. He censured the Romans for re-electing the same men: 'You will be thought not to deem your offices worth much, or else not to deem many men worthy of your offices.'

Contra Ser. Galbam pro direptis Lusitanis. See p. 235. Frg. 186 M.: 'multa me dehortata sunt huc prodire, anni, aetas, vox, vires, senectus; verum enimvero cum tantam rem peragier arbitrarer.' 187 M.: 'tamen dicunt deficere voluisse. ego me nunc volo ius pontificium optime scire; iamne ea causa pontifex capiar? si volo augurium optime tenere, ecquis me ob rem eam augurem capiat?'

De Ptolemaeo minore contra Thermum sive De Thermi quaestione. See p. 237. Frg. 76 M.: 'sed si omnia dolo fecit, omnia avaritiae atque pecuniae causa fecit, eiusmodi scelera nefaria, quae neque fando neque legendo audivimus, supplicium pro factis dare oportet.' 77 M.: 'quantoque suam vitam superiorem atque ampliorem atque antiquiorem animum inducent esse quam innoxiiorem.' 78 M.: 'per deos immortalis, nolite vos atque.' 79 M.: 'rege optimo atque beneficissimo.' 80 M.: 'tu otiosus ambulas, qui apud regem fuisti, donicum ille tibi interdixit rem capitalem.'

De rege Attalo et vectigalibus Asiae. Fraccaro has shown (*Stud. Stor.* 1910, 281 ff.) that this speech belongs to c. 151/0 (see p. 238). If the C. Licinius mentioned in the only fragment (180 M.: 'C. Licinio praetore remiges scribti cives Romani sub portisculum, sub flagrum conscribti veniere passim') is the praetor of 172 (the fragment corresponds with what L. xlii. 27, records about him) a *terminus post quem* is fixed, which can be brought down to 159 since Cato would hardly refer to Attalus as *rex* until the death of Eumenes; the *terminus ante quem* is Cato's death (149). The speech was probably delivered on the occasion of Prusias' appeal and the *vectigalia* are the sums due to Attalus; there can be no question of money paid to Rome at this period (cf. L. xxxvii. 55. 6). E. V. Hansen (*The Attalids of Pergamon*, 128) writes: 'Cato, still cherishing his antipathy against the Attalids, spoke in opposition to the king of Pergamon and the indemnity.' But Cato had shown his dislike of Eumenes, not Attalus (above, p. 238). The dispute was now between Attalus and Prusias; in view of the latter's earlier aggression and self-indulgent character ('he lived by day and night the barbarous life of a Sardanapallus': for Polybius' unflattering portrait see xxxvi. 15), Cato is likely to have supported Attalus' claim. E. V. Hansen may have been influenced by the word *dissuasio* ('Cato in dissuasione de rege Attalo et vectigalibus Asiae', Festus, 266 L.), but the *dissuasio* can well be a speech in which Cato *dissuasit* the appeal of Prusias (cf. Malcovati, *ORF*, p. 74 n. 5).

De Achaeis. See above, p. 239. In the only fragment (177 M.: 'cumque Hannibal terram Italiam laceraret atque vexaret', cf. Plut. *Cato*, 1. 6), Cato may have been referring to the neutrality of the Achaean League during the Hannibalic War.

De bello Carthaginiensi. See pp. 240 ff. and 288. Frg. 181 M.: 'pueri atque mulieres extrudebantur fami causa.' 182 M.: 'aures nobis calliscerunt ad iniurias.' 183 M.: 'homines defoderunt in terram dimidiatos ignemque circumposuerunt: ita interfecerunt.' Frg. 185, see p. 271.

(d) Orationes incerti temporis

In Lentulum apud censores. See p. 13. The speech cannot be dated, while the number of Cornelii Lentuli of this period makes any certain identification impossible. Presumably Lentulus had neglected his duty as a guardian or patron and was prosecuted by Cato for this breach of the *mos maiorum.* Frg. 190 M.: 'quod maiores sanctius habuere defendi pupillos quam clientem non fallere. adversus cognatos pro cliente testatur, testimonium adversus clientem nemo dicit. patrem primum, postea patronum proximum nomen habuere.'

In C. Pisonem. The only fragment (195 M.: 'video hac tempestate concurrisse omnes adversarios') might suggest the attack that was made on Cato after his censorship: see above, p. 164, and cf. p. 151.

NOTES, POLITICAL AND PERSONAL

I. *The Roman Electorate*

THE evidence for assessing the size of the electorate at the time of the Hannibalic War allows only a very general estimate (cf. p. 20). In 233 B.C. there were 270,713 adult male citizens, including non-voting *cives sine suffragio* (Livy, *Epit.* 20. Cf. the evidence of P. ii. 24. On the meaning of the census figures see T. Frank, *AJP*, 1930, 313). Perhaps one-third of this total lived in or around Rome (cf. Frank, *CAH*, viii. 345; *Econ. Surv.* i. 75). Of these 90,000 men the majority would possess the *ius suffragii*, but some would often be serving in the army abroad (e.g. some 22,000, i.e. 4 legions of 5,500 men each). The number of citizens from other parts of Italy attending the elections was probably very small in normal circumstances. Thus the potential maximum of voters actually in Rome at any election was well under 100,000. This number was not exceeded before 169 B.C., and was often much lower, e.g. in 204 B.C. there were 214,000 citizens of whom perhaps 70,000 lived near Rome, but 19 legions (i.e. 95,000 men) were in the field of whom, say, 32,000 came from Rome, and some citizens served with the fleet. This leaves only 38,000 voters in Rome itself. As war-time conditions would scarcely encourage many country voters to go to Rome, the potential electorate in Rome in 204 B.C. may have been between 40,000 and 50,000.

II. *Consuls and Commissioners, 221–218 B.C.*

The Consular Fasti, 221–219. The consular Fasti and Livy fail for the triennium 221–219. Two variations upon the list given on p. 39 have been suggested: (*a*) Since Livy (xxiii. 30. 15; xxix. 11. 3) says that M. Aemilius Lepidus (*cos.* 232) was consul twice, the suggestion has been made that he was *consul suffectus* in 221, 220, or 219 (cf. Klebs, *PW*, s.v. Aemilius n. 66, and A. Degrassi, *Inscr. Ital.* XIII. i, p. 117), but the awkwardness of fitting him in seems to create almost more difficulty than the supposition that Livy has simply made a mistake (cf. Münzer, *RA*, 168). (*b*) The Chronographer *anno 354* (see *Inscr. Ital.* XIII. i, p. 442) asserts, contrary to all other sources, that Laevinus and Scaevola were consuls in 220. Scaevola will have been Q. Mucius Scaevola, praetor of 215 (the holding of a consulship before a praetorship would not be unprecedented). Further, Livy (xxix. 11. 3; xxx. 23. 5) and the consular Fasti (*Inscr. Ital.* XIII. i, p. 46) record that M. Valerius Laevinus (*cos.* 210) was twice consul. Accepting this evidence, Degrassi (ibid. 119) believes that Valerius and Scaevola were the first consuls of 220, that they were declared *vitio facti* and abdicated, and were followed by Veturius and Lutatius as *consules suffecti*. If this view is right, it would seem that a hostile faction tried to break up the Aemilian-Scipionic predominance and failed.

The Colonial Commissioners of 219. Of the commissioners appointed to establish Latin colonies at Placentia and Cremona (see p. 42) Polybius (iii. 40. 9) names only Lutatius and 'two men of praetorian rank'. Livy (xxi. 25. 3–4) gives

Lutatius, Servilius, and Annius, but mentions alternatives to the last two which he found in other annals: either M'. Acilius and C. Herennius or P. Cornelius Asina and C. Papirius Maso. If Polybius' statement is accepted, the two last names may be rejected, because Asina and Maso were *consulares*. Servilius (*pr. c.* 220) may be accepted in view of his subsequent career (L. xxx. 19. 6). All these men seem to have belonged to the same group: for the Servilii see Schur, *Scipio*, 122, 129 f.; Acilii, Münzer, *RA*, 91 f.; Papirii, ibid. 110 ff. Little is known about the Annii, but a certain C. Annius was linked with an Aemilius in a dedicatory inscription of the time of the Hannibalic War: '⟨Aem⟩ilio M. f., C. An⟨nio C. f. $\frac{quaes}{prae}$⟩toris pro po⟨plod vic. par⟩ti Diove dede⟨re⟩': *CIL*, i², 20. On such administrative triumviral commissions, see E. T. Sage and A. J. Wegner, *CP*, 1936, 23 ff. Normally they appear to have comprised two senior and one junior member. No doubt they were a means by which young men could be tested in public life, and membership would be keenly contested among the nobility.

Did Fabius Maximus go to Carthage in 218? Among the five senatorial *legati* sent to Carthage in 218 (see p. 42) was a Fabius. Livy (xxi. 18. 1) gives Q. Fabius; Florus (i. 27. 7) and Silius Italicus (ii. 3, 369, 382) give simply Fabius; but Dio Cassius (frg. 54. 10) and Zon. (viii. 2. 2) give M. Fabius. Here Willems's suggestion that Μάρκος is a corruption of Μάξιμος is an unnecessary cutting of the knot. De Sanctis (iii. ii. 1) prefers Marcus, because a later annalist might well substitute the famous Q. Fabius Maximus Cunctator for the more obscure M. Fabius, although in 218 the latter was an outstanding personality (*cos.* 245, censor in 241, and the oldest living *censorius* in 218). Ed. Meyer (*Kl. Schr.* ii. 367), followed by E. Groag (*Hannibal*, 72 n. 5) doubts the historicity of the ambassadors' names, but this scepticism is not justified. As the leader was a Fabius, Fabius Pictor may well have had a hand in the preservation of the names. True, a threat of prosecution was hanging over Livius Salinator and Aemilius Paullus, but they may have been allowed to carry through this short mission first, just as Alcibiades was allowed to sail with the Sicilian expedition.

III. *The Dictatorships of Fabius*

That Fabius was dictator twice is attested by his *elogium* (*Inscr. Ital.* XIII. iii, n. 80), the Fasti Consulares (ibid. i, p. 44), Livy (xxii. 9. 7), and Valerius Maximus (i. 1. 5). For his appointment in 217 see L. xxii. 8, who later contradicts his own statement by saying (ibid. 31) that Fabius was only *pro dictatore*, a false conjecture due to late jurists and refuted by the *elogium*, &c. The Fasti Cap. curiously, and erroneously, state that he was appointed 'interregni caussa': see De Sanctis, III. ii. 45 n. 67. The date of Fabius' first dictatorship, which will have been *comitiorum habendorum caussa*, probably falls in the triennium 221–219, for which the Fasti are missing. According to Valerius Maximus, Fabius' *magister equitum* was C. Flaminius, a curious pair. Plutarch (*Marcell.* 5. 6), who also gives Flaminius, says that the dictator was Minucius, but Μινουκίου might be a textual corruption of Μαξίμου. Religious objections (the squeaking of a mouse, cf. p. 27 n. 2), however, forced the dictator to abdicate.

The details of Livy's account (xxii. 25–6) *de aequando imperio*, whereby in 217

Minucius was made co-dictator with Fabius (see p. 46), may be mainly fictitious, but there can be no doubt about the fact. Pareti's hypothesis (*Riv. Fil.* 1912, 559 ff.) that Minucius was made successor to, not co-ordinate with, Fabius may be rejected, since Polybius (iii. 103) is explicit and Livy or his source may have been confused by a juristically-minded annalist. Cf. De Sanctis, III. ii. 53 n. 84 and p. 122.

IV. *The Election of Aemilius Paullus*

M. L. Patterson (*TAPA*, 1942, 323–4) emphasizes that the election of L. Aemilius Paullus as consul for 216 was mainly due to the realization by the nobles that none of their existing candidates was a sufficiently strong counterweight to Varro, and so they forced Paullus to stand (cf. L. xxii. 35. 3). Doubtless the need for experienced men was realized (as is shown also by the election of so strong a college of praetors), but this in itself does not explain the choice of Paullus (see above, p. 51). He had been successful enough in the Illyrian War, but other men had equal or greater claims, e.g. T. Manlius Torquatus, already twice consul (235, 224) and censor (231), with victories over Sardinians and Boii to his credit and willing to serve his country even in a subordinate capacity (he won a victory in Sardinia in 215 as praetor); L. Postumius Albinus, twice consul (234, 229) and elected praetor for 216; Q. Fulvius Flaccus, twice consul (237, 224) and censor (231); Sp. Carvilius Maximus (*cos.* 234, 228); M. Claudius Marcellus (*cos.* I, 222); P. Furius Philus (*cos.* 227); finally even Fabius himself, twice consul and censor. In fact of the 35 consuls of the previous twenty years (237–218; five men held office twice) at least 28 are known to have been living in 217 and more may have been; nor need some of the men who held the office before 237 be considered too old for active service since Q. Fulvius Flaccus, the consul of 237, campaigned with vigour in his third consulship in 212 and did not die until about 205. Thus there was no shortage of experienced men. Why, then, was it considered necessary, as M. L. Patterson suggests, to wait until Aemilius Paullus could be persuaded to stand? The cause of the delay in the elections was more complex, and the election of Paullus, as opposed to other possible outstanding adherents of the Fabian or Claudian groups, was a victory for the Aemilian group.

V. *The Position of Postumius*

The precise status of Postumius is uncertain (see p. 57). There is no doubt that he was elected consul. This is categorically stated in the Fasti Capitolini: 'L. Postumius A. f. A. n. Albinus III', with the note that 'in praetura in Gall. occis. est quod antequam ciretur . . .'. Polybius (iii. 118. 6) says that he was killed a few days after Cannae, i.e. in August 216. Livy (xxiii. 24) refers his death to the end of the winter of 216/15 after his election to the consulship and shortly before he and Sempronius were due to enter office. To square these accounts De Sanctis (III. ii. 327–9) has suggested that Postumius was not *consul designatus* for 215, but *consul suffectus* of 216 elected in place of Aemilius Paullus who fell at Cannae; he did not, however, actually enter office, because the dictator Iunius did not give up his office until it was too late for Postumius to function. In this situation Livy or his source may well have confused *consul suffectus* and *designatus*: confusion is more probable than a deliberate falsification for which there is no obvious purpose.

The objection to De Sanctis's view is that it contradicts Livy who gives a reasonable and consistent account, that it is unlikely that a *consul suffectus* would be appointed when there was a dictator already in office, and that if Postumius was *consul suffectus* he would surely have been referred to as consul and not 'in praetura' in the Fasti. If De Sanctis is right, the consuls elected for 215 must have been Sempronius and Marcellus, the two men who had had some slight success in the field. But in any case Marcellus resigned and Fabius took his place.

vi. *The Licinii*

The Licinii (see Münzer, *RA*, 183 ff., and above, p. 67), who had been pro-minent at the time of the Licinian-Sextian Rogations, sank into comparative obscurity until they re-emerged after the First Punic War, doubtless with the help of the Cornelii. C. Licinius Varus reached the consulship in 236 together with P. Cornelius Lentulus Caudinus; the latter's more important elder brother, Lucius (later *princeps senatus* and Pontifex Maximus, who died in 213), was Licinius' predecessor in 237. Licinius Varus doubtless owed his advancement to these two Lentuli; his son, P. Licinius Varus, who did not advance beyond the praetorship (208), is mentioned in an anecdote in connexion with Scipio Africanus (Cic. *De orat.* ii. 250). P. Licinius Crassus derived from a collateral branch of the family, being the eldest son of P. Licinius Crassus who was a brother of C. Licinius Varus (*cos.* 236).

vii. *The Legal Position of C. Servilius Geminus in 209*

Trouble arose about the legality of the position of the aedile C. Servilius Geminus (see p. 62 n. 2) when news came that his father, the land-commissioner of 218 who was believed to have been killed by the Boii (p. 42 n. 5), was in fact alive and a prisoner. Later, during his consulship in 203, Geminus rescued his father and brought him back to Rome where the People passed a measure relieving the consul from penalties for having acted illegally as tribune and plebeian aedile while his father who had held curule office was, unknown to him, still alive.[1] This statement by Livy has given rise to considerable speculation. Mommsen suggested that Livy formulated the legal difficulty inaccurately and that it arose not from the fact that the father had held curule office but because he was a patrician and had not at the right time authorized his son's adoption of plebeian status: thinking that his father was dead and desiring the tribunate the son had carried through a *transitio ad plebem*, only to find in 209 that his father was alive. But Münzer has shown that the *transitio* probably occurred before 218 and that it was carried through by the father before his captivity rather than by the son; he therefore suggests that the son's right to office was questioned because the father had lost his citizen status as a prisoner of war.[2]

It is, however, possible to believe that Livy's statement is correct and that a

---

[1] L. xxx. 19. 9: 'latum ad populum est, ne C. Servilio fraudi esset, quod patre, qui sella curuli sedisset, vivo, cum id ignoraret, tribunus plebis atque aedilis plebis fuisset, contra quam sanctum legibus erat.'

[2] Mommsen, *Staatsr.* i. 487 n. 2 (*Dr. publ.* ii. 135 n. 2). Münzer, *RA*, 137 ff.; *PW*, s.v. Servilius n. 59. A. Aymard (*Rev. Ét. Anc.* 1943, 204 ff.), who has demolished these views, points out *inter alia* that a law of indemnity was unnecessary as soon as the father returned to Rome since he then regained all his rights by virtue of *postliminium*.

law existed which closed the two plebeian offices of tribune and plebeian aedile to sons of curule magistrates while their fathers were still living. Such a law may have been passed during the years when Flaminius had influence (232–218) and would have been an anti-senatorial measure in line with his *lex agraria* and the lex Claudia, designed to enable more new men to gain plebeian office and to hinder undue co-operation between the nobility and the tribunate.[1] The fact that Servilius had unwittingly broken this law was revealed to him in 209 and may explain the slowness of his subsequent career. Perhaps foreseeing the possibility of prosecution for illegal tenure of plebeian offices (he had been tribune probably in 212 and plebeian aedile in 209) he proceeded slowly as a proof of his good faith in an attempt to gain popular favour;[2] he held the curule aedileship and was *magister equitum* in 208, but did not step straight into the consulship like so many *magistri equitum*; he was praetor in 206 and consul finally in 203.

VIII. *The Dictatorship of Manlius Torquatus*

In the new fragment of the Fasti Capitolini (*Bull. Com. Arch.*, 1926, 267 ff.; *Inscr. Ital.* XIII. i, p. 46) Manlius (see above, p. 71) is named *dictator rei gerundae*: 'T. Quinctius L. f. L. n. Crispin⟨us⟩ ex vol⟨nere mortuus est⟩. T. Manlius T. f. T. n. Torquatus dict⟨ator⟩ reig⟨erundae⟩ et c⟨omitiorum habendorum caussa⟩.' The phrase 'reigerundae et', to which Livy makes no reference, was probably added later together with the phrase 'ex volnere', to indicate that on the death of Crispinus supreme power was transmitted from him to Manlius who became in fact, if not in law, *dictator reigerundae caussa*. The death of a consul was recorded in the Fasti only when the name of the *suffectus* is added. As the consuls had died near the end of the year, *suffecti* were not elected, but the power passed for a short period to the dictator who was legally nominated by the dying Crispinus. A lesser reason for the dictator's appointment was 'ludorum faciendorum causa' (see L. xxvii. 33. 8); this is not mentioned in the Fasti, any more than is the fact that C. Servilius, who was *dictator comitiorum caussa* in 202, celebrated the Ludi Ceriales. Cichorius (*Röm. Stud.* 55 f.) refers a line of Naevius to Manlius: 'dictator ubi currum insidet, pervehitur usque ad oppidum' (*oppidum* means the barrier of a circus, i.e. *carceres*: Varro, *LL*, v. 153).

IX. *The Servilii and Scipio*

Opposition to Scipio in 203 (see p. 79). R. M. Haywood (*Scipio*, 56–7) attempts to deny the Servilian opposition to Scipio: 'Caepio was not trying to oust Scipio from his command in Africa by an indirect method. It was only natural for him to feel that his province was not Bruttium but wherever Hannibal was, and that his duty was to pursue the enemy whom the Senate had sent him to oppose.' This is surely special pleading. It is not clear that a magistrate had any legal right to vacate his province without further instru ctionsfrom the Senate, and there is no indication that Caepio would have subordinated himself to Scipio in Africa; his arrival would therefore have been regarded as a hindrance rather than as a

---

[1] See De Sanctis, IV. i. 538. This view has been developed by Aymard (loc. cit.) who suggests that the law was repealed early in the second century (*c.* 179 or later), when nobles wanted their sons to hold plebeian offices during their own lifetimes in order that they might reach higher office quickly (since after 196 plebeian aediles rose quicker than curule aediles) and to keep out obscurer families. [2] Cf. ibid. 217.

help. Whatever reliance can be put on the details of the intrigues of the Servilii, it would strain the evidence to the breaking-point to suggest that they and others were agitating to cross to Africa in 203 and 202 in order to *help* Scipio. If they were not, then their action must have been politically hostile to him. Similarly in connexion with the senatorial debate on the peace-embassy in 203, when Metellus urged the acceptance of Scipio's terms and Livius Salinator urged delay until one of the Servilii returned, it is difficult to believe with Haywood that 'Salinator's views on this occasion do not show that his support of Scipio was weakening'.

Opposition in 202 (see pp. 79 f.). Again Haywood (op. cit. 57 f.) dismisses any idea of hostility between the consuls of 202 and Scipio: 'prolonged commands were not the Roman system . . . the Senate and consuls probably felt that it was a normal change for one of them to succeed Scipio now that Hannibal had moved to Africa.' A. Aymard (*Rev. Ét. Anc.* 1944, esp. 239 n. 7 and 240 n. 1) supports this rejection of the idea that the Servilii Gemini were hostile to Scipio. He refers to a remark of Mommsen (*Staatsr.* i². 25 n. 3) that if the consul (Ti. Claudius) received a province *pari imperio* with the proconsul (Scipio) the measure was favourable to the latter, whose authority was normally inferior to that of the consul: a remark which Mommsen omitted from the third edition of his *Staatsrecht.* Aymard believes that since an army command was the normal function of a consul (especially for one with a good military record like C. Servilius), any desire to command the only existing army of any importance was a legitimate ambition, unaffected by jealousy. This view is difficult to accept. Circumstances were not normal. Scipio, who had a far greater military record than M. Servilius, let alone Cn. Servilius Caepio (whose battle with Hannibal in 203 is an invention of Valerius Antias: L. xxx. 19. 11) or Ti. Claudius Nero, might reasonably count on being allowed to strike the final blow, especially as Hannibal was at large in north Africa. Scipio's prolonged command, his long series of victories in Spain and Africa, the tactical skill which he had infused into the Roman army, the devotion of his troops, the success of his strategy—all these factors gave him a claim which no other commander could equal. Thus it is difficult to believe that legitimate ambition rather than personal or political jealousy lay behind the attempts to supersede him or hamper him with a colleague. It would seem more reasonable to reject the whole annalistic tradition about these attempts than to try to explain away any implied political or personal hostility; but that desperate solution is unnecessary. Details may be suspect, but behind the tradition there appears to lie the fact of political intrigue against Scipio. J. H. Thiel (*Roman Sea-Power,* 176 ff.) believes that the Senate decided to reinforce the weak fleet in Africa, in case Scipio should be defeated by land: then the need for evacuation or to keep the war within Africa would require stronger Roman command of African waters. He believes that Claudius failed to win the African land command for himself, but was granted the naval command as a consolation prize: regarding this as a slight to his consular dignity, Claudius deliberately delayed sailing to Africa.

x. *The Dictatorship of Servilius*

One difficulty in Livy's account of the puzzling episode of Servilius' dictatorship (see above, pp. 80 f.) is the fact that the plebeian aediles were forced to abdicate eight months after their entry into office (i.e. after they had held the Plebeian Games in Nov. 202). To meet this and other difficulties A. Aymard (*Rev. Ét. Anc.* 1944, esp. 252 ff.) has put forward an ingenious theory that Livy has interchanged the two Games: the aediles celebrated the Cerialia in April *202* and were later forced to abdicate; when November came, the celebration of the Plebeian Games and the Epulum Iovis (i.e. not the Cerialia) was entrusted to Servilius by a SC. The delay in holding the elections is to be explained not with Schur as due to political intrigue on the part of Scipio's friends; Münzer is more reasonable in suggesting that Servilius wanted to maintain his influence longer. But both Schur's and Münzer's views are based upon an untenable interpretation of Livy: since Servilius did not celebrate the Cerialia of 201, no one knows how long he remained dictator after 15 March 201 nor when the new magistrates were finally elected; if he had become dictator in Nov. 202, he could still legally be dictator in April 201 (*contra* Mommsen). Why was the dictatorship of Servilius the last one in the old sense in Roman history? Not because of any supposed illegal prolongation, but rather through aristocratic disgust at the manner in which the Servilii had exercised power during these two years; also the end of war-conditions in Italy rendered *dictatores com. hab.* less necessary. Thus Servilius' conduct was the occasion rather than the real cause of the end of an institution of which the authentic form had ended in 216 with the last *dictator reigerundae caussa.*

It is impossible briefly to do justice to Aymard's elaborate argument, but some may not find it more difficult to believe that magistrates were forced to abdicate eight months after entering office (admittedly an unprecedented period) than that at this early period elections could be so postponed; if conditions permitted, and if the Servilii had the political power to achieve, such serious interference with the constitution, then exceptionally bold wire-pulling by the augural college might well go unchallenged. If Livy's statement that the consular elections were postponed until after 15 March 201 is to be accepted (as it is by Aymard, who, however, asserts the legality of Servilius' position), then it would not appear difficult to accept his implication about the abdication of the plebeian aediles.

XI. *A Senatorial Debate on Carthage in 201*

Appian (*Lib.* 57–65) records a senatorial debate in 201 on the fate of Carthage, in which a friend of Scipio's urged moderation and rejected alternative solutions such as destroying it, handing it over to Masinissa, turning it into a province, or colonizing it (see p. 81). The case for destruction and vengeance was put by a relative of the consul Cn. Cornelius Lentulus, named Publius (he probably was not his cousin P. Cornelius Lentulus Caudinus, the praetor of 203, who may not have returned from Sardinia (L. xxx. 41. 2), but was perhaps P. Cornelius Lentulus, praetor in 214). The fact that Diodorus (xxvii. 13–17 and 18) also gives extracts from these speeches shows that they were not invented by Appian, but go back to the common source of Appian and Diodorus. This in all probability was Polybius (who in fact records a discussion in the Carthaginian Senate). The omission of the debate by Livy is to be explained, as suggested by A. H. McDonald, by the probability that Livy was not using Polybius here: in fact he uses him only for the East, and where other parts appear Polybian they probably go back to the senatorial historians who were also used by Polybius. But in view of the loss of the relevant part of Polybius and the possibility that the substance of the speeches as given by Appian may have been affected by arguments used in the debates which preceded the Third Punic War (cf. pp. 240 ff.), it is safer not to build too much upon their detailed arguments. No doubt some senators did argue for the application of harsher terms than those demanded by Scipio, and it is possible that Cato shared their desire, but there is no evidence to prove Cato's support for such a step.

XII. *Senior Senators in 201 B.C.*

The senior senators who were certainly or probably alive in 201 were the following:

Dictatorius patricius	P. Sulpicius Galba (*cos.* I, 211; dict. 203)
Dictatorii plebeii	Q. Caecilius Metellus (*cos.* 206; dict. 205)
	C. Servilius Geminus (*cos.* 203; dict. 202)
Censorii patricii	P. Licinius Crassus (*cos.* 210; cens. 205)
	M. Cornelius Cethegus (*cos.* 204; cens. 209)
	C. Claudius Nero (*cos.* 207; cens. 204)
Censorius plebeius	P. Sempronius Tuditanus (*cos.* 204; cens. 209)
Consulares patricii	M. Valerius Laevinus (*cos.* 210)
	L. Veturius Philo (*cos.* 206)
	P. Cornelius Scipio Africanus (*cos.* 205)
	Cn. Servilius Caepio (*cos.* 203)
	Ti. Claudius Nero (*cos.* 202)
	Cn. Cornelius Lentulus (*cos.* 201)
Consulares plebeii	C. Terentius Varro (*cos.* 216)
	M. Servilius Geminus (*cos.* 202)
	P. Aelius Paetus (*cos.* 201)

The following list of *praetorii*, with the gentile names in alphabetical order, contains the names of many men who may in fact not have survived until 201. Those definitely living in 201 are marked with an asterisk.

Praetorii patricii	*L. Aemilius Papus (praetor 205)
	L. Cornelius Lentulus (211)
	P. Cornelius Lentulus (214)
	*P. Cornelius Lentulus Caudinus (203)
	P. Cornelius Merenda (stood for *cos.* 217)
	P. Cornelius Sulla (212)
	*M. Fabius Buteo (201)
	Sex. Iulius Caesar (208)
	*L. Manlius Acidinus (210)
	*P. Quinctilius Varus (203)
	*C. Sulpicius Galba (? Galus. ?= pontifex who died in 199)
	*M. Valerius Falto (201)

Praetorii plebeii   *P. Aelius Tubero (201)
     M. Atilius (Regulus: Serranus?) (213)
     C. Atilius Serranus (218)
     *C. Aurelius Cotta (202)
     C. Aurunculeius (209)
     M. Caecilius Metellus (206)
     C. Calpurnius Piso (211)
     L. Cincius Alimentus (210)
     Q. Claudius (208)
     Ti. Claudius Asellus (206)
     A. Cornelius Mammula (217)
     Cn. Fulvius Flaccus (212; in exile?)
     *A. Hostilius Cato (207)
     *L. Hostilius Cato (207)
     C. Hostilius Tubulus (209)
     *M. Iunius Pennus (201)
     M. Iunius Silanus (212)
     *C. Laetorius (210)
     P. Licinius Varus (208)
     *C. Livius Salinator (202)
     *Sp. Lucretius (205)
     *C. Mamilius Atellus (207)
     Q. Mamilius Turrinus (206)
     M. Marcius Ralla (204)
     *Cn. Octavius (205)
     M. Pomponius Matho (204)
     L. Porcius Licinus (207)
     L. Scribonius Libo (204)
     M. Sextius Sabinus (202)
     Cn. Tremellius Flaccus (202)
     *P. Villius Tappulus (203)

Aedilicii curules patricii   Ser. Sulpicius Galba (209)
     L. Cornelius Lentulus Caudinus (209; but probably
       to be identified with the praetor of 203)
     Ser. Cornelius Lentulus (207)
     L. Quinctius Flamininus (201)
     L. Valerius Flaccus (201)

Aedilicii curules plebeii   L. Licinius Lucullus (202)
     Q. Fulvius Gillo (202)

Aedilicii plebis   M. Fundanius Fundulus (213)
     Q. Catius (210)
     Ti. Claudius Asellus (205)
     L. Laetorius (202)
     L. Apustius Fullo (201)
     Q. Minucius Rufus (201)

XIII. *The Speech of Ti. Gracchus against Scipio*

Livy (xxxviii. 56) himself had some doubt about the authenticity of Gracchus' speech (see p. 84). The main arguments against it are that (1) it was unknown to Cicero (*Brutus*, 79), and (2) Scipio's alleged violence to the tribunes and his refusal of a perpetual consulship and dictatorship are more typical of the end of the Republic than of the mid-Republic. Mommsen (*Röm. Forsch.* ii. 502) maintained that it was a forgery derived from a pamphlet of the Caesarean period, circulated in 49 to counteract the threat of a dictorship. Ed. Meyer (*Caes. Monarchie*, 531) dated it to *c.* 44 on the ground that its purpose was to induce Caesar to resign his dictatorship. R. M. Haywood (*Scipio*, 15 ff.), however, defends its authenticity on the ground that (1) Cicero's ignorance of it could be explained by its discovery, after the time of his writing, by Varro when collecting for Caesar's new library, and (2) that we have no right to decide on general grounds that Scipio would not have laid hands on a tribune, while it is not impossible that in the wave of relief and gratitude which followed the end of the Hannibalic War exceptional honours might have been proposed for Rome's deliverer. De Sanctis (*Riv. Fil.* 1936, 189 ff.) rejects these arguments and suggests that the speech is a falsification which would suit the time of Sulla even better than that of Caesar: Sulla was a Cornelius, had killed a tribune in office (Sulpicius), and had renounced his dictatorship. It was introduced as a speech by a Sullan annalist in accordance with the ordinary practice of Roman historians and was later circulated for party purposes; this would explain why it was not known to Cicero. Whether De Sanctis's view is to be preferred to Mommsen's, the authenticity of the speech must remain extremely doubtful. One argument in favour of its basic reliability, which its champions appear to have neglected, would be Polybius' statement that 'Scipio again and again rejected . . . the power of a king' (x. 40. 9; cf. p. 85 f.). But the whole impression which the speech makes is that of later conditions. Thus in the absence of any other specific reference it is safer to reject the idea that any definite offer of a dictatorship was made to Scipio.

XIV. *Some Praetors and Praetorii* (*200–199, 185–181*)

The Sergii. The *cognomen* of C. Sergius, praetor in 200 (see above, p. 93) was Plancus or Plautus (cf. *PW*, s.v. Sergius, n. 36). What little evidence there is points to the Sergii being friendly to the Scipios. L. Sergius (*PW.* n. 11) was sent by Scipio in 202 to Carthage about the armistice (P. xvi. 1). M. Sergius (*PW*, n. 19) was a military tribune who was sent by Scipio to Locri (L. xxix. 6; 9; 18; 19). Silius Italicus (xv. 448) mentions or invents a (Sergius) Catilina in Scipio's army in Spain. Little is known of M. Sergius Silus (*PW*, n. 40) the praetor urbanus of 197, except that though in 218 he lost his right hand, which was replaced by an iron one, he fought four times against the Carthaginians, and is depicted on a later coin (see Frontispiece, No. 15) as a horseman holding in his left hand a sword and the head of a foe. Another M. Sergius Silus (*PW*, 41), a legate of Aemilius Paullus at Pydna, was probably his son (L. xliv. 40).

Praetorian candidates for the consulship of 199 (cf. p. 96). A glance at the praetorian Fasti shows that the number of patrician *praetorii*, who could have stood hopefully as consular candidates for 199, was small. If the praetors who had held office before 210 are omitted on the ground that they would have little chance of success after so long an interval, and if those who reached the consulship before 199 are also eliminated, the number of patrician ex-praetors until 201 is eight. Little is known about the subsequent careers of six of these (P. Manlius Vulso, praetor 210; Sex. Iulius Caesar, 208; L. Aemilius Papus, 205; P. Quinctilius Varus, 203; M. Valerius Falto, 201; and M. Fabius Buteo, 201); these therefore may be presumed not to have been particularly able. The other two, L. Manlius Acidinus (*pr.* 210 and later the colleague of L. Lentulus in Spain) and P. Cornelius Lentulus Caudinus (*pr.* in 203 and cousin of Gnaeus and Publius Cornelius Lentulus), were probably not *personae gratae* to the Claudian-Servilian coalition: Manlius was a member of an old pro-Fabian *gens* and in any case he was still in Spain, while P. Lentulus, who had helped Scipio in the African campaign (203–202), may not have followed his cousins in their desertion of Africanus. Thus there were few serious rivals to L. Cornelius Lentulus, who had several years of efficient service in Spain to his credit. This relatively small number of outstanding patrician *praetorii* should be borne in mind when the subsequent consular elections are considered.

Later Careers of the Praetors of 185–181. The *collegia*, which are discussed above on p. 185, were as follows:

185 B.C. Two patricians reached the consulship, P. Cornelius Cethegus in 181 and A. Postumius Albinus (with his cousin conducting the elections) in 180. One patrician, L. Postumius Tempsanus, and two plebeians, C. Afranius and C. Atilius Serranus, got no farther, nor perhaps did M. Claudius (the consul of 183 could be this man or the praetor of 188).

184 B.C. None became consul. C. Decimius and P. Sempronius Longus died respectively in 184 and 183. C. Sempronius Blaesus survived until 170 and A. Terentius Varro until 167, but neither they nor their colleagues Naevius Matho and P. Cornelius Cethegus (the only patrician) succeeded.

183 B.C. Only Sp. Postumius Albinus became consul, and that not until 174. Cn. Sicinius obtained a second praetorship in 172. C. Valerius Flaccus as Flamen Dialis could not easily be consul. P. Cornelius Sisenna, L. Iulius, and L. Pupius were never consuls.

182 B.C. Only Q. Fulvius Flaccus Q. f. became consul, and that after only two years. P. Manlius had died by 180, but M. Valerius Laevinus was alive until after 171. The plebeian praetors, L. Caecilius Denter, M. Ogulnius Gallus, and C. Terentius Istra, are not heard of again.

181 B.C. Only Q. Petillius Spurinus became consul, in 176. The three patrician praetors, Q. Fabius Maximus, Q. Fabius Buteo, and Ti. Claudius Nero, were never consuls.

The praetors of 178 B.C. were not outstanding; none of them ever reached the consulship, and only Ti. Claudius Nero came from a distinguished family. Some of the others (T. Fonteius Capito, M. Aebutius Carrus, C. Cluvius Saxula, M. Titinius Curvus, and M. Titinius) may have been Fulvian nominees. Livy records Ti. Nero, Titinius Curvus, and Fonteius (xl. 59. 5), and T. Aebutius Carrus (xli. 6. 5). As there is no good reason to reject the fact that Cluvius was praetor II in 173, he must have been praetor I before 175; as the lists for 177 and 176 are complete, he should be assigned to 178. Münzer has shown (*RA*, 218; *contra* E. Maxis, *Die Praetoren Roms*, 51) that two Titinii should be distinguished: M. Titinius, praetor urbanus (L. xli. 5. 7), and M. Titinius Curvus, praetor in Hispania Citerior (xli. 9. 3; 15. 11; 26. 1; xliii. 2. 6; cf. *CIL*, i, pp. 48 and 341).

xv. *The Flight of Hannibal*

Nepos (*Han.* 7) and Appian (*Syr.* 4) place Hannibal's flight from Carthage in 196 (i.e. he was sufete in 197), but Livy (xxxiii. 46; cf. Justin, xxxi. 3. 5) puts it in 195. To the arguments advanced in favour of Livy's date (e.g. by Holleaux, *Hermes*, 1908, p. 296; 1913, p. 87; Ed. Meyer, *Meister d. Politik*, i. 139; Gsell, *Hist. anc. de l'Afrique du Nord*, ii. 275; Groag *Hannibal*, 114 n. 4) may be added a consideration arising from the composition of the Roman embassy (cf. p. 114). If M. Claudius Marcellus is the consul of 196, he is unlikely to have left Italy during his year of office as he was fighting in north Italy or before his triumph on 4 March 195. De Sanctis argues (IV. i. 115 n. 3) that there are two or three M. Claudii Marcelli who might suit, but this is doubtful. A certain M. Claudius Marcellus (*PW*, n. 221) who had been plebeian aedile in 216 (L. xxiii. 30. 17) is not heard of again. There are two others whom it is difficult to distinguish, one praetor in 188, the other in 185, one of them being consul in 183. But these men were too young in 195 for so important a mission. If it be objected that Terentius Culleo was not praetor until 187, it must be remembered that he had been a prisoner in Carthage and was probably included in the embassy because of his local knowledge and to represent the interests of Scipio to whom he was closely attached. Further, if the aedile of 216 survived the Hannibalic War, he was apparently of little weight as he attained no other office. The commission more probably consisted of two men of consular rank, Servilius and Marcellus, while Terentius was added for the reasons given above. If Marcellus, then, was the consul of 196, Hannibal's flight must be dated 195.

XVI. *Scipio Africanus on L. Scipio's Staff*

A slightly different version about the position of Scipio Africanus from that given by Cic. *Phil.* xi. 7 (cf. above, p. 128) is found in Cic. *Pro Mur.* 32: 'neque vero cum P. Africano senatus egisset, ut legatus fratri proficisceretur . . . nisi illud grave bellum et vehemens putaretur.' There is little to commend the view of B. Niese (*Gesch. d. gr. u. maked. Staaten*, ii. 721, and *Grundriss*[4], 133 n. 1) that Africanus was not legate to his brother, but was granted proconsular power. It rests upon two texts: (*a*) P. xxi. 10. 11, in which Aemilius Regillus told Antiochus that peace could not be made πρὸ τοῦ τὸν ἀνθύπατον ἐλθεῖν. But Livy (xxxvii. 19. 6) translates this passage as 'ante consulis adventum de pace agi non posse', while Polybius himself earlier in the same chapter (§ 7) refers to ὕπατον, and in ch. 8. 1 (παρὰ τοῦ Λευκίου τοῦ τὴν ὕπατον ἀρχὴν ἔχοντος καὶ παρὰ Ποπλίου Σκιπίωνος) he hardly could have avoided reference to a proconsulship if it had been granted. It is better to follow Reiske's correction of ὕπατον for ἀνθύπατον in § 11 and refer it to L. Scipio. (*b*) Memnon of Heraclea *apud* Photium (*FHG*, iii. 539) quotes a letter of Σκιπίων στρατηγὸς ἀνθύπατος confirming his goodwill to Heraclea Pontica. This is referred by Photius, followed by Niese, to Africanus, but it would more naturally allude to L. Scipio, since the next sentence runs τὰ αὐτὰ δὲ Λευκίῳ Πόπλιος Κορνήλιος Σκιπίων ὁ ἀδελφὸς καὶ στρατηγὸς τοῦ ναυτικοῦ τοῖς Ἡρακλεώταις διαπρεσβευσαμένοις ἀνέγραψε. In any case the title στρατηγὸς ἀνθὕπατος (proconsul) causes difficulty because the term ἀνθύπατος began to be used only from the middle of the second century in literary sources and inscriptions, and a reference in an inscription of this time might be expected to allude to a proconsul as στρατηγὸς ὕπατος (Flamininus is so called, though a proconsul, in Dittenberger, *Syll.* i, n. 276. See in general M. Holleaux, Στρατηγὸς ὕπατος (1918).) It is better to assume that ἀνθύπατος is simply a textual error for ὕπατος and that the reference is to Lucius. If the letter quoted by Memnon is genuine (and this is uncertain), the title might of course have been altered to accord with later usage, but only on the assumption that the reviser knew that Scipio was proconsul, and this is unlikely. In view of the fact that in the Scipios' letters to Colophon and Heraclea-by-Latmus (cf. above, pp. 131 f.) Africanus is given no title, it would be unsafe to allow Memnon's doubtful evidence to outweigh the tradition which Cicero and Livy knew, nor is it probable that a grant of proconsular *imperium* would have been recorded nowhere else in extant literature. See further Fraccaro, *Processi*, 358 n. 4. Memnon's suggestion that the brothers divided their spheres of influence and that Africanus was in command at sea should be rejected. (See also F. Jacoby, *FGH*, iii B (1950), p. 350.)

XVII. *The Trial of Glabrio and the Election of Censors (189)*

Livy implies that the trial of Acilius Glabrio (see p. 137) was held in January 189 (between the *deductio* of Bononia in December 190 and the triumph of Regillus which he seems to place on 1 February 189) and that the censorial elections followed immediately afterwards. But the elections were almost certainly later, as Mommsen pointed out (*Staatsr.* ii³. 352; for the cause of Livy's error see rather Fraccaro, *Processi*, 369 n. 3). Candidates usually handed in their names some months before the actual elections; at the time of the trial the names had already been given in, as Cato spoke *in toga candida* (hence the scandal). But it is not in fact necessary to fix the trial before 1 February 189, since Regillus' triumph was probably misplaced by Livy and took place in February 188, i.e. mid-November 189 by the Julian calendar (see De Sanctis, IV. 395, and abóve, p. 139 n. 1). The trial therefore may be placed nearer the elections. Cato's movements do not contribute any conclusive evidence. He was in Greece for a considerable part of the year (frg. 71 M.), though in Rome for both trial and elections. If it is unlikely that he left Greece twice, either the trial was early in 189 before he left Rome (in which case he would seek leave to return for the elections) or the trial and elections took place within a fairly short period later in the year, in which case also Cato need have left Greece only once. Alternatively, if he was not sent to Greece until after his failure at the elections his *legatio* has no bearing on the chronological problem.

XVIII. *Changes in the Priesthoods in 174 B.C.* (cf. p. 193)

The pontiffs Servilius Caepio (*cos.* 203, pontiff since 213 and father of the praetor of 174) and M. Sempronius Tuditanus (*cos.* 185) died, the former being replaced by C. Sulpicius Galba (*pr.* 171); the name of Tuditanus' successor is not recorded. The augur P. Aelius Paetus (censor 199) was replaced by his son Q. Aelius Paetus (*cos.* 167), and Ti. Sempronius Gracchus (probably a son of the consul of 215; he is not to be confused with the consul of 177 and father of the Gracchi) by T. Veturius Gracchus Sempronianus, who was probably a son of a Sempronius Gracchus adopted by one of the patrician Veturii Philones (on the difficulties of the identification see Mommsen, *Röm. Forsch.* i. 120, and Münzer, *RA*, 130–1). C. Sempronius Longus became *decemvir sacrorum* in place of Ti. Sempronius Longus (*cos.* 194), probably his father. C. Scribonius Curio (*pr.* 193) became the second plebeian Curio Maximus in succession to C. Mamilius Atellus (*pr.* 207) who had been the first plebeian to gain this office despite considerable patrician opposition. Finally, a certain Cn. Cornelius became Flamen Dialis, but he was soon succeeded by P. Cornelius Scipio, son of Africanus, probably in 171 (L. xli. 28. 7). An inscription from the tomb of the Scipios (*CIL*, i. 33) bewails the early death of Publius and a line which was added later names him Flamen Dialis. It has been argued that this does not apply to Publius since he is not named augur, an office which he undoubtedly held (L. xl. 42. 13). But although Publius is not named as Flamen in the extant part of Livy, a reference to his election may have occurred in the gap early in book xliii (171 B.C.). If so, the tenure of the office by Cn. Scipio will have been brief. Cf. Münzer, *PW,* s.v. Cornelius, nn. 22 and 331.

xix. *M. Fulvius Flaccus*

The identification of the brother of Q. Fulvius Flaccus who was expelled from the Senate by Postumius Albinus in 174 is difficult: 'insignes notae fuerunt M. Corneli . . . et L. Fulvi, qui frater germanus et, ut Valerius Antias tradit, consors etiam censoris erat' (L. xli. 27. 2; cf. above, p. 192). Velleius (i. 10. 6) gives Cn. Fulvius. Mommsen therefore rejected Livy's Lucius because the *praenomen* is not found elsewhere among the Fulvii Flacci, and accepted Gnaeus. But Cn. Fulvius (*pr.* 190) was probably the elder brother of Q. Fulvius Cn. f. (*cos. suff.* 180) and not the brother of Q. Fulvius Q. f. the censor of 174. Therefore both *praenomina*, L. and Cn., are equally suspicious. Münzer (*PW*, s.v. Fulvius n. 57) has shown that the man was probably M. Fulvius Flaccus, who served under his elder brother (the censor of 174) in Spain in 181 (L. xl. 30. 4). There is no reason why he should not be the military tribune of 180, who was probably M. Fulvius Flaccus, not M. Fulvius Nobilior (as ibid. 41. 7; see above, p. 178). Livy's 'frater Q. Fulvi M. Fulvius' will then mean the brother not of the *consul suffectus* (Q. Fulvius Cn. f.) but of the Spanish governor (Q. Fulvius Q. f.) of the same year. A. Postumius Albinus, who as consul and colleague of the elder Q. Fulvius Flaccus in 180 had punished the military tribune, now in his censorship expelled him from the Senate; the reason is obscure. This M. Fulvius Flaccus can scarcely be the same M. Fulvius who went to Aquileia in 171 (L. xliii. 1. 12) or the M. Fulvius Flaccus who went to Macedonia in 170 (ibid. 11. 2), since these ambassadors must have been senators.

xx. *The Eumenes–Perseus Talks*

Polybius (xxix. 5–9), who was interested in these negotiations (see p. 214), accepted the view that some serious intriguing did take place as the best explanation of the later alienation of Rome from Eumenes (6. 4). But in proportion as a more cynical view of the purpose of Rome's treatment of Eumenes is taken, so the value of the rumours of his dealings with Perseus declines. Some senators might accept vague rumours at their face value, if they wished deliberately to weaken Eumenes' position in Asia Minor. The extent to which Roman tradition sought to whitewash Roman conduct is seen in Valerius Antias (L. xliv. 13. 12) who contrasts the support which Marcius Philippus received from Attalus in 169 with Eumenes' alleged refusal to co-operate with him or his praetor Marcius Figulus. When Eumenes returned to Asia, Attalus remained with the consul, and Antias adds that 'sinceram eius fidem aequali tenore egregiamque operam in eo bello fuisse'. In this biased account lies a valuable hint as to which senators favoured Attalus. But the fact that after careful investigation Polybius refused to dismiss the rumours of Eumenes' dealings with Perseus should suggest that they cannot have arisen merely from the tradition of Roman self-justification nor that the subject of the interchange was unimportant (e.g. an exchange of prisoners), as De Sanctis tends to believe (IV. i. 359). It may be that if Perseus rather than Eumenes initiated the talks, he vented his annoyance at their failure by circulating a rumour that it was Eumenes that had first suggested them. Cf. B. Niese, *Gesch. d. gr. u. maked. Staaten*, iii. 198 n. 4, and E. V. Hansen, *The Attalids of Pergamum*, 111.

XXI. *Q. Marcius Philippus and the Rhodians*

When the question of declaring war on Rhodes was debated in Rome in 167 (see pp. 216 f.), it is likely that Q. Marcius Philippus, though absent in Greece, had a finger in the pie and that the praetor Iuventius Thalna, who urged war, was acting in his interest. Thalna perhaps owed his consulship in 163 to the influence of Philippus who was censor in 164. Philippus may have used the method of a direct appeal to the People in order to force the Senate to discuss the issue, thinking that otherwise there might not be enough pressure within the Senate. Another connexion is possible. In 169 the Rhodians had sent one embassy to the Senate and a second to Philippus in Greece in an attempt to improve relations. These moves were successful and Philippus even privately urged one of the ambassadors to mediate in the war between Egypt and Syria. Polybius (xxviii. 16–17) was puzzled about Philippus' motive: was it due to fear that if the Macedonian war was long protracted Antiochus might capture Alexandria and prove dangerous to Rome, or was it because he was confident of a quick victory over Perseus and so wanted an excuse to interfere farther afield? Polybius inclined towards the second explanation. It would appear that Philippus was skilfully attempting to use the Rhodians as pawns in order to check the Egypto-Syrian quarrel without exposing Rome's temporizing policy to the light of day. At the same time he may have been laying some trap for the Rhodians. True, Polybius must have received this secret information from Rhodian informants, whose account would naturally be apologetic, and he only published it after the death of Philippus, who could not then deny it, but whatever the extent of these private negotiations Philippus' attitude may well have encouraged the Rhodians to make their unfortunate attempt at mediation in 168; after that fiasco had placed them in a false position, the next move was to get Thalna to propose an attack on Rhodes and to show the Senate how strong a popular backing he enjoyed.

XXII. *Cato and Carthage*

Cato's Visit to Carthage. Certainty cannot be reached regarding when and how many Roman commissions were sent to Carthage (see p. 240). Livy's *Periochae* give several episodes, but no fixed dates; they perhaps contain a doublet and certainly represent in part Roman annalists who tried to justify Roman behaviour, while it is difficult to equate the incidents they give with those recorded by other authors. For the date of Cato's mission see Gsell, *Hist. anc. de l'Afrique du Nord*, iii. 321, and Bilz, *Scipio Aemilianus*, 18 n. 37; the latter rejects the attempt by Gelzer (*Philol.* 1931, 260 ff.) to identify Cato's mission with that of Nasica. Cato's visit (Appian, *Lib.* 69, and Plut. *Cato*, 26) is probably to be identified with the anonymous mission at the end of Livy, *Perioch.* xlvii ('legati ad disceptandum . . . deprehendisse').

Cato's Speeches on Carthage. According to Livy (*Perioch.* xlviii) Cato made three speeches urging the declaration of war on Carthage, of which only one appears to have been published (Gellius, ix. 14. 9; Nonius, p. 128 L.). The date of delivery is uncertain. Malcovati (*ORF*, i. 75) assigns it to 150, apparently on the ground that it must have been delivered in the year when war was actually declared, but F. E. Adcock (*CHJ*, 1946, 124) points out that frg. 184 (Carthage preparing to be an enemy; cf. above, pp. 241 f.) presupposes that no positive infringement of the treaty of 201 had yet been made by Carthage, i.e. the speech must fall between Cato's visit to Carthage (153) and the Carthaginian breach of the treaty (150). It is of course possible, though unlikely, that in frg. 184 Cato was quoting in 150 a remark that he had made earlier (a trick he had used before in his speech, *De sumptu suo*; cf. above, p. 221); if so, the speech could still be set in 150.

The Senatorial Debate of 153. The result of this debate (cf. p. 240) is obscure. According to Appian (*Lib.* 69) the Senate decided upon war, but still needed a pretext and meanwhile concealed its determination. Bilz (op. cit. 19 ff.) believes that this passage, together with P. xxxvi. 4 and Diod. xxxii. 1, proves that the better tradition recorded an actual resolution of the Senate for war in 153, which was kept secret until a πρόφασις could be found; this came with the attack by Carthage on Masinissa in 150, the αἰτία of the war being Roman φόβος. The annalistic account in the interest of Roman honour suppressed all reference to this secret decision and gave the Polybian πρόφασις as the αἰτία: Punic perfidy seemed a better cause than Roman fear. But it is difficult to see why Cato should have persisted in his importunate public advocacy of war, if a secret senatorial decision had been reached; surely in that case the less said the better, so that Rome's intentions should not be advertised and when the excuse to intervene offered itself Rome could gain the benefits of surprise. The truth behind the passage of Appian may not be more than that in 153 a considerable number of senators realized that war was desirable or necessary, but the opposition to this view was not negligible, as witness the subsequent debates which would have lacked a sense of reality if all those taking part knew that the war had been decided upon.

Carthaginian Rearmament. In 150 Carthage could arm a great number of men (58,000 according to Appian), while even after her defeat in that year her arsenals were not empty (cf. the list of the arms surrendered in 149: App. *Lib.* 80). But Carthage probably had not acquired a large navy in defiance of the treaty of 201 which allowed her only ten warships, although the Livian tradition harps upon the *navalis materia*. The passages of Appian (*Lib.* 76 and 79) which imply that in 149 Carthage had no navy perhaps should outweigh other passages (92 and 134; Zon. ix. 26; Livy, *Per.* xlvii, xlviii; Florus, i. 31. 7; Oros. iv. 22. 2) which suggest the opposite, since the latter may result from Roman attempts at self-justification; cf. Gsell, op. cit. iii. 334 n. 3. Possibly Cato may have seen at Carthage supplies of timber, &c., which were intended for the merchant fleet, but which he feared would be used for military purposes, as in fact they ultimately may have been when Rome forced the issue (unless the Senate ordered their destruction, as is suggested by F. E. Adcock, op. cit. 118; this would presumably have been done in 152). The existence of a large fleet in 153 would surely have given Cato the very πρόφασις that he required for the declaration of war. Despite the fact that by 191 Carthage had sufficiently recovered from the Hannibalic War to offer to repay her outstanding indemnity in one lump sum, and that her agriculture was flourishing, her economic prosperity was on the wane: see, for example, L. Zancan, *Le cause della terza guerra punica*, 566–72.

Carthage and Masinissa. The theory of Kahrstedt (*Gesch. Karthager*, iii. 615–17), that fear of Masinissa drove Rome to destroy Carthage (cf. above, p. 244), is attractive. Cf. Gsell, op. cit. iii. 329, 335; B. L. Hallward, *CAH*, viii. 476; Schur, *PW*, s.v. Masinissa. True, there is little direct support for it in the ancient sources (unless, as may well be, the speech which Appian, *Lib.* 61, puts in the mouth of a speaker at the end of the Hannibalic War really reflects views current before the Third Punic War), but if Rome really intended to kill two birds with one stone, she would hardly advertise the fact that one of them was her friend and ally of fifty years' standing; thus references to Masinissa's part would scarcely be writ large in the sources.

Kahrstedt's theory can hardly be said to have been demolished by the arguments of Zancan, op. cit. 577, or Bilz, op. cit. 29 ff. F. E. Adcock, op. cit. 118 f., who finds it 'seductive', refuses, however, to capitulate to it, and pertinently observes that 'it would be the traditional statecraft of Rome to check Numidian expansion the moment it seemed dangerous, rather than to create a vacuum which Rome's legions might have to defend. A Numidian king with Utica in his hands might prove a danger even if Carthage was destroyed, so that with the destruction of Carthage the danger would not be finally conjured.' But it is difficult to see how, short of military operations, Rome could effectively have checked Masinissa's expansion except by encouraging Carthaginian resistance to his claims, and such a policy, which Nasica probably advocated, would be generally unpopular. Nor is it easy to believe that if Rome had been forced to destroy Carthage for fear of Numidia she would have allowed Masinissa to advance and occupy Utica: in the event she did not. Kahrstedt's view cannot of course be more than a hypothesis, but in the light of the changing balance of power in Africa some Romans, as Nasica, may have hoped to redress the balance by giving Carthage a little more encouragement, while Cato's blind hatred may have driven him to urge a more drastic solution and to use Masinissa's increasing power as an excuse. But even if fear of Masinissa or readiness to assume responsibility for a new province in Africa (cf. Adcock, op. cit. 119) may explain why the Senate was ready to enforce the *deditio* of Carthage, they scarcely explain why the Senate decided to destroy the city and move the population inland: this must surely be attributed to a 'phase of that irrational impatience that historians have, if reluctantly, to recognise as a factor in historical causation' (Adcock, 128).

APPENDIX IV

THE TRIALS OF THE SCIPIOS

I. *The Sources*[1]

THE 'trials' of the Scipios are among the most confused and uncertain episodes of Roman history.[2] With an early authoritative account lacking and with abundant later evidence of doubtful value, the main problem is to decide to what extent the surgeon's knife must be used on the later tradition. In the absence of contemporary evidence,[3] the main source is Polybius, who relates two relevant anecdotes when recording the death and character of Africanus. This Polybian chapter, brief, anecdotal, and not beyond criticism, must nevertheless be the final criterion for all later accounts, but as it is stripped of all details which would not suit Polybius' universal history, it may legitimately be supplemented with material which is in itself intrinsically probable. After Polybius comes the better and older annalistic tradition, which is represented by Nepos (*apud* Gellium), Cicero, and part of Livy (xxxviii. 55. 9–57. 8). Gellius records the two Polybian anecdotes in more detail, refers to the authority of the *veteres annales*, and above all makes it clear that there were three episodes, one in the Senate (iv. 18) and two

---

[1] Polybius, xxiii. 14; Livy, xxxviii. 50. 4–60 (50, 4–55. 7 and 58–60 derive from Valerius Antias); xxxix. 52; Cicero, *De or.* ii. 249; *De prov. cons.* 18; Gellius, iv. 18; vi (vii). 19 (follows Nepos); Diodorus, xxix. 21; Valerius Maximus, iii. 7. 1; iv. 1. 8; 2. 3; v. 3. 2; 8. 1; Plutarch, *Cato Maior*, 15, *Apophthegm.* ii. 7, 8, 10; Dio Cassius, frg. 63; Zonaras, 9. 20; Appian, *Syr.* 39; *De vir. illustr.* 49. 15–18; 53. 2; Seneca, *Dial.* x (*de brev. vit.*) 17. 6, xi (*ad Pol.*) 14. 4, xii (*ad Helv.*) 12. 6; *Contr.* v. 2. 3; Pliny, *Praef.* 10; Orosius, iv. 20, 29; Ampelius, *Lib. mem.* 19. 3.

BIBLIOGRAPHY: Th. Mommsen, *Hermes*, i (1866), 161–216; reprinted with additions in *Röm. Forschungen*, ii. 417–510 (1879); B. Niese, *De Annalibus Romanis observationes alterae* (1888); Anspach, *Jahrb. f. Philol.* cxxxix (1889), 355, on references in Plautus, *Bacchides*; C. Pascal, *Studi Romani*, I. iii (Turin, 1896); L. Holzapfel, *Berl. Philol. Wochenschr.* xvi. 1587 f., xvii. 627 f. (review of Pascal); G. Kirner, *Rassegna di antichità classica*, 1896, 199 f. (review of Pascal); C. Pascal, *Rivista di storia antica*, ii (1897), 64 (reply to reviews); Kniep, *Societas publicanorum* (1896), 146 f., 154 f. (on legal question); C. Niccolini, *Rivista di stor. ant.* iii (1898), 28; C. Pascal, ibid. iv (1899), 268 (again replies); F. Münzer, *PW*, s.v. Cornelius 337 (1900); C. Pascal, *Fatti e leggende di Roma antica* (1903), 53 f., edited by Le Monnier; G. Bloch, *Revue des études anciennes*, 1906, 93–110, 191–228, 287–322; P. Fraccaro, 'I Processi degli Scipioni', *Studi storici per l'antichità classica*, iv (1911), 217–414; also published separately; C. Pascal, *Athenaeum*, iii–iv (1915), 451; W. Drumann–P. Groebe, *Geschichte Roms*, v² (1919), 119–22; De Regibus, *Il Processo degli Scipioni* (1921); De Sanctis, *Storia dei Romani*, IV. i (1923), 591–8; T. Frank, *Cambr. Anc. Hist.* viii (1930), 371; R. M. Haywood, *Studies on Scipio Africanus* (1933), ch. v; P. Fraccaro, *Athenaeum*, 1939, 3 ff.

[2] The foundations of modern studies of the problem were well and truly laid by Mommsen, who first adequately emphasized the legal aspect and exposed the falsifications of the annalists. Among other modern writers P. Fraccaro gives the best statement, in the judgement of the present writer: the following pages owe much to his work. The short account by T. Frank (*CAH*, viii. 371) is not above criticism: see Fraccaro, *Athenaeum*, 1931, 466.

[3] Attempts to find references in Plautus or Ennius are not conclusive, e.g. *Bacchides*, 321, or Ennius, *Sat.* 8–9: 63 Vahlen, *Scip.* 1–2, 8–9 V., *Scen.* 423 V.

distinct trials (iv. 18; vi. 19). The rest of Livy reproduces Valerius Antias, who heads the inferior later annalistic tradition and displays his usual disregard for truth in the interests of rhetoric and dramatic effect, but amid his falsifications there are still some details worth preserving.[1]

11. The Attack in the Senate (187 B.C.)

According to Polybius someone in the Senate demanded that Publius Scipio should give an account of the money he had received before the treaty from Antiochus for the pay of his army. Africanus replied that he had the account book, but ought not to be called to account by anyone. When the questioner persisted, he bade his brother bring the book and, tearing it to pieces, he told his critic to look in the fragments. He asked the rest of the Senate how they could demand the items of expenditure of 3,000 talents and not ask by whose agency 15,000 talents from Antiochus had come into the Treasury, nor how they had become masters of Asia, Africa, and Spain. This speech reduced the questioner to silence.

Three small difficulties arise. Polybius relates the incident after an accusation before the People, while there is reason to suppose that it must have taken place first; but since Polybius was recounting anecdotes to illustrate Scipio's character, a correct chronological sequence was not necessary. Secondly, Publius Scipio was not directly responsible for the money in question. We must assume that at first the demand was made of Lucius, that Publius, who was *princeps senatus* and knew the attack was really aimed at him, intervened in the discussion, and that Polybius kept the more important figure in the centre. Thirdly, the Scipios were concerned with only 500 talents; the remaining 2,500 were the responsibility of their successor, Vulso. Either Polybius has made a slip, or else Africanus refused to limit his reply and tried to vindicate the financial independence of commanders in general.

Nepos follows Polybius closely, but adds that the accusation was made by two tribunes, named Petillius, and that they were instigated by Cato.[2] Although he exaggerates still more the part played by Publius, he adds in parenthesis that Publius had been his brother's legate, thus showing that he realized that Publius was not directly responsible but at the same time demonstrating that the attack was really aimed behind Lucius at Publius. Nepos also adds that Publius was called to account not only for the 'pecunia Antiochena' but also for 'praeda quae

[1] R. M. Haywood (*Scipio*, 86 ff.) has tried to find more reliable material in Antias than is usually admitted: Antias used annalists of the time of Piso (*cos.* 133) who in turn had extracted some evidence relating to the trials (SC, *leges, plebiscita*) from the State archives. But this view must be rejected because of the unreliability of the documents themselves as well as the historian's general untrustworthiness: see further De Sanctis, *Riv. Fil.* 1936, 195; Fraccaro, *Athen.* 1939, 10.

[2] Livy (xxxviii. 50. 5) gives 'duo Q. Petillii'; if this *praenomen* is correct, the men must have been cousins, not brothers. One was probably Q. Petillius Spurinus (*pr.* 181, *cos.* 176). The text of *De vir. ill.* 49. 15, which refers to Petillius Ateius, is uncertain and should not be accepted. Haywood (*Scipio*, 88 n. 11) suggests that there may have been only one Petillius on the ground that in, for instance, Cato's speech the final -us may have been dropped (this form occurs e.g. in the contemporary *SC de Bacchanalibus*, as Claudi(us) and Valeri(us): Dessau, *ILS*, 18) and that later this form was taken as nominative plural instead of singular. This assumption is perhaps unnecessary and unlikely, because the name would presumably occur as the subject of a verb, the number of which might have kept the writer from such an error.

eo in bello capta erat'; this is almost certainly incorrect. Livy refers very briefly to the incident, but the version given by Valerius Maximus (iii. 7. 1) is very reasonable: the accusation is made against Lucius about the money from Antiochus, there is no mention of *praeda*, the subordinate position and irregular conduct of Publius are noted, together with the distinction between the responsibility he claimed and the responsibility he actually could incur.

In each incident of the 'trials' the points to determine are the date, court, accusers, accused, accusation, procedure, and the verdict and its justice. The fact that the first episode, which is usually dated 187,[1] took place in the Senate which was not a court of justice, precludes any idea of a legal trial. Any senator could draw attention to anything of interest to the State, and when public attention had been arrested, the Senate could as the result of a public demand decree an inquiry which might lead to a trial before the People. Thus the episode was the first movement of the political enemies of the Scipios to stir up trouble. The attack came from the Petillii, instigated by Cato. The accused was probably Lucius Scipio, but at some point in the debate his brother intervened and Lucius dropped into the background. The accusation was probably that Lucius should give an account of 500 talents which he had received from Antiochus after Magnesia as a condition of the armistice: the indemnity which Scipio had proposed was 15,000 talents, of which 500 were to be paid at once, 2,500 on the ratification of the terms, the rest in twelve annual instalments. The 2,500 passed through the hands of Scipio's successor Vulso, but probably they were mentioned by Scipio in the debate together with the 500 for which his brother was responsible. The result of the demand was that Africanus disdainfully tore up the account-books and the matter was dropped. The Senate, however jealous some members might be of the Scipios, made it clear that it would still remain loyal to its Princeps. No other result could be expected, except damage to Scipio's prestige. Africanus' high-handed conduct had averted the blow, but in doing this he had harmed more than his popularity: in tearing up the books he had destroyed the evidence that could vindicate the honesty of his brother's administration. Suspicion, engendered by his autocratic bearing, could now flourish unchecked.

Was Scipio under legal obligation to account for the money? The financial responsibility of generals is not clearly defined. A consul naturally was responsible for State funds voted to him by the Senate; he could also obtain money from the Treasury without a special decree of the Senate because he acted through a quaestor who was responsible and gave account of sums paid from the Treasury to his officer and also of sums raised by the general from taxes. Generals were less accountable for money won from the enemy. Booty was probably handled by their *praefecti fabrum* rather than by their military quaestors. They could use it freely in the interests of their army or public utility, without having to render an account, which perhaps strictly could be enforced, but which in fact was seldom claimed; presumably they would normally keep accounts of receipts and payments for their personal use. Any surplus would normally be paid into the

---

[1] The only definite date for the incident in the Senate is that the Antian account implies 187; there is no reason to doubt this date which is accepted by most modern writers. The Petillii launched their attack after Vulso's return to Rome; discussions about his financial arrangements would pave the way for a request that the Scipios should render their accounts.

Treasury, while a general could be charged with peculation if suspected of undue personal profit.[1]

Thus a distinction must be drawn between State funds administered by responsible quaestors, and *praeda*, which was controlled by the general directly or his agent. But into which division do the 500 talents fall? The fact that Scipio had demanded and received the sum from Antiochus to pay his troops[2] would lend colour to the view that it was *praeda* at the general's disposal. But the fact that the Senate and the Roman People approved it by including the sum in the terms of the armistice would support the view that it was State funds. It was a matter of definition. Scipio maintained that it was *praeda*, for which no account should be given, whereas the opposition under Cato classed it as a contribution of war.

It is unlikely that, at this stage, there was any suggestion that L. Scipio had administered the money incorrectly or that there had been some leakage; Lucius was merely asked to put the matter in order and in accordance with constitutional practice. The Senate was very jealous of its financial rights, and would be quick to question an act by which a general had administered personally, and not through a quaestor, a part of the indemnity which they had approved. When the Roman annalists say that the demand concerned not merely the *pecunia Antiochena* but also *praeda*, they miss the subtlety of the attack; for if *praeda* had been mentioned, then Scipio would have been within his rights. Thus it is hardly possible or legitimate to say whether Scipio was right or wrong. He indignantly asserted the correctness of his position (οὐ δεῖν δ' αὐτὸν ὑποσχεῖν οὐδενὶ λόγον), while the opposition could equally well press their point. Scipio won the day, since the Senate probably recognized that it would be harsh to narrow down a political attack in a way that would infringe the rights of one who was still at least in name their leader, and while they might grudge the consuls too much freedom, they disliked still more bold tribunician interference in financial matters.

III. *The Trial of Lucius Scipio*

The subsequent attacks on the Scipios are more difficult to follow. While Polybius merely refers to a trial of Africanus before the People, Livy (Antias) has devoted nine chapters to this and the trial of Lucius. It is, in fact, far from clear whether Africanus was ever formally accused or the attack on him was only an incident in the legal trial of his brother. But before these two episodes can be interrelated, falsifications must be recognized and removed, and a bare minimum

---

[1] A general's responsibilities may have varied in respect of different categories of booty. The precise definition of the terms *praeda* and *manubiae* is not very certain. Gellius (xii. 25. 28) defines *manubiae* as revenue gained from the sale of booty ('pecunia per quaestorem populi Romani ex praeda vendita contracta'), although it more probably was that part of the booty which was reserved for the general ('manubiae . . . sunt praeda imperatoris pro portione de hostibus capta': Ps.-Asc. *in* Cic. *Verr.* ii. 1. 54). It is uncertain whether *manubiae* included certain categories of spoil (e.g. *capita libera*) and excluded others (as works of art), as is suggested by Cato's charge against Glabrio. In general see Mommsen, *Röm. Forsch.* ii. 443; Marquardt, *Röm. Staatsverwalt.* ii. 277; Lammert, *PW*, xv, col. 1361; Ph. Fabia, Daremberg–Saglio, iii. 2. 1582; Fraccaro, *Processi*, 376.

[2] P. xxiii. 14. 7. A rough estimate of the annual requirements of Scipio's army in Asia suggests that it may have needed some 380 talents. Thus the 500 from Antiochus should have been ample for Scipio's immediate needs or, as his political opponents might allege, more than ample.

of fact established. The trial of Lucius must be considered first, because it either preceded the attack on Africanus or formed the main drama in which this attack was only one act. The matter cannot be discussed fully here, but the following notes may be added.

The account by Valerius Antias. Lucius' trial is placed (wrongly) after Africanus had been accused, had won a temporary success, and had withdrawn to Liternum where he died. Antias' account may be summarized: the accused was L. Scipio and his staff; the accusation, his use of the money received from Antiochus to bring about an easier peace; the court was a special *quaestio* under a praetor set up as the result of a *rogatio* brought by the Petillii before the People (Cato supporting the *rogatio* in a speech which 'is still extant', and Terentius Culleo conducting the inquiry); the verdict was 'guilty'; the sentence, a heavy fine; the result, the fine was paid only after Lucius had refused to give surety and had been saved from prison by a tribune, Sempronius Gracchus; the sequel was that when Lucius' property was found insufficient to cover the fine, this was paid by his relatives, and popular feeling turned against the prosecution.

This account of the procedure and establishment of a *quaestio* must be rejected because it is flatly contradicted by the simple statement of Nepos, based on the authority of the early annalists, that a tribune, C. Minucius Augurinus, fined (*multam inrogavit*) Lucius and on that account demanded surety (*praedes poscebat*). The most likely explanation of the reason of this falsification by Antias is that having recounted all the references to Africanus' trial before he came to deal with Lucius, Antias preferred not to repeat another tribunician trial and so invented the *quaestio*; that is, he was exhausting his material and thought a little variety might quicken his readers' interest. Also, if his sources were not very precise, he may have reconstructed procedure from that of his own day without fully realizing how false this would be for the earlier period. To do this he may have taken some names from an accurate list of magistrates and thus have given a greater appearance of truth to his version (e.g. the Mummii, tribunes who had tried to veto the *rogatio*, or the names of Scipio's staff officers[1]). Also Cato's speech, to which he refers, was doubtless genuine, although he has probably wrongly assigned it to this occasion.

Further, Antias' statements of the charge are confused: he gives both *peculatus* and *repetundarum*, so that there is implicit in his version the ludicrous situation of Lucius being accused of not having paid into the Treasury the bribes he had received. The alleged charge of corruption or treason may be dismissed; Polybius does not hint that Lucius was involved in the rumours that arose from Africanus' interview with Antiochus' agent: the meeting was private. Also Antias wrote after and under the influence of the Jugurthine War when accusations of corruption had often been made and substantiated.

The account by Nepos and Aulus Gellius. Nepos' account, that a tribune Minucius imposed a fine on Lucius and demanded surety, may be accepted. It does

---

[1] A. and L. Hostilius Cato and C. Furius Aculeo. The Hostilii had served on the land-commission in 201 and may have been friendly with the Scipios, but it is not known whether in fact they were legates of Lucius. No other Furius Aculeo is known, while in the Ciceronian age the *cognomen* Aculeo belonged to the Visellii. On the two traditions about Terentius Culleo, that he was either friendly or hostile (Antias) to the Scipios (L. xxxviii. 55), see Fraccaro, *Processi*, 297.

not necessarily presuppose even a charge of peculation. Rather, Scipio's enemies, having failed to win their point in the Senate, took steps to enforce it elsewhere; they found a tribune willing to support Cato's stricter interpretation of the category to which the money belonged and to demand that Lucius should render his account and to fine him when he refused. Why Lucius refused can only be surmised. Perhaps Africanus' haughty spirit would not allow his brother to respond to a demand which he had refused in the Senate and thus tacitly to admit that their interpretation there had been wrong. Also the account-books had been destroyed; unless they were kept in duplicate, an accurate account might now be impossible. Again, Africanus would hardly suppose that his prestige had sunk so low that none of the other tribunes could be found to veto their colleague's proposal.

There were five stages in a tribunician action: the summons (*diei dictio*), the inquiry (*anquisitio*), the magistrate's verdict (*iudicatio* or *multae irrogatio*), an appeal to the People by the condemned (*provocatio*), and the verdict of the People (*iudicium populi*). Mommsen believed that Minucius demanded surety from Lucius after the final stage, but it was more probably after the third stage, that is, before the magistrate's verdict was referred to the People. His action no doubt was perfectly legal, but in this age was harsh.

Gellius records that Africanus then appealed on behalf of his brother (i.e. *alieno nomine*) to the tribunician college, eight of whom issued a decree which Gellius reproduces *verbatim*. But its official form does not make it authentic. The only real test is its content. It has been demonstrated (by Fraccaro, *Processi*, 254) that the phrases of the first part (dealing with the grounds of Africanus' appeal) reflect conditions of the later revolutionary period. The second half (the tribunes' decision) is equally suspect. The tribunes declare that if Asiaticus pays the surety they will prevent his arrest. But there was no question of arrest if he did pay; imprisonment was to be the penalty of non-payment. It is only the next clause, that the tribunes will let justice take its course if the surety is not paid, that has any importance. Thus this imposing-looking document represents in an official form an earlier annalistic narrative account, elaborated with ideas of a later period. All that results is that the tribunes rejected Africanus' appeal. It is not really clear on what ground the appeal was based; presumably that the demand for surety was unnecessarily harsh.

The sequel, according to Gellius, was that when Lucius refused to pay surety, Minucius ordered his arrest, but Gracchus, who had not supported the tribunician decree, issued another decree protecting Lucius from imprisonment, on the ground that it was unworthy of the State to treat in this way a general who had triumphed. Gracchus, who was Africanus' personal enemy, took an oath that his action did not involve a renewal of friendship with Africanus. The form of this second tribunician decree must be rejected, but its content should be weighed.

The relation of the Scipios with Gracchus. The fact of Gracchus' intervention can be questioned only by a baseless scepticism, but his motive (concern for the dignity of the State) is less certain.[1] Perhaps it arose from the strict relationship

---

[1] 'Cum L. Cornelius Scipio Asiaticus triumphans hostium duces in carcerem coniectarit . . . .' There is no evidence that Lucius had imprisoned enemy generals (unless it is implied in L. xxxvii. 59. 5). Cf. Cicero (*De prov. cons.* 18) who refers to the decree in an indirect form.

which existed between an ex-officer and members of his staff: Gracchus had served under L. Scipio in Greece and Asia in 190.[1] His attitude to the Scipios has been coloured and even distorted because of the political differences between his more famous sons and Africanus' grandson, Scipio Aemilianus. Further, the aristocratic literary tradition persistently contrasted the conduct of the elder Gracchus with his degenerate and revolutionary sons.[2] Thus when later writers came to record the relations of the elder Gracchus and Africanus they could not but be influenced by events of the revolutionary period. Not only was the hostility of the two families projected back into an earlier generation, but there was also a conscious attempt to contrast the degeneracy of young Tiberius, who had even deposed a fellow tribune, with the generosity of his father who had intervened to save a political opponent from imprisonment when the dignity of the State demanded it. Therefore the view has been advanced that this tradition of hostility between the Scipios and the elder Gracchus should be rejected.[3] The fact that they entrusted him with an important and confidential mission to Philip of Macedon when he was still young suggests, though it does not prove, a friendly relationship.[4] Further, both Dio Cassius (frg. 65. 1) and an anecdote preserved by Valerius Maximus (iii. 7. 7) represent Gracchus as a fierce opponent of Cato. Nor is it likely that a young man with no great record behind him would have gained a reputation as a serious opponent of Africanus.[5] But although evidence for personal enmity, which derives mainly from the episodes of the 'trials', may have been unduly influenced by later events, political rivalry existed: the Sempronii in general supported the Claudii rather than the Cornelii, and although Sempronius Longus had been friendly to Africanus, Gracchus seems to have turned towards the middle senatorial group, and he may well have interposed his veto on behalf of L. Scipio from a sense of duty towards his superior officer.

Africanus' Command in Etruria. Livy gives a different account of the end of the trial. He says that Africanus, who was serving in a subordinate command in Etruria when he heard of his brother's misfortune, hurried back to Rome and even used violence towards the tribunes in an attempt to rescue Lucius who was being haled to prison. Gracchus intervened to protect Lucius, but condemned the conduct of Africanus and contrasted it with his earlier moderation when he rebuked the People for wishing to make him perpetual consul and dictator. The genuineness of Gracchus' speech is generally rejected (p. 282) and this may be done the more readily when it is recognized that the circumstances which it was nominally written to adorn are totally unhistorical; Mommsen, who rejected the

---

[1] Fraccaro (*Processi*, 259–65) has elaborated this point.

[2] Cic. *De prov. cons.* 18, *De orat.* i. 38; Plut. *Ti. Gracch.* 14. 3, *C. Gracch.* 10. 4; Cic. *De amicit.* 41, *De rep.* vi. 12.

[3] See Fraccaro, op. cit. 260–4, and J. Carcopino, *Autour des Gracques*, 47 ff. For a reply see R. M. Geer, *TAPA*, 1939, 381 ff. The tradition that the reconciliation, which followed Gracchus' help to the Scipios, was sealed by his marriage to Cornelia, Africanus' daughter, can be rejected. Carcopino shows that as the marriage occurred *c.* 175 B.C., after Africanus' death, it had no connexion with the reconciliation.

[4] Carcopino has shown that Gracchus was about a dozen years younger than was generally thought.

[5] Geer, op. cit. 385 n. 10, argues that Gracchus did not enter the Senate before 184 and possibly not until 181; he reaches no decision (383 n. 7) about whether Gracchus held the quaestorship.

speech, failed to take this further step of demolishing the background as well. The supposed legation of Africanus in Etruria is in itself improbable; he would scarcely accept such a commission merely to avoid trouble, while such commissions became more frequent later during the revolutionary period (e.g. of Nasica, who killed Ti. Gracchus). The incident was invented merely to create a dramatic situation in order that Africanus might suddenly intervene at his brother's arrest.[1] Otherwise, if he was in Etruria only a few days from Rome, why had he not returned during the trial itself, which would not be finished for at least a month after the first stage? Or if it was only news of the condemnation that caused him to return, how did he get there in time to interfere in the actual arrest which would immediately follow Lucius' refusal to pay the guarantee? Thus Fraccaro would abolish the Etrurian commission entirely, but Africanus may have held such a commission during his last years and the annalists may have used this fact to create a false background for a false speech.

The date. Antias apparently placed Lucius' trial in 187 together with the incident in the Senate, but he falsely transferred the trial of Africanus from 184 to 187. Might he not also have transferred Lucius' trial from some other date (? 184) to 187? Mommsen (*Röm. Forsch.* 481 n. 135) thought so and suggested that the trial of Africanus preceded that of Lucius and that Antias changed the order. His views, which have been rejected by Fraccaro (*Processi*, 389 n. 2), need not be discussed at length, but a few points may be noted. Mommsen's contention that the reference to Africanus' *legatio* in Etruria (which he believes was granted to Africanus in order to suspend his trial) proves that Africanus had been tried before Lucius was accused is not sound, if, as is probable, the Etrurian *legatio* should be rejected. Further, it would be natural for Cato to attack Lucius before venturing to make a direct assault upon Africanus himself, while if Africanus had already been forced into exile there was less point in pressing home the charge against Lucius. Finally, there is no ground to question the intervention of Africanus at Lucius' trial, which therefore preceded his own and was thus probably before 184.

Both the intervention of Gracchus and the role of Minucius as accuser should be accepted as facts, but the date of the tribunate of neither is known. Mommsen and Münzer (*PW*, s.v. Sempronius) argue for 184, but 187 would suit Gracchus' career well and is accepted by Niccolini (*Fasti d. Trib.* 111, 115). Further, Gracchus intervened in the discussion on the triumph of Fulvius Nobilior over the Aetolians (L. xxxix. 5. 1) which was celebrated on 23 December 187 (see above, p. 144). The discussion in the Senate was therefore probably before 10 December 187, the date when the new tribunes for 186 entered office. Unless the record of Gracchus' intervention is rejected, his tribunate must be placed in 187.

Thus the only date provided by the ancient authorities may be tentatively accepted, i.e. 187. This in itself is more probable than 184, since if the charge against Lucius was the same as that made in the Senate, namely, that he should render his accounts, then it is likely that it would follow soon after the first incident and not be postponed for three years.

Summary. It is fairly sure that the accuser was the tribune Minucius, backed by Cato; the accusation, that Scipio, when so requested, refused to render his

[1] Fraccaro, *Processi*, 315.

accounts; this led to suspicion, but probably not to any direct charge of peculation; the procedure was the imposition of a tribunician fine and a demand for
surety which Lucius refused; the result was that before the tribune's judgement
was confirmed by the Tribes and when Lucius was threatened with drastic
treatment, Africanus persuaded Gracchus to veto proceedings, so that the matter
fell through. The question of Lucius' guilt hardly arises. As in the case of
Africanus the justice of the demand that the accounts should be rendered was
a matter of definition; in strict law such a demand may have been allowed and
could be enforced, though custom was against it. If the charge had been peculation and Lucius' guilt probable, it is unlikely that Cato would have allowed the
matter to rest there.

iv. *The Attack on Scipio Africanus*

For this episode the main authority is an anecdote in Polybius, and by this all
other accounts must be judged.[1] To demonstrate Scipio's popularity Polybius
says 'that when someone took upon himself to bring Scipio to trial before the
People in the manner usual at Rome, and produced many bitter accusations
against him, he came forward and said nothing but that it ill became the Roman
People to listen to accusations against P. Cornelius Scipio, to whom the accusers
owed it that they had the power of speech at all. At this the populace dispersed
and quitting the assembly left the accuser alone.' This account leaves some
critical points unanswered. The accuser is anonymous (τις); the accusation is
vague (πολλὰ καὶ πικρῶς); the ultimate result is uncertain; and Polybius may be
guilty of slight dramatic exaggeration, since Cato and his followers would scarcely
desert the accuser in this way. But the account must be accepted as substantially
correct.

Gellius (iv. 18) provides some important additions. The accuser is the tribune
M. Naevius; the accusation is that Scipio 'had received money from Antiochus
in order that peace might be made with him in the name of the Roman People
on more favourable and easier conditions; and certain other charges unworthy
of such a man'. Scipio made a few remarks 'quae dignitas vitae suae atque
gloria postulabat', and recalling that it was the anniversary of Zama, he moved
(*censere*) that all should leave the trifler (*nebulo*) and go and give thanks to Iuppiter
Optimus Maximus; the whole meeting then followed him to the Capitol. Gellius
adds 'the speech which is believed to have been delivered by Scipio that day is
extant; those who deny that it is genuine at least admit that these were the words
of Scipio which I have given'. Thus the additions to Polybius' account are the
name of the accuser, the accusation, Scipio's reference to Zama, the substance
of his speech, and a reference to a surviving speech in addition to the speech or
account from which Gellius derived the words which he quotes.

The reference to Zama is improbable: such a dramatic coincidence would
hardly have been overlooked by Polybius. The annalists probably elaborated the
reference to the 'crowning mercy' of Zama implied in the words 'Africanus to

---

[1] P. xxiii. 14. A tantalizing fragment of an inscription has come to light in the Forum
of Nerva: *Inscr. Ital.* xiii. 3, *Elogia* n. 22. It reads: '[. . .]u[. . .]ium q[. . . p]lebis m[. . .
quaestione? i]niudic[ata . . .]cere vo[. . .] tr[ibuni] pl[ebis] le[. . . conse?]nsu post[. . .].' It
might be part of an *elogium* of Africanus and refer to his trial, but the editor, Degrassi,
believes that such a conjecture is 'admodum incertam'.

whom the accusers owed it that they had the power of speech at all'; it would then be a short step to suggest that the accusation actually fell on the anniversary. But even if true, the story would not help to date the episode, because the date of Zama is uncertain.[1] The then extant speech of Africanus, although accepted by some modern writers, must be considered a forgery: Polybius' witness that Africanus ἀλλὰ μὲν οὐδὲν εἶπεν προελθών must be final.[2] Also Gellius' version of the upshot is inferior, because a proposal to leave the court would have been a serious act of contempt towards the tribune's right *agere cum plebe*.

Despite its falsifications, the version of Antias must be briefly considered. The two Petillii instituted proceedings before the People against Africanus, who on the first day of the trial made no allusion to the charges but spoke only of his services to Rome. The accusation apparently was 'pecunia capta', based on suspicions rather than direct proof. Other charges were raked up and added: the winter-quarters at Syracuse; the conduct of Pleminius; the restoration by Antiochus of Scipio's son without ransom; Scipio's own autocratic and almost monarchical bearing. Proceedings were adjourned, and on the next day, the anniversary of Zama, Scipio won a success similar to that recorded by Gellius. After a long adjournment had been arranged, Scipio retired to Liternum; when the day came, Lucius apologized for his brother's absence on the ground of ill health. The prosecuting tribunes objected, but the rest of the college accepted the excuse; Gracchus went farther and carried a resolution that he would protect Scipio, if he returned, because it was unworthy of Rome to treat her saviour so. Proceedings were dropped and Scipio died soon afterwards.

Much of this account can be dismissed out of hand. For instance, the trial will have been extended to two days in order to give more scope to Scipio's oratory and importance. Also the intervention of L. Scipio and Gracchus may be rejected as a doublet of the end of the trial of L. Scipio: here Lucius takes the part played by his cousin Nasica at his own trial, while Gracchus' role is similar in both cases. But Antias makes some positive contributions: the name of the accuser (the Petillii), the accusation (*pecunia capta*), and the date (187). These may all be wrong, but they merit some consideration.

The name of the accuser is of paramount importance because it helps to fix the date of the episode, and according as the episode is fitted chronologically into a wider series of events, so these events must influence our judgement of the episode itself. Three possibilities appear: the accusers were the Petillii and the date was 187 (Antias); the accuser Naevius and the date 184 (Gellius); the accuser's name is unknown and the date was 187. A fourth possibility, that the accuser's name is unknown and the date was 184, can be dismissed because the reason for supporting the later date is the part played by Naevius.

Unfortunately, little is known about M. Naevius. The name occurred in the tribunician Fasti for 184 (L. xxxix. 52. 4: 'in magistratuum libris'), and also doubtless

---

[1] Valerius Maximus also gives the Zama version (iii. 7. 1e); otherwise his account of the episode is surprisingly sane.

[2] Cf. Cic. *De off.* iii. 4; L. xxxviii. 56. 5. Even if Ennius' line ('illic est nugator, nihili non nauci ⟨est⟩ homo', frg. 37 V.) does refer to the incident, it does not prove the authenticity of the speech; at most it supports the words quoted by Nepos and suggests their source. The suggestion that Scipio's jest ('quod hoc Naevio ignavius?': Cic. *De orat.* ii. 249) might derive from this speech of Africanus is not very cogent; it might equally well come from an earlier reply by Scipio to the poet Naevius (cf. p. 254).

in the annalists used by the forger of Africanus' speech.[1] But many modern historians believe that Naevius' name was introduced into the tradition of the trial by annalists who, finding it in the Fasti and knowing the anecdote of the enmity of Africanus and the poet Naevius, decided that the tribune must have shared the poet's political outlook. Those who maintain this view[2] and still believe in a trial of Africanus base their arguments on the assumption that the trial occurred in 187; consequently, having to explain why some annalists placed it in 184, they question the truth of Naevius' role. But if their assumption is not admitted, their explanation is unnecessary. Their assumption is supported only by Antias' statement that the Petillii were the accusers. But since all agree that Antias has transferred Africanus' death from 184/3 to 187, it is unreasonable to accept his other statement without compelling proof; and such is hardly to be found in the circular argument which tries to dispose of Naevius, whose name, as Mommsen (*Röm. Forsch.* 466) and Fraccaro (*Athenaeum*, 1939, 7) believe, is one of the few rocks amid the shifting sands of unreliable evidence. In short, the assumption that the trial of Africanus occurred in 187 involves the arbitrary dismissal of Naevius and an unnecessary assumption of unscrupulousness on the part of the annalists.

But was there ever a trial of Africanus? Those who place the incident in 187 for the most part think not. De Sanctis, for example, tries to explain away Polybius' reference to Africanus being accused before the People as follows: the Petillii, after their failure in the Senate, presented a *rogatio* for an inquiry concerning the money paid by Antiochus to the Roman commanders (i.e. L. Scipio and Manlius). In one of the subsequent *contiones*, where Cato delivered his *De pecunia regis Antiochi*, the presiding tribune disregarded L. Scipio and attacked the man who was really responsible; when thus called upon to explain, Africanus uttered the proud words ascribed to him by Polybius and carried out a *coup de théâtre*; the tribunes then dropped the *rogatio* as useless.[3] De Regibus links Africanus' outburst with an inquiry about the indemnity and the subsequent trial of L. Scipio for peculation; it was apparently at one of the stages of the trial (the *anquisitio*, before the voting) that Africanus intervened, after which he withdrew and the trial was dropped.

In view of his close connexion with the Scipionic family Polybius must surely have known the real facts, but does he mean literally what he says: that Africanus was brought to trial before the People in the manner usual at Rome? If he could say that someone demanded that Africanus, not Lucius, should produce his accounts in the Senate, may he not be misleading here also, as is apparently

---

[1] Livy (xxxviii. 56. 6) reveals the history of the forgery: 'The index of the speech of P. Scipio has the name of the tribune M. Naevius; the speech itself is without the name of the accuser; he calls him sometimes a knave, sometimes a trifler (modo nebulonem, modo nugatorem).' Münzer (*PW*, s.v. Naevius) says that Naevius was represented as Africanus' accuser because of the speech with the index. But probably the name on the index came from the annalists and was authentic: see Fraccaro, *Athenaeum*, 1939, 6 f.

[2] e.g. Niese, De Regibus (p. 18), De Sanctis, iv. i. 594. The last two, however, believe that there was no trial of Africanus.

[3] De Sanctis's reconstruction thus contradicts the tribunician trial for a fine (given by Gellius and the *veteres annales*) and rests on Antias' *rogatio Petillia* and a trial for 'peculatus ob Antiochenam pecuniam', which Gellius expressly denies and which in Livy (chs. 54–5) De Sanctis himself condemns as 'one of the most impudent of Antias' falsifications' (p. 595, n. 274).

thought by those who deny the trial? Could not his statement be merely a para-
phrase of the fact that Africanus intervened when his brother was being tried for
peculation or when an attempt was being made to establish an inquiry about the
indemnity? Such suggestions can scarcely be disproved, but it is not justifiable
to reject Polybius' plain statement without very strong reasons, stronger, for
instance, than De Sanctis' belief (p. 595 n.) that Polybius would not have quoted
the anecdote as an example of Africanus' popularity with the People if it had
been immediately followed by Scipio's withdrawal to Liternum where he was
left in peace only by the intervention of Gracchus. But by the same token would
Polybius have quoted it if, as De Sanctis supposes, the result of his action was
the continuation of the trial and virtual condemnation of his brother Lucius?
Surely the difficulty is at least no greater if Africanus' action obtained a victory
at his own trial, even if he did decide to withdraw afterwards to Liternum, where
he was allowed to pass his remaining days, not through any apocryphal intervention of Gracchus (which is merely an historical doublet) but because his
political opponents did not press the point in view of his retirement and his
popularity with the masses. To support his modification of the Polybian trial to
a *rogatio*, De Sanctis says that the approval of an inquiry was morally a condemnation, while a parallel is found in Sulpicius Galba about whose conduct in
Spain an inquiry was demanded, though the best sources say he was accused
before the People and acquitted. Further, De Sanctis refers Cato's speech to this
rogatio—'M. Cato suasit rogationem . . . exstat oratio eius' (L. xxxviii. 54. 11).
But only in Antias' version is it connected with a *rogatio*, and even then it must
be disassociated from the circumstances because there was certainly no *rogatio* to
set up a *quaestio* as Antias says. In fact it need have nothing to do with a *rogatio*
at all, but have been delivered at the *anquisitio* which followed the imposition
of a fine on L. Scipio. Finally, it may be suspected that the reason why De
Sanctis suggests a *rogatio* and rejects Polybius' statement of a trial is the difficulty
of fitting a trial into the sequence of events in 187. A formal trial of both brothers
in this year is unlikely, since if both had been virtually condemned and had left
Rome, Lucius would scarcely have been able to raise his head again the next
year. If the incident *must* be placed in 187, then the explanations of De Sanctis
or De Regibus are plausible. But if the tradition about Naevius is accepted and
in consequence the trial of Africanus is placed in 184, then Polybius' plain statement can also be accepted.[1]

If, then, Africanus was formally accused by Naevius, what was the accusation?
The sources vary: many things (Polybius); receiving money from Antiochus to
negotiate a more favourable peace (Nepos); receiving bribes, based on suspicion
rather than evidence, together with the return of his son unransomed and Scipio's
autocratic behaviour in the East (Antias); corruption and treachery (Appian); *repetundae* (*De vir. ill.*); having made easier terms on account of his son (Zonaras).
If, as is probable, the trial was a political move rather than a legal necessity,
the precise charge may have been formulated somewhat slowly. Africanus'

---

[1] Some form of trial, however embroidered with fictions, is at the base of all accounts.
See Appian, *Syr.* 40; Zon. 9. 20; Diodor. xxix. 21; Plut. *Cato*, 15, *Apophth.* ii. 10; *De
vir. ill.* 49. 15. It is difficult to follow T. Frank (*CAH*, viii. 371) who rejects the trial of
Africanus and yet retains Naevius and makes him the accuser of Lucius in 184 before
the Concilium Plebis. This surely is to make confusion worse confounded.

political opponents would begin to organize all the rumours and suspicions that were rife about him. The question of the indemnity or of peculation was a charge which legally could be brought against Lucius alone: it had been brought and the matter had fallen through. It would be useless to try to revive it as a handle against Africanus, so the Catonians chose more subtle weapons. Africanus' personal dealings with Antiochus had been private: exact information about what had occurred would not be current knowledge. Any dealings with the enemy in time of war could be represented in a bad light, especially when rumours could be based on the undeniable fact of the return of Scipio's son. Further, Scipio had in accordance with his imperial views granted easy terms to Antiochus. This was totally opposed to the foreign policy of Cato who would represent Scipio's generosity as treasonable. Any suspicion of treason, however groundless, would make a good political weapon. Thus there seems little reason to reject the view that Africanus was actually accused of *proditio*, with the object of discrediting his position (more particularly before the censorial elections of 184) rather than with any real hope of substantiating the charge. Cato had used the method before against Glabrio in 189. It was easy to fabricate an accusation against Africanus which he rebutted once but which he did not attempt through illness and disgust to answer a second time. Scipio's withdrawal was all the victory Cato wished.

If, then, a trial of Africanus is possible or even probable, what form did it take? What was the procedure and penalty proposed? Did the case come before the Comitia Centuriata or the Comitia Tributa? The accusation and penalty can sometimes be deduced from the procedure, because capital cases came before the Centuries while cases involving fines came before the Tribes.[1] But the process cannot be reversed and the procedure and penalty deduced from the accusation, because the magistrate at his own discretion could decide the penal category, the penalty, and the procedure. It is true that Diodorus and Plutarch both say that Africanus was accused on a capital charge, but though they use the word 'death' their evidence should not be taken to mean that condemnation would have involved the death-penalty; the most they imply is loss of civil status.[2] Antias gives a tribunician prosecution before the Tribes, and although his account is enveloped in falsification this basic fact may be true. Of the rival claims of Comitia Tributa and Centuriata, the former is perhaps slightly the stronger,[3] but the fact that the debate occurred in the Forum and at the Rostrum proves little, because even in a capital trial the preliminary discussions could take place in the Forum, and only the decisive stage, when the People voted *centuriatim*, was held in the Campus Martius. Certainty is unobtainable, but probably Africanus was accused by a tribune before the Tribes with the proposed sentence of a fine.

Two subsidiary points may be adduced to support this view: the motives which led to the chronological alterations and secondly the historical background. If the incident occurred in 187, it is difficult to see why it was transferred by some authorities to 184. The answer, that it was in order to connect it with the name of Naevius, is not adequate. It is conceivable that if the trial occurred in 184 an

---

[1] Cf. Fraccaro, *Processi*, 397.

[2] The statement of Diodorus and Plutarch might have arisen from a misunderstanding of a Latin text in which *caput* meant loss of *existimatio* and *fama*. If it is unlikely that Diodorus consulted a Latin text, he may simply have developed Polybius' word πικρῶς.

[3] Bloch (op. cit. 201 ff.) after a long examination concludes in favour of the Tributa.

annalist on finding the name of Naevius among the tribunes of the year might cast a part for him similar to that played by the poet Naevius, but it is hardly credible that any annalist would transfer the episode from three years earlier merely to bolster up a fiction which there was no apparent reason ever to have created. On the other hand, it is far easier to explain why, if the incident happened in 184, it was transferred to 187. First, some annalists (e.g. Antias) transferred the death of Africanus to 187, so that they had automatically to antedate the trial also, unless the half-hour allotted by nursery rhyme to King Charles was to be increased to three years in the case of Africanus. Secondly, an annalist, recounting the attacks on the Scipios, might transfer the final incident to the same year, in order to recount the fall of the Scipios as an artistic unit, rather than leave the matter in the air and then later have to revive the reader's interest.

Secondly, the framework of events points to 184 rather than to 187. If Africanus was accused in 187, it is unlikely that his brother would have recovered ground so quickly in 186. To obviate such a difficulty, the attacks on Africanus have to be subordinated as a mere incident in the trial of his brother (if it is to be placed in 187), but this forces the evidence of our primary authority. On the other hand the situation early in 184 suits the facts well. Asiaticus had been attacked in 187, but was saved by his brother's influence. Because Africanus retained his position, Asiaticus was able to recover quickly and hoped to complete his political career by winning the censorship in 184. Although the effect of Lucius' Games might have worn off by then, it was useless to try to prosecute him again. This time the attack was aimed at Africanus, without whose help Lucius could never succeed; and this time the attack was successful. After a momentary set-back, when Africanus stirred the dying embers of his popularity into sudden flame, his enemies pressed home the charge; now ageing and ill, he decided to withdraw and leave the field to them. With Africanus' downfall his brother naturally failed at the elections. Thus the placing of the incident in 184 fits the general situation and reveals the tactics of the opposition.

To sum up: the evidence points to the reliability of the name Naevius and a trial of Africanus. This, then, must be placed in the year 184 in accordance with the better annalists (Nepos) and contrary to the worst ones (Antias)—a date which is supported by a consideration of the annalists' methods and by the historical circumstances of the time.

CONSULS AND CENSORS[1]

222 Cn. Cornelius Scipio Calvus — M. Claudius Marcellus
221 P. Cornelius Scipio Asina — M. Minucius Rufus
220 L. Veturius Philo — C. Lutatius Catulus
Censors: L. Aemilius Papus — C. Flaminius
219 L. Aemilius Paullus — M. Livius Salinator
218 P. Cornelius Scipio — Ti. Sempronius Longus
217 Cn. Servilius Geminus — C. Flaminius II
216 L. Aemilius Paullus II — C. Terentius Varro
215 Q. Fabius Maximus III — Ti. Sempronius Gracchus
214 Q. Fabius Maximus IV — M. Claudius Marcellus III
Censors: M. Atilius Regulus — P. Furius Philus
213 Q. Fabius Maximus — Ti. Sempronius Gracchus II
212 Ap. Claudius Pulcher — Q. Fulvius Flaccus III
211 P. Sulpicius Galba Maximus — Cn. Fulvius Centumalus Maximus
210 M. Valerius Laevinus (II) — M. Claudius Marcellus IV
Censors: L. Veturius Philo — P. Licinius Crassus Dives
209 Q. Fabius Maximus V — Q. Fulvius Flaccus IV
Censors: M. Cornelius Cethegus — P. Sempronius Tuditanus
208 T. Quinctius Crispinus — M. Claudius Marcellus V
207 C. Claudius Nero — M. Livius Salinator II
206 L. Veturius Philo — Q. Caecilius Metellus
205 P. Cornelius Scipio — P. Licinius Crassus Dives
204 M. Cornelius Cethegus — P. Sempronius Tuditanus
Censors: C. Claudius Nero — M. Livius Salinator
203 Cn. Servilius Caepio — C. Servilius (Geminus)
202 Ti. Claudius Nero — M. Servilius Pulex Geminus
201 Cn. Cornelius Lentulus — P. Aelius Paetus
200 P. Sulpicius Galba II — C. Aurelius Cotta
199 L. Cornelius Lentulus — P. Villius Tappulus
Censors: P. Cornelius Scipio — P. Aelius Paetus
198 T. Quinctius Flamininus — Sex. Aelius Paetus Catus
197 C. Cornelius Cethegus — Q. Minucius Rufus
196 L. Furius Purpureo — M. Claudius Marcellus
195 L. Valerius Flaccus — M. Porcius Cato
194 P. Cornelius Scipio II — Ti. Sempronius Longus
Censors: C. Cornelius Cethegus — Sex. Aelius Paetus
193 L. Cornelius Merula — Q. Minucius Thermus
192 L. Quinctius Flamininus — Cn. Domitius Ahenobarbus
191 P. Cornelius Scipio Nasica — M'. Acilius Glabrio
190 L. Cornelius Scipio — C. Laelius
189 Cn. Manlius Vulso — M. Fulvius Nobilior
Censors: T. Quinctius Flamini- — M. Claudius Marcellus
nus
188 M. Valerius Messalla — C. Livius Salinator
187 M. Aemilius Lepidus — C. Flaminius
186 Sp. Postumius Albinus — Q. Marcius Philippus
185 Ap. Claudius Pulcher — M. Sempronius Tuditanus

[1] For the Fasti of 221–219 see p. 273, of 216–215 see p. 275.

184 P. Claudius Pulcher
    Censors: L. Valerius Flaccus
183 Q. Fabius Labeo
182 L. Aemilius Paullus
181 P. Cornelius Cethegus
180 A. Postumius Albinus Luscus

179 L. Manlius Acidinus Fulvianus
    Censors: M. Aemilius Lepidus
178 A. Manlius Vulso
177 C. Claudius Pulcher
176 Cn. Cornelius Scipio Hispallus
    C. Valerius Laevinus, *suffectus*
175 M. Aemilius Lepidus II
174 Sp. Postumius Albinus Paullulus
    Censors: A. Postumius Albinus
173 L. Postumius Albinus
172 P. Aelius Ligus
171 P. Licinius Crassus
170 A. Atilius Serranus
169 Cn. Servilius Caepio
    Censors: C. Claudius Pulcher
168 L. Aemilius Paullus II
167 Q. Aelius Paetus
166 C. Sulpicius Gallus
165 T. Manlius Torquatus
164 A. Manlius Torquatus
    Censors: L. Aemilius Paullus
163 Ti. Sempronius Gracchus II
162 P. Cornelius Scipio Nasica abd.
    P. Cornelius Lentulus
161 M. Valerius Messalla
160 M. Cornelius Cethegus
159 Cn. Cornelius Dolabella
    Censors: P. Cornelius Scipio
    Nasica
158 M. Aemilius Lepidus
157 Sex. Iulius Caesar
156 L. Cornelius Lentulus Lupus
155 P. Cornelius Scipio Nasica II
154 L. Postumius Albinus
    Censors: M. Valerius Messalla
153 Q. Fulvius Nobilior
152 L. Valerius Flaccus
151 A. Postumius Albinus
150 T. Quinctius Flamininus
149 L. Marcius Censorinus
148 Sp. Postumius Albinus Magnus
147 P. Cornelius Scipio Aemilianus
    Censors: L. Cornelius Lentulus
    Lupus
146 Cn. Cornelius Lentulus

L. Porcius Licinus
    M. Porcius Cato
M. Claudius Marcellus
Cn. Baebius Tamphilus
M. Baebius Tamphilus
C. Calpurnius Piso
Q. Fulvius Flaccus, *suffectus*
Q. Fulvius Flaccus Q. f.
    M. Fulvius Nobilior
M. Iunius Brutus
Ti. Sempronius Gracchus
Q. Petillius Spurinus

P. Mucius Scaevola
Q. Mucius Scaevola
    Q. Fulvius Flaccus
M. Popillius Laenas
C. Popillius Laenas
C. Cassius Longinus
A. Hostilius Mancinus
Q. Marcius Philippus II
    Ti. Sempronius Gracchus
C. Licinius Crassus
M. Iunius Pennus
M. Claudius Marcellus
Cn. Octavius
Q. Cassius Longinus
    Q. Marcius Philippus
M'. Iuventius Thalna
C. Marcius Figulus abd.
Cn. Domitius Ahenobarbus
C. Fannius Strabo
L. Anicius Gallus
M. Fulvius Nobilior
    M. Popillius Laenas

C. Popillius Laenas II
L. Aurelius Orestes
C. Marcius Figulus II
M. Claudius Marcellus II
Q. Opimius. *Suff.* M'. Acilius Glabrio
    C. Cassius Longinus
T. Annius Luscus
M. Claudius Marcellus III
L. Licinius Lucullus
M'. Acilius Balbus
M'. Manilius
L. Calpurnius Piso Caesoninus
C. Livius Drusus
    L. Marcius Censorinus

L. Mummius

218 L. Manlius Vulso
    M. Aemilius Lepidus (I)
217 T. Otacilius Crassus I
    M. Pomponius Matho I
216 M. Claudius Marcellus II (*cos.* I, 222)
    L. Postumius Albinus II (*cos.* I, 234)
215 M. Valerius Laevinus II (*cos.* 210)
    Ap. Claudius Pulcher (*cos.* 212)

214 Q. Fulvius Flaccus (III) (*cos.* 237)
    T. Otacilius Crassus II
213 P. Sempronius Tuditanus (*cos.* 204)
    Cn. Fulvius Centumalus (*cos.* 211)
212 Cn. Fulvius Flaccus
    C. Claudius Nero (*cos.* 207)
211 L. Cornelius Lentulus
    M. Cornelius Cethegus (*cos.* 204)
210 P. Manlius Vulso
    L. Manlius Acidinus
209 L. Veturius Philo (*cos.* 206)
    T. Quinctius Crispinus (*cos.* 208)
208 P. Licinius Crassus Dives (*cos.* 205)
    P. Licinius Varus
207 L. Porcius Licinus
    C. Mamilius Atellus
206 C. Servilius (Geminus) (*cos.* 203)
    M. Caecilius Metellus
205 Sp. Lucretius
    Cn. Octavius
204 Ti. Claudius Nero (*cos.* 202)
    M. Marcius Ralla
203 P. Cornelius Lentulus
    P. Quinctilius Varus
202 M. Sextius Sabinus
    Cn. Tremellius Flaccus
201 M. Iunius Pennus
    M. Valerius Falto
200 Q. Minucius Rufus (*cos.* 197)
    L. Furius Purpureo (*cos.* 196)
199 L. Quinctius Flamininus (*cos.* 192)
    L. Valerius Flaccus (*cos.* 195)
198 L. Cornelius Merula (*cos.* 193)
    M. Claudius Marcellus (*cos.* 196)
197 L. Manlius Vulso
    C. Sempronius Tuditanus
    M. Sergius Silus
196 Q. Fabius Buteo

C. Terentius Varro (*cos.* 216)
C. Atilius Serranus
M. Aemilius (Regillus)
A. Cornelius Mammula
M. Pomponius Matho II

P. Furius Philus II (*cos.* 223)
Q. Fulvius Flaccus (II) (*cos.* 237)
Q. Mucius Scaevola
T. Manlius Torquatus, *suffectus*
Q. Fabius Maximus (*cos.* 213)
P. Cornelius Lentulus
M. Atilius (Regulus)
M. Aemilius Lepidus (II)
M. Iunius Silanus
P. Cornelius Sulla
C. Sulpicius (Galus)
C. Calpurnius Piso
C. Laetorius
L. Cincius Alimentus
C. Hostilius Tubulus
C. Aurunculeius
Sex. Iulius Caesar
Q. Claudius Flamen
C. Hostilius Cato
A. Hostilius Cato
Ti. Claudius Asellus
Q. Mamilius Turrinus
Cn. Servilius Caepio
L. Aemilius Papus
L. Scribonius Libo
M. Pomponius Matho
P. Aelius Paetus (*cos.* 201)
P. Villius Tappulus (*cos.* 199)
C. Livius Salinator (*cos.* 188)
C. Aurelius Cotta (*cos.* 200)
M. Fabius Buteo
P. Aelius Tubero
Q. Fulvius Gillo
Q. Sergius Plancus
L. Villius Tappulus
Cn. Baebius Tamphilus (*cos.* 182)
M. Porcius Cato (*cos.* 195)
C. Helvius
M. Helvius
M. Minucius Rufus
L. Atilius
M'. Acilius Glabrio (*cos.* 191)

Ti. Sempronius Longus (*cos.* 194)

Q. Minucius Thermus (*cos.* 193)

195 Cn. Manlius Vulso (*cos.* 189)

Ap. Claudius Nero

P. Porcius Laeca

194 P. Cornelius Scipio Nasica (*cos.* 191)

Cn. Cornelius Merenda

Cn. Cornelius Blasio

193 L. Cornelius Scipio (*cos.* 190)

M. Fulvius Nobilior (*cos.* 189)

C. Scribonius

192 L. Scribonius Libo

M. Fulvius Centumalus

A. Atilius Serranus I

191 L. Aemilius Paullus (*cos.* 182)

M. Aemilius Lepidus (*cos.* 187)

M. Iunius Brutus (*cos.* 178)

190 M. Tuccius

L. Aurunculeius

Cn. Fulvius

189 Q. Fabius Labeo (*cos.* 183)

Q. Fabius Pictor

M. Sempronius Tuditanus (*cos.*185)

188 Q. Marcius Philippus

M. Claudius Marcellus (? *cos.* 183)

C. Stertinius

187 Ap. Claudius Pulcher (*cos.* 185)

Ser. Sulpicius Galba

Q. Terentius Culleo

186 T. Maenius

P. Cornelius Sulla

C. Calpurnius Piso (*cos.* 180)

185 P. Cornelius Cethegus (*cos.* 181)

A. Postumius Albinus (*cos.* 180)

C. Afranius Stellio

184 C. Decimius Flavus

P. Sempronius Longus

P. Cornelius Cethegus

183 C. Valerius Flaccus

Sp. Postumius Albinus (*cos.* 174)

P. Cornelius Sisenna

182 Q. Fulvius Flaccus (*cos.* 179)

M. Valerius Laevinus

P. Manlius II

181 Q. Fabius Maximus

Q. Fabius Buteo

Ti. Claudius Nero

180 Ti. Sempronius Gracchus (*cos.* 177)

L. Postumius Albinus (*cos.* 173)

P. Cornelius Mammula

179 Cn. Cornelius Scipio Hispallus (*cos.* 176)

L. Apustius Fullo

C. Laelius (*cos.* 190)

C. Fabricius Luscinus

C. Atinius Labeo

P. Manlius I

Cn. Domitius Ahenobarbus (*cos.* 192)

Sex. Digitius

T. Iuventius Thalna

M. Valerius Messalla (*cos.* 188)

L. Porcius Licinus (*cos.* 184)

C. Flaminius (*cos.* 187)

M. Baebius Tamphilus

L. Valerius Tappo

Q. Salonius Sarra

A. Cornelius Mammula

C. Livius Salinator (*cos.* 188)

L. Oppius Salinator

L. Aemilius Regillus

P. Iunius Brutus

C. Atinius Labeo

Sp. Postumius Albinus (*cos.* 186)

L. Plautius Hypsaeus

L. Baebius Dives

C. Atinius

P. Claudius Pulcher (*cos.* 184)

L. Manlius Acidinus (*cos.* 179)

L. Terentius Massiliota

Q. Fulvius Flaccus (*cos. suff.* 180)

M. Furius Crassipes I

M. Licinius Lucullus

C. Aurelius Scaurus

L. Quinctius Crispinus

C. Atilius Serranus

L. Postumius Tempsanus

M. Claudius (? *cos.* 183)

Q. Naevius Matho

C. Sempronius Blaesus

A. Terentius Varro

L. Pupius

L. Iulius Caesar

Cn. Sicinius I

M. Ogulnius Gallus

L. Caecilius Denter

C. Terentius Istra

Q. Petillius Spurinus (*cos.* 176)

M. Pinarius Rusca

L. Duronius

Ti. Minucius Molliculus

C. Claudius Pulcher (*cos.* 177), *suffectus*

A. Hostilius Mancinus (*cos.* 170)

C. Maenius

P. Mucius Scaevola (*cos.* 175)

C. Valerius Laevinus (*cos. suff.* 176)

178 M. Titinius Curvus
Ti. Claudius Nero
T. Fonteius Capito

177 P. Aelius Tubero
C. Quinctius Flamininus

176 M. Popillius Laenas (*cos.* 173)
P. Licinius Crassus (*cos.* 171)
M. Cornelius Scipio

175 (Ser.) Cornelius (Sulla)
C. Popillius Laenas
(?) Cn. Lutatius Cerco

174 M. Atilius Serranus
Cn. Servilius Caepio (*cos.* 169)
P. Furius Philus

173 N. Fabius Buteo
C. Matienus
C. Cicereius

172 C. Licinius Crassus (*cos.* 168)
M. Iunius Pennus (*cos.* 167)
Sp. Lucretius

171 C. Sulpicius Galba
L. Furius Philus
L. Canuleius Dives

170 L. Hortensius
Q. Maenius
(?) Q. Aelius Paetus (*cos.* 167)

169 C. Decimius
M. Claudius Marcellus (*cos.* 166)
C. Sulpicius Gallus (*cos.* 166)

168 Cn. Baebius Tamphilus
L. Anicius Gallus (*cos.* 160)
Cn. Octavius (*cos.* 165)

167 Q. Cassius Longinus (*cos.* 164)
M'. Iuventius Thalna (*cos.* 163)
Ti. Claudius Nero

166 L. Iulius (Caesar)
L. Appuleius Saturninus
A. Licinius Nerva

Q. Mucius Scaevola (*cos.* 174)
T. Aebutius Carrus (Parrus)
C. Cluvius Saxula
M. Titinius
C. Numisius
L. Mummius
L. Papirius Maso
M. Aburius
L. Aquillius Gallus
Ap. Claudius Centho
P. Aelius Ligus
(?) Q. Baebius Sulca
L. Claudius
L. Cornelius Scipio
(?) C. Cassius Longinus (*cos.* 171)
M. Furius Crassipes II
A. Atilius Serranus II
C. Cluvius Saxula II
Sp. Cluvius
Cn. Sicinius II
C. Memmius
C. Lucretius Gallus
C. Caninius Rebilus
L. Villius Annalis
M. Raecius

(?) T. Manlius Torquatus (*cos.* 165)
C. Marcius Figulus (*cos.* 162)
Ser. Cornelius Lentulus
P. Fonteius Capito
P. Fonteius Balbus
M. Aebutius Helva
C. Papirius Carbo
Cn. Fulvius Flaccus
C. Licinius Nerva
A. Manlius Torquatus (*cos.* 164)
P. Rutilius Calvus
P. Quinctilius Varus
M. Fonteius

THE CORNELII SCIPIONES, ETC.

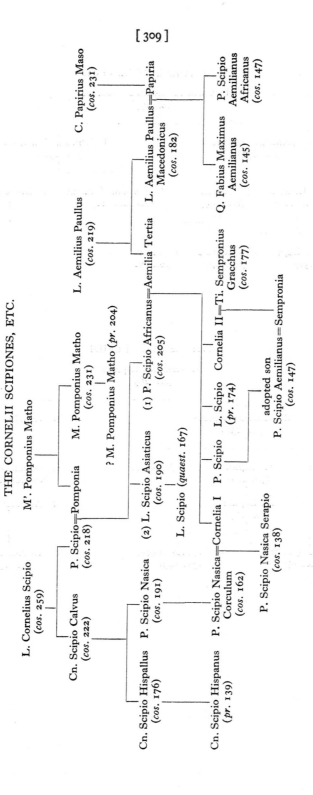

THE CORNELII LENTULI

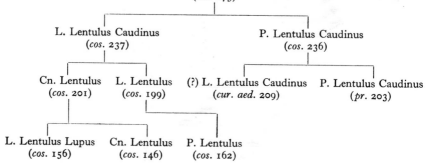

L. Cornelius Lentulus Caudinus
(*cos.* 275)

L. Lentulus Caudinus
(*cos.* 237)

P. Lentulus Caudinus
(*cos.* 236)

Cn. Lentulus
(*cos.* 201)

L. Lentulus
(*cos.* 199)

(?) L. Lentulus Caudinus
(*cur. aed.* 209)

P. Lentulus Caudinus
(*pr.* 203)

L. Lentulus Lupus
(*cos.* 156)

Cn. Lentulus
(*cos.* 146)

P. Lentulus
(*cos.* 162)

THE AEMILII LEPIDI

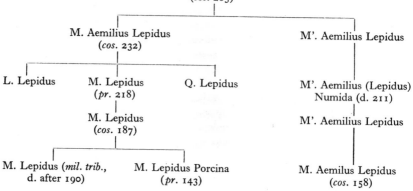

M. Aemilius Lepidus
(*cos.* 285)

M. Aemilius Lepidus
(*cos.* 232)

M'. Aemilius Lepidus

L. Lepidus

M. Lepidus
(*pr.* 218)

Q. Lepidus

M'. Aemilius (Lepidus)
Numida (d. 211)

M. Lepidus
(*cos.* 187)

M'. Aemilius Lepidus

M. Lepidus (*mil. trib.*,
d. after 190)

M. Lepidus Porcina
(*pr.* 143)

M. Aemilus Lepidus
(*cos.* 158)

THE SERVILII

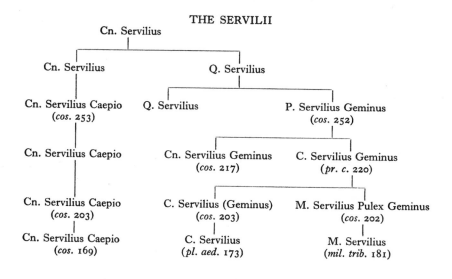

Cn. Servilius

Cn. Servilius   Q. Servilius

Cn. Servilius Caepio
(*cos.* 253)

Q. Servilius   P. Servilius Geminus
(*cos.* 252)

Cn. Servilius Caepio

Cn. Servilius Geminus
(*cos.* 217)

C. Servilius Geminus
(*pr. c.* 220)

Cn. Servilius Caepio
(*cos.* 203)

C. Servilius (Geminus)
(*cos.* 203)

M. Servilius Pulex Geminus
(*cos.* 202)

Cn. Servilius Caepio
(*cos.* 169)

C. Servilius
(*pl. aed.* 173)

M. Servilius
(*mil. trib.* 181)

THE LICINII

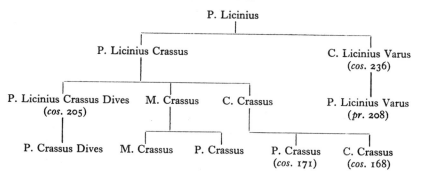

P. Licinius

P. Licinius Crassus

C. Licinius Varus
(*cos.* 236)

P. Licinius Crassus Dives
(*cos.* 205)

M. Crassus   C. Crassus

P. Licinius Varus
(*pr.* 208)

P. Crassus Dives   M. Crassus   P. Crassus

P. Crassus
(*cos.* 171)

C. Crassus
(*cos.* 168)

THE CLAUDII

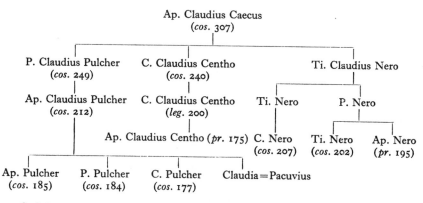

Ap. Claudius Caecus
(*cos.* 307)

P. Claudius Pulcher
(*cos.* 249)

C. Claudius Centho
(*cos.* 240)

Ti. Claudius Nero

Ap. Claudius Pulcher
(*cos.* 212)

C. Claudius Centho
(*leg.* 200)

Ti. Nero   P. Nero

Ap. Claudius Centho (*pr.* 175)

C. Nero
(*cos.* 207)

Ti. Nero
(*cos.* 202)

Ap. Nero
(*pr.* 195)

Ap. Pulcher
(*cos.* 185)

P. Pulcher
(*cos.* 184)

C. Pulcher
(*cos.* 177)

Claudia = Pacuvius

THE FULVII

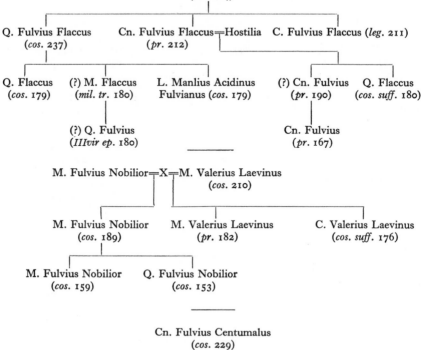

M. Fulvius Flaccus
(*cos.* 264)

Q. Fulvius Flaccus   Cn. Fulvius Flaccus⹀Hostilia   C. Fulvius Flaccus (*leg.* 211)
(*cos.* 237)   (*pr.* 212)

Q. Flaccus   (?) M. Flaccus   L. Manlius Acidinus   (?) Cn. Fulvius   Q. Flaccus
(*cos.* 179)   (*mil. tr.* 180)   Fulvianus (*cos.* 179)   (*pr.* 190)   (*cos. suff.* 180)

(?) Q. Fulvius   Cn. Fulvius
(*IIIvir ep.* 180)   (*pr.* 167)

M. Fulvius Nobilior⹀X⹀M. Valerius Laevinus
(*cos.* 210)

M. Fulvius Nobilior   M. Valerius Laevinus   C. Valerius Laevinus
(*cos.* 189)   (*pr.* 182)   (*cos. suff.* 176)

M. Fulvius Nobilior   Q. Fulvius Nobilior
(*cos.* 159)   (*cos.* 153)

Cn. Fulvius Centumalus
(*cos.* 229)

(?) Cn. Fulvius Centumalus Maximus
(*cos.* 211)

M. Fulvius Centumalus
(*pr.* 192)

INDEX

A fairly full list of persons is given; they are entered under their gentile names (e.g. for Cato *see* Porcius). But in general the aim of this Index is usefulness rather than completeness.